HANDBOOK OF ALTERNATIVE TH ECONOMIC GROWTH

Handbook of Alternative Theories of Economic Growth

Edited by

Mark Setterfield

Trinity College, USA

Edward Elgar
Cheltenham, UK • Northampton, MA, USA

Published by
Edward Elgar Publishing Limited
The Lypiatts
15 Lansdown Road
Cheltenham
Glos GL50 2JA
UK

Edward Elgar Publishing, Inc.
William Pratt House
9 Dewey Court
Northampton
Massachusetts 01060
USA

A catalogue record for this book
is available from the British Library

Library of Congress Control Number: 2009938384

Mixed Sources
Product group from well-managed
forests and other controlled sources
www.fsc.org Cert no. SA-COC-1565
© 1996 Forest Stewardship Council

ISBN 978 1 84720 402 8 (cased)

Printed and bound by MPG Books Group, UK

Contents

Contributors

Robert A. Blecker, American University, USA

Gérard Duménil, University of Paris X, France

Amitava Krishna Dutt, University of Notre Dame, USA

Jesus Felipe, Asian Development Bank, Philippines

Peter Flaschel, University of Bielefeld, Germany

Duncan K. Foley, New School For Social Research, USA

John Foster, University of Queensland, Australia

Bill Gibson, University of Vermont, Burlington, USA

Alfred Greiner, University of Bielefeld, Germany

Davide Gualerzi, University of Padua, Italy

Eckhard Hein, Berlin School of Economics and Law, Germany

John E. King, La Trobe University, Australia

Heinz D. Kurz, University of Graz, Austria

Matteo Lanzafame, University of Messina, Italy

Marc Lavoie, University of Ottawa, Canada

Miguel A. León-Ledesma, University of Kent, UK

Dominique Lévy, PSE-CNRS, France

Gilberto Tadeu Lima, University of São Paulo, Brazil

John McCombie, Cambridge University, UK

J. Stan Metcalfe, University of Manchester, UK

Thomas R. Michl, Colgate University, USA

Juan Carlos Moreno Brid, United Nations, Mexico

C.W.M. Naastepad, Delft University of Technology, Netherlands

Thomas I. Palley, Economics for Democratic and Open Societies, USA

Esteban Pérez Caldentey, United Nations, Chile

Arslan Razmi, University of Massachusetts, Amherst, USA

Mark Roberts, Cambridge University, UK

Neri Salvadori, University of Pisa, Italy

Stephanie Seguino, University of Vermont, USA

Mark Setterfield, Trinity College, USA

Peter Skott, University of Massachusetts, Amherst, USA

Servaas Storm, Delft University of Technology, Netherlands

Till van Treeck, Macroeconomic Policy Institute, Germany

An introduction to alternative theories of economic growth
Mark Setterfield

It has become commonplace for leading textbooks on growth theory to characterize the historical development of the subject as a simple progression from first- to second-generation neoclassical growth theory, punctuated only by a brief hiatus during the 1970s when inflation became the cause célèbre of macrodynamics (for representative examples, see Barro and Sala-i-Martin, 1995; Jones, 2002; Aghion and Howitt, 2009). But as has been remarked elsewhere (Setterfield, 2002, 2003), these "stylized facts" are more apparent than real. They conceal a rich history of alternative theories of economic growth, that both parallels and interacts with the development of neoclassical theory. The purpose of this Handbook is to provide a comprehensive overview of these alternative theories – one that both surveys major sub-fields of alternative theories of economic growth (including, but not limited to, Classical, Kaleckian, Evolutionary, and Kaldorian growth theories) and draws attention to frontier issues in the field. The ambition of this introduction is to orient the reader towards the content that follows.

1 Common themes in alternative theories of economic growth

Economic theories that depart from one or more of the "hard core" presuppositions of neoclassical economics (such as optimizing behaviour by decision makers, or the marginal productivity theory of value and distribution) are often said to be defined chiefly in terms of their opposition to neoclassical theory – that is, in terms of what they are *not*. As is obvious from what has already been said above, it is tempting to lapse into the same habit of thought when characterizing alternative theories of economic growth. Fortunately, however, it is not necessary to succumb to this habit. Despite their differences, alternative theories of economic growth exhibit many commonalities. Ultimately, they constitute a "broad church" characterized by numerous shared preconceptions. And even if these preconceptions cannot all be combined in a single synthetic model of growth, distribution and technical change, they are nevertheless suggestive of a "common research program rather than a gulf of irreconcilable scientific differences" (see Foley and Michl, Chapter 2, this volume). In this section, five broad features of the research programme common to alternative theories of economic growth are highlighted, with a view to emphasizing what the corpus of alternative theories of economic growth *is*, rather than what it is *not*.

1.1 The role of aggregate demand in the long run

An enduring theme in alternative theories of economic growth – one that was inspired by the Keynesian revolution in macroeconomics and, in particular, such seminal contributions to growth theory as Harrod (1939) and Robinson (1956) – is the role of aggregate demand in the long run. This is not to say that all alternative theories of growth identify a causal role for aggregate demand in the long run, but rather that there is a shared tradition of taking the demand side of the economy seriously. This is every bit as evident in the Classical tradition, in which aggregate demand is ultimately found to matter only in the short or medium run (see, for example, Duménil and Lévy, 1999), as it is in the contemporary theories of demand-led growth associated with the Kaleckian and Kaldorian traditions.

1.2   Value and distribution

The value-theoretic foundations of alternative theories of economic growth are typically rooted in the Classical surplus approach rather than marginal productivity theory. This helps to explain the prominence of distributional outcomes in alternative growth theories – not just as potential causes of, for example, technical change or the precise rate of growth, but also as something of interest and importance in and of themselves. This latter concern arises from the likelihood that distributional outcomes will reflect inequities in the functioning of capitalist economies, rather than simply benign forms of inequality.

1.3   The theory of production

Alternative theories of economic growth generally postulate that the technical structure of production is best characterized by Leontieff (fixed coefficient) technology, rather than the possibility of continuous substitution between factors of production. It is also common to regard the state of technology as being embodied in factors of production, so that technical change requires factor accumulation accompanied by discrete change in the technique of production.

1.4   Technical change

The embodied technical change described above is generally understood to be caused by growth and distribution outcomes themselves. In other words, technical change is not just endogenous in the sense of being explained within the model (the key innovation that distinguishes second-generation neoclassical endogenous growth theory from the first-generation neoclassical growth model associated with Solow (1956)). It is also endogenous to the very outcomes (growth and distribution) with which alternative theories of economic growth are ultimately concerned. Examples of these mechanisms of endogenous technical change include the Verdoorn Law (see, for example McCombie and Thirlwall, 1994, Chapter 2; McCombie et al., 2003) and the Classical theory of induced, factor-biased technical change (see, for example, Foley and Michl, 1999; Sasaki, 2008).

1.5   Methodology

An enduring question in growth theory is how best to characterize (and hence model) capitalist growth? The dominant view – reinforced by Kaldor's (1961) oft-repeated stylized facts – is that growth is a steady and balanced process. This view lends itself to steady-state equilibrium analysis, which does proliferate in alternative theories of economic growth. But historically the latter have also shown concern with different visions of what the growth process involves and hence how it should be modelled. These include the possibility that long-run growth is best conceived as innately cyclical (rather than as a steady process punctuated by short-run disturbances), and that long-run growth is inherently unbalanced, involving structural change in the composition of output, employment, consumer demand and so forth.

2   Emerging themes in alternative theories of economic growth

The themes highlighted above can be regarded as well-rehearsed features of alternative theories of economic growth. As such, it will not surprise the reader to learn that they recur throughout this volume. But the chapters that follow also serve to highlight a variety of other "emerging" themes which, if not all strictly new, are nevertheless associated with what are currently frontier research issues in alternative theories of economic growth. One of these emerging themes concerns the precise adjustment mechanism – or combination of such mechanisms – that describes the response of a growing economy to conditions of excess aggregate demand. Does it involve changes in prices (and hence the mark up/profit share) as, for example, in the classic Cambridge models of growth associated with Robinson, Kaldor and Pasinetti? Or does it involve changes in output (and hence the rate of capacity utilization), as in the canonical Kaleckian model of growth? Or is it the case that some combination of these mechanisms – which are by no means mutually exclusive – renders them simultaneously operative? This seemingly narrow, technical issue has profound implications for growth theory, not the least of which is its impact on the very stability of equilibrium in some steady-state models. As such, it is not surprising to find that it is extensively discussed in the chapters that follow, including those by Kurz and Salvadori, Skott, Lavoie and Gibson (see Chapter 4, 5, 6 and 1).[1]

A second prominent emerging theme is the relationship between the actual and the potential (i.e. Harrodian natural) rates of growth. One concern here is with the endogeneity of the latter to the former, something that transforms the natural rate of growth from an exogenously given ceiling into a path-dependent constraint on the expansion of the economy. A second concern is with the reconciliation of the two growth rates in a steady-state framework. The importance of this issue is easily seen by reference to the following, simple measure of resource capacity utilization (E):

$$E = \frac{Y}{Y_p} \tag{1}$$

where Y is the actual level of real output and Y_p is the potential level of real output. It follows from the expression above that:

$$e = y - y_p \tag{2}$$

where lower case letters denote the rates of growth of upper case variables. Since it is obvious by inspection of (1) that E is bounded above and below, it follows from (2) that any steady growth equilibrium also requires balanced growth of the form:

$$y = y_p \tag{3}$$

in order for the steady-state growth equilibrium to be sustainable in the long run. In short, the actual and potential growth rates must be reconciled in a steady-state framework in order to avoid illogical claims regarding the rate of resource utilization, E. This problem persists even if the natural rate of growth is endogenous to the actual rate.

Hence note that, beginning from a situation in which equation (3) is satisfied and conjecturing an increase in y, the endogeneity of y_p to y is not, in and of itself, sufficient to restore the condition in (3). Instead any increase (decrease) in y must induce an equal proportional increase (decrease) in y_p in order for (3) to be maintained. In other words we require an elasticity of aggregate supply (i.e. potential output) with respect to aggregate demand (i.e. actual output) of exactly one (Cornwall, 1972). If this is not observed (and estimates of, for example, the Verdoorn law suggest that in general it will not be), then some other mechanism must be postulated to bring the actual and natural rates of growth back into alignment. The chapters by Dutt, León-Ledesma and Lanzafame, and Seguino and Setterfield (Chapters 11, 10 and 18) all address the relationship between the actual and natural rates of growth.

Another emerging theme in alternative theories of economic growth concerns the potential importance of endogenous variation in labour costs for the stability of the growth process. This theme is complementary to the concern with "output versus price adjustment" discussed earlier and, as such, it is not surprising to find that it is taken up in Chapters 5 and 6 by Skott and Lavoie, in the context of Harrodian and Kaleckian growth models, respectively. But the importance of endogenous variation in labour costs also has a long pedigree in the Classical tradition. This is reflected, for example, in its centrality to the cyclical growth process described by Goodwin (1967). Chapter 16 by Flaschel and Greiner in this volume further advances this tradition, by examining whether or not the stabilizing role of wages in Goodwin-type growth dynamics can be replaced with mechanisms that are more compatible with a social-democratic variant of capitalism.

Finally, the interaction of finance and growth has emerged as a pressing theme in alternative theories of economic growth, in view of the increased "financialization" of capitalism in recent decades. The novelty and significance of this topic is amply demonstrated in Chapters 13 and 14 by Hein and van Treeck, and Palley. Having previously been likened to "Hamlet without the Prince" by virtue of their neglect of money and finance (Kregel, 1985), alternative theories of economic growth have now embraced the search for processes that make sense of how growth is affected by financial variables (such as interest rates, stocks of debt, debt-servicing commitments, and so forth) and the very institutional structure of finance and its relationship to industry.

It is important to emphasize that the issues discussed above are not the only emerging themes in contemporary alternative theories of economic growth. Moreover, they are by no means the only *important* themes, whether emerging or already well established. As such, the purpose of the foregoing discussion is not to privilege certain issues relative to others. Instead, the point is to draw attention to the fact that, in addition to reviewing the existing state of the art in alternative theories of economic growth, a second objective of this Handbook is to highlight frontier issues in the field. The themes discussed above serve no greater purpose than to exemplify this aspect of the project. It is hoped that they suffice to give the reader at least a sense of the two-fold ambition of the volume; that is, both to take stock of and to point towards promising avenues for advancing alternative theories of economic growth.

3   The structure of this Handbook
The organization of this volume reflects the fact that there are numerous sources of overlap between the chapters that follow. Some chapters are similar by virtue of their

structure, surveying themes associated with a particular approach to analysing growth. Others utilize a common framework or model in their analysis of what might otherwise be putatively different issues. And some chapters share an interest in a particular topic, regardless of the framework of analysis they adopt. The sequence of chapters with which the reader is presented represents an effort to balance these various cross-cuts in a manner that makes the Handbook readable from beginning to end. But those who are interested in, for example, a particular alternative theory of growth, or a particular issue in growth theory, or even in simply coming to grips with the "nuts and bolts" of the different approaches that comprise alternative theories of economic growth, may find it profitable – and are actively encouraged – to read the chapters out of sequence.

3.1 Alternative theories of economic growth: an overview
The volume begins with a series of eight chapters that survey the main approaches that comprise alternative theories of economic growth. In the opening chapter, Bill Gibson analyses structuralist growth theory relative to its neoclassical counterpart. In a salient lesson for growth theorists of all stripes, Gibson shows how both neoclassical and structuralist models can be developed in a common analytical framework that highlights the similarities of orthodox and alternative growth theories – in particular, the dependence of their steady-state solutions on a single, key variable (the rate of growth of the labour force in the neoclassical model, the rate of growth of autonomous demand in the structuralist model). The chapter then investigates efforts to make investment – the key component of autonomous demand in the structuralist tradition – endogenous to the rate of capacity utilization. It is shown that, as compared to the neoclassical model, which requires relatively few plausible assumptions for steady growth to emerge, variants of the structuralist model in which investment is endogenous to capacity utilization face potential instability problems. Gibson then shows how these problems can be ameliorated by reconsidering the role of the profit share in the determination of investment. The chapter concludes by noting – with some irony – that while the stability of the neoclassical model is structurally determined, it is necessary for structuralists to pay more attention to agency – in particular, the investment behaviour of firms – in order for their models to generate stable, steady-state growth paths.

In Chapter 2, Duncan Foley and Tom Michl provide an account of the Classical tradition in growth theory, in relation to both neoclassical and Keynesian theories of growth. To this end, they review the main features of the Classical, neoclassical and Keynesian approaches to growth, before explicitly comparing and contrasting the neoclassical and Keynesian theories with the core tenets of the Classical tradition. Foley and Michl argue that the main debate between Classical and Keynesian growth theorists concerns the applicability of Keynesian results (such as the paradoxes of thrift and costs) in the long run – a controversy that can be summarized in terms of how these competing theories envisage the reconciliation of the actual and normal rates of capacity utilization. But the authors also draw attention to similarities between Classical and Keynesian growth theories, including their treatment of labour as a chronically under-utilized resource, and of labour supply and technical change (and hence the natural rate of growth) as endogenous to the actual rate of growth. After reviewing exogenous, semi-endogenous and endogenous variants of neoclassical growth theory, Foley and Michl highlight the important differences between the Classical and neoclassical traditions in growth theory. These include contrasting treatments of production and technical change in Classical and neoclassical growth analysis. Of particular importance in this regard is the interplay of distribution and technical change in Classical growth theory, a relationship that is overlooked in the legalistic-cum-technocratic treatment of technical progress typical of neoclassical growth theory.

The third chapter, by Stan Metcalfe and John Foster, identifies the cumulative, two-way interaction between economic growth and the growth of knowledge as central to evolutionary growth theory – an approach that the authors also associate with emphases on unbalanced growth, non-equilibrating adjustment processes, and an attention to heterogeneity at the microeconomic level (particularly with regard to the conduct of entrepreneurs and the process of innovation). After discussing the stylized facts of economic growth, Metcalfe and Foster develop a model of evolutionary growth in which aggregate growth outcomes arise from the interaction of two essential processes operating at lower levels of aggregation: technical progress, and changes in the composition of demand. Both of these processes are, themselves, endogenous to economic growth – the first thanks to the Smith-Young-Kaldor dictum that "the division of labour depends on the extent of the market", and the second to a generalization of Engel's Law. The upshot is a model of non-equilibrium and non-equilibrating growth – or "restless capitalism" – that shows how evolutionary growth theory can reconcile Kaldor's (1961) stylized facts of constancy and balance in the growth record with those of Clark (1944) and Kuznets (1971), which emphasize structural change.

Chapter 4, by Heinz Kurz and Neri Salvadori, surveys theories of growth and distribution based on what Kaldor (1955–56, p. 95) termed the "Keynesian hypothesis", that investment is determined independently of saving and that saving adjusts to investment to create a situation of equilibrium. The authors identify two different adjustment mechanisms consistent with this Keynesian hypothesis. One involves the adjustment of saving to investment by means of changes in prices relative to wages (i.e. through a redistribution of income between profits and wages) and is usually associated with models of full capacity utilization and full employment. The second involves changes in capacity utilization and employment (and in the long run, the rate of accumulation) with the distribution of income taken as given. Kurz and Salvadori survey models based on both mechanisms, identifying the former primarily with the work of Kaldor and Pasinetti, and the latter with the class of models that is now conventionally referred to as Kaleckian. With respect to the former, the authors pay particular attention to the conditions necessary for the existence of a two-class economy; with respect to the latter, they focus attention on the plausibility of the underlying adjustment mechanism and its importance in the analysis of long-run growth.

Chapter 5, by Peter Skott, sets out to develop and contrast Kaleckian and Harrodian models of growth and distribution. The chapter begins by outlining the canonical Kaleckian growth model. By calibrating the equilibrium solution of this model to actual data, Skott argues that the Kaleckian model predicts a variability in the rate of capacity utilization that is at odds with what is observed in reality. He traces this problem to two key theoretical features of the Kaleckian model: its assumption of a constant mark up (and hence profit share); and its treatment of investment as relatively insensitive to the rate of capacity utilization. Skott then proceeds to develop a variety of Harrodian models of growth that eschew the two key theoretical features of the Kaleckian approach. In these models, it is variously assumed that the supply of labour is either perfectly elastic or else constrains the long-run growth rate, and that either the profit share or output adjust rapidly in response to variations in aggregate demand. Ultimately, Skott argues that Harrodian models are based on behavioural foundations that are superior to those of the Kaleckian model. He also calls attention to the potential instability of the Harrodian warranted rate as providing a framework suitable for the analysis of both trend *and* cycle.

Marc Lavoie's survey of Kaleckian growth theory in Chapter 6 places particular emphasis on the stability properties of the Kaleckian model, in both the short run and the long run. The chapter begins by studying short-run stability dynamics – that is, the process of adjustment towards equilibrium rates of growth and capacity utilization. Two adjustment processes are considered: a pure Keynesian adjustment process involving changes in capacity utilization; and a dual adjustment process involving changes in both capacity utilization and profit margins. The first depends on the traditional Kaleckian stability condition, but the latter does not. Lavoie thus argues that the robustness of Kaleckian stability results is greater than some critics of this model suggest. Attention is then turned to long-run stability dynamics – that is, the reconciliation of the actual (equilibrium) rate of capacity utilization and its normal or desired rate. Lavoie rebuts Duménil and Lévy's (1999) claim as to the necessity of being "Keynesian in the short run and Classical in the long run", showing that with appropriate dynamic adjustment mechanisms, key Kaleckian results (such as the paradox of thrift and paradox of costs) carry over to the long run.

Following the Harrodian and Kaleckian emphases of the two preceding chapters, it is fitting that in Chapter 7, John King surveys the Kaldorian approach to growth theory, as exemplified both by Kaldor himself and his followers. Four variants of Kaldor's own growth analysis are discussed. The first two (pre-1966) variants focus on the relationships between distribution, technical change, and growth in a closed, one-sector economy. The two remaining (post-1966) variants are principally concerned with multi-sector and/or open economy issues, and their impact on growth conceived as a historical (path-dependent) rather than an equilibrium process. Kaldorian growth theory, meanwhile, is shown to build largely on Kaldor's post-1966 contributions. Three interrelated variants are identified: balance-of-payments-constrained growth models; models based on the principle of cumulative causation; and North–South models that feature sectoral (agriculture and industry) interactions. A key conclusion that emerges from King's survey is that modern Kaldorian growth theory comprises various overlapping strands rather than a single, unified (i.e. general) theory of growth – much like the work of Kaldor himself.

Davide Gualerzi's chapter (Chapter 8) brings the opening section of the volume to a close by discussing transformational growth theory, which he identifies as an analysis centred on explaining growth and structural change in terms of both the rate of expansion and changes in the composition of aggregate demand. Gualerzi locates transformational growth theory within the broad corpus of demand-led growth theory, but argues that it transcends the dominant (e.g. Kaleckian and Kaldorian) approaches to demand-led growth by seeking to better explain how demand is generated by the process of growth and development itself, along the course of an unbalanced growth path. He outlines a theory of endogenous demand creation centred on the evolution of basic social structures (such as the household and the firm) and imbalances created by the process of uneven development. Gualerzi also highlights the role played by historical evidence and stylized facts in the methodology of transformational growth theory. His chapter culminates with an analysis of the seeming exhaustion of the process of transformational growth by the early 1970s, and its subsequent resurgence in the guise of the information economy during the 1990s.

3.2   Aggregate demand, aggregate supply and long-run growth
Chapters 1 through 8 having thus outlined the major approaches characteristic of alternative theories of economic growth, the remainder of the volume is organized thematically, focusing on a variety of issues in which alternative theories of economic growth express a shared interest. Each of the three chapters in Part II of the Handbook is concerned with the treatment and/or interaction of aggregate demand and aggregate supply in the analysis of long-run growth. In Chapter 9, Jesus Felipe and John McCombie begin by noting the ubiquity of and central role played by continuous aggregate production functions in neoclassical growth theory. The authors argue that because of the severe theoretical difficulties associated with aggregation and the results of the Cambridge capital controversies, the best defence of the aggregate production function is an instrumentalist one: it is useful because it predicts well. Felipe and McCombie's chapter is devoted to illustrating that this claim is unsustainable. The problem lies in the fact that all data against which aggregate production functions are tested satisfy an accounting identity (relating total value added to the sum of wages and profits) that can be re-written so that it resembles an aggregate production function with constant returns to scale and output elasticities equivalent to factor shares. Hence any hypothesized production function with these features will provide a near perfect fit with the data *regardless* of the production technology that *actually* characterizes the economy, simply because of the way that the data are compiled. To illustrate this point, Felipe and McCombie discuss four simulations in which data are generated by specific and known structures of production. In each case, a Cobb-Douglas production function is shown to provide a perfectly good – but entirely spurious – fit to the data. Because the aggregate production function is the centrepiece of neoclassical growth theory, the authors conclude that their results call into question the capacity of neoclassical theory to furnish answers to even the most basic questions in macrodynamics, such as what determines growth and why growth rates differ.

As its title suggests, Chapter 10 by Miguel León-Ledesma and Matteo Lanzafame is concerned with the endogeneity of the natural rate of growth – specifically, the propensity of the latter to be influenced by variations in the *actual* rate of growth. The authors identify the notion of an endogenous natural rate with the Kaldorian tradition in growth theory, in which there is a long-standing emphasis on path dependency in the growth process according to which both the equilibrium *and* the potential rates of growth may be influenced by the actual rate. But León-Ledesma and Lanzafame note that neoclassical growth theory – in which the natural and equilibrium rates of growth are one and the same – has also begun to emphasize mechanisms through which the natural rate is endogenous to the actual rate. There is thus an emerging consensus within the growth literature on the interplay of trend and cycle. The authors go on to survey recent empirical evidence on the link between the actual and natural rates of growth. They conclude that this has largely strengthened the original findings of León-Ledesma and Thirlwall

(2000, 2002), but that in so doing it has drawn attention to the likely impact of structural features of the economy (such as the sectoral composition of employment and the structure of the financial system) on the relationship between the actual and natural rates of growth.

The final chapter in this section of the Handbook, by Amitava Dutt, begins with the observation that, historically, growth theory has been "partitioned" into theories of supply-determined growth (associated with the Classical and neoclassical traditions) and theories of demand-led growth (associated with the Keynesian tradition) with the former, in its neoclassical guise, having become the dominant mode of analysis. The central premise of Dutt's chapter is that *both* demand and supply factors play a role in the determination of growth, and that value therefore attaches to theories that seek to reconcile demand and supply in the analysis of long-run growth. The author reviews the essential architecture of both Classical and neoclassical theories of supply-led growth, and Keynesian theories of demand-led growth. He then describes two existing attempts to integrate aggregate demand and aggregate supply in the theory of long-run growth, deriving from the Classical and neoclassical traditions respectively. The chief shortcoming of these models, Dutt argues, is that aggregate demand is significant only in the short run: it plays no role in the determination of long-run growth in what therefore remain quintessentially supply-determined growth models. Dutt then draws attention to the stringency of the assumptions necessary to produce these results and shows how, by relaxing these assumptions, it is possible to develop models that involve a richer and more satisfactory reconciliation of the roles played by aggregate demand and aggregate supply in the determination of long-run growth.

3.3 Economic growth and technical change

Although technical change is a theme that recurs throughout this Handbook, Part III of the volume features a chapter that is devoted exclusively to the development and application of a particular theory of technical change – specifically, the Classical theory of induced, factor biased technical change. Gérard Duménil and Dominique Lévy build a dynamical model of this process, central to which is the choice of technique by firms, based on the criterion of comparative profitability. In each period, firms select from among available techniques in an environment of random technical innovation. Despite its apparent simplicity, the authors show that their model can be used to explain trends in technology and the distribution of income in the US since the mid-nineteenth century, and many of the "laws of motion" attributed to capitalism by Marx. Especially important in this latter regard is the secular behaviour of the rate of profit, which Duménil and Lévy associate with the conditions of innovation and, in particular, the *difficulty* of innovating (as represented by an innovation set that provides too few opportunities for profitable changes in technique). Finally, the authors reflect on the Marxian pedigree of their model, its relationship to evolutionary theorizing in economics, and the differences between their model and neoclassical analysis based on continuous aggregate production functions.

3.4 Money, finance and growth

As intimated earlier, money and finance have traditionally been regarded as "missing pieces" in the analysis of long-run growth – even in models associated with the Keynesian tradition, in which the intrinsically monetary nature of the economy is a central tenet. The two chapters in Part IV of the volume go some way towards rectifying this error of omission. Eckhard Hein and Till van Treeck begin their chapter with a survey of the effects of "financialization" in post-Keynesian models of growth and distribution. Financialization is a notoriously imprecise concept (see, for example, Epstein, 2005, p. 3, for a broad definition), but the authors circumvent this problem by focusing on three specific channels through which financial processes can affect the economy: the objectives of and constraints faced by firms; the accumulation of financial assets and liabilities by households; and the distribution of income. The principal question addressed by the chapter is: are the effects of financialization expansionary in the short run and/ or long run? Hein and van Treeck show that the answer to this question is ambiguous. Depending on the precise form and relative strength of the three channels identified above, financialization may have either expansionary or contractionary effects on the economy. However, the authors caution that even when financialization has expansionary effects, the resulting growth path may be associated with the gradual build-up of, for example, stock-flow imbalances. In other words, the economy may grow rapidly but also become more financially fragile, which raises questions about the *sustainability* of a financialized accumulation process.

In the following chapter, Tom Palley examines the effects of private sector debt accumulation on growth, thus focusing on a particular aspect of the broader process of financialization discussed by Hein and van Treeck. Once again, Palley's particular concern is with the question as to whether or not the dynamics of private sector debt accumulation are likely to raise the rate of growth. This concern becomes pressing once it is recognized that, from the perspective of demand-led growth theory, debt accumulation is a "double-edged sword". On one hand, in an endogenous money environment where some forms of lending create money, debt accumulation relaxes the constraint on aggregate expenditures (and hence economic expansion) that would otherwise be imposed by current income and previously accumulated wealth. This assists demand formation and boosts growth. On the other hand, once accumulated, debt must be serviced. The resulting transfer payments to creditors can diminish growth, by raising the value of the average propensity to save. However, Palley shows that this latter result is most likely in the event that debtors are households: debt service payments by corporations can, in principle, *increase* aggregate spending and growth. The overall conclusion of the chapter is, therefore, that private sector debt accumulation has theoretically ambiguous effects on long-run growth – a conclusion that, as the preceding chapter illustrates, is very much of a piece with those reached by the financialization literature as a whole.

3.5   *Growth and distribution*
As previously discussed, the interplay of distribution and growth is an issue of long-standing concern in alternative theories of economic growth. Part V, the penultimate section of the Handbook, revisits the relationship between growth and distribution, its four chapters drawing attention to new avenues of research associated with this well established theme.

The first two chapters in this section are both concerned with the potential benefits of egalitarian labour market policies in a growing economy, as analysed from the perspective of Keynesian and Classical growth theories, respectively. The point of departure in Chapter 15, by Ro Naastepad and Servaas Storm, is the conventional wisdom that there exists a trade-off between efficiency and equality – or, more precisely, between rapid growth and low unemployment on one hand, and egalitarian labour market policies that enhance employment security and the rate of growth of wages on the other. The authors contend that the models under-girding this conventional wisdom are mis-specified, in that they neglect the Kaleckian influence of the wage share on the rate of growth, the Kaldorian influence of growth on technical progress, and the Marxian influence of the wage share on technical progress. Naastepad and Storm construct a growth model consistent with each of these principles, and use it to investigate the hypothesis that real wage restraint and/or labour market "flexibility" will unambiguously improve growth and employment performance. The authors reject this hypothesis, showing that even when wage restraint and labour market "flexibility" produce "conventional" results (faster employment growth and falling unemployment), these seemingly benefi-cial labour market outcomes may result from regressive growth outcomes (specifically, slower productivity growth). They conclude that egalitarian or "high road" growth paths associated with both rapid growth and secure, well-paid employment are both desirable and economically feasible.

The premise of the chapter by Peter Flaschel and Alfred Greiner is that any form of capitalism that is made self-regulating (and therefore sustainable in the long run) by periodic bouts of mass unemployment (as, for example, in Goodwin, 1967) is socially unacceptable. The authors posit that in a democratic society, the Marxian reserve army mechanism must be replaced by an alternative mechanism that reconciles full employ-ment with the reproduction of capitalist relations of production in the long run. Indeed, Flaschel and Greiner show that a Goodwin-type model augmented by "environmental feedbacks" (in which the availability of natural resources positively influences the value of the capital–output ratio, while high (low) values of the latter degrade (replenish) the environment) generates unstable growth cycles, making the need to transcend Goodwin-type dynamics all the more pressing. To this end, the authors construct a model of flexicurity capitalism, in which labour is hired and fired at will in the private sector, but in which workers are always guaranteed a job in a second (state-backed) labour market. They demonstrate that such a system is capable of generating steady growth outcomes consistent with protection of the environment. In this way, and similar to the previous chapter, Flaschel and Greiner show that it is possible to create a variant of capitalism that is both sustainable in the long run *and* provides income security for the whole of society.

In the penultimate chapter of this section of the Handbook, Gilberto Lima argues that examining the impact of profit sharing schemes on distribution and growth represents a natural extension of the traditional concern with distribution and growth in alternative theories of economic growth. Lima modifies a standard Kaleckian model of growth so that workers receive compensation in the form of both wages and a share of total profits. Several different specifications of the investment and savings functions are considered in order to ensure that any general conclusions drawn from the analysis are robust with respect to the most obvious plausible changes in household and firm behaviour. Lima focuses attention on the comparative static effects of income redistribution (resulting from *either* a change in the real wage *or* a change in workers' share of total profits) on capacity utilization, growth and the various (class-specific and aggregate) rates of profit to which his model gives rise. He finds that these are sensitive to the different assumptions made about investment and saving behaviour – but in the process, he is able to identify in what precise circumstances the Kaleckian model corroborates Weitzman's (1983, 1984, 1985) neoclassical arguments regarding the beneficial macroeconomic effects of profit sharing schemes.

In Chapter 18, Stephanie Seguino and Mark Setterfield examine the impact of reduced gender wage inequality on long-run growth in developing economies. Using a balance-of-payments-constrained growth model, the authors identify a variety of possible effects of gender wage inequality on growth. They note, however, that if women work in predominantly cost-sensitive, export-oriented industries, then increasing the growth of women's wages in the pursuit of reduced gender inequality is likely to reduce the equilibrium rate of growth. Seguino and Setterfield then go on to show that even if increasing gender wage equality *does* reduce growth, lower growth can be an unequivocally good thing – even in economies whose low standards of living make rapid growth desirable. This result turns on the need, discussed earlier, to reconcile the actual rate of growth with the potential rate of growth if steady growth is to be sustainable in the long run. The authors identify two key labour market mechanisms that, if brought about by judicious policy intervention, would mean that growth in excess of the natural rate automatically reduces gender wage inequality and hence lowers the actual rate of growth towards the potential rate of growth. In this way, it is shown that mechanisms designed to reduce gender wage inequality can contribute to a "long-run soft landing", by reconciling the actual and potential rates of growth and thereby increasing the sustainability of the growth process.

3.6 International and regional dimensions of growth

Each of the three chapters in Part VI, the final section of the book, addresses international and/or regional dimensions of the growth process. Robert Blecker and Arslan Razmi begin their chapter with an empirical observation: despite the success of export-led growth strategies in the East Asian "tiger" economies (and, more recently, in India and China), the majority of developing countries that have sought to raise their rates of growth by specializing in exports of manufactures have not met with great success. One hypothesis that purports to explain this observation rests on the notion of a "fallacy of composition" (FOC) in export-led growth: developing economies cannot simultaneously prosper by exporting the same manufactures to the same developed-economy markets. Blecker and Razmi subject this hypothesis and its policy implications to closer examination. The authors identify and test three distinct FOC hypotheses: the idea that exports from one developing country directly displace or "crowd out" exports from other countries; the idea that price competition among export-oriented, developing countries erodes the gains that might otherwise accrue to those countries individually; and the idea that real exchange devaluation relative to the currencies of its export-market competitors will boost the growth rate of a developing economy. They find empirical evidence for all three of these hypotheses. Blecker and Razmi conclude that since industrialized countries seem not to have grown fast enough to facilitate successful export-led growth by all developing economies, development policy must place more emphasis on internal markets and domestic demand. They note that this affords opportunities as well as challenges – including the possibility that wages come to be seen more as a source of demand

and hence "homespun" growth, and less as simply a cost of production that must be minimized in the pursuit of export markets.

Chapter 20, by Juan Carlos Moreno Brid and Esteban Pérez Caldentey, analyses the relationship between trade and growth from a Latin American perspective. The authors argue that popular understanding of the nature of the trade–growth relationship in Latin America has changed significantly over the past 60 years. Five distinct stages in the evolution of this popular understanding are identified, which have taken Latin America from an initial rejection of free trade and an emphasis on state-led development as the key to sustained growth, through an "orthodox" phase during which free trade and free markets were emphasized as essential drivers of growth, to a contemporary position of scepticism regarding the importance of trade liberalization for growth. In the process of discussing the different approaches to trade and growth that have, at different times, dominated Latin America since the 1940s, the authors pay particular attention to economic rhetoric and the efforts that each approach has made to present itself as the "correct" view, both theoretically and in terms of Latin American reality. At the same time – and echoing the general observation made by Blecker and Razmi in Chapter 19 – Moreno Brid and Pérez Caldentey draw attention to the fact that during the period they study, no robust relationship between trade and growth is discernable in Latin America. They suggest that overcoming this state of affairs is one of the most important challenges confronting contemporary Latin American economies.

In the final chapter of the Handbook, Mark Roberts and Mark Setterfield critically assess the now burgeoning literature on the spatial application of endogenous growth theory. Following a brief discussion of various issues of measurement and definition, the authors draw attention to the variety of ways in which the principles of endogenous growth theory have been linked to urban and regional development. Next, they identify and assess two main strands in the empirical literature on endogenous regional growth: a predominantly North American strand associated with the "new economics of urban and regional growth" (see, for example, Glaeser et al., 1992); and a predominantly European strand that focuses on either regional economic convergence or estimation of the Verdoorn law. Finally, Roberts and Setterfield identify avenues for future research motivated by the observation that there is much that North American and European researchers can learn from one another. Foremost among these is the need for greater recognition that endogenous growth can be either "neoclassical" (i.e. supply-led) or "Keynesian" (demand-led) in character – a distinction that, at present, surfaces only in the branch of the European empirical literature that focuses on estimation of the Verdoorn law. The authors note that the differences between demand- and supply-led endogenous growth have important implications for what is understood to be the ultimate *source* of growth (and hence how regional development policy should be conducted), and for our understanding of why the sources of growth are geographically confined and why, as a result, the growth process has an inherently spatial dimension.

4   Conclusion

By way of conclusion, it only remains to be said that alternative theories of economic growth represent a vibrant and ongoing research effort to understand the macrodynamics of capitalist economies. Above all else, then, it is hoped that this Handbook will provide both a fillip to and a valuable springboard for further research that will continue the development of these theories, inspiring both existing researchers and those new to the field to build on the body of work to date that the volume represents.

Note

1. The theme also emerges in the chapter by Metcalfe and Foster (Chapter 3), although theirs is an evolutionary model of growth in which adjustments are an ongoing feature of the growth process, rather than a transitory property of movement towards a steady state.

References

Aghion, P. and P. Howitt (2009) *The Economics of Growth*, Cambridge, MA: MIT Press.

Barro, R.J. and X. Sala-i-Martin (1995) *Economic Growth*, New York: McGraw-Hill.

Clark, C. (1944) *The Conditions of Economic Progress*, London: Macmillan.

Cornwall, J. (1972) *Growth and Stability in a Mature Economy*, London: Martin Robertson.

Duménil, G. and D. Lévy (1999) "Being Keynesian in the short term and classical in the long term: the traverse to classical long-term equilibrium", *The Manchester School*, 67, 684–716.

Epstein, G.A. (ed.) (2005) *Financialization in the World Economy*, Cheltenham, UK and Northampton, MA, USA: Edward Elgar.

Foley, D and T. Michl (1999) *Growth and Distribution*, Cambridge, MA: Harvard University Press.

Glaeser, E.L., H.D. Kallal, J.A. Scheinkman and A. Shleifer (1992) "Growth in cities", *Journal of Political Economy*, 100, 1126–52.

Goodwin, R. (1967) "A growth cycle", in C.H. Feinstein (ed.) *Socialism, Capitalism and Economic Growth*, Cambridge: Cambridge University Press.

Harrod, R.F. (1939) "An essay in dynamic theory", *Economic Journal*, 49, 14–33.

Jones, C.I. (2002) *Introduction to Economic Growth*, 2nd edn, New York: W.W. Norton.

Kaldor, N. (1955–56) "Alternative theories of distribution", *Review of Economic Studies*, 23, 83–100.

Kaldor, N. (1961) "Capital accumulation and economic growth", in F.A. Lutz and D.C. Hague (eds) *The Theory of Capital*, London: Macmillan.

Kregel, J.A. (1985) "Hamlet without the Prince: Cambridge macroeconomics without money", *American Economic Review*, 75, 133–9.

Kuznets, S. (1971) *Economic Growth of Nations*, Cambridge, MA: Belknap Press, Harvard University.

León-Ledesma, M. and A.P. Thirlwall (2000) "Is the natural rate of growth exogenous", *Banca Nazionale Del Lavoro Quarterly Review*, 215, 433–45.

León-Ledesma, M. and A.P. Thirlwall (2002) "The endogeneity of the natural rate of growth", *Cambridge Journal of Economics*, 26, 441–59.

McCombie, J.S.L. and A.P. Thirlwall (1994) *Economic Growth and the Balance of Payments Constraint*, London: Macmillan.

McCombie, J.S.L., M. Pugno and B. Soro (eds) (2003) *Productivity Growth and Economic Performance: Essays on Verdoorn's Law*, London: Palgrave Macmillan.

Robinson, J. (1956) *The Accumulation of Capital*, London: Macmillan.

Sasaki, H. (2008) "Classical biased technical change approach and its relevance to reality", *International Review of Applied Economics*, 22, 77–91.

Setterfield, M. (2002) "Introduction: a dissenter's view of the development of growth theory and the importance of demand-led growth", in M. Setterfield (ed.) *The Economics of Demand-Led Growth: Challenging the Supply Side Vision of the Long Run*, Cheltenham, UK and Northampton, MA, USA: Edward Elgar (2002) and Madrid: Ediciones Akal, S.A. (2005).

Setterfield, M. (2003) "Supply *and* demand in the theory of long-run growth: introduction to a symposium on demand-led growth", *Review of Political Economy*, 15, 23–32, reprinted in *Circus: Revista Argentina de Economia*, 1, 1, 38–50 (2007).

Solow, R. (1956) "A contribution to the theory of economic growth", *Quarterly Journal of Economics*, 70, 65–94.

Weitzman, M.L. (1983) "Some alternative implications of alternative compensation systems", *Economic Journal*, 93, 763–83.

Weitzman, M.L. (1984) *The Share Economy*, Cambridge, MA: Harvard University Press.

Weitzman, M.L. (1985) "The simple macroeconomics of profit sharing", *American Economic Review*, 95, 937–53.

PART I

ALTERNATIVE THEORIES OF ECONOMIC GROWTH: AN OVERVIEW

1 The structuralist growth model
Bill Gibson[1]

1 Introduction

The structuralist growth model (SGM) has its roots in the *General Theory* of Keynes (1936), Kalecki (1971) and efforts by Robinson (1956), Harrod (1937), Domar (1946), Pasinetti (1962) and others to extend the Keynesian principle of effective demand to the long run. The central concept of growth models in this tradition is the *dual* role played by investment, both as a component of aggregate demand and as a flow that augments the stock of capital. The basic structuralist model has been extended to cover a wide variety of topics, including foreign exchange constraints, human capital (Dutt, 2008; Gibson, 2005), the informal sector and macroeconomic policy analysis (Lima and Setterfield, 2008). The model has served as a foundation for large-scale computable general equilibrium models (Taylor, 1990; Gibson and van Seventer, 2000).

This chapter reviews the logic of the basic SGM and some of its variants and compares and contrasts the SGM with the standard growth models of Solow (1956) and developments thereafter (Barro and Sala-i-Martin, 2004). Both the structuralist and standard growth models are solved within a common mathematical framework and it is seen that each relies on an exogenously given rate of growth of a key variable. In the case of the standard model it is the labor force, and for the structuralists it is the growth of effective demand. In both cases these variables are taken as given for good reason: they are notoriously difficult to model accurately. It is seen that when structuralists attempt to endogenize effective demand in a meaningful way, thorny problems arise and structuralists increasingly rely on models of agency rather than structure.

The chapter is organized as follows. After some general observations on the nature of the SGM and its standard counterpart in the second section, the third discusses the basic mathematical framework of the two models and attention is drawn to the effort to endogenize investment growth via dependence on capacity utilization. The fourth section introduces the functional distribution of income and shows how it can solve the problems of instability generated by the attempt to endogenize investment. A concluding section offers some final thoughts on the project of comparing the two models.

2 Perspectives on the SGM

As the Keynesian model has fallen out of fashion in the profession as a whole, so too has interest in SGMs, per se, outside of a small community of authors. But this is not to say that the questions addressed by the structuralists are unimportant or passé. Modern endogenous growth models, for example, are highly structural in nature, if structure is defined as a shared context in which individual decisions about production and consumption are made (Aghion and Howitt, 1998; Zamparelli, 2008).

In challenging the orthodoxy of the time, early structuralists confronted the profession with a range of unanswered questions, from why there is still mass unemployment in many countries of the world to how financial crises emerge and propagate (Gibson, 2003a). Early structuralists proposed the antithesis to the accepted wisdom of the perfectly competitive general equilibrium model and the welfare propositions that logically flowed from it. It is not an exaggeration to say that much of the standard literature today that focuses on innovation and spillovers, strategic interaction, asymmetric information and the like, is a synthesis of the naive competitive model and its critique offered by Marxist, post-Keynesian and other heterodox challenges, including structuralists (Gibson, 2003b). To the extent that the early structuralists had a contribution to make, it was to identify contours of empirical reality that had been omitted in the rush to coherent reasoning about how an economy functions.

This is not to say that structuralists necessarily were or *are* content with the way that standard economic theory has appropriated their insights. The orthodoxy perhaps errs in its overemphasis of agency in the same way the early structuralist work seemed to deny it. But in venturing into the area of growth, structuralists risked a serious confrontation with their own view of how models were properly constructed. It is one thing to say that the level of effective demand is *given* in the short run, determined by a multiplier process on investment, which in turn depends on "animal spirits." But ultimately structure is nothing more than accumulated or fossilized agency. Taking animal spirits as a long-run explanation is therefore tantamount to saying that structure itself cannot be resolved theoretically. Some structuralists do seem to be comfortable with this implication, but this is hardly a satisfying position, and possibly the denouement of the structuralist approach. Recent efforts to incorporate hysteresis and remanence into structuralist models are necessarily drawn to more sophisticated models of microeconomic agent behavior. Good models of accumulation must have good models of agency at their core.

For the SGM, the process begins with the very definition of the independent investment function. Structuralists generally hold that investment should be modeled as co-dependent on a wholly exogenous animal spirits term and some endogenous motivational variable, usually capacity utilization or the rate (or share) of profit. The problem is that capacity utilization introduces dynamic instability into the model, as shall be seen in detail below, and some other economic process must be introduced to counteract the destabilizing force. Moreover, there is no guarantee that the rate of capacity utilization will converge to one (or any other specific number) in the long run. Whether from the labor market, the financial environment, the trade regime, fiscal and monetary policy or simply the mechanics of monopoly and competition, some force must come into play in order to arrest the tendency of the economy to self-destruct, increasing at an increasing rate or the opposite, until the structure disintegrates.

This implies that structuralists must think hard about factors *other* than structure when it comes to growth models. In the short run, agency is constrained by structure, but in the long run, agency must determine structure, simply because there is nothing else. As we shall see, there is a tendency to deny this basic fact among structuralist writers and it can lead to results that are wildly at variance with the data on how actual economies accumulate capital. Few structuralist models, for example, deal effectively with technical progress and diffusion and most deal with a representative firm and two social classes, eliminating the possibility of *emergent properties* from the interaction of agents at the micro level.[2]

3 Dynamic models

Lavoie (1992) notes that the key components in post-Keynesian and structuralist models are the roles of effective demand and time. The role of effective demand certainly distinguishes the SGM, but all dynamic models must treat time carefully. Indeed, the central concept of any dynamic economic model is the *stock-flow* relationship. Economic models built on a mathematical chassis break up the flow of time into discrete units so that it is possible to talk about time "within the period" versus "between periods." Within periods variables *jump* into equilibrium, while variables that describe the *state* of the environment change between periods. Thus, models are thought to have enough time to get into a temporary equilibrium within a period. This implies that markets clear, by way of prices, quantities or some combination of the two, and that savings are equal to investment at the aggregate level. But within the period, the economy does not arrive at a fully adjusted equilibrium, since the forces that drive the state variables have not had time to do their work. Expectations of future events may influence behavior but there is no time for agents to determine if their expectations are indeed correct. While it is analytically simpler to think in terms of discrete time models, it is mathematically simpler to solve continuous time models. The latter come about as we shrink the discrete units of time and periods get too short to allow much to happen that is not contemporaneous. Adjustment between periods occurs at the same pace as adjustment within the period. While analytical models are usually, but not always, solved in continuous time, computer simulation of applied models must take place in discrete time.

Much of the discussion of macroeconomic models is about how the economy gets into short-run equilibrium. The "closure debate" of the last century focused on whether savings drive investment or vice versa. In the standard model of dynamic economics, capacity utilization is always equal to one and so there is no role for effective demand. Factor availability determines output through a sequence of adjustment in goods and factor prices. In the structuralist view, price is a state variable and *quantity* adjustments, within the period, bring the economy to a temporary equilibrium. The principal role of the price variable is to determine the distribution of income. It is roughly correct to say, then, that in the standard model, the jump variables are prices, while in the structuralist model it is quantities. In the former model, factor quantities adjust between periods, while in the latter, prices, and thus income distribution, adjust.

Figure 1.1 is a schematic of a generic growth model in which output and investment growth are linked. Factors of production are combined to produce output, Q. Some fraction, α, of the output is accumulated as capital, which increases the quantity of capital by ΔK, after accounting for depreciation. This process takes some time, during which the other factor of production, labor, also expands by ΔL.

The standard model adheres to this schematic very closely. Once the factor inputs are known, the outputs are determined by way of a production function. Flexible prices ensure that all that can be produced from the factors of production is used for either consumption or investment. The fraction of output reinvested is not determined endogenously, but taken as a given parameter. This is also true of the growth rate of the labor force, n, as well as the underlying technology.

The SGM is, in many ways, more complex. As noted, there is an independent investment function that is not tied directly to output through a savings propensity. The links between the factors of production and output in Figure 1.1 can be broken in the transient

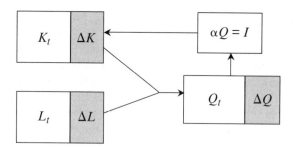

Figure 1.1   Accumulation of capital

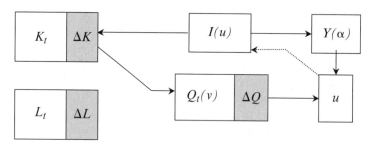

Figure 1.2   Structure of the investment constrained structuralist model

state. The arrows in the diagram are still present, but now represent constraints that may or may not have slack. If the capital constraint does not bind, then there is excess capacity and if there is slack in the labor constraint, there is unemployment. Either one or both can be present in structuralist models.

When neither of the constraints binds, the SGM takes on the configuration shown in Figure 1.2. Investment is at the center of the model as it generates both demand and the change in the capital stock. The latter determines the capacity, Q, by way of a fixed capital-output ratio, v.[3] Since capacity utilization, u, is the ratio of aggregate demand to capacity, investment directly or indirectly determines *all* the variables of the model.

Depending on the relative strength of investment to create demand or capacity, u rises or falls in the transient state. The feedback loop from u that affects investment growth is shown by the dotted line in Figure 1.2. When capacity utilization is high, investment accelerates to generate more capacity. But since the same investment also creates proportionately more demand, an explosive cycle can easily result. The solution, adopted by most structuralists, is to weaken the effect of capacity utilization on investment, in order to enhance the stability of the system. This sequence may well conflict with actual data: Chapter 5 by Skott in this volume points out a savings shock in the canonical Kaleckian model produces very large changes in utilization, but negative changes in utilization do not seem to be correlated with big savings shocks in US data. The take-away point from Figures 1.1 and 1.2 is that investment is the independent variable of the SGM, whereas it is derivative of factor growth in the standard model. Investment in the SGM may depend on u recursively, but it certainly cannot be defined as a homogeneous function of capacity utilization. Something more must be given, usually referred to as "animal spirits." Most SGM investment functions rely on a (positive) constant to capture the

Table 1.1   A social accounting matrix

	Firms	Households	Investment	Total
Firms		C	I	Y
Households	V_A			Y_h
profits	π			Y_π
wages	λ			Y_λ
Savings		S		S
Total	Y	Y_h	I	

effect of animal spirits and then repress the effect of capacity utilization on investment in the calibration of the model.

3.1   Model calibration

For applied discrete models it is approximately correct to think of each time period as described by a social accounting matrix (SAM). Dynamic linkages then join a sequence of SAMs. In the simplified SAM of Table 1.1, there is no government or foreign sector, only firms and households. GDP is then firm income, Y, the sum of consumption and investment. Household income, Y_h, is value added, V_A, the sum of wages and profits, and total savings, S, is equal to total investment I.

The SAM provides a *boundary condition*, some point in the time trajectory through which the model must pass. Typically these are the initial conditions for the dynamic model. In principle, the SAM could describe any point along the trajectory, even a long-run steady state. It is impossible to tell if the economy of the SAM of Table 1.1 is growing without knowing the composition of investment. The latter is decomposed into *replacement* and *net* investment, I_n, defined as

$$I_n = I - \delta K \tag{1}$$

where replacement investment is δK. Here δ is the fraction of the capital stock lost to wear and tear or obsolescence during the period. If I is less than replacement investment, the economy is contracting; if I is equal to replacement investment, it is in the *stationary state*. In the latter case, investment just balances the charge for depreciation, δK, and so *net* investment is zero. If there is net investment, the economy of the SAM is expanding.

The SAM is constructed for time t and the capital stock at the beginning of the period is K_t. The capital stock for the next period is given by the difference equation

$$K_{t+1} = K_t(1 - \delta) + I_t \tag{2}$$

If the time-path of investment is known, this is a simple dynamical system in one variable, K. Define equilibrium in the path as the time period t in which the change in the capital stock is zero. This will occur when

$$\delta K_t = I_t \tag{3}$$

This is the mathematical definition of the stationary state. To define *steady-state growth*, rewrite equation (2) as

$$\hat{K} = \frac{I_t}{K_t} - \delta \tag{4}$$

where the "hat" notation refers to growth rates.[4]

Now it is evident from equation (4) that if I_t/K_t were constant, so too would $\hat{K}$ be constant. Thus steady-state growth implies that

$$\hat{I} = \hat{K} \tag{5}$$

that is, the rate of growth of investment must equal that of the capital stock.[5] Note, however, that equation (5) does *not* define any particular rate of growth for these two magnitudes. That depends on the *level* of I/K at which the growth rates of the numerator and denominator come into equilibrium. This critical ratio can be re-expressed as

$$\frac{I}{K} = \frac{I}{Q}\frac{Q}{K} = \frac{\alpha}{v} \tag{6}$$

where Q is output, α is the share of investment in output and v is the capital–output ratio. If v were known and it could be assumed that the economy were fully utilizing its capital stock, the steady-state growth rate could be determined by reading α directly from the SAM.[6]

Now let the growth rate of investment, $\hat{I}$, be known and denote it as γ. It is then possible to derive a continuous approximation to the time path of the economy that satisfies equation (4). Rewriting that equation

$$\frac{dK}{dt} + \delta K = I_0 e^{\gamma t}. \tag{7}$$

To solve this differential equation, an integrating factor of $e^{\int \delta dt}$ is introduced. Multiplying both sides

$$\frac{dK}{dt}e^{\int \delta dt} + \delta K e^{\int \delta dt} = I_0 e^{\gamma t}e^{\int \delta dt}$$

where $e^{\int \delta dt} = e^{\delta t}$. So that

$$K\delta e^{\delta t} + e^{\delta t}\frac{dK}{dt} = I_0 e^{(\gamma + \delta)t}$$

the left-hand side of which can be seen as a derivative using the product rule

$$\frac{d}{dt}(Ke^{\delta t}) = I_0 e^{(\gamma + \delta)t}.$$

This can be integrated by separation of variables to yield

$$Ke^{\delta t} = \frac{I_0 e^{(\gamma + \delta)t}}{\gamma + \delta} + C$$

where C is an arbitrary constant. Simplifying

$$K(t) = \frac{I_0 e^{\gamma t}}{\gamma + \delta} + C e^{-\delta t}. \tag{8}$$

Since at $t = 0$, $K = K_0$, we can evaluate $C = K_0 - I_0/(\gamma + \delta)$. The constant is positive if the initial growth of investment is greater than the growth rate of the capital stock and vice versa.[7] Equation (8) has two terms. As t grows large, the second term on the right, the transient part of the solution, gets smaller and eventually goes to zero. Thereafter, the solution consists of only the steady-state part, the first term on the right, with the growth rate of the capital stock equal to the growth rate of investment, γ. The ratio of investment to capital stock is constant at $\gamma + \delta$. The fixed capital–output ratio ensures that output and the capital stock are growing at the same rate and thus the share of output devoted to accumulation remains constant as well.

The solution to this differential equation is general and it will be seen that the standard and structuralist models are special cases of it. If the rate of growth of investment is the same in the two models, the paths for the capital stock followed will be identical, as defined by equation (8). The structuralist and standard models differ in how the rate of investment is determined, but once established, the capital stock and output must follow the same path.

Moreover, so long as both the standard and structuralist economies pass through the same SAM and the rate of depreciation is the same, the steady-state path of *output* will also be the same. To see this, note that by definition, the rates of growth of investment and the capital stock are the same in the steady-state and thus I/K must be the same as the models pass through the SAM. With the same investment, as read from the SAM, the capital–output ratios must then be identical.[8]

But will v and α remain constant in each model? The answer is yes in both cases, so long as there are constant returns to scale. In the structuralist model, the capital–output ratio is fixed by assumption, but it is also true that in the standard model, the capital–output ratio remains constant since capital and labor must both be growing at the same rate. To see that, consider Figure 1.3. Let us say that the SAM above is for period 0. At the beginning of that

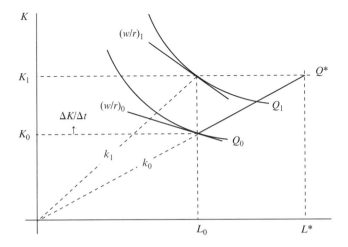

Figure 1.3   Adjustment process

period, there was available capital at level K_0 and labor at L_0. These factors combined to produce real output on isoquant Q_0. During the period, the SAM shows that investment at rate I took place. With a given rate of depreciation, say that the capital stock increased from K_0 to K_1. If labor does not grow, output rises only to Q_1. The capital–labor ratio increases from k_0 to k_1. Because there is more capital per unit of labor, *diminishing returns* to capital sets in and output cannot grow in proportion to the capital stock. The capital–output ratio must then rise to something above the base level v. Only if labor grows in proportion to the capital stock, from L_0 to L^* will diminishing returns be avoided. Assuming constant returns to scale, output will grow at the same rate as the factors of production. The steady-state capital–output ratio remains constant for the standard model as well.

The distribution of factor income also remains fixed in both models. In the structuralist model, distribution is given and therefore independent of the rates of growth of capital and labor. For the standard model, Figure 1.3 shows that when labor is constant at L_0, the wage–rental ratio rises from $(w/r)_0$ to $(w/r)_1$. But when labor expands proportionately, there is no change in the distribution of income between wages and profits. Factor demand grows at the same rate as factor supply, so the market-clearing factor prices remain fixed.

In steady-state equilibrium, there is evidently little to distinguish the two models. The essential difference must then lie in how investment behaves as the models approach the steady state.

3.2   Investment growth

It could be argued that taking the rate of growth of investment as the independent variable of the system begs one of the central questions of economic analysis, viz. how is γ determined. Keynes famously held that since investment undertaken by individual agents depends on irresolvable uncertainty about the future, aggregate investment *must* be taken as the independent variable of the macroeconomic system. One might object that even with "animal spirits" in control of the path of investment, current period output must, at a minimum, impose an upper bound on current investment. But since current output depends on the Keynesian multiplier, the system would seem to support *any* rate of growth of investment. If output did constrain the structuralist model, the difference would shrink even outside the steady state, since the fraction of output devoted to accumulation is not explained within the standard model. But output does not constrain investment in the SGM for two fundamental reasons: *first*, since the model is "demand driven" any spare output, in excess of what is needed for consumption and accumulation, would not have been produced in the first place. And, of course, output that was never produced cannot be saved. Thus, the SGM provides a highly subjective account of the accumulation process, dependent for the most part on how agents perceive the future in regard to profitability. Investment growth is in no way "structural" and requires deep thinking, not only about agency, but about how the agents interact. Keynes's arresting analogy of a "beauty contest," in which investors seek shares in firms only because they believe others will find them attractive, is the key. Clearly, agency rather than structure rules here, but not the atomistic agency of the standard approach. *Second*, output cannot determine investment because the subjective nature of the investment decision would not allow it. As just noted, perceptions of profitability are key to the structuralist account of investment, and the additional capacity that would have been generated by spare output would surely *reduce* the inducement to invest, which itself would prevent any spare output from arising in the first place. Since structuralists do not attempt to model the "beauty contest" in any serious way, it follows that for the SGM, investment must remain the independent variable of the system.[9]

Paradoxically, the standard model relies even more on structure to close the loop. There, investment growth depends on output, which in turn is limited by the growth of the factors of production. The model then depends on adjustments in the functional distribution of income to ensure that any spare capacity be fully utilized. Investment growth is endogenized, but the model still depends, in a fundamental way, on a variable given outside the system, the rate of growth of employment.

The standard model can be solved for the time path of the capital stock and we now do so in a way that will be easily compared to that of the SGM above. With the investment to output ratio given, it is a simple matter to rewrite equation (4) in continuous time as

$$\frac{dK}{dt} + \delta K = \frac{\alpha}{v(K)} K \tag{9}$$

where v is expressed as a function of the capital stock to allow for out-of-equilibrium dynamics, as depicted in Figure 1.3.

Note that the path of $v(K)$ depends crucially on what happens to labor and how labor is substituted for capital along the path. This means that we must have some functional form to describe the curvature of the isoquants in Figure 1.3. Take, for example, the standard Cobb-Douglas production function. There the capital–output ratio is given by

$$v = \left(\frac{K}{L}\right)^{(1-\beta)} \tag{10}$$

where β is the elasticity of output with respect to the capital stock, that is, the exponent on the capital stock in the Cobb-Douglas equation or share of capital in total output. Assume that we know the time path of L as $L_0 e^{nt}$, with n as the rate of growth of labor. Substituting equation (10) into equation (9), we have

$$\frac{dK'}{dt} + \delta' K' = L_0' e^{n't} \tag{11}$$

where $K' = K^{1-\beta}$, $\delta' = (1-\beta)\delta$, $L_0' = \alpha(1-\beta)L_0^{1-\beta}$ and $n' = n(1-\beta)$. The transformation is made in order to emphasize the basic similarity with equation (7). Note that the variables on the left-hand side are only slightly transformed versions of the originals, while on the right *labor* has taken the place of investment.[10]

Since equations (11) and (7) have the same form, it follows that the solution will be the same as well. Therefore, we can immediately write

$$K'(t) = \frac{L_0' e^{n't}}{n' + \delta'} + C' e^{-\delta't} \tag{12}$$

where C' is a constant similar to C in equation (8). Since the rates of growth $\hat{K}'$ and $\hat{K}$ are the same by virtue of the constancy of β, we conclude that the constant C' is positive if the *adjusted* rate of growth of labor $(1-\beta)n$ is greater than the rate of growth of the capital stock and vice versa.

Despite their having different drivers, investment growth in the case of the SGM and

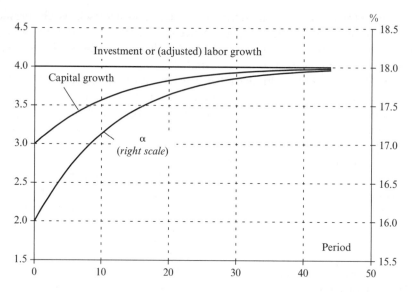

Figure 1.4   Adjustment to the steady state in the SGM and standard model

labor for the standard model, the models are strikingly similar. Both rely on the exogenous determination of crucial variables of the system, parameters that are taken as given
rather than modeled explicitly as an agent-based decision-making process.

3.3   Transition to the steady state

We have seen that the two models are equivalent in the steady state, but how do they
behave in the transient part of the solution? Figure 1.4 shows that in fact the two models
approach the steady state in equivalent ways, with both C and $C' > 0$. For the structuralist model, the horizontal line is the rate of growth of investment. That same line
represents the adjusted rate of growth of labor, $n(1-\beta)$ for the standard model. Again,
the similarity is evident; in both models, the capital stock adjusts to an exogenously
given rate of growth. As we have seen, the major difference is that the exogenous factor
in the case of the standard model, L, drives the growth rate of investment *through* the
production function. In the Cobb-Douglas production function the elasticity of output
with respect to labor growth is $1 - \beta$. Since investment and output grow at the same
rate, investment in the standard model must then grow at $(1 - \beta)n$. In Figure 1.4 these
are equal by construction; therefore, the time path of the capital stock must be the same
for both models. Figure 1.4 shows the time path of the capital stock. How does output
respond in each of the two models? In the standard model, output grows as a weighted
average of labor and capital stock growth, with the weights as the marginal products of
the two factors of production. We then have

$$\hat{Q} = Q_K \hat{K} + Q_L \hat{L}$$

where subscripts indicate partial derivatives. With $C' > 0$, labor growth is faster than
capital growth, so output growth is somewhere in between for the standard model along

the time path. In the SGM, however, the fixed capital–output ratio ensures that output growth is always exactly equal that of the capital stock. If the capital stock approaches investment growth from below, then output must be growing more slowly than γ and vice versa if from above. In Figure 1.4, then, the standard model must be growing *faster* than the SGM, and this turns out to be a fundamental difference between the two approaches.

It is easy to see how this difference arises. In the SGM, the rate of growth of the labor force must exceed γ, otherwise the labor constraint would eventually bind. Normally, surplus labor accumulates without having any effect on output whatsoever. The standard model, by contrast, economizes on the scarce resource, capital, and will progressively switch to a more labor-intensive growth path. With the same addition to capital stock, but more labor, its firms will produce more than SGM. With more output available to invest, the rate of growth of investment will accelerate. This transition will continue until the rate of growth of the capital stock is just equal to that of the labor force. If the two models pass through the same SAM on the way to the steady state, output per unit of capital will necessarily be higher after the transition in the standard model. Evidently, output lags behind in the SGM because it does not fully utilize available labor. We shall see below that the SGM will lag even further if it fails to fully utilize capital, that is, if capacity utilization is less than one.

3.4   Stability

With the growth rate of investment γ taken as given, the SGM converges nicely to a steady state, just as the standard model. In the standard model α is usually taken as fixed, as the savings rate. In the SGM, however, the ratio of investment to capacity output, Q, must be *rising* over time for $C > 0$ (and vice versa). Since $\alpha = I/Q$ and Q grows at the same rate as K because of the assumption of the fixed capital–output ratio, it must be the case that α rises to an asymptote, as seen in Figure 1.4.

This movement of α is crucial to the stability of the SGM. If α were constant, the inflow of investment into the capital stock would increase with the capital stock in exact proportion. Since depreciation is also a fixed percentage of the capital stock, the capital growth rate would be a *constant* $\alpha/v - \delta$. It is immediately obvious that there is no mechanism to bring this growth rate into equality with γ, unless by fluke. This is the famous "knife-edge problem" that goes back to Harrod (1937). In a capital constrained SGM, a fixed percentage of output cannot be plowed back as investment *unless the model is already in the steady state*.

This raises the question of why must γ be given. Could the level of investment be given instead? Clearly, if the level of investment were a given constant, then its growth rate would be zero. The economy would then be in a stationary state with capital stock growth equal to zero. But what if investment were given as, say, a fraction of capacity output? In that case, we would have the right-hand side of equation (6) constant, which would immediately imply $\hat{I} = \hat{K}$. The model is then *already in the steady state*. Is the system stable in the sense that if K departs from the growth path momentarily, growing either faster or slower than its steady-state value, will forces then emerge to return it to the steady state? The answer to this question is, unfortunately, no. If the capital stock were to rise, then so too would capacity. If investment stood in fixed proportion to capacity, it would also rise and $\hat{K}$ would increase. Now investment and the capital stock are again

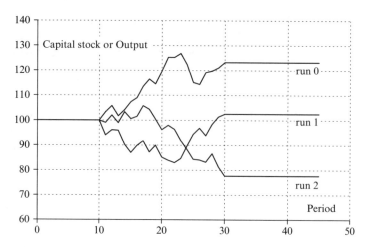

Figure 1.5   Instability in the capital-constrained SGM

growing at the same rate and the economy is in a steady state, but *different* from the one from which it momentarily departed. Apparently, for a meaningful transient part of the solution, the rate of growth of investment, not its level, must be given.

The instability is illustrated in the simulations of Figure 1.5. There the economy is in a stationary state for the first ten periods. Between periods ten and thirty, a random shock is introduced on α, altering the rate of growth of the capital stock. It is clear from the figure that the shock sends the economy on a random walk. In the thirty-first period, the shock is removed and the economy stabilizes again, but at significantly different levels of the capital stock. This is the permanent effect of changes in the parameters of the model that is much discussed in the literature (Skott, 2008).[11]

We conclude that the standard model achieves stability through flexibility in the capital–output ratio while the capital-constrained SGM does the same by way of a variable α. We have for the steady state

$$\frac{\alpha}{v} - \delta = \begin{cases} n' & \text{if standard, } \alpha \text{ constant, } v \text{ variable} \\ \gamma & \text{if capital constrained SGM, } v \text{ constant, } \alpha \text{ variable} \end{cases} \tag{13}$$

It could be argued that both models produce unrealistic results. In the standard model, capital intensity will decline until all those willing to work at the market wage rate are employed. This is, of course, seemingly inconsistent with the experience of developing countries, prior to the Lewis turning point. High unemployment rates can persist for decades, despite low wages and surplus labor. The structuralist model, on the other hand, does produce results consistent with high levels of unemployment. The problem is that with a fixed capital–labor ratio, employment must grow at the same rate as investment γ. With γ less than n, the unemployment rate goes to 100 percent. At the end of every period, more labor will have accumulated than the capital necessary to employ it.

3.5   Variable investment growth

So far it has been assumed that in the structuralist model, γ is constant. A constant γ is consistent with the Keynesian notion that investment is the independent variable of the system, but some SGMs allow γ to vary, at least within a narrow range. In this section, we show that this is only feasible to the extent that γ is bounded. If the rate of growth of investment is higher than that of the capital stock, γ must be bounded from above. If γ is less than $\hat{K}$, γ must be bounded from below.

The most common arguments in the γ function are capacity utilization, u, and some measure of income distribution, either the wage–rental ratio or the profit share. We address these sequentially beginning with capacity utilization. If there is no trend in u in the long run, it follows that $\hat{Y} - \hat{Q}$. Any variation in γ because of changes in u can then only occur on the transient path.[12] Before the steady state equation (6) shows that $\hat{u}$ can only be non-zero when γ differs from $\hat{K}$. When the former exceeds the latter, capacity utilization is rising, and vice versa.[13] Hence, a variable rate of investment growth along the adjustment path does not upset the comparability of the two models in the steady state undertaken above.

Outside the steady state, the γ function is almost always assumed to rise with u; the exception is when commodity, labor or financial costs rise as well, reducing the rate of profit and thus the incentive to invest, even though extra capital is needed. For the moment, assume

$$\gamma = \gamma(u) \text{ with } \gamma'(u) > 0$$

As utilization rises, employment also increases and with it savings of firms or by households for retirement or to educate their children. Rising demand provides an incentive for firms to expand investment, to add productive capacity or accumulate inventories. But the first effect on savings must be stronger than the second on investment. Were it not, an increase in investment would itself raise capacity utilization, which would, in turn, raise investment producing an explosive cycle. Capacity utilization would quickly exceed its unitary bound. That consumption does not grow in proportion to income is known as the standard Keynesian short-run stability condition and is usually assumed in SGMs (Taylor, 1983). Hence we have a continuous approximation

$$I = I_0 e^{\gamma(u)t}$$

where γ *must* be defined by a functional form that follows

$$\gamma = \begin{cases} \bar{\gamma} & \text{if } u = 1 \\ \gamma(u) & \text{if } u < 1 \end{cases} \tag{14}$$

where $\lim_{u \to 1} \gamma(u) = \bar{\gamma}$.

If γ depends on capacity utilization, then the investment growth line could shift up as shown in Figure 1.6. For the first ten periods, γ is 3 percent, but then increases to 4 percent. The figure shows a smooth transition as capital stock growth also rises to 4 percent. In the process, capacity utilization rises from 80 to 90 percent. As u approaches one, γ approaches its limiting value, $\bar{\gamma}$. Thus a variable γ is consistent with the basic SGM, so long as it has an upper bound as described in the conditions shown just above.

One way to ensure that the conditions above are indeed satisfied is to use the discrete logistic function

$$\gamma_{t+1} = \phi \gamma_t (1 - \gamma_t)$$

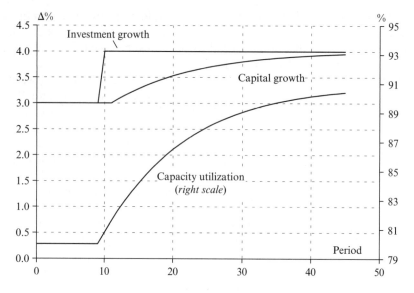

Figure 1.6   Growth of investment depends on capacity utilization

where φ is an adjustment parameter. When γ is small, the quadratic term is close to zero and γ approximates an exponential growth path. If $C > 0$, an increase in the growth rate of investment causes the growth rate of the capital stock to accelerate, but not proportionately, according to equation (4). With a constant α, actual output *does* increase proportionately and, thus, capacity utilization rises. This in turn causes γ to rise.[14] The logistic equation ensures that γ will not rise indefinitely. As γ approaches its maximum, $\bar{\gamma}$, growth in γ slows. Figure 1.7 shows a family of curves that could describe the adjustment path of γ. They start with different initial values, the lowest at $\gamma(0) = 0.01$.

The logistic equation can be calibrated to give $u = 1$ at the steady-state growth rate of investment as follows. Taking account of equation (6) with $u = 1$, the upper bound must be

$$\bar{\gamma} = \frac{\alpha}{v} - \delta.$$

And now convergence is simply a matter of calibrating the logistic function to this bound. The logistic difference equation has a fixed point at

$$\gamma_t = \phi \gamma_\tau (1 - \gamma_t).$$

If γ is taken as given at $\gamma = \bar{\gamma}$, we need only solve for φ to calibrate the model; we have

$$\phi = \frac{1}{1 - \bar{\gamma}}$$

So we need not specify a constant rate of growth of investment for a coherent SGM; all that is necessary is a steady-state rate of growth of investment and the capacity utiliza-

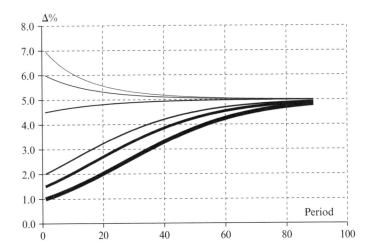

Figure 1.7   Logistic equation for γ

tion term generates no instability. Further if $\bar{\gamma}$ is set to equal the rate of growth of the labor force, n, the standard model and SGM converge to the same steady-state level of the capital stock and look very similar indeed. The SGM allows for less than full capacity utilization along the transient path yet converges to long-run equilibrium with the rate of growth of the capital stock equal to the growth of the labor force. This would eliminate the main objection to the SGM noted above, viz., that the rate of unemployment is 100 percent in the long run.[15]

3.6   Example
In this example, we calibrate an investment function that follows a logistic path such that $u = 1$ when the economy is growing at 5 percent. Figure 1.8 shows the trajectories for the growth rate of investment and capital stock, together with capacity utilization when γ grows according to the logistic function. The model passes through the base SAM, in Table 1.2, with an initial capacity utilization of 0.8, and depreciation rate, $\delta = 0.05$. The share of investment in output is calibrated from the SAM at $\alpha = 0.2$. The fixed point of the discrete logistic function is $\varphi = 1.0526$ so that investment growth converges to $\bar{\gamma} = 0.05$. In the figure, the γ function of the model follows the lowest of the family of curves in Figure 1.7, that is, with an initial value of $\gamma(0) = 0.01$. After 80 periods, there is still a gap between investment growth and the capital stock, but it narrows and capacity utilization converges toward one.

3.7   The investment constrained SGM
So far we have argued that a fully coherent SGM must take the rate of growth of investment as the independent variable and that there are a variety of ways in which variable capacity utilization can be built into the model. Since a time path for γ implies a time path for the share of investment in GDP, α, why not simply take α as given and let the rate of growth of investment and capital stock adjust? In the capital constrained SGM, we have seen that this deprives the model of a meaningful transition to the steady state. Is

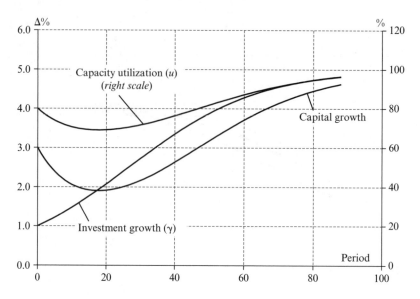

Figure 1.8   Adjustment with a logistic equation for γ

Table 1.2   A social accounting matrix

	Firms	Households	Investment	Total
Firms		400	100	500
Households	500			500
Savings		100		100
Total	500	500	100	

Source: Author's calculations.

the same true when the model is investment constrained, that is, when the rate of capacity utilization is variable?

To begin to address this question, rewrite equation (4) as

$$\hat{K} = \frac{I}{K} - \delta = \frac{\alpha u}{v} - \delta \qquad (15)$$

Once capacity utilization is less than full, no constraint binds. Is it then meaningless to talk about an upper bound on investment given by how much the economy produces? The usual account is that investment growth simply adjusts to subjectively determined perceptions of future profitability. Typically the investment function takes the form

$$I = (a + bu)K \qquad (16)$$

where *a* and *b* are given constants that (supposedly) capture "animal spirits" and the responsiveness of investment to capacity utilization. Substituting the definition of capacity utilization

$$I = [a + b(Y/Q)]K$$

but since $Y = I/\alpha$ and $Q = K/v$, we have

$$I = \frac{a}{1 - bv/\alpha}K \qquad (17)$$

Thus, if α is constant, it is immediately evident that $\hat{I} = \hat{K}$, the condition for steady growth. Again, the model seems to be stuck in the steady state from birth, at least as configured in equation (16). Any change in u or α will cause the model to move to a new equilibrium, which will again be a steady state, as illustrated in Figure 1.6 above. Introducing variable capacity utilization does not alter the character of the SGM, so long as α is constant.

So if α is indeed variable, how might it be determined? First, there are obvious bounds on α that must be respected; in particular capacity utilization must be *non-negative* with an upper bound of 1. Thus I/K must be in the range corresponding to $u = [0, 1]$

$$(a + b) \geq \frac{I}{K} \geq a$$

which implies that $1 \geq \alpha \geq (a + b)v$. The smaller the level of α the larger is I/K, so $(a + b)v$ puts an upper limit on $\hat{K}$. Since γ cannot exceed $\hat{K}$ in the steady state, full capacity utilization provides an upper limit on investment growth.

Stability is more problematic. In the SGM, output adjusts to investment according to the rule that if savings exceeds investment, output falls and when investment exceeds savings, output rises. Stability is ensured by the restriction that savings respond to an increase in capacity utilization more than investment. Savings are usually taken to be a function of output, so might the stability condition effectively put a bound on the γ function? This possibility is discussed by Dutt (1997). Consider a steady-state equilibrium in which capacity utilization is less than one. An instantaneous uptick in capacity will increase γ and cause $\hat{K}$ to accelerate. What forces are available to return the capacity utilization to its initial level? Nothing really, as we have seen, the higher γ will cause the capital stock to adjust to a higher I/K in a new steady-state equilibrium. The only available variable in the model that could restore the initial capacity utilization is α. Differentiating equation (17), with α variable

$$\hat{I} = \frac{-bv}{\alpha - bv}\hat{\alpha} + \hat{K}$$

where the denominator of the first term on the right is positive by the Keynesian stability condition. It now is obvious that α must increase so that the rate of growth of investment *falls*. The underlying economic reasoning for why this must occur is not usually spelled out, but the impact is clear: for stability, a rise in capacity utilization in the steady state must cause γ to *fall* even though this is inconsistent with the assumed motivation for investment, that is, that investment respond positively to higher capacity utilization. If investment rose faster than output, α would increase and the model would move to another equilibrium as discussed above.

We conclude that the standard stability condition does indeed effectively provide a bound for γ, but does so in a way that is no less arbitrary than exogenously imposing an upper bound on the γ function, as for example, does the logistic function studied above. Moreover, the standard stability condition similarly deprives the system of any meaningful adjustment process to the steady state, since it ensures that *any* equilibrium is a steady-state. Imposing a stabilizing path on α means that any deviations from the equilibrium level of capacity utilization will be restored. The short-term stability condition is at once a long-run stability condition, since the long run for the SGM is nothing more than a sequence of short runs. This certainly distinguishes the two models, since in the standard model, the transient part of the path can last for many periods, often in the 100–150 range. It must be concluded that the steady state plays a much bigger role in the overall character of the SGM relative to the standard model.

It also seems fair to say that capacity utilization in the SGM is *not* a fundamental determinant of investment since its range of variation is necessarily narrow. Changes in capacity utilization provide an extra burst of growth when there is an independent investment function. But unlike diminishing returns in the standard model, the independent investment function works the wrong way, causing instability in the adjustment process. The SGM is now clearly distinguished from the standard model in an important respect. The second main difference, its treatment of labor, is discussed in more detail in the following section.

4   The distribution of income

The functional distribution of income may provide the solution to the stability problem, reducing the incentive to invest as factor supplies become less abundant, raising costs and thereby reducing profit per unit of capacity. In the standard model, the treatment of the functional income distribution is straightforward. If the rate of growth of one factor exceeds that of the other, its relative return falls. Profit maximization ensures that more of the abundant factor will be employed in production. Diminishing returns guide the combination of factors to its correct level, with the marginal increment in costs equal to the marginal increase in the value of output for each factor. Income distribution thus plays a crucial role in the standard model, regulating the rate of growth of the capital stock so that it eventually comes to equal the growth rate of labor.

Normally investment in the standard model depends on output, but when capital accumulation is linked to profit rather than output as a whole, the standard model adjusts more rapidly to differences in the relative rates of factor growth. If labor is growing too fast, the marginal product of capital increases and with it the mass of profits from which investment flows (and vice versa if labor is growing too slowly). Rather than get in the way, income distribution assists the equilibrating process.

In the SGM, income distribution does not always move in a beneficial way. Say, for example, that labor growth outstrips that of capital. With wages determined outside the model, there is no natural mechanism by which capital accumulation can accelerate to accommodate more abundant labor. The fixed relationship between capital and output prevents stepped up utilization of labor. In the worst case, labor accumulates ad infinitum, as noted above, while capital accumulation proceeds unfazed.

In the standard model, factor shares are usually taken as given, either directly or through a calibrated elasticity of substitution. In the SGM, initial factor shares are calculated from the base SAM. The factor shares in the SAM also determine mark-up, τ. This results from the simple price equation in the SGM. This usually takes the form

$$p = (1 + \tau)wl$$

where p is the price level and l is unit labor demand. Thus, if the rate of profit, r, is total profit divided by the value of capital stock

$$r = \frac{\tau w l Y}{pK} = \beta \frac{u}{v}$$

where β is the share of capital

$$\beta = \frac{\tau}{1 + \tau}$$

so that fixing the mark-up determines the profit share and vice versa. Profitability depends on both the profit share *and* capacity utilization. The wage–rental ratio, $\omega = (w/p)/r$, for the SGM can then be expressed as

$$\omega = \frac{1 - \beta}{\beta} \frac{v}{lu}. \qquad (18)$$

As either the profit share or capacity utilization rises, the wage–rental ratio falls. A rise in u in turn implies that $\hat{I}$ must be greater than $\hat{K}$. Once at full capacity utilization, the wage–rental ratio is fixed and again the SGM closely resembles the standard model. In the latter model, with Cobb-Douglas technology, the wage–rental ratio depends on the fixed capital–labor ratio and the shares of income of the factors of production

$$\omega = \frac{(1 - \beta)}{\beta} k \qquad (19)$$

where $k = K/L$. But since v/l is also k, equations (18) and (19) give the same value for ω when $u = 1$.

Thus, with a constant β, the wage–rental ratio normally declines with u. But the profit share might also erode due to increased costs as utilization increases. If so, ω can increase as the model approaches the steady state, and even overwhelm the effect of rising capacity utilization. Rising costs would then reduce γ, enhancing the stability of the system. In that case, SGM would come to more closely resemble the standard model, with class conflict replacing diminishing returns to ensure the stability of the system.

Bhaduri and Marglin (1990) note that any increase in the real wage will depress the profit margin, that is, the mark-up, and thus the profit share. Aggregate demand will rise or fall depending on the impact of the falling β on investment. A lower profit share will weaken the incentive to invest, so that a higher wage rate increases consumption, but reduces investment. The balance of these forces determines the effect of an increase of the real wage on output. The derivative u_β is said to depend on deep structural features of the economy called, somewhat infelicitously[16]

$$u_\beta = \begin{cases} < 0 & \text{stagnationist or wage-led} \\ > 0 & \text{exhilarationist or profit-led.} \end{cases}$$

Since neither β nor u can have a trend, these structural features only matter in the short run. Moreover, exhilarationist configurations are stabilizing but stagnationist ones are not. To see this, consider an economy in the steady state with full capacity utilization. Now introduce a negative demand shock, so that $u < 1$. This lowers employment and output. If there is a strong investment response to the rising profit share, the economy will return to full capacity utilization. If the economy is stagnationist, the demand shock is more likely to be permanent and capacity utilization will remain below one on a new steady growth path.

The theory of how the profit share moves is not well defined in the structuralist framework. It is not, for example, tied to the capital–labor ratio as in the standard model. There might be a "target" ω, that corresponds to a "normal" profit share that occurs at full capacity utilization, but it is not clear how that target is determined or, in particular, why it would be respected.[17] It is sometimes argued that ω is given by some exogenous process, such as the "class struggle," or that the real wage is fixed by some biological minimum, as in the classical Marxian model. There, increases in the share of profits cannot be tolerated, since starvation would reduce the supply of workers, eventually causing the labor constraint to bind. Since the labor constraint does not bind in the structuralist model, it follows that β is exogenously bounded at some upper limit.

An early SGM that employs a variable profit share is due to Taylor (1983). In this model, labor is initially in excess supply, but then eventually becomes scarce, driving up the wage as capacity utilization nears one.[18] Investment growth then converges to its steady-state equality with capital stock growth. The key to the stability of this model is to make investment more sensitive to the profit share than to capacity utilization so that near full capacity utilization γ falls.

As in the previous section, investment is first defined as a level rather than by way of its growth rate γ

$$\frac{I}{K} = f(\beta) \text{ or } \gamma = \hat{f} + \hat{K} \tag{20}$$

where $\hat{f}$ must be equal to zero in equilibrium. Accumulation is set as a fraction of profit, which is in turn a fraction of income. Practically, this amounts to the same thing as setting α, since the fraction of profits devoted to accumulation is usually taken as a fixed and given constant. Thus, the multiplier depends *only* on the profit share β, which is distinguished from α as a share of total output.[19]

With the multiplier in hand and the constant labor coefficient, l, employment relative to full employment $\overline{L}$ can be defined as

$$L/\overline{L} = l\frac{I}{\beta I}$$

where the fully employed labor force is assumed to be growing at some constant rate n. Substituting equation 20 normalized by $\overline{L}$

$$\frac{L}{I} = l\frac{f(\beta)k}{\beta}$$

where $k = K/\overline{L}$. The crucial assumption is that as the employment fraction approaches one, labor's improved bargaining position causes the share of profits, β, to fall. Thus the equation of motion for β is

$$\dot{\beta} = \theta\left[1 - l\frac{f(\beta)k}{\beta}\right] \tag{21}$$

with $\theta > 0$ as the adjustment coefficient. Taylor notes that there must be a strong positive investment response for stability, and we shall see that this is indeed true. As β increases, $f(\beta)/\beta$ must increase, rather than fall, if employment is to rise. For employment to increase with a rise in profit share requires, then[20]

$$\frac{d[f(\beta)/\beta]}{d\beta} = \frac{\beta f'(\beta) - f(\beta)}{\beta^2} > 0$$

or

$$\varepsilon = \frac{\beta f'(\beta)}{f(\beta)} > 1$$

where ε is the elasticity of f with respect to the profit share.

Finally, we normalize equation (4) to the full employed labor force, $\overline{L}$, so that all variables are expressed on a per capita basis. This is often done in the standard model and makes for easy comparison. The SGM can now be expressed as a simultaneous system of differential equations[21]

$$\frac{\dot{k}}{k} = f(\beta) - \delta - n \tag{22}$$

$$\dot{\beta} = \theta\left[1 - l\frac{kf(\beta)}{\beta}\right] \tag{23}$$

where n is the growth rate of the labor force.[22]

The state variables of this system are the capital–labor ratio $k = K/\overline{L}$ and profit share β, while the jump variable is $I/K = f(\beta)$. Thus, at the beginning of each period, k and β are known from the previous period and generate new levels of investment and employment for the current period.

The long-run solution to the system of equations for the model is obtained by setting the right-hand side of equations (22) and (23) equal to zero

$$f(\beta) = \delta + n$$
$$k = \frac{\beta}{lf(\beta)} \tag{24}$$

where a functional form for f must be assumed in order to get an explicit solution. Figure 1.9 shows a calibrated example, with $f(\beta)$ as described in the example below. In the model with a constant β, the system would come to rest somewhere along the $\dot{k} = 0$ isocline in Figure 1.9. But with a variable β, if it turned out that there was less than full employment, the profit share would increase. This would in turn stimulate investment, which through the multiplier would raise income and, with a constant labor coefficient, employment. At the same time, investment raises the capital stock at some growth rate $\hat{K}$. If this latter rate exceeds n, the capital–labor ratio increases. The solution trajectory then departs the $\dot{k} = 0$ isocline to the northeast.

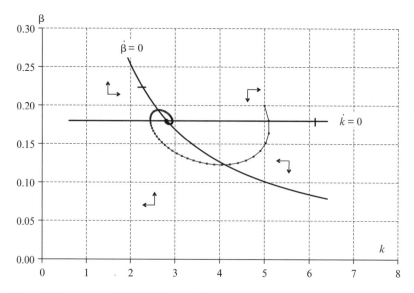

Figure 1.9   Adjustment in the SGM

Equilibrium occurs when the rate of growth of investment and capital are *both* equal to the exogenously given rate of growth of the labor force, *n*. At that point, the capital–labor ratio is constant and there is full employment of the labor force. As a result there is no tendency for income shares to change.

The Jacobian matrix of the right-hand side of the system of equations (22) and (23) is used to formally evaluate the local stability of the system around the steady state. Thus, the Jacobian is evaluated at full employment and full capacity utilization

$$
J = \begin{bmatrix} f(\beta) - \delta - n & f'(\beta) \\ -\theta\dfrac{lf(\beta)}{\beta} & -\theta l\dfrac{f(\beta)}{\beta^2}(\varepsilon - 1) \end{bmatrix}
$$

where the J_{11} term of the Jacobian is zero in the steady state. Local stability depends on two conditions, first that the trace of the Jacobian is negative; that is, $J_{11} + J_{22} < 0$. For this condition to hold, we must have $\varepsilon > 1$. The second condition is that the determinant $J_{11}J_{22} - J_{12}J_{21} = f'/k > 0$, which is automatically satisfied, so long as the economy is exhilarationist.

Figure 1.10 shows the time paths for the rates of growth of investment and capital stock implied by the adjustment process shown in Figure 1.9. The figure shows that the initial values of *k* and β are far from their steady-state values. While the trajectories exhibit significant variability initially, they eventually settle down and begin to come together by the fiftieth period. Employment and capacity utilization also converge as well, both to 100 percent.

There is a counterpart to this adjustment process in the standard model. Consider what happens there when the steady state is perturbed in Figure 1.3. The perturbation might take the form of the destruction of some part of the capital stock. The model then starts

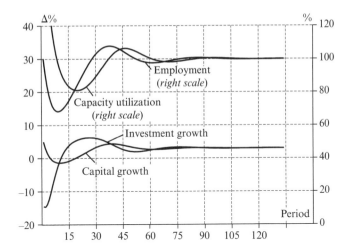

Figure 1.10   Adjustment in the structuralist model

at L_0, K_0 and during the following period, capital expands to K_1, because of the investment during the year. In the diagram, labor is held fixed and so capital obviously grows more rapidly than labor. The relative factor–price line must rotate in a clockwise fashion, increasing the wage–rental ratio. With a constant share of output devoted to capital accumulation, the rate of growth of capital declines until it again equals that of labor.

In the SGM example, the process is very closely related. All profit is invested, but profit itself is driven lower as wages rise with higher employment, and capital stock growth slows as a result. Figure 1.9 shows that the system follows a stable focus with both the profit share and capital–labor ratio first rising and then falling as the equilibrium is approached. What prevents monotonic adjustment to the new steady state? It is essentially that in the structuralist model, investment responds to profitability rather than output as a whole and is therefore more volatile. In Figure 1.3, investment drives the capital stock from K_0 to K_1, but the wage–rental rate increases so much that the next increment to the capital stock is less and may even fall. If labor growth is constant, employment fluctuates dramatically as shown in Figure 1.9. Instead of a smooth increase in the capital–labor ratio, k also increases rapidly and then falls back as the capital stock and labor growth rates come together. Of course the fall in β would not affect profitability so dramatically, were the labor coefficient, l, and capital–output ratios not constant.

It is probably fair to say that this version of the SGM meets the standard model more than half way, in that it allows for full employment in the long run but with less than full capacity utilization in the short run. We might therefore want to refer to the model as a hybrid structuralist–standard model since like the standard model, it must ultimately adjust to an externally given rate of growth of the labor force.

4.1   Example
Consider the SAM in Table 1.3 and the additional information in Table 1.4. How can an SGM be calibrated to this data that converges to full employment and capacity utilization? The first step is to specify a functional form for $f(\beta)$. There is very little

Table 1.3   A social accounting matrix

	Firms	Households	Invest	Total
Firms		400	100	500
Households				500
wages	400			
profits	100			
Savings		100		100
Total	500	500	100	

Table 1.4   Additional data for calibration

	Base SAM	Steady state
Capacity utilization	0.8	1
Growth of the labor force	0.03	0.03
Adjustment parameter θ	0.015	0.015
Employment ratio	0.8	1
Depreciation rate	0.05	0.05

Source: Author's calculations.

guidance here from theory and indeed there is no guarantee that the function actually exists. But suppose that an econometric exercise were able to establish that the elasticity of investment with respect to the profit share was equal to 2. A simple functional form might then be

$$f(\beta) = z\beta^2 \tag{25}$$

where z is a calibration constant. With full capacity utilization, the steady-state f is constant and equal to $\delta + n = 0.08$. We also know that

$$\frac{\beta_\infty}{v} = 0.08$$

where β_∞ is the steady-state value for β. Since equation (25) must also hold for this β, we can eliminate β_∞ to find

$$v^2 z = \frac{1}{\delta + n}$$

The initial SAM must also be consistent with equation (25), however, and that requires that the capital–output ratio be set in the calibration process. It must be true that

$$\frac{I_0}{K_0} = z\beta_0^2$$

where the zero subscript indicates the value in the base SAM. With knowledge of the initial value of capacity utilization, we have

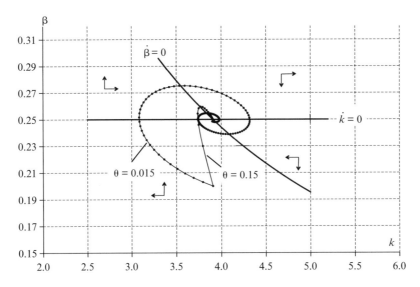

Figure 1.11   Different adjustment speeds

$$zv = \frac{u_0}{\beta_0}$$

where the initial profit share, β_0, can be read from the SAM, and is 0.2. Solving these last two equations simultaneously, we find that $v = 3.13$ and $z = 1.28$.[23] From these two parameters, the rest of the model can be calibrated. The initial level of capital is $K = vQ = vY_0/u_0$ or 1953.1, where Y_0 and u_0 can be read from the data tables. The labor force is then $400/0.8 = 500$ so the initial capital–labor ratio is $k = 3.9$. Figures 1.11 and 1.12 show the results. These figures plot two adjustment speeds, one for $\theta = 0.15$, and a slower one with $\theta = 0.015$. Note the significant impact on the trajectory that the adjustment speed has. In the fast case there is very little overshooting of capacity utilization or employment compared to Figure 1.9, even more in line with the standard model.

4.2   Other stabilizing mechanisms

The Taylor model is just one of many structuralist examples in which some additional mechanism is employed to reverse the instability introduced by the capacity utilization term. In an early model by Dutt, for example, monopoly power is used to set β in a stabilizing fashion (Dutt, 1984). There the mark-up follows a concave path with respect to capacity utilization, rising first as industries are concentrated. The mark-up then falls as excess profits attract entry and foreign competition, or state imposed anti-trust mechanisms take effect.

Similarly, Taylor offers a model in which inflation is introduced directly into the investment function in order to arrest the explosive effect of capacity utilization (Taylor, 1991). There, full capacity utilization causes inflation to accelerate and this effect overcomes that of rising u. Skott introduces the cost of finance, through a "financialization" effect to serve the same purpose. Setterfield and Lima have central bank policy, through

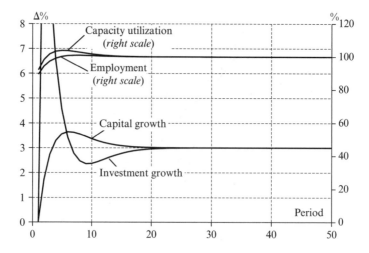

Figure 1.12   Fast adjustment of the profit share

the effect of inflation targeting, playing the role of rising wages in the canonical model of Taylor (1983).

Anytime an adjustment speed is introduced, the path of the model will depend on *both* the initial conditions and the adjustment parameter. In principle then, this adjustment parameter should be explained within the structural theory of the model, although it rarely is. Frequently, the stability properties of the model depend on the size of the adjustment parameter, in that it cannot be "too big." A stable adjustment process with an appropriately sized parameter is then just another way to impose a bound on the growth rate of investment.[24] One can calibrate the model to actual data to deduce its value. The path then depends on the initial SAM as well as how fast the adjusting variables dampen out.

4.3   Path dependence, multiple equilibria and hysteresis

Dutt argues that path dependency is an important characteristic of realistic models, since intuitively, "the destination depends on what happens along the way" (Dutt, 2005). While this assertion is hardly self-evident, Dutt marshals a number of convincing arguments that hysteresis, or irreversibility, is common in most real economies. Hysteresis, first applied to magnetism, implies *remanence*: a shock to an economy, followed by an equal and opposite shock, will *not* restore the model to its original equilibrium. This will be generally true in models for which the initial conditions play a role in the determination of the steady state of the model. Since shocks alter the effect of the original initial conditions, it follows that the model will not necessarily return to its original equilibrium of when the shock is reversed. Initial conditions are also important when there are multiple equilibria, since they can determine which of the equilibria are selected.

The standard model does not exhibit any of these characteristics since it converges to a unique globally stable equilibrium. More generally, the standard model is ergodic in that it "shakes free" from the influence of its past state, even when its parameters are stochastic (David, 2000). Ergodicity is usually considered an important characteristic of stochastic models, since it is then possible to reach any state of the model from any other state. Where one starts does not exclude any particular destination. Data collected from ergodic simulations are therefore free of any bias imposed on the model by its initial conditions. Ergodic models are free from bias in a more profound sense: nothing that the underlying agents do is affected by anything other than the behavior of the agents themselves, either collectively or individually. Hysteresis can still be present, but there is nothing that guides the behavior of the model from above. The standard model is, of course, constrained from above by the rate of growth of the labor force. A fully ergodic model would have the decision of whether to join the labor force, or indeed population growth itself, would be determined from the ground up, that is, by the agents themselves.

Dutt notes that in order for structural history to matter, it is necessary for a model to have either multiple equilibria, a continuum of equilibria or exhibit hysteresis. The first and third rely on a detailed analysis of agent behavior, while the second, as we have seen, is a property of the pure structuralist approach, with investment growth linked to capacity utilization (see Figure 1.5). Dutt goes further to argue that hysteresis is very common, with the absence of hysteresis "a rarity." Hysteresis is grounded in individual agent decision-making, rather than imposed structure. Hysteresis derives from hysterons, model elements that switch on or off depending on local circumstances, neighborhood effects, time delays, biases arising from the availability heuristic and other forms of bounded rationality. Irreversibility due to loss aversion means that the direction of change influences the magnitude of change. These arguments are based on behavioral regularities rather than aggregate structural features. Apparently for structure to really matter, agency must be considered in very careful ways.[25]

Practical structuralist models are calibrated to an initial SAM and then adjustments are made to the behavioral parameters until the model tracks historical data reasonably well (Gibson and van Seventer, 2000; Lovinsky and Gibson, 2005; Taylor, 1990). Policy analysis can then be conducted around the calibrated path and recommendations tailored to the relevant structural constraints of the target economy can then be made. Indeed, this is why structuralist models are structuralist. A model with an investment function calibrated in this way is ipso facto "path dependent" in that were it adjusted to track a different set of data, it would have a different γ and therefore converge to a different steady state. Whether the logistic equation is engineered to produce full capacity utilization in the steady state, as above, depends on the time frame for which the model is to be employed.

The discrete logistic γ function is just one of many functional forms that might be used to describe the time path of investment. It has two fixed points, a trivial one at zero and one at $\gamma = (k - 1)/k$, as seen above. The first is a repeller, that is unstable, while the second is an attractor, or stable equilibrium. Since there is only one attractor, the initial conditions do not matter; all roads lead to the same destination. Iterative models that have attracting fixed points, found by way of numerical simulations, allow calibrated parameters to determine the steady state. Small changes in policy variables do not send the model off on wholly different trajectories, and thankfully so.[26] Other plausible functions to describe investment growth may well have more than one attractor and thus the initial conditions would indeed matter. Depending on the initial SAM to which the model is calibrated, a difference equation simulation could converge to one of any number of equilibria. Examples include tangent and pitchfork bifurcations, in which fixed (or periodic points) appear for certain parameter values, come together and then disappear for others. Parameter changes can change a repelling fixed point into an attracting or neutral one, or vice versa.

"Lock-in" that derives from coordination failure has been discussed by Setterfield and others (Setterfield, 1997).[27] Lock-in is a stronger property than remanence and hysteresis in that it refers to how equations of motion are themselves formulated. It is one thing to say that hysterons lead to non-ergodicity in models so that when the model arrives at some states, other states are not available (Durlauf, 1996). It is another to ignore forces that might build to break out of the locked-in equilibrium. Indeed, lock-in has been challenged by Liebowitz and Margolis, among others, on the grounds that if the "unavailable" states were Pareto superior, then presumably they could be found (Liebowitz and Margolis, 1994). Random experimentation in reinforcement learning models can bring this about (Sutton and Barto, 1998), as well as the standard compensation principle to allow trading to the new equilibrium even when some agents are locally worse off.

Good modeling is good modeling and so it is incumbent upon both structuralists and those attracted to the standard approach to think more deeply about the component parts of the model. Structuralists should strive to model precisely how the decisions of agents in the past have produced the structures that constrain agents of the present. These may be rational, or indeed, "predictably irrational" to borrow a fashionable term from behavioral economics, but they most assuredly must be predictable to some degree. The standard model clearly requires more attention to bounds on rationality and the speed with which markets adjust.

Finally, there is nothing to say that the SGM really needs to focus on the adjustment process to a steady-growth full employment, full capacity utilization equilibrium. The structuralist model, shorn of these moorings, is a fine model with which to simulate an economy. Fine, so long as one is confident in the forecast for the investment path as well as the structural rigidity of the productive structure. Above all, labor can have no meaningful role in determining output and the rate of unemployment can increase or decrease with no direct feedback on the capital–output ratio. These are all significant assumptions, of course, and probably explain why the structuralist model is often referred to as a *medium*-run model, that is, not really designed to capture the "long run", in which the economy is fully adjusted to factor availability.

5   Conclusions

What then is the essential ingredient that makes a model structuralist? It has been argued here that both the standard and structuralist models rely on an exogenous independent variable. In the case of the standard model, it is the growth of the labor force. For the structuralist model, it is rather the animal spirits component in the growth of investment. In the case of the latter model, part of the structure is the investment climate, but it is not amenable to full theoretical treatment. It is inherently subjective, historical or otherwise, locally determined and not subject to treatment within the standard optimization framework.

The capital stock will only achieve steady growth when investment and the capital stock are growing at the same rate, and this is true for models of either stripe. Steady growth of the capital stock, at whatever rate, therefore necessarily implies steady growth of investment. All the feedback that arises from the short-run equilibrium between savings and investment must therefore dampen out when the model reaches the steady state. One of the major hurdles of the structuralist framework is getting the effect of capacity utilization on the growth path of investment to dampen out as the model reaches *full* capacity utilization. Here the shortage of capacity is at its greatest and one would expect that investment would surge. In fact, other forces must always come into play to keep investment in check.

The irony of the structuralist model is that these forces are themselves rooted in short-run reactions of variables with significant degrees of freedom, variables that cannot be determined structurally. Agency must intervene and structuralists have conceded to this point to various degrees and in a multiplicity of ways. Other contributions to this volume show this can be done in interesting and creative ways, but it has been the purpose of this chapter to show more precisely how and why a comprehensive theory of individual agents making investment decisions is necessary.

Notes

1. Thanks to Diane Flaherty, Mark Setterfield, Roberto Veneziani and the members of the Analytical Political Economy group, Queen Mary University, London, for invaluable comments in the preparation of this chapter.
2. An important exception to this is Setterfield and Budd (2008). See also Gibson (2007).
3. Most structuralists, post-Keynesian and Kaleckian writers, ignore factor substitution or the choice of technique problem. There are exceptions, see for example Skott (1989). Mostly, however, the production function that governs the path of the capital–output ratio in the standard model is absent and without a production function, the default option is to assume a *constant* capital–output ratio. Unfortunately, this assumption is flatly contradicted by the historical record; see Mohun (2008) and references cited therein.
4. That is, $\hat{K}$ is the growth rate of the capital stock, or $K_{t+1}/K_t - 1$.
5. The stationary state is then just a special case of the steady-state growth in which the growth rate is zero.
6. Alternatively, if we knew the growth rate of investment, say from the SAM in the following period, we could determine the capital–output ratio. If, for example, investment is growing at 4 percent per year and depreciation is 5 percent, I/K must be 9 percent. If α can be read from the SAM, say at 18 percent of GDP, then the capital–output ratio would be 2 percent for steady growth.
7. Proof: $C > 0 \rightarrow K_0 - I_0/(\gamma + \delta) > 0 \rightarrow \gamma > \frac{I_0}{K_0} - \delta$. If the growth rate of investment is *less* than that of the capital stock, then the constant is negative and the growth rate of the capital stock is slowing down as the system approaches equilibrium.
8. Let v' be the capital–output ratio for the standard model and v be that of the structuralist model. From equation (2) we have

$$\frac{\alpha}{v'} = \frac{\alpha}{v}$$

so if they pass through the same SAM, $v = v'$.
9. It is possible to define a *capital constrained* SGM for which the two Keynesian principles are held in abeyance, such that income is determined by the time path of the capital stock. We will see shortly, however, that it is not possible to have a constant fraction of output devoted to accumulation in the capital-constrained model without introducing instability. See section 3.6 below.
10. But why is labor multiplied by the factor $(1 - \beta)$? One way to think of this is that in the SGM, investment had a direct effect on K, but now labor growth must be filtered through the production function before it affects the growth of the capital stock. The production function must be reduced by α to get to investment. The growth rate n is reduced for the same reason: the impact of labor growth on capital accumulation is diminished by its co-participation in production.
11. Some structuralists view this as an advantage of the methodology, that there is path dependence in the model, in that where the economy ends up depends on the path taken (Dutt, 2005). See section 4.3 for further discussion.
12. It makes no conceptual difference whether full capacity utilization is defined as $u = 1$ or $u = \bar{u}$, where the latter is defined as some "normal" or "desired" utilization rate. Lavoie et al. (2004) have argued

that the desired rate can be determined endogenously, but in each case the long-run equilibrium is defined exogenously. Actual utilization deviates from desired by some rule that reduces desired utilization until it is consistent with the expected γ. Skott (2008) notes that this generates a stable two-equation system that converges to some γ and $\bar{u}$. But this adds nothing to the determination of γ since whether u converges to one or some other given number makes no difference to the necessity that it converge.

13. While it would be formally possible to have $\hat{u}$ just equal to the difference between γ and $\hat{K}$, this cannot persist in the steady state since u would display a trend. Since u is bounded by one, a trend in u seems infeasible. Critically damped cycles are, however, possible and would give rise to cyclical behavior of u.

14. When $C < 0$, the process unfolds in reverse and u falls continuously.

15. The logistic approach is but one way to impose the order on the γ function that all SGMs must do. It is, for example, possible to make γ_t follow a path that explicitly depends on u, but with the effect dying out asymptotically. This can be accomplished with the negative exponential function.

$$\gamma = \bar{\gamma}[1 + \varphi(e^{-1} - e^{-u})]$$

where φ is an adjustment factor. Note that when $u = 1$ the rate of growth of investment is $\bar{\gamma}$. Simulation of a model that employs this functional form produces results similar to Figure 1.6, except that there is some curvature in the investment growth rate.

16. The distinction does not normally arise in the standard model, but it can. If investment is taken to be a share of profits, as it is for example, in its golden rule version, then the standard model is by definition exhilarationist or profit led (Barro and Sala-i-Martin, 2004). But if investment rises with the share of labor, then the standard model can also be stagnationist. The usual way in which the standard model is designed produces neither result, since investment is a fraction of total output and is not responsive to changes in its distributive components.

17. One argument is that competition, domestic or foreign, imposes limits on the movement of ω, which in turn implies limits on the profit share. Another is that profit and wage shares are structurally determined and evidence from the historical record is adduced to support the idea that they are constant and do not fluctuate much. This argument is somewhat self-referential since shares cannot, by definition, have a time trend.

18. See Ros (2003) who uses imported inflation to the same effect, arresting the growth in investment as capacity utilization nears one.

19. Note that f can be written as function of β alone without loss of generality since now

$$f(\beta) = I/K = \beta u/v$$

from which u is determined as a function of β. The wage–rental ratio is also implicitly present, since with both β and u known, ω is determined by equation (18).

20. This says that the response of investment to the profit share is very large. If β is 20 percent, moving from a profit share of 0.4 to 0.41 would have to give more than a 5 percent increase in the rate of growth of investment and from 0.4 to 0.5 would give an increase of 50 percent.

21. The original model is embedded in this system of equations. Drop the second equation and hold β constant, as it usually is, and the equilibrium condition reduces to equation (2) with $\gamma = \hat{K}$. If γ is greater than n, unemployment must be falling. The second equation slows down the growth of investment, given that a rise in I/k reduces β. The negative relationship between β and γ is then stabilizing.

22. The first of these two equations is strikingly similar to the standard growth differential equation, expressed in per capita terms

$$\hat{k} = sf(k) - n - \delta \tag{23}$$

where the term $sf(k)$ simply describes how much of total output is saved on a per capita basis.

23. The solutions are

$$v = \frac{\beta_0}{u_0(\delta + n)} \text{ and } z = \frac{u_0}{v\beta_0}.$$

24. Dutt shows that this can be done when introducing the expected rather than actual rate of profit into the I/K function (Dutt, 2005). He lets

$$\frac{dr^e}{dt} = \theta(r - r^e)$$

be the adjustment of the expected profit rate , r^e to the actual, r.

25. Setterfield and others have raised the question of whether models that solve simultaneously for all variables can be path dependent in the same way, as say a random walk (Setterfield, 2001).

26. Consider this:

> The existence of sensitive dependence in dynamical systems has profound implications for scientists and mathematicians who use difference or differential equations as mathematical models. If a given system exhibits sensitive dependence on initial conditions, then numerical predictions about the fate of orbits are to be *totally distrusted* [emphasis added]. For we can never know the exact seed or initial condition for our orbit or solution because we cannot make physical [or indeed social! BG] measurements with infinite precision. Even if we had exact measurements, we could never carry out the necessary computations. The small numerical errors that are always introduced in such numerical procedures throw us off our original orbit and onto another whose ultimate behavior may be radically different (Blanchard et al., 2002, p. 685).

27. See Setterfield (2001) and references cited therein.

References

Aghion, P. and P. Howitt (1998). *Endogenous Growth Theory*. Cambridge, MA: MIT Press.

Barro, R. and X. Sala-i-Martin (2004). *Economic Growth*. New York: McGraw-Hill.

Bhaduri, A. and S. Marglin (1990). "Unemployment and the real wage: The economic basis for contesting political ideologies." *Cambridge Journal of Economics*, **14** (4), 375–93.

Blanchard, P., R.L. Devaney, and G.R. Hall (2002). *Differential Equations* (2 edn). Pacific Grove, CA: Brooks-Cole.

David, P.A. (2000). "Path dependence, its critics and the quest for 'historical economics'." In P. Garrouste and S. Ioannides (eds.), *Evolution and Path Dependence in Economic Ideas: Past and Present*. Cheltenham, UK and Northampton, MA, USA: Edward Elgar.

Domar, E.D. (1946). "Capital expansion, rate of growth and employment." *Econometrica*, **14**, 137–47.

Durlauf, S.N. (1996). "A theory of persistent income inequality." *Journal of Economic Growth*, **1** (1), 75–93.

Dutt, A.K. (1984). "Stagnation, income distribution and monopoly power." *Cambridge Journal of Economics*, **8**, 25–40.

Dutt, A.K. (1997). "Equilibrium, path dependence and hysteresis in post-Keynesian models." In P. Arestis, G. Palma, and M. Sawyer (eds), *Capital Controversy, Post-Keynesian Economics and the History of Economic Thought: Essays in Honour of Geoff Harcourt*. London: Routledge.

Dutt, A.K. (2005). "Robinson, history and equilibrium." In B. Gibson (ed.), *Joan Robinson's Economics: A Centennial Celebration*. Cheltenham, UK and Northampton, MA, USA: Edward Elgar.

Dutt, A.K. (2008). "Education, growth and distribution: a heterodox macrodynamic perspective." Department of Economics, University of Notre Dame.

Gibson, B. (2003a). "An essay on late structuralism." In A. Dutt and J. Ros (eds), *Development Economics and Structuralist Macroeconomics: Essays in Honor of Lance Taylor*. Cheltenham, UK and Northampton, MA, USA: Edward Elgar, pp. 52–76.

Gibson, B. (2003b). "Thinking outside the Walrasian box." *International Journal of Political Economy*, **33** (2), 36–46.

Gibson, B. (2005). "The transition to a globalized economy: Poverty, human capital and the informal sector in a structuralist CGE model." *Journal of Development Economics*, **78** (1), 60–94.

Gibson, B. (2007). "A multi-agent systems approach to microeconomic foundations of macro." University of Massachusetts, Department of Economics Working Paper Series.

Gibson, B. and D.E. van Seventer (2000). "A tale of two models: Comparing structuralist and neoclassical computable general equilibrium models for South Africa." *International Review of Applied Economics*, **14** (2), 149–71.

Harrod, R. (1937). "An essay in dynamic theory." *Economic Journal*, **49**, 14–33.

Kalecki, M. (1971). *Selected Essays on the Dynamics of the Capitalist Economy*. Cambridge, UK: Cambridge Univerisity Press.

Keynes, J.M. (1936). *The General Theory of Employment, Interest and Money*. London: Macmillan.

Lavoie, M. (1992). *Foundation of Post-Keynesian Economic Analysis*. Aldershot, UK and Brookfield, USA: Edward Elgar.

Lavoie, M., G. Rodríguez, and M. Seccareccia (2004). "Similitudes and discrepancies in post-Keynesian and Marxist theories of investment: A theoretical and empirical investigation." *International Review of Applied Economics*, **18** (2), 127–49.

Liebowitz, S.J. and S.E. Margolis (1994). "Network externality: an uncommon tragedy." *Journal of Economic Perspectives*, **8** (2), 133–50.

Lima, G.T. and M. Setterfield (2008, April). "Inflation targeting and macroeconomic stability in a post Keynesian economy." *Journal of Post Keynesian Economics*, **30** (3), 435–61.

Lovinsky, J. and B. Gibson (2005). "A Robinson model for Argentina." In B. Gibson (ed.), *Joan Robinson's Economics: A Centennial Celebration*. Cheltenham, UK and Northampton, MA, USA: Edward Elgar, pp. 225–44.

Mohun, S. (2008). "Aggregate capital productivity in the U.S. economy." Queen Mary, University of London.

Pasinetti, L.L. (1962). "Rate of profit and income distribution in relation to the rate of economic growth." *Review of Economic Studies*, **29**, 267–79.

Robinson, J. (1956). *The Accumulation of Capital*. London: Macmillan.

Ros, J. (2003). "Stabilization, adjustment and growth." In A.K. Dutt and J. Ros (eds), *Development Economics and Structuralist Macroeconomics: Essays in Honor of Lance Taylor*. Cheltenham, UK, and Northampton, MA, USA: Edward Elgar.

Setterfield, M. (1997). "History versus equilibrium' and the theory of economic growth." *Cambridge Journal of Economics*, **21**, 365–78.

Setterfield, M. (2001). "Cumulative causation, interrelatedness and the theory of economic growth: A reply to Argyrous and Toner." *Cambridge Journal of Economics*, **25** (1), 107–12.

Setterfield, M. and A. Budd (2008). "A Keynes-Kalecki model of cyclical growth with agent-based features." Department of Economics, Trinity College.

Skott, P. (1989). *Conflict and Effective Demand in Economic Growth*. Cambridge, UK: Cambridge University Press.

Skott, P. (2008). "Investment functions, stability and the reserve army of labor." University of Massachusetts Working Paper Series.

Solow, R.M. (1956). "A contribution to the theory of economic growth." *Quarterly Journal of Economic*, **70** (1), 65–94.

Sutton, R.S. and A.G. Barto (1998). *Reinforcement Learning*. Cambridge, MA and London: MIT Press.

Taylor, L. (1983). *Structuralist Macroeconomics*. Boston, MA: Basic Books.

Taylor, L. (ed.) (1990). *Socially Relevant Policy Analysis*. Cambridge, MA: Massachusetts Institute of Technology.

Taylor, L. (1991). *Income Distribution, Inflation, and Growth*. Cambridge, MA: MIT Press.

Zamparelli, L. (2008). "Direction and intensity of technical change: a micro model." New School for Social Research.

2   The classical theory of growth and distribution
Duncan K. Foley and Thomas R. Michl

Since the purpose of this chapter is to locate the classical theory of economic growth in relation to both Keynesian and mainstream neoclassical theories of growth, we begin with an overview of the problem before elaborating the theoretical frameworks and examining their interrelationships.

Economic growth is the cumulative increase in the productive power of human labor effort to meet human needs through changes in the scale and technology of production, the acquisition of skills and knowledge, and the accumulation of means of production such as tools, buildings, and transportation systems.

Economic growth was slow and irregular for most of human existence, up to the emergence of industrial capitalism in Europe starting in the fourteenth to sixteenth centuries CE, though the comparison of the Roman or Chinese empires with Stone Age societies shows that substantial economic growth cumulated over many millennia. A dramatic acceleration of world economic growth occurred starting in Europe at the end of the Middle Ages, which has spread to the whole world economy over the last 500 years. Economic growth in this period is based on the organization of a complex division of labor through the exchange of products as commodities bought and sold in monetized markets, the spread of the institution of free wage labor, the establishment of private property rights in means of production including land and natural resources, the emergence of strong national states with effective legal and regulatory systems, and the systematic application of scientific methods to the improvement of productive technology.

It is useful to classify theories of economic growth in terms of the key factor that they identify as limiting or constraining growth. The main candidates for limitations on growth are natural resources (land), human resources (skilled and knowledgeable workers), produced resources (capital), and aggregate monetary demand. The early classical economists emphasized constraints arising naturally, such as the limited availability of fertile land, but their analytical framework envisions growth as a self-regulating activity in the absence of such external constraints, limited only by the ability of the economy to manufacture its own resources on an expanded scale. This vision of growth as a kind of bootstrap operation remains vibrant among modern followers of the classical economists. To a lesser extent, it also informs the New Endogenous Growth theorists that have broken off from the mainstream neoclassical model. The mainstream neoclassical theory of growth takes human resources as the ultimate constraint on growth. A central tenet of neoclassical growth theory is that capitalist economies fully employ the available labor force in the long run and that the labor force evolves independently of economic growth. The rise of Keynesian economics in the last century introduced a new potential constraint on growth: insufficient growth of aggregate demand. While both the modern classical economists and the neoclassical economists acknowledge this constraint over short time horizons, a substantial school of demand-constrained growth theorists insists that aggregate demand cannot be ignored, even in the long run.

1   Classical political economy

Classical political economy, whose outstanding figures are Adam Smith, Thomas Malthus, and David Ricardo, building on the analytical foundations provided by its physiocratic predecessors, developed a comprehensive theory of economic growth within the framework of capitalist economic institutions. The basis of this theory is the organization of production through a division of labor sustained by the exchange of products on markets. Through their ownership of means of production (factories, mills, mines, transport) capitalists organize the productive effort of workers hired on wage contracts. Because wages on average represent a fractional claim on real production (and a smaller money value than the whole value created through production) capitalists can appropriate a profit. Competition among capitalists leads them to re-invest a large fraction of these profits in expanding production, which increases employment, extends the social division of labor, and raises the productive power of labor. This virtuous cycle explains the surge in economic growth associated with industrial capitalism. Individual capitalists also have strong incentives to seek out cost-reducing technical innovations, which secure higher-than-average profits to their first adopters. Thus industrial capitalism institutionalizes the process of technical change, eventually leading to the systematic organization of scientific and engineering effort toward strategic cost-reductions in the economy. High wages tend to channel technical change toward labor-saving innovations which reduce labor costs to capitalists.

In this classical political economy perspective, the growth of human population is a consequence of economic growth. To the extent that the accumulation of capital outpaces labor-saving innovations, the demand for labor grows, leading to higher wages, and hence to an increase in population by reducing infant mortality and attracting migration from less-productive regions and societies. Improvements in nutrition, sanitation, and basic medical care that accompany industrial capitalism also reduce mortality and increase population.

Classical political economy is divided in its projection of the long-run tendencies of economic growth based on capital accumulation. Smith foresaw a gradual rise in wages keeping pace with labor productivity, and hoped that the widening division of labor and technical ingenuity could overcome resource limitations on economic growth indefinitely. Malthus and Ricardo emphasized the limits to growth inherent in limited supplies of land and other natural resources that could eventually choke off economic growth through the operation of diminishing returns that cannot be offset by a widening division of labor and technical innovation. Karl Marx, who based his theory of revolutionary change on the classical political economic analysis of capital accumulation, foresaw limits to capitalist economic growth arising from the social class divisions on which industrial capitalism rested, and leading to a new phase of economic growth organized through socialism.

The central regulating factor in the classical political economists' theory of economic growth is the division of value created (or value-added) in production between wages and profits. Economic growth paths on which the wage share in value added continually rises or falls are not sustainable. If wages grow less rapidly than labor productivity, the wage share approaches zero, and the social contradictions of capitalism become unmanageable as workers' contribution to aggregate demand vanishes. If wages grow more rapidly than labor productivity, the wage share approaches unity and the profitability of production vanishes, taking with it the incentives to organize and improve production that drive economic growth. The average rate of profit, r, which regulates the capitalist economic growth process, can be expressed as the product of the profit share (which is one minus the wage share, denoted by the Greek letter ω) multiplied by the ratio of value-added to the value of the capital stock (sometimes called the productivity of capital), denoted by the Greek letter ρ:

$$r = (1 - \omega)\rho \qquad (1)$$

If the proportion of profits reinvested is s_p, the rate of growth of the capital stock is

$$g = s_p\, r = s_p\, (1 - \omega)\rho \qquad (2)$$

The rate of growth of employment, e, which ultimately regulates the rate of growth of population, n, in the classical theory of economic growth, is the rate of growth of the capital stock less the rate of labor-saving technical innovation, γ (assuming a constant productivity of capital):

$$e = g - \gamma \qquad (3)$$

This three-equation framework in seven variables can be elaborated as a determinate model of economic growth paths under assumptions of closure specifying the mechanisms determining four of the variables (ω, ρ, s_p, and γ), either as exogenously given parameters or as outcomes of more complex economic interactions. For example, the rate of labor-saving technical change may be treated as exogenously given or as endogenously regulated by the availability of labor.

Modern theorists often utilize the concept of the effective labor force, which is the natural labor force adjusted for any changes in technology that enhance the productive power of each actual worker. We will make frequent reference to the rate of growth of effective employment ($e + \gamma$) and the rate of growth of the effective labor force ($n + \gamma$).

Classical political economy sees economic growth primarily as a process of transformation of individual economies. International trade and investment bind separate economies into a single world economic system, and mediate the differences in pace and intensity of economic growth in individual economies. The world economy grows because its component individual economies grow. Marx in particular is prescient in recognizing that economic growth of individual capitalist economies can only be understood as aspects of a world-wide process of social transformation of production.

2 Keynesian growth theories

The theory of economic growth, with a few important exceptions, such as work in the Marxist tradition, Allyn Young's interest in increasing returns phenomena, and the work of the German historical school on the institutional foundations of capitalist economic growth, went into eclipse in the final decades of the nineteenth and the first decades of the twentieth centuries. Theoretical interest in economic growth revived, however, with the appearance of Keynesian economics on the intellectual stage as a response to the world-wide economic crisis of the depression of the 1930s. Keynes's *General Theory of Employment, Interest, and Money* proposes a theory of the determination of employment and economic output based on the analysis of aggregate demand, rather than on the analysis of the growth of inputs to production and improvements in technology. Keynes takes the utilization of productive capacity, u, as a variable fraction between 0 and 1. The actual value of net output per unit of capital value thus becomes $u\rho$, and is determined in the short run by the demand for consumption goods on the part of workers and capitalists, and the demand of capitalists for investment (abstracting from government spending and international trade). If workers' propensity to save out of wage income, $\omega u\rho$ is s_w, workers' consumption is $(1 - s_w)\omega u\rho$, and capitalists' consumption $(1 - s_p)(1 - \omega)u\rho$, both expressed per unit value of the capital stock. Keynes's innovation is to argue that capitalists' decisions to invest are independent of social saving, so that the growth rate of the capital stock (abstracting from depreciation), g, is exogenously given in the short run. The actual net output per unit value of capital thus satisfies the equation $u\rho = (1 - s_w)\omega u\rho + (1 - s_p)(1 - \omega)u\rho + g$, which can be solved:

$$u\rho = g/(s_w\omega + s_p(1 - \omega)) = g/s \tag{4}$$

Here $s = s_w\omega + s_p(1 - \omega)$ is the social marginal (and, in this case, average) propensity to save out of income, and $1/s$ is the Keynesian multiplier, the ratio of aggregate demand to autonomous spending (in this case investment). Only one rate of growth of the capital stock is compatible with a given level of capacity utilization (say $u = 1$), social saving propensity, and productivity of capital, the warranted rate of growth:

$$g_w = s\rho$$

Following Keynes's discovery of the role of aggregate demand in determining employment levels in the short run, Roy Harrod and Evsey Domar raised two questions about the compatibility of this warranted rate of growth with a natural rate of growth of the effective labor force, $n + \gamma$, that depends on exogenously given growth in labor supply and labor productivity. The first is simply whether it is possible for the warranted rate to adjust to the natural rate, recognizing that the warranted rate is determined by two parameters that do not have any self-evident connection to the natural rate. This is the existence question. The second is whether growth at the warranted rate would be stable (even if the warranted and natural rates happened to correspond). This is the stability question. If the actual growth rate differs from the warranted rate, what process will force the actual rate to converge toward the warranted rate? If the warranted rate exceeds the natural rate, Harrod argues that the failure of the economy actually to grow at the warranted rate will (somewhat counterintuitively) depress the rate of capacity utilization, discourage investment, and lead through a chronic deficiency of aggregate demand to economic stagnation. If the warranted rate falls short of the natural rate, the tendency of the economy to grow faster than the warranted rate will induce a chronic shortage of capital, excess aggregate demand, and structural inflation. These observations posed the question of what mechanisms in real economies might operate to bring the actual, warranted and natural rates of growth into line, to allow balanced growth with full employment in the context of exogenously given rates of growth of the labor force and labor productivity. Most of the attention of growth theorists has been devoted to the existence question, taking the growth path as stable.

Nicholas Kaldor and Luigi Pasinetti, returning to classical political economic themes linking distribution and growth, proposed a model in which changes in the distribution of income between wages and profits raise or lower the social saving propensity for a given exogenous productivity of capital to bring the warranted rate of growth to equality with the natural rate and resolve the existence question. If the propensity to save out of profit income is higher than the propensity to save out of wage income, $s_p > s_w$, when the warranted rate is lower than the natural rate, the pressure of structural unemployment on wages will lower the wage share and raise the warranted rate, stabilizing the economy toward a balanced growth path.

Pasinetti discovered that the relationship between the rate of growth and the rate of profit in the steady state would be fully described by equation (2), a remarkable fact given that it does not contain any reference to workers' saving, as does equation (4). This result is called the Cambridge Theorem. It is surprising that an increase in workers' saving has no long-run effect on the distribution of income, assuming a given natural rate of growth. An increase in workers' saving will have only a temporary effect on income distribution; its permanent effect, raising the share of capital wealth held by workers, accounts for the absence of any long-run effect of workers' saving on the rate of profit. (To see this, as Pasinetti discovered, equation (4) needs to be amended to allow workers to save out of the returns to the capital they own.) The Cambridge Theorem points toward the classical theme that capitalist agents occupy a privileged position in the class structure of accumulation. As Michl (2009) argues, this theorem has important implications for the political economy of fiscal policies involving public debt and pension systems.

The Kaldor–Pasinetti model of long-run growth is essentially a classical growth model specialized by the assumption of full employment of a predetermined labor supply. The Goodwin (1967) model is a classical growth model lying intermediate between Kaldor–Pasinetti and the traditional classical model. In Goodwin's model, the effective labor force is assumed to grow independently at a natural rate. The employment rate (share of workers employed) then evolves with the capital stock that provides jobs. Goodwin assumes that the growth rate of the wage share is a positive (and linear) function of the employment rate. The rest of his model is identical to the classical model outlined above (with no worker saving). Thus a period of high employment creates the conditions for its own demise, because the wage share rises, shrinking the rate of profit and the growth of capital. Eventually the employment rate will have to decline as the growth of capital dips below the natural rate of growth. This model creates growth that cycles around the (predetermined) natural rate of growth, with corresponding cycles in the employment and unemployment rates. These cycles have the same mathematical form (the Lotka–Volterra equations) as biological models of predator–prey dynamics. A reserve of unemployed workers emerges as a natural accompaniment to the accumulation process that modulates and contains the conflict over the distribution of value added.

Yet another resolution to Harrod's existence question has been to return to the classical conception that the growth of the labor force accommodates changes in capital accumulation. In this case, if the warranted and actual growth rates were below the natural rate for an extended period of time, potential workers would be discouraged from entering the labor force, perhaps choosing non-market activity or emigration. Modern post-Keynesian economists, such as Lance Taylor (2004), following Michal Kalecki and Joseph Steindl, have pursued models of demand-constrained growth that incorporate this resolution. Because they recognize the Keynesian independence of investment and saving, these models exhibit the paradox of thrift. An increase in the saving rate will, in itself, increase the warranted rate of growth. But as argued above, that will express itself in economic stagnation, depressing the rate of utilization below unity because of the decline in consumer demand. If the presence of unused capacity has a further dampening effect on investment spending, it will also depress the actual rate of growth. In terms of equation (4), the increase in the saving rate leads to a combination of lower growth and lower utilization (the paradox of thrift). When the increase in the saving rate is the result of a redistribution of income toward profits, this is called the paradox of cost because lower wages have (counterintuitively) reduced the level of activity. This class of model is sometimes called wage-led or stagnationist to emphasize the tendency for growth to bog down without injections of demand.

3   The relationship between classical and Keynesian theory

The classical and Keynesian theories of growth have a complex relationship with one another. The stagnationist models, with their paradoxes of cost and thrift, seem to represent a dramatically different paradigm, and although there are other important types of Keynesian growth models (see, for example, McCombie and Thirlwall, 1994), the stagnationist models provide a particularly clear contrast with the classical theory. It comes as no surprise that lively debates have erupted between representatives of the stagnationist and classical approaches. At their heart stand two different interpretations of the rate of profit. In the classical theory, the rate of profit regulates the rate of growth in a direct and transparent fashion through equation (2). Any change in technology or the distribution of income, such as a wage decrease, that improves profitability can be expected to stimulate capital accumulation. In the Keynesian theory, the profit rate both regulates growth, through the investment equation, and reflects growth in aggregate demand through the effect of utilization on profitability. It is not inconceivable that a wage cut would reduce both aggregate demand and profitability from this vantage point.

This difference is dramatized by the paradox of cost, a variant of the paradox of thrift in which a decrease in the real wage results in a reduction in the rate of utilization rather than an increase in the rates of profit and growth. In the Keynesian system, the rate of profit is defined as $r = u(1 - \omega)\rho$, so that it is algebraically possible for a simultaneous decline in ω and u to lower r or leave it invariant.

The central issue in these debates is the meaning of an equilibrium in which firms operate with excess or underutilized capacity. The stagnationist theorists work with an investment equation of the form

$$g^i = g(\rho, \omega, \hat{u})$$

where $\hat{u}$ represents the utilization gap between normal or desired utilization and actual utilization. The hypothesis is that an increase in utilization signals that entrepreneurs need to expand their capital stock to avoid capacity shortages. The remaining variables indicate that entrepreneurs respond to the expected profitability of capital in formulating their plans. Anything that improves the profit rate can be expected to arouse their appetite for more investment and expansion. With this kind of investment equation coupled with a saving equation like equation (2), the stagnationist model generates an equilibrium in which there can be a permanent gap between actual and desired utilization. A demand shock, such as an increase in capitalist consumption (equivalently a reduced capitalist saving rate), will raise utilization and reduce the gap. In effect, this kind of system can accommodate a surge in demand by utilizing its existing capacity more fully, without having to accumulate more capital resources.

The criticism raised by classical economists has been that in the long run, we would expect capitalist entrepreneurs to adjust their capital stock so that they operate at their normal or desired rate of utilization. In this interpretation, the stagnationist theory is not incorrect on its own terms. Rather, it describes an equilibrium that is only partial, since the firms remain out of balance in terms of the utilization gap. Recent attempts to explain how a system like this achieves a fully adjusted equilibrium include Duménil and Lévy (1999). They argue that (1) the presence of a central bank which regulates the value of money, (2) the sensitivity of the price level to the utilization rate and (3) the presence of financial influences on investment together can explain why the stagnationist investment equation could describe the short-run behavior of an economy that gravitates toward a fully adjusted equilibrium with utilization at desired or normal levels in the long run. For example, a temporary equilibrium with a large utilization gap would generate a declining price level, inducing a looser monetary policy that stimulates investment spending. The resulting acceleration in demand will increase utilization, closing the utilization gap. A model with this kind of adjustment mechanism exhibits Keynesian properties like the paradox of thrift in the short run, but operates more like the classical model in the long run; in particular, its long-run growth rate is described by the saving equation (2) alone since the investment equation adjusts to close the utilization gap.

For their part, the stagnationist theorists have responded to this criticism by insisting that the basic insights of their model can be preserved, even in a fully adjusted long run with no utilization gap. One argument, advanced independently by Lavoie (1995) and Dutt (1997), is that the normal level of utilization is inherently subjective, and that it evolves in an adaptive way, much like habit formation. This provides an alternative mechanism for eliminating a utilization gap. For example, a temporary equilibrium with a large utilization gap would generate changes in the norms of entrepreneurs. As they become accustomed to operating with more unused capacity, their standards change and the desired or normal level declines until the gap is eliminated. A model with this kind of adaptive mechanism exhibits the key hallmarks of the stagnationist paradigm, such as the paradoxes of thrift and cost. This subjective treatment of the normal rate of utilization calls to mind Keynes's notion that capitalist entrepreneurs are motivated to invest in new business ventures more by their animal spirits than by their spirit of rational calculation.

The paradox of cost, really a corollary of the paradox of thrift, has been shown to depend on special assumptions about the worker saving rate and other details of the model, as explained by Blecker (2002). Thus, the main disagreement between these two models revolves around the paradox of thrift. Despite some heroic efforts (Pollin, 1997) to resolve this question empirically, it is very difficult to imagine how national income data can ever distinguish the direction of causality between saving and investment since the realizations of these categories are equalized by accounting convention.

While these alternative resolutions seem diametrically opposed, it would be a mistake to overlook their deep commonalities. Both schools of thought are skeptical of the neoclassical belief that the long run is defined by full employment of a predetermined labor force (see below), in favor of the belief that the long run is defined by full or normal utilization of the capital stock. Both deploy a methodology that seeks to identify and understand the macroeconomic foundations of economic behavior in such structural features as social class or the corporate form of business enterprise, eschewing the methodological individualism of neoclassical theory. And both envision the level of employment as a consequence rather than a cause of the amount of capital and its rate of utilization. In short, they both see the accumulation of capital as the animating force of capitalism. In the Duménil-Lévy resolution, a demand shock that does not affect equation (2), say an autonomous decrease in investment, will temporarily reduce the rate of capital accumulation. The system will recover its original rate of growth after undergoing the adjustment process described above, but at a lower level of capital and employment than it would achieve in the absence of the original shock. In the Dutt–Lavoie resolution, the same demand shock might permanently reduce the growth rate (by depressing the rate of utilization). Both resolutions recognize that demand shocks can have permanent effects. In this case they disagree about whether these are growth rate effects or level effects. Given the shared preconceptions that unite the classical and stagnationist economists, it is tempting to conclude that the disagreements that remain chart a common research program rather than a gulf of irreconcilable scientific differences. In other words, some kind of hybridization or synthesis between Keynesian and classical theory seems almost natural.

Because these theories treat the supply of effective labor as an endogenous response to accumulation, they would explain the relative stability of the unemployment rate over long spans of historical time as the result of adjustments in the supply of labor rather than a reflection of the accommodation of accumulation to the growth of the labor force as in the Kaldor–Pasinetti or Goodwin models described above. But this remains an incomplete part of the heterodox research program. For example, it is not clear to what extent the adjustment mechanism relies on changes in the rate of technical change induced by labor shortages (which augments the effectiveness of an existing supply of labor) as opposed to changes in the actual labor force induced by the flows into and out of the reserves of labor, although there is some good evidence (Thirwall, 2002) that one or both of these mechanisms operates at business cycle frequencies in advanced capitalist economies.

4 Neoclassical growth theory

Robert Solow (and independently, Trevor Swan) proposed a different mechanism to guarantee the convergence of the warranted rate to a given natural rate, the substitution of capital for labor leading to a change in capital productivity, ρ. Full employment is achieved in every period in the Solow–Swan model through the flexibility of wages leading to the substitution of capital for labor in just the proportions necessary to employ the existing labor force with the existing capital stock. If the resulting warranted rate of growth is higher than the natural rate of growth, the potential excess capital is absorbed in the next period through a rise in the wage, and a consequent increase in capital employed per worker and fall in the productivity of capital. This process continues over time until the warranted rate declines through intensive capital accumulation to the given natural rate, at a steady-state balanced growth path. While this process is compatible with the wage share, and hence the social saving propensity, changing as the wage rises or falls, expositions of the Solow–Swan model emphasize the case where the elasticity of substitution between capital and labor with respect to the wage is unity, so that the shares of wages and profit are technologically fixed (the Cobb-Douglas production function). This scenario emphasizes the ability of capital–labor substitution to bring about convergence of the warranted growth rate to a given natural growth rate with a fixed social propensity to save. The role of the social saving rate in the Solow–Swan model is to determine the steady-state capital intensity, and thus the productivity of effective labor (adjusted for labor productivity changes) on the steady-state growth path.

This model predicts that economies with the same technology, natural rate of growth, and social savings rate will converge on the same steady-state growth path. Extensive statistical study of this convergence thesis has provided limited evidence to support convergence among a group of high-income economies, but the evidence to support convergence in conditional form (controlling for differences in saving rates and natural growth rates) in the world economy as a whole has been mixed.

On the one hand, it does seem true that controlling for these differences brings out an inverse relationship between a country's initial level of output per worker and its rate of growth. While that finding is consistent with a convergence effect, it is important to note that other explanations besides those arising from the neoclassical growth model are also consistent with conditional convergence. For example, Mark Roberts (2007) has shown that the hypothesis of dynamic economies of scale, ultimately due to Adam Smith, can also generate conditional convergence of a similar type when it is embedded in a Keynesian growth model. Foley and Michl (1999, Chapter 7) point out that these convergence patterns could also reflect the diffusion of technology from the advanced industrialized countries to the emerging countries that are identified by the high saving rates that accompany rapid capitalist development.

On the other hand, there are two difficulties with the evidence. First, the magnitude of the effect is not consistent with the observed shares of profit and wages in national income accounts. The observed profit share of around one-third implies that diminishing returns to capital are quite strong. A poor country or region whose workers are equipped with little capital should enjoy relatively high productivity of capital that will enable it to accumulate capital rapidly and converge quickly towards the rich countries. The conditional convergence that has been observed, however, proceeds relatively slowly. The estimated rates of convergence typically imply much weaker diminishing returns to capital that are consistent with a profit share of around two-thirds, much higher than the share of one-third typically observed in real economies. One resolution to this problem offered by Gregory Mankiw, David Romer, and David Weil has been to broaden the definition of capital to include the acquired productive skills of workers, often called human capital. This can be accomplished fairly easily within the Solow–Swan framework by adding human capital to the production function while maintaining the assumption of constant returns to scale. Second, much of the catching-up seems to be the result of transfers of technology from rich to poor countries rather than the capital deepening along a common production function predicted by the Solow–Swan model. Instead of acting as a form of capital that enters into the production process like an ordinary resource or factor of production, human skills may play a central role in facilitating the transfer of technology, possibly undermining Mankiw, Romer, and Weil's resolution of the first problem. The evidence that catching-up is driven by technology transfer provides some of the motivation for theories of endogenous technical change discussed below.

The Solow–Swan model has been criticized on the ground that the assumption of smooth macroeconomic substitutability between capital and labor on which it rests presumes that the value of capital goods can be used as a measure of capital intensity, which is not true for general disaggregated models of production. Despite the fact that this Cambridge critique has proved to be theoretically well founded, the Solow–Swan production function model became the paradigm for neoclassical investigations of economic growth. The historical statistics of an economy that grows with steady rates of increase in labor and capital productivity and relatively constant wage and profit shares in income (the pattern most industrialized capitalist economies tend to produce) will fit the Cobb-Douglas production function very well, even if there is no substitutability between labor and capital. Indeed, as Anwar Shaikh (1974) demonstrated, under these conditions a good econometric fit of the Cobb-Douglas function is guaranteed by virtue of the fact that it can be derived algebraically from the national income identity between value added and the sum of wages and profits.

The Cobb-Douglas production function provides a framework for the statistical aggregation of labor and capital (and potentially other) inputs to economic production. Solow's concept of total factor productivity rests on this mathematical-statistical method. The Cobb-Douglas production function represents the value of output in a period t, Y_t, as proportional to a geometrical weighted average of labor and capital inputs in the same period, K_t and N_t:

$$Y_t = A_t K_t^\alpha N_t^{1-\alpha} \tag{5}$$

Neoclassical economic theory predicts that the profit and wage shares of an economy will be equal to the weights α and $(1 - \alpha)$. With these assumptions equation (5) can be used to construct an index of changes in total factor productivity, A_t, given statistics on the value of output, the value of capital, and the labor input. (The index of total factor productivity is the weighted average of the separate indexes of average capital and labor productivity, using profit and wage shares as weights.) Studies based on this methodology tend to attribute a large proportion, in the order of 80 percent, of historical increases in output to rises in total factor productivity, and a relatively small proportion to increases in inputs to production.

5   Semi-endogenous economic growth

The assumption of strictly exogenous technical change can be relaxed in order to extend the Solow–Swan model by positing the existence of a distinct research and development sector that produces new knowledge according to its own production function. New knowledge is assumed to increase total factor productivity, A. The rate of production of knowledge can be measured by the change per unit of time of total factor productivity, or mathematically, by the time derivative, symbolically represented by placing a dot over a variable, $\dot{A}$. The production function for the research and development sector can thus be written:

$$\dot{A}_t = a R_t A_t^\theta \qquad \theta \le 1$$

In this equation, *a* is a scaling parameter, R_t represents resources devoted to R&D (in the simplest case the number of scientists and engineers), and the coefficient θ is a parameter representing the returns to technology, whose presence was suggested by Charles Jones. For example, if fundamental discoveries like calculus empower future scientists to make more rapid progress, this parameter will exceed zero. But the parameter will be negative if making new breakthroughs becomes progressively more difficult as the stock of possible discoveries is depleted.

Some early efforts to construct a model of endogenous growth (discussed more fully below) assumed that θ is exactly unity. In this case, the rate of technical change will depend on the number of scientists. An increase in the proportion of a fixed labor force that works in the research sector would permanently increase the rate of growth. This formulation was vulnerable to the critique of Charles Jones: the rising number of scientists and engineers in the developed economies should be generating steadily rising rates of technical change, and there is no sign of that happening. If instead, θ is taken to be strictly less than unity, the rate of technical change (that is, the rate of growth of total factor productivity) will stabilize around a steady state value given by:

$$\frac{\dot{A}_t}{A_t} = \frac{n}{1 - \theta}$$

This equation has been derived by recognizing that in a steady state, the proportion of the labor force working in the research sector will be constant (by the definition of a steady state) so that the number of scientists and engineers, R_t, will rise at the same rate as the population, *n*. This equation demonstrates that even when technology has been rendered endogenous, its growth rate can depend on the rate of population growth (which is still exogenous) for the simple reason that new ideas require people (scientists and engineers) to discover them. An increase in the proportion of workers who are scientists and engineers will only increase the rate of technical change temporarily; eventually it will return to its original rate given by the equation above. The *level* of total factor productivity will be endogenously determined, even though its *rate of growth* is not; hence this extension of the Solow–Swan model is called a semi-endogenous growth model.

6   Endogenous economic growth

The structure of the Solow–Swan model implies that the rate of long-term growth of an economy converges to its natural growth rate, *n* + γ, the sum of the rates of growth of the labor force and labor productivity. An economy that saves and invests more of its output will grow faster in the short run, but as its capital stock grows faster than the effective supply of labor, diminishing returns will set in and its growth rate in the steady state will return to the underlying natural rate. Even the semi-endogenous extension of the Solow–Swan model ultimately succumbs to the law of diminishing returns. In this respect the Solow–Swan model echoes Ricardo's analysis of capitalist growth as limited by the finite availability of land and natural resources, with labor constraints taking over the role of land (and wages being determined by relative scarcity, like Ricardian rents to land). The classical political economic vision, on the other hand, sees economic growth as a self-sustaining interaction of economic decisions to produce, invest, and innovate. Furthermore, the statistical implication of the Solow–Swan approach, that most economic growth actually results from residual increases in total factor productivity due to unexplained changes in the efficiency of labor and capital inputs in production, greatly diminishes the explanatory power of the theory.

Attempts to transcend the exogeneity of the growth rate in the Solow–Swan model have led to the revival of classical themes in a spectrum of endogenous growth models, as Heinz Kurz and Neri Salvadori (1998) have pointed out.

Human skills and knowledge accumulate as the result of investment in education and research. If we include this investment in human capital in the Solow–Swan framework, it has the effect of raising the labor input. But investment in human capital is part of overall social saving. Human capital, H, can be incorporated in a Cobb-Douglas production function:

$$Y_t = A_t K_t^\alpha (H_t N_t)^{1-\alpha} = A_t K_t^\alpha H_t^{1-\alpha} N_t^{1-\alpha} \tag{6}$$

In this formulation there are no diminishing returns to the combination of physical and human capital, as there are in the Mankiw, Romer, and Weil extension of the Solow–Swan model discussed above. Since both human capital and physical capital are accumulated by saving out of output, the steady-state growth rate of an economy that saves more of its output will be higher.

Variants of this idea overcome the limitation of diminishing returns in the Solow–Swann model in other ways. For example, if the accumulation of physical capital also produces an accumulation of knowledge and experience that augments the productivity of labor, it may be that each individual productive enterprise, i, has a production function:

$$Y_{it} = A_t \overline{K}_t^\beta K_{it}^\alpha N_{it}^{1-\alpha} \tag{7}$$

Here total factor productivity depends on the average social accumulation of capital, $\overline{K}$. Though each enterprise sees diminishing returns to physical capital accumulation given labor input, the economy as a whole may, if the coefficient β is large enough, experience constant or even increasing returns to the accumulation of physical capital. These modifications to the Solow–Swan model bring it into a form very similar to the classical political economists' vision of economic growth based on the endogenous accumulation of productive capital.

In some versions of this story, the average stock of social capital is interpreted as an accumulated stock of knowledge from investment in research and development. Because of the inherent increasing returns to scale in the accumulation of knowledge in these models, the paradigm of price-taking perfect competition among enterprises breaks down. Considerable ingenuity (as in the models of Paul Romer, Robert Lucas, and Phillipe Aghion and Peter Howitt) has been expended in adapting models of monopolistic competition to allow for the calculation of market equilibrium in the production of knowledge in a way that is compatible with these increasing returns to research activity.

Any economic activity, such as research, which has effects on production that extend beyond the enterprise that undertakes the activity, implies a discrepancy between the private marginal costs and benefits perceived by decision makers in the enterprise, and the social marginal costs and benefits of the activity. In the case of research in endogenous growth models, this externality has the form of positive spillovers, which imply that in equilibrium private markets will allocate too few resources to research. Thus endogenous growth models of this class suggest some intervention in market outcomes to correct this pervasive (and possibly extremely large) externality, such as government subsidies to research or the creation of property rights in spillovers to internalize the costs and benefits of research.

Endogenous growth models also call into question the presumption in the Solow–Swan framework that each economy undergoes economic growth as a separate unit. Developing countries often acquire new technology not by developing it themselves, but by adopting it from other more advanced economies, either through attracting foreign investment that embodies the new technologies, or by imitation. This perspective suggests that it is necessary to conceptualize economic growth as a unified process of transformation of the world economy, operating through individual economies. A small number of advanced economies specialize in the production of new knowledge and supply the world with the raw material for productivity-enhancing innovation.

7　The relation between classical and neoclassical growth theories

From the classical perspective, the neoclassical approach to economic growth, either in its original Solow–Swan form, its more modern semi-endogenous form, or even its more radical endogenous form, rests on several questionable preconceptions. First, the neoclassical theories all presume the full employment of labor, and this assumption is supported by their free use of the Cobb-Douglas or similar aggregate production function. With this kind of function, any excess demand or supply of labor can be eliminated by a change in the wage rate that induces firms to change the capital–labor ratio in the direction needed to eliminate the excess demand or supply. For example, an excess supply of labor will depress real wages, incentivize the use of more labor-intensive techniques, and thus soak up the unemployed labor resources. Another way of putting this is that with the Cobb-Douglas assumption, there can never be too little capital to support full employment. While classical models of full employment (Kaldor–Pasinetti) or labor-constrained growth (Goodwin) do exist as we have seen, these are treated more like special, polar cases since the natural presumption in classical theory is that growth is constrained by capital rather than by labor.

Second, the neoclassical theories rely on the marginal productivity theory of income distribution, in which the real wage and profit rate are equal to the marginal products of labor and capital. The Cambridge critique of the aggregate production function attacks both of these foundation stones of neoclassical theory. Since the value of capital per worker does not have a predictable relationship with the real wage in a general disaggregated model of production, the first presumption cannot stand because there may be no mechanism that will guarantee that the capital stock is sufficient to support full employment of a predetermined labor force. Similarly, in a disaggregated model of production, it will generally be impossible to define a marginal product of capital or labor, rendering the marginal productivity theory moot. In the classical theory, capital is treated first and foremost as a social relationship between workers and the owners of productive wealth. From this perspective, the marginal productivity theory obscures or distorts the nature of this relationship by reifying capital, treating it as a productive resource (factor of production) on a par with labor-power or land. Without the crutch provided by the neoclassical production function, there seems to be no resolution to the existence problem posed by Harrod and Domar, except returning to the classical assumption of a class structure of saving rates (which is just another expression of the idea that capital is in essence a social relationship), or to the classical assumption of an endogenously generated effective labor force.

The classical alternative to the neoclassical production function emphasizes the incentives for technical change that are internal to capitalist property relations. The well-established fact that the output elasticity of capital exceeds the profit share by a wide margin, for example, is analytically equivalent to a wage that exceeds the apparent marginal product of labor (Foley and Michl, 1999). (The apparent marginal product is equal to the hypothetical wage that would make a new technique and the old technique it replaces equally profitable.) Under these conditions, capitalists have an incentive to introduce more capital-intensive techniques, even if these reduce capital productivity, because they increase the rate of profit for the innovating firm. And the technical dynamism of the capitalist mode of production depends on the increases in real wages that are necessary in order to reproduce this inequality between the wage and the apparent marginal product of labor. In this way, the classical approach emphasizes the role of capital as a social relationship per se in ushering in the modern capitalist era of technical dynamism, unlike neoclassical economists such as Lucas (2002) who emphasize the emergence of intellectual property and individual investments in human capital.

Many modern classical models of growth (Foley, 2003) treat the relationship between wages and technical change as reciprocal. Rising wages not only reflect rising labor productivity, but also induce capitalists to seek more technical improvements that can further raise labor productivity, a hypothesis that has been explored empirically by Marquetti (2004). In this tradition, the neoclassical separation between capital deepening (moving along a production function) and technical change (shifts in the production function) is replaced by the view that capital accumulation and technical change are both aspects of the same dynamic process of development and growth. The hypothesis of induced technical change provides a specific mechanism through which the effective labor force can be considered an endogenous resource that adjusts to the requirements of capital accumulation. Rapid accumulation that depletes the reserves of available labor and bids up wages as a result will create powerful incentives for capitalists to intensify their search for labor-saving technical changes that ultimately reduce the demand for workers and overcome the labor shortages. In this way, the original classical vision of capital accumulation as a self-contained process of development and transformation finds expression in the modern conversation of economic theory.

Bibliography

Aghion, Phillipe and Peter Howitt (1998), *Endogenous Growth Theory*, Cambridge, MA: The MIT Press.
Barro, Robert J. and Xavier Sala-i-Martin (2004), *Economic Growth*, 2nd edn, Cambridge, MA: The MIT Press.
Blecker, Robert A. (2002), "Distribution, demand and growth in neo-Kaleckian macro-models", in Mark Setterfield (ed.), *The Economics of Demand-Led Growth: Challenging the Supply-Side Vision of the Long Run*, Cheltenham, UK and Northampton, MA, USA: Edward Elgar, pp. 129–52.
Cohen, Avi and Geoff Harcourt (2003), "Retrospectives: whatever happened to the Cambridge capital theory controversy?", *Journal of Economic Perspectives*, **17**(1), 199–214.
Duménil, Gerard and Dominique Lévy (1999), "Being Keynesian in the short term and classical in the long term: the traverse to classical long-term equilibrium", *The Manchester School*, **67**(6), 648–716.
Dutt, Amitava K. (1997), "Equilibrium, path dependence and hysteresis in post-Keynesian models", in Philip Arestis and Malcolm Sawyer (eds), *Essays in Honour of G.C. Harcourt: Markets, Unemployment and Economic Policy*, London: Routledge, pp. 238–53.

Eltis, Walter (2000), *The Classical Theory of Economic Growth*, 2nd edn, New York: Palgrave.

Foley, Duncan K. (2003), "Endogenous technical change with externalities in a classical growth model", *Journal of Economic Behavior and Organization*, **52**(2), 167–89.

Foley, Duncan K. and Thomas R. Michl (1999), *Growth and Distribution*, Cambridge, MA: Harvard University Press.

Goodwin, Richard M. (1967), "A growth cycle", in C.H. Feinstein (ed.), *Socialism, Capitalism and Growth*, Cambridge, UK: Cambridge University Press, pp. 54–8.

Harrod, Roy (1942), *Toward a Dynamic Economics*, London: Macmillan.

Helpman, Elhanan (2004), *The Mystery of Economic Growth*, Cambridge, MA: Harvard University Press.

Heston, Alan, Robert Summers and Bettina Aten (2002), "Penn World Table Version 6.1", Center for International Comparisons at the University of Pennsylvania (CICUP).

Jones, Charles I. (2002), *Introduction to Economic Growth*, 2nd edn. New York: W.W. Norton.

Kaldor, Nicholas (1956), "Alternative theories of distribution", *Review of Economic Studies*, **23**(2), 83–100.

Kurz, Heinz-Dieter and Neri Salvadori (eds) (1998), *Understanding "Classical" Economics: Studies in Long-Period Theory*, London and New York: Routledge.

Lavoie, Marc (1995), "The Kaleckian model of growth and distribution and its neo-Ricardian and neo-Marxian critiques", *Cambridge Journal of Economics*, **19**(6), 798–818.

Lucas, Robert E. Jr (2002), *Lectures on Economic Growth*, Cambridge, MA: Harvard University Press.

McCombie, J.S.L. and A.P. Thirlwall (1994), *Economic Growth and the Balance-of-Payments Constraint*, London: Macmillan.

Mankiw, N. Gregory, David Romer and David Weil (1992), "A contribution to the empirics of economic growth", *Quarterly Journal of Economics*, **107**(2), 407–37.

Marquetti, Adalmir (2004), "Do rising real wages increase the rate of labor-saving technical change? Some econometric evidence", *Metroeconomica*, **55**(4), 432–41.

Michl, Thomas R. (2009), *Capitalists, Workers, and Fiscal Policy: A Classical Model of Growth and Distribution*, Cambridge, MA: Harvard University Press.

Pasinetti, Luigi L. (1974), *Growth and Income Distribution: Essays in Economic Theory*, Cambridge, UK: Cambridge University Press.

Pollin, Robert (1997), *The Macroeconomics of Saving, Finance, and Investment*, Ann Arbor, MI: University of Michigan Press.

Roberts, Mark (2007), "The conditional convergence properties of simple Kaldorian growth models", *International Review of Applied Economics*, **21** (5), 619–32.

Romer, Paul M. (1994), "The origins of endogenous growth", *Journal of Economic Perspectives*, **8**(1), 3–22.

Shaikh, Anwar (1974), "Laws of production and laws of algebra: the humbug production function", *Review of Economics and Statistics*, **56** (1), 115–20.

Solow, Robert (2000), *Growth Theory: An Exposition*, Oxford: Oxford University Press.

Taylor, Lance (2004), *Reconstructing Macroeconomics: Structuralist Proposals and Critiques of the Mainstream*, Cambridge, MA: Harvard University Press.

Thirlwall, Anthony P. (2002), *The Nature of Economic Growth*, Cheltenham, UK and Northampton, MA, USA: Edward Elgar.

Young, Allyn (1928), "Increasing returns and economic progress", *Economic Journal*, **38**(152), 527–42.

3 Evolutionary growth theory
J. Stan Metcalfe and John Foster

> Our general conclusion must be that in the field of economic progress the notion of tendency towards equilibrium is definitely inapplicable to particular elements of growth and with reference to progress as a unitary process or system of interconnected changes is of such limited and partial application as to be misleading rather than useful. (Knight, 1935/1997, p. 176)

1 Introduction

An evolutionary theory of economic growth is naturally designed to answer the all-important question "How is wealth created from knowledge?" No serious economist doubts that the growth of per capita income and welfare is a consequence of the growth of understanding about the human built and natural worlds, but how useful knowledge is created and translated into economic development is a matter of great complexity. At the heart of this problem is the need for a disaggregated framework of understanding that explains much more than the rate of growth of aggregate economic activity and the evolution of broad macroeconomic ratios. Of course, many different theoretical frames can be consistent with the same broad aggregate facts, but they must also be consistent with many more disaggregated facts about the way a capitalist economy develops, particularly those facts that are ultimately traceable to the role of enterprise and creative thought in economic growth.[1] Inventive creativity is part of this process, as is its relationship to the development of formal, general scientific and technological knowledge. But invention alone is insufficient; it must be translated into innovation, which depends greatly on specific knowledge of time and place and conjectures of market opportunity, quite different dimensions of knowing. Moreover, if innovations are to have significant growth effects, the allocation of resources and patterns of demand must adapt to the possibilities opened up by new methods and new goods and services. Market processes loom large in this scheme but so do other instituted systems, such as the science and technology system or the education system.[2] The interplay between these different forms of organisation leads to a two-way interaction between economic growth and the growth of knowledge that fully deserves to be labelled an endogenous growth theory. It is the nature of the two-way interaction that is the primary focus of this chapter. It is certainly not a comprehensive treatment of evolutionary growth theory but rather an exposition of some of the links between technical progress and structural change in an evolving economy. The foundations are Schumpeterian, and there are strong elements of Marshall too. We build on these foundations in a way which renders compatible the diverse circumstances of innovation and investment with aggregate patterns of economic change.[3] How innovations in firms and markets "add up" to constitute industry and whole economy level adaptations is the evolutionary problem that we are addressing.

There are three themes to this chapter that follow from its evolutionary perspective. The first is that capitalist economies grow as they develop, so that growth cannot be treated meaningfully by a concept of uniform expansion in which all the components of an economy expand at the same proportionate rate. Balanced growth is a chimera, it is the heterogeneity of growth rates within the economy that needs to be explained, and differential rates of growth lead us directly to structural change and development. It follows that an aggregate rate of growth or an aggregate ratio has no more substance than the individual components from which it is constructed by the observer. Indeed, even in a multi-sector economy, there may be no activity that grows at the aggregate, average rate. Consequently, the evolutionary modes of explanation used below are essentially statistical in nature and relate to changes in population ensembles. Second, as the epigraph to this chapter indicates, growth is not an equilibrium process and cannot be if it is knowledge based, for what sense is there in the idea that the growth of knowledge is an equilibrium process?[4] Yet the possibility of evolution depends on order and on the organising processes that generate coherent structures of economic activity, whether in firms, in markets or in other organisational forms that sit within the wider set of evolved and instituted rules of the game (Abramovitz, 1989; Nelson, 2005). Thus there is a paradox at the centre of capitalism: the presence of order depends on stabilising forces that give coherence and durability to patterns of organisation, but the development of the system requires that the prevailing order is open to invasion by economic novelty, and to this degree it is marked by instability.[5] It is the inherent openness of the market system to the challenge contained in novel economic conjectures, its capacity to stimulate and resolve disagreement about better ways to allocate resources and meet changing needs, which gives innovation and the entrepreneur such a powerful role to play in evolutionary growth theory. This is Schumpeter's argument but it was surely also Marshall's point when he identified knowledge and organisation as "our most powerful engine of production" (1920, p. 138). Third, like Nelson and Winter (1982), we believe that aggregate explanations of economic growth should be compatible with the vast diversity of micro level, historical evidence concerning the events and processes that equate to the notions of "innovation" and "enterprise". Technical progress has measurable aggregate effects but it is not generated by any aggregate process. Thus, any respectable evolutionary explanation of growth should connect to the rich literatures that study innovation and its management, the history of technology and business organisation, and the developing capabilities of firms and other institutions that jointly influence the growth and application of knowledge. These literatures are natural complements to an evolutionary theory of economic growth; they frame our understanding of the processes generating and limiting innovation, and they provide countless empirical examples to shape our thinking on the knowledge–growth connection.

Several formal consequences follow that differentiate an evolutionary account from modern equilibrium growth theory, endogenous or otherwise. First, we make no appeal to the representative agent, or more accurately described "the uniform agent". What is statistically representative cannot be chosen on a priori grounds. Rather, representative action is an emergent, developing consequence of the economic process, and no evolutionary theory can operate by eliminating diversity in economic behaviour. Indeed, our whole scheme generates growth because of non-representative behaviour. Second, while our economy is competitive, we do not mean by this a state of perfect competition but rather a process of competition within and between industries, the grand themes of Marshallian flux and Schumpeterian enterprise. The importance of competition is not to be understood narrowly, in terms of optimal resource allocation but, broadly, in terms of the connection between technical progress and the widespread diffusion of gains in real income through reductions in the prices of goods and services. Finally, we make no sharp separation between factor substitution within a given technique and changes in technique, for the two phenomena are inseparable. All change in methods requires some new understanding that is only obtained by investing resources in problem-solving activities. In part this is because we do not accept the neoclassical production function as a frame of analysis (Bliss, 1975; Harcourt, 1972), but more fundamentally it is because we do not reason in terms of aggregate stocks of knowledge. There is no metric to reduce knowledge and its changes to a meaningful real aggregate, and the attempt to construct such an aggregate serves only to disguise the role of new knowledge in the process of development. What matters is the uneven development and ever changing heterogeneity of what is known and understood (Kurz, 2008; Steedman, 2003; Metcalfe, 2001). This does not mean that capital accumulation is reduced to a relatively minor, passive role in the growth process, far from it. The accumulation of capabilities through the embodiment of new understanding in the labour force and in the stock of capital structures is a central channel of economic growth, and we place great emphasis on investment processes as the vehicle of change (Nelson et al., 1967). It is important to recognise that these problems are treated here at a price. It is that we enter the argument at the level of the industry, suppressing all the lower level evolution that is occurring between and within firms, the evolution that is the epitome of enterprise and innovation. The origins of economic development and growth are not to be found at the aggregate level, even though there are high level constraints on the evolution of firms and industries. At most we have half an argument, but nonetheless an interesting half that allows us to draw together previously unrelated strands of thought in classical and evolutionary reasoning.

The remainder of this chapter is structured as follows. We begin by outlining competing stylised facts about economic growth and then set out the relations between structural change and aggregate productivity growth contingent on the evolution of the pattern of demand. We then introduce the concept of an industry level technical progress function, and show how rates of technical progress are mutually determined as a consequence of increasing returns and the changing distribution of demand. We next sketch a macroeconomic closure of the evolutionary process, expressed in terms of the mutual determination of rates of capital accumulation and rates of productivity growth. This takes us to the final section where we elaborate on the restless nature of innovation-based economic growth and the conditions under which Kaldor's stylised facts are compatible with the Clark–Kuznets stylised facts.

We may summarise our perspective quite sharply. What distinguishes modern capitalism is not only its order-imposing properties that lead to the self-organisation of the economy, but also the self-transforming properties that create wealth from knowledge and in so doing induce the further development of useful knowledge. It is the manner in which self-organisation and self-transformation interact that is at the core of this chapter.[6]

2   The competing stylised facts of growth and development

We have alluded above to the fact that economic evolution arises at multiple levels throughout an economy of which the aggregate, whole economy level, is only one element in the total picture. Indeed, prior to the Keynesian revolution and Harrod's formulation of aggregate growth theory in the late 1930s, a rich empirical and theoretical literature had developed on the problem of secular economic change, a literature that posed the problem of economic growth in terms of a set of meso level stylised facts relating to growth rate diversity, structural change, innovation and the development of demand in different industries. When growth theory turned "macro", economists largely forgot about the between and within industry detail and replaced one set of stylised facts with a quite different set, expressed in terms of aggregate growth rates and ratios. The two very different, and on the surface incompatible, sets of facts are those most usually associated with Colin Clark and Simon Kuznets on the one hand and Nicholas Kaldor on the other. The Clark–Kuznets facts relate to patterns of growth in different industries and point to the large-scale changes in economic structure that accompany economic growth.[7] This is transparent in terms of the movements in the relative importance of the "high aggregates" such as agriculture, industry and services[8] but it becomes even more manifest when we consider the economy at more disaggregated levels where, for example, there are greater differences in rates of growth of individual industries relative to the manufacturing average, and even greater differences in the growth rates of individual firms relative to an industry average. Consequently there are large inter- and intra-sectoral shifts in shares in output, employment and capital stocks over time that reflect a wide dispersion of growth rates around the economy-wide averages.[9] These shifts are also associated with the entry of new industries and the elimination of old industries along the lines that leading economic historians rightly emphasise (Sayers, 1950; Landes, 1969; Mokyr, 1990, 2002). On this the historical record is absolutely clear; measured economic growth flows from a process of structural change driven by long sequences of innovations in technique and organisation that may usefully be summarised as distinct technical epochs (Freeman and Louçã, 2001).

However, this uneven pattern of the growth record is only part of the picture. Simon Kuznets (1929) and Arthur Burns (1934) also identified a further regularity in the process of restless growth, namely retardation, the persistent tendency of industry growth rates to decline over time from the inception of the industry. Solomon Fabricant (1940, 1942) found compelling evidence on the retardation of growth in American manufacturing output and employment over the period 1899 to 1939. Further studies, by Hoffman (1949), Stigler (1947) and Gaston (1961) also investigated the empirical basis of the retardation thesis in different bodies of industrial data but without any further development of the underlying theory. Taken together these authors might be described as espousing "a moving frontier" view of economic growth and structural change, in which, in Kuznets' words,

> As we observe various industries within a given national economy, we see that the lead in development shifts from one branch to another. A rapidly developing industry does not retain its vigorous growth forever but slackens and is overtaken by others whose period of rapid development is beginning. Within one country we can observe a succession of different branches of activity in the vanguard of the country's economic development, and within each industry we can notice a conspicuous slackening in the rate of increase. (Kuznets, 1929/1954, p. 254).

By contrast, Kaldor's (1961) stylised facts refer to the rough constancy of the growth rates of aggregate output and capital stocks together with the constancy of several key aggregate ratios, particularly the capital output ratio, the shares of profits and contractual incomes in GDP, and the overall rate of profits (Maddison, 1991). To understand the relation between these very different facts is a major challenge to our thinking about economic growth, not least because the familiar devices of semi-stationary growth (Bliss, 1975), or proportional dynamics (Pasinetti, 1993) are no more than ways to hide from view the Clark–Kuznets facts, as if the relative proportions of different activities are frozen in time.[10] There is neither structural change nor retardation in these contrived macro worlds, only uniform expansion or, just as readily, uniform contraction. In approaching the analysis of economic growth in this way, we effectively rule out any meaningful connection between the growth of knowledge and the growth of the economy. Several recent contributions have addressed this problem of reconciliation by developing frameworks in which rates of growth of demand and/or rates of technical progress differ sector by sector. In many of these frameworks the rates of technical progress are treated exogenously, and that is to us an unhelpful restriction that is certain to misrepresent the relation between the growth of knowledge and the development of the economy.[11]

The important insight here is not that structural change and the growth of aggregate measures occur together, for that would be quite compatible with the idea of structural change as a passive, inessential by-product of growth. If that were all that were at stake, a macro, single-sector approach would be a plausible first step. Unfortunately, this is not so; for structural change is not only a consequence of differential growth, it is a cause of that differential growth. This process is autocatalytic – progress generates progress, structural change generates structural change – which is what we take Schumpeter to have meant when he wrote of "development from within", or what Frank Knight meant when he described growth in capitalism as a "self-exciting" process. Precisely what one might expect to occur in an economy whose long-run evolution is driven by new knowledge, by entrepreneurial conjecture and by the reallocation of resources to take advantage of the opportunities immanent in innovation.

To term this an evolutionary process is entirely appropriate. Structural change is a product of differential growth, and the mutual determination of growth rate differences within a population is a leading characteristic of evolutionary theory. Moreover, the more we disaggregate any given population into its component subpopulations the more we find evidence for differential growth over any given period, and the longer that period the greater the diversity of growth experience. Thus there is a simple evolutionist's maxim that must always be borne in mind, namely, "the more we aggregate the more we hide the evidence for and causes of economic evolution". The evolutionary question is "Why do rates of growth differ across activities and over time?" not the question "Why are they uniform and stable?"

It is because a macro perspective hides the very processes that explain the differential growth of productivity and output that we cannot confront many of the most important stylised facts of modern economic growth (Kuznets, 1954, 1971, 1977; Harberger, 1998). Nor can we incorporate the role of demand in shaping growth patterns between industries; indeed it is remarkable how the modern growth story is a predominately supply side account of the expansion of productivity and inputs. Changes in the composition of demand are ignored and the coordinating role of markets in the growth process is lost from view. Our approach therefore places two processes at the heart of evolutionary growth, the endogenous generation of industry-specific rates of technical progress, and the endogenous evolution of demand as growing per capita income is reallocated across different lines of expenditure. Let us consider each one in turn.

At the core of any theory of endogenous growth we find some hypothesis about the origination of innovation and its impact on methods of production. Our approach develops the notion of an industry-specific technical progress function that follows from Adam Smith's central idea linking technical progress to the changing division of labour within and between activities, and its subsequent elaboration by Allyn Young (1928). Developing from roots in Smith and Marshall, Young articulated the view that the extension of the market causes and is caused by the exploitation of new technological opportunities. We shall suggest below that this is precisely the insight needed to capture the link between structural change and aggregate growth. Of course, the scope of Young's argument was much broader than the linking of growth of market and technical progress *within* a single industry. What mattered was the reciprocal dependence between different industries in which "inventions" in one sphere initiate "responses elsewhere in the industrial structure which in turn have further unsettling effect" (Young, 1928, p. 532). For Young, for Schumpeter and for Marshall, progress is systemic and the idea of capitalism as a system in equilibrium did not hold much appeal.[12]

As soon as we abandon the equi-proportional method there is immediate scope for giving demand side forces a key role in the explanation of structural change, and for giving far more attention to the role of demand in the connection between growth and technical change. As Pasinetti has expressed it, "any investigation into technical progress must necessarily imply some hypotheses . . . on the evolution of consumer preferences as income increases", while "increases in productivity and increases in income are two facets of the same phenomenon, since the first implies the second, and the *composition* of the second determines the relevance of the first, the one cannot be considered if the other is ignored" (our emphasis, 1981, p. 69). This is the territory marked out by Engel's law, not only in terms of the broad aggregates in relation to agriculture, industry and services but also in terms of income elasticities for the more narrowly defined outputs of specific industries (Kindleberger, 1989).

The mutual interdependence between the differential growth of demand and the differential incidence of technical progress is at the centre of our evolutionary account of growth and development. But we are not free to propose any pattern of economic evolution independently of the constraints implicit in the requirement that aggregate saving equals aggregate investment. This leads to the central importance of Harrod's insight that the aggregate rate of growth also depends on the interaction between capital productivity and thrift. This is what our frame is meant to capture in terms of the simultaneous evolution of the macro and the sectoral such that the one cannot be explained independently of the other. It is a frame that because it is both "bottom up" and "top down" allows us to render compatible the competing stylised facts.

3 The population method: accounting for structural change and economic growth

An economy with many industries in which each industry engages in many different activities is of a level of complexity that places a great challenge to any growth theory. Yet, if we understand an economy to be a population of different activities, a method of analysis immediately becomes apparent, one that is central to all evolutionary theories of a variation-cum-selective retention kind. This is the method that we call population analysis. In it an evolutionary population is represented by a set of differentiated entities that are acted on by common causal forces to transform the population, either by changing the constituent entities or by changing their relative importance. In our case the entities are distinct industries. The common causal forces are the reallocation of demand across the industries as per capita income increases, the different rates of technical progress in each industry and the constraint imposed by the equality of saving and investment in the aggregate. One of the immediate advantages of the population method is that it can be conducted at multiple, interconnected levels so that change at one level correlates with change at other levels. Thus we could also treat each industry as a population of different branches of "similar but not identical" activities, and each such branch as a further population of closely competing firms. In this way an economy becomes a population of populations of populations. Even the firm could be analysed as a population of different activities under unified managerial control if we wanted to conduct the argument at its most refined level. For expositional reasons we must suppress the below industry level of aggregation, recognising that a full account of technical progress at the level of the industry necessarily requires an analysis of the differential innovation performance of firms and their differential rates of growth. All we need say here is that our knowledge-based economy is coordinated in the sense that the average price within an industry is a long-run normal price, set to maintain full capacity utilisation over time. Short period deviations from full capacity working are ignored, as seems appropriate in a treatment of sustainable growth. What we lose is any account of the within-industry determinants of prices and profitability and thus of the within-industry role of dynamic coordination through competition. However, intra-industry analysis is already well developed in evolutionary economic theory, whereas the aspects treated here are not (Andersen, 2004; Witt, 2003; Dosi, 2000; Metcalfe, 1998; Nelson and Winter, 1982).

One of the principal attributes of the population method is its connection with the statistical method of analysis that is common ground in modern evolutionary theory. This is reflected in the fact that the rate and direction of evolution in a population depend on statistical measures of the variety that are defined over that population. In the presence of pervasive heterogeneity we use the population moments of various industry characteristics (means, variances, covariances and so on), to understand the rate and direction of evolutionary change in that population. Here the three principal characteristics in which the industries vary are their prevailing levels of productivity, their income elasticities of demand, and their technical progress functions. Additional dimensions of differentiation are not ruled out; indeed the greater the number of dimensions of variation the richer is the evolutionary analysis in prospect. The population moments that play a central role in the evolutionary approach are always weighted moments, where the weights are the appropriate measures of the relative importance of each industry in the population. The weights capture the immediate structure of the population and change in response to the divergent rates of growth within that population. Moreover, because the weights are changing so are the moments that they are used to construct. The system is restless and we do not need to assume that its motion is governed by a stable attractor to which it is converging: which is fortunate, for the very process of movement necessarily revises the terms and conditions for future movement.

Within the total population of industries that defines our economy we identify three classes of structural change: there is the differential growth of the industries that continue in operation over some time interval; there is the entry of new industries; and there is the exit of existing industries. Over a short interval of time the aggregate growth of the whole population is accounted for by $g = g_c + n - e$, where g is the growth rate of the ensemble of total activity, g_c is the growth rate of the aggregate of the continuing industries, n is the proportionate increase in output associated with newly created industries (the industry birth rate), and e is the proportionate loss of output associated with industries that disappear (the industry death rate).[13] For short intervals of time these birth and death rates may be of negligible importance but over longer intervals they may make up the bulk of the explanation of population level change. Indeed, for sufficiently long intervals the output of continuing industries may be of negligible importance: that is to say, the sets of industries that define the economy at any two census dates may have few elements in common. However, any newly born industries can only increase their relative importance if they grow more quickly than the average population, just as the industries that have disappeared will have grown less rapidly than the economy as a whole. Entry and exit matter qualitatively but they only matter quantitatively in terms of the subsequent and antecedent rates of differential expansion. Hence we shall focus exclusively on this factor of differential expansion and contraction, considering rates of growth defined over short intervals and setting the net industry entry rate equal to zero.

We must now be precise about the characteristics of each vertically integrated industry. Each one consists of a group of firms supplying final output ready to be consumed or invested, together with a group of firms supplying the produced means of production to produce the final goods. When we speak of employment or investment, we refer to the total quantities in the supply chain that support the current output of the final good, including investments to expand capacity to produce the requisite intermediate goods. The technology of each vertically integrated industry is reflected in a pattern of division of labour and specialisation that in turn reflects the different technological and organisational knowledge bases of each component activity. In relation to technology and organisation, the capital coefficient, b_j (the ratio of capital stock in the whole integrate industry to the capacity output for the final good) is assumed to be different for each industry. Moreover, all innovations are assumed to be Harrod neutral process improvements; progress is purely labour augmenting within the entire supply chain. Let a_j be defined as unit labour requirements within the supply chain required to produce full capacity output, then labour productivity for the industry, again measured in terms of capacity output, is $q_j = 1/a_j$. Notice carefully that at levels of aggregation above the industry, the ensemble input proportions will change in response to the different final output growth rates of the various integrated industries. However, this is not factor substitution in the traditional sense, for there is no smooth industry production function, it is instead factor reallocation or between-industry adaptation and it is the reallocation or adaptation effects that play a central role in this evolutionary growth theory.

3.1 *Measures of population structure*
We need just two measures of population structure to capture the relative importance of each vertically integrated industry – one in terms of its share of aggregate employment, e_j, the other in terms of its share in aggregate capacity output, z_j.[14] Once we know the population structure we can immediately translate industry labour efficiency (and its inverse labour productivity) into their population equivalents: reflecting the fact that each

industry contributes to aggregate productivity in proportion to its share in total employment, and to aggregate unit labour requirements (efficiency) in proportion to its share in capacity output. It follows that the average unit labour requirement is $a_z = \Sigma z_i a_i$ and average labour productivity is $q_e = \Sigma e_j q_j$, from which it follows that, $a_z q_e = 1$.

Some elementary but important aspects of population accounting now follow from these definitions. First there is a structural consistency condition

$$e_j q_j = z_j q_e \text{ and } z_j a_j = e_j a_z. \tag{1A}$$

From (1A) it follows immediately that the employment structure will differ from the output structure as individual productivity or efficiency levels deviate from their population averages. It also follows that the proportional rates of change in these measures are related by the conservation conditions[15]

$$\hat{q}_e = -\hat{a}_z \tag{1B}$$

$$\hat{e}_j + \hat{q}_j = \hat{z}_j + \hat{q}_e \text{ and } \hat{z}_j + \hat{a}_j = \hat{e}_j + \hat{a}_z \tag{1C}$$

This is the dynamic counterpart to the proposition that the employment and output share weights for any industry are equal only when it has a *level of productivity* equal to the population average. We can see immediately that proportional growth necessarily implies the absence of structural change, structure is frozen, and from this it follows that each industry must have the same rate of productivity and efficiency increase, a requirement that is not conformable to the facts. One immediate corollary is that if, say, we hold the employment share constant in some industry then, in general, the corresponding output share cannot be constant. The converse is also true. Notice also, that the wider the spread of productivity levels in the population the greater the difference between output shares and employment shares.[16]

These accounting relations are no more than bookkeeping devices but they provide the necessary connections between investment, technical progress and the changing pattern of demand as we can now establish. Investment is important in three complementary ways: as the means to expand productive capacity; as a generator of aggregate demand; and as the carrier of new knowledge and a stimulant to productivity growth. This is the sense in which we have a long-run growth theory; it is a theory dependent on the determinants and consequences of investment activity. However, by the long run we do not mean some date far into the hypothetical future when the economy has converged to a steady expansion path but rather the immediate present when long-run forces of investment and technical progress are active. As in Marshall's analysis, different causal forces are working at every moment but with different velocities, and the different velocities are the generators of structural change and evolution.

3.2　Demand and aggregate productivity growth

Just as the production side of the economy can be analysed as a population of industries, so the demand side can be analysed as a population of final consumers, such that the final demand for the output of any one industry depends on the number of consumers it has and the rate at which they consume. We assume that the driving causal processes behind changes in the pattern of demand are employment growth in relation to the number of consumers, and the growth of per capita income (the consequence of the growth of aggregate productivity) in relation to their rates of consumption. In this scheme, productivity growth reduces prices relative to money incomes, and the consequent increase in real income generates a redistribution of expenditure over the different industries – the Engel law effects that we referred to above. That the rates of growth of demand differ across industries, differences that would become more marked the lower the level at which we construct our industry aggregates, is not only one of the most important empirical regularities in economics, it is the reason why proportional growth models cannot capture the process of economic growth in a substantial way.[17]

Let the per capita income elasticities for each industry, ψ_j, be defined as the ratio of the growth in per capita demand for the output of each industry to the growth rate of aggregate per capita income, thus

$$\psi_j = \frac{g_j - n}{g_z - n} \tag{2}$$

where n is the rate of growth of total employment, and $g_z = \Sigma z_j g_j$ is the rate of growth of aggregate output.[18] These elasticities provide us with the basis for a selection process across the set of industries since they give rise to different growth rates of demand and output. The simplification, that employment growth is neutral in its demand composition effects, is precisely that, a convenient simplification. What matters is that per capita income growth and population growth have differential demand effects and this is what we have captured in equation (2) and in its consequences below. Of course, in emphasising the role of income elasticities in the inter-industry selection process, we should not be deluded into thinking that we have said anything terribly profound. The elasticities are averages taken across the population of consumers, contingent on the distribution of tastes, on the distribution of income (both personal and functional) and on the particular prevailing pattern of expenditure across very different commodities. What we need is some empirical and conceptual understanding of the determinants of income elasticities in general, their relation to the distribution of income, and how they change in relation to innovation and the entry of new industries. This we do not yet have, nor do we need it for immediate purposes.[19]

From equation (2) we can write the rate of output growth of each industry as

$$g_j = n + \psi_j \hat{q}_e \tag{3}$$

where $\hat{q}_e = (d/dt)\log q_e$ is the, yet to be constructed, aggregate rate of productivity increase. The immediate consequence of this formulation is that the rate of growth of each industry cannot be determined before we have determined the rates of growth of employment and productivity across the entire population ensemble. Thus, the pattern of industry growth rates that emerges is simultaneously determined with the aggregate rate of growth of employment and of productivity.

The pattern of structural change in terms of output follows immediately from equation (3) since

$$\dot{z}_j = z_j(g_j - g_z) = z_j(\psi_j - \psi_z)\hat{q}_e \tag{4A}$$

An industry gains or loses relative importance in the ensemble of total (capacity) output as its income elasticity is greater or less than the population average income elasticity, which, of course, necessarily takes the numerical value of one. However, the proximate driver of the changes in structure is the growth of average per capita income; without technical progress the output structure of the population and its employment structure are frozen in time.

Relation (4A) is our first example of the use of the replicator dynamic principle, in which the changing economic weight of an industry depends on how its characteristics compare to the population average of those characteristics.[20] The importance of the replicator dynamic is that it provides a way of analysing economic change that is independent of any assumption of the existence of a long-run attractor towards which the economy is converging. In an open, knowledge-driven economy there cannot reasonably be expected to be any such stable attractor, for the very movement towards it would create new knowledge and new entrepreneurial conjectures, and thus change the foundations of that attractor. Replicator dynamics sidesteps these inherent difficulties by making the relevant rates of change dependent on the distributions of industry characteristics around their current population averages, while simultaneously providing an explanation of how those averages are changing. We have already pointed out that evolutionary analysis is inherently statistical in the sense that it relates different statistical moments within a causal structure, and an immediate illustration of this principle can be found in the relation between the variance of the industry growth rates and the variance in the income elasticities of demand, which, making use of (4A) is given by

$$\sum z_i (g_i - g_z)^2 = V_z(g) = \hat{q}_e^2 V_z(\psi) \tag{4B}$$

where $V_z(\psi_j)$ is the capacity-weighted variance in the income elasticities of demand. The greater the rate of productivity growth the greater is the variance in the industry growth rates for a given variance in the income elasticities, and the greater is the resultant turbulence in the capacity shares.

There is an implication of the replicator principle that is worth drawing out at this point. It is that the income elasticities of demand cannot all be constant in a progressive economy, unless, trivially, they are all equal to one, the necessary condition for proportional growth. This is a deduction that is already implicit in Engel's law in which the elasticities decline with increases in per capita income. It follows because the population average elasticity $\psi_z = 1$ is a constant even though the structure of demand is evolving according to equation (3). Consequently,

$$\sum \dot{z}_j \psi_j + \sum z_j \dot{\psi}_j = 0$$

and from (4B) this becomes

$$\sum z_j \dot{\psi}_j = -\hat{q}_e \sum z_j (\psi_j - \psi_z) \psi_j = -\hat{q}_e V_z(\psi_j)$$

It follows that $\sum z_j \dot{\psi}_j = 0$ if, and only if, productivity growth is zero or if all income elasticities are the same (unity in value). The former assumption rules out technical progress, the latter rules out structural change. Hence we are left with the requirement that in a progressive economy $\sum z_j \hat{\psi}_j < 0$. On average the income elasticities must decline as productivity grows, although this constraint is quite consistent with some of them increasing. This result is an example of what evolutionists call Fisher's principle, after the eminent biologist who first formulated some of the statistical rules of population dynamics.[21] It will recur in many different guises below.

3.3 Aggregate productivity growth

We can now explore the implications for the relation between productivity growth in the individual industries and productivity growth for the entire economy. This is not as straightforward as it might seem, because the movement in the ensemble averages for productivity or efficiency is composed of two components, technical progress in each industry and structural change. Thus, for example, since $q_e = \sum e_j q_j$, it follows from equation (1A) that the aggregate rate of productivity growth is given by

$$\hat{q}_e = \sum z_j \hat{a}_j + \sum z_j \hat{e}_j \qquad (5A)$$

With a similar expression applying to the change in average efficiency, thus

$$\hat{a}_z = \sum e_j \hat{a}_j + \sum e_j \hat{z}_j \qquad (5B)$$

In relations (5A) and (5B) the aggregate rate of change is the sum of the average technical progress effect and the average structural change effect; two terms that are often called the "within-industry effect" and the "between-industry effect" in modern productivity accounting exercises.[22] However, our hypothesis on demand dynamics allows us to elaborate further the structural change effect and to write $\hat{q}_e$ as proportional to the weighted sum of the industry productivity growth rates.[23] Since n_j is the rate of growth of employment in industry j and $g_j = n_j + \hat{q}_j$, it follows that $n_j - n = \psi_j \hat{q}_e - \hat{q}_j$. If we weight this last expression by the employment shares e_j and sum across the population of industries we find that

$$\sum e_j(n_j - n) = \left(\sum e_j \psi_j\right)\hat{q}_e - \sum e_j \hat{q}_j = 0$$

since $\sum e_j n_j = n$ by definition. Thus, our weighting scheme is provided by

$$\hat{q}_e = \frac{1}{\sum e_j \psi_j} \sum e_j \hat{q}_j \qquad (6A)$$

Unless $\sum e_j \psi_j = 1$, these weights do not sum to unity. Indeed, it follows immediately that the employment-weighted income elasticity is given by

$$\sum e_j \psi_j = \psi_e = 1 - \frac{C_e(\psi_j, q_j)}{q_e} \qquad (6B)$$

where $C_e(\psi_j, q_j)$ is the "e"-weighted covariance between productivity levels and income elasticities across the population of industries. Thus, the employment-weighted average of the income elasticities coincides with the output-weighted average only if this covariance is zero.

By an analogous argument, the rate of decline in unit labour requirements is given by

$$\hat{a}_z = \frac{\sum e_j \hat{a}_j}{\psi_e} \tag{7A}$$

And here we can express the employment weighted income elasticity as

$$\sum e_j \psi_j = 1 + \frac{C_z(\psi_j, a_j)}{a_z} \tag{7B}$$

where $C_z(\psi_j, a_j)$ is the corresponding "z"-weighted covariance between industry income elasticities and average unit labour requirements in each industry.[24] The employment-weighted average income elasticity plays an important role in our analysis of aggregate growth and structural change, a result that could not be readily anticipated.

To explore this point further, we can establish how much of the overall growth of productivity or efficiency is a result of structural change and how much is a result of technical progress proper. Consider first the decomposition of changes in $\hat{a}_z$. Let σ_a be defined as the proportion of the rate of change in aggregate efficiency that is a result of output structural change. Then we find from (5B) and (7B) that $\sigma_a = 1 - \psi_e$. It follows that the corresponding proportion of aggregate labour efficiency change that is a result of technical progress, $1 - \sigma_a$ is equal to ψ_e. Consequently if $C_z(\psi_j, a_j) = 0$, that is, the income elasticities and efficiency levels are uncorrelated when weighted by output shares ($\psi_e = 1$), then the contribution of structural change to average efficiency growth will be zero even though the output structure is changing. Moreover, if this covariance is positive, then changes in the structure of output are offsetting the effect of technical progress in the generation of average efficiency change, because demand is shifting relatively in favour of industries that have above average unit labour requirements.

How much structural change in total is generated for this population of industries? One measure of this is obtained by adding together the weighted changes in the employment and output shares so that[25]

$$\sum z_j \hat{e}_j + \sum e_j \hat{z}_j = -\frac{C_e(q_j, \hat{q}_j)}{q_e} = -\frac{C_z(a_j, \hat{a}_j)}{a_z} \tag{8}$$

In (8) the statistic $C_e(q_j, \hat{q}_j)$ is the employment-weighted covariance between levels of productivity and rates of productivity change across the population of industries, while $C_z(a_j, \hat{a}_j)$ is the corresponding output-weighted covariance between levels and rates of change in efficiency. When these covariances are zero, it follows that the average amount of structural change is zero. These covariances play an important role in constraining the patterns of change in the population. As one might expect, the way the pattern of productivity change correlates with the pattern of productivity levels is an important determinant of the overall pattern of evolution.[26]

It is less straightforward to establish how much of the change in aggregate labour productivity is a result of structural change in the pattern of employment, because this depends on the co-movements of output and productivity. However, if we define σ_q as the proportional contribution of structural change in employment to total productivity growth then it follows from equation (8) that

$$(\sigma_q - \sigma_a)\hat{q}_e = -\frac{C_e(q_j, \hat{q}_j)}{q_e} \tag{9}$$

From equation (9) we see that σ_q and σ_a are different whenever levels and rates of change of productivity are correlated, and that $\sigma_q < \sigma_a$ whenever this correlation is positive. This is an important result in evolutionary productivity accounting. Since the output structure and the employment structure evolve differently, one would expect that their changes make different structural contributions to aggregate productivity and efficiency change (Metcalfe and Ramlogan, 2006). Thus, for example, to discover empirically that changes in employment structure make a negligible contribution to aggregate productivity growth, $\sigma_q = 0$, would be consistent with the simultaneous finding that changes in the output structure made a large contribution to aggregate efficiency growth and by implication productivity growth.

From equation (8) we can also decompose the aggregate rate of productivity growth in a different but illuminating way in terms of the average rate of technical progress and the average amount of structural change in the population. Let the average rate of technical progress be defined as $T_z = \Sigma z_j \hat{q}_j = -\Sigma z_j \hat{a}_j$ from which it follows that

$$\hat{q}_e = \frac{1}{\psi_e}\left[T_z - \frac{C_e(q_j, \hat{q}_j)}{q_e} \right] \tag{10}$$

When $C_e(q_j, \hat{q}_j) = 0$ then $T_z = \psi_e \hat{q}_e$ and the employment-weighted average income elasticity exactly measures the proportion of aggregate productivity growth that is contributed by technical progress alone.

Having spelt out the population accounting relations between structural change and productivity change, we turn next to the determinants of productivity growth at the industry level, for this is the fundamental driving force in this evolutionary frame. Structural change in demand, operating through the differentiated income elasticities, matters, but it only operates in response to these more fundamental forces that create wealth from knowledge. Since we reject any reference to a neoclassical production function and to changes in aggregate knowledge, how can we build an account of the self-transformation of industries and economies? Such an account should generate the transformation process "from within", it should connect with the sector-specific growth of knowledge and it should emphasise the fundamental features of enterprise in relation to investment and innovation. If we are to choose any principle that draws together these desiderata it is that the division of labour is limited by, and in turn limits, the extent of the market. Changes in the division of labour require changes in technology in the broad, and extension of the market requires the growth of per capita income. No other principle would seem to have the ability to unify the transformation of production methods and the extension of demand to create an endogenous theory of enterprise and economic transformation.

4   Investment and a technical progress function

In a remarkable empirical investigation into the growth of manufacturing in the USA over the period 1899–1939, Solomon Fabricant (1942) drew attention to the fact that rapidly growing output in an industry is usually associated with rising employment and increasing labour productivity and that when output is in decline so is productivity. Across industries, there are wide variations both in levels of productivity and in growth rates of productivity, so Fabricant saw that the way was open to explain these differences in terms of the differential growth of the markets for different groups of products.

Moreover, growth of output is usually associated with net investment, and conversely, such output growth usually implies the growth of measured capital per worker. The significance of this argument is not only that investment creates the capacity to serve a growing market but that it is a major channel through which technical advances "cut into unit labour requirements" (p. 96).

By investment, we mean any use of resources that improves the capacity of productive assets of any kind, assets being defined in the conventional way, by their ability to yield future income streams. From this perspective, investment is the activity that enhances productive economic capabilities, and it is much broader than the laying down of new plant and physical infrastructure. Investments in human capital, in research and development, in improvements in the organisation of firms are all of importance alongside the development of new plants and structures. Investment can then be interpreted as the cost of making the arrangements to improve capabilities and thus the cost of generating improvements in productivity (Scott, 1989). Of course, any change in such capabilities will require the growth of knowledge somewhere in the economy but the kinds of knowledge required tend to vary enormously and cannot be reduced to any simple metric or common denominator. Following Harrod (1948) we can distinguish two broad classes of investment that realise productivity improvements. One is the investment that adds capacity at the margin of production, and the other is rather more diffuse and includes any investment that serves to raise efficiency in existing plants without changing their capacity output. We call the second the "improvement effect" (operating on existing capacity), and the first the "best practice" effect (operating at the margin of new capacity), following Salter (1960).

We now introduce the concept of a technical progress function, to connect the rate of productivity growth to the rate of gross investment industry by industry (Kaldor, 1957). This function is the realisation of the prevailing scope and scale of innovation and enterprise in a vertically integrated industry, and is thus the realisation of the opportunities opened up by the growth of knowledge throughout the entire vertically integrated supply chain (Pasinetti, 1981). It combines the two classes of investment such that an industry's overall rate of productivity growth is necessarily a weighted average of their different effects. In general, the relative incidence of the two types of investment will vary industry by industry, reflecting the particular composition of its vertically integrated supply chain and the rates of progress in the component parts of that supply chain. However, in all cases, the faster the growth rate of capacity the faster is the rate of productivity growth and the greater is relative importance of investment in "best practice" compared to the investment in improving the existing population of plants.

Let α_j denote the proportionate improvement effect on existing plants inclusive of the retirement of marginal capacity, and let β_j denote the proportionate rate of improvement in best practice design as embodied in new plants. Both these coefficients are averages struck across each vertically integrated industry to reflect technical change at plant level, and the wider effects of reorganisation and differentiation of the supply chain as a market grows. Then we can write each vertically integrated technical progress function as[27]

$$\hat{q}_j = \alpha_j + \beta_j g_j \tag{11A}$$

which is equivalent to

$$\hat{q}_j = \alpha_j + \omega_j\left(\frac{I}{Q_c}\right)_j \tag{11B}$$

where I/Q_c is the vertically integrated ratio of investment in new plant to physical capacity and $\omega_j = \beta_j/b_j$ is the coefficient that translates that investment into productivity growth.[28] This specification informs us immediately that structural change has feedback effects on the industry rates of productivity growth, because each industry growth rate is arithmetically equal to the sum of the population average output growth rate and the proportionate rate of change in the output share of that industry. Hence the core evolutionary principle that productivity growth induces structural change, which induces further productivity growth without limit provided that knowledge continues to develop.

Relations (11) are fundamental to understanding everything that follows; they are the basic building blocks of our investment-led evolutionary theory of growth and development. Indeed the key point about any endogenous growth theory is that it requires some specification of the economic determinants of technical progress, some link between new knowledge and its economic application. We should note immediately that the same relation has been introduced by Kaldor (1972), in his exposition of the Verdoorn law, although Verdoorn's original account has very different foundations from those articulated by Kaldor or Fabricant.[29]

5 Increasing returns and the interdependence of rates of productivity growth

The immediate consequence of combining the technical progress functions with the population analysis of productivity growth is to find that the industry rates of productivity growth are interdependent. Here we are following the line of enquiry that is traced from Adam Smith, through Alfred Marshall to Allyn Young (1928), to the effect that increasing returns and the extension of the market generate reciprocal interdependences of productivity growth between the different industries. As Young put it, "[e]very important advance in the organisation of production alters the conditions of industrial activity and initiates responses elsewhere in the industrial structure which in turn have a further unsettling effect" (p. 533). The precise forms those changes in organisation and technique take within each supply chain are not the issue in question, rather it is their reciprocal effects on productivity growth that matter. There is an organic unity to the pattern of technical progress, a unity that is conditioned by the structure of the economy and that changes as that structure changes.

The interdependence of productivity growth rates follows directly from the technical progress functions (11), the relations between the growth of each industry and the overall rate of productivity growth (3), and the relation between the aggregate and the industry productivity growth rates (6A). Thus we can translate each technical progress function into the corresponding increasing returns function to integrate the evolution of technology with the evolution of demand,

$$\hat{q}_j = \alpha_j + \beta_j\left[n + \psi_j\left(\frac{\sum e_j\hat{q}_j}{\sum e_j\psi_j}\right)\right] \tag{12}$$

This expresses the central point of the Smith/Marshall/Young approach, which is that productivity growth in any one sector increases with productivity growth in all other sectors provided that its output is a normal good. The productivity growth rates are

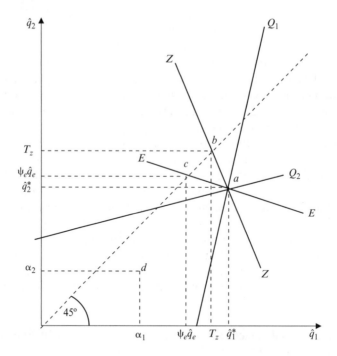

Figure 3.1   The distributed pattern of technical progress

mutually determined through the coordination of demand and capacity in the market process, industry by industry. Equation (12) generates an ensemble of simultaneous productivity growth equations, and the solution in the two-industry case is sketched in Figure 3.1. The schedules Q_1 and Q_2 are the reciprocal increasing returns functions for each industry, and they intersect at a to determine the market coordinated rates of technical progress, in each industry, $\hat{q}_1^*$ and $\hat{q}_2^*$.

The position and slope of each increasing returns function depends on the structure of the aggregate population and this structure is captured by the weights $u_j = e_j \psi_j / \psi_e$ which measure the contribution each industry makes to the employment-weighted average income elasticity of demand.[30] The coordinated rates of technical progress thus depend on the structure of the economy but in the subtle way embodied in the weights, u_j. Any change in employment structure, as mediated by the distribution of income elasticities, implies a different pattern of technical progress across the population of industries, and it also implies a different aggregate rate of technical progress. Thus structure shapes the pattern of progress, and the pattern of progress reshapes the structure.

Now draw through point a in Figure 3.1 the straight line $Z - Z$ with slope, $- z_1/z_2$ (the relative capacity output shares) to intersect the 45° line at b. This point measures the rate of aggregate technical progress, $T_z = \Sigma z_j \hat{q}_j^*$ and, as drawn, $\hat{q}_1^* > T_z > \hat{q}_2^*$. This differs from the aggregate rate of productivity growth by the contribution made by employment structural change, as given in equation (10) above. Hence, if we also draw the line $E - E$ through point a with slope $- e_1/e_2$, it intersects the 45° degree line at c to measure $\psi_e \hat{q}_e$. One can see immediately how the average rate of structural change in employment and output combined is determined jointly with the pattern of productivity growth, because the distance between points b and c measures the covariance statistic $C_e(q_j, \hat{q}_j)/q_e$. As drawn in Figure 3.1, $T_z > \psi_e \hat{q}_e$, so this covariance is positive,[31] and the overall pattern of structural change is acting to reduce aggregate productivity growth below the average rate of technical progress. The converse case means that this covariance statistic is negative. When the industry levels of productivity and rates of productivity growth are uncorrelated then points b and c coincide and the covariance is zero. Here there are two relevant possibilities. Either the levels of labour productivity are the same in each industry so that the schedules $Z - Z$ and $E - E$ coincide, or the two increasing returns functions happen to intersect on the 45° line, to equate the industry rates of productivity growth. Now consider point d. This depicts the pattern of productivity growth when the best practice rates of design improvement β_j are equal to zero, so eliminating the possibility of increasing returns and the mutual interdependence of rates of technical progress. The difference between points d and a reflects the importance of increasing returns in this population and of reciprocal interdependence in the growth process: it measures what we shall term the "Young effect"; the stimulus to growth generated by the autocatalytic nature of technical progress and the growth of per capita income. The point about positive feedback, as Young emphasised, is that it augments growth within and between sectors, amplifying the wellspring of progress, provided by the enterprise-based relations between processes of innovation and investment.[32] In this way, we can comprehend his insistence that changes in one industry induce changes in other industries, mutually reinforcing the growth of productivity within the entire population of industries.[33]

Having dwelt extensively on the relation between industry rates of technical progress and aggregate productivity growth we should also draw attention to the other lessons contained in Figure 3.1. The first is that the industry pattern of technical progress depends on the rate of growth of total employment, and the faster is total employment growth the faster are the rates of technical progress industry by industry. The second relates to the fact that the technical progress functions are defined in terms of sets of supply chain relationships, with the likelihood that different industries have elements of their respective supply chains in common. Thus, for example, an improvement in steel or plastics technology will influence the increasing returns functions of all the vertically integrated industries that utilise steel and plastics in their supply chains. Such a technological breakthrough of a "general purpose" kind will shift outwards both the increasing returns functions in Figure 3.1, and induce further technical progress, according to the pattern of weights u_j.

Notice carefully, that Figure 3.1 represents a process of growth coordination at a point in time. It does not represent growth equilibrium interpreted in some more general sense, as a fixed attractor on which productivity patterns converge and stabilise. Indeed, it is a fundamental assumption of our evolutionary perspective that growth is open-ended, that there is not any state of dynamic rest in the presence of innovation-driven growth. Thus, points a and b, c and d are continually "on the move" as the relative employment shares vary over time.

We can now derive the appropriate expressions for the aggregate rate of productivity growth and the aggregate rate of technical progress. For the former, we weight each increasing returns function (12) by the corresponding employment share weights and sum to yield the following relation between aggregate productivity growth and the rate of growth of total employment

$$\hat{q}_e = \frac{\alpha_e + \beta_e \cdot n}{\psi_e(1 - \beta_u)} \tag{13A}$$

In (13A), $\alpha_e = \Sigma e_j \alpha_j$ is the average rate improvement to existing plant, $\beta_e = \Sigma e_j \beta_j$ is the average progress elasticity constructed with the employment shares, while $\beta_u = \Sigma u_j \beta_j$ is the average progress elasticity, derived from the weights u_j.[34] The conditions for Fabricant's law to hold in the aggregate are $\beta_e < 1$, and $\beta_u < 1$, which are certainly satisfied if the individual rates of best practice design improvement are less than unity. Then we are assured that growth is autocatalytic, with demand, output and productivity growth mutually reinforcing one another.

To derive the average rate of technical progress, T_z, we net out the contribution of structural change to productivity growth by multiplying each increasing returns function by the capacity output weights z_j, to obtain the relation[35]

$$T_z = \left[\alpha_z + \frac{\alpha_e \beta_w}{\psi_e(1 - \beta_u)} \right] + \left[\beta_z + \frac{\beta_e \beta_w}{\psi_e(1 - \beta_n)} \right] n \tag{13B}$$

where $\beta_z = \Sigma z_j \beta_j$ and $\beta_w = \Sigma w_j \beta_j$ are appropriately weighted best practice effect elasticities.[36]

The formulations in equations (13) map directly into Figure 3.1 because they take as given the rate of employment growth. However, from our viewpoint the rate of growth of employment is not an arbitrary given but is rather a derived consequence of the difference between aggregate output growth and aggregate productivity growth. Rearranging (13A) we can thus express Young's law across the ensemble of industries, as the aggregate relation between productivity growth and output growth, thus[37]

$$\hat{q}_e = \frac{\alpha_e + \beta_e g_z}{\psi_e(1 - \beta_u) + \beta_e} \tag{14}$$

Equation (14) is the aggregate increasing returns function for this population of industries. It reflects the implicit growth of knowledge and its rate of application industry by industry, and it captures the fundamental point that average productivity growth cannot be independent of the structure of the ensemble of industries and how that structure is changing. The economy is simultaneously coordinated and restless, as all knowledge-based economies must be. We shall take up the restless theme in our final section but we must turn first to the interdependence between aggregate output growth and aggregate productivity growth.[38]

6   Closing the system: accumulation and increasing returns

We have shown how productivity growth differences at the industry level and the aggregate rate of productivity growth are simultaneously determined. However, we have yet to determine what the aggregate rate of output and productivity growth will be, for the individual industry growth rates are ultimately constrained by the requirement that aggregate investment is equal to aggregate saving. That is to say, there are limits to the exploitation of increasing returns and these are naturally set by limits to the aggregate growth of the market. As Kaldor (1972) pointed out, there is a missing element in the

Young approach that can only be dealt with by an explanation of the relation between capital accumulation and effective demand in the aggregate.

To express this more formally, relation (14) provides only one relation to determine two unknowns. A relation is missing and here there are at least two possibilities. The first is to claim that the rate of growth of employment, n, is given by virtue of arguments in relation to the growth of population, labour migration, changing gender composition of the population, and changes in institutional rules in relation to the market for labour. Whatever the rationale, the full employment value of 'n' determines $\hat{q}_e$ through (13A) and correspondingly determines the growth rate of output, g_z. This is the route explicitly followed by Arrow (1962) and Jones (1995a and 1995b) in their very different accounts of endogenous growth, for they both end up with the claim that steady state productivity growth is proportional to the growth in population. Consequently, a stationary population implies an end to progress, which seems an unduly tough restriction on the growth of knowledge and its transfer into the growth of productivity. Instead we follow a different approach; one grounded in Harrod's pioneering treatment of endogenous growth in terms of aggregate saving and investment. In this view, the requirements for macroeconomic coordination set the aggregate constraints on the relations between growth rates at industry level. In following this approach, some hypothesis has to be adopted on the nature of capital markets, investment and saving behaviour.[39]

We start by assuming that all profits are distributed, all investment is funded via the capital market, and that the aggregate saving ratio of households is a constant, s.[40] The ratio of saving to capacity output is then equal to sx_z where $x_z = \Sigma z_j x_j$ is the average degree of capacity utilisation and x_j is the degree of capacity utilisation (the ratio of actual to capacity output) in each industry. Long-run normal prices are set to keep each industry operating at full capacity, $x_j = x_z = 1$, and thus ensure that the rate of growth of capacity is equal to the rate of growth of demand, given each industry's propensity to invest. Coordination of the capital market requires that the aggregate saving ratio must equal the aggregate investment ratio for the economy, but here we must introduce the two kinds of investment that we alluded to in constructing each technical progress function. First there is investment that expands capacity. Since capacity is fully employed in each industry, the ratio of this kind of investment to the industry's output is $(I/Q)_j = b_j g_j$. It follows that the aggregate ratio of capacity expanding investment to capacity is given by

$$\frac{I}{Q} = \Sigma z_j b_j g_j = b_z g_v$$

where $g_v = \Sigma v_j g_j$ is the rate of growth of the aggregate capital stock, defined using the weights $v_j b_z = z_j b_j$. The weights v_j measure the share of each industry in the total capital stock, which is equal to the proportionate contribution that each industry makes to the aggregate capital output ratio. Second, there is improvement investment that enhances the efficiency with which current capacity is operated, and we let μ denote the aggregate ratio of this kind of investment to capacity expanding investment.[41] From this, we immediately obtain a version of the familiar Harrod condition

$$g_v = \frac{s}{(1 + \mu)b_z} \tag{15A}$$

Given our assumptions about capacity utilization rates, this is the familiar Harrod formula, taking account of the distinction between the two kinds of investment. Clearly, the greater the fraction of investment that is devoted to improvement rather than capacity expansion, the smaller will be the rate of growth of the aggregate capital stock.

However, g_v in this formula is not the growth rate of aggregate capacity output as normally defined, which is $g_z = \Sigma z_j g_j$, the output share weighted average of the industry growth rates. The two growth rates would only be equivalent in conditions of proportional growth, *that is, when growth is not associated with development*, but here they are logically different and are related by the condition

$$g_z = g_v - \frac{C_z(g_j, b_j)}{\overline{b}_z}$$

In this expression $C_z(g_j, b_j)$ is a secondary covariance since the growth rates are endogenously determined. However, because of the relationship between the distribution of demand growth and aggregate productivity growth it follows that this secondary covariance is equal to $C_z(\psi_j, b_j) \cdot \hat{q}_e$, where $C_z(\psi_j, b_j)$ is the capacity output weighted primary covariance between the industry capital output ratios and the industry income elasticities of demand. Thus, the aggregate rate of output growth becomes

$$g_z = g_v - \frac{C_z(\psi_j, b_j)}{b_z}\hat{q}_e$$

and it follows that the aggregate growth rate of output is related to the aggregate growth rate of productivity by

$$g_z = \frac{s}{(1 + \mu)b_z} - \left[\frac{C_e(\psi_j, b_j)}{b_z}\right]\hat{q}_e \tag{15B}$$

That is to say, the aggregate growth rate of output is not independent of the forces, making for uneven rates of growth in the individual sectors.

Now, if we combine together the accumulation relation (15B) with Young's law (14), we can simultaneously determine the mutually consistent values for the growth of aggregate output and the growth of aggregate productivity. This solution is sketched in Figure 3.2. The accumulation schedule labelled H shows the rates of growth of output associated with different rates of productivity growth when aggregate saving equals aggregate investment. It is a schedule of regular advance as Harrod put it. We have assumed for purposes of illustration that $C_z(\psi_j, b_j)$ is positive. The resulting negative association between the rates of growth of output and productivity reflects the "least favourable case", in that the industries with above average income elasticities of demand are also the industries with below average capital productivity. Productivity growth consequently has a retarding effect on output growth since it concentrates the latter in industries with relatively lower productivity of invested capital.[42] The increasing returns schedule, labelled Y, imposes a positive association between the two rates of growth, and so the mutually dependent aggregate solutions for g_z and $\hat{q}_e$ follow, and are shown in Figure 3.2 by point y. The solution at y is the "Young" solution, with mutual interdependence of productivity and output growth. By contrast, the point labelled h is the traditional "Harrod" solution, with output growth equal to capital stock growth and productivity growth independent of output growth. The diagram also depicts the aggregate rate of

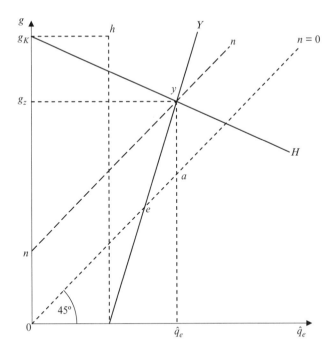

Figure 3.2 The coordination of aggregate productivity growth, output growth and employment growth

employment growth. The 45 degree line in Figure 3.2 shows all combinations of output and productivity growth that generate a zero rate of growth of aggregate employment. The distance $ya = 0n$ measures the positive rate of employment growth consistent with the solution at point y. Notice also that point e denotes the minimum rate of productivity growth consistent with non-negative employment growth. That the joint distributions of income elasticities of demand, productivity levels, and capital output ratios matter for this outcome, is entirely a product of our evolutionary framework. Structure and variety matter in an essential way for the performance of the system and our solutions in Figure 3.2 show how.

Some rather obvious comparative static exercises now fall into place with the help of Figure 3.2. Thus comparing two economies that are identical except for their savings ratios, we find that the high saving economy has faster growth rates of output, productivity and employment. Similarly comparing two economies, one of which is technically more progressive, the latter will have a higher rate of productivity growth, a lower rate of output growth and a lower rate of employment growth. A more difficult exercise is to consider the effects of an increase in μ, the ratio of improvement to capacity expanding investment. This notional change shifts the H schedule downwards and reduces the growth rate and the rate of productivity growth for a given aggregate increasing returns function. However, the expectation is that an increase in the resources devoted to improvement investment, for example, through more R&D or training, will also shift this schedule to the right, increasing the rate of productivity growth but further reducing the rate of output growth. How this works out in full will depend on how the investments pay off in terms of improved productivity growth, and this is a question that can only be addressed industry by industry and firm by firm. This is beyond our remit but at least we know where to look to see how investments in knowledge generation are translated into additional wealth, and it is not at the macroeconomic level.

The pattern of coordination in Figure 3.2 represents a perfectly plausible "model" of evolutionary growth without making any assumptions that the point of coordination is a stable long-run attractor for the economy. Quite the contrary, what makes this approach evolutionary is that the determinants of the point of coordination are restless; they evolve in response to the structural changes that are induced by the processes of economic coordination at aggregate and industry levels. It is not a system in equilibrium; indeed, capitalism in equilibrium seems from this point of view a contradiction in terms. There are always reasons and incentives to change prevailing arrangements, and every change opens up new opportunities for further change, ad infinitum. This is the powerful message first stated by Smith, refined by Marshall and Young, and given empirical content by Fabricant, Schumpeter, Kaldor and modern evolutionary economists. What can we say on the nature of restless development and growth and the relation between the different stylised facts? The discussion is necessarily brief but we hope that it points to deeper questions about evolutionary growth.

7   Restless capitalism and the stylised facts

We begin by reminding ourselves of the basic dynamics of structural change. An industry is increasing its share of aggregate output precisely to the degree that its income elasticity of demand exceeds a value of unity, the population average income elasticity. Nothing more needs to be said, but when we come to the changes in employment shares, the outcome is a little less transparent, for employment and output shares do not automatically move in step. An industry is increasing its share of employment if $n_j > n$, which is equivalent to the requirement, $\hat{q}_e \psi_j > \hat{q}_j$. That is to say, the ratio of industry to average productivity growth has to be less than the income elasticity of demand for that industry. We can decompose this requirement even further using the increasing returns functions, so that an industry's employment share is increasing whenever

$$\frac{\psi_j(1 - \beta_j)}{\psi_e(1 - \beta_u)} > \frac{\alpha_j + \beta_j n}{\alpha_e + \beta_e n}$$

This is a condition that captures with neat symmetry the relation between industry and population characteristics in relation to technical progress and structural change.

Since the shares in output and employment are in continual flux, it is not at all obvious that the aggregate growth rate can be constant – a definitive test for states of steady state, balanced growth. For it is immediately apparent that when industry growth rates differ there may be no industry that grows at the average rate, and consequently the average growth rate cannot be constant. How does it change? This is where we reconnect with the work of Kuznets and Burns on retardation and growth rate divergence discussed in section 2 above. Using (4B) we find that the change in the aggregate growth rate is

$$\frac{dg_z}{dt} = \dot{g}_z = \sum \dot{z}_j g_j + \sum z_j \dot{g}_j$$

$$= \sum z_j(g_j - g_z)g_j + \sum z_j\hat{g}_j$$

$$= V_z(\psi)\hat{q}_e + R_z \tag{16}$$

The variance in income elasticities multiplied by the productivity growth rate captures the structural change effect, while $R_z = \sum z_j\hat{g}_j$ is the average rate of change in the individual growth rates, and measures the retardation effect. If all the individual growth rates are constant this second term vanishes and the average growth rate is necessarily increasing because it is converging on the largest of the given industry growth rates at a rate that equals the population variance in the industry growth rates.[43] Consequently, the only way the average growth rate can remain constant is if the individual growth rates are declining, that is to say that the Kuznets/Burns retardation principle holds on average. If it should happen that the average output growth rate is indeed constant then the required average rate of retardation is given by $R_z = -V_z(\psi)\hat{q}_e$, which increases with the average rate of productivity growth. Thus the Kuznets and Burns analysis of individual industries has its aggregate counterpart in relations (15).[44]

Principal among the aggregate stylised facts is the constancy over time of the aggregate capital output ratio. Within our framework there is no necessity for it to be constant since the given capital output ratios differ industry by industry. Consequently the aggregate capital output ratio evolves with the output structure according to the relation

$$\hat{b}_z = g_v - g_z = \left[\frac{C_z(\psi_j, b_j)}{b_z} \right] \hat{q}_e \tag{17A}$$

Only if the distributions of capital output ratios and income elasticities of demand are uncorrelated at the prevailing output structure will the aggregate capital output ratio be constant. This is an important clue to the nature of the evolutionary process; its aggregate consequences are conditional not only on the variety within the fundamental data of the economy but on their degree of correlation as well. Thus, as a general rule in an evolving economy, Harrod neutrality at industry level will not produce Harrod neutrality at the aggregate economy level, and the purpose of the aggregation procedure is to identify how and why the emergent aggregate properties do not mimic the corresponding properties at industry level. Of course, Figure 3.2 shows a case where the capital output ratio is increasing over time, so that structural change imposes an "evolutionary load" on the aggregate rate of growth.

Constancy of the industry capital output ratios also means that each industry's capital labour ratio, k_j, will be increasing at the same rate as labour productivity in that industry. At the population level this means that the aggregate capital labour ratio, is $k_e = \sum e_j k_j = b_z q_e$, so its movement depends on the changing patterns of employment and output. Consequently, from (16a) the growth in the aggregate capital labour ratio is

$$\hat{k}_e = \left[1 + \frac{C_z(\psi_j, b_j)}{b_z} \right] \hat{q}_e \tag{17B}$$

Notice that in the case of the movement of both of the average ratios in (17A) and (17B), the rate of change increases with the rate of average productivity growth, precisely because the rates of structural change increase with the rate of average productivity growth.

Of course, we are not ruling out the possibility that Kaldor's stylised facts will hold in respect of these ratios (although the evidence in their favour is problematic). If they are validated empirically, it will not be because of the absence of structural change but rather because of the particular correlation structure between technology and demand across the ensemble of industries.[45] There is no necessity for steady growth to apply in an evolving economy; if it does it will be the result of an averaging process and to this degree an emergent ensemble property of the economy.

It should now be apparent that the point of coordination in Figure 3.2 is a restless position. It is restless because the economy-wide averages that determine the positions of the accumulation and technical progress schedules are continually evolving. We have seen this in respect of the capital output ratio and the "Harrod" schedule, so let us conclude with a second example, which relates to the change in the "Young" schedule. Consider then the change in the average rate of improvement on existing plants, α_e. This is a more complicated story. The rate at which this average changes has two components, one reflecting the impact of the changing employment structure, and the other reflecting any changes (accelerations or decelerations) in the industry-specific rates of improvement in existing plants and capital structures, α_j. Thus

$$\frac{d\alpha_e}{dt} = \dot{\alpha}_e = \sum \dot{e}_j \alpha_j + \sum e_j \dot{\alpha}_j$$

About the second term we have little to say, since it is a sum of changes arising below the industry level and is ruled out of our discussion for this reason. However, the structural effect in the first term is far more amenable to analysis. By familiar steps it follows immediately that $\sum \dot{e}_j \alpha_j = C_e(\alpha_j, n_j)$. If this covariance is positive then the employment structure is increasingly concentrated on those industries with above average rates of improvement, necessarily increasing the population average rate of improvement. Taking account of the fact that the distribution of the employment growth rates around their average, $n_j - n$, is equal to $\psi_j \hat{q}_e - \hat{q}_j$, it follows that

$$C_e(\alpha_j, n_j) = C_e(\alpha_j, \psi_j) \cdot \hat{q}_e - C_e(\alpha_j, \hat{q}_j)$$

This is a typical product of evolutionary economic reasoning, in that the covariation between an endogenous variable (in this case n_j) and an exogenous variable (in this case α_j) reflects the deeper causal structure underlying the changing patterns of output and employment. This deeper structure is reflected in the covariation between income elasticities and rates of improvement and between rates of productivity growth and rates of improvement. The system is restless because of the variety contained within it and because of the correlation between those different dimensions of economic variety. All is flux, the product of variation, selection and the ongoing development of productivity within the causal structure of demand and output coordination, industry by industry and in the aggregate.[46]

8   Concluding remarks

When the uneven growth of the economy is driven by and drives the uneven growth of useful human knowledge, we can neither restrict our analysis of growth to the aggregate economy nor can we treat structural change as a passive epiphenomenon. Innovation and technical progress cause and are caused by the patterns of economic restructuring and differential growth in the economy. At its most fundamental level the system evolves because of the non-representative behaviours contained within it. Unfortunately, a full treatment of the origins of wealth from knowledge must necessarily delve below the level of the industry to the connections between innovation and the competitive perform-ance of rival firms. This further step will reinforce our claim that capitalism is restless because knowledge is restless; that capitalism grows unevenly because knowledge grows unevenly, precisely what Schumpeter meant by creative destruction. Diversity and cor-relation of determining characteristics are the keys to adaptive, restless capitalism; and it is the diversity in the conditions of technical progress, in capital output ratios, and in income elasticities of demand that we have shown to sustain the essential unity of our two sets of stylised facts. Aggregate growth and structural self-transformation are one and the same problem. Needless to add, in an open economy these evolutionary forces are further amplified through international trade and investment, although that really must be another story.

Acknowledgments

This chapter is an extension and revision of Metcalfe, Foster and Ramlogan, 2006. We thank Cristiano Antonelli, Harry Bloch, Dick Nelson, and Mark Setterfield for their comments and suggestions on earlier drafts. JSM gratefully acknowledges the generous support of Curtin University of Technology and its School of Economics and Finance, where much of the initial drafting was carried out.

Notes

1. See for example Nelson and Winter (1974) where an evolutionary model of innovation is used to replicate the aggregate behaviour of a Solow-type, neoclassical growth model. The two theoretical worlds are poles apart, yet they are consistent with the same aggregate facts. See Fagerberg and Verspagen (1999) for further elaboration.
2. For a powerful exposition of knowledge-related factors in economic growth, together with the impor-tance of distinguishing different kinds of knowledge, and an understanding of the instituted context in which useful knowledge is developed and applied, see Mokyr (2002).
3. Schumpeter (1912) and (1928) are the key texts here, and Marshall (1919) is at least as significant as Marshall (1920).
4. For alternative, complementary approaches to out of equilibrium growth theory, see Amendola and Gaffard (1988, 1998), and Silverberg and Verspagen (1998).
5. A stationary state is in this sense a closed economic system, a system without history as Schumpeter pointed out.
6. That an economic order is self-transforming is not to be taken for granted but depends on wider instituted and encultured factors that overcome the conserving tendencies which reinforce the prevailing order. See Mokyr (2002) Chapter 6 for an extended discussion, and Nelson (2005) Chapters 5 and 8.
7. See Colin Clark (1944) and Kuznets (1971) for original statements of the relation between aggregate growth and large-scale structural change. Saviotti and Pyka (2004) simulate industry entry and exit effects in an evolutionary growth model.
8. For some interesting commentary see Baumol et al. (1989, Chapter 3). The idea that development is a process of reducing the relative importance of agriculture is a common theme among development econo-mists.
9. See Kuznets (1971) Chapter 7 for the details, particularly Table 4.
10. This is not to deny that proportional dynamics has its uses as, for example, in the Von Neumann growth model. However, this method seems entirely incapable of addressing the two-way relation between the growth of knowledge and the growth of economic activity. Does any economic historian ever find pro-portional dynamics a useful device with which to order the record of the past? We think not.
11. See for example, Kongsamut et al. (2001), Ngai and Pissarides (2004), Echevarria (1997), and Acemoglu and Guerrieri (2008). For a very good synopsis of the developing literature, and of the different kinds of

stylised facts, the reader is referred to the paper by Bonatti and Felice (2008). This latter paper is more closely connected to our approach than any of the other papers referred to above, since the authors incorporate endogenous technical progress into their two-sector model by effectively assuming a Kaldor style technical progress function (as do we). They also assume non-homothetic preferences, equivalent to our reliance on Engel's Law, and differentiated income elasticities of demand, sector by sector. Nonetheless our approaches to the broad problem are very different.

12.   For an excellent account of Young's approach and its relation to the wider literature on economic development and cumulative causation see Toner (1999). The problem of cumulative causation is precisely the problem addressed here in terms of the disaggregated connections between increasing returns and the aggregate growth of per capita income.

13.   See Metcalfe (2008) for a more detailed examination of the statistical nature of evolutionary population analysis.

14.   The measure of output shares is contingent on the particular set of price weights used to construct the aggregate measure of capacity output, just as the employment shares are contingent on the prices of different kinds of labour within the employment aggregate. The shares in final output are different from the shares in value added industry by industry. The two differ by the product of the economy-wide ratio of intermediate to final output and the fraction of the value of total intermediate output used by an industry.

15.   We use a carat over a variable to indicate its logarithmic rate of change, and a dot above a variable to indicate its differential rate of change.

16.   Carlin et al. (2001) point out that the 90th decile of the UK manufacturing productivity distribution is almost five times more productive in labour productivity terms than the 10th decile.

17.   That we ignore pure substitution effects but not the income effects of price changes is simply a consequence of not delving below the level of the industry where prices are determined. See note 38 for further comment on the role of pure substitution effects.

18.   If we distinguish two final uses for each good, in consumption and in investment, we can further decompose these total elasticities as follows

$$z_j \psi_j = (1 - s)c_j \psi_{cj} + s i_j \psi_{Ij}$$

where s is the aggregate saving ratio, c_j is the fraction of the industry's output absorbed in consumption, and i_j is the corresponding fraction absorbed in investment ($c_j + i_j = 1$). Thus ψ_{cj} is the per capita consumption elasticity, and ψ_{Ij} is the per capita investment elasticity for industry j. Summing across the industries yields the relation

$$\psi_z = \sum z_j \psi_j = 1 = (1 - s)\psi_c + s\psi_I$$

A constant saving ratio, as assumed below, implies a unitary income elasticity of demand for wealth. See Laitner (2000) for an analysis of non-unitary income elasticities for assets and the growth process.

19.   See Bianchi (1998) and Saviotti (2001) for a very useful discussion of innovation and consumer behaviour relevant to these questions.

20.   See Montobbio (2002) for an exposition of the replicator principle in the context of industry dynamics.

21.   See Andersen (2004), Foster (2000), Knudsen (2004) and Metcalfe (2008) for further analysis and critical discussion of Fisher's principle. Aldrich et al. (2008) provide a detailed, general discussion of evolutionary variation-cum-selection dynamics.

22.   There is an extensive literature on this topic. See Bartelsman and Doms (2000), Disney et al. (2003), Baldwin and Gu (2005), and for an evolutionary perspective, Nelson (1989) and Metcalfe and Ramlogan (2006).

23.   See Cornwall and Cornwall (2002) for a closely related derivation.

24.   To derive this result, write, $\sum e_j \psi_j = \sum z_j \psi_j + \sum (e_j - z_j) \psi_j$ and recall that $e_j a_z = z_j a_j$, with $a_z = \sum z_j a_j$. The analogous result in equation (6B) is proved similarly.

25.   Using the fact that $\hat{q}_e = -\hat{a}_z$ we can rearrange equations (1A) and (1B) to derive (8).

26.   Another way to express (8) is to note that $\sum z_j \hat{e}_j = (C_e(n_j, q_j))/(q_e)$ and that $\sum e_j \hat{z}_j = (C_z(g_j, a_j))/(a_z)$, results that make use of the relations between output shares and employment shares noted above in equation (1).

27.   It is easily shown that the weight applied to the improvement effect, α_j, is $(1 + g_j)^{-1}$ and the weight applied to the best practice effect, β_j, is $g_j \cdot (1 + g_j)^{-1}$. When the growth rate, g_j, is small, and the time interval short, we can approximate the technical progress function by (11A) of the text.

28.   See Eltis (1973) Chapter 6 for an extended discussion of analogous technical progress functions. If we express the rate of productivity growth in terms of actual output ($\hat{q}'_j$) rather than capacity output ($\hat{q}_j$), then $\hat{q}'_j = \hat{q}_j + \hat{x}_j$, where $\hat{x}_j$ is the rate of change of the average degree of capacity utilisation in the industry. For

reasons that we have already made clear it is appropriate in a long-run analysis to hold capacity utilisation constant.

29. For outstanding reviews of this literature see Scott (1989), Toner (1999), Bairam (1987) and McCombie (1986).

30. These weights change according to the rule $\hat{u}_i = \hat{e}_i - \hat{\psi}_e$. Since $\Sigma \dot{u}_i = 0$, it follows that $\hat{\psi}_e = \Sigma u_i \hat{e}_i$. If we consider the increasing returns function for industry one we find that its slope is equal to $u_2 \beta_1 (\psi_1/\psi_2)[1 - u_1\beta_1]^{-1}$ and that the intercept is equal to $(\alpha_1 + \beta_1 n)[1 - u_1\beta_1]^{-1}$, with corresponding expressions for industry two.

31. That is to say, $\hat{q}_1^* > \hat{q}_2^*$, implies that $q_1 > q_2$, which implies that $e_1/z_1 < e_2/z_2$.

32. Of course, it is trivially obvious that without innovation there would be no technical progress functions, no positive feedback and no productivity growth. We haven't yet escaped from Usher's (1980) warning, that no progress means no growth.

33. The reader can visualise this in terms of shifts in each increasing returns function in Figure 3.1.

34. Neither of the aggregate progress elasticities β_e and β_u are constants; they vary with each change in the structure of employment. Exactly as one should expect, the dynamic properties of the economy change as its structure changes. A little manipulation establishes, for example, that $d\beta_u/dt = C_u(\beta, g)$ and that $d\beta_e/dt = C_e(\beta, g)$, and that these secondary covariances can be expressed in primary terms as in the case of relations (17) below.

35. Summing each technical progress function by the output shares gives $T_z^* = \alpha_z + \beta_z n + \beta_u \hat{q}_e$. The rate of growth of productivity is eliminated using (13A).

36. The weights $w_j = z_j \psi_j$ measure the contribution that each industry makes to the output-weighted income elasticity of demand, remembering that $\psi_z = 1$. We can always reduce a difference between the differently weighted means of a variable to an appropriate covariance Thus, for example, $q_e(\alpha_z - \alpha_e) = C_e(q_j, \alpha_j)$ expresses the difference between the different weighted averages for the industry rates of improvement. Similarly, $q_e(\beta_z - \beta_e) = C_e(q_j, \beta_j)$ and $\beta_w - \beta_z = C_z(\psi_j, \beta_j)$. If desired, the reader can, for example, rewrite (13B) in terms of various covariances to eliminate all the averages except those constructed using the employment weights.

37. An analogous expression in terms of the aggregate growth rate of output can be derived for (13B).

38. Technical progress has such a powerful effect on some relative prices, that the reader may rightly wonder how the results are changed if we give pure substitution effects a more explicit role. Briefly, we can state that the full analysis of relative price effects requires that (3) be replaced by $g_j = n + \psi_j \hat{q}_e - \Sigma_k \chi_{jk}(\hat{p}_k - \hat{p}_z)$, where the χ_{jk} are the own and cross (pure) price substitution elasticities of demand for industry j with respect to each industry price, the $\hat{p}_k$ are the proportional rates of change in the industry prices, and $\hat{p}_z = \Sigma_k z_k \hat{p}_k$ is the rate of change in the average price level – the standard of value. The aggregate income equals expenditure constraint and homogeneity ensure that the elasticities "add up" to give $g_z = n + \hat{q}_e$ so that the relative price effects net out to zero in the aggregate. That is to say, $\Sigma_k z_k \chi_{ki} = 0$ for the effect of changes in the price of industry i across all industries, and $\Sigma_k \chi_{ik} = 0$ for the effect of changes in all prices on the demand for industry i. To go further requires a theory of price formation and change at the industry level and this is why we do not take the discussion any further here. However, if one assumes that the dominant factor in changing prices is technical progress then one could, for example, approximate and set $\hat{p}_k = -\hat{q}_k$ and find that the analysis of Figure 3.1 is reproduced, but with the slopes and positions of the Q schedules depending on the own and cross price substitution elasticities as well as on the income elasticities.

39. The Harrod model is a more sophisticated version of the so-called AK model of endogenous growth, by virtue of requiring an independent investment function. The crucial change introduced by Solow's growth model was not the assumption of a variable capital output ratio but rather the disappearance of an independent investment function. It is Say's law model in which savings and investment are automatically equal in all economic circumstances. See Kurz and Salvadori (1998) for an elaboration and critique. Other, post-Keynesian, approaches differentiating savings by type of income are equally applicable but would take us too far afield in this preliminary exposition.

40. As noted above, this is tantamount to assuming a unitary income elasticity of demand for per capita wealth.

41. The distinction was first made in relation to growth theory by Harrod (1948, p. 79).

42. The converse case of a negative value for the covariance between capital output ratios and income elasticities we leave to the reader to explore. The comparative static exercises below are contingent on the assumed positive value of this covariance.

43. This is a straightforward consequence of Fisher's principle in which the change in one statistical moment is related to the value of other statistical moments. Just as the average is not in general stationary, neither is the variance, for the average is changing along with the output weights, and additionally the income elasticities have already been shown not to be constants in section 3 above. A little manipulation shows that $(dV_z(\psi))/(dt) = S_z(\psi_j) + 2C_z(\psi_j, \dot{\psi}_j)$. In this expression, $S_z(\psi_j)$ is the third moment of the income

elasticities around their population average, and $C_z(\psi_j, \dot{\psi}_j)$ is the output-weighted covariance between the elasticities and their rates of change.

44. The reader can work through the consequences for other aggregate growth rates, for example the growth rate of the capital stock, $g_K = \Sigma v_j g_j$. Because $g_l = g_K - \hat{g}_K$ it follows that the rate of change of the aggregate accumulation rate can be expressed as $\hat{g}_K = -[(C_z(\psi_j, b_j))/(k_z)\hat{q}_e + V_v(g_j)]$. In this expression, $V_v(g_j)$ is the variance of the industry capital stock growth rates constructed using each industry's share in the aggregate capital stock as weights. This variance effect reduces the growth rate of the capital stock, but the covariance term may work either way. In Figure 3.2, the two effects are in the same direction since the covariance is there assumed to be positive.

45. We leave it to the reader to explore the movements in the aggregate rate of profits, in the share of profits in income and in the rate of change of the average rate of technical progress, $T_z = \Sigma z_j \hat{q}_j^*$.

46. The reader can go further and eliminate the endogenous productivity growth rates in $C_e(\alpha_j, \hat{q}_j)$ by using the increasing returns functions (11). After some manipulation, using the different weighting schemes introduced above, we find that this is reduced to the rather complicated but readily intelligible expression $C_e(\alpha_j, n_j) = -V_e(\alpha_j) - nC_e(\alpha_j, \beta_j) + \hat{q}_e[C_e(\psi_j, \alpha_j)(1 - \beta_n) - \psi_e C_u(\alpha_j, \beta_j)]$. A special case arises when the primary elements, α, β, ψ, are uncorrelated one with the other. Then this expression reduces to $C_e(\alpha_j, n_j) = -V_e(\alpha_j)$, the latter being the employment-weighted variance in the rates of improvement. In this case, the effects of structural change result in a decline in the average rate of improvement.

References

Abramovitz, M. (1989), *Thinking about Economic Growth: And other Essays on Economic Growth and Welfare*, Cambridge: Cambridge University Press.

Acemoglu, D. and Guerrieri, V. (2008), "Capital deepening and nonbalanced economic growth", *Journal of Political Economy*, **116**(3), 467–98.

Aldrich, H.E., Hodgson, G.M., Hull, D.L., Knudsen, T., Mokyr, J. and Vanberg, V. (2008), "In defence of generalised Darwinism", *Journal of Evolutionary Economics*, **18**, 577–96.

Amendola, M. and Gaffard, J.L. (1988), *The Innovative Choice*, Oxford: Blackwell.

Amendola, M. and Gaffard, J.L. (1998), *Out of Equilibrium*, Oxford: Oxford University Press.

Andersen, E.S. (2004), "Population thinking, Price's equation and the analysis of economic evolution", *Evolutionary and Institutional Economics Review*, **1**, 127–48.

Arrow, K.J. (1962), "The economic implications of learning by doing", *Review of Economic Studies*, **29**, 155–73.

Bairam, E.I. (1987), "The Verdoorn law, returns to scale and industrial growth: a review of the literature", *Australian Economic Papers*, **26**, 20–42.

Baldwin, J.R. and Gu, W. (2005), "Competition, firm turnover and productivity growth", mimeo, Ottowa, Micro Economic Analysis Division, Statistics Canada.

Bartelsman, E.J. and Doms, M. (2000), "Understanding productivity: lessons from longitudinal data", *Journal of Economic Literature*, **38**, 569–94.

Baumol, W.J., Blackman, S.A.B. and Wolff, E.N. (1989), *Productivity and American Leadership*, Cambridge, MA: MIT Press.

Bianchi, M. (ed.) (1998), *The Active Consumer*, London: Routledge.

Bliss, C. (1975), *Capital Theory and the Distribution of Income*, New York: Elsevier.

Bonatti, L. and Felice, G. (2008), "Endogenous growth and changing sectoral composition in advanced economies", *Structural Change and Economic Dynamics*, **19**, 109–31.

Burns, A.F. (1934), *Production Trends in the United States Since 1870*, Boston, MA: NBER.

Carlin, W., Haskel, J. and Seabright, P. (2001), "Understanding 'The essential fact about capitalism': markets, competition and creative destruction", *National Institute Economic Review*, **175**, 67–84.

Clark, C. (1944), *The Conditions of Economic Progress*, London: Macmillan.

Cornwall, J. and Cornwall, W. (2002), "A demand and supply analysis of productivity growth", *Structural Change and Economic Dynamics*, **13**, 203–30.

Disney, R., Haskel, J. and Heden, Y. (2003), "Restructuring and productivity growth in UK manufacturing", *Economic Journal*, **113**, 666–94.

Dosi, G. (2000), *Innovation, Organisation and Economic Dynamics*, Cheltenham, UK and Northampton, MA, USA: Edward Elgar.

Echevarria, C. (1997), "Changes in sectoral composition associated with economic growth", *International Economic Review*, **38**(2), 431–52.

Eltis, W. (1973), *Growth and Distribution*, London: Macmillan.

Fabricant, S. (1940), *The Output of Manufacturing Industries: 1899–1937*, New York: NBER.

Fabricant, S. (1942), *Employment in Manufacturing: 1899–1937*, New York: NBER.

Fagerberg, J. and Verspagen, B. (1999), "Vision and fact: a critical essay on the growth literature", in J.

Madrick (ed.), *Unconventional Wisdom: Alternative Perspectives on the New Economy*, New York: The Century Foundation Press.

Foster, J. (2000), "Competitive selection, self-organisation and Joseph A. Schumpeter", *Journal of Evolutionary Economics*, **10**, 311–28.

Freeman, C. and Louça, C. (2001), *As Time Goes By: From the Industrial Revolutions to the Information Revolution*, Oxford: Oxford University Press.

Gaston, J.F. (1961), *Growth Patterns in Industry: A Re-examination*, New York: National Industrial Conference Board.

Harberger, A.C. (1998), "A vision of the growth process", *American Economic Review*, **88**, 1–32.

Harcourt, G.C. (1972), *Some Cambridge Controversies in the Theory of Capital*, Cambridge: Cambridge University Press.

Harrod, R.F. (1948), *Towards a Dynamic Economics*, London: Macmillan.

Hoffman, W.G. (1949), "The growth of industrial production in Great Britain. A quantitative survey", *Economic History Review*, **2**, 162–80.

Jones, C.I. (1995a), "RandD-based models of economic growth", *Journal of Political Economy*, **103**, 759–804.

Jones, C.I. (1995b), "Time series tests of endogenous growth models", *Quarterly Journal of Economics*, **110**, 495–525.

Kaldor, N. (1957), "A model of economic growth", *Economic Journal*, **67**, 591–624.

Kaldor, N. (1961), "Capital accumulation and economic growth", in F.A. Lutz and D.C. Hague (eds), *The Theory of Capital*, London: Macmillan.

Kaldor, N. (1972), "The irrelevance of equilibrium economics", *Economic Journal*, **82**, 1237–55.

Kindleberger, C.P. (1989), *Economic Laws and Economic History*, The Raffaelle Mattioli Lectures, Cambridge: Cambridge University Press.

Knight, F.H. (1935/1977), "Statics and dynamics", in *The Ethics of Competition*, New Brunswick, NJ: Transactions Publishers.

Knudsen, T. (2004), "General selection theory and economic evolution: the Price equation and the replicator/interactor distinction", *Journal of Economic Methodology*, **11**, 147–73.

Kongsamut, P., Rebelo, S. and Xie, D. (2001), "Beyond balanced growth", *The Review of Economic Studies*, **4**, 869–82.

Kurz, H. (2008), "On the growth of knowledge about the role of knowledge in economic growth", mimeo, University of Graz.

Kurz, H. and Salvadori, N. (1998), "The 'new' growth theory: old wine in new goatskins", in F. Coricelli, M. Di Matteo and F. Hahn (eds), *New Theories in Growth and Development*, London: Macmillan.

Kuznets, S. (1929), *Secular Movements of Production and Prices*, Boston, MA: Houghton Miflin.

Kuznets, S. (1954), *Economic Change*, London: Heinemann.

Kuznets, S. (1971), *Economic Growth of Nations*, Cambridge, MA: Belknap, Harvard.

Kuznets, S. (1977), "Two centuries of economic growth: reflections on US experience", *American Economic Review*, **67**, 1–14.

Laitner, J. (2000), "Structural change and economic growth", *Review of Economic Studies*, **67**(3), 545–61.

Landes, D.S. (1969), *The Unbound Prometheus*, Cambridge: Cambridge University Press.

McCombie, J.S.L. (1986), "On some interpretations of the relationship between productivity and output growth", *Applied Economics*, **18**, 1215–25.

Maddison, A. (1991), *Dynamic Forces in Capitalist Development*, Oxford: Oxford University Press.

Marshall, A. (1919), *Industry and Trade*, London: Macmillan.

Marshall. A. (1920), *Principles of Economics*, 8th (variorum) edn, London: Macmillan.

Metcalfe, J.S. (1998), *Evolutionary Economics and Creative Destruction*, London: Routledge.

Metcalfe, J.S. (2001), "Institutions and progress", *Industrial and Corporate Change*, **10**, 561–86.

Metcalfe, J.S. (2008), "Accounting for economic evolution: fitness and the population method", *Journal of Bioeconomics*, **10**, 23–50.

Metcalfe, J.S. and Ramlogan, R. (2006), "Creative destruction and the measurement of productivity change", in *Revue, de L'OFCE*, Paris: Observatoire Francais des Conjunctures Economiques, Presses de Science Po.

Metcalfe, J.S., Foster, J. and Ramlogan, R. (2006), "Adaptive economic growth", *Cambridge Journal of Economics*, **30**(1), 7–32.

Mokyr, J. (1990), *The Lever of Riches*, Oxford: Oxford University Press.

Mokyr, J. (2002), *The Gifts of Athena*, Princeton, NJ: Princeton University Press.

Montobbio, F. (2002), "An evolutionary model of industrial growth and structural change", *Structural Change and Economic Dynamics*, **13**(4), 387–414.

Nelson, R. (1989), "Industry growth accounts and production functions when techniques are idiosyncratic", *Journal of Economic Behaviour and Organisation*, **11**, 323–41.

Nelson, R. (2005), *Technology, Institutions and Economic Growth*, Cambridge, MA: Harvard University Press.

Nelson, R. and Winter, S. (1974), "Neoclassical vs. evolutionary theories of economic growth: critique and prospectus", *Economic Journal*, **84**, 886–905.

Nelson, R. and Winter, S. (1982), *An Evolutionary Theory of Economic Change*, Cambridge, MA: Harvard, Belknap Press.

Nelson, R., Peck, M. and Kalachek, E.D. (1967), *Technology, Economic Growth and Public Policy*, Washington, DC: The Brookings Institution.

Ngai, L.R. and Pissarides, C.A. (2004), "Structural change in a multi-sector growth model", mimeo, CEPR, London School of Economics.

Pasinetti, L.L. (1981), *Structural Change and Economic Growth*, Cambridge: Cambridge University Press.

Pasinetti, L.L. (1993), *Structural Economic Dynamics*, Cambridge: Cambridge University Press.

Salter, W.E.G. (1960), *Productivity and Technical Change*, Cambridge: Cambridge University Press.

Saviotti, P. (2001), "Variety, growth and demand", *Journal of Evolutionary Economics*, **11**(1), 119–42.

Saviotti, P. and Pyka, A. (2004), "Economic development by the creation of new sectors", *Journal of Evolutionary Economics*, **14**(1), 1–36.

Sayers, R.S. (1950), "The springs of technical progress in Britain, 1919–1939", *Economic Journal*, **60**, 275–91.

Schumpeter, J.A. (1912/1934), *The Theory of Economic Development*, Oxford: Oxford University Press.

Schumpeter, J. (1928), "The instability of capitalism", *Economic Journal*, **38**, 361–86.

Scott, M. F.G. (1989), *A New View of Economic Growth*, Oxford: Oxford University Press.

Silverberg, G. and Verspagen, B. (1998), "Economic growth as an evolutionary process", in J. Lesourne and A. Orlean (eds), *Advances in Self-Organisation and Evolutionary Economics*, Paris: Economica.

Steedman, I. (2003), "On measuring knowledge in new (endogenous) growth theory", in N. Salvadori (ed.), *Old and New Growth Theories: An Assessment*, Cheltenham, UK and Northampton, MA, USA: Edward Elgar.

Stigler, G.J. (1947), *Trends in Output and Employment*, New York: NBER.

Toner, P. (1999), *Main Currents in Cumulative Causation*, London: Macmillan Press.

Usher, D. (1980), *The Measurement of Economic Growth*, London: Blackwell.

Witt, U. (2003), *The Evolving Economy*, Cheltenham, UK and Northampton, MA, USA: Edward Elgar.

Young, A.A. (1928), "Increasing returns and economic progress", *Economic Journal*, **38**, 527–42.

4 The post-Keynesian theories of growth and distribution: a survey*
Heinz D. Kurz and Neri Salvadori

1 Introduction

The main idea underlying the post- or neo-Keynesian theories of growth and distribution is that of aggregate savings adjusting to an independently given volume of aggregate investment. The adjustment of savings to investment, rather than the other way round, is seen to be a central, if not *the* central, message of Keynes's *General Theory* (see Keynes, *CW*, VII). As Keynes emphasized in the year following the publication of his book, "the initial novelty" of *The General Theory* "lies in my maintaining that it is not the rate of interest, but the level of income which ensures equality between saving and investment" (Keynes, 1937, p. 250). The idea that investment, governed by "animal spirits", is independent of savings, was dubbed the "Keynesian hypothesis" by Nicholas Kaldor (1955–56, p. 95). The following argument will be largely based on this hypothesis. Since many of the ideas that play an important role in the field of research surveyed in this chapter can be traced back to contributions by Michal Kalecki, one could also speak of a post-Kaleckian theory. The post-Keynesian theories of growth and distribution are essentially an offspring of the principle of the multiplier, developed by Richard Kahn (1931) and then adopted by Keynes (*CW*, VII, Chapter 10). There are essentially two channels by means of which the adjustment of savings to investment can take place. As Kaldor pointed out, the principle of the multiplier can be "alternatively applied to a determination of the relation between prices and wages, if the level of output is taken as given, or to the determination of the level of employment, if distribution (i.e., the relation between prices and wages) is taken as given" (Kaldor, 1955–56, p. 94). That is to say, in conditions of continually full capital utilization and full employment of labour, the adjustment of savings to investment is envisaged to be effected via prices changing relative to money wages and thus a redistribution of income between wages and profits or classes of income recipients. In conditions of less than full utilization of the capital stock and of the labour force, on the other hand, savings can adjust to investment via a change in the degree of capital utilization and the level of employment, without any marked change in the real wage rate, at least within limits. This case is, however, not restricted to the short run with which Keynes was mainly concerned. It applies also to the long run, with the average degree of capital utilization and the average rate of employment reflecting different levels of pressure of effective aggregate demand. While in the short run the adjustment takes place via changing levels in the utilization of given productive capacity, in the long run it takes place via changes in the average degree of capital utilization and/or in the rate of growth of productive capacity.

The idea that the long-term rate of accumulation determines the distribution of income is frequently traced back to the so-called "widow's cruse" parable in Keynes's *Treatise on Money*:

> If entrepreneurs choose to spend a portion of their profit on consumption . . . the effect is to *increase* the profit on the sale of liquid consumption goods by an amount exactly equal to the amount of profits which have been thus expended. . . . Thus, however, much of their profits entrepreneurs spend on consumption, the increment of wealth belonging to entrepreneurs remains the same as before. Thus profits, as a source of capital increment for entrepreneurs, are a widow's cruse which remains undepleted however much of them may be devoted to riotous living. (Keynes, *CW*, V, p. 125)

While in the *Treatise* an excess of investment over saving is reflected in a change in the general price level only, given the level of output and employment, Kalecki in his early contributions, that is, prior to Keynes's *General Theory*, developed essentially the same idea but allowed for quantity adjustments (see Laski, 1987). He emphasized that investment "finances itself" (Kalecki, 1954, pp. 49–50) via changes in economic activity and total profits. By assuming that workers consume all their wages while capitalists consume only a fraction of their profits, Kalecki (1938, p. 76) arrived at the conclusion that total profits are equal to investment plus capitalists' consumption. In a subsequent paper, he interpreted this equality by saying that it is capitalists' "investment and consumption decisions which determine profits, and not the other way round" (Kalecki, 1942, p. 259). However, both Keynes's analysis in the *General Theory* and Kalecki's are predominantly short-run.

In this chapter we deal first with the post-Keynesian theory of value and distribution in conditions of full utilization of productive capacity (section 2). This variant of the theory is associated especially with the names of Nicholas Kaldor and Luigi Pasinetti. It has became prominent in the 1950s and early 1960s and has triggered a rich literature dealing with various aspects of the problems under consideration. The section provides an overview of the most important contributions to this line of thought. We then turn to a brief summary account of approaches that dispense with the assumption of the full utilization of productive resources (section 3). In such conditions the interplay between economic growth and income distribution is more complex and also more interesting. The approaches under consideration can be traced back to Keynes himself and then especially to contributions by Michal Kalecki. The latter saw levels of utilization of productive capacity below full utilization as reflecting both failures of effective aggregate demand and expressions of oligopolistic and monopolistic structures in the economy, with firms deliberately keeping margins of excess capacity in order to deter potential competitors from entering the market.

2 Full employment and full capacity utilization

2.1 Kaldor's contribution
The full employment version of the post-Keynesian theory of growth and distribution was first proposed by Kaldor (1955–56). Kaldor called his new theory "Keynesian", even if, he emphasized, Keynes had never developed it himself. The theory, as mentioned, is derived from the principle of the multiplier. Kaldor's original presentation is characterized by a distinction of groups of income-earners, whose saving habits are homogeneous within each group and are differentiated among the groups. Kaldor made a distinction between wage-earners and profit-earners, noticing that the propensity to save of the first group can be assumed to be smaller than that of the second group, simply as a conse-

quence of the fact that the bulk of profits accrues in the form of company profits and a high proportion of these profits is put to reserve (see Kaldor, 1955–56, pp. 95 fn.). In a later contribution Kaldor (1966, pp. 310–11) confirmed his intention to refer to a situation in which profits were generated by companies with a high propensity to save (i.e. a high quota of undistributed profits to favour self-finance). Kaldor's saving function is, therefore,

$$S = s_\omega W + s_\pi P,$$

where S is total savings of a given economy, and W and P are total wages and total profits. Since, in equilibrium, planned saving equals planned investment, and since wages plus profits equal the national income, it is possible to write

$$I = (s_\pi - s_\omega)P + s_\omega Y,$$

where I is net investment and Y is net national income. Finally, because of "the 'Keynesian' hypothesis that investment, or rather, the ratio of investment to output, can be treated as an independent variable" (Kaldor, 1955–56, p. 95),

$$\frac{P}{Y} = \frac{1}{s_\pi - s_\omega} \frac{I}{Y} - \frac{s_\omega}{s_\pi - s_\omega}. \tag{1}$$

The rate of profits is then obtained by multiplying equation (1) by the output–capital ratio, Y/K, which Kaldor (1955–56) assumed to be constant with respect to changes in distribution:

$$\frac{P}{K} = \frac{1}{s_\pi - s_\omega} \frac{I}{K} - \frac{s_\omega}{s_\pi - s_\omega} \frac{Y}{K}, \tag{2}$$

where I/K is the rate of capital accumulation. Since a fairly constant capital-to-output ratio, K/Y, is taken to be a "stylized fact" of recent economic history, the rate of growth of output equals the rate of capital accumulation.

As early as in the 1930s, Kaldor had analysed the relationship between the rate of profits and the rate of growth (see Kaldor, 1937). However, he did not think at that time of reversing the causal link between the former and the latter variable. A "great deal of stimulus" to move in this direction was provided, according to Kaldor (1955–56, p. 94 fn.), by a paper published by Kalecki (1942) and by some discussions he had with Joan Robinson who was then working on her book *The Accumulation of Capital* (Robinson, 1956). The links with the Kaleckian aphorism that "capitalists earn what they spend, and workers spend what they earn" are clearly apparent in the special case in which $s_\omega = 0$ since equations (1) and (2) then become:

$$\frac{P}{Y} = \frac{1}{s_\pi} \frac{I}{Y},$$

$$\frac{P}{K} = \frac{1}{s_\pi} \frac{I}{K}.$$

2.2 The contributions of Pasinetti

In contradistinction to Kaldor, Luigi L. Pasinetti (1962) regarded steady growth analysis "as a system of necessary relations to achieve full employment" (Pasinetti, 1962, p. 267), thus avoiding any reference to the working of actual economies. Besides, he dealt with *classes* (capitalists and workers) rather than with *income groups*, suggesting the use of the following saving functions, which assume that the propensity to save out of the profits earned by the capitalist class, s_c, differs from the propensity to save out of the profits earned by the working class, s_w:

$$S_w = s_w(W + P_w),$$

$$S_c = s_c P_c.$$

Further, Pasinetti explicitly introduced the dynamic equilibrium conditions, according to which capitalists' and workers' capitals, like all variables changing through time, must, in the steady state, grow at the same rate as the economy as a whole. In addition, he pointed out that, since those who save out of wages must receive a part of the profit as interest for what they lend to capitalists, to determine the rate of profits it is necessary to specify the relationship between the rate of interest and the rate of profits in steady growth. He maintained that "in a long-run equilibrium model, the obvious hypothesis to make is that of a rate of interest equal to the rate of profit" (Pasinetti, 1962, pp. 271–72).

Let us now present what became known as the threefold savings ratio model. This model, introduced by Chiang (1973), has the property of being general in the sense that both the Kaldor model of 1955–56 and the Pasinetti model of 1962 can be obtained from it by an appropriate choice of parameters.

There are two social classes: workers and capitalists. Workers' earnings comprise wages (W) and profits (P_w) as interest on loans to capitalists. Capitalists receive only profits (P_c). Workers' and capitalists' savings (S_w and S_c, respectively) are defined by the following linear functions

$$S_w = s_{ww}W + s_{pw}P_w$$

$$S_c = s_c P_c.$$

It will also be assumed that

$$0 < s_{ww} \leq s_{pw} \leq s_c < 1.$$

Furthermore, steady-state growth is assumed. Then workers' and capitalists' capitals grow at the same rate g. That is, the following constraints hold:

$$s_{ww}W + s_{pw}P_w = gK_w \tag{3}$$

$$s_c P_c = gK_c, \tag{4}$$

where K_w is workers' capital loaned to the capitalists, and K_c is capitalists' own capital ($K_w + K_c = K$).

If it is assumed that interest and profit rates coincide, then $P_c = rK_c$ and $P_w = rK_w$. If, moreover, $K_c > 0$, then the rate of profits is immediately obtained from equation (4):

$$r = \frac{g}{s_c}. \tag{5}$$

If $K_c > 0$, then equation (3) merely serves the purpose of determining the capital shares (K_w/K and K_c/K) via the K_w/W ratio. In fact, from equation (3) we obtain

$$\frac{K_w}{W} = \frac{s_{ww}}{g - s_{pw}r}.$$

Therefore

$$\frac{K_w}{K} = \frac{W}{K}\frac{K_w}{W} = \frac{1 - rv}{v}\frac{s_{ww}}{g - s_{pw}r},$$

where v is the capital–output ratio. Hence, $K_w/K \le 1$ if and only if

$$\frac{1}{v} \le r + \frac{g - s_{pw}r}{s_{ww}}. \tag{6}$$

Let us now investigate the case in which $K_c = 0$. Equation (4) is satisfied whatever the value of r and $K_w = K$, since capitalists have disappeared. Therefore, equation (3) determines a relationship between $1/v$ and r:

$$\frac{1}{v} = r + \frac{g - s_{pw}r}{s_{ww}}. \tag{7}$$

The above analysis is presented diagrammatically in Figure 4.1, where the horizontal axis gives the rate of profits r and the vertical axis the output–capital ratio ($1/v$). The 45° line OD cuts the first quadrant in two parts: only above the line OD are wages positive ($W > 0$); along OD wages vanish ($W = 0$). Curve AD represents equation (7). Because of inequality (6), capitalists' capital is positive only below curve AD. Line BC represents equation (5). Steady-state growth is only feasible either along the segment AD or along the segment BC.

Taking into consideration the technological relationship between v and r, a long-run equilibrium exists whenever the technological relationship cuts segment AD or segment BC.[1] If this relationship meets BC at C, then only capitalists earn income. If it cuts AD (point B included) then there is a one-class long-run equilibrium in which capitalists' capital equals zero. A two-class long-run equilibrium is only possible if the technological relationship cuts the segment BC, excluding the extreme points B and C. Hence a two-class economy exists if and only if the technological relationship satisfies the following inequalities[2]

$$\frac{s_{ww}}{s_c + s_{ww} - s_{pw}} < \frac{g}{s_c}v^* < 1,$$

where (g/s_c, v^*) is a point of the technological relationship.

Equation (5) is a direct consequence of the assumption that the rate of interest is equal

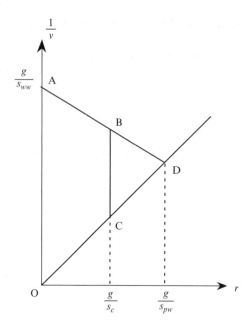

Figure 4.1   Steady-state growth and income distribution

to the rate of profits and is totally independent of any assumption about workers' saving habits. This assumption, though clearly stated by Pasinetti (1962, p. 272), has not always been properly taken into account. Samuelson and Modigliani (1966b, p. 269), for instance, failed to mention it when presenting the so-called "Pasinetti theorem". The same failure can be found in the Introduction to Volume 5 of Kaldor's *Collected Economic Essays* (Kaldor, 1978, p. xv) and in more recent literature. Marglin (1984, p. 121), for instance, claims that the "Cambridge equation" was obtained by lowering the propensity to save on the profit "that accrues to workers from s_c to s_w". He does not mention at all Pasinetti's assumption of equality between the rate of interest and the rate of profits.

The fact that Kaldor obtained a different result for the rate of profits (see equations 2 and 6) calls for an explanation. Pasinetti (1962) suggested that Kaldor had slipped on the simple truism that people who save accumulate capital and then obtain profits. But Samuelson and Modigliani (1966a) remarked that there need not be a "logical slip" in the Kaldorian model, as long as it is assumed that the propensity to save out of income from capital is s_c whether that income is received by capitalists or by workers. This hypothesis, which may or may not be empirically sound, is certainly not logically self-contradictory. Following this remark, Gupta (1977) and Mückl (1978), rectifying Maneschi (1974), clarified that, if the rate of interest is equal to the rate of profits, the saving habits in Kaldor's analysis require that

$$s_w W K_c = 0,$$

where s_w is the saving ratio out of wages; and Fazi and Salvadori (1981) have shown that if the rate of interest is lower than the rate of profits, then the Kaldorian model is perfectly consistent (see also Fazi and Salvadori, 1985, and Salvadori, 1991). This means that even if Kaldor's formulation of the theory does not need to specify the relationship between the rate of interest and the rate of profits in order to determine the latter, nevertheless a two-class economy with Kaldorian saving functions can exist in long-run equilibrium only if the rate of interest is lower than the rate of profits.

In subsequent writings, Pasinetti himself (1974, 1983) and other authors (Laing, 1969; Balestra and Baranzini, 1971; Moore, 1974; Fazi and Salvadori, 1981, 1985; and Salvadori, 1988, 1991) examined the implications for post-Keynesian theory of a rate of interest lower than the rate of profits, meaning by that a ratio of workers' profits to their capital lower than the ratio of total profits to total capital. This assumption makes it possible that capitalists and workers hold shares and bonds in different proportions and that the rates of return on these assets are different.

2.3   The "Pasinetti theorem"
The "Pasinetti theorem" gave rise to a large debate that turned around the limits of Pasinetti's result: see Meade (1963, 1966), Meade and Hahn (1965), Samuelson and Modigliani (1966a, 1966b), Pasinetti (1962, 1966a, 1966b, 1974), Kaldor (1966), and Robinson (1966). Meade (1963) and Samuelson and Modigliani (1966a) deserve credit for having drawn attention to the case in which $K_c = 0$, and therefore to the problem of the existence of a two-class economy.

The alternative saving functions advocated by Kaldor and Pasinetti suggests that a more general formulation including them as special cases can be found. As mentioned above, Chiang (1973) introduced the threefold savings ratio model. This model has also been utilized by Maneschi (1974), Gupta (1977), Pasinetti (1983), and others. Fazi and Salvadori (1985) have presented a formulation where workers' and capitalists' savings are defined by the following functions:

$$S_w = F(P_w, W),$$

$$S_c = G(P_c).$$

More recently, Salvadori (2004) has proposed a formulation that considers also capitalists' and workers' wealth as arguments of the saving functions:

$$S_w = F(P_w, W, K_w),$$

$$S_c = G(P_c, K_c).$$

As mentioned above, in order to close the model, a technological relationship between the rate of profit r and the capital–output ratio v has to be considered. The neoclassical participants in the debate often assumed that the technological relationship has all the properties generated by a typical neoclassical production function. Kaldor (1955–56, p. 98) assumed that the capital–output ratio is constant with respect to the rate of profits.[3] Franke (1985) and Salvadori (1988) clarified some aspects concerning the construction of this technological relationship. (They also added some remarks on the case in which there is joint production.) Morishima (1964, 1969) was probably the first economist who inserted Pasinetti's saving functions in a von Neumann-type model. This route was then followed by people interested in generalizing the post-Keynesian theory of distribution in order to take into account joint production and fixed capital. Bidard and Hosoda (1987), Bidard and Franke (1987), and Salvadori (1980) worked out this problem under different assumptions about technology and consumption habits.

2.4 The technological relationship

Let us clarify how the technological relationship mentioned above is built up. First of all such a relationship is a correspondence, $v \in V(r)$, since at the levels of the rate of profits that are switchpoints there is a range of values v can assume. Such a relationship depends on (i) the technology, (ii) the growth rate, (iii) workers' consumption habits, (iv) workers' saving habits, and (v) capitalists' consumption habits. It is built up in the following way on the assumption that single production prevails.

For a given rate of profits r lower than the maximum one, R, there exists a cost-minimizing technique $(\mathbf{A}, \mathbf{l})$, where $\mathbf{A}$ is the material input matrix and $\mathbf{l}$ is the labour input vector. If more than one cost-minimizing technique exists – which is the case at the switchpoint levels of r – let us apply the following procedure to each cost-minimizing technique. The price vector $\mathbf{p}$ is determined by the equation

$$\mathbf{p} = (1 + r)\mathbf{A}\mathbf{p} + w\mathbf{l}$$

and by the equation stating the numeraire, whereas the intensity vector $\mathbf{q}$ is determined by the equation

$$\mathbf{q}^T = (1 + g)\mathbf{q}^T\mathbf{A} + \frac{[W + (r - g)K_w]}{\mathbf{b}_w^T\mathbf{p}}\mathbf{b}_w^T + \frac{(r - g)K_c}{\mathbf{b}_c^T\mathbf{p}}\mathbf{b}_c^T$$

where

$$W = w\mathbf{q}^T\mathbf{l}, \quad K_w = \frac{s_{ww}}{g - s_{pw}r}(w\mathbf{q}^T\mathbf{l}), \quad K_c = \mathbf{q}^T\mathbf{A}\mathbf{p} - \frac{s_{ww}}{g - s_{pw}r}(w\mathbf{q}^T\mathbf{l}),$$

and workers consume commodities in proportion to vector $\mathbf{b}_w^T$, whereas capitalists consume commodities in proportion to vector $\mathbf{b}_c^T$. (We do not exclude the possibility that $\mathbf{b}_w^T$ and $\mathbf{b}_c^T$ are functions of vector $\mathbf{p}$.) If r is a switchpoint, then vector $\mathbf{p}$ is still uniquely determined, but for each cost-minimizing technique a vector $\mathbf{q}$ can be calculated. Then

$$v = \frac{\mathbf{q}^T\mathbf{A}\mathbf{p}}{\mathbf{q}^T(\mathbf{I} - \mathbf{A})\mathbf{p}} \equiv \frac{\mathbf{q}^T\mathbf{A}\mathbf{p}}{w\mathbf{q}^T\mathbf{l} + r\mathbf{q}^T\mathbf{A}\mathbf{p}}.$$

At a switchpoint more than one vector $\mathbf{q}$ can be determined, and therefore more than one v. In this case $V(r)$ coincides with the range limited by the possible values of v. Otherwise, $V(r) = \{v\}$. Obviously, $V(r)$ depends on s_{ww}, s_{pw}, $\mathbf{b}_c^T$ and $\mathbf{b}_w^T$ unless $\mathbf{b}_c^T \equiv \mathbf{b}_w^T$ or $r = g$ (i.e. $s_c = 1$).

The technological relationship $v \in V(r)$ is utilized in order to determine: (i) the capital shares in the case in which two classes exist; (ii) whether one or two classes exist; and (iii) the profit rate if only workers exist. Obviously, if capitalists do not exist, that is, $K_c = 0$ and $K_w = K = \mathbf{q}^T\mathbf{A}\mathbf{p}$, then s_{ww}, s_{pw}, and $\mathbf{b}_c^T$ do not matter in determining the technological relationship. It is possible to prove that these data may be excluded from the construction of the technological relationship when it is utilized to determine whether one or two classes exist. This can be relevant with respect to two facts. First, in comparative static analysis the technological relationship can remain unchanged if workers' saving habits or capitalists' consumption habits change. Second, from a theoretical point of view, whether one or two classes exist is independent of capitalists' consumption habits: a two-class economy exists if and only if the one-class economy cannot save enough to sustain growth at rate g and at the rate of profits g/s_c.

It is possible to show that if fixed capital is introduced into the picture, then there is no other complication than that concerning the positivity of capitalists' capital. But if general joint production is allowed for, then the problem of the choice of technique cannot be separated from the determination of quantities produced.

3   Less than full employment and full capacity utilization

Several critics have pointed out that the assumptions of full capacity utilization and full employment are difficult to reconcile with the assumption of downward flexible real wages. This is, however, what Kaldor implied in his profit inflation argument: with a rise in the rate of accumulation, g, the rate of profits, r, will rise and the real wage rate, w, will correspondingly fall. It is via this mechanism, which implies a variable overall savings rate, that savings are taken to adjust to investment. To this Joseph Steindl (1979), among others, objected that a situation of full employment can hardly be supposed to favour a shift away from wages towards profits if accumulation is speeded up. Trade unions can be expected to be strong in conditions of full employment and thus able to ward off any pressure on real wages. Money prices may rise, but money wages will follow swiftly, annihilating any tendency of real wages to fall. In conditions of full employment it is considered even more probable that real wages rather than the rate of profits will rise, because firms, competing for scarce labour, can be expected to bid up wages. Hence, Kaldor's argument is not all that convincing and actually finds little empirical support.

According to some critics, the Kaldorian theory is also difficult to reconcile with Keynes's more mature point of view. Keynes in *The General Theory*, it is true, adopted the traditional hypothesis that the marginal product of labour is inversely related to the amount of employment, which, in turn, paved the way for acceptance of what he called the first "classical" postulate, that is, the real wage is equal to the marginal product of labour (see Keynes, *CW*, Vol. VII, p. 5). This implied that even in the short run an increase in employment as a result of an increase in investment is accompanied by a reduction in the real wage rate(s). From this perspective Kaldor's theory may be considered a faithful extension of Keynes's theory from the short to the long run. However, as is well known, in response to several critics, in particular J.G. Dunlop, L. Tarshis and M. Kalecki, Keynes in his article "Relative movements of real wages and output", published in 1939, retracted his previous opinion and argued: "We should all agree that if we start from a level of output very greatly below capacity, so that even the most efficient plant and labour are only partially employed, marginal real cost may be expected to decline with increasing output, or, at the worst, remain constant" (ibid., p. 405). An increase in employment would therefore be possible "without seriously affecting real hourly wages" (ibid., p. 401).

When a similar criticism was put forward against the full employment version of the post-Keynesian theory of growth and distribution, its major advocates responded in a similar way. Both Kaldor (1964, pp. xvi–xvii) and Robinson (1969, pp. 261–2) admitted that their models were deficient because they focused attention on adjustments in prices and income distribution rather than in quantities. They also implied that one ought to distinguish between the *normal* rate of profits and the actual or *realized* rate. For a given real wage rate the former will obtain when productive capacity is utilized at its desired degree, whereas at lower degrees of utilization a below normal rate will be realized.

Ever since, a large number of macroeconomic and multisectoral models allowing for below normal degrees of utilization of productive capacity both in the short and in the long run have been elaborated and refined. Early contributions came from, among others, Rowthorn (1981), Kurz (1986, 1990), Dutt (1986), Kalmbach and Kurz (1988) and Marglin and Bhaduri (1990). More recent works include Lavoie (2003). We do not have the space to provide a detailed account of the various directions in which the theory based on the Keynesian hypothesis within a non-full employment of resources framework developed (but see Blecker, 2002 and Lavoie Chapter 6 in this volume, for surveys). It must instead suffice to emphasize the basic idea that underlies the theory.

In the case in which there are sufficiently large margins of spare capacity, an increase in investment activity may indeed increase the rate of profits without any decrease in the real wage rate. A simple macroeconomic argument may illustrate this case. In obvious notation we have

$$Y = W + P = wL + rK$$

Dividing by Y and calling the desired (or "optimal") labour–output ratio and the desired (or "optimal") capital–output ratio l^* and v^*, where $l^* = L/Y^*$ and $v^* = K/Y^*$, with Y^* giving capacity (or "potential") output, we get

$$1 = w\frac{L}{Y^*}\frac{Y^*}{Y} + r\frac{K}{Y^*}\frac{Y^*}{Y} = \frac{wl^*}{u} + \frac{rv^*}{u} \tag{8}$$

or

$$r = \frac{u - wl^*}{v^*},$$

where $u = Y/Y^*$ is the degree of utilization of productive capacity. Since u depends on the rate of accumulation, so does the rate of profits, where in our simple case

$$\frac{\partial r}{\partial u} = \frac{1}{v^*}$$

In the case in which firms are able to hire and fire workers at will, they could always realize the desired labour–output ratio and instead of equation (8) we would have

$$1 = w\frac{L}{Y^*} + r\frac{K}{Y^*}\frac{Y^*}{Y} = wl^* + \frac{rv^*}{u} \tag{9}$$

While in the case depicted by equation (8) the share of wages would fall as the degree of utilization increases, in the case of equation (9) it would remain constant (at a level to which in the former case the share of wages would tend as the system approaches full utilization).

A schematic extension of the argument to the long run is close at hand. Assume two identical economies except for the fact that one, because of a better stabilization policy, manages to realize on average, over a succession of booms and slumps, a higher average rate of capacity utilization than the other economy. With s as the overall savings rate and v now as the actual, or realized, capital-to-output ratio, we have $g_i = (S/Y)(Y/K) = s/v = (S/Y)(Y^*/K)(Y/Y^*) = (s/v^*)u_i$ $(i = 1, 2)$.

Assume, for example, that $s = 0.2$ and $v^* = 2$, but $u_1 = 0.8$ and $u_2 = 0.7$. Then the first economy would grow at 8 per cent per year, whereas the second would grow at only 7 per cent. This may seem a trifling matter, and in the short run it surely is, but according to the compound (instantaneous) interest formula, after about 70 years the first economy would be larger than the second one by the amount of their (common) size at the beginning of our consideration. Hence effective demand matters.

Experience also suggests that there is no reason to presume that actual savings can be expected to move sufficiently close around full employment and full capacity savings. Persistently high rates of unemployment in many countries, both developed and less developed, strongly indicate that the problems of growth and development cannot adequately be dealt with in terms of the full employment and full capacity utilization assumptions.

In the long run investment cannot sensibly be taken as given. It is safe to assume that investment behaviour will be shaped by what is happening in the economy. Taking up suggestions by Keynes, Kalecki and others, there have been attempts to model more carefully investment behaviour. The presence of an "investment function" in addition to, and independently of, the savings function is indeed a characteristic feature of the class of Keynesian models under consideration. This has led to a class of investment-led growth models, in which growth is typically seen to depend on two main, but interrelated factors: profitability and effective demand. As regards the second factor there is wide agreement and strong empirical evidence that investment responds positively (negatively) to rising (falling) levels of capacity utilization. Indeed, the old accelerator model does not perform too badly in empirical studies. Profitability, in turn, is governed by the innovative potential that can be exploited at a given moment of time and by income distribution. Put in a nutshell, the type of investment function typically employed is as follows

$$\gamma = \gamma(\rho, \rho^e, i, u)$$

where γ is the share of investment, I/Y, ρ the current rate of profit as an indicator of the possibilities of internal financing, ρ^e the expected rate of profit, i the long-term rate of interest, and u the degree of capacity utilization. There are three essential characteristic features of these models. First, income distribution and growth are simultaneously determined. Second, the "paradox of thrift" is not limited to the short run: an increase in the overall propensity to save, other things being equal, may in certain circumstances reduce both the rate of growth and the rate of profit. This is exactly the opposite of what neoclassical models typically predict. Finally, the rate of growth depends negatively on the real wage rate provided the system is in what is called a "profit-led growth regime". However, this need not be the case. There exist constellations of the parameters which give the model an "underconsumptionist" flavour, with the growth rate rising together with the real wage rate over a certain range. For a summary account of this class of models, see Commendatore et al. (2003).

Notes

*   We should like to thank Mark Setterfield for valuable comments on an earlier version of this chapter. All remaining errors are, of course, our responsibility.
1.   On such a technological relationship, see subsection 2.4 below.
2.   Since $C \equiv (g/s_c, g/s_c)$ and $B \equiv (g/s_c, (g/s_c) + (gs_c - s_{pw}g)/s_{ww}s_c)$, a two-class economy exists if and only if

$$\frac{g}{s_c} < \frac{1}{v^*} < \frac{g}{s_c} + \frac{gs_c - s_{pw}g}{s_{ww}s_c}$$

from which the inequalities in the text are obtained.
3.   Kaldor did not deny that the capital–output ratio can vary with the rate of profits. He opined however "that technical innovations . . . are far more influential on the chosen v than price relationships" (1955–56, p. 98 fn.)

References

Balestra, P. and Baranzini, M. (1971). "Some optimal aspects in a two class growth model with a differentiated interest rate", *Kyklos*, **24**, 240–56.
Bidard, Ch. and Franke, R. (1987). "On the existence of long-term equilibria in the two-class Pasinetti-Morishima model", *Ricerche Economiche*, **41**, 3–21.
Bidard, Ch. and Hosoda, E. (1987). "On consumption baskets in a generalized von Neumann model", *International Economic Review*, **28**, 509–19.
Blecker, R. (2002). "Distribution, demand and growth in neo-Kaleckian macro-models", in M. Setterfield (ed.), *The Economics of Demand-led Growth: Challenging the Supply-side Vision of the Long Run*, Cheltenham, UK and Northampton, MA, USA: Edward Elgar, pp. 129–52.
Chiang, A.C. (1973). "A simple generalization of the Kaldor-Pasinetti theory of profit rate and income distribution", *Economica*, **40**, 311–13.
Commendatore, P., D'Acunto, S., Panico, C. and Pinto, A. (2003). "Keynesian theories of growth", in N. Salvadori, (ed.), *The Theory of Economic Growth: A Classical Perspective*, Cheltenham, UK and Northampton, MA, USA: Edward Elgar, pp. 104–39.
Dutt, A.K. (1986). "Growth, distribution and technological change", *Metroeconomica*, **38**, 113–33.
Fazi, E. and Salvadori, N. (1981). "The existence of a two-class economy in the Kaldor model of growth and distribution", *Kyklos*, **34**, 582–92.
Fazi, E. and Salvadori, N. (1985). "The existence of a two-class economy in a general Cambridge model of growth and distribution", *Cambridge Journal of Economics*, **9**, 155–64.
Franke, R. (1985). "On the upper- and lower-bounds of workers' propensity to save in a two-class Pasinetti economy", *Australian Economic Papers*, **24**, 271–77.
Gupta, K.L. (1977). "On the existence of a two-class economy in the Kaldor and Pasinetti models of growth and distribution", *Jahrbücher für Nationalökonomie und Statistik*, **192**, 68–72.
Kahn, R. (1931). "The relation of home investment to unemployment", *Economic Journal*, **41**(2), 173–98.
Kaldor, N. (1937). "Annual survey of economic theory: the recent controversy on the theory of capital", *Econometrica*, **5**, 201–33.
Kaldor, N. (1955–56). "Alternative theories of distribution", *Review of Economic Studies*, **23**, 83–100.
Kaldor, N. (1964). *Essays on Economic Policy*, Vol. I, London: Duckworth.
Kaldor, N. (1966). "Marginal productivity and the macro-economic theories of distribution", *Review of Economic Studies*, **33**, 309–19.
Kaldor, N. (1978). "Introduction", in N. Kaldor, *Further Essays on Economic Theory*, Vol. 5 of *Collected Economic Essays*, London: Duckworth, pp. vii–xxix.
Kalecki, M. (1938). *Essays in the Theory of Economic Fluctuation*, London: Allen & Unwin.
Kalecki, M. (1942). "A theory of profit", *Economic Journal*, **52**, 258–66.
Kalecki, M. (1954). *Theory of Economic Dynamics; An Essay on Cyclical and Long-run Changes in Capitalist Economy*, London: Allen & Unwin.
Kalmbach, P. and Kurz, H.D. (1988). "Einige Überlegungen zu Akkumulation und Einkommensverteilung in keynesianischer Perspektive", *Ökonomie und Gesellschaft*, **6**, 22–45.
Keynes, J.M. (1937). "Alternative theories of the rate of interest", *Economic Journal*, **47**, 241–52.
Keynes, J.M. (1973 ssq.). *The Collected Writings of John Maynard Keynes*, 32 vols, managing eds A. Robinson and D. Moggridge, London: Macmillan. In the text referred to as *CW*, volume number and page number.
Kurz, H. D. (1986). "'Normal' positions and capital utilization", *Political Economy*, **2**, 37–54.
Kurz, H.D. (1990). "Technical change, growth and distribution: a steady-state approach to 'unsteady' growth", in H.D. Kurz, *Capital, Distribution and Effective Demand*, London: Polity Press, pp. 210–39.

Laing, N.F. (1969). "Two notes on Pasinetti's theorem", *Economic Record*, **45**, 373–85.
Laski, K. (1987). "Kalecki, Michal", in J. Eatwell, M. Milgate and P. Newman (eds), *The New Palgrave. A Dictionary of Economics*, vol. 3, pp. 8–14.
Lavoie, M. (2003). "Kaleckian effective demand and Sraffian normal prices: towards a reconciliation", *Review of Political Economy*, **15**(1), 53–74.
Maneschi, A. (1974). "The existence of a two-class economy in the Kaldor and Pasinetti models of growth and distribution", *Review of Economic Studies*, **41**, 149–50.
Marglin, S.A. (1984). *Growth, Distribution, and Prices*, Cambridge, MA: Harvard University Press.
Marglin, S.A. and Bhaduri, A. (1990). "Unemployment and real wage: the economic basis for contesting political ideologies", *Cambridge Journal of Economics*, **14**, 375–93.
Meade, J.E. (1963). "The rate of profit in a growing economy", *Economic Journal*, **73**, 665–74.
Meade, J.E. (1966). "The outcome of the Pasinetti-process: a note", *Economic Journal*, **76**, 161–4.
Meade, J.E. and Hahn, F.H. (1965). "The rate of profit in a growing economy", *Economic Journal*, **75**, 445–8.
Moore, B.J. (1974). "The Pasinetti paradox revisited", *Review of Economic Studies*, **41**, 297–9.
Morishima, M. (1964). *Equilibrium, Stability and Growth*, Oxford: Clarendon Press.
Morishima, M. (1969). *Theory of Economic Growth*, Oxford: Clarendon Press.
Mückl, W.J. (1978). "On the existence of a two-class economy in the Cambridge models of growth and distribution", *Jahrbücher für Nationalökonomie und Statistik*, **193**, 508–17.
Pasinetti, L.L. (1962). "Rate of profit and income distribution in relation to the rate of economic growth", *Review of Economic Studies*, **29**, 267–79.
Pasinetti, L.L. (1966a). "Changes in the rate of profit and switches of techniques", *Quarterly Journal of Economics*, **80**, 503–17.
Pasinetti, L.L. (1966b). "New results in an old framework", *Review of Economic Studies*, **33**, 303–6.
Pasinetti, L.L. (1974). *Growth and Income Distribution. Essays in Economic Theory*, Cambridge: Cambridge University Press.
Pasinetti, L.L. (1983). "Conditions of existence of a two-class economy in the Kaldor and more general models of growth and distribution", *Kyklos*, **36**, 91–102.
Robinson, J.V. (1956). *The Accumulation of Capital*, London: Macmillan.
Robinson, J.V. (1966). "Comment on P.A. Samuelson and F. Modigliani", *Review of Economic Studies*, **33**, 307–8.
Robinson, J.V. (1969). "A further note", *Review of Economic Studies*, **36**, 260–62.
Rowthorn, R. (1981). "Demand, real wages and economic growth", in *Thames Papers in Political Economy*, London: Thames Polytechnic.
Salvadori, N. (1980). "On a generalized von Neumann model", *Metroeconomica*, **32**, 51–62.
Salvadori, N. (1988). "The existence of a two-class economy in a general Cambridge model of growth and distribution: an addendum", *Cambridge Journal of Economics*, **12**, 273–8.
Salvadori, N. (1991). "Post-Keynesian theory of distribution in the long run", in E. Nell and W. Semmler (eds), *Nicholas Kaldor and Mainstream Economics: Confrontation or Convergence*, New York: St. Martins Press, pp. 164–89.
Salvadori, N. (ed.) (2003). *The Theory of Economic Growth: A Classical Perspective*, Cheltenham, UK and Northampton, MA, USA: Edward Elgar.
Salvadori, N. (2004). "Wealth in the post-Keynesian theory of growth and distribution", in G. Argyrous, M. Forstater and G. Mongiovi (eds), *Growth, Distribution, and Effective Demand. Alternatives to Economic Orthodoxy*, Armonk and London: M.E. Sharpe, pp. 61–80.
Samuelson, P.A. and Modigliani, F. (1966a). "The Pasinetti paradox in neoclassical and more general models", *Review of Economic Studies*, **33**, 321–30.
Samuelson, P.A. and Modigliani, F. (1966b). "Reply to Pasinetti and Robinson", *Review of Economic Studies*, **33**, 269–302.
Steindl, J. (1979). "Stagnation theory and stagnation policy", *Cambridge Journal of Economics*, **3**(1), 1–14.

5 Growth, instability and cycles: Harrodian and Kaleckian models of accumulation and income distribution*

Peter Skott

1 Introduction

Post-Keynesian theory is sometimes seen as encompassing almost anything "non-mainstream". Following the seminal contributions by Rowthorn (1981), Dutt (1984) and Taylor (1985), however, Kaleckian models with stable steady-growth paths have come to dominate post-Keynesian and structuralist macroeconomics. These models are characterized by a low sensitivity of accumulation to variations in utilization, and with a given markup, the utilization rate becomes an accommodating variable in both the short and the long run. Thus, the steady-growth value of the utilization rate is not, as in Harrodian or Robinsonian models, tied to a structurally determined desired rate. Instead, shocks to demand (changes in saving rates, for instance) can have large, permanent effects on utilization.

A substantial literature discusses the long-run relation between actual and desired utilization rates. Kurz (1986), Committeri (1986), Duménil and Lévy (1993), and Auerbach and Skott (1988) are among those who have faulted Kaleckian models for their failure to ensure that actual utilization and desired utilization coincide in steady growth.[1] A Kaleckian response has been articulated by Lavoie (1995, 1996), Amadeo (1986), Dutt (1997), and Lavoie et al. (2004). I find the Kaleckian response unconvincing (see Skott 2008 for details), and in this chapter I shall argue that an alternative Harrodian approach is both promising and analytically tractable. The chapter goes over some of the same ground as Lavoie's interesting and influential 1995 article, but the conclusions are rather different.

Harrodian models are more complex than the standard Kaleckian formulation. They require a distinction between short-run and long-run accumulation functions and may generate unstable "warranted growth paths". Despite these complexities, the analysis remains tractable and the complexities bring significant rewards. The Harrodian assumptions, first, can be given clear behavioral justifications. The Kaleckian stability condition, by contrast, is usually introduced for instrumental reasons to ensure stability, stability being seen (implicitly but mistakenly) as imperative for the real-world relevance of the model. Harrodian investment functions, second, can be compatible with multiple steady-growth solutions, some of which may be stable, and the existence of multiple solutions carries interesting implications. The (local) instability of a warranted growth path, third, quite naturally leads to an integration of growth and cycles. As emphasized by Frisch, Slutsky and Kalecki in the 1930s and 1940s as well as by most contemporary theories of the business cycle, stochastic shocks may play a role in the generation of cyclical movements. But the presence of shocks does not exclude endogenous mechanisms, and Harrodian instability provides a powerful foundation for endogenous cycles.[2]

Section 2 outlines a basic Kaleckian model. A Harrodian perspective is presented in section 3. Drawing on Skott (1989a, 1989b) and Nakatani and Skott (2007), section 4 analyses a Kaldor/Marshall version of the Harrodian model. Two different cases are considered: a "dual-economy" case in which the labor supply is perfectly elastic and the growth of the economy can be determined without any reference to the labor market, and a "mature" economy in which the labor supply constrains the long-run rate of growth. The relaxation of the standard Kaleckian assumption of a fixed markup is a key element in the analysis of both dual-economy and mature cases. In the Kaldor/Marshall version, the fixed markup is replaced by fast, demand-determined adjustments in the profit share and sluggish movements of output. An alternative Robinson/Steindl version assumes sluggish adjustments in prices and the profit share but fast output adjustments. This version is considered in section 5, which draws on Skott (2005a) and Flaschel and Skott (2006). Section 6 contains a few concluding comments.

2   A Kaleckian benchmark model

Kaleckian models have been extended and modified in many ways. Some extensions have introduced a government sector and an explicit analysis of policy issues (e.g. Lima and Setterfield, 2008); others add financial variables or open-economy complications (e.g. Blecker 1989, 1999; Lavoie and Godley 2001–02; Dos Santos and Zezza, 2008; Hein and van Treeck, 2007). For present purposes, however, a stripped-down model of a closed economy without public sector and without financial constraints on investment will suffice.

Algebraically, the canonical Kaleckian model is exceedingly simple:

$$\frac{I}{K} = \alpha + \beta u + \gamma r \tag{1}$$

$$\frac{S}{K} = s(\pi) u \sigma \tag{2}$$

$$\frac{I}{K} = \frac{S}{K} \tag{3}$$

$$r = \pi u \sigma \tag{4}$$

$$\pi = \overline{\pi} \tag{5}$$

$$g = \hat{K} = \frac{I}{K} - \delta \tag{6}$$

Using standard notation, equations (1)–(2) are the investment and saving functions. Investment is increasing in utilization (u) and the profit rate (r), and the saving rate out of income ($s(\pi)$) is an increasing function of the profit share (π); σ denotes the technical output–capital ratio. Equation (3) is the equilibrium condition for the product market; equation (4) defines the profit rate as the product of the profit share, the utilization rate and the technical output–capital ratio. Equation (5) is the pricing equation with the profit share fixed by a markup on marginal cost, the latter assumed constant and equal to unit labor cost. Equation (6) sets the growth rate of the capital stock ($g = \hat{K}$) equal to gross accumulation minus the rate of depreciation, δ. All parameters are assumed positive and the Keynesian stability condition is supposed to hold,

$$\frac{\partial(I/K)}{\partial u} = \beta + \gamma\overline{\pi}\sigma < s(\overline{\pi})\sigma = \frac{\partial(S/K)}{\partial u} \tag{7}$$

Simple manipulations of equations (1)–(6) imply that

$$u^* = \frac{\alpha}{s(\overline{\pi})\sigma - \beta - \gamma\overline{\pi}\sigma} \tag{8}$$

$$g^* = \frac{\alpha s(\overline{\pi})\sigma}{s(\overline{\pi})\sigma - \beta - \gamma\overline{\pi}\sigma} - \delta \tag{9}$$

It is readily seen that if the saving function is linear ($s(\pi) = s\pi$), the stability condition (7) implies that

$$\frac{\partial u^*}{\partial\overline{\pi}} < 0 \tag{10}$$

$$\frac{\partial g^*}{\partial\overline{\pi}} < 0 \tag{11}$$

Thus, the economy is both "stagnationist" (equation (10)) and "wage led" (equation (11)) in the terminology of Marglin and Bhaduri (1990).[3]

Marglin and Bhaduri challenged these implications of the model and suggested that the investment function be recast with accumulation as a function of utilization and the profit share, rather than utilization and the profit rate,

$$\frac{I}{K} = \alpha + \beta u + \gamma\pi \tag{12}$$

Using this alternative specification of the investment function, they showed that the Keynesian stability condition need not produce stagnationist and wage-led regimes. The utilization rate remains an accommodating variable, however, and the main difference between the investment functions (1) and (12) is that the sensitivity of investment to changes in utilization has been *reduced*, relative to the sensitivity with respect to the profit share. The non-stagnationist outcomes become possible precisely because, using (12) instead of (1), we may have $(\partial(I/K))/(\partial\overline{\pi}) > (\partial(S/K))/(\partial\overline{\pi})$, even when the Keynesian stability condition is satisfied, something that cannot occur when the investment function is given by (1) and the saving function is linear ($s(\pi) = s\pi$). Equivalently, equation (12) does not exclude the possibility that, holding constant the rate of profit, an increase in utilization may reduce accumulation. This is in sharp contrast to Harrodian formulations. Thus, although both the Marglin–Bhaduri formulation and the Harrodian models below may produce profit-led outcomes, the behavioral assumptions are very different, and from a Harrodian perspective the Marglin–Bhaduri specification suffers from the same problems as the original Kaleckian model.

To simplify the exposition I shall set γ equal to zero. In this special case, the two investment functions (1) and (12) coincide, the Keynesian stability condition can be written $s(\overline{\pi})\sigma > \beta$, and the equilibrium solutions for u^* and g^* take the form

$$u^* = \frac{\alpha}{s(\overline{\pi})\sigma - \beta} \tag{13}$$

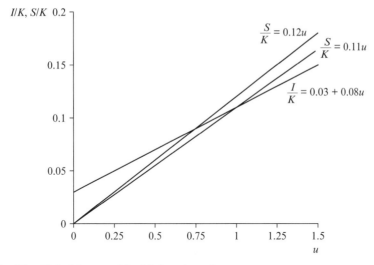

Figure 5.1   The Kaleckian model with benchmark parameters

$$g^* = \frac{\alpha s(\bar{\pi})\sigma}{s(\bar{\pi})\sigma - \beta} - \delta \tag{14}$$

The model is illustrated graphically in Figure 5.1. Unlike most illustrations, which focus on the qualitative properties, Figure 5.1 is based on Kaleckian benchmark values. Empirically, the gross saving rate $s(\pi)$ typically falls in the range 0.15–0.3 and the technical output–capital ratio in the range 1–3. Figure 5.1 uses $s(\pi)\sigma = 0.12$; $\beta = 0.08$ and $\alpha = 0.03$; yielding an equilibrium utilization rate of $u^* = \alpha/(s(\bar{\pi})\sigma - \beta) = 0.75$.

Figure 5.1 and the numerical example illustrate one of the main weaknesses of the Kaleckian analysis. Assume that the saving rate drops slightly, with $s(\bar{\pi})\sigma$ falling from 0.12 to 0.11. As a result, the growth rate increases by 2 percentage points while the utilization rate jumps from 75 percent to 100 percent. This strong sensitivity of utilization to variations in parameters is an intrinsic property of the Kaleckian model. For any reasonable specification of the saving function, the Kaleckian stability condition puts a very low ceiling on the maximum value of β (about 0.1). Shocks to the saving function therefore give rise to fluctuations in utilization rates that are at least about ten times larger than those in accumulation. Shocks to the accumulation function (changes in α) produce movements along the saving function and (given the stability condition) the ratio of variations in utilization to variations in the growth rate is slightly larger, but still unlikely to be much below ten. These implications do not fit the data. Utilization rates are difficult to measure, but existing data suggest modest long-run variations. As shown in Figure 5.2a, utilization rates for US manufacturing industry fluctuate significantly in the short run (as one would expect) but the long-run trend is quite flat, and the ratio of long-run variations in utilization to long-run variations in growth is nowhere near the values suggested by the Kaleckian model (Figure 5.2b gives growth rates of capital capacity in US manufacturing).

From a theoretical perspective the problems with the Kaleckian specifications arise from the combination of an exogenous markup with the extension to the long run of a

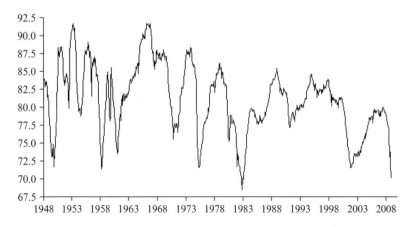

Source: Federal Reserve.

Figure 5.2a   Utilization rates, US manufacturing

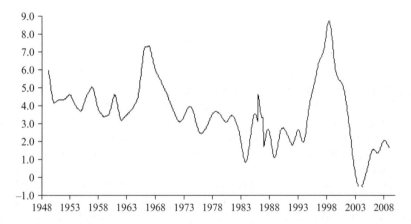

Source: Federal Reserve.

Figure 5.2b   US manufacturing capacity; annual growth rate

standard, Keynesian short-run stability condition: the relative insensitivity of investment to variations in aggregate demand.[4] A Harrodian approach addresses these issues.

3   A Harrodian alternative
A Harrodian specification of the investment function makes a distinction between the short-run and the long-run sensitivity of investment to changes in aggregate demand. The insensitivity is plausible in the short run, but changes in aggregate demand have lagged effects on investment, and a weak impact effect (which is required for the stability of the short-run Keynesian equilibrium) does not guarantee that the long-term effects of a sustained increase in aggregate demand and utilization will be weak as well.

In a discrete-time framework (and still assuming, for simplicity, that only utilization matters for investment), the presence of lags can be captured by a general specification,

$$\left(\frac{I}{K}\right)t = f\left(u_t, u_{t-1}, \ldots, u_{t-m}, \left(\frac{I}{K}\right)_{t-1}, \left(\frac{I}{K}\right)_{t-2}, \ldots, \left(\frac{I}{K}\right)_{t-n}\right)$$ (15)

The short-run effect of utilization on accumulation is given by the partial derivative $\partial f/\partial u_t$, and the Keynesian stability condition can be written

$$s(\pi)\sigma > \frac{\partial f}{\partial u_t}$$ (16)

The long-run effect of changes in utilization, on the other hand, is given by

$$\hat{K} = \frac{I}{K} - \delta = \phi(u)$$ (17)

with

$$\phi'(u) = \frac{d\frac{I}{K}}{du\big|_{u_t = u_{t-p}, \frac{I}{K_t} = \frac{I}{K_{t-k}}}} = \frac{\displaystyle\sum_{i=0}^{m} \frac{\partial f}{\partial u_{t-i}}}{1 - \displaystyle\sum_{j=1}^{n} \frac{\partial f}{\partial\left(\frac{I}{K}\right)_{t-j}}}$$ (18)

The short-run condition (16) carries no implications for the relation between the long-run sensitivity, ϕ', and $s(\pi)\sigma$.

The significance of the distinction between short-run and long-run specifications depends on the magnitude of the lagged effects. According to Harrod the lagged effects are large and $\phi'(u) \gg s(\pi)\sigma$. This condition is satisfied by the following special case of (15):

$$\left(\frac{I}{K}\right)t = \lambda(u_t - u^d) + \left(\frac{I}{K}\right)t - 1$$ (19)

or, in continuous time,

$$\dot{g} = \frac{d}{dt}\hat{K} = \lambda(u - u^d)$$ (20)

where u^d is the desired rate of utilization. The standard Harrodian specification in equation (20) implies that the accumulation rate becomes a state variable and that there is no immediate impact of changes in utilization on investment. In the long run, by contrast, accumulation is perfectly elastic: utilization must be at the desired rate in steady growth, but as long as this condition is satisfied, the accumulation function imposes no constraints on the growth rate. Thus, the specification (20) implies a particularly simple (even if unconventional) steady-growth accumulation function:

$$u = u^d$$ (21)

Equation (21) is a special case of (17) with $\phi' = \infty$ at $u = u^d$.

The behavioral story behind the Harrodian specification is quite straightforward.

Firms have a well-defined objective (to maximize profits) and this objective implies a desired utilization rate. Since capital stocks adjust slowly and demand expectations are not always met, actual utilization may deviate from desired rates in the short run. It would be unreasonable, however, to assume that demand expectations can be persistently and systematically falsified in steady growth. Consequently, it is hard to conceive of a steady-growth scenario in which firms are content to accumulate at a constant rate despite having significantly more (or less) excess capacity than they desire. From a behavioral perspective the only real question concerns the determination of the desired rate of utilization.[5]

The desired utilization rate may deviate from unity. A firm may want to hold excess capacity to deter entry or to enable the firm to respond quickly to variations in demand; or excess capacity may exist simply as a result of indivisibilities of investment (non-convexities in adjustment costs). The desired degree of excess capacity, second, need not be constant over time; changes in the degree of product market competition or in the volatility of demand, for instance, could affect desired utilization rates. Managerial constraints or other bottlenecks, third, may make it difficult or costly to expand capacity at a rapid pace, and the desired utilization rate, consequently, may depend, inter alia, on the rate of accumulation. This case can be represented by equation (17) which specifies a long-run relation between accumulation and desired utilization. If the long-run accumulation function is given by (17) with $0 < \phi' < \infty$, the counterpart to (20) is

$$\dot{g} = \lambda(u - \phi^{-1}(g)) \tag{22}$$

Using (22) instead of the Kaleckian investment function (1), the steady growth solutions for u and g are determined by

$$g^* = \phi(u^*) = s(\bar{\pi})u^*\sigma - \delta \tag{23}$$

and the economy is "exhilarationist" and profit led in the long run: by assumption $\phi' > s(\bar{\pi})\sigma$ and hence

$$\frac{du^*}{d\pi} = \frac{s'(\bar{\pi})\sigma u^*}{\phi'(u^*) - s(\bar{\pi})\sigma} > 0; \quad \frac{dg^*}{d\pi} = \phi'(u^*)\frac{du^*}{d\pi} > 0 \tag{24}$$

A Harrodian steady-growth path, however, may be unstable. This, indeed, is the case with the simple model based on (2)–(3) and (22). The accumulation rate is predetermined at any moment and the short-run Keynesian equilibrium is stable, but the trajectory of Keynesian equilibria does not converge to the steady-growth path. Combining (2)–(3) and (22), we get a one-dimensional differential equation with an unstable stationary solution:[6]

$$\dot{g} = \lambda\left[\frac{g + \delta}{s(\bar{\pi})\sigma} - \phi^{-1}(g)\right] \tag{25}$$

and (since $\phi' > s(\bar{\pi})\sigma$)

$$\frac{d\dot{g}}{dg} = \lambda\left[\frac{1}{s(\bar{\pi})\sigma} - \frac{1}{\phi'(g)}\right] > 0 \tag{26}$$

The instability of a Harrodian warranted growth path has been viewed as a powerful argument against this approach. The argument may not be spelled out in any detail but it is suggested, implicitly, that stability is needed for the model to make sense and/or for the properties of the steady-growth path to be empirically relevant (e.g. Lavoie, 1995, p. 794). There are several possible answers to these implicit claims. As argued in sections 4.1 and 5.1, stability may be achieved without abandoning a Harrodian investment function if the fixed markup is abandoned. More importantly, the steady growth path may be relevant even in the absence of asymptotic stability. Local instability is consistent with endogenously generated, bounded fluctuations around a steady-growth solution, and an unstable steady-growth path may provide a good approximation to average outcomes in the medium to long run.[7] Sections 4.2 and 5.2 consider how boundedness may be generated by a Marxian employment effect, but the general argument does not depend on this particular mechanism.

4   Harrodian instability: a Kaldor/Marshall analysis

Kaldorian models from the 1950s and early 1960s include endogenous adjustments in the profit share. Since the profit share is determined by the pricing equation, this calls for a reconsideration of firms' price and output decisions.

In the Keynesian literature – both old and new – it is often assumed that firms set prices and that output adjusts instantaneously and costlessly to match demand. The empirical evidence in favor of significant price rigidity is quite weak, however,[8] and output does not adjust instantaneously. Production is subject to a production lag, and increases in production and employment typically give rise to substantial search, hiring and training costs; firing or layoffs also involve costs, both explicit costs like redundancy payments and hidden costs in the form of deteriorating industrial relations and morale. Based on these considerations, a Kaldor/Marshall approach assumes fast price adjustments and sluggish output movements: shocks to aggregate demand are accommodated initially by movements in prices and profit shares, rather than in output and utilization.

In a continuous-time setting the effects of lags and adjustment costs for output can be approximated by assuming that output is predetermined at each moment and that firms choose the rate of growth of output, rather than the level of output. If firms maximize profits (or pursue some other well-defined objectives), the growth of output is chosen so as to balance the costs of changes against the benefits of moving toward a preferred level of output and employment; (expected) costs and benefits, in turn, are determined by the demand and cost signals that firms receive from product and labor markets.

4.1   A dual economy

Consider first a dual economy in which there is a perfectly elastic supply of labor to the capitalist sector. Endogenous changes in the cost signal from input markets may be ignored in this kind of economy. A perfectly elastic labor supply, to be sure, does not rule out shifts in the perceived costs of changes in output. Exogenous shifts in worker militancy, for instance, may affect these perceived costs, but the dual-economy assumption implies that labor market conditions do not change endogenously as a result of firms' output and investment decisions.

The demand signal from product markets, by contrast, is endogenously determined. If prices are fully flexible, this signal can be captured by the prevailing profit share.

By assumption the level of output is predetermined, and a rise in demand leads to an increase in the price of output. Wage contracts are cast in terms of money wages, and it may be assumed that there is neither perfect foresight nor instantaneous feedbacks from output prices to money-wage rates. The real wage rate and the share of profits in income therefore respond to unanticipated movements in prices: a positive demand shock generates a rise in the profit share, and firms respond to this rise by increasing the growth rate of output.[9]

Algebraically, we get a generic growth function[10]

$$\hat{Y} = h(\pi); h_\pi > 0 \qquad (27)$$

The growth function (27) replaces the pricing equation (5) and may, as the pricing equation, be influenced by the sectoral composition of the economy and the degree of competition in the product markets. In general, the function is likely to be highly non-linear. It seems reasonable to suppose that the adjustment costs for output are convex as a function of $\hat{Y}$, and there may also be upper and lower limits on the rate of growth, $g^{min} \leq \hat{Y} \leq g^{max}$. Thus, the growth rate will be more sensitive to variations in the profit share for intermediate values of the profit share than for very high or very low values.

In a Kaldor/Marshall model, aggregate demand shocks are accommodated through variations in prices and the profit share. This accommodation is possible since a rise in the profit share raises aggregate saving and reduces excess demand, as in Keynes (1930) and Kaldor (1956). Using a linear version of equation (2),

$$\frac{S}{K} = s\pi u\sigma \qquad (28)$$

the equilibrium condition for the product market yields the following solution for the profit share

$$\pi = \frac{g + \delta}{su\sigma} \qquad (29)$$

where both $g = \hat{K}$ and u are predetermined, given a Harrodian investment function and sluggish output adjustment.

In order to close the model, equations (28)–(29) need to be combined with a specification of the accumulation function. Consider first the standard specification in equation (20). Using the saving function (28), the steady-growth condition $u = u^d$ (implied by (20)), and the equilibrium condition for the product market, the set of steady-growth solutions for (π, g) is characterized by

$$h(\pi^*) = su^d\sigma\pi^* - \delta \qquad (30)$$

$$g^* = h(\pi^*) \qquad (31)$$

The non-linearity of the h-function implies that there may be multiple steady-growth solutions, as in Figure 5.3b. Outcomes with a unique solution are also possible (Figures 5.3a and 5.3c), and a case without steady-growth solutions can be obtained when the lower limit on $\hat{Y}$ is abandoned ($g^{min} = -\infty$); this case is illustrated in Figure 5.3d.

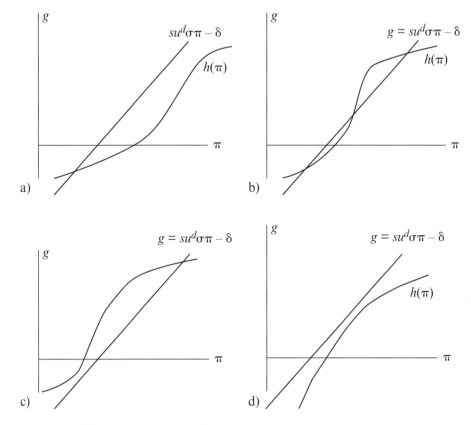

Figure 5.3   A Harrodian model of a dual economy

Essentially, the cases in 5.3a and 5.3d are identical since with negative growth rates, there can be capitalist development in neither case.

Figure 5.3b represents the most interesting case. At the two extreme equilibria we have $h' < s\sigma u^d$; at the intermediate equilibrium this inequality is reversed. Not surprisingly, the inequality is closely related to stability conditions. The profit share at any moment is given by equation (29), and substituting (29) into the growth function (27), we get an equation of motion for the utilization rate

$$\hat{u} = \hat{Y} - \hat{K} = h\left(\frac{g + \delta}{su\sigma}\right) - g \tag{32}$$

Equations (20) and (32) define a two-dimensional system of differential equations. Evaluated at a stationary point, the Jacobian of the system is given by

$$J(g, u) = \begin{bmatrix} 0 & \lambda \\ u\left(\dfrac{h'}{s\sigma u} - 1\right) & -uh'\dfrac{g + \delta}{s\sigma u^2} \end{bmatrix} \tag{33}$$

and

$$\text{tr}(J) = -uh'\frac{g + \delta}{s\sigma u} < 0$$

$$\det(J) = -\lambda u\left(\frac{h'}{s\sigma u} - 1\right) > 0 \quad \text{iff} \quad h' < s\sigma u$$

It follows that a steady-growth path is locally asymptotically stable if and only if $h'(\pi^*) < su^d\sigma$. The stability condition is satisfied at the two extreme solutions in Figure 5.3b; the intermediate solution on the other hand will be unstable.

Similar results can be obtained if investment is described by the static equation (17). At first sight, this may seem a peculiar accumulation function in a Harrodian analysis, but since utilization is treated as a state variable, the seemingly static specification (17) embodies the main Harrodian principle.[11] By assumption the impact effect of changes in aggregate demand falls entirely on prices and the profit share, and the insensitivity of investment to short-run fluctuations in demand is satisfied by (17); a strong long-run sensitivity follows if $\phi'(u)$ is "large". Using (17) and (27)–(28), the steady-growth conditions are given by

$$g^* = h(\pi^*) = s\sigma u^*\pi^* - \delta = \phi(u^*) \tag{34}$$

These equations can be described using a modified Figure 5.3; the only difference is that the *IS*-curve (the solutions to the last equation in (34) for given π) will now be non-linear in a (π, g)-space; see Figure 5.4 which corresponds to 5.3b when the ϕ-function takes the form $\phi(u) = \mu(u - u_0)$.[12] This specification of the model produces a one-dimensional dynamic system

$$\hat{u} = h\left(\frac{\phi(u) + \delta}{su\sigma}\right) - \phi(u) \tag{35}$$

and local stability, again, is achieved at the two extreme solutions.[13]

The above analysis of a dual economy has several noteworthy implications. The existence of multiple steady-growth paths, first, implies that countries that initially seem quite similar may follow very different growth trajectories and that temporary aggregate demand policy may raise the long-run rate of growth. Suppose, for instance, that initially an economy is at the low growth path in Figure 5.3b (an analogous argument applies to the specifications underlying Figure 5.4): Using a trivial extension of the model to include a government sector, expansionary policy can reduce the average saving rate. The result is a rise in the profit share for any given growth rate or, equivalently, a downward shift in the *IS*-curve (the $g = s\pi u^d\sigma - \delta$ line in Figure 5.3b). If the shift is large enough, the new configuration will be as in Figure 5.3c, and a move to the high steady-growth equilibrium may get under way. Once at the high-growth path, the expansionary policy is no longer needed. Following a return to the old saving rate, the economy may now grow at the rate associated with the high solution.

Shifts in the h- or s-functions or in the desired utilization rate u^d (more generally, in the accumulation function ϕ), second, have permanent growth effects. An increase in animal spirits, for instance, may be reflected in an upward shift in the h-function (an increase in

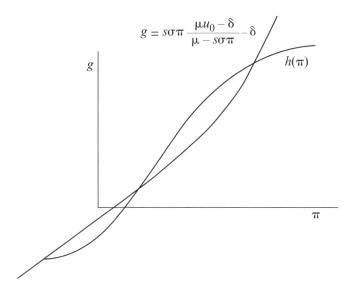

$$g = s\sigma\pi \frac{\mu u_0 - \delta}{\mu - s\sigma\pi} - \delta$$

$h(\pi)$

Figure 5.4 The Harrodian model with a static investment function

the growth of output for any given profit share) and/or a fall in the desired utilization rate (corresponding to an upward shift in the investment function). At a stable growth path, not surprisingly, these shifts are unambiguously expansionary. A downward shift in the *s*-function also raises the steady-growth solutions for both π and $\hat{Y}$ if the initial position is at a stable steady-growth path. Since the profit share is endogenous, there is no direct counterpart to the stagnationist Kaleckian "paradox of cost" but an increase in the concentration rate and decline in competition will be associated with a downward shift in the growth function and, starting from a stable growth path, a decline in the growth rate.

   The high steady-growth solution may have empirical counterparts in the experience of successful developing countries, including Japan, Korea and China during their years of miracle growth (it should be noted in this context that the average growth rate for a successful developing economy with a large reserve of hidden unemployment understates the growth of the modern, capitalist sector). Empirical counterparts to the low-growth trap are not hard to find either, and the Japanese stagnation since about 1990 and its relation to the present framework are discussed in Nakatani and Skott (2007). But established industrialized countries without significant reserves of hidden unemployment and with relatively stable growth rates in the 1–5 percent range fit neither the low nor the high equilibrium. The intermediate solution might seem more promising, but the dual-economy assumption is questionable for these economies and the model needs to be modified.

4.2 The reserve army of labor
Many writers (including Steindl, 1952, Kaldor, 1966, 1978 and Marglin, 1984) have regarded capitalist accumulation as essentially unconstrained by the growth of the labor force, a position that is reflected also in the canonical Kaleckian model. This dual-economy assumption is reasonable for many LDCs (less developed country) and NICs (newly industrialized country) where the existence of hidden unemployment

makes the rate of open unemployment largely irrelevant as an indicator of conditions in the labor market. In most OECD countries, however, measured employment provides important information about the state of the labor market, and the growth function in section 4.1 needs to be extended: the cost of output variations can no longer be taken as independent of the employment rate.[14]

The employment rate influences the costs of changing output through its effects on the availability of labor with the desired qualifications. Labor markets are not perfectly competitive and it is harder for a firm to attract and retain workers when unemployment is low. Thus, high employment rates increase the costs of recruitment and since the quit rate tends to rise when labor markets are tight, the gross recruitment needs associated with any given rate of expansion increase at a time when low unemployment makes it difficult to attract new workers. A high turnover of the labor force, on the other hand, allows firms to reduce production and employment more rapidly without large adjustment costs when the employment rate is high. These standard microeconomic effects may be reinforced by broader Marxian effects on the social relations of production. A high rate of employment strengthens workers vis-à-vis management. This shift in the balance of power may lead to increased worker militancy, and increased monitoring and additional managerial input may also be needed in order to maintain discipline and prevent shirking. As noted by Kalecki (1943), high employment is bad for business because "the self assurance and class consciousness of the working class" will grow and "the social position of the boss" will be undermined (quoted from Kalecki, 1971, p. 140–41). Overall, one would expect the general deterioration of the business climate associated with high employment rates to put a damper on firms' expansion plans.

These considerations suggest a reformulation of the growth function for a "mature economy": the growth of production now responds to signals from both goods and labor markets. Other input or cost signals could play a role but for simplicity intermediate inputs are left out and firms typically maintain excess capital capacity. As far as production decisions are concerned, the labor market therefore provides the relevant signal, and the employment rate is used as an indicator of the state of the labor market. Thus, the growth function for a mature economy includes two arguments, the profit share (π) and the employment rate (e):[15]

$$\hat{Y} = h(\pi, e); h_\pi > 0, h_e < 0. \tag{36}$$

As argued above, the key element in the Harrodian approach is the distinction between a small short-run and large long-run sensitivity of investment to variations in aggregate demand and with utilization as a state variable, this distinction can be captured by a static relation between the accumulation rate and the rate of utilization:

$$\hat{K} = \phi(u) \tag{37}$$

where ϕ describes the relation between accumulation and desired utilization, and $\phi' \gg s\sigma\pi$. Using (36)–(37) we have the following two-dimensional system:

$$\hat{u} = \hat{Y} - \hat{K} = h(\pi, e) - \phi(u) \tag{38}$$

$$\hat{e} = h(\pi, e) - n \tag{39}$$

where n is the growth rate of the labor force. For simplicity I take n as exogenous; a straightforward extension allows n to depend positively on the employment rate e.[16] Retaining the linear saving function (28) and using a Kaldor/Marshall approach, the profit share is still determined by the equilibrium condition for the product market, as in (29)

$$\pi = \frac{\phi(u) + \delta}{s\sigma u} = \psi(u) \tag{40}$$

The strong long-run sensitivity of accumulation to variations in utilization ($\phi' > s\sigma\pi$) implies that $\psi' > 0$.

A (non-trivial) stationary solution satisfies $\hat{u} = \hat{e} = 0$, and it follows that $\phi(u) = n$. With $\phi(u) = n$, equation (40) determines a unique value of π,

$$\pi^* = \frac{n + \delta}{s\sigma\phi^{-1}(n)} \tag{41}$$

Substituting this value into the growth function, there is at most one steady-growth solution for e: A solution in the admissible range ($0 \leq e \leq 1$) exists if and only if

$$h(\pi^*, 0) \geq n \geq h(\pi^*, 1) \tag{42}$$

The second inequality in (42) must be satisfied: as e increases it becomes progressively more difficult to expand employment, and if $e = 1$ it is logically impossible for the rate of growth of employment to exceed the rate of growth of the labor force. The first inequality, however, need not be satisfied: firms may be insufficiently dynamic and, as a result, a capitalist economy may not be capable of growth at the natural rate. The likelihood of this outcome increases if π^* is small, that is, for low values of the natural rate and high saving rates. As argued by Nakatani and Skott (2007), Japan's stagnation since about 1990 may be related to structural demand problems of this kind: with the exhaustion of hidden unemployment, the growth rate had to come down, but a high saving rate and low natural growth rate precluded a smooth transition to a path with minor fluctuations around a new steady-growth solution with $g = n$.

Assuming the existence of a steady-growth solution, the local stability is determined by the Jacobian,

$$J(u, e) = \begin{bmatrix} u[h_\pi\psi' - \phi'] & uh_e \\ eh_\pi\psi' & eh_e \end{bmatrix} \tag{43}$$

with

$$\det(J) = -ue\phi'h_e > 0$$

$$\text{tr}(J) = u[h_\pi\psi' - \phi'] + eh_e$$

The determinant is unambiguously positive and the trace must become negative if the employment effect is sufficiently strong. An outcome with a negative trace may require employment effects that are implausibly strong, but a weaker employment effect is sufficient to generate a stable limit cycle and bounded fluctuations around the locally

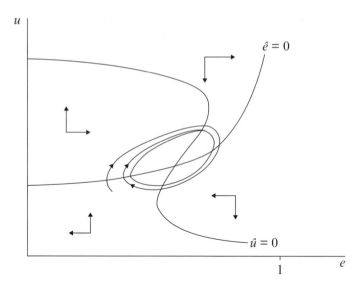

Figure 5.5   Growth cycles in a mature economy

unstable, stationary solution (see Skott, 1989a, 1989b). The negative feedback effect from employment to the growth rate of output mirrors the homeostatic mechanism in Goodwin's (1967) formalization of a Marxian growth cycle. Goodwin's model excludes Keynesian effective demand problems, but the same basic feedback effects tend to stabilize the Harrodian system.

The phase diagram in Figure 5.5 illustrates the dynamics. The model produces clockwise movements in an (e, u)-space (or equivalently, since $\pi = \psi(u)$, in (e, π)-space). The predicted movements in employment, utilization and profitability are broadly consistent with the stylized facts, and the marriage of destabilizing Harrodian effects with stabilizing Marxian mechanisms provides a unified explanation of growth and cycles.

The boundedness of the fluctuations implies that the (locally) unstable steady-growth solution becomes relevant for the long-run effects of changes in parameters and exogenous variables. The average values of e, u and π in the long run need not be exactly equal to the steady-growth solutions, but the comparative statics of the steady-growth solution will give a good approximation to changes in the average values.[17] Using the steady-growth conditions, it is readily seen that improved animal spirits (an upward shift in the accumulation and/or growth function) will be expansionary. But since the growth rate is pinned down by the growth of the labor force, there is only a level effect: the employment rate goes up following a rise in animal spirits, as does the profit share if the accumulation function shifts up.[18] Analogously, a decline in the saving rate raises both the profit share and the rate of employment. An increase in labor militancy will be reflected in a downward shift in the growth function and, as in the Goodwin model, the result is a decline in the steady-growth value of the employment rate.

5 A Robinson/Steindl approach

Essentially, the Harrodian instability is curtailed in section 4 by abandoning the instantaneous output adjustments at a given markup and, in the mature economy, by variations in the reserve army of labor. I have referred to the models as Kaldorian or Marshallian since demand-determined variations in prices and income distribution are at the heart of the analysis, but the analysis in section 4 also has affinities with the work of Robinson (1956, 1962) and Steindl (1952).[19]

5.1 Dual economies

Robinson set up models with multiple steady-growth paths. The utilization rate is at the desired rate in these models but the mechanism is different from the one in section 4. Accumulation is a non-linear function of profitability while price competition, she suggested, keeps utilization at the desired rate.[20]

Her verbal argument (1962, p. 47) implies that the accumulation function takes the form

$$g = \frac{I}{K} = f(r^e) \tag{44}$$

where r^e is the expected future rate of profit on new investment and $f' > 0$. Retaining the linear saving function (28), the current rate of profit is determined by the market-clearing condition for the product market,

$$s\sigma u\pi = sr = g \tag{45}$$

In steady growth we have $r^e = r$, and assuming that the investment function f is strictly concave, the well-known "banana diagram" emerges with two steady-growth solutions.

The stability properties of these steady-growth solutions depend on the formation of profit expectations, and most of Robinson's analysis seems to rely on static expectations. Under conditions of imperfect competition, however, firms' expected profit rate, r^e, cannot be independent of their investment decisions. Thus, implicitly, the specification in equation (44) seems to assume perfect competition. This assumption is logically consistent but unattractive, both theoretically and empirically, and Robinson acknowledges as much. She notes that "in reality, of course, markets for manufacturers are highly imperfect, prices are fairly sticky and changes in investment are generally accompanied by changes in output and employment" (Robinson, 1962, p. 65). The sluggish adjustment in prices can be formalized by letting the profit share, π, adjust to the difference between actual and desired capacity utilization

$$\dot{\pi} = v(u - u^d) \tag{46}$$

where $v > 0$ is the adjustment speed. With slow price adjustment it is now instantaneous movements in the utilization rate u that ensure the equalization of saving and investment in the short run. The saving–investment balance and the definition of the profit rate, $r = \pi u \sigma$, imply that

$$u = \frac{g + \delta}{s\pi\sigma} = \xi(g, \pi) \tag{47}$$

where

$$\xi_g = \frac{1}{s\sigma\pi} = \frac{u}{g + \delta} > 0 \text{ and } \xi_\pi = -\frac{g + \delta}{s\sigma\pi^2} = -s\sigma\frac{u^2}{g + \delta} < 0.$$

Turning to the specification of the investment function outside steady growth, the distinction between expected and actual profitability in Robinson's argument essentially serves to introduce sluggish adjustments in accumulation. In a continuous-time setting, this can be achieved by a dynamic version of the investment function (44),[21]

$$\dot{g} = \lambda[f(u, \pi) - g] \tag{48}$$

where $\lambda > 0$ and $f_u > 0$, $f\pi > 0$, and where the ill-defined variable r^e has been replaced by the current values of the utilization rate and the profit share.

Equations (48) and (46) yield a two-dimensional dynamic system in the growth rate of the capital stock and the profit share

$$\dot{g} = \lambda\{f[\xi(g, \pi), \pi] - g\} \tag{49}$$

$$\dot{\pi} = v[\xi(g, \pi) - u^d] \tag{50}$$

Stationary solutions satisfy $u = u^d$ (using (46)) and $g = f(u^d, \pi) = f(u^d, \frac{g}{s\sigma u^d})$ (using (47)–(48) and $u = u^d$). Turning to local stability, the Jacobian is given by

$$J(g, \pi) = \begin{bmatrix} \lambda(f_u\xi_g - 1) & \lambda(f_\pi + f_u\xi_\pi) \\ v\xi_g & v\xi_\pi \end{bmatrix} \tag{51}$$

and, evaluated at the stationary point, we have

$$\det(J) = -\lambda v(\xi_\pi + f_\pi\xi_g) = \lambda v\frac{u^d}{g^* + \delta}(s\sigma u^d - f_\pi) \tag{52}$$

$$\mathrm{tr}(J) = \left[\lambda\left(f_u\frac{u^d}{g^* + \delta} - 1\right)\right] - \left[v\frac{u^d}{g^* + \delta}s\sigma u^d\right] \tag{53}$$

The Robinsonian stability condition – desired investment being less sensitive than saving to changes in the profit share – ensures that det(J) is positive. This condition is satisfied at the high equilibrium in the banana diagram, ruling out saddlepoint instability. Local asymptotic stability of the high solution depends on the sign of the trace. In the expression for the trace, the first term in square brackets may be either positive or negative, but local stability is assured if the adjustment speed for prices is fast (relative to the adjustment speed of investment). Thus, the explicit introduction of pricing dynamics confirms Robinson's main conclusion in a setting without perfect competition.

5.2   Mature economies
The high and stable solution in the banana diagram satisfies the "Robinsonian stability condition": investment is less sensitive than saving to variations in profitability. This

condition (as the corresponding condition with respect to the growth function in section 4) may be plausible at growth rates that are empirically relevant for successful developing countries, but the model and the high solution seem less promising for mature economies with modest growth rates. As in section 4, variations in the reserve army can be included explicitly in the analysis of these mature economies: employment effects may stabilize the otherwise unstable low solution in the banana diagram.

The size of the reserve army could influence accumulation and/or pricing. As an example consider the following extension of the dual-economy model:[22]

$$\dot{g} = \lambda\,[f(u, \pi, e) - g]; \ f_u > 0, f_\pi > 0, f_e < 0 \tag{54}$$

$$\dot{\pi} = v(u - u^d) \tag{55}$$

$$\hat{k} = g - n \tag{56}$$

where the new state variable k describes the ratio of the capital stock to the labor force. The ratio k is definitionally related to employment and utilization, and – normalizing units so that labor productivity is equal to one – we have

$$e = u\sigma k \tag{57}$$

The pricing equation (55) is unchanged (but re-stated for convenience). The innovation compared to the dual economy is the introduction of the employment rate e as a determinant of the long-run accumulation function f in (54). The utilization rate adjusts to clear the product market and is still given by (47).

A stationary solution satisfies

$$u = u^d \tag{58}$$

$$g = n \tag{59}$$

$$\pi = \frac{n + \delta}{\sigma u^d} \tag{60}$$

$$f(u^d, \pi, k) = n \tag{61}$$

Equations (58)–(60) give explicit and unique solutions for u, g and π, and substituting these solutions into (61) we get a unique solution for k and thereby (using (57)) for e.

Local stability is determined by the Jacobian

$$J(g,\pi,k) = \begin{bmatrix} \lambda\,[(f_u + \sigma k f_e)\frac{1}{\sigma\pi} - 1] & -\lambda\,[(f_u + \sigma k f_e)\frac{g+\delta}{\sigma\pi^2} - f_\pi] & \lambda f_e \frac{g+\delta}{\sigma\pi}\sigma \\ v\frac{1}{\sigma\pi} & -v\frac{g+\delta}{\sigma\pi^2} & 0 \\ k & 0 & 0 \end{bmatrix} \tag{62}$$

The necessary and sufficient Routh-Hurwitz conditions for local stability are that, evaluated at the equilibrium,

1. $\text{tr}(J) = \lambda[(f_u + \sigma kf_e)\frac{1}{s\sigma\pi} - 1] - v\frac{g+\delta}{s\sigma\pi^2} < 0$
2. $\det(J_1) + \det(J_2) + \det(J_3) = [\lambda v\frac{g+\delta}{s\sigma\pi^2} - \lambda f_\pi v\frac{1}{s\sigma\pi}] - k\sigma\lambda f_e\frac{g+\sigma}{s\sigma\pi} > 0$
3. $\det(J) = v\lambda k\frac{g+\delta}{s\sigma\pi^2}f_e\frac{g+\delta}{s\sigma\pi}\sigma < 0$
4. $-\text{tr}(J)[\det(J_1) + \det(J_2) + \det(J_3)] + \det(J) > 0$

The third condition is always satisfied, and straightforward calculations show that the other three conditions must be satisfied if the employment effect f_e is sufficiently strong.[23]

Comparing the Robinsonian and Kaldorian formulations in sections 4–5, the steady-growth equality between desired and actual utilization – equation (21) – is based on pricing/output behavior in Robinson and on accumulation in Kaldor; to get a steady-growth relation between growth and profitability, conversely, the Robinsonian model uses capital accumulation instead of output growth, as in the Kaldorian equation (27). From a steady-growth perspective these changes in the assignment of pricing and accumulation make no difference.[24] The relative adjustment speeds for output and prices are reversed in the two models, and this reversal affects the short-run dynamics. Both versions, however, have utilization at the desired rate in steady growth, both versions endogenize the profit share and use this endogenization as a stabilizing factor, and both versions yield multiple steady-growth solutions for a dual economy.[25,26]

In behavioral terms I find the Kaldorian version more persuasive and its short-run dynamics fit some important stylized facts. A more detailed discussion of the relative merits of the two versions, however, is beyond the scope of this chapter.

6   Conclusion

The Kaleckian growth model has become a standard work-horse for the analysis of growth and distribution. The model is simple and tractable and it lends itself to extensions in many directions. The simplicity and tractability, however, come at a cost. The model includes a questionable stability condition and key predictions of the model, including the accommodating long-run variations in utilization, find little support in empirical evidence. At a methodological level, moreover, the standard Kaleckian approach may have unfortunate consequences since it plays down the need to "think dynamically".

Dynamic issues were at the heart of the Keynesian revolution. The fundamental proposition of the General Theory is that even with flexible prices and wages, the market mechanism can not be expected to ensure full employment. A market-clearing neoclassical general equilibrium may exist but is unlikely to be stable, even under hypothetical conditions of highly flexible prices and wages.[27] Harrod extended the dynamic analysis to movements over time of a Keynesian economy, his basic approach consisting "in a marriage of the 'acceleration principle' and the 'multiplier' theory" (Harrod, 1939, p. 14). A number of early contributors (including Samuelson, 1939; Kaldor, 1940; Hicks, 1950 and Goodwin, 1951), formalized these interactions and although in some ways primitive, the fundamental insights remain valid: steady growth paths of a mature capitalist economy are likely to be locally unstable.

These dynamic issues are glossed over by the standard Kaleckian macro model with its emphasis on stable steady-growth paths, its neglect of lags and its use of utilization rates as an accommodating variable, in the long as well as the short run. The predominant focus in Kaleckian theory on dual economy regimes, moreover, may threaten the relevance of the analysis with respect to most OECD economies.

This chapter has discussed alternatives to the Kaleckian model. Sections 4–5 used endogenous variations in income distribution and employment to stabilize an otherwise unstable economy. I consider these mechanisms theoretically and empirically plausible but other solutions to the Harrodian "instability problem" have been suggested. Shaikh (2007), for instance, denies the inherently unstable tendency in Harrod's argument while Duménil and Lévy (1999) accept the instability tendency but suggest that the stabilizing force comes from monetary policy.[28,29]

In general, the Harrodian alternatives are more complex than the Kaleckian model. They remain tractable, however, and the basic models in this chapter can be (and have been) extended in a number of ways; Skott and Ryoo (2008), for instance, analyze the implications of financialization, using models that include explicit financial stocks. Most importantly, in my view, the Harrodian-inspired models tell a behavioral story that is more convincing and that fits the empirical evidence better than the Kaleckian model.[30] The current dominance of the Kaleckian model therefore is unfortunate.

Notes

*   I thank Paul Auerbach, Martin Rapetti, Ben Zipperer and participants in the Analytical Political Economy workshop at Queen Mary University London, May 2008, for helpful comments on a longer study that included an early draft of this chapter.

1. The desired rate of utilization is sometimes referred to as the "normal" rate or the "target" rate.
2. Other mechanisms may play a role as well. An example is endogenous, Minsky-type changes in financial behavior.
3. The canonical model need not be stagnationist if the saving function is nonlinear (or just affine, $s(\pi) = s_0 + s\pi$ with $s_0 > 0$) since in this case the "Robinsonian stability" condition $((\partial I)/(\partial\pi) < (\partial S)/(\partial\pi))$ can be violated even if the "Keynesian stability" condition $((\partial I)/(\partial u) < (\partial S)/(\partial u))$ is met. This point, which may have been noted in the literature, was made by Ben Zipperer in comments on an early draft of this chapter.
4. Skott (2008) discusses the theoretical and empirical case against the Kaleckian investment function in greater detail.
5. Chick and Caserta (1997) suggest that although the utilization rate must be at (or near) the desired rate in long-run steady growth, deviations could last for significant periods of time. Long-lasting deviations, however, do not justify a depiction of this medium-run scenario as a self-sustaining equilibrium without internal forces for change.
6. The instability of the "warranted growth path" was emphasized by Harrod himself although he rejected the knife-edge metaphor (Harrod, 1973, p. 33).
7. Using the simple Harrodian specification in (20), it is readily seen that if the fluctuations in the accumulation rate $\hat{K}$ are bounded, the time-average of the utilization rate ratio u must be approximately equal to u^d when the average is taken over a long period. To show this, integrate (20) to get $\bar{u} - u^d = (\hat{K}_{t_1} - \hat{K}_{t_0})/(\lambda(t_1 - t_0))$ where $\bar{u}$ is the average utilization rate over the interval $[t_0; t_1]$. If $|\hat{K}_{t_1} - \hat{K}_{t_0}|$ is bounded below some constant for all (t_0, t_1), it follows that $\bar{u}$ converges to u^* for $t_1 - t_0$ going to infinity.
8. The study by Levy et al. (1997) of menu costs in five supermarkets, for instance, is often cited in support of menu costs and price stickiness (e.g. Romer, 2001, pp. 315–16). This study found that on average 16 percent of all prices were changed each *week*. These frequent changes in prices were not costless but the finding that menu costs constitute a significant proportion of net profits is largely irrelevant for an evaluation of price flexibility. With prohibitively high menu costs, for instance, there would be no price changes and the share of menu cost in revenue would be zero; negligible menu costs on the other hand may allow firms to change prices frequently as part of their marketing strategies, and the observed share of menu costs in net profits could be very high in this case.
9. Demand signals could also be reflected in inventories. For the aggregate economy, however, changes in inventories tend to amplify fluctuations in other demand components over the cycle. Thus, the need for price adjustments would remain, even if inventories were included.
10. The behavioral foundations of the function are discussed in greater detail by Skott (1989a, Chapter 4), who used the term "output expansion function".

11. The distinction between short- and long-run effects is observed as long as accumulation depends on a state variable. In the Robinsonian model below, utilization adjusts instantaneously but the profit share becomes a state variable.
12. Assuming a linear accumulation function,

$$g = \varphi(u) = \mu(u - u_0)$$

the equilibrium condition $I = S$ implies

$$g = s\sigma\pi\frac{\mu u_0 - \delta}{\mu - s\sigma\pi} - \delta$$

13. Local stability requires

$$h'\left[\frac{\varphi' - \pi s\sigma}{su\sigma}\right] - \varphi' < 0$$

or, equivalently,

$$h' < \frac{dg^*}{d\pi}$$

where g^* is the growth rate that clears the product market for a given profit share, π.
14. A dual-economy scenario fits the OECD countries at an earlier stage of their development. Kaldor's rejection in the mid-1960s of his own labor-constrained models should be seen in the context of agricultural employment shares that were still above 25 percent in countries like Japan and Italy and at or above 20 percent in France; West Germany had a smaller share (just over 10 percent) but had been experiencing massive immigration in the 1950s (Kuznets, 1971).

 Arguably, the assumption still applies to the world economy as a whole, but a one-sector model of the world economy without spatial disaggregation has obvious limitations.
15. A static counterpart to this equation can be obtained by setting $\hat{Y} = 0$. The equation then defines the profit share as an increasing function of the employment rate. A short-run equilibrium relation of this kind could be derived from profit maximization if firms have monopsony power and the (perceived) elasticity of labor supply to the individual firm is decreasing as a function of the aggregate rate of employment. Manning (2003) provides an extended analysis of monopsonistic features of the labor market.
16. High employment rates may stimulate the growth of the labor force in several ways. Immigration is an obvious mechanism in open economies; for a closed economy, changes in participation rates may affect the growth of the labor force in the medium run, and high employment and incipient labor shortages may serve as incentives for labor saving innovation in the long run. The argument could be formalized by assuming that $n = n(e)$, $n'(e) \geq 0$.
17. The results will be biased only insofar as changes in a parameter affect the magnitude of the deviation between steady-growth solution and time-average. The existence of an unchanged deviation between the two generates no errors.
18. The absence of a well-defined *NAIRU* is standard in post-Keynesian and structuralist theory. My own take on this issue is discussed in Skott (1999, 2005b).
19. Flaschel and Skott (2006) discuss Steindl's analysis.
20. She assumes that "competition (in the short-period sense) is sufficiently keen to keep prices at the level at which normal capacity output can be sold" (Robinson, 1962, p. 46).
21. Mathematically this formulation is closely related to Robinson's own analysis. The equilibrium condition for the product market implies that $r = g/s$. If $g = f(r^e)$ and $\frac{d}{dt}r^e = \dot{r}^e = \lambda(r - r^e)$, it follows that

$$\dot{r}^e = \lambda\left(\frac{f(r^e)}{s} - r^e\right)$$

and hence,

$$\dot{g} = f'(r^e)\dot{r}^e = f'(r^e)\lambda\left[\frac{g}{s} - f^{-1}(g)\right]$$

Since $f' > 0$, this equation has the same stability properties as the equation

$$\dot{g} = \lambda\left[f\left(\frac{g}{s}\right) - g\right] = \lambda[f(r) - g]$$

The latter equation, in turn, is a special case of equation (48).
22. This example retains the "dynamic" specification of the investment function in equation (48). It is

straightforward to set up a two-dimensional analogue to the model in section 4.2. Having employment enter negatively in the growth function (36) corresponds to an inverse effect of employment on accumulation in this setting, and this effect can be captured by letting desired utilization depend positively on employment in (55). Thus, let

$$\dot{\pi} = H(u, e) = v(u - u^d) = v(u - \theta(e)), \quad \theta' > 0$$

$$\hat{k} = \hat{K} - n = f(\pi) - n$$

$$u = \frac{f(\pi) + \delta}{s\sigma\pi}$$

The accumulation function $f(\pi)$ conforms to the Harrodian principle since the profit share is now a state variable. The Jacobian for this two-dimensional system is given by

$$J(\pi, k) = \begin{bmatrix} v(u_\pi - \theta'\sigma k u_\pi) & -v\theta'u\sigma \\ kf' & 0 \end{bmatrix}$$

and

$$\det(J) = kf'v\theta'u\sigma > 0$$

$$\text{tr}(J) = vu_\pi(1 - \theta'\sigma k)$$

The derivative u_π is positive at the low, unstable solution in the banana diagram, and stability requires that the employment effect on "desired utilization" in the equation for $\dot{\pi}$ be sufficiently strong.

23. The expression in condition 4 is quadratic in f_e.
24. Steindl (1952) also set up models with multiple steady-growth paths, focusing on the stable high-growth solution. Steindl's verbal argument is close to Robinson's and includes sluggish adjustments in the markup. As shown by Flaschel and Skott (2006), however, his focus on a high-growth solution in a formal model with a fixed markup seems misplaced.
25. Chiarella et al. (2005) pursue specifications with sluggishness in both prices and output.
26. Behavioral relations between growth and profitability have been discussed by many other writers, including Penrose (1959), Wood (1975) and Eichner (1976).
27. "Old Keynesians" like Tobin have emphasized this point (Tobin, 1986).
28. I do not find Shaikh's argument convincing. Leaving out some minor twists, Shaikh (2007) specifies the following investment function

$$\hat{K} = \hat{Y}^e + k(u - u^d) \tag{63}$$

Assuming that short-run expectations are being met (that is, $\hat{Y} = \hat{Y}^e$) and that the technical output–capital coefficient and the desired utilization rate are constant, this equation implies a stable differential equation for u,

$$\hat{u} = -k(u - u^d) \tag{64}$$

and utilization will converge to the desired rate.
  This argument is correct but it is based on the assumption of fulfilled expectation at all times, and the Harrodian instability argument is precisely that when all firms reduce investment in order to raise their utilization rate, the outcome will be an unanticipated decline in aggregate demand and a fall in the utilization rate. Shaikh circumvents the instability by *assuming* that the economy is always on a warranted path with $\hat{Y} = \hat{Y}^e$, and his argument shows not the stability of warranted growth but the convergence of a warranted growth path to steady growth with $u = u^d$.
29. The Duménil and Lévy argument has been discussed in relation to standard Taylor rules by Lavoie and Kriesler (2007). An emphasis on policy is in line with Harrod's analysis but he also suggested that the instability would be bounded even "without the application of monetary and fiscal restoratives" (Harrod, 1973, p. 36).
30. To avoid misunderstanding, let me emphasize that contributors to the post-Keynesian and structuralist literature cannot be neatly categorized into groups of "Kaleckians", "Harrodians", "Robinsonians", etc. Some of the main contributors to the Kaleckian literature have also produced important studies that incorporate Harrodian instability. Conversely, writers, myself included, that may be thought of as critical of the Kaleckian model have used the Kaleckian model in some of their own work.

References

Amadeo, E. (1986) "The role of capacity utilization in long-period analysis". *Political Economy*, **2** (2), 147–85.

Auerbach, P. and Skott, P. (1988) "Concentration, competition and distribution". *International Review of Applied Economics*, **2**, 42–61.

Blecker, R. (1989) "International competition, income distribution and economic growth". *Cambridge Journal of Economics*, **14**, 375–93.

Blecker, R. (1999) "Kaleckian macro models for open economies". In Johan Deprez and John T. Harvey (eds) *Foundations of International Economics: Post Keynesian Perspectives*. London: Routledge.

Chiarella, C., Flaschel, P. and Franke, R. (2005) *Foundations for a Disequilibrium Theory of the Business Cycle*. Cambridge: Cambridge University Press.

Chick, V. and Caserta, M. (1997) "Provisional equilibrium in macroeconomic theory". In P. Arestis, G. Palma and M. Sawyer (eds) *Capital Controversy, Post-Keynesian Economics and the History of Economic Thought: Essays in Honour of Geoff Harcourt*, Vol. II. London: Routledge.

Committeri, M. (1986) "Some comments on recent contributions on capital accumulation, income distribution and capacity utilization". *Political Economy*, **2**, 161–86.

Dos Santos, C.H. and Zezza, G. (2008) "A simplified, 'benchmark', stock–flow consistent post-Keynesian growth model". *Metroeconomica*, **59** (3), 441–78.

Duménil, G. and Lévy, D. (1993) *The Economics of the Profit Rate*. Aldershot, UK and Brookfield, USA: Edward Elgar.

Duménil, G. and Lévy, D. (1999) "Being Keynesian in the short term and classical in the long term: the traverse to classical long term equilibrium". *The Manchester School*, **67** (6), 684–716.

Dutt, A.K. (1984) "Stagnation, income distribution and monopoly power". *Cambridge Journal of Economics*, **8**, 25–40.

Dutt, A.K. (1997) "Equilibrium, path dependence and hysteresis in post-Keynesian models". In P. Arestis, G. Palma and M. Sawyer (eds) *Capital Controversy, Post-Keynesian Economics and the History of Economic Thought: Essays in Honour of Geoff Harcourt*, London: Routledge.

Eichner, A. (1976) *The Megacorp and Oligopoly*. Cambridge: Cambridge University Press.

Flaschel, P. and Skott, P. (2006) "Steindlian models of growth and stagnation". *Metroeconomica*, **57** (3), 303–38.

Goodwin, R.M. (1951) "The nonlinear accelerator and the persistence of business cycles". *Econometrica*, **19**, 1–17.

Goodwin, R.M. (1967) "A growth cycle". In C.H. Feinstein (ed.) *Socialism, Capitalism and Growth*, Cambridge: Cambridge University Press.

Harrod, R. (1939) "An essay in dynamic theory". *Economic Journal*, **49**, 14–33.

Harrod, R. (1973) *Economic Dynamics*. London and Basingstoke: Macmillan.

Hein, E. and van Treeck, T. (2007) "'Financialisation' in Kaleckian/post-Kaleckian models of distribution and growth". Working Paper 7/2007, Hans Boeckler Stiftung.

Hicks, J.R. (1950) *A Contribution to the Theory of the Trade Cycle*. Oxford: Oxford University Press.

Kaldor, N. (1940) "A model of the trade cycle". *Economic Journal*, **50**, 78–92.

Kaldor, N. (1956) "Alternative theories of distribution". *Review of Economic Studies*, **23**, 83–100.

Kaldor, N. (1966) *Causes of the Slow Rate of Economic Growth in the UK*. Cambridge: Cambridge University Press.

Kaldor, N. (1978) "Introduction". In N. Kaldor, *Further Essays on Economic Theory*. London: Duckworth.

Kalecki, M. (1943) "Political aspects of full employment". Reprinted in M. Kalecki, *Selected Essays on the Dynamics of the Capitalist Economy*, Cambridge: Cambridge University Press, 1971.

Keynes, J.M. (1930) *A Treatise on Money*. London and Basingstoke: Macmillan.

Kurz, H. (1986) "Normal positions and capital utilization". *Political Economy*, **2** (1), 37–54.

Kuznets, S. (1971) *Economic Growth of Nations: Total Output and Production Structure*. Cambridge, MA: Harvard University Press.

Lavoie, M. (1995) "The Kaleckian model of growth and distribution and its neo-Ricardian and neo-Marxian critiques". *Cambridge Journal of Economics*, **19**, 789–818.

Lavoie, M. (1996) "Traverse, hysteresis, and normal rates of capacity utilization in Kaleckian models of growth and distribution". *Review of Radical Political Economics*, **28** (4), 113–47.

Lavoie, M. and Godley, W. (2001–02) "Kaleckian models of growth in a coherent stock-flow monetary framework: a Kaldorian view". *Journal of Post Keynesian Economics*, **24** (2), 277–311.

Lavoie, M. and Kriesler, P. (2007) "Capacity utilization, inflation, and monetary policy: the Dumenil and Lévy macro model and the new Keynesian consensus". *Review of Radical Political Economics*, **39** (4), 586–98.

Lavoie, M., Rodriquez, G. and Seccareccia, M. (2004) "Similarities and discrepancies in post-Keynesian and

Marxist theories of investment: a theoretical and empirical investigation". *International Review of Applied Economics*, **18** (2), 127–49.

Levy, D., Bergen, M., Dutta, S. and Venable, R. (1997) "The magnitude of menu costs: direct evidence from large U.S. supermarket chains". *Quarterly Journal of Economics*, **112**, 791–825.

Lima, G.T. and Setterfield, M. (2008) "Inflation targeting and macroeconomic stability in a post Keynesian economy". *Journal of Post Keynesian Economics*, **30**, 435–61.

Manning, A. (2003) *Monopsony in Motion.* Princeton, NJ: Princeton University Press.

Marglin, S. (1984) "Growth, distribution, and inflation: a centennial synthesis". *Cambridge Journal of Economics*, **8**, 115–44.

Marglin, S. and Bhaduri, A. (1990) "Profit squeeze and Keynesian theory". In S. Marglin and J. Schor (eds) *The Golden Age of Capitalism – Reinterpreting the Postwar Experience.* Oxford: Clarendon.

Nakatani, T. and Skott, P. (2007) "Japanese growth and stagnation". *Structural Change and Economic Dynamics*, **18** (3), 306–32.

Penrose, E.T. (1959) *The Theory of the Growth of the Firm.* Oxford: Oxford University Press.

Robinson, J. (1956) *The Accumulation of Capital.* London and Basingstoke: Macmillan.

Robinson, J. (1962) *Essays on the Theory of Economic Growth.* London and Basingstoke: Macmillan.

Romer, D. (2001) *Advanced Macroeconomics*, 2nd edn. London: McGraw-Hill.

Rowthorn, B. (1981) "Demand, real wages and economic growth". In *Thames Papers in Political Economy.* London: Thames Polytechnic.

Samuelson, P.A. (1939) "A synthesis of the principle of acceleration and the multiplier". *Journal of Political Economy*, 786–97.

Shaikh, A. (2007) "Economic policy in a growth context: a classical synthesis of Keynes and Harrod". Mimeo.

Skott, P. (1989a) *Conflict and Effective Demand in Economic Growth.* Cambridge: Cambridge University Press.

Skott, P. (1989b) "Effective demand, class struggle and cyclical growth". *International Economic Review*, **30**, 231–47.

Skott, P. (1999) "Wage formation and the (non-)existence of the NAIRU". *Economic Issues*, **March**, 77–92.

Skott, P. (2005a) "Equilibrium, stability and economic growth". In B. Gibson (ed.) *Joan Robinson's Economics: A Centennial Celebration.* Cheltenham, UK and Northampton, MA, USA: Edward Elgar.

Skott, P. (2005b) "Fairness as a source of hysteresis in employment and relative wages". *Journal of Economic Behavior and Organization*, **57**, 305–31.

Skott, P. (2008) "Theoretical and empirical shortcomings of the Kaleckian investment function". Mimeo.

Skott, P. and Ryoo, S. (2008) "Macroeconomic implications of financialization". *Cambridge Journal of Economics*, **32**, 827–62.

Steindl, J. (1952) *Maturity and Stagnation in American Capitalism.* Oxford: Blackwell.

Taylor, L. (1985) "A stagnationist model of economic growth". *Cambridge Journal of Economics*, **9**, 383–403.

Tobin, J. (1986) "The future of Keynesian economics". *Eastern Economic Journal*, **12** (4), 347–56.

Wood, A. (1975) *A Theory of Profits.* Cambridge: Cambridge University Press.

6 Surveying short-run and long-run stability issues with the Kaleckian model of growth[1]

Marc Lavoie

1 Introduction

Writing a survey on the Kaleckian model of growth and distribution is a difficult task in view of the existence of the excellent survey that has already been provided by Blecker (2002). Since then, another survey, just as complete, has been written in French by Allain (2009). In addition, at least three other chapters in the present book deal with complications involving the Kaleckian model. As a result the present chapter will deal with elementary issues of stability, both in the short run and in the long run. We start with the former, before addressing the long run in the second half of the chapter. In both cases, we will show that the generality of Kaleckian results is greater than many critics of the Kaleckian model have suggested.

2 The standard Kaleckian model

The usual Kaleckian model is made up of three equations: an investment equation, a saving equation, and a pricing equation. Each of these equations can be made more complicated at will, as will be shown in other chapters, and of course we may wish to add other equations, for instance equations defining inflation determination (Cassetti, 2002; Lavoie, 1992, Chapter 7), or central bank reaction functions (Lavoie and Kriesler, 2007). Here we stick to the basic model.

$$r = mu/v \tag{1}$$

$$g^s = s_p r \tag{2}$$

$$g^i = \gamma + \gamma_u u + \gamma_r m \tag{3}$$

We assume away overhead labour (but see Rowthorn, 1981 and Lavoie, 1992), so that the pricing function in terms of the profit rate r depends simply on the profit share m, the rate of capacity utilization u, and v the capital to capacity ratio. The higher m, the lower the real wage. We assume no saving out of wages, so that the saving function in growth terms depends only on the profit rate and the propensity to save out of profits s_p.[2]

Finally there is the contentious issue of the investment function. We adopt a linear variant of the popular Bhaduri and Marglin (1990) function, which can also be attributed to Kurz (1990), so that investment depends on some constant, the rate of capacity utilization, and the share of profit (or more likely on the normal profit rate, as we shall see later), with γ, γ_u and γ_r being three parameters. The advantage of this investment function, as is now well known, is that it provides for richer possibilities. In addition, the function can be easily tested empirically, since statistics on both the rate of utilization and the profit share can easily be obtained. A drawback of this function is that it is not really clear why investing entrepreneurs would care about the profit share, in contrast to the profit rate, which is usually the third component of the canonical Kaleckian growth model. In addition, in a model with overhead labour, the profit share becomes an endogenous variable, which depends on the actual rate of utilization, so that it cannot in general be considered as given, resulting from the relative bargaining strength of workers and firms.

A way out is to argue, from a purely theoretical standpoint, that what Bhaduri and Marglin really have in mind is that investment depends on expected profitability, computed at normal prices, based on the normal rate of capacity utilization – a point made frequently by Sraffian authors such as Ciconne (1986, p. 26), Vianello (1989), and Kurz (1990). This expected profitability at the normal rate of capacity utilization, which we call u_n, is the normal profit rate, which we denote as r_n. We may thus rewrite equations (1) and (3) in a way that is amenable to this reinterpretation:

$$r = (r_n/u_n)u \tag{1A}$$

$$g^i = \gamma + \gamma_u u + \gamma_r r_n \tag{3A}$$

Obviously, $r_n = mu_n/v$ where v is the capital to output capacity ratio, and it makes little difference whether we use one or the other of these formulations.[3] Combining equations (1), (2), and (3) to obtain the equilibrium rate of utilization, we get:

$$u^* = \frac{\gamma + \gamma_r m}{s_p(m/v) - \gamma_u} \tag{4}$$

Whereas combining equations (1A), (2) and (3A), we obtain:

$$u^* = \frac{\gamma + \gamma_r r_n}{s_p(r_n/u_n) - \gamma_u} \tag{4A}$$

To make economic sense u^* must be positive. Hence, if the denominator is positive, its numerator must also be positive; and if the denominator is negative, the numerator must be negative, which then implies (since $\gamma_r m$ is necessarily positive) that the γ parameter must be negative and its absolute value sufficiently large.[4] These conditions will play a role in our analysis of stability.

3 Some preliminaries

The first issue we wish to tackle is that of short-run stability. For that problem to exist, there must exist some discrepancy between aggregate demand and aggregate supply, or at least intended aggregate demand and supply. There are a few ways out.

(a) We may suppose that output, or capacity utilization, is given, and that an adjustment occurs within the period, through changes in profit margins or changes in prices at given nominal wage rates. In this case aggregate demand immediately adapts to aggregate supply. This is sometimes associated with a so-called *ultra-short* or *market* period. Some say that this is what Keynes had in mind in some passages of the *General Theory* (Dutt, 1987; Hartwig, 2007). This mechanism can be found in very few heterodox works (e.g. Skott, 1989). It is also the standard Walrasian adjustment mechanism. We assume away this mechanism.

(b) By contrast, we may suppose that the short period is sufficiently long for firms to change output and capacity utilization in line with aggregate demand. In this case, it is now aggregate supply that very quickly adapts to aggregate demand. The adjustment is a pure quantity adjustment. This is the standard interpretation of Keynes, and it is sometimes considered to be his key contribution (Leijonhufvud, 1968, p. 52). Keynesian and Kaleckian authors usually make use of this assumption in their models, and for this reason Duménil and Lévy (1987, p. 136) call it the *Keynesian adjustment process*. But because aggregate supply is being equated to aggregate demand in each and every period, they also call these models, *equilibrium dynamics models*.

(c) Finally, another possibility is to assume no market clearing in the short period. Ideally, one should then take into account the evolution of inventories and their impact on rates of capacity utilization as firms try to bring them back to their normal levels (Duménil and Lévy, 1987, 1993; Godley and Lavoie, 2007). But a less demanding strategy is to assume that the adjustment towards aggregate demand and supply equality is only gradual, and is being done through changes in both profit margins and rates of capacity utilization, without keeping track of inventories. This is what we shall do here.

4   The pure Keynesian adjustment process

As a start, let us consider the pure Keynesian adjustment process, the so-called equilibrium dynamics. To do so, let us distinguish between the realized rate of capacity utilization u and the expected rate of capacity utilization u^e, that is, the rate of capacity utilization that entrepreneurs expect to realize in the current period when supply responds to demand. We may presume that entrepreneurs will invest in the current period as a function of the share of profits (the normal profit rate) and the rate of capacity utilization that they expect to be realized as firms modify output in response to sales. In this case, the investment function needs to be slightly modified to:

$$g^i = \gamma + \gamma_u u^e + \gamma_r m \tag{3B}$$

The investment function now depends on the *expected* rate of capacity utilization, whereas the saving function depends on the *realized* rate of capacity utilization, which, combining equations (1), (2), and (3B), is given by:

$$u^K = \frac{\gamma + \gamma_r m + \gamma_u u^e}{s_p(m/v)} \tag{4B}$$

We denote by u^K this short-period equilibrium rate of capacity utilization, to indicate its Keynesian or Kaleckian pedigree. Visually, two cases can be distinguished, depending on the slopes of the investment and saving functions. As we shall see, Figure 6.1 corresponds to the case of *Keynesian stability*, or *stability in dimension* as Duménil and Lévy (1993) like to call it, with the slope of the investment function being smaller than that of the saving function. The Keynesian stability condition holds when the following inequality is verified:

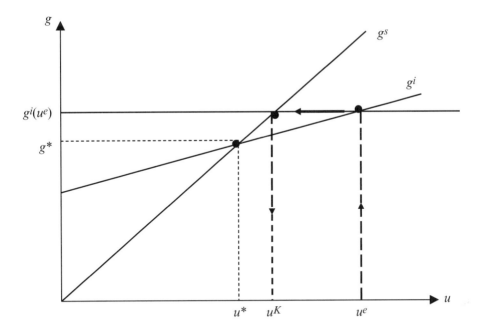

Figure 6.1 Keynesian stability

$$\gamma_u - s_p m/v < 0 \tag{5}$$

On the basis of the expected rate of capacity utilization, firms engage in investment expenditures corresponding to $g^i(u^e)$. At that level of capital accumulation, and with the given propensity to save out of profits, aggregate demand will be such that sales will induce a rate of capacity utilization equal to u^K – the short-run Keynesian equilibrium – as shown in Figure 6.1. A very similar process is described with the help of Figure 6.2 that corresponds to the case of Keynesian instability, and where the slope of the investment function is larger than that of the saving function, such that:

$$\gamma_u - s_p m/v > 0 \tag{5A}$$

Why does Figure 6.1 illustrate Keynesian stability whereas Figure 6.2 illustrates Keynesian instability? With adaptive expectations about capacity utilization, the evolution of the expected rate of capacity utilization is described by the following differential equation:

$$\dot{u}^e = \theta(u^K - u^e) \tag{6}$$

In Figure 6.1, the expected and the realized short-run rates of capacity utilization will converge towards the equilibrium rate of capacity utilization u^*, as entrepreneurs realize that they were overly optimistic. In Figure 6.2, entrepreneurs overestimate the equilibrium rate of capacity utilization ($u^e > u^*$), but the realized short-run rate of utilization

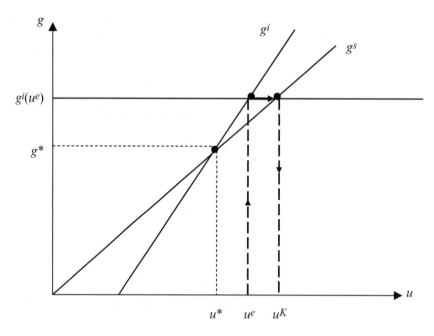

Figure 6.2   Keynesian instability

is even higher than the overestimated rate ($u^K > u^e$), so that entrepreneurs are induced to raise the expected rate of utilization still further more, thus moving away from the equilibrium defined by equation (4).

Thus, if we adopt the pure Keynesian adjustment mechanism, condition (5) must hold, unless other dynamic adjustment mechanisms are put in place.

5   A dual adjustment process

5.1   *Questioning Keynesian stability*

It has recently been argued by some post-Keynesian authors, most notably Dallery (2007) and Skott (2008), that the Keynesian stability condition was unlikely to be met for calibrated values of the main parameters of the model. This can be readily seen. The main problem is that for utilization rates and growth rates to move within a reasonable range of values, one needs the γ_u parameter in equation (3) to be around 0.30. In this case, rates of utilization varying between 75 and 85 per cent, as they have done historically, will generate growth rates between 1 per cent and 4 per cent – a range of values that has been observed within industrialized economies. But the problem is that, even with generous estimates of $s_p = 0.8$, $m = 0.4$, and $v = 2$, the term $s_p m/v$ is no higher than 0.16 and hence the stability condition given by equation (5) is not met. A possible answer would be to say that the saving of workers has been omitted, and that adding this saving component would help salvage a modified stability condition, as the saving equation would include an additional term that is sensitive to changes in the rate of utilization, helping to fulfil the stability condition. One would have:

$$g^s = s_p mu/v + s_w(1 - m)u/v \tag{2A}$$

where s_w is the propensity to save out of wages, with $(1 - m)$ being the share of wages.

5.2   Getting away from the equilibrium dynamic model

Whether Keynesian stability is likely to hold or not, is there any way for Kaleckian models to retain stability, despite the failure of the Keynesian stability condition given by equation (5)? One possibility has been explored by Bruno (1999) and Bhaduri (2006, 2008), and is the subject of this section.

Both Bruno and Bhaduri start away from the equilibrium dynamics model, assuming the absence of market clearing in the short period. Thus, in the short (or ultra-short) period, (intended) investment and saving are not equal. Capacity utilization is fixed, as are profit margins. But let us assume that both quantities and prices react to disequilibria, so that two adjustment mechanisms get going simultaneously, as shown in equations (6A) and (7):

$$\dot{u} = \mu(g^i - g^s) \qquad \text{with } \mu > 0 \tag{6A}$$

$$\dot{m} = \psi(g^i - g^s) \tag{7}$$

Equation (6A) represents the quantity adjustment mechanism. Firms increase capacity utilization whenever investment surpasses saving, that is, whenever output demand is above production. Equation (7) is the price adjustment mechanism. One would presume that the ψ parameter is necessarily positive. When output demand is above production ($g^i > g^s$), prices and profit margins rise, thus leading to a rise in the profit share m (or in the normal profit rate r_n). This case corresponds to the standard classical price adjustment mechanism, and it also corresponds to the Cambridge adjustment mechanism, found in the earlier post-Keynesian growth models à la Kaldor and Robinson, and associated with forced saving. Bhaduri (2008) however argues that the alternative, with $\psi < 0$, is not inconceivable. With excess demand, firms must raise rates of capacity utilization and hence employment rises faster than capacity, and this may generate a stronger bargaining position for workers. Thus, in some circumstances, when output demand is above production, it may be that real wages rise and hence that profit margins and the profit share m falls. We shall call this the Radical case, since this kind of profit-squeeze behaviour has been underlined mostly by Radical economists.

Because equations (6A) and (7) turn out to be non-linear when one takes into account their explicit form through equations (1), (2), and (3), we examine the local stability of this system of differential equations by linearizing the system, making use of the partial derivatives, and computing its Jacobian matrix evaluated at the equilibrium (u^*, m^*). The Jacobian matrix J so obtained, is given by:

$$J = \begin{bmatrix} \mu(\gamma_u - s_p m/v) & \mu(\gamma_r - s_p u/v) \\ \psi(\gamma_u - s_p m/v) & \psi(\gamma_r - s_p u/v) \end{bmatrix}_{(u^*, m^*)} \tag{8}$$

The determinant of the matrix is zero, implying that this system has a zero root and hence that there is a multiplicity of equilibria on a single demarcation line. Whether this locus of equilibria is stable or not depends on the sign of the trace of the matrix. The model as modified is stable whenever the trace is negative, and it is unstable whenever the trace is positive. The trace of the matrix is equal to the sum of the two diagonal terms:

$$\text{Tr } J = \mu(\gamma_u - s_p m/v) + \psi(\gamma_r - s_p u/v)$$

Keynesian stability, or *stability in dimension*, requires that the first term of the trace be negative. Given that $\mu > 0$, it means that equation (5) is verified, as in the Keynesian adjustment process. Stability *in proportion* requires that the second term, associated with changes in profit margins, be negative. In the case of the classical or Cambridge adjustment process (with $\psi > 0$), this will occur whenever investment does not react too briskly to changes in profit margins, that is, when:

$$\gamma_r - s_p u/v < 0 \tag{9}$$

This condition is called the Robinsonian stability condition by Marglin and Bhaduri (1991, p. 138). When equation (9) is verified, excess demand leads to an increase in profit margins and profit shares, with a moderate positive impact on investment, and a more important impact on saving, thus bringing together saving and investment, and thus bringing the economy towards equilibrium – a point made early on by Pasinetti (1962). With no quantity adjustment (with $\mu = 0$), this process through price adjustment guarantees the stability of the system.

By contrast, in the Radical case, with $\psi < 0$, excess demand leads to a fall in profit margins and profit shares. To reduce the discrepancy between investment and saving, investment must react strongly to the fall in the profit share, decreasing faster than saving does, and thus in this alternative case, stability in proportion requires that equation (10) be fulfilled:

$$\gamma_r - s_p u/v > 0 \tag{10}$$

With both the quantity and the price mechanisms in action, no fewer than eight cases, all shown in Table 6.1, become possible. With stability in both dimension and proportion, the trace is necessarily negative, and stability is unconditional. Symmetrically, with instability both in dimension and proportion, the trace is necessarily positive, and the model is unstable. In the other four cases, stability is conditional. Thus, in the absence of Keynesian stability, the Kaleckian growth model may still be stable.

5.3 Profit-led and wage-led regimes

Table 6.1 also highlights the fact that, using the terminology of Blecker (2002), whether the economy is wage-led or profit-led in terms of aggregate demand, that is, relative to the rate of utilization, depends on the signs of the first two columns.[5] This can be seen by taking the total differentials of the combination of equations (1) and (2), and of equation (3), each evaluated at a position of equilibrium ($g^i = g^s$), which gives us:

$$dg^s = s_p(m/v)du^* + s_p(u/v)dm^*$$

Table 6.1   Stability or instability in dimension and in proportion, Cambridge vs profit-squeeze price adjustment mechanisms, and wage-led vs profit-led regimes

Sign of $\gamma_u - s_p m/v$	Sign of $\gamma_r - s_p u/v$	Classical or Cambridge case: $\psi > 0$	Radical case: $\psi < 0$	$du^*/dm^* = \dfrac{\gamma_u - s_p m/v}{\gamma_r - s_p u/v}$
(−) Stability in dimension	(−)	(A) $\psi(\gamma_r - s_p u/v) < 0$ Stability in proportion Tr $J < 0$ Unconditional stability	(B) $\psi(\gamma_r - s_p u/v) > 0$ Instability in proportion Tr $J = ?$ Conditional stability if μ is large	(−) Wage-led locus
	(+)	(C) $\psi(\gamma_r - s_p u/v) > 0$ Instability in proportion Tr $J = ?$ Conditional stability if μ is large	(D) $\psi(\gamma_r - s_p u/v) < 0$ Stability in proportion Tr $J < 0$ Unconditional stability	(+) Profit-led locus
(+) Instability in dimension	(−)	(E) $\psi(\gamma_r - s_p u/v) < 0$ Stability in proportion Tr $J = ?$ Conditional stability if ψ is large	(F) $\psi(\gamma_r - s_p u/v) > 0$ Instability in proportion Tr $J > 0$ Unconditional instability	(+) Profit-led locus
	(+)	(G) $\psi(\gamma_r - s_p u/v) > 0$ Instability in proportion Tr $J > 0$ Unconditional instability	(H) $\psi(\gamma_r - s_p u/v) < 0$ Stability in proportion Tr $J = ?$ Conditional stability if ψ is large	(−) Wage-led locus

$$dg^i = \gamma_u du^* + \gamma_r dm^*$$

Equating the above two expressions, we obtain the equation that is in the last column of Table 6.1. Thus, unless we have a priori opinions about the values taken by the parameters in the investment and saving functions, a wage-led aggregate demand regime is as likely as a profit-led regime.[6] It is interesting to note that some configurations are impossible. For instance, a stable wage-led (in aggregate demand or in growth) economy with a classical or Cambridge price adjustment mechanism is only compatible with stability in dimension. Similarly, a stable profit-led economy with a Radical or profit-squeeze price adjustment mechanism requires stability in dimension. Note also that the cases of stability in dimension are easy to interpret intuitively. For instance, when the economy is wage led, an increase in the real wage leads to higher rates of utilization, but this effect tends to bring the real wage back towards its initial position through the Cambridge price mechanism, thus ensuring unconditional overall stability. By contrast, with the Radical price mechanism, the initial increase in the real wage generates a further increase in the real wage as the increase in the rate of utilization strengthens the bargaining power of workers, thus leading only to conditional stability. However, when the economy is profit led, unconditional stability will be achieved with the Radical price mechanism, as an initial increase in the real wage leads to lower rates of utilization, which in turn tends to reduce the real wage rate towards its initial value.

5.4   Graphical illustrations of the dynamics
Figures 6.3 to 6.6 illustrate the transition dynamics in the various cases. Figures 6.3 and 6.4 illustrate the Keynesian or dimension stability cases. When there is excess demand, the rate of utilization rises, and this will tend to bring the economy towards the equilibrium locus in the Keynesian stability case. When the economy is wage-led, the addition of the Cambridge price adjustment mechanism (rising profit margins with excess demand) will reinforce this tendency, as shown with the A arrow in Figure 6.3 (which corresponds to the A entry in Table 6.1). But with a Radical price adjustment mechanism (falling profit margins with excess demand), stability may either occur (arrow B_S) or not occur (arrow B_U). When the economy is profit-led, the reverse occurs. With the addition of the Cambridge price adjustment mechanism, convergence may either occur (arrow C_S) or not occur (arrow C_U), whereas it will always occur with the addition of a Radical price adjustment mechanism (arrow D).

Keynesian instability is illustrated in Figures 6.5 and 6.6. This time, when there is excess demand, increases in rates of utilization are driving away the economy from the equilibrium locus. When the economy is profit-led, the addition of a Cambridge price adjustment mechanism provides for conditional stability (arrow E_S), whereas the addition of a Radical mechanism makes the model completely unstable (arrow F). With a wage-led regime, it is the Cambridge price adjustment mechanism that will make the model unconditionally unstable (arrow G). With a Radical mechanism, convergence may either arise (arrow H_S) or not occur (arrow H_U).

It could be interesting to link these disequilibrium dynamics to the standard representation of the Kaleckian growth model. This is done in Figures 6.7 and 6.8. Figure 6.7 illustrates the Keynesian stability case. In the initial steady state, the rate of capacity utilization is given by u_0. We then assume an upward shift in the γ parameter of the investment function, so that the investment curve g^i shifts up, so that now we have $g^i > g^s$. With the pure Keynesian adjustment process, the economy would move to a new steady state, at the higher rate of utilization u_1. This rate of utilization is the same rate u_1 that can be found in Figures 6.3 and 6.4. However, with the dual adjustment process, profit margins will change. Assuming a classical or Cambridge adjustment process, profit margins and profit shares go up, so that the saving function rotates upwards while the investment function shifts up. In the case of the wage-led economy, with $\gamma_r - s_p u/v < 0$, the shift in the investment function will be small relative to the shift in the saving function, so that the new equilibrium will be u_{wl}, below the equilibrium u_1 that would have existed without the increase in profit margins. This corresponds to the u_{wl} point found in Figure 6.3. In the case of the profit-led economy, with $\gamma_r - s_p u/v > 0$, the shift in the investment function

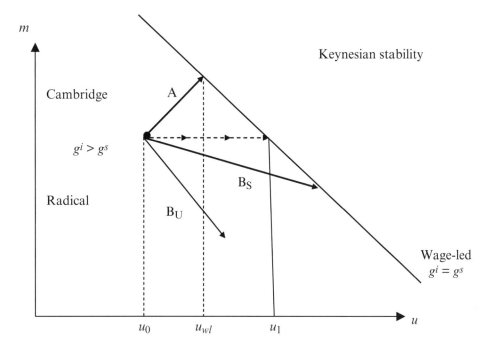

Figure 6.3 A wage-led regime with stability in dimension

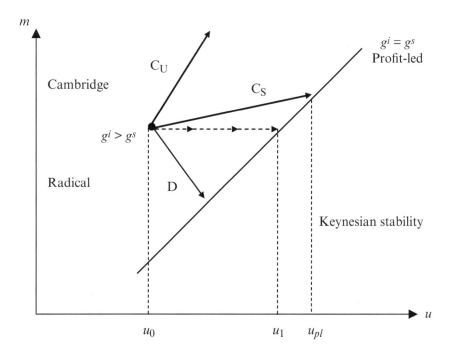

Figure 6.4 A profit-led regime with stability in dimension

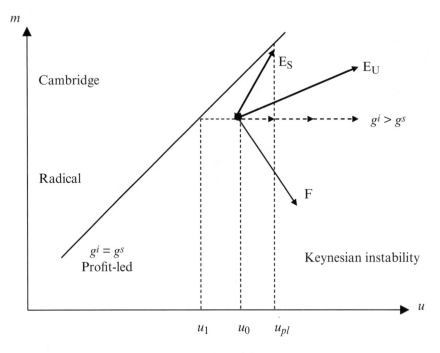

Figure 6.5   A profit-led regime with instability in dimension

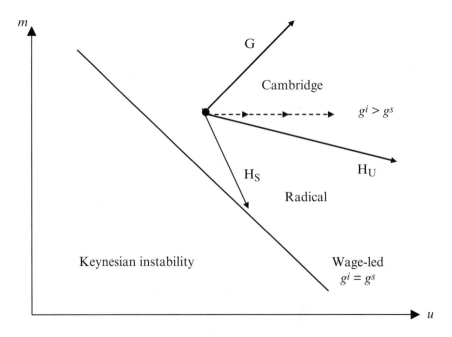

Figure 6.6   A wage-led regime with instability in dimension

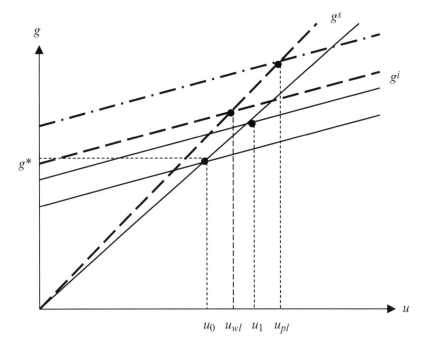

Figure 6.7   The impact of higher animal spirits with stability in dimension

will be relatively large, so that the new equilibrium will be u_{pl}, above the equilibrium u_1 that would have existed without the increase in profit margins. This corresponds to the u_{pl} rate found in Figure 6.4.

A similar exercise can be conducted with Keynesian instability, illustrated with Figure 6.8. The economy, initially, stands at u_0. There follows a positive shock on the investment function, shifting the investment curve upwards. With no change in profit margins, the new equilibrium ought to be at u_1. However, this could only be a virtual equilibrium, for no economic forces will drive the economy towards it. On the basis of the Keynesian adjustment, u_1 is not a stable equilibrium, because, with $g^i > g^s$ at the initial rate of utilization u_0, the rate of utilization tends to rise, moving away from u_1. However, with the addition of a classical price adjustment mechanism, the economy converges conditionally towards a new equilibrium, at the rate of utilization u_{pl} for instance. This rate corresponds to the rate u_{pl} of Figure 6.5. In this case, the economy is profit-led, because a higher rate of utilization is associated in equilibrium with a higher profit margin.

6   Kaleckian in the short run, classical in the long run?

Several economists would argue that, so far, the analysis has been confined to the short and medium runs, or to provisional equilibria, as Chick and Caserta (1997) would call them. In the long run, critics of the Kaleckian model would say, two things are likely to happen. First, the rate of utilization should come back to its normal value. Second, the actual rate of growth of the economy should approximate the natural rate of growth, for otherwise the rate of unemployment would keep rising or falling without limit. The latter

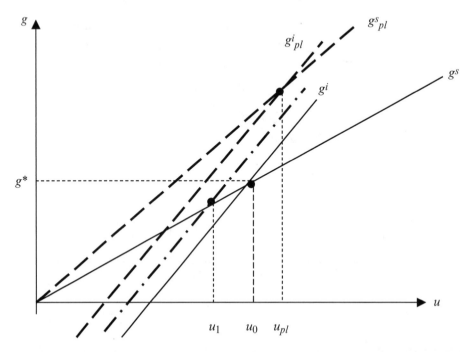

Figure 6.8   The impact of higher animal spirits with stability in dimension

problem has been brought up and tackled more recently, and is handled elsewhere in this book (Dutt, Chapter 11, this volume); the former problem was first noted more than 20 years ago (Kurz, 1986; Committeri, 1986, 1987; Auerbach and Skott, 1988). In dealing with this issue, we shall assume that Keynesian stability holds.

Now one could argue that the normal rate of capacity utilization is more a norm than a target, and hence that firms may be quite content to run their production capacity at rates of utilization that are within an acceptable range of the normal rate of utilization. If this is correct, then the analysis pursued so far would still be valid in the long run, as long as the rate of capacity utilization remains within the acceptable range (Dutt, 1990, p. 59).

But let us admit for discussion purposes that this range is very limited. What mechanisms could exist that would bring back the economy towards a normal rate of utilization of capacity, or towards what Sraffians would call fully adjusted positions (Vianello, 1985)? Two French economists, Duménil and Lévy (1999), have long argued that Keynesian economists are mistaken in applying to the long run those results arising from the short run. Their claim, in short, is that one should be Kaleckian or Keynesian in the short run, but classical in the long run. What they mean by this is that, in the long run, the economy will be brought back to normal rates of utilization – fully adjusted positions as the Sraffians would say – and that in the long run classical economics will be relevant again. Put briefly, this implies that in the long run a lower propensity to save will drive down the rate of growth of the economy, and that a lower normal profit rate (that is higher real wages and a lower profit share for a given technology), will also drive down the rate of accumulation. These authors thus reject the paradox of thrift and the paradox of costs, with the latter implying that a reduction in profit margins leads to a higher realized profit rate.

In view of the investment function proposed by Kurz (1990) and by Bhaduri and Marglin (1990), a rejection of the paradox of costs is only incompatible with the canonical Kaleckian model, which does not include a profit share or normal profit variable in its investment function. In addition, various authors have shown that the paradox of costs is weakened by the introduction of saving by wage recipients (Blecker, 2002; Lavoie, 1992, p. 344). On the other hand the paradox of thrift is considered to be a robust component of the Kaleckian growth model. Thus one could say that the paradox of thrift is the crucial relationship at stake here.

Duménil and Lévy (1999) provide a simple mechanism that ought to bring the economy back to normal rates of capacity utilization. They consider that monetary policy is that mechanism. Their model, as shown by Lavoie (2003) and Lavoie and Kriesler (2007), is strongly reminiscent of the New Consensus model, but there is also a great deal of resemblance with Joan Robinson's inflation barrier and the reaction of the monetary authorities that she describes (1956, p. 238; 1962, p. 60). We can write their model as equations (1A), (2), which we rewrite here for convenience, and equations (3C), (11) and (12):

$$r = r_n u / u_n \tag{1A}$$

$$g_s = s_p r \tag{2}$$

$$g^i = \gamma + \gamma_u u - \gamma_r i \tag{3C}$$

$$\pi = \chi(u - u_n) \tag{11}$$

$$\Delta i = \varepsilon \pi \tag{12}$$

where i is the real rate of interest and π is the rate of inflation. Thus equation (11) is some sort of non-vertical Phillips curve, while equation (12) is a differential equation that represents the central bank's reaction function.[7]

Suppose that this economy is subjected to a Keynesian adjustment mechanism, and that inflation kicks off with a lag. A decrease in the propensity to save will rotate the saving function downwards in Figure 6.9, bringing the rate of capacity utilization from u_n to u_1. Through equation (11), this generates demand inflation, which induces the central bank to raise real interest rates, as shown by equation (12). Interest rates will keep on rising as long as inflation is not brought back to zero. As a consequence, the investment function g^i shifts down gradually. It will stop shifting only when it hits the normal rate of utilization u_n, because this is where inflation is brought back to zero. The end result, however, as can be read off Figure 6.9, is that the economy now grows at a slower rate, g_2 instead of g_0.

The lesson drawn from this graph is that the economy might be demand-led in the short

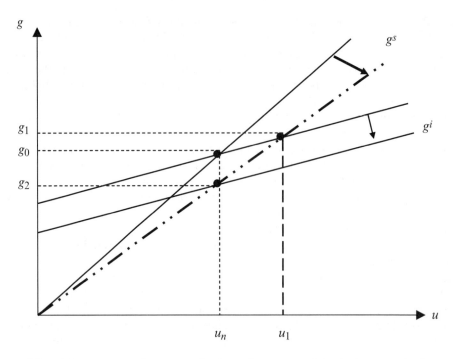

Figure 6.9   A lower propensity to save leads to slower growth in the long run in the Duménil and Lévy (1999) model

run, but in the long run it is supply-led. In the long run, the growth rate is determined by the saving function, calculated at the normal rate of capacity utilization, and hence calculated at the normal profit rate: $g^s = s_p r_n$. Thus, a reduction in s_p or r_n, in the propensity to save or the normal profit rate, induces a slowdown of the rate of accumulation in the long run. We are back to the *dismal* science.

7   The Cambridge price mechanism on its own: cul-de-sac or way out?

Are there any alternatives to the return of the dismal science? The old Cambridge story – the one provided by Joan Robinson (1956, 1962) – provides a fully adjusted position without giving up the paradox of thrift. As is well known, her suggested investment function is a function of the expected profit rate, itself determined by past realized profit rates, so that, as a simplification we may write:

$$g^i = \gamma + \gamma_r r \tag{3D}$$

Suppose again that the propensity to save decreases, thus generating the paradox of thrift by bringing the accumulation rate from g_0 to g_1 while the rate of utilization slides up from u_n to u_1, as shown in Figure 6.10, thus allowing the rate of profit to rise from r_0 to r_1. Robinson and the Cambridge economists thought however that the economy would be back at its normal rate of utilization in the long run. Their proposed adjustment mechanism is a variant of what we have called the Cambridge price adjustment mecha-

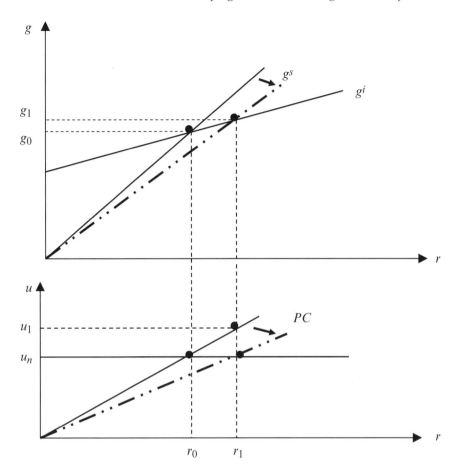

Figure 6.10   A lower propensity to save leads to faster growth in the long run in the Joan Robinson model

nism (equation (7)), and, recalling equation (1A), it can be written either as equation (13) or equation (13A).

$$\dot{r}_n = \phi(u - u_n) \qquad \text{with } \phi > 0 \tag{13}$$

$$\dot{r}_n = \phi\frac{u_n}{r_n}(r - r_n) \text{ with } \phi > 0 \tag{13A}$$

With above-normal rates of utilization, profit margins rise.[8] As a result, the profit curve *PC*, as given by equation (1A), rotates down in the lower part of Figure 6.10, bringing back the actual rate of utilization towards u_n. Since the Cambridge investment function depends on the profit rate, it is impervious to the change in the profit margin, so that the growth rate and the profit rate remain at their higher values, g_1 and r_1. Despite the fully adjusted position, the paradox of thrift is sustained in the long run. Thus, as pointed out by Marglin (1984, p. 125), in the early Cambridge model, "the key assumption is that the rate of capacity utilisation varies on the path between steady-state configurations, but not across steady-growth states". This means however that there exists a necessary negative relationship (for a given technology) between real wages and accumulation in the long run.

8   Path dependence in the long run: back to Kaleckian results

In a number of places, I have argued that the paradoxes of thrift and costs, as well as the long-run endogeneity of the rate of capacity utilization, could be salvaged even when adopting this kind of Cambridge price adjustment mechanism for the long run (Lavoie, 1992, pp. 417–21; 2003). The reason is that, with bargaining between firms and labour unions, one must distinguish between the normal rate of profit r_n, as assessed by firms, and the target rate of return r_s which is incorporated into prices. What the Cambridge price adjustment mechanism of equation (13A) tells us is that the normal rate of profit will change in line with the realized rate of profit. In the long run, these two rates will equate each other, so that $r_n = r$. However, through bargaining and real wage resistance, the target rate of return embodied in the pricing equation will be different from the normal rate of profit as assessed by firms, so that $r_s \neq r_n$ even in the long run.[9] As a consequence, the rate of capacity utilization does not converge to the normal rate of capacity utilization in the long run despite the assumed price adjustment mechanism.

The endogeneity of the actual rate of capacity utilization is thus preserved in both the short and the long run, and the standard Kaleckian results – such as the paradox of thrift, or the paradox of costs if it holds in the assumed configuration – are still vindicated. The above is also consistent with Steindl's rejection of the intuitive belief that planned excess capacity ought to equal actual long-term excess capacity, as he concluded that "the degree of utilization actually obtaining in the long run is no safe indication of the planned level of utilization" (Steindl, 1952, p. 12).

I have taken a different approach in another paper (Lavoie, 1996), introducing two adjustment mechanisms at once instead of a single one, as was done in the previous section that dealt with the dual adjustment process. In that paper, one has to distinguish between fast and slow processes. In the short run, we have a dynamic equilibrium model, based on a pure Keynesian adjustment process. Thus, in the short period aggregate supply adjusts quickly enough to aggregate demand for aggregate demand to be at all times equal to aggregate supply. Keynesian stability is thus assumed. But there is also a slow adjustment process that operates in the long run, and that involves two variables. Depending on the exact model being considered, and on the exact adjustment processes being taken into account, various conclusions can be drawn. Cassetti (2006) uses a similar method, but drawing on an adjustment process that involves four variables, including the rate of capital scrapping, which is not considered here.

8.1   Price only dynamics

Let us first start with an even simpler Kaleckian model, where investment only depends on the rate of utilization, as sometimes recommended by Dutt (1990, p. 59). We have the following three equations:

$$r = (r_n/u_n)u \tag{1A}$$

$$g^s = s_p r \tag{2}$$

$$g^i = \gamma + \gamma_u u \text{ with } \gamma > 0 \tag{3E}$$

accompanied by the following two long-run adjustment processes, which, with the present model, obviously only have an impact on the pricing and saving equations:

$$\dot{r}_n = \phi(r^* - r_n) = \phi(r_n/u_n)(u^* - u_n) \tag{14}$$

$$\dot{u}_n = \sigma(u^* - u_n) \tag{15}$$

where u^* and r^* are the medium-run values of the model.

With equation (3E) we set aside for the moment the complications that could arise from considering the shape of the investment function. Whereas I presume that most of my colleagues would accept the notion that the normal rate of profit would be influenced by past realized profit rates, as suggested in equation (13A), certain authors, such as Skott (2008), are rather reluctant to accept the argument that the normal rate of capacity utilization will also be influenced by past realized rates of utilization, as proposed in equation (15). While I have some sympathy for their objections, having myself argued that the normal rate of capacity utilization may be more influenced by the past variance of actual rates of utilization than by their past realized values (Lavoie, 1992, p. 330), there is nevertheless some evidence that normal rates of utilization are influenced by past realized values. For instance, Clifton (1983, p. 26) remarks that cost-plus prices are based on standard volumes of utilization taken from historical data that cover several business cycles. In addition, Joan Robinson has herself argued that normal rates of profit and of capacity utilization were subjected to adaptive adjustment processes, as the following quote shows:

> Where fluctuations in output are expected and regarded as normal, the subjective-normal price may be calculated upon the basis of an average or standard rate of output, rather than capacity. . . . Profits may exceed or fall short of the level on the basis of which the subjective-normal prices were conceived. Then experience gradually modifies the views of entrepreneurs about what level of profit is obtainable, or what the average utilization of plant is likely to be over its lifetime, and so reacts upon subjective-normal prices for the future. (Robinson, 1956, pp. 186, 190)

Looking now at equations (14) and (15), we see that what we have is a model that is a particular case of the dual adjustment mechanism that we described earlier and that gave rise to Table 6.1. Keynesian stability is assumed, and since $\gamma_r = 0$, the slope of du^*/dm^* is necessarily negative, implying a wage-led model. The relative size of the adjustments to the normal profit rate and the normal utilization rate explain whether the model is driven by a Cambridge price adjustment process or by a Radical price adjustment process. Thus, this model corresponds to entries A and B in Table 6.1.

The model reaches its long-run equilibrium – its fully adjusted position – when $\dot{u} = \dot{r} = 0$, that is when $u^* - u_n = 0$. Using equation (4A) with $\gamma_r = 0$, we can compute that this will occur along the demarcation line defined by:

$$r_n^{**} = (\gamma_u u_n^{**} + \gamma)/s_p \tag{16}$$

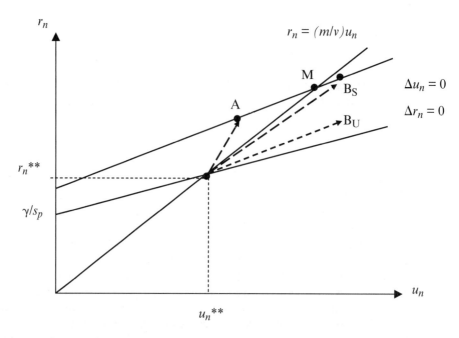

Figure 6.11   Long-run adjustment processes of the normal rate of capacity utilization and the normal rate of profit in the pricing equation, following a decrease in the propensity to save

Figure 6.11 illustrates this slow adjustment process that occurs in the long run. The economy is initially in a fully adjusted position at $u_n{}^{**}$ and $r_n{}^{**}$ on the lower demarcation line. Then there is a decrease in the propensity to save, which shifts up the demarcation line, raising both the short-run actual rate of profit and rate of capacity utilization. The other upward sloping line, marked as $r_n = (m/v)u_n$, represents the relationship between the normal rate of profit and the normal rate of utilization when profit margins don't change. With the slow adjusting mechanism associated with normal values, the economy will move to point A, corresponding to entry A in Table 6.1, if the normal profit rate rises faster than the normal rate of utilization (that is if $\varphi > \sigma$). In this case, as shown in the figure, profit margins are rising, and this corresponds to a kind of Cambridge price adjustment mechanism. If profit margins remain constant while normal rates of profit and of capacity utilization rise, then the economy gets to point M (if $\varphi = \sigma$). Finally, if the normal profit rate rises more slowly than the normal rate of utilization (if $\varphi < \sigma$), the economy will move to point B_S in the stable case, while it will move along the B_U arrowhead in the unstable case. Instability will occur if the slope of the trajectory towards the new fully adjusted position is less steep than the slope of the new demarcation line, given by equation (13), that is if: $dr_n/du_n = (\varphi/\sigma)(r_n/u_n) < \gamma_u/s_p$ or if $(\varphi/\sigma) < (\gamma_u u_n)/(s_p r_n)$.

An interesting characteristic of the present model is that it features what Setterfield (1993) calls *deep endogeneity*. The new fully adjusted position depends on the previous fully adjusted position. Very clearly, it also depends on the reaction parameters during the transition or traverse process, and hence we may also say that it is path-dependent.

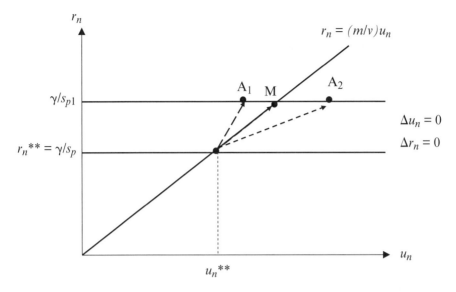

Figure 6.12 *Long-run adjustment processes of the normal rate of capacity utilization and the normal rate of profit in the pricing and investment equation, following a decrease in the propensity to save*

It retains the main properties of the canonical Kaleckian growth model, as shown here with the paradox of thrift.

8.2 Combining price and investment dynamics

We now examine another variant of the Kaleckian model, by assuming that entrepreneurs entertain the same value of the normal rate of capacity utilization, both in the pricing equation and in the investment equation. To take this into consideration, we must modify the investment equation yet again, adopting an equation that is often found in the literature. With equations (1A), (2), (11) and (12), we have:

$$g^i = \gamma + \gamma_u(u - u_n) \text{ with } \gamma > 0 \qquad (3F)$$

While such a model would seem to be more complicated than the previous one, in fact it is the opposite. What happens is that the fully adjusted position gets simplified, thanks to equation (3F), because $\dot{u} = \dot{r} = 0$ when $u^* - u_n = 0$, which means that $g^{**} = \gamma$ in the fully adjusted position. Using equation (2), this implies that:

$$r_n^{**} = \gamma/s_p \qquad (17)$$

Once more we can illustrate the slow long-run adjustment process, with Figure 6.12, which is a degenerate version of Figure 6.11. The demarcation line is now a simple horizontal line, given by equation (17), which shifts up when the propensity to save is lower (or animal spirits, as proxied by γ, are higher). Both the normal profit rate and the normal rate of utilization rise under such a change. The model is unconditionally stable, but there is a cost to this: since the growth rate of the economy is stuck at γ in the long run, the paradox of thrift no longer applies to fully adjusted positions, although lower propensities to save will generate higher normal rates of profit and higher normal rates of capacity utilization.

8.3   *Investment dynamics*

Finally, one may wish to focus on the long-run dynamics involving only the investment function, as in Dutt (1997, pp. 245–8). In this case, we consider once again investment function (3F), along with equations (1) and (2):

$$r = mu/v \tag{1}$$

$$g^s = s_p r \tag{2}$$

$$g^i = \gamma + \gamma_u(u - u_n) \text{ with } \gamma > 0 \tag{3F}$$

The γ parameter in investment function (3F) is often interpreted as the secular growth rate of the economy, or the expected growth rate of sales. Firms speed up accumulation, relative to this secular growth rate, when current capacity utilization exceeds the target, thus trying to catch up. One would also think that the expected trend growth rate is influenced by past values of the actual growth rate. With normal rates of capacity utilization also being influenced by past actual rates, the two dynamic equations are given by:

$$\dot{u}_n = \sigma(u^* - u_n) \tag{15}$$

$$\dot{\gamma} = \Omega(g^* - \gamma) \tag{18}$$

Making the proper substitutions, these two equations can be rewritten as:

$$\dot{u}_n = \frac{\sigma(\gamma - \alpha u_n)}{\alpha - \gamma_u} \tag{15A}$$

$$\dot{\gamma} = \frac{\Omega\gamma_u(\gamma - \alpha u_n)}{\alpha - \gamma_u} \tag{18A}$$

with $\alpha = s_p m/v$, and hence the differential function relevant to the perceived growth trend is:

$$\dot{\gamma} = \frac{\Omega\gamma_u}{\sigma}\dot{u} \tag{18B}$$

Thus once again we have a continuum of equilibria, such that $\dot{u}_n = \dot{\gamma} = 0$ when $\gamma = \alpha u_n = (s_p m/v)u_n$ as shown in Figure 6.13. With a decrease in the propensity to save, the continuum of long-run equilibria rotates downward, and two cases arise. Either the dynamic equations (15) and (18) describe a stabilizing process, in which case the normal rate of utilization and the perceived growth trend rise up to a point such as A_S in Figure

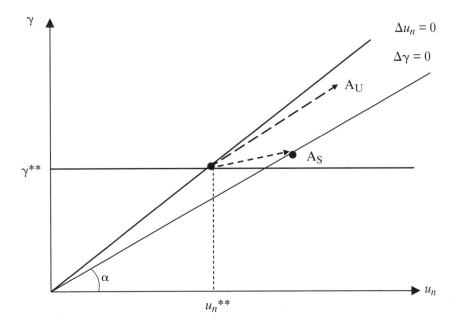

Figure 6.13 *Long-run adjustment processes of the normal rate of capacity utilization and the secular growth rate of the economy in the investment equation, following a decrease in the propensity to save*

6.13, or the process is unstable, as shown by arrowhead A_U. The process will be stable provided the transitional path has a smaller slope than that of the new demarcation line, that is provided we have $d\gamma/du_n = \Omega\gamma_u/\sigma < \alpha$, which means that $s_p m/v > (\Omega/\sigma)\gamma_u$. If the Keynesian stability condition holds, that is if $s_p m/v > \gamma_u$, then a sufficient condition for dynamic stability is simply $\sigma > \Omega$. In other words, the Harrodian instability effect, represented by equation (18), which tells us that entrepreneurs will raise their expectations about future growth rates whenever current realized growth rates exceed the current trend estimate, must not be too large.

Other mechanisms have recently been proposed to tame Harrodian instability or to bring the Kaleckian model back to normal rates of capacity utilization (Shaikh, 2009), but the discussion of these mechanisms would overly extend the present chapter. They are studied at length in Hein, Lavoie and van Treeck (2008).

9 Conclusion

The Kaleckian growth model has proven to be highly flexible and fruitful, being able to incorporate the concerns of several different schools of thought. I have not dealt with the important question of the discrepancy between the rate of accumulation as determined by the Kaleckian model and the natural rate of growth. Neither have I dealt with finance, debt, or stock-flow issues (Taylor, 2004, pp. 272–8). But all these questions can be addressed in the Kaleckian framework and, indeed, are discussed elsewhere in this book (Dutt, Chapter 11, and Hein and van Treeck, Chapter 13, in this volume).

Notes

1. Many thanks for the comments provided by Eckhard Hein, Till van Treeck, and Franck Van de Velde, as well as the mathematical and stylistic corrections provided by Mark Setterfield.
2. We could assume that there is consumption out of wealth, but this would barely change things, as the saving function would become: $g^s = s_p r - c_w$, with c_w the propensity to consume out of wealth. But it shows that the saving function need not arise from the origin.
3. If one considers that equation (3A) is the most correct investment equation, then equation (3) should really be rewritten as: $g^i = \gamma + \gamma_u u + \gamma_r (m u_n / v)$. But we will leave it at that.
4. Although this is a trivial point, both Blecker (2002, p. 137) and Bruno (1999, p. 135) introduce unwarranted restrictions by forgetting that the γ parameter could be negative even when the numerator of equations (4) or (4A) is positive. Lavoie (1992, pp. 341–3) shows that a negative γ can also enrich the range of possible results in a model with overhead labour.
5. Bhaduri and Marglin (1990) call these *stagnationism* and *exhilarationism* regimes, while Kurz (1990) uses the expressions *underconsumption* and *supply-side* regimes.
6. With the same two differential equations, one can also assess the conditions under which the economy is in a *wage-led growth* regime or a *profit-led growth* regime. As one would expect, in the case of Keynesian stability, a wage-led growth regime is more likely when investment is mainly sensitive to utilization rates and less so to profit shares. The sign of dg/dm depends on the following expression:

$$\frac{\gamma_u u - \gamma_r m}{\gamma_u - s_p m / v}$$

7. More exactly this precise formulation can be found in the earlier working paper that gave rise to Duménil and Lévy (1999). For a truly New Consensus model, with a vertical Phillips curve, one would need the *change* in inflation to depend on the discrepancy between the actual and the normal rates of utilization. In this case, to avoid a limit cycle, one would need the central bank reaction function to be a function of both the level of inflation (relative to the target inflation rate) and the change in inflation.
8. Earlier Cambridge economists such as Robinson, Kaldor and Pasinetti thought that this would occur through some competitive process, whereas Cambridge economists in the 1970s, for instance Alfred Eichner, Wynne Godley, G.C. Harcourt and Adrian Wood, thought that this would occur through a price-setting mechanism whereby oligopolistic firms would raise profit margins when trend growth was faster. Kaldor also came to adopt this point of view later in his life.
9. Dallery and van Treeck (2008) develop this idea in exciting new directions.

References

Allain, O. (2009) "La modération salariale: le point de vue (néo-)kaleckien", *Revue économique*, **60** (1), 81–108.
Auerbach, P. and P. Skott (1988) "Concentration, competition and distribution", *International Review of Applied Economics*, **2** (1), 42–61.
Bhaduri, A. (2006) "The dynamics of profit- and wage-led expansion: a note", in E. Hein, A. Heise and A. Truger (eds), *Wages, Employment, Distribution and Growth*, London: Macmillan/Palgrave, pp. 247–53.
Bhaduri, A. (2008) "On the dynamics of profit-led and wage-led growth", *Cambridge Journal of Economics*, **32** (1), 147–60.
Bhaduri, A. and S. Marglin (1990) "Unemployment and the real wage: the economic basis for contesting political ideologies", *Cambridge Journal of Economics*, **14** (4), 375–93.
Blecker, R.A. (2002) "Distribution, demand and growth in neo-Kaleckian macro-models", in M. Setterfield (ed.), *The Economics of Demand-led Growth: Challenging the Supply-side Vision of the Long Run*, Cheltenham, UK and Northampton, MA, USA: Edward Elgar, pp. 129–52.
Bruno, O. (1999) "Long-run positions and short-run dynamics in a classical growth model", *Metroeconomica*, **50** (1), 119–37.
Cassetti, M. (2002) "Conflict, inflation, distribution and terms of trade in the Kaleckian model", in M. Setterfield (ed.), *The Economics of Demand-led Growth: Challenging the Supply-side Vision of the Long Run*, Cheltenham, UK and Northampton, MA, USA: Edward Elgar, pp. 189–211.
Cassetti, M. (2006) "A note on the long-run behaviour of Kaleckian models", *Review of Political Economy*, **18** (4), 497–508.
Chick, V. and M. Caserta (1997) "Provisional equilibrium in macroeconomic theory", in P. Arestis, G. Palma and M. Sawyer (eds), *Capital Controversy, Post-Keynesian Economics and the History of Economic Thought: Essays in Honour of Geoff Harcourt*, vol. 2, London: Routledge, pp. 223–37.
Ciccone, R. (1986) "Accumulation and capacity utilization: some critical considerations on Joan Robinson's theory of distribution", *Political Economy*, **2** (1), 17–36.

Clifton, J.A. (1983) "Administered prices in the context of capitalist development", *Contributions to Political Economy*, **2**, 23–38.

Committeri, M. (1986) "Some comments on recent contributions on capital accumulation, income distribution and capacity utilization", *Political Economy*, **2** (2), 161–86.

Committeri, M. (1987) "Capacity utilization, distribution and accumulation: a rejoinder to Amadeo", *Political Economy*, **3** (1), 91–5.

Dallery, T. (2007) "Kaleckian models of growth and distribution revisited: evaluating their relevance through simulations", paper presented at the 11th Workshop of the Research Network *Macroeconomic Policies*, Berlin, October 2007.

Dallery, T. and T. van Treeck (2008) "Conflicting claims and equilibrium adjustment processes in a stock–flow consistent macroeconomic model", IMK working paper 9/2008, Hans Böckler Stiftung, Düsseldorf.

Duménil, G. and D. Lévy (1987) "The dynamics of competition: a restoration of the classical analysis", *Cambridge Journal of Economics*, **11** (2), 133–64.

Duménil, G. and D. Lévy (1993) *The Economics of the Profit Rate*, Aldershot, UK and Brookfield, USA: Edward Elgar.

Duménil, G. and D. Lévy (1999) "Being Keynesian in the short term and classical in the long term: the traverse to classical long-term equilibrium", *The Manchester School*, **67** (6), 684–716.

Dutt, A.K. (1987) "Keynes with a perfectly competitive goods market", *Australian Economic Papers*, December, 275–93.

Dutt, A.K. (1990) *Growth, Distribution and Uneven Development*, Cambridge: Cambridge University Press.

Dutt, A.K (1997) "Equilibrium, path dependence and hysteresis in post-Keynesian models", in P. Arestis, G. Palma and M. Sawyer (eds), *Markets, Unemployment and Economic Policy: Essays in Honour of Geoff Harcourt*, Vol. 2, London: Routledge, pp. 238–53.

Godley, W. and M. Lavoie (2007) *Monetary Economics: An Integrated Approach to Credit, Money, Income, Production and Wealth*, London: Palgrave/Macmillan.

Hartwig, J. (2007) "Keynes versus the post Keynesians on the principle of effective demand", *European Journal of the History of Economic Thought*, **14** (4), 725–39.

Hein, E., M. Lavoie and T. van Treeck (2008) "Some instability puzzles in Kaleckian models of growth and distribution: a critical survey", IMK working paper 19/2008, Hans Böckler Stiftung, Düsseldorf.

Kurz, H.D. (1986) "Normal positions and capital utilization", *Political Economy*, **2** (1), 37–54.

Kurz, H.D. (1990) "Technical change, growth and distribution: a steady state approach to unsteady growth", in H.D. Kurz, *Capital, Distribution and Effective Demand: Studies in the Classical Approach to Economic Theory*, Cambridge: Polity Press, pp. 210–39.

Lavoie, M. (1992) *Foundations of Post-Keynesian Economic Analysis*, Aldershot, UK and Brookfield, USA: Edward Elgar.

Lavoie, M. (1996) "Traverse, hysteresis and normal rates of capacity utilization in Kaleckian models of growth and distribution", *Review of Radical Political Economics*, **28** (4), 113–47.

Lavoie, M. (2003) "Kaleckian effective demand and Sraffian normal prices: towards a reconciliation", *Review of Political Economy*, **15** (1), 53–74.

Lavoie, M. and P. Kriesler (2007) "Capacity utilization, inflation and monetary policy: the Duménil and Lévy macro model and the new consensus", *Review of Radical Political Economics*, **39** (4), 586–98.

Leijonhufvud, A. (1968) *On Keynesian Economics and the Economics of Keynes*, New York: Oxford University Press.

Marglin, S. (1984), "Growth, distribution and inflation: a centennial synthesis", *Cambridge Journal of Economics*, **8**, 115–44.

Marglin, S.A. and A. Bhaduri (1991) "Profit squeeze and Keynesian theory", in E.J. Nell and W. Semmler (eds), *Nicholas Kalder and Mainstream Economics: Confrontation or Convergence?*, London: Macmillan, pp. 123–63.

Pasinetti, L.L. (1962) "Rate of profit and income distribution in relation to the rate of economic growth", *Review of Economic Studies*, **29** (4), 267–79.

Robinson, J. (1956) *The Accumulation of Capital*, London: Macmillan.

Robinson, J. (1962) *Essays in the Theory of Economic Growth*, London: Macmillan.

Rowthorn, B. (1981) "Demand, real wages and economic growth", in *Thames Papers in Political Economy*, London, Thames Polytechnic.

Setterfield, M. (1993) "Towards a long-run theory of effective demand: modeling macroeconomic systems with hysteresis", *Journal of Post Keynesian Economics*, **15** (3), 347–64.

Shaikh, A. (2009) "Economic policy in a growth context: a classical synthesis of Keynes and Harrod", *Metroeconomica*, **60** (3), 455–94.

Skott, P. (1989) *Conflict and Effective Demand in Economic Growth*, Cambridge: Cambridge University Press.

Skott, P. (2008) "Investment functions, stability and the reserve army of labor", Working Paper, University of Massachusetts in Amherst.

Steindl, J. (1952) *Maturity and Stagnation in American Capitalism*, New York: Monthly Review Press.

Taylor, L. (2004) *Reconstructing Macroeconomics: Structuralist Proposals and Critiques of the Mainstream*, Cambridge, MA: Harvard University Press.

Vianello, F. (1985) "The pace of accumulation", *Political Economy: Studies in the Surplus Approach*, **1** (1), 69–87.

Vianello, F. (1989) "Effective demand and the rate of profits: some thoughts on Marx, Kalecki and Sraffa", in M. Sebastiani (ed.), *Kalecki's Relevance Today*, New York: St Martin's Press, pp. 164–90.

7 Kaldor and the Kaldorians
John E. King

1 Kaldor

1.1 Introduction

Nicholas Kaldor was born in Budapest in 1908. He was educated at the University of Berlin and the London School of Economics, where he spent 20 years (1927–47) as undergraduate, research student and lecturer. After two years at the United Nations Economic Commission for Europe in Geneva he returned to academic life in October 1949 as Fellow of King's College, Cambridge. Kaldor was appointed to a personal chair in 1966. He retired in 1975 but remained very active in research and policy advocacy right up to his death in 1986. There are three intellectual biographies (Thirlwall, 1987; Targetti, 1992; King, 2009).

Kaldor's thinking on economic growth passed through four phases, which are detailed below. His ideas were distinctly "alternative" throughout. He maintained that economic theorists must never take refuge in imaginary worlds of their own creation, but must locate their analysis of growth in actual historical experience and should aim to explain the "stylised facts" of real-world capitalist economies. Kaldor rejected both the marginal productivity theory of distribution and the use of aggregate production functions, denying the validity of growth accounting exercises based on them. He also made no attempt to provide neoclassical microeconomic foundations for his growth models, and his own microeconomics was Marshallian, not Walrasian. He emphasised the diversity of economic agents; the crucial role of capitalist expenditure decisions and the relative unimportance of classless individual consumers; the prevalence of oligopoly in the product market; the pervasiveness of uncertainty, which rendered vacuous the maximisation of any objective function; and the powerful forces of circular and cumulative causation that undermined any form of equilibrium analysis. This last point was reinforced by his insistence that supply curves were irreversible, so that the process of economic growth was necessarily path-dependent.

1.2 Kaldor's growth theories: Mark I and Mark II

Kaldor's work on the economics of growth began soon after his arrival in Cambridge, as part of the efforts by British and American Keynesians to "generalise the *General Theory*" (King, 2002; Harcourt, 2006). Keynes had deliberately confined his analysis to the short period, in which investment was allowed to increase aggregate demand but not to add to productive capacity. It was a simplifying assumption, made in order to keep the argument manageable in much the same way that he had also restricted his analysis to the unrealistic but much more tractable case of a closed economy. The first attempt to extend the analysis to the long period came from Roy Harrod, who distinguished the actual rate of growth from the maximum or "natural" rate (given by population growth and technical progress), and both the actual and natural rates from what he termed the "warranted rate" (that rate of growth at which entrepreneurs were satisfied with the outcome of their investment decisions). There was no obvious reason why these three rates of growth should be equal.

The neoclassical solution to this problem was developed independently by Robert Solow and Trevor Swan, who relied on capital–labour substitution in response to changes in relative factor prices. In Harrod's growth equation, $g = s/v$, where g is the rate of growth, s the savings ratio and v the capital–output ratio, and both s and v are assumed to be constant. In the Solow–Swan growth model v becomes a variable, and this facilitates the adjustment of the warranted to the natural rate of growth. The underlying causal mechanism is Say's Law: saving drives investment, so that the capital stock (and the labour force) is always fully employed.

In the Cambridge (UK), "Anglo-Italian" or "Post-Keynesian" solution to Harrod's problem, developed by Nicholas Kaldor and Joan Robinson, it is s that varies, not v. Capitalists have a much higher propensity to save than workers, so that a redistribution of income from wages to profits, which might be expected to occur in a strong boom, will raise the average propensity to save, and this is what facilitates the adjustment of the warranted to the natural growth rate. Robinson always regarded the equality of the two growth rates as an unlikely accident that would occur in what she sardonically described as a "golden age". Between 1945 and 1973 the OECD countries did in fact enjoy rapid growth with more or less continuous full employment, and with hindsight this has often been described as "the golden age of capitalism". In his Mark I and Mark II growth models Kaldor assumed full employment of labour and capital, without ever really providing a convincing account of the causal mechanism that brought the warranted and natural growth rates into equality.

He set out his own, avowedly "Keynesian" theory in simple algebra. The model describes a capitalist economy in which total income (Y) is distributed between wages (W) and profits (P); investment (I) is equal to saving (S), which is the sum of saving out of profits (S_p) and out of wages (S_w). Kaldor thus wrote three identities: $Y \equiv W + P$, $I \equiv S$ and $S \equiv S_p + S_w$. With s_p and s_w as the propensities to save out of profits and wages respectively (both assumed to be constant), it can easily be shown that

$$P/Y = 1/(s_p - s_w).\ I/Y - s_w/(s_p - s_w).$$

"Thus", Kaldor concluded, "given the wage-earners' and the capitalists' propensities to save, the share of profits in income depends simply on the ratio of investment to output" (Kaldor, 1956a, p. 95). As he noted, the model works only if $s_p > s_w$. In the special case where $s_w = 0$, the profit share depends only on the savings propensity of the capitalists and the ratio of investment to income. In this case, $P/Y = 1/s_p.\ I/Y$. "The critical assumption", Kaldor continued, "is that the investment–output ratio is an independent variable" (Kaldor, 1956a, p. 96). He provided a simple numerical example. If I/Y is 20 per cent, $s_w = 0$ and $s_p = 50$ per cent, it follows that $P/Y = 40$ per cent; an increase in I/Y to 21 per cent will thus increase P/Y to 42 per cent (ibid., p. 96, n. 2).

In the context of economic growth, the investment–output ratio becomes a variable, given by the relationship between the rate of growth of capacity (G) and the capital–output ratio (v). Since $v = K/Y$ and $G = I/K$, $I/Y = Gv$. This was Harrod's first growth equation. Kaldor rewrote Harrod's second equation, $s = I/Y$, in terms of his own theory of distribution, that is, as $I/Y = (s_p - s_w). P/Y + s_w$. "Hence the 'warranted' and 'natural' rates of growth are not independent of one another; the former will adjust itself to the latter through a consequential change in P/Y" (ibid., p. 97).This did not mean that steady growth was inevitable. On the contrary, "the process of growth" might break down, in which case "the economy will relapse into a state of stagnation". This, Kaldor argued, might occur for several reasons. Entrepreneurs might be too pessimistic; an excessive degree of liquidity preference might put too high a floor under the rate of profit on capital, which (owing to uncertainty) must always exceed the rate of interest; and inadequate competition might lead to "over-saving" because of excessive profit margins. If none of these difficulties arose, "there will be an inherent tendency to growth and an inherent tendency to full employment. Indeed, the two are closely linked to each other" (ibid., p. 99). This last point was to prove extremely contentious, in what was supposed to be a "Keynesian" model of distribution and growth.

In the following year Kaldor published his first model of the growth process. The first and most controversial of the "basic properties" of the model was the assumption of full employment. As in 1956, he asserted baldly that "an equilibrium of steady growth is inconsistent with an under-employment equilibrium" (Kaldor, 1957, p. 594), since the process of growth must be treated as "a prolonged boom". The second basic property of the model was that Kaldor now rejected "any distinction between changes in techniques (and in productivity) which are induced by changes in the supply of capital relative to labour and those induced by technical invention or innovation". More capital per worker, he argued, almost inevitably involved improved technology, while technical progress generally had to be embodied in new capital equipment. Thus the orthodox distinction between movements along a given production function, and a shift in the function as a result of technical progress, was "arbitrary and artificial" (Kaldor, 1957, p. 596). He therefore replaced the static production function by a new Technical Progress Function, which related the rate of growth of output per worker to the rate of growth of capital per worker. Kaldor claimed that "the system will always tend towards the point where the growth in capital and the growth in productivity are equal" (Kaldor, 1957, pp. 597–8), which gave one of the historical constancies, or "stylised facts", that any growth theory had to be able to explain: a constant capital–output ratio. With constant savings propensities for both capitalists and workers, both the wage and profit shares and the rate of profit were also constant; these were additional "stylised facts". The profit rate itself "depends only on the rate of economic growth and the division of capitalists' income between consumption and saving, and is independent of everything else" (ibid., p. 613). This became known as the "Cambridge equation": $r = g/s_p$.

In 1962 Kaldor published a new, Mark II model of economic growth, retaining the full employment assumption of the Mark I analysis. But this did not entail full capacity utilisation, since markets were assumed to be imperfectly competitive and each entrepreneur "prefers to maintain an appreciable amount of excess capacity so as to be able to exploit any chance increase in his selling power either by increasing his share of the market or by invading other markets" (Kaldor and Mirrlees, 1962, p. 176). Thus full employment of labour did not mean full employment of capital. There was one further, and much more radical, change. The new model avoided "the notion of a quantity of capital, and its corollary, the rate of capital accumulation, as variables of the system; it operates solely with the value of current gross investment (gross (fixed) capital expenditure per unit of time) and its rate of change in time" (ibid., p. 175). Hence the Technical Progress Function was redefined. It now expressed the relationship between "the annual rate of growth of productivity per worker *operating on new equipment*" (ibid., p. 176; emphasis in the original), and the rate of growth of investment per worker (*not* the rate of growth of capital per worker, as in the 1957 model). It was still effectively a one-sector model, however, since the rate of technical progress was assumed to be the same in all sectors.

Even more than in the Mark I model, in Mark II technical progress was now

> the main engine of economic growth . . . determining not only the rate of growth of productivity but – together with some other parameters – also the rate of obsolescence, the average lifetime of equipment, the share of investment in income, the share of profits, and the relationship between investment and potential output (the "capital/output ratio" on new capital). (Kaldor and Mirrlees, 1962, p. 188)

The model was Keynesian in the important sense that entrepreneurs' expenditure decisions were primary, and it was "severely *non*-neo-classical" in denying any role to marginal productivities or marginal substitution ratios. There was no aggregate production function. "Everything depends on past history, on how the collection of equipment goods which comprises K_t has been built up" (ibid., p. 188). At this point Kaldor reverted to a theme that he had emphasised back in 1934 and then allowed to fade from view (Setterfield, 2003). It would later form an essential part of Kaldor's attack on the irrelevance of equilibrium economics.

1.3   Kaldor's growth theories: Mark III and Mark IV
The 1962 model was set at a very high level of abstraction, in an idealised one-commodity, one-country world where no distinction was made between the agricultural, manufacturing and service sectors and there were no balance of payments problems. It seems likely that Kaldor had become dissatisfied with it almost before it was published. His doubts intensified after 1964, when he became special adviser to the Chancellor of the Exchequer in the newly elected Labour government. In Whitehall Kaldor was forced to reflect on the real problems of the British economy – slow growth, the "stop–go cycle", chronic balance of payments problems and an overvalued currency – which seemed to have only the loosest connection with either his Mark I or Mark II models of growth.

In 1966 Kaldor gave a public lecture on "Causes of the Slow Rate of Growth in the United Kingdom". His analysis was quite different from anything he had previously published. Kaldor began by noting that between 1950 and 1965 output in the UK had grown much more slowly than in most other advanced capitalist economies. The principal reason for this was the "maturity" of the British economy, which he defined as "a state of affairs where real income per head has reached broadly the same level in the different sectors of the economy" (Kaldor, 1966, p. 3). This was significant because, almost alone among the industrialised countries, the UK had no reserves of surplus labour in low-productivity agriculture that could be transferred to the manufacturing sector. There was, Kaldor argued, a strong positive relationship between the rate of growth of total output and the rate of growth of output in manufacturing. This reflected the importance of increasing returns to scale, which had been emphasised by Adam Smith, by Alfred Marshall and above all by Kaldor's old teacher at the LSE, Allyn Young. For Young, increasing returns were dynamic rather than static in nature; they were related to the *growth* of output, not the *level* of output. They were connected with learning, which was itself the product of experience, and they were a "macro-phenomenon", since each industry benefited from the expansion not just of its own output but of output as a whole (ibid., p. 9). Increasing returns were found in the secondary sector (public utilities, construction and manufacturing), but *not* in the primary or tertiary sectors. Kaldor now introduced the Verdoorn Law, discovered by the Dutch economist P.J. Verdoorn (1949): productivity growth is a function of output growth. Regressing the rate of growth of labour productivity in manufacturing on the rate of growth of manufacturing output in 12 countries between 1953–54 and 1963–64, Kaldor reported, revealed that it was the slow growth of manufacturing output that had been primarily responsible for Britain's slow productivity growth rate.

What was it, then, that had constrained manufacturing output growth? Kaldor emphasised supply rather than demand, and distinguished two types of supply constraint: commodities and labour. For any individual country, commodity supply problems tended to take the form of a balance of payments constraint, since otherwise the necessary commodities could simply be imported. Even in the absence of balance of payments difficulties, however, the labour constraint would have been binding. "In post-war Britain", Kaldor claimed, "periods of faster growth in manufacturing industry invariably led to severe labour shortages which slowed down the growth of output and which continued for some time after production reached its cyclical peak" (ibid., p. 25). This, in turn, was a reflection of the country's economic maturity.

Kaldor's new model was ignored by the economic historians and won little support from his fellow economists. Characteristically, Kaldor himself soon abandoned the labour shortage explanation of Britain's slow rate of growth, instead emphasising poor export performance. This was reinforced by his reading of British economic history. Here he drew on his understanding of the lessons of global development over the previous two centuries, which showed that "both the level and the rate of growth of output of the capitalist sector are dependent on the level, or rate of growth, of the effective demand for its products coming from *outside* the capitalist sector" (Kaldor, 1977, p. 198; emphasis in the original). This led him to another fundamental proposition, namely "the doctrine of the 'foreign trade multiplier', according to which the production of a country will be determined by the *external* demand for its products and will tend to be that multiple of such demand which is represented by the reciprocal of the proportion of *internal* incomes spent on imports". This, Kaldor continued, pointed to a demand-side theory of growth, in which the availability of capital and labour was the result of "the growth of external demand over a long series of past periods" (ibid., p. 199).

Kaldor did not really offer a model of this process. He did not even write the formula for the (static) foreign trade multiplier, which Harrod had done back in 1933: $Y = 1/m.X$, where Y is the level of output and m is the propensity to import. Still less did Kaldor provide any formal analysis of the determinants of m. To be fair, this was not the purpose of the paper, which was instead to offer a new interpretation of British economic history in which the nation's industrial growth had been export-led from a very early date. After 1945, Kaldor noted, Germany, Italy and Japan had enjoyed the benefits of export-led growth, while Britain had again lagged behind because it had been replaced by consumption-led growth (Kaldor, 1977, pp. 202–203). This was partly the fault of the early Keynesians, including Kaldor himself, who had worked from a closed economy model that was not appropriate for an open economy like Britain. They had "treated the problem of full employment and (implicitly) of growth as one of internal demand management, and not [as] one of exports and of international competitiveness" (Kaldor, 1971, p. 5).

He had made similar points in an influential paper on the case for regional policies, which began by noting that the huge discrepancy in growth rates between rich and poor nations since 1750 could be regarded as a regional issue, albeit on a global scale (Kaldor, 1970). It could not, however, be explained in terms of different resource endowments. A growing capital stock, in particular, was as much the result of rapid economic development as its cause. Kaldor invoked Gunnar Myrdal's principle of "circular and cumulative causation" (Myrdal, 1957), according to which any initial advantage that one region might possess, relative to other regions, tended to increase when trade was opened up between them, rather than diminishing, as orthodox theory would lead one to expect. Hence there was a need for regional policies to induce convergence (instead of divergence) between advantaged and disadvantaged regions. Kaldor again invoked Verdoorn's Law, but with a new twist. The growth of productivity in manufacturing was positively related to the rate of growth of manufacturing output, which in turn – and this was the novel aspect – depended solely on the rate of growth of exports. The case for regional policies followed directly from this analysis.

1.4   North and South

Some of the themes that Kaldor emphasised in his post-1966 work on growth had already emerged in his thinking on economic development. Why, he asked, had Western Europe and North America pulled away from the rest of the world so dramatically after 1750? What was responsible for the enormous differences between rich and poor countries in real income per head? Kaldor denied that the answer lay in excessive population growth, lagging technical innovation or inadequate rates of saving and capital accumulation. These were all *consequences* of slow economic growth, and not the fundamental cause, which was the changing human attitude to risk-taking and profit-making. Kaldor pointed to the survival, especially in agriculture, of a "traditionalist outlook" that discouraged risk-taking and profit-making (Kaldor, 1956b).

Although Kaldor was a strong advocate of industrial development, he did not support the import substitution industrialisation that had been adopted by many developing countries in response to the collapse of their export markets in the Great Depression. He had no objection to the principle of import substitution or to the protection of infant industries, but protective measures must be moderate, discriminating and selectively applied, first encouraging the development of "light industries" (such as textiles), with "heavy industries" (such as chemicals, steel and engineering) coming later. This was a veiled – but presumably deliberate – attack on the Stalinist approach to industrialisation, in which consumer goods production was sacrificed to the rapid expansion of the capital stock, so that priority was given to "heavy" over "light" industry. The Latin American countries, Kaldor argued, had implemented indiscriminate protection, encouraging the growth of high-cost industries that were unable to compete in export markets; this explained the continent's chronic balance of payments problems. Although he was not a free trader, Kaldor's vision of industrialisation in the Third World was always outward-looking, with growing exports of manufactured goods invariably at the heart of his policy prescriptions (Kaldor, 1974).

The fate of the global South was, of course, inextricably linked with the growth performance of the global North. The "golden age" of the world capitalist economy came to a sudden end in 1973 as inflation accelerated, output fell and unemployment increased in all the rich countries, with dramatic consequences for the rest (all except those that were large net exporters of oil). Kaldor's explanation of the great stagflation began in the global North, but emphasised the importance of primary product prices and hence of the global South. He concluded that global macroeconomics must be done in terms of two-sector models, and must place the terms of trade between primary products and manufactured goods at the centre of the analysis. International commodity price agreements were essential to provide price stability, Kaldor maintained; they should be supported by the holding of substantial buffer stocks of the most important foodstuffs and raw materials, and these stocks should be used as backing for a new international currency (Kaldor, 1976).

In his 1984 Mattioli lectures, published posthumously, Kaldor formalised the argument somewhat, without adding anything substantial to it (Kaldor, 1996, pp. 39–54). Finally, in his 1985 Hicks lecture, he returned to the important question of the long-run trend in commodity prices, rejecting the neo-Malthusian approach taken by the Club of Rome and reaffirming his support for the Prébisch-Singer thesis that the long-run tendency in the relative price of primary products in terms of manufactures was downwards. Land-saving technical change in agriculture, combined with fierce price competition between producing nations which ensured that "the benefits of technical progress of *both* [industry and agriculture] tend to accrue to the *industrial* sector", cast serious doubt on the fears of the neo-Malthusians (Kaldor, 1986, p. 197; emphasis in the original).

1.5 *The irrelevancy of equilibrium economics*

For Kaldor, the Mark III and Mark IV growth models had fundamental methodological implications. Myrdal's principle of circular and cumulative causation demonstrated the limitations of equilibrium analysis and the necessity for growth theory to be nested in a deeper understanding of the social and political framework of each individual country. Kaldor developed an aversion to the closed-system modelling that appealed so strongly to the great majority of mainstream economists. He attacked "the irrelevance of equilibrium economics", criticising Walrasian theory as "barren and irrelevant as an apparatus of thought to deal with the manner of operation of economic forces, or as an instrument for non-trivial predictions concerning the effects of economic changes, whether induced by political action or by other causes" (Kaldor, 1972, p. 1237).

Far from making progress, Kaldor maintained, economics had been going backwards in terms of its scientific status ever since "the theory of value took over the centre of the stage – which meant focusing attention on the *allocative* functions of markets to the exclusion of their *creative* functions – as the instrument for transmitting impulses to economic change" (ibid., p. 1240; emphasis in the original). Economic change was inescapably path-dependent. This entailed that technical progress was endogenous, undermining Harrod's notion of a "natural" rate of growth determined by the supposedly exogenous growth rates of the labour force and of technical change (Kaldor, 1996, p. 36). Thus macroeconomic theory could not be timeless, derived from a set of universal axioms about rational human behaviour, but must instead be historically specific (Kaldor, 1996, pp. 4, 41–2). It followed that economists should be modest about their ability to predict, which "becomes progressively less as we consider the more distant future as against the nearer future" (Kaldor, 1985, p. 62).

1.6   Kaldor and his critics

Kaldor's macroeconomic theory of distribution provoked a torrent of criticism from the defenders of neoclassical orthodoxy, who objected that his results were valid only under particular (and unrealistic) values of his parameters (Harcourt, 1972, Chapter 5). His early growth theories were also heavily criticised for lacking "the discipline of a coherent, consistent macroeconomic model" (Dorfman, 1961, p. 496) and relying on "extreme over-simplification" (Baumol, 1961, p. 411). There was also friendly fire, with Geoff Harcourt (1963) objecting to the full employment assumption and Kurt Rothschild (1959) complaining about the limited number of variables that Kaldor considered, the simplicity of their functional relationships and the neglect of historical, sociological and institutional factors. Jan Kregel summarised the differences between Joan Robinson's approach to the theory of economic growth and that of Kaldor. "For Kaldor stability is a natural property of long-period analysis", Kregel noted, while "for Professor Robinson it is a myth" (Kregel, 1973, p. 187). This led Kaldor to his highly contentious assumptions of full employment and neutral technical progress. These strictures are relevant to the Mark I and Mark II models but not to Kaldor's later thinking on growth, and it is possible that Robinson's criticisms, faithfully reflected in Kregel's summary, did finally sink home. His later writings on growth do reflect the profound suspicion of equilibrium theorising that he had revealed in one of his very first papers (Kaldor, 1934), but had subsequently forgotten.

Kaldor's post-1966 interpretation of the "lessons from Britain's experience" was not shared by the majority of economic historians. Nicholas Crafts rejected his analysis, attributing the country's slow growth after 1945 to supply-side factors, including poor industrial relations, low and misdirected spending on research and development, poor technical education and poor management. Similar factors also accounted for the poor growth record of the UK in the much longer term, from 1870 to 1950 (Crafts, 1991, pp. 270–81). The emergence of so-called "new growth theory" in the years immediately before his death was, however, a substantial vindication of Kaldor's insistence that technical change could not be treated as exogenous and that returns to scale were increasing, not decreasing (at least in manufacturing). But the neoclassical proponents of "endogenous growth" also made many of the serious errors that he had identified many years before, disinterring the aggregate production function and resurrecting the marginal productivity theory of distribution, both of which should have been laid to rest in 1966 when the Cambridge (US) side conceded defeat in the great capital controversies.

But there were real problems with Kaldor's own ideas on growth. First, he always assumed that dynamic increasing returns to scale reflected the special role of manufacturing. But these are two separate propositions. There may well be increasing returns to scale in modern corporate agriculture – Kaldor never took account of the great differences between agribusiness and peasant farming – and in many business service activities that have themselves become very closely integrated with manufacturing, more narrowly defined. A second and related criticism concerns the increasing diversity of the activities that Kaldor lumped together as "manufacturing", which range from elementary "screwdriver assembly" operations carried out by unskilled workers to the production of "elaborately transformed manufactures" with a very high input of scientific and technical knowledge. Related to this was Kaldor's failure to take into account in his thinking on growth the "new international division of labour", in which low-skilled manufacturing operations have increasingly moved to the global South. "Who needs manufacturing?", Kaldor's mainstream critics ask. "Leave it to the Chinese". At any rate, the word "manufacturing" probably conceals as much as it reveals. For this reason all empirical work on Kaldor's growth laws may prove to have been mis-specified.

A third, and again related, criticism is that Kaldor entirely ignored intellectual property and the income accruing from its ownership, which was important in his lifetime and has become massively more important since his death. It is also true that he did not especially emphasise the role of human capital (as opposed to physical capital) in thinking about economic growth. Fourth, and finally, there is a very important question about the direction of causation (Caves, 1968). Does output growth cause productivity growth, through scale economies and the reduction of the average age of the capital stock? Or does productivity growth cause output growth by shifting supply curves outwards, reducing prices and increasing sales? Or both? And in what proportions?

To summarise: Kaldor's writings did not add up to a comprehensive and coherent alternative to mainstream economic theory, and indeed he himself never really aspired to anything of the sort. But he did supply a large set of rich and provocative ideas, positive as well as negative, to be used in the construction of an alternative economics of growth.

2 The Kaldorians

2.1 Introduction
Three classes of growth theory can legitimately be termed Kaldorian. These are the balance-of-payments-constrained growth models of A.P. Thirlwall and his co-authors; models of increasing returns and circular and cumulative causation in the tradition of Young, Verdoorn and Myrdal; and elaborations of Kaldor's own global, North–South model. The three theories overlap to a considerable extent, but it will be convenient to treat them separately. In conclusion, brief reference will be made to some points of contact between Kaldorian and other non-mainstream thinking on growth.

2.2 Balance-of-payments-constrained growth
The Harrod trade multiplier, discussed in section 1.2 above, was a short-period, static construction. It was extended to the long period and applied to theory of economic growth by Kaldor's first biographer, A.P. Thirlwall (1979), who has published extensively on these matters. The essential reference is McCombie and Thirlwall (1994); an excellent short summary is provided by McCombie and Roberts (2002).

Thirlwall's Law states that, for any individual country (or region), the balance-of-payments-constrained growth rate is

$$g_B = \varepsilon z / \pi, \qquad (1)$$

where ε is the world's income-elasticity of demand for the country's exports; π is its own income-elasticity of demand for imports; and z is the rate of growth of world income. This can be expressed as

$$g_B = x/\pi, \tag{2}$$

where x $(=\varepsilon z)$ is the rate of growth of exports. Equations (1) and (2) can also be written in a more complicated version that incorporates the price-elasticities of demand for exports and imports, but most advocates of Thirlwall's Law follow Kaldor in assuming that non-price competition is fundamentally important in international trade, with the implication that fluctuations in exchange rates cannot be relied on to restore balance of payments equilibrium. Thus the parameters ε and π depend more on product quality, innovation, marketing and after-sales service than on relative prices. Kaldor himself noted that, in the 1950s and 1960s, those industrialised countries whose currencies depreciated had a declining share of world trade; this has been described as "Kaldor's paradox" (McCombie and Thirlwall, 1994, pp. 298–99).

Equations (1) and (2) give the maximum rate of growth that is consistent with balance of payments equilibrium (that is, a zero current account deficit). Sensitivity analysis reveals that international capital flows do not make much difference to the balance of payments constraint on economic growth (McCombie and Roberts, 2002, pp. 92–6). The analysis does not, of course, entail that the constraint will be binding on all countries, at all points in time. A useful taxonomy of the six possible cases, involving all the relevant combinations of the warranted, natural and balance-of-payments-constrained growth rates, is provided by Thirlwall (2001).

How, exactly, does the constraint operate? Three mechanisms can be distinguished. First, in extreme cases like Cuba in the 1990s and Zimbabwe in the 2000s, a shortage of foreign exchange makes it impossible fully to operate the existing capital stock (since spare parts can no longer be imported), and growth declines or becomes negative. Second, during the fixed exchange rate regime imposed by the Bretton Woods system (1945–73), governments were forced to implement deflationary monetary and fiscal policies to protect the currency in face of often quite small payments deficits. This generated the "stop–go" cycle that Kaldor regarded as the principal cause of Britain's poor growth performance in this period. Third, in a floating exchange rate regime, the principal constraint on output growth is the rate of growth of export demand. Kaldor himself came to believe that exports were the *only* source of autonomous aggregate demand, since all other categories of expenditure were fully determined by income: consumption directly, investment indirectly through the accelerator coefficient, and government spending indirectly through taxation receipts, themselves a function of income. This is a characteristically extreme position, which is difficult to justify. But it is not necessary to deny the existence of *some* autonomous consumption, investment and government spending in order to recognise the importance of export demand as a factor in economic growth. For most small countries, and for all regions within countries, exports are indeed the most important factor.

Three (related) questions remain contentious. First, what are the policy implications of the model? Second, what determines the values of the two crucial parameters, ε and π? Third, are we really dealing here with a demand-side theory of growth, or have Crafts's supply-side factors been smuggled back in to the analysis once again, as determinants of ε and π?

2.3 Beyond Verdoorn

Thirlwall's Law is an equilibrium relationship, which sits uneasily with Kaldor's own categorical rejection of equilibrium economics. To be genuinely Kaldorian, some elements of circular and cumulative causation, increasing returns and path-dependence must be introduced into the balance-of-payments-constrained growth model. The first attempt to do so was by Dixon and Thirlwall (1975), who sought to provide an analytical basis for constant (that is, neither converging nor diverging) *regional* growth rate differences; the model can, however, easily be applied also to national differences. There is a strong flavour of balance-of-payments-constrained growth: "All investment is induced" in this model, with exports as the only source of autonomous demand (Dixon and Thirlwall, 1975, p. 203, n.5). The Verdoorn relation is written as

$$r_t = r_a + \lambda(g)_t, \tag{3}$$

where r_t is the average rate of growth of labour productivity; g_t is the rate of growth of output; r_a is the rate of "autonomous" productivity growth (that is, the rate at which productivity would grow if output were constant); and λ is the Verdoorn coefficient. The final expression for g_t is much more complicated than this (ibid., p. 205, equation 8), but the underlying argument is simple. Differences between regions in the Verdoorn coefficient (λ) lead to differences in regional growth rates. Even if λ does not vary across regions, it will amplify any inter-regional differences in the other parameters: "once a region obtains a growth advantage, it will keep it. . . In models of cumulative causation, this is the essence of the theory of divergence between 'centre' and 'periphery' and between industrial and agricultural regions" (ibid., pp. 205–206). The policy implications are also clear. To raise a region's growth rate it is necessary to make it more competitive in inter-regional trade and/or to change the industrial structure in favour of industries with a higher income-elasticity of demand. The same arguments apply across countries. Dixon and Thirlwall conclude that devaluation is likely to ossify the industrial structure, and instead propose export promotion and "import substitution properly directed" to stimulate growth in lagging regions and countries (ibid., p. 211).

This has become the "standard model" of cumulative causation in the Kaldor tradition (McCombie, 2002, p. 83). It has been criticised for failing adequately to encapsulate the spirit of Kaldorian path-dependency, though it can be extended to analyse the traverse from the initial to the ultimate growth rate, with the parameters changing over time in what is intended to be a model of "evolutionary hysteresis" (Setterfield, 2002, p. 216). This might overcome objections to the equilibrium nature of the Dixon–Thirlwall model, given Kaldor's own strong opposition to all equilibrium theorising. Empirical evidence on the Verdoorn coefficient is summarised in McCombie et al. (2002); see also Pieper (2003) and Reinert (2005). Some measurement problems are discussed by McCombie (2002, pp. 95–9). They include the possibility of simultaneous equation bias and the difficulty of distinguishing Verdoorn's Law (a long-run relation between output growth and productivity growth) from Okun's Law (a short-run, cyclical relationship between the levels of output and productivity).

Verdoorn's Law itself has been subject to a variety of explanations, which are not necessarily inconsistent with each other. It "may result from a combination of 'learning by doing' and increasing returns at the firm level, together with an increasing degree of specialisation at the inter-firm or inter-industry level" (McCombie, 2002, p. 75). There are obvious parallels both with the early Smithian analysis of increasing returns by Allyn Young (1928) and with post-1975 mainstream developments in "new" or endogenous growth theory, though Chandra and Sandilands (2005) argue convincingly that that the latter fails adequately to represent many of Young's fundamental insights, subsequently adopted by Kaldor. As intimated by Dixon's and Thirlwall's allusion to "centre" and "periphery", these insights are also highly relevant to the third set of Kaldorian growth models, which have a global or North–South emphasis.

2.4   North-South growth models

The informal character of Kaldor's own work on this question has often been noted. He "provides a suggestive sketch of a model but it is merely a sketch" (Skott, 1999, p. 366). Early formalisations of the North–South model came from David Canning, Amitava Dutt, Hassan Molana and David Vines, Ferdinando Targetti and A.P. Thirlwall (King, 1994, Part IV). More recently, in an extended review of Kaldor's (1996) Mattioli lectures, Peter Skott (1999) set out an elaborate model of a world economy with diminishing returns in agriculture and increasing returns in industry. Sustained growth is possible in this model, avoiding the dangers of a Malthusian trap, so long as the "average" returns to scale, taking primary and secondary production together, are non-decreasing. The effects of agricultural supply shocks are more complicated. A negative shock will induce global stagflation, as Kaldor argued, but the consequences of a positive shock (that is, one that reduces the price of agricultural products in terms of manufactures) depend on the precise assumptions made about the determinants of investment in the agricultural sector. Almost certainly Skott makes more concessions to mainstream thinking than Kaldor would have found acceptable. His aim is to establish an equilibrium growth path. There are aggregate production functions in both sectors, with neoclassical technology in agriculture and Leontief (fixed-coefficient) technology in industry. The positive effect of increased saving on the growth rate is obviously non-Keynesian (Skott, 1999, pp. 362–3). Although Skott does invoke Verdoorn's Law (ibid., p. 359, equation 7), there is also little or no cumulative causation, path dependence or hysteresis in his model.

An alternative version, closer to the spirit of Kaldor's work, takes as its starting-point W. Arthur Lewis's model of economic development, in which the surplus product in agriculture operates as a binding supply constraint. In the model of Amit Bhaduri and Rune Skarstein, in contrast to Skott, "the availability of agricultural surplus . . . is exogenous, but the extent of its *realisation* into purchasing power is governed endogenously by demand from industry" (Bhaduri and Skarstein, 2003, p. 588, italics in the original). In the short run an increase in the demand from the industrial sector for primary products generates higher purchasing power in agriculture and expands the sector's capacity to import, setting in motion the familiar Harrod trade multiplier process. In the long run the dynamic (Thirlwall) trade multiplier applies, slightly revised to express the relative growth rates of the two sectors as functions of the "purchasing power elasticities of imports by agriculture and industry, respectively" (ibid., p. 590). Engel's Law suggests that industry will grow more rapidly than agriculture, but whether this will shift the long-run terms of trade in favour of primary products depends also on the strength of real wage resistance, and the forces preserving profit mark-ups, in the industrial sector.

Bhaduri and Skarstein conclude, with some justice, that their version of the

North–South model incorporates two of Kaldor's most important insights. First, industrial growth is generated by agriculture's demand for manufactured exports, not by industrial investment (still less by saving in the industrial sector). Thus Kaldor's insistence on the trade multiplier and agricultural demand for industrial output as the central mechanisms for analysing the problem of industrial growth is confirmed. Second, industry may benefit from an *adverse* movement in the terms of trade, since less favourable terms of trade for industry increase the purchasing power of agriculture over industrial goods, thereby expanding the market for industrial exports (ibid., p. 592). As with Skott, however, this is an equilibrium analysis that lacks any significant element of cumulative causation or path dependence. It also neglects Kaldor's emphasis on speculative price volatility in the primary sector as a powerful negative influence on global growth. It would be fair to conclude that, while some aspects of his thinking have found their way into later models of North–South growth, many of Kaldor's theoretical insights have proved immune to systematic analysis or comprehensive formalisation.

2.5 Kaldor and other non-mainstream approaches

There are several points of overlap between Kaldorian and Schumpeterian (or neo-evolutionary) thinking on growth. Kaldor himself expressed strong interest in some of Schumpeter's ideas, in particular on the role of entrepreneurship and social institutions (Kaldor, 1956b), and of course on the overriding importance of technological change. However, neither Kaldor nor his followers have used explicit evolutionary analogies or attempted to model evolutionary processes. Kaldorian growth theory has little or nothing to say about the diffusion of innovations, and its predominantly macroeconomic focus is rather different from the microeconomic perspective of the Schumpeterians.

The Kaldorians are much closer to Kaleckian thinking on growth. There is the same insistence on modelling the real features of actual capitalist economies, with emphasis placed on the different resources and behaviour of capitalists and workers and the crucial role of profits as the driver of investment and growth. Kaldor and Kalecki both took a strong interest in economic development, and the Polish economist's emphasis on the external constraints on growth in poor countries is very similar to the balance-of-payments-constrained growth models of the Kaldorians. There are also significant differences, including Kaldor's dismissal of the degree of monopoly theory of income distribution as a tautology (Kaldor, 1956a, p. 92) and his rather orthodox views on incomes policy, which imply a rejection of the Kaleckian "paradox of costs".

Despite Kaldor's own vigorous criticism of Karl Marx, there are also similarities between Kaldorian and Marxian models of growth. Both agree that economic theory must be historically and socially specific, and should focus on the profit-driven investment decisions of capitalists rather than the consumption decisions of "representative agents". The Cambridge growth equation (see section 1.2 above) can be derived very easily from the extended reproduction models of *Capital*, Volume II, and Marx would certainly have approved of Kaldor's insistence on the unstable and inherently cyclical character of capitalist growth. Marxians would, however, be dismayed by Kaldor's hostility to the labour theory of value, and critical of his "stylised facts" that rule out any tendency for the profit share to increase or the profit rate to fall in the process of capitalist growth. Just possibly the Kaldorian North–South models might form the basis for a modern theory of imperialism, but Marxians have taken very little interest in them, thus far.

One original attempt to reconcile Kaldor and Marx is that of Mark Setterfield and John Cornwall, who take ideas from the French "regulation school" and the US "social structure of accumulation" approach to Marxian political economy, and derive a "neo-Kaldorian" model to explain the slowdown in global growth at the end of the golden age (1945–73). In this model a central role is played by the *macroeconomic regime* in each episode of growth, which involves "a process of income generation embedded within a historically specific institutional framework". Institutional change leads to discrete parameter changes and thence to variations in the rate of growth, bringing about "distinct and relatively enduring growth episodes" (Setterfield and Cornwall, 2002, p. 67).

2.6   Kaldorian growth policy
For Kaldor and the Kaldorians, economics is fundamentally a policy science, grounded in the reality ("stylised facts") of the global capitalist economy and with a distinctly practical focus. They reject the mainstream dichotomy between short-period and long-period analysis. Path dependency entails that "history matters", in the short period no less than the long period. Growth is not a stable process, and the historical phenomena of stop–go cycles (in the 1950s and 1960s) and stagflationary crises (in the 1970s and – almost – the late 2000s) illustrate just how important it is to "get the short period right". Thus Kaldor (1996) argued for expansionary fiscal policy and cheap money to restore full employment, an incomes policy to control inflation, international agreements to stabilise commodity prices, and also import controls where necessary to maintain growth in countries with severe balance of payments difficulties. He was strongly opposed to monetarism and other free market excesses, but also rejected both Stalinist and Fabian varieties of centralised state socialism.

In the long period, Kaldorians favour industrial policies to promote growth, paying special attention to export promotion and the problems of backward regions within advanced economies; this is sometimes described as "supply-side Keynesianism". For developing economies they propose a strategy of export-led industrialisation, with a system of dual exchange rates and perhaps also import controls to relieve the balance of payments constraint on economic growth. Kaldorian policies are thus quite distinctive, and involve strong criticism of mainstream economics, neoliberal globalisation and the Washington Consensus.

2.7   Kaldor and the Kaldorians
Evidently there is no single, definitive Kaldorian model of economic growth. Kaldor himself changed his mind repeatedly in the course of his long career, and his followers have thus been able to draw on a wide range of different, and sometimes inconsistent, ideas that can all be found in his extensive writings on growth. Nonetheless, some important common themes can be discerned in the Kaldorian literature. Some are methodological: the need for realism in theory construction; the significance of cumulative causation, increasing returns to scale and path-dependence; the dangers of equilibrium theorising. Others are substantive: the analysis of a capitalist economy, in which business expenditure decisions are central; the importance of demand constraints on growth; the critical role of export demand in determining the growth rate. The Kaldorians also

share some unorthodox views on policy with respect to growth, both domestic (doubts as to the effectiveness of currency depreciation; the need for industry policy) and international (the case for primary product price stabilisation agreements). It is their focus on growth as a problem of the global economy, however, that is perhaps the most distinctive characteristic of this important group of heterodox theorists.

References

Baumol, W.J. (1961). "Review of N. Kaldor, *Essays on Value and Distribution* and *Essays on Economic Stability and Growth*", *American Economic Review*, **51**(3), 409–13.

Bhaduri, A. and Skarstein, R. (2003). "Effective demand and the terms of trade in a dual economy: a Kaldorian perspective", *Cambridge Journal of Economics*, **27**(4), 583–95.

Caves, R.E. (1968). "Market organization, performance, and public policy", in R.E. Caves and associates, *Britain's Economic Prospects*, Washington, DC: Brookings Institution, pp. 279–323.

Chandra, R. and Sandilands, R. (2005). "Does modern endogenous growth theory adequately represent Allyn Young?", *Cambridge Journal of Economics*, **29**(3), 463–73.

Crafts, N.F.R. (1991). "Economic growth", in N.F.R. Crafts and N.W.C. Woodward (eds), *The British Economy Since 1951*, Oxford: Clarendon Press, pp. 261–90.

Dixon, R.J. and Thirlwall, A.P. (1975). "A model of regional growth-rate differences on Kaldorian lines", *Oxford Economic Papers*, **27**(2), 201–14.

Dorfman, R. (1961). "Review of N. Kaldor, *Essays on Economic Stability and Growth* and *Essays on Value and Distribution*", *Journal of Political Economy*, **69**(5), 495–7.

Harcourt, G.C. (1963). "A critique of Mr. Kaldor's model of income distribution and economic growth", *Australian Economic Papers*, **2**(1), 20–36.

Harcourt, G.C. (1972). *Some Cambridge Controversies in the Theory of Capital*. Cambridge: Cambridge University Press.

Harcourt, G.C. (2006). *The Structure of Post-Keynesian Economics*. Cambridge: Cambridge University Press.

Kaldor, N. (1934). "A classificatory note on the determinateness of equilibrium", *Review of Economic Studies*, **1**, 122–36.

Kaldor, N. (1956a). "Alternative theories of distribution", *Review of Economic Studies*, **23**(2), 83–100.

Kaldor, N. (1956b). "Characteristics of economic development", *Asian Studies*, **1**(1), 19–23.

Kaldor, N. (1957). "A model of economic growth", *Economic Journal*, **67**(268), 591–624.

Kaldor, N. (1966). *Causes of the Slow Rate of Economic Growth of the United Kingdom: An Inaugural Lecture*, Cambridge: Cambridge University Press.

Kaldor, N. (1970). "The case for regional policies", *Scottish Journal of Political Economy*, **17**(3), 337–48.

Kaldor, N. (1971). "Conflicts in national economic objectives", *Economic Journal*, **81**(321), 1–16.

Kaldor, N. (1972). "The irrelevance of equilibrium economics", *Economic Journal*, **82**(328), 1237–55.

Kaldor, N. (1974). "The role of industrialization in Latin American inflation", in D.T. Geithman (ed.), *Fiscal Policy for Industrialization and Development in Latin America*, Gainesville, FL: University of Florida Press, pp. 14–28.

Kaldor, N. (1976). "Inflation and recession in the world economy", *Economic Journal*, **86**(344), 703–14.

Kaldor, N. (1977). "Capitalism and industrial development: some lessons from Britain's experience", *Cambridge Journal of Economics*, **1**(2), 193–204.

Kaldor, N. (1985). *Economics Without Equilibrium*. Cardiff: University College of Cardiff Press.

Kaldor, N. (1986). "Limits on growth", *Oxford Economic Papers*, **38**(2), 187–98.

Kaldor, N. (1996). *Causes of Growth and Stagnation in the World Economy*. Cambridge: Cambridge University Press.

Kaldor, N. and Mirrlees, J. (1962). "A new model of economic growth", *Review of Economic Studies*, **29**(3), 174–92.

King, J.E. (ed.) (1994). *Economic Growth in Theory and Practice: A Kaldorian Perspective*. Aldershot, UK and Brookfield, USA: Edward Elgar.

King, J.E. (2002). *A History of Post Keynesian Economics Since 1936*. Cheltenham, UK, Northampton, MA, USA: Edward Elgar.

King, J.E. (2009). *Nicholas Kaldor*. Basingstoke: Palgrave Macmillan.

Kregel, J.A. (1973). *A Reconstruction of Political Economy*. London: Macmillan.

McCombie, J. (2002). "Increasing returns and the Verdoorn Law from a Kaldorian perspective", in J. McCombie, M. Pugno and B. Soro (eds), *Productivity Growth and Economic Performance: Essays on Verdoorn's Law*. Basingstoke: Palgrave Macmillan, pp. 64–114.

McCombie, J.S.L. and Roberts, M. (2002). "The role of the balance of payments in economic growth", in M.

Setterfield (ed.), *The Economics of Demand-Led Growth: Challenging the Supply-Side Vision of the Long-Run*. Cheltenham, UK and Northampton, MA, USA: Edward Elgar, pp. 87–114.

McCombie, J.S.L. and Thirlwall, A.P. (1994). *Economic Growth and the Balance-of-Payments Constraint*. Basingstoke: Macmillan.

McCombie, J., Pugno, M. and Soro, B. (2002). "Introduction", in J. McCombie, M. Pugno and B. Soro (eds), *Productivity Growth and Economic Performance: Essays on Verdoorn's Law*. Basingstoke: Palgrave Macmillan. pp. 1–27.

Myrdal, G. (1957). *Economic Theory and Underdeveloped Regions*. London: Duckworth.

Pieper, U. (2003). "Sectoral regularities of productivity growth in developing countries: a Kaldorian interpretation", *Cambridge Journal of Economics*, **27**(6), 831–50.

Reinert, E.S. (2005). "Development and social goals: balancing aid and development to prevent 'welfare colonialism'", *Post-autistic Economics Review*, **30**, 21 March 2005, article 1, available at http://www.paecon.net/PAEReview/issue30/Reinert30.htm

Rothschild, K.W. (1959). "The limitations of economic growth models: critical remarks on some aspects of Mr. Kaldor's model", *Kyklos*, **12**(4), 567–86.

Setterfield, M. (ed.) (2002). *The Economics of Demand-led Growth: Challenging the Supply-Side Vision of the Long-run*. Cheltenham, UK and Northampton, MA, USA: Edward Elgar.

Setterfield, M. (2003). "A model of Kaldorian traverse: cumulative causation, structural change and evolutionary hysteresis", in J. McCombie, M. Pugno and B. Soro (eds), *Productivity Growth and Economic Performance: Essays on Verdoorn's Law*. Basingstoke: Macmillan, pp. 215–33.

Setterfield, M. and Cornwall, J. (2002). "A neo-Kaldorian perspective on the rise and decline of the Golden Age", in Setterfield (ed.), *The Economics of Demand-led Growth: Challenging the Supply-Side Vision of the Long-run*, Cheltenham, UK and Northampton, MA, USA: Edward Elgar, pp. 67–86.

Skott, P. (1999). "Growth and stagnation in a two-sector model: Kaldor's Mattioli lectures", *Cambridge Journal of Economics*, **23**(3), 353–70.

Targetti, F. (1992). *Nicholas Kaldor: The Economics and Politics of Capitalism as a Dynamic System*. Oxford: Clarendon Press.

Thirlwall, A.P. (1979). "The balance of payments constraint as an explanation of international growth rate differences", *Banca Nazionale del Lavoro Quarterly Review*, **128**, 45–53.

Thirlwall, A.P. (1987). *Nicholas Kaldor*. Brighton: Harvester.

Thirlwall, A.P. (2001). "The relation between the warranted growth rate, the natural rate, and the balance of payments equilibrium growth rate", *Journal of Post Keynesian Economics*, **24**(1), 81–7.

Verdoorn, P.J. (2002 [1949]). "Factors that determine the growth of labour productivity", in J. McCombie, M. Pugno and B. Soro (eds), *Productivity Growth and Economic Performance: Essays on Verdoorn's Law*. Basingstoke: Macmillan, pp. 28–36.

Young, A.A. (1928). "Increasing returns and economic progress", *Economic Journal*, **38**(152), 527–42.

8 The paths of transformational growth

Davide Gualerzi

1 Introduction

Transformational growth is the key concept of a long-term theory centered on structural transformation and the growth of the market. It defines an approach to the analysis of the growth pattern that has characterized the development of advanced industrial economies as a result of the operations of the market. The focus, however, is not on the allocation function of the market, but rather on its mode of operation as an institution of change determining *the forms of economic development and their evolution*. At the same time, the structure of the market, its "structural development", is the object of the analysis. Transformation is the key to the main question, the growth of the market, an issue that (a) addresses the problem of the demand side of economic development; and (b) changes the very outlook on the process of growth and the role of the market in development. Transformational growth is, then, a particular perspective from which to analyze growth patterns, with their inherent uncertainties and periodical tendencies towards stagnation. We have an established history of this process, which the theory aims at interpreting, but the future directions it can take are ultimately open-ended. The question of the paths of transformational growth is of great importance for advanced market economies, and helps to put into perspective the ultimate causes of the severe recession that we now face at the end of the 2000s.

The dynamics of transformation affect many aspects of the economic analysis of industrial systems, most notably the role of government, the functions of money and credit, and the evolution of the general institutional framework. The theory of transformational growth (TG) thus deals with the crucial questions addressed by economic theory. Ultimately, it is no less than a basis for the analysis of the operations of the market, and this explains its particular methodology, which brings together stylized facts, field work, and historical-empirical evidence in support of abstract theorizing.

Transformational growth theory was developed by Edward J. Nell, and those who have since followed the direction set out by his work. The approach is the topic of several existing contributions, including three books (Nell, 1988, 1992, 1998) and various research articles (see, in particular, Nell, 2002). Its distinguishing feature is that technical progress and structural evolution are discussed in the context of the growth of demand. TG therefore deals with themes central to the analysis of growth and structural change, a topic that, although discussed in a large literature, remains outside the mainstream of modern growth theory.[1]

2 Demand-led growth and transformational growth

2.1 Demand-led growth

To better understand the transformational growth approach it is useful to first examine the particular position it occupies within the theoretical framework of demand-led growth.

In a recent book, Thirlwall (2002) discusses the laws of development from a demand-led perspective, focusing on cumulative causation and export-led growth. He emphasizes that "It has been a central feature of most of my own work on growth to try and put demand back into growth theory" (p. 66). He argues that demand-led growth can better explain economic performance and convergence, therefore providing an alternative to neoclassical growth theory and its close associate new growth theory, both supply determined and highly aggregative. The differential growth performance of nations is better understood in terms of the idea that demand determines its own supply, rather than the pre-Keynesian view of supply creates its own demand.

In another book, Setterfield (2002) points out the various research lines originating from the criticism of the dominant supply-determined approach to growth. The rejection of Say's law is the first step, which leads in the different directions of various demand-led growth models. Despite the different vantage points from which one can look at the question, the fundamental challenge unifying these models is to show why and how demand matters in the long run, beyond the short-run framework in which Keynes discusses the principle of effective demand. The point, says Setterfield, is to bring back to the center of the discussion the great puzzle of effective demand. Thus, Nicholas Kaldor's contribution, which is the basis of Thirlwall's approach, is examined side by side with those of Keynes and Kalecki in a broader attempt to define a demand-side perspective on growth.

The contributions in these two books are quite successful at placing demand at the center of the analysis of growth and economic development. They do not, however, delve deeply into the question that the long-run process of development raises, that of the sources of demand within the growth process.

Where does Thirlwall's autonomous demand come from? Initially, demand comes from the development of agriculture, but later it is the demand for exports that matters, fueled by foreign income dynamics and the pattern of specialization of the economy. But if one looks closely at the growth-development process, the challenge confronting a theory of growth based on demand is to explain how demand comes about *endogenously*, as a result of the growth process, generating and regenerating demand. This is where cumulative causation appears incomplete.

Similarly, the central role played by effective demand in demand-led models suggests that a central question is: what determines investment in the long run? According to Halevi and Taouil (2002), investment, as a source of effective demand, is exogenous, the first mover of expansion. But isn't this peculiar, to take as exogenous the very fundamental stimulus to growth? Clearly, the source of demand must ultimately be seen as endogenous, resulting from an interaction between technology, development dynamics and other economic variables.

The theory of demand-led growth would therefore be strengthened if fundamental demand variables were not treated as exogenous (except for certain limited purposes). In other words, though clearly referring to endogenous processes originating within the dynamics of development, demand-led growth does not elaborate on the link between economic development and demand. This aspect is left largely uninvestigated theoretically, in favor of simply emphasizing the causal role of demand in the determination of long-run growth.

2.2 A theory of the growth of demand

Although sharing the fundamental focus on the demand side of economic development, the approach of transformational growth is rather broader than most other demand-led models. Specifically, it allows for analysis of the questions raised above concerning the origins of demand. Transformational growth, then, occupies a peculiar position in the framework of demand-led growth, contributing to that framework a theory of long-term transformation. Its distinguishing characteristic is its focus on structural change and the growth of demand.

In *The General Theory of Transformational Growth*, Nell (1998) argues that when looking at accumulation in a manner in keeping with Keynesian premises, we need to focus on demand growth. This is clearly a long-run issue and its understanding is necessary to put demand at the center of an alternative approach to growth. Getting to the question was difficult for the traditional growth model, that in essence is a "real economy model". Overlooking the role of finance made it plausible to concentrate the analysis on supply, since "there must be an expansion in the supply of some other goods with which to pay for the newly demanded set" (Nell, 2002, p. 251).

For a theory of effective demand and the sources of autonomous demand, what matters is the *theory of the growth of demand*. In other words, we may well agree that demand leads growth and economic development, and therefore have a theory of growth based on demand. But we need to explain where demand comes from. Structural change, an issue little discussed in demand led models,[2] is clearly fundamental to this question. Thus, a theory of the transformation of the economy, articulated in specific stages of development, is the key to unlocking the problem. Bringing demand back into growth theory requires, then, a theory of the growth of demand, explaining how demand grows in the long run and how it is generated endogenously by economic development.

2.3 Steady state and structural change

The notion of transformational growth represents the culmination of a key criticism of steady growth, leading ultimately to an alternative approach to growth theory. Steady growth, Nell (1982) argues, is not only virtually impossible, it would inevitably lead to stagnation. Transformational growth is then the process by which capitalism can, at least up to a certain point, sustain itself in the long run: "To work properly the system must grow, and to grow it must continually transform itself through the introduction of new products and new processes, creating new life-styles, redistributing income and generating new markets" (Nell, 1988, p. 159). Growth, therefore, depends on a complex process of change, which involves innovation, income redistribution and market expansion.[3]

Structural change, then, emerges as the key issue: there can be no growth without change in the structure of the economy, contrary to what is at least implicitly assumed by steady growth models. Moreover, structural change is clearly a fundamental aspect of the transformation through which demand grows. Nevertheless, structural change has received relatively little attention in the growth literature.

As pointed out by Pasinetti (1981, 1993, 2007), the other major theorist who has placed structural change at the center of the analysis of growth, proportional growth, which leaves sectoral proportions unaltered, is the only abstraction consistent with steady growth. But this, he argues, is "pseudo dynamics". Whereas Pasinetti's structural dynamics is held together by reference to a growth path maintaining full employment, transformational growth addresses the question of the actual pattern of transformation and how it can sustain itself in the long run. This is why, unlike the work of Pasinetti, the analysis of structural dynamics is combined with an analysis of institutional change and the stylized facts of historical transformation in the theory of transformational growth.

2.4   The growth of demand and new markets
A theory of demand growth inevitably leads us to examine the evolution of demand, and in particular changes in its composition and the creation of new markets.

Argyrous (2002) has pointed out that, despite "the often stated desire to use history rather than equilibrium as the methodological guidepost for the analysis" (p. 237), post-Keynesian theory has little to offer by way of an explanation for the evolution of effective demand and the consequent growth of markets. To fully confront the neoclassical view that demand is extraneous to the analysis, we need to analyze the development of markets from a historical perspective, as in the theory of transformational growth. Argyrous examines the ways in which "productivity growth induces an expansion of demand" (p. 241), the influences on demand expansion resulting from changes in its composition, and lastly the importance of the development of the capital goods sector. He concludes that the process of endogenous growth may encounter limits – for example, as services grow and manufacturing loses its role as engine of growth – and suggests a focus on changes in the structure of production and consumption. This appears necessary to complement the reference to the "mutually reinforcing feed-back between technology and market expansion" (p. 241), as articulated by Allyn Young in the 1920s, and models of cumulative causation centered on manufacturing in the Kaldorian tradition.

Nell (2002, p. 252) has observed that, once we recognize that "a separate account of the demand side is required" the work of reconstruction begins from a full appreciation of the distinction between investment decisions and investment spending, with the former determined by "the anticipated growth of markets" (p. 254). The expansion of existing markets (more or less mature) can be explained by the diffusion path of new products, shaped by the product life cycle, and the income-driven dynamics associated with the Engel curve. The more difficult problem is that of the creation of new markets (p. 257). That requires innovation, and an understanding of an ongoing process of structural transformation.

As we will see there are two major sources of new markets: the evolution of the social structure, with its effects on the structure of demand; and development scenarios driven by major facts of historical transformation or, in more abstract terms, by structural imbalances.

3   The issue: the creation of demand
Transformational growth most clearly indicates that the ultimate question for *demand-led growth* is the creation of demand and how that links up with the process of structural change. The theory should speak to the question: where does demand growth come from? Supply is obviously the result of productive capacity, however defined. The question is: what determines this capacity and why does it grow? The traditional answer is saving, and the motivation is profit. Introducing demand into the picture raises complications. Demand is spending, and spending appears a dominated rather than a dominating element. Moreover, while Keynes explained that investment leads savings, he developed

the principle of effective demand in a short-run framework. That has made it seem almost reasonable to argue that a long-run equilibrium will depend only on the overall supply of productive resources but the analysis of accumulation requires a demand side. Thus, the challenge for demand-led growth is to show that demand matters in the long run, that is, to develop a long-run theory of demand. The particular way in which transformational growth looks at the problem is to argue that what is ultimately required is a theory of the sources of demand growth. Demand grows because of new markets, which expand the market in the aggregate. This opens up a new direction of research and adds a fundamentally new dimension to demand-led growth theory.

Consider first how new markets emerge from the process of transformation. The starting point of such a process is the introduction of a "new principle", which means "a new way of accomplishing some general social purpose" (Nell, 1988, p. 160) identified with the fundamental necessities of social life, such as food, clothing, shelter, and so on. The application of this new principle "tends to generate an interlocked set of new products and processes, which create new activities and new social patterns, which in turn combine to create new ways of living, new forms of social life." The result is "the development of many new industries, and the expansion and modification of many old ones, to supply the needs of both new industries and new ways of living" (ibid.) Thus, transformational growth "tends to be expansive" since it stimulates investment (although that does not rule out the possibility of constraints emanating from the availability of labor). Along with changes in the structure of the economy as a result of the growth of new industries and the new technological requirements of production, the result is growth "creating new markets in the process" (ibid., p. 161).

This differs from what is customarily offered by economic theory, in which markets expand because of population and income growth – a view of the growth process that can be accommodated within a steady state growth framework. But Nell (1998, p. 17) argues that "there is another, more interesting way in which markets may expand" that has to do with transformation, which is thus revealed as not merely an additional feature of the growth process, but its very essence and engine.

Market expansion is examined with respect to a secular trend underlying the growth of capitalist economies, associated with the "conquest of domestic production" (ibid., p. 18) that takes place in the transition from craft- and family-based production to modern, factory-based mass production. This is an endogenous source of demand growth, at least until mass production reaches the mature stage.

> For the past century perhaps the chief impetus to growth has been the progressive invasion by industrial capitalism of the traditional province of the family. This has created the great consumer markets of the advanced West . . . The market and the state . . . have taken over most of the functions previously performed by the family. (1988, pp. 168–9)

As a result of this process, mass produced products have been substituted for those emanating from domestic and handicraft production. This has transformed the industrial structure *and* sustained market creation and accumulation.

There are, however, a number of reasons to think that the peak of this type of development was reached during the 1960s, and that the growth slowdown of the 1970s has a much deeper cause than that usually associated with the analysis of stagflation. Hence according to Nell (1988, p. 170):

> That, for better or worse has been the process of transformational growth. And, evidently, it has come to an end. Given the distribution of income, and in the absence of a major attempt to create new incomes for the poor, there is nothing left to transform.

The reasons why "transformation draws to an end" stem from the direction of structural evolution and its capacity to sustain the growth of demand.

> It is not a matter of a "shortage" of new inventions or of new technologies; in fact we are in an era of almost unprecedented technological innovation, coupled, paradoxically, with stagnation in investment. This is because many of these innovations tend to be labor displacing or market destroying, rather than expansionary. (ibid.)

Thus, the viability of transformational growth appears to depend on specific conditions. In particular, its future depends on the response to the tendencies towards secular stagnation that resurfaced with the crisis of mass production in the 1970s, when an alternative path of transformational growth was nowhere in sight.

4   The general theory of transformational growth

In *The General Theory of Transformational Growth*, Nell (1998) returns to this fundamental theme, presenting a theory of demand growth articulated in the context of a long-term general theory of transformation. This completes and supercedes his previous work on the same topic, bringing together theory and the use of empirical evidence in an alternative methodology for the analysis of macrodynamics.

Transformational growth is first contrasted with the main theoretical abstraction of modern growth theory, steady state growth. But it is not only the unsteady or non-proportional character of growth that is the defining feature of transformational growth, but also its combination of growth with "structural development" (p. 14). At the very root of the problem is the question "How can we explain the change from a traditional society in a stable condition of natural order to a growing society operating in a regularly progressive mode?" The question does not concern "historical details or specific events . . . It is a matter of theory and the issue is causality", namely, what caused the change from one to the other mode of operation of the economy, and what are the differences between the two. The answer is that "Broadly speaking . . . it was the development of the market" (p. 15). Is the latter the same thing as the growth of demand? To a large extent, yes. The question then is: *how does the market develop, fueling demand growth?*

At the core of the regularly progressive mode of economic activity is innovation, promoted by the generalization of the competitive pressures associated with the spread of the market. "This suggests that a universal competitive market system causes the economy to grow" (p. 16), but there are two qualifications, the market economy must be a capitalist economy. Second, "the markets must be expanding . . . Why should anyone invest and build more capacity, if there is no additional demand expected?" But this poses the fundamental problem: *what causes market expansion?*

It was noted earlier that the conventionally cited reasons for market expansion are population and/or income growth, which can be accommodated by a steady growth framework. The reasons for secular, but unsteady, market expansion relate to the way that markets take over "functions that were formerly carried out through non-market procedures" (p. 17). The conquest of domestic production by the market tells much of the story of the development of advanced industrial economies during the nineteenth century and even for the best part of the twentieth century. But still we need to explain: "how this invasion of the domestic sphere by the market began, and what forces kept it going" (p. 18). In general, it is an "imbalance in the economy", a structural imbalance, rooted in historical facts, such as the enclosure movement during the early stage of capitalism, which brings forward a response that fuels expansion. In the case of the enclosures, it was the creation of an urban-industrial setting, where new markets, and therefore new jobs, were created. "But this is not a one-time, exogenously caused imbalance; it is an imbalance which results from an ongoing process, an imbalance which will be reproduced if corrected" (p. 19). Transformational growth is then the long-term tendency of the economy to evolve by changing its sectoral composition.

There are stages in the process of transformational development. Nell defines four of them, from the period of early industry to that of computerized production, but a number of stylized facts suggest we can identify two patterns of growth, defined as pure types, these being the "craft" and the "industrial" economy (p. 30). In the craft system "growth simply replicates existing stationary relationships . . . By contrast, in the mass production system growth is a major agent of innovation and change and it is central to the normal working of markets . . . it is part of the competitive process" (p. 34). The reason for the different pressures to grow that characterize the two systems "lies in the different relationship of technology to competition in the two cases" (p. 31). This is reflected in different rules for price-setting in the two different systems.

The endogenous creation of demand, that is, the theory of demand growth, is the common element running through all of the stages of transformational development. Thus, while in "The long run growth of demand is governed by the development of the markets" (p. 34), the operation of the market, and more specifically market adjustment and the role of prices, must be analyzed with respect to the stylized facts of the old and new business cycle, distinguished by the different rules governing craft and mass production. But to analyze market expansion "We need to take a closer look at demand in a modern industrial economy" (p. 34).

Nell elaborates on the question of demand later on in the volume, focusing on the relationship between demand, pricing and investment plans (Chapter 10). Consistent with what was said above, the analysis distinguishes between two eras: "investment in Craft economies could be broadly described as supply driven, that is, governed by the natural rate. But in Mass production economies investment will be governed by technical progress and the expected growth of demand" (p. 467). In other words, in the era of mass production, growth is *demand-driven*. For that we need "an understanding of how and why markets grow, to provide the basis on which business can develop firm expectations of market expansion" (p. 465). Thus, while the very mechanism of growth in mass production underscores the role of the growth of demand, the latter flows from within the growth process and specifically from the forms it takes. Its investigation encompasses the analysis of household behavior and its relationship to growth.

Demand evolves following a complex pattern, in which the effects of prices are intertwined with the role played by changes in the social structure and investment in self-improvement. To analyze the growth of demand Nell distinguishes two classes, "the professional and managerial, and the working class" (p. 469) and focuses on spending on learning and the acquisition of skills as a way of gaining status. In fact, "households compete for status" (p. 473). Within the limits set by class income, it is the spread of a dominant lifestyle that fuels demand growth, although, in the long term, technology and rising income will lead to changes in lifestyle. The point is that assuming "a general increase in the level of real wages and salaries . . . could be expected to lift a section of the upper level of the working class to a level where they could command the resources to invest in 'self-betterment'" (p. 476). Furthermore, "the very investment in self-improvement that generates growth in demand will also increase productivity, causing the consumption–growth trade-off to shift out and up" (p. 477).

While the positive relation between the real wage and demand growth is a fundamental characteristic of the approach, it is only part of the story. Nell elaborates on various demand growth scenarios, one based on "colonies and/or the frontier for economies of the last century", and one based on the "Welfare State" for the post-war period concerning "spending on education, pensions, and health" (p. 480). But there is a third scenario, where differences between sectoral growth rates are the basis for the rise of new markets, so that "At the macrolevel the growth of demand results from changes in the structure of the economy" (p. 481).

These scenarios are associated with what Nell calls "'normal' growth of demand", that is, a rate of growth that can be reasonably expected as a central tendency, given the conditions defining the scenario. In the last scenario, however, the question is more complicated, since the relationship between new markets and current markets appears indeterminate. The role of marketing studies would be precisely that of analyzing the relationship between the two. The course of development implies that the normal rate of growth of demand will be progressively undermined and taken over by a new one, as the process of structural change unfolds, completes itself and is reproduced. "Thus, the history of capitalism will be the history of growth, driven by market expansions generated by structural changes, where the effect of the market expansion is to bring about further structural changes" (p. 482).

5   Long-term transformation: history, theory and method
Transformational growth focuses attention on the interdependence of structural change, demand composition and the growth of demand. The question then is: how does the market develop?

In this respect we must take notice of the historical circumstances that are relevant to the development of the market. A previously cited example is that of enclosures, which were central to the first stage of TG – that of the transition to craft production. Another example is the dynamics set in motion by migrations. Migration, of course, raises questions about the employment and income of immigrants, but can also provide a tremendous stimulus to market expansion. This created the pressure for mechanized production, and thus the onset of the industrial revolution.[4]

Historical circumstances, however, are not by themselves theoretical propositions. Those recalled above are indeed dramatic instances of long-run transformation. They suggest that "For growth to start up the economy must become imbalanced . . . [when] a structural imbalance is regularly reproduced it becomes a trend" (Nell, 1998, p. 19). This creates an incentive and an opportunity for innovation of a specific type. Initially this will happen in a few industries and in a few places and these will become centers of innovation and investment (ibid., p. 20).

The point is the following: examination of historical facts and empirical evidence leads to theoretical propositions. An intermediate step is the particular use of the notion of stylized facts. Stylized facts are a step up towards abstraction. They are based on observed trends and capture the most relevant characteristics of the process of change in the stages of transformational growth. They are associated with the behavior of markets and the effects on growth of the main economic variables (Nell, 1998, p. 41). Thus, transformational growth suggests that economic rules, adjustment processes and institutions change according to the phases of the process of transformation. They help to shape the concrete form taken by the emergence of new markets and new opportunities for investment, but also the limits within which transformation may continue.

This exemplifies the *method* of theorizing. On the one hand, starting from the observation of development trends, which are empirically confirmed by historical facts, such as the enclosure movement and migration from the countryside, Nell derives the theoretical propositions that substantiate the mechanism of growth and therefore the general theory of the transformation. On the other hand, a series of stylized facts define each era of transformational development, allowing for the analysis of economic relations, such as those pertaining to market adjustment, the monetary system and characteristics of financial markets. These stylized facts are then the manifestation of the underlying economic structure and institutions that characterize the old (up to World War I) and the new (post-World War II) business cycle. A consistent feature of the analysis is that history, not equilibrium, is at the basis of the analysis.

Thus, the TG approach contributes to two additional themes for the study of economic dynamics and demand-led growth: the relationship between theory and historical evidence and the role of stylized facts. Bringing together theorizing, stylized facts and long-term transformation defines an alternative methodology for the analysis of dynamics. Both the theory and method of TG constitute a criticism of the mainstream approach to macrodynamics, though the purpose is emphatically not criticism, but positive theory.

6   Demand, investment and technical change

The theory of transformational growth makes ample reference to history and stylized facts. Nevertheless, it focuses on theory. This is true both in the sense of addressing the theoretical questions underlying the particular view of Keynes after the reconstruction of the classical approach by Sraffa, and in the sense of defining the theoretical propositions that substantiate the mechanism of growth and therefore *the general theory of the transformation*. The ultimate focus of this constructive task is the rate of growth of demand and so, as stated earlier, a theory of the growth of demand.

The rate of growth of demand depends on the development of the market and in particular on the rise of new markets. Indeed, new markets are indispensable in determining new and higher levels of normal demand. It was suggested above that the analysis of new markets takes two main directions: one is linked to the evolution of the social structure, which affects the structure of demand; the other draws on the response to structural imbalances generated from within the growth process. A closer examination of all this will lead us directly to the question of the paths of transformational growth.

6.1   Demand theory
In Chapter 10 of *The General Theory of Transformational Growth*, Nell examines the foundations of a theory of consumer demand and then proceeds to outline the relationship of a changing composition of demand to growth.

As pointed out above, an evolving social structure is the result of the demand for new skills coming from production. Learning and the acquisition of skills, and investment in education and self-improvement especially, change the structure of final demand. This is associated with the spread of new ways of life, which creates the possibility of new markets. In this way, household budget decisions affect the composition of demand and productivity growth, and ultimately the growth of demand.[5] Nell (2002) elaborates on this theme. With a rising real wage, combined with "a Verdoon-Kaldor relationship, relating productivity growth to output growth and real wages" (p. 262), the effort of families to improve their social status explains changes in demand composition that will sustain demand expansion.

One of the main long-term consequences is the growth of expenditure on "collective goods and interactive services" (p. 264), such as education and communication, which in turn affects the volume and role of government expenditure.

But new markets arise not only from changes in the social structure, but also as a response to structural imbalances, an ongoing dynamic phenomenon, with the possibility of the two phenomena feeding back and reinforcing one another. Particularly important in this regard is a development scenario where differences between sectoral growth rates are the basis for the rise of new markets.

As pointed out above, this case highlights a complication, since the relationship between new markets and current markets appears indeterminate. Nell suggest that marketing studies – that is, studies of the actual (historical) creation of new markets – could help illuminate the balance between the two sets of markets. This also poses the question as to whether new markets, and thus the direction taken by the structural development of the market, are such as to ensure *market creation* to an extent capable of sustaining an adequate growth of demand?

6.2   Technical progress, investment and new markets
The question raised above is fundamental and concerns, above all else, investment decisions. If, in the era of mass production, growth is demand-driven, then investment plans depend on the expected growth of the market. This implies an investment theory that is essentially a generalization of the "accelerator" principle. Investment is driven by expected market expansion. Hence the fundamental importance of the scenarios of development on which these expectations, and investment decisions, are based. But how exactly do structural imbalances result in new markets? What should the marketing studies described above focus on?

The TG theory centered on market growth also clarifies the notion that technical change is a demand-led phenomenon. The direction of transformational growth is not technologically determined. Rather, technological change is driven by the same logic that shapes the development of the market, thus determining the possibility of new markets and market expansion, which in turn drives economic growth. Technology and innovation, which are typically treated as supply-side phenomena, thus become demand-led phenomena because of their association with *investment*.

This is an important change of perspective. Unless we think of innovation purely in terms of cost-cutting, the association between investment and innovation leads inevitably to consideration of new products and new industries. Differences in sectoral growth rates underscore changes in the pattern of investment, with new investment unevenly distributed towards innovative sectors. The result is a changing industrial structure. This suggests that our focus should be on what drives changes in the composition of investment. It must be some form of autonomous investment, and the question is then: what motivates this autonomous investment? Although essentially a bet on the future, autonomous investment necessitates a rather different view of the relationship between expected demand and investment spending. This relationship cannot be the same as the one underlying "traditional" induced investment, for the simple reason that demands for final output have yet to be articulated, but are instead discovered and made actual only subsequently.

We do not need to question the notion of expected demand that is at the basis of induced investment, but simply distinguish between induced and autonomous investment. In the process of market development, which accounts for the growth of demand, there are stages (Gualerzi, 2001) and in the first of these stages expected demand is no more than a potential to be transformed in actual markets by investment in new products and the rise of new industries. This is why we can speak of potential demand, rather than expected demand. In successive stages, investment can be more directly determined by the growth of demand, as postulated by the fundamental idea behind the accelerator.

Technical progress and structural change are a demand-led phenomenon not only because they respond to expected market growth, but also because they serve the very process of constructing the market (Gualerzi, 2001). This, in turn, highlights the particular role of investment in responding to structural imbalances: taking advantage of technical progress to create new markets. It follows that investment in new products and new industries is a major force in shaping new markets through the process of structural transformation. The two notions of expected demand can be brought together in a consistent view of the structural development of the market. In the process, they become the key to the directions taken by the process of transformational growth, a crucial issue, particularly in the period since the crisis of mass production.

7   The paths of transformational growth

7.1   The end of transformational growth?

The paths of transformational growth are the possibilities inscribed into the transformation as we have observed it so far and the directions it can take. This emphasizes the capacity of the approach to address, from a theoretical perspective, fundamental issues relating to the prospects for long-run growth in advanced market economies, which follow from the less than robust growth performance of these economies (compared to that of the 1960s or that of emerging economies) in recent decades.

While the transformation associated with the transition from family-based artisan and domestic production to modern industrial production is the paradigmatic example of long-run transformation sustaining the development of the market and thus the growth of demand, how did that extend into the decades following the 1970s crisis?

Nell argues that transformational growth is the process underlying the restructuring of industrial capitalism and in particular it is "the kind of growth the US experienced during the 1920s, during the war and for the twenty years after the war" (1988, p. 162). It is based on a process whereby expansion tends to be self-sustaining.

> With new products and new processes coming on line generating new ways of life and new markets employment will be high, productivity and real wages will be growing, profits will be high and capital will be accumulating rapidly, while prices will tend to be stable as cost cutting will tend to offset increases due to high demand. A high level of investment spending means a boom in the investment goods sector; with high employment and high wages in the capital goods sector, the consumer goods sector will also prosper. And the effects will be cumulative. . . . Transformational growth, then, tends to encourage a boom. (Nell, 1988, p. 163)

Following the general idea that development scenarios are associated with a "normal" growth of demand, continuously reproduced by the rise of new markets – that is, the structural development of the market – we could say that mass consumption led market expansion up to the 1960s, and that the 1970s growth slowdown was largely caused by the lack of further dynamism of consumption patterns, thus weakening the process of transformational growth. Up to the 1960s markets grew in tandem with the rising prosperity of new social classes and subclasses. But by the 1970s the ability of mass production to create and expand markets had largely run its course. The sources of growth had become largely exhausted and new ones were not in place yet.

So the question is: what is the pattern of growth in the advanced industrial economies following the end of mass production (consumption) of the post-war period? The theory of long-term transformation and demand growth can guide the effort of analyzing and speculating on these questions. What comes to light is the possibility of interpreting the expansive cycles after the 1970s, and in particular the 1980s recovery and the hi-tech boom of the 1990s. Indeed, even the slowdown that followed and the new crisis in the 2000s can be seen in a new light.

7.2 The 1980s and the 1990s
To pursue the analysis of the paths of transformational growth we ought to discuss the specifics of the expansion cycles of the 1980s and the 1990s and how the response to the crisis of mass production was articulated during these two decades.

The end of transformational growth seems to depend on the lack of any clear alternative to mass production. Indeed when growth entered a period of stagnation "the setting up of the information economy, had hardly begun" (1988, p. 171). Conservative public policy only made things worse.[6] On the other hand, the importance of a growing new hi-tech sector (Nell, 1998, p. 34) is associated with a fourth stage of transformational growth, identified with computerized production and biotech agriculture. The last 20 years have seen a progressively clearer articulation of this stage and in particular of a now more clearly defined scenario associated with the "information economy" (1998, p. 701).

One of the major trends of transformation concerns the growing impact of new information and communication technologies (ICTs) on the economy. ICTs fueled the boom during the second half of the 1990s, and what has been called the new economy. Focusing on technological advances involves nothing more than analyzing the fundamental relationships between technology, structural change and new markets that are at the core of the TG approach.[7]

Seemingly the distinguishing novelty of the 1990s, the theme of hi-tech had already characterized the debate on growth and industrial restructuring during the 1980s, but with differences that are worth analyzing. In the 1980s the new information technologies were still not able to create the conditions for new markets at a sufficient rate. But the emerging consumption patterns were quite different from those of mass consumption. In the era of mass production, social groups whose incomes were rising and who usually had a common form of employment, became self-aware and adopted new lifestyles. This created a mass market, and encouraged an investment boom. During the 1980s, however, innovation in consumption took the form of new upgraded goods and services for the wealthy, leading to an evolution of consumption associated with glamorous modes of life and "consumption deepening" (Gualerzi, 2001). But a glamor boom for the wealthy is not the answer to the end of mass consumption; this will not re-establish high growth rates.

Nevertheless, the boom of the ICT sector in the 1990s should be seen as the result of the maturing of a technological trajectory involving the advances of basic science in the fields of electronics and computer science and the rise of a hi-tech industrial complex that stretches back to the 1980s. The dominance of ICTs in the 1990s was incubated during the preceding decade. But the structural change and dynamics of consumption, as well as the effects on market creation and macro-performance, were different.

ICTs flowered during the second Clinton administration (1996–2000), allowing at least *a first glimpse of a new pattern of development*. Indeed, the ICT sector seemed to cause an acceleration of growth during this period. It is well known that the expansion culminated in a phase of high growth rates and stock market euphoria. The return to high growth rates (by post-war standards) seemed to have convinced some that we had entered a phase of *unlimited growth*. But the dramatic correction in the stock market and the uncertain prospects of the economy at the end of the 1990s cooled this enthusiasm for the prospects of hi-tech driven growth.

The problem is that, together with the possibilities of new markets, the transformation soon signaled the limits to an "internet scenario of development", that is, the difficulties of combining a sustained process of market creation and income growth with a pattern of growth centered on ICTs (Gualerzi, 2010). It is not yet clear whether, after more than 20 years, the information economy is a sufficient alternative to mass production to ensure an adequate growth of demand. Thus, the questions posed at the end of the 1990s expansion concern: (a) the long-run consequences of new technology as measured by their stimulus to market growth; (b) the difficulty of articulating a new stage of transformational growth and the open-ended question of the directions it can take. Answering these questions is made all the more problematic by the fact that the further expansion of debt that followed the bursting of the ICT bubble seems to have created the worse growth scenario since the Great Depression.

Thus, considering the particular circumstances facing the US economy and advanced market economies in general, transformational growth appears most useful precisely because it directly leads to analysis of variations in growth and the nature of the problems underlying tendencies towards stagnation. Rather than technological development per se, it suggests that the main issue is that of the opportunities and limitations for the creation of new markets based on technology advances. TG theory can help to better understand the obstacles standing in the way of the "knowledge economy". These include problems of institutional development and appropriate policies for addressing the questions arising from structural transformation. Indeed, a neglected aspect of full employment policies might be precisely asking the question of the sources of demand in the long run, together with the institutional arrangements most conducive to a transformation of consumption patterns along socially desirable lines. Salvation is not ensured, but this only makes investigation of the pattern of long-term transformational growth and the directions it can take all the more compelling.

Notes

1. The approach bears some fundamental similarities to that of John Cornwall (see, for example, Cornwall and Cornwall, 2001).
2. There is, of course, recognition that structural change is imbedded in the process of development, as pointed out by the role played by manufacturing in cumulative causation. It would therefore be incorrect to say that growth remains an entirely aggregate notion; nevertheless, structural change is hardly a central element of the analysis.
3. "A capitalist industrial system, being inherently dynamic, has two and only two long run options – transformational growth or stagnation. . . . These two choices tend to alternate, giving rise to the appearance of 'long waves' in economic life" (Nell, 1988, p. 163).
4. Note that the focus on the development of the market from a historical perspective echoes the debate on the transition from feudalism to capitalism, and Dobb's argument about the rise of trade and towns progressively undermining the system centered on serfdom and feudal social relations (Dobb, 1963).
5. Notice that in this way changes in the composition of demand more effectively establish the link between consumption and growth than discussions of "variety" in consumption found in neoclassical endogenous growth theory.
6. A massive attack on poverty might well have created new markets on the scale needed; but the War on Poverty failed, and redistribution ran in the opposite direction, starting in the 1980s.
7. This is not to say that other factors were not also influential on the boom and bust (Gualerzi and Nell, 2010).

References

Argyrous, G. (2002). "Endogenous demand in the theory of transformational growth", in M. Setterfield (ed.), *The Economics of Demand-Led Growth*. Cheltenham, UK and Northampton, MA, USA: Edward Elgar.
Cornwall, J. and Cornwall, W. (2001). *Capitalist Development in the Twentieth Century*. Cambridge: Cambridge University Press.
Dobb, M. (1963). *Studies in the Development of Capitalism*. New York: International Publishers.
Gualerzi, D. (2001). *Consumption and Growth: Recovery and Structural Change in the U.S. Economy*. Cheltenham, UK and Northampton, MA, USA: Edward Elgar.
Gualerzi, D. (2010). *The Coming of Age of Information Technologies and the Path of Transformational Growth*. London: Routledge.
Gualerzi, D and Nell, E. (2010). "Transformational growth in the 1990s: government, finance and hi-tech". *Review of Political Economy*, **22**, 97–117.
Halevi, J. and Taouil, R. (2002). "The exogeneity of investment: from systemic laws of accumulation and growth to effective demand conditions", in M. Setterfield, (ed.), *The Economics of Demand-Led Growth*. Cheltenham, UK and Northampton, MA, USA: Edward Elgar.
Nell, Edward J. (1982). "Growth, distribution and inflation, *Journal of Post Keynesian Economics*, **5** (1), 104–13.
Nell, Edward J. (1988). *Prosperity and Public Spending*. London: Allen & Unwin.
Nell, Edward J. (1992). *Transformational Growth and Effective Demand*. New York: New York University Press.
Nell, Edward J. (1998). *The General Theory of Transformational Growth*. Cambridge: Cambridge University Press.
Nell, Edward J. (2002). "Notes on the transformational growth of demand", in Setterfield, *The Economics of Demand-Led Growth*. Cheltenham, UK and Northampton, MA, USA: Edward Elgar.
Pasinetti, L.L. (1981). *Structural Change and Economic Growth*. Cambridge: Cambridge University Press.
Pasinetti, L.L. (1993). *Structural Economic Dynamics*. Cambridge: Cambridge University Press.
Pasinetti, L.L. (2007). *Keynes and the Cambridge Keynesians. A "Revolution in Economics" to be Accomplished*. Cambridge: Cambridge University Press.
Setterfield, M. (2002). *The Economics of Demand-Led Growth*. Cheltenham, UK and Northampton, MA, USA: Edward Elgar.
Thirlwall, A.P. (2002). *The Nature of Economic Growth. An Alternative Framework for Understanding the Performance of Nations*. Cheltenham, UK and Northampton, MA, USA: Edward Elgar.

PART II

AGGREGATE DEMAND, AGGREGATE SUPPLY AND LONG-RUN GROWTH

9 On accounting identities, simulation experiments and aggregate production functions: a cautionary tale for (neoclassical) growth theorists
Jesus Felipe and John McCombie[1]

1 Introduction

A *sine qua non* of neoclassical growth theory is the existence of an aggregate production function. It is the very first equation of Solow's (1957) seminal paper. The widely used growth accounting approach, following Solow's (1957) seminal work, as well as the recent developments in endogenous growth theory, are grounded in the aggregate production function. (See, for example, Barro and Sala-i-Martin, 2004, especially Chapters 4 and 10.) Yet it has been known for a long time just how flimsy are its theoretical foundations. Indeed, Solow (1957, p. 312) himself conceded that "it takes something more than the usual 'willing suspension of disbelief' to talk seriously of the aggregate production function". But this reservation was quickly glossed over – it "is only a little less legitimate a concept than, say, the aggregate consumption function".

The theoretical criticisms of the aggregate production function involve both the "aggregation problem" that dates from the 1940s and the Cambridge capital theory controversies of the 1960s and 1970s. Fisher (1992) has shown with respect to the former that the problems of aggregation are so severe that the aggregate production cannot be said to exist – not even as an approximation.[2] The Cambridge capital theory controversies proved to be more controversial and generated a great deal of heated debate in the leading academic journals. Fisher (2003) has argued that the issues involved are merely a subset of a more general aggregation problem, although Cohen and Harcourt (2003a, 2003b) consider that there is more to it than that. Nevertheless, whatever viewpoint one subscribes to, both serve to demonstrate the shortcomings of the neoclassical production function.

It is remarkable that although these arguments have been around for over half a century and while they were briefly acknowledged in textbooks and surveys in the 1970s, any reference to them has all but completely disappeared from the current literature. This is notwithstanding that there has been no convincing refutation of these criticisms. They have simply been assumed away or ignored.

So why is the aggregate production function so widely and uncritically used? The answer seems to involve a form of Friedman's (1951) methodological instrumentalism. All theories, so the argument goes, involve heroic abstraction and unrealistic assumptions, but what matters is their predictive ability. The aggregate production function, it is argued, passes this test with flying colours. The problem with this defence, as we shall show, is that the estimation of a putative aggregate production function using constant-price monetary (value) data cannot provide any inferences about the values of the putative parameters of the production function (output elasticities, aggregate elasticity of substitution) or the rate of technical progress. The reason is that there is an underlying accounting identity that relates these variables. This identity can be easily rewritten in a form that resembles a production function. This precludes any meaningful estimation of the "production function" and interpretation of the coefficients as estimates of an underlying technology. This critique is arguably the most damaging for the aggregate production function, because it applies even if there were no aggregation problems.

This is not a new critique, but first came to prominence in a rudimentary form in Phelps Brown's (1957) criticism of Douglas's cross-industry regression results (see, for example, Douglas, 1948), and elements of it can be traced back to Bronfenbrenner (1944) and Marshak and Andrews (1944). The critique was later formalised by Simon and Levy (1963) and Shaikh (1974, 1980, 1987) generalised it to time-series estimation of production functions. Simon (1979a) also considered the criticism in the context of both cross-section and time-series data and thought it serious enough to mention it in his Nobel prize lecture (Simon, 1979b). The criticism was re-examined and extended by Felipe and Adams (2005), Felipe and McCombie (2001, 2003, 2005a, 2005b, 2006, 2007), Felipe (2001a, 2001b), Felipe and Holz (2001), McCombie (1987, 1998a, 1998b, 2000–01, 2001), McCombie and Dixon (1991) and McCombie and Thirlwall (1994). The critique as applied to cross-section data was also "rediscovered" by Samuelson (1979).

While Cramer (1969), Wallis (1979) and Intriligator (1978) in their econometric textbooks, and Walters (1963) in his survey on production and cost functions, have mentioned the argument, none pushed it to its logical conclusion: namely, that it invalidates any attempt to test, or estimate, the aggregate production function, per se. (See McCombie, 1998a, for a discussion.) Solow (1974, 1987), it is true, did attempt refutations of a couple of aspects of the critique, but these are not compelling (Shaikh, 1980, McCombie, 2001, Felipe and McCombie, 2005a).

The implications of the critique are far reaching. It implies that all those areas of neoclassical macroeconomics that use the aggregate production function (with, or without, the assumption that factors are paid their marginal products) have no theoretical or empirical basis. Because of the accounting identity, any estimation of a putative aggregate production function can be made, through a suitable specification, to give a perfect fit to the data with constant returns to scale and with the output elasticities equalling the respective factor shares. This is true even though the aggregate production function does not exist and, for example, individual firms may be subject to substantial returns to scale. Consequently, the estimation of aggregate production functions is problematic, to say the least.

One way of forcefully illustrating the critique is to use simulation experiments. The advantage of this approach is that it allows us to know precisely what is the underlying micro-structure of the economy. Suppose, for example, the Cobb-Douglas production function gives a good fit to the aggregated data when we know that either the underlying technology of the firms in no way resembles the Cobb-Douglas production function, or, if it does, the conditions for successful aggregation are (deliberately) violated. This should at least give us reason to pause for thought. To this end, we review four simulation exercises that clearly demonstrate just how flimsy are the foundations of the aggregate production function and, hence, neoclassical growth theory. First, however, we briefly review the critique.

2 Aggregate production functions and the accounting identity

The standard analysis of neoclassical production theory is well known and so is only briefly recapitulated here. The production function, which is essentially a microeconomic concept, in a general form is written as:

$$Q_t = f(K_t, L_t, t) \tag{1}$$

where Q, K, L, and t are output, capital, labour and a time trend that acts as a proxy for technical change. Theoretically, Q and K should be measured in *homogeneous physical units* as equation (1) is a technological relationship (Ferguson, 1971). Equation (1) may be expressed in growth rates as:

$$\hat{Q}_t = \lambda_t + \alpha_t \hat{K}_t + \beta_t \hat{L}_t \tag{2}$$

The symbol ^ above a variable denotes a growth rate, α and β are the technologically determined output elasticities of capital and labour and λ is the rate of technical change, all of which may change over time.

If there is perfect competition and firms are paid their marginal products, then it can be simply shown that the following holds:

$$\hat{Q}_t = \lambda_t + a_t \hat{K}_t + (1 - a_t) \hat{L}_t \tag{3}$$

where a_t and $(1 - a_t)$ are the factor shares.

From Euler's theorem, using equation (1), output may be written in constant-price value terms as:

$$p_0 Q_t = p_0 f_{Kt} K_t + p_0 f_{Lt} L_t = \rho_t K_t + w_t L_t \tag{4}$$

where ρ is the rental price of each machine (i.e. the price per unit of time) and w is the wage rate, both measured in constant-price money terms and p_0 is the base-year price. From the dual, given the usual neoclassical assumptions, equation (3) can be derived by differentiating equation (4) as:

$$\hat{Q}_t = a_t \hat{\rho}_t + (1 - a_t) \hat{w}_t + a_t \hat{K}_t + (1 - a_t) \hat{L}_t \tag{5}$$

where $\lambda_t = a_t \hat{\rho}_t + (1 - a_t) \hat{w}_t$.

Such a discussion appears in all standard microeconomic textbooks and is carried seamlessly over into macroeconomic textbooks with no discussion of the problems involved in applying this analysis to the whole economy or a particular industry.

But, as we noted above, constant-price monetary data have to be used empirically to measure both output and capital, and it is here that an insurmountable difficulty arises both at the firm and industry levels. From the national accounts, the following identity must always hold at any level of aggregation:[3]

$$V_t \equiv r_t J_t + w_t L_t \tag{6}$$

where r is the rate of profit (a pure number) and w is the average real wage rate. V is value added and J is the constant price value of the capital stock, usually calculated by using the perpetual inventory method. We use V instead of Q and J instead of K to emphasise the distinction between constant-price monetary values and physical units. The total compensation of capital is given by the rate of profit (which in competitive capital markets equals the rate of interest) multiplied by the constant price value of the capital stock, that is, $r_t J_t$. It also equals the rental price of capital multiplied by the number of machines, that is, $\rho_t K_t$. Consequently, the relationship between J_t and K_t is $J_t = (\rho_t/r_t)K_t$.[4] In other words, from equation (6), the sum of total profits and the total compensation of labour *must* equal value added. Equation (6) can also be written, in growth rates, as:

$$\hat{V}_t \equiv a_t\hat{r}_t + (1 - a_t)\hat{w}_t + a_t\hat{J}_t + (1 - a_t)\hat{L}_t \tag{7}$$

It can readily be seen that equation (7) is formally equivalent to equation (5) when the latter is summed over firms and Q and K are expressed in constant prices.[5] In these circumstances, $\hat{r}_t$, which is the growth of the rate of profit (a pure number), equals $\hat{\rho}_t$. But it should be noted that equation (7) does not require *any* of the neoclassical assumptions used to derive equation (5), including the existence of an aggregate production function. Thus, equation (5), when expressed using monetary values for output and capital, must always hold by virtue of the identity given by equation (6), and may give the misleading impression that equation (5) holds for any level of the economy, notwithstanding the aggregation problems, which are erroneously assumed to be negligible.

Neoclassical production theory generally uses a specific functional form for equation (1), such as a Cobb-Douglas, CES, or translog production function. This is then estimated to derive values for the parameters of interest, such as the aggregate elasticity of substitution. This does not affect the argument. If equation (6) is expressed in *instantaneous* growth rates and then integrated, we derive, purely as a result of a mathematical transformation, the result that at a specific time τ:

$$V_\tau \equiv r_\tau J_\tau + w_\tau L_\tau \tag{8}$$

$$\equiv B_0 r_\tau^{a_\tau} w_\tau^{(1-a_\tau)} J_\tau^{a_\tau} L_\tau^{(1-a_\tau)} \tag{9}$$

$$\equiv A_\tau J_\tau^{a_\tau} L_\tau^{(1-a_\tau)} \tag{10}$$

B is the constant of integration and is equal to $a_\tau^{-a_\tau}(1 - a_\tau)^{-(1-a_\tau)}$. The shares are "constant" because only one point of time (τ) is being considered. Consequently, if we use data for an economy or industry for, say, any one year, then the right-hand side of equations (8), (9) and (10) will give *identical* values for value added. Consequently, at any point of time, a Cobb-Douglas will always give a good fit to the data, simply as an alternative mathematical way of writing the identity given by equation (6). More generally, if several periods are considered, equation (10) is an alternative way of writing the accounting identity if factor shares are constant over the time periods being considered.

If we use cross-industry or cross-regional data and estimate $V_i = AJ_i^\alpha L_i^\beta$ in logarithmic form, it follows from equation (10) that we should find an almost perfect fit to the extent that the variation in the logarithm of the wage rate and the rate of profit is small and the factor shares do not greatly differ across observations. This is precisely what Douglas's many cross-sectional regressions in the 1930s found, with the coefficients on capital and labour nearly identical to their factor shares. Although, of course, this result is purely an artefact of the accounting identity, Douglas (erroneously) concluded that it proved the neoclassical theory of distribution and refuted the Marxian theory (Douglas, 1976).

Returning to time-series estimation, a stylised fact is that there is no discernible trend in the rate of profit, that is, $\hat{r}_t = 0$, over the long run and the growth of the real wage grows at a roughly constant rate, that is, $\hat{w}_t = \hat{w}$. Moreover, it is generally found that factor shares are roughly constant over time, that is, $a_t = a$ and $1 - a_t = 1 - a$. (A constant mark-up pricing policy will, inter alia, give this result.)[6] Hence the identity given by equation (6) may be expressed as:

$$V_t \equiv r_t J_t + w_t L_t \equiv A_o e^{\lambda t} J_t^a L_t^{(1-a)} \tag{11}$$

where $\lambda = (1 - a)\hat{w}$. Equation (11) is nothing more than the accounting identity, but resembles a Cobb-Douglas relationship where $\alpha \equiv a$ and $(1 - \alpha) \equiv (1 - a)$.

But why do estimations of production functions not always give good statistical fits? The fact that they do not may give the impression that production functions are actually behavioural equations. The poor regression results could be because of two reasons. First, factor shares may vary considerably over the estimation period and, second, the path over time of the weighted rate of profit and the wage rate $(a_t \hat{r}_t + (1 - a_t)\hat{w}_t)$ may not be sufficiently accurately proxied by a linear time-trend (λ). In other words, the two assumptions to transform equation (6) into equation (11) may be empirically incorrect. Using simulation analyses, McCombie (1998a) and Felipe and Holz (2001) have shown that variations in factor shares do not prevent the Cobb-Douglas form from generally yielding acceptable results.

It is the second assumption, that is, the approximation of $(a_t \hat{r}_t + (1 - a_t)\hat{w}_t)$ through a linear trend that is more often incorrect, and this can significantly bias the coefficients on the capital and labour variables and can even be responsible for suggesting, for example, that there are increasing returns to scale. But the fit to the identity can always be improved by the introduction of a suitable non-linear time trend (and there is nothing in neoclassical production theory that says technical progress has to be a linear function of time). Alternatively, including a suitable capacity utilisation variable or adjusting the capital and labour input for the intensity of use can have the same effect. If factor shares vary over time, then a functional form that is more flexible than the Cobb-Douglas (such as a Box-Cox transformation, which turns out to be similar to the CES) could always be used. This implies that if the path of the factor shares is not assumed to be constant, equation (6) can be transformed into functional forms that resemble CES or translog production functions. See, for example, Felipe and McCombie (2001) for the derivation of the CES from the identity.

The argument is simple and devastating. There is no point in estimating production functions using value (monetary) data. There are qualifications, such as the difference between the ex post rate of profit used in the identity and the neoclassical concept of the rental price of capital, but this does not significantly affect the argument and will not be considered here (see Felipe and McCombie, 2007).

The argument for the Cobb-Douglas production function is summarised in Table 9.1

Table 9.1   The relationship between the accounting identity and the aggregate Cobb-Douglas production function using time-series data

The accounting identity	The neoclassical production function
Prices are a mark-up on unit labour costs for firm i:	The micro production function with constant returns to scale is given by:
$$p_i = (1 + \pi_i)\frac{w_i L_i}{Q_i}$$	$$Q_i = A_0 e^{\lambda t} K_i^\alpha L_i^{(1-\alpha)}$$
A constant mark-up gives constant shares of capital (a) and labour ($1 - a$) in total value added, regardless of the underlying technology.	Aggregation problems and the Cambridge capital theory controversies show that theoretically the aggregate production function does not exist. Nevertheless, it is assumed that:
$a_i = \pi_i/(1 + \pi_i)$ and $(1 - a_i) = 1/(1 + \pi_i)$	$$\sum_i Q_i = Q = A_0 e^{\lambda t} K^\alpha L^{(1-\alpha)}$$
The accounting identity is given by:	Assuming (i) perfect competition and (ii) the aggregate marginal productivity theory of factor pricing gives:
$$p_i Q_i \equiv V_i \equiv r_i J_i + w_i L_i$$	$$p\frac{\partial Q}{\partial K} = p f_K = \rho \text{ and } p\frac{\partial Q}{\partial L} = p f_L = w$$
where $r_i = (p_i Q_i - w_i L_i)/J_i$	
Summing over industries gives:	From Euler's theorem:
$$V = \sum_i p_i Q_i = rJ + wL$$	$$Q = f_K K + f_L L$$
There are no serious aggregation problems. Aggregation may actually reduce the variability of the aggregate factor share compared with the individual factor shares.	and the cost identity is:
	$$pQ = \rho K + wL \text{ or } Q = (\rho/p)K + (w/p)L$$
By definition (and making no assumption about the state of competition or the mechanism by which factors are rewarded) the following conditions hold:	where ρ/p and w/p are physical measures and equal f_K and f_L. It is assumed for empirical analysis that $pQ = V$ and $(\rho/r)K = J$ where r is the rate of interest, which is assumed to equal the rate of profit.
$$\frac{\partial V}{\partial J} \equiv r \text{ and } \frac{\partial V}{\partial L} \equiv w$$	
Given constant factor shares, the accounting identity at time t may be written as:	Using time-series data and estimating $\ln V_t = c + b_1 t + b_2 \ln J_t + b_3 \ln L_t$ provides estimates of b_2 and b_3, which are the aggregate output elasticities of labour and capital. If a good statistical fit is found, it is inferred that the estimation has not refuted the hypothesis of the existence of the aggregate production function.
$$V_t = Br_t^a w_t^{(1-a)} J_t^a L_t^{(1-a)}$$	
or, assuming the stylised fact that $a\hat{r}_t + (1 - a)\hat{w}_t = (1 - a)\hat{w} = \lambda$, as:	The estimates of b_2 and b_3 equal the observed factor shares, i.e.,
$$V_t = Be^{\lambda t} J_t^a L_t^{(1-a)}$$	$$b_2 = \alpha = a \text{ and}$$
Estimating $\ln V_t = c + b_1 t + b_2 \ln J_t + b_3 \ln L_t$ gives estimates of b_2 and b_3 exactly	$$b_3 = (1 - \alpha) = (1 - a)$$

Table 9.1 (continued)

The accounting identity	The neoclassical production function
equal to the factor shares for *definitional* reasons: i.e. $b_2 = a$, and $b_3 = (1 - a)$. It is always possible to find an approximation that will give a perfect statistical fit to the data.	if assumptions (i) and (ii) above hold. If this is found to occur, it constitutes a failure to refute the theory that markets are competitive and factors are paid their marginal products.

Estimating $\ln V = c + b_1 t + b_2 \ln J + b_3 \ln L$ will always give a perfect fit to the data, provided that factor shares are constant and the stylised fact $a\hat{r}_t + (1 - a)\hat{w}_t = (1 - a)\hat{w} = \lambda$ holds. This is the case irrespective of whether there is a "true" underlying aggregate Cobb-Douglas production function (no matter how theoretically implausible this may be) or no aggregate production function exists at all. The data cannot discriminate between these two cases. (The same result holds using growth rates.) If the condition of constant factor shares and a constant growth of the weighted wage and profit rates is not met, it is still possible to obtain a perfect fit by a more flexible approximation to the accounting identity than that given by the Cobb-Douglas. It is, therefore, not possible empirically to test the existence of the aggregate production function or the aggregate marginal productivity theory of factor pricing.

Source: Felipe and McCombie (2005a), reproduced with permission.

where it is assumed that constant factor shares result from a constant mark-up pricing policy (although there are other reasons why factor shares do not show much variation over time).

We next turn to a consideration of four simulation exercises that illustrate the issues involved.

3 Four simulation exercises[7]

3.1 Fisher's (1971) "Aggregate production functions and the explanation of wages"[8]

Fisher's (1971) approach in his simulation experiments was to start with well-defined Cobb-Douglas micro-production functions at the firm or industry level. Having constructed the data for these separate firm production functions annually over a 20-year period, the statistics were then summed and used to estimate an aggregate production function. A proxy for the aggregate capital stock was constructed, but this suffered from an aggregation problem. When the macroeconomic data were used to estimate an aggregate production function, Fisher, to his evident surprise, found the results were remarkably well determined and the data gave a good prediction of the wage rate, even though the aggregate production function did not exist.

To elaborate: Fisher proceeded by constructing a large number of hypothetical economies, each comprising two, four, or eight "firms", depending on the experiment. The micro Cobb-Douglas production functions of each firm exhibited constant returns to scale. Perfect competition was assumed to prevail. Hence, the underlying economy was quintessentially neoclassical. The individual firms had different output elasticities; in one series of experiments the values of labour's output elasticities were chosen to be uniformly spread over the range of 0.7 to 0.8 and, in the other, over the range of 0.6 to 0.9, so that in the four-firm case the values were 0.6, 0.7, 0.8 and 0.9. The unweighted average in all cases was 0.75.

The labour force and the capital stock were constructed to grow at predetermined rates over the 20-year period. Technical change occurred at a constant rate that differed between firms, or was absent. Output was homogeneous and capital was heterogeneous and firm specific. Given this latter constraint, labour was allocated between firms such that the marginal product of labour was constant across firms. The heterogeneous capital was *not* allocated between firms so that the marginal dollar invested in each firm was the same. Moreover, as the capital stocks were heterogeneous, they could not be simply added together, so an index, with all its attendant aggregation problems, had to be constructed.

Consequently, there were a number of reasons for anticipating that the aggregate Cobb-Douglas production function would not give a good fit to the generated data.

- The exponents of the individual Cobb-Douglas micro-productions differed.
- Capital was firm specific and not allocated optimally between firms.
- The heterogeneity of the capital stock meant that an index of capital had to be constructed, with the consequent aggregation problems.
- The firm data were summed arithmetically to give the aggregate variables.

Fisher ran 830 simulations using a number of different assumptions and estimated the following relationships using time-series data aggregated across the individual firms:

$$lnV_t = c + b_4t + b_5lnJ_t^* + b_6lnL_t \tag{12}$$

$$ln(V_t/L_t) = c + b_4t + b_5ln(J_t^*/L_t) \tag{13}$$

where V is aggregate value added[9] and J^* is an index of capital, which will be discussed below. Note that it differs from J used earlier in equation (6). (The time trend was dropped for the experiments where no technical change was introduced.)

Fisher found uniformly high R^2s of generally around 0.99, a value not untypical of R^2s found using real, as opposed to hypothetical, data. Generally speaking, the aggregate production functions gave well-defined estimates, especially when constant returns were imposed to remove the multicollinearity between lnL and lnJ^* (equation (13)).

However, the main focus of the study was on the degree to which the aggregated production function succeeded in explaining the generated wage data. It was found that, in the main, there were exceptionally good statistical fits, much to Fisher's surprise.

We should not expect the prediction of wages to be very accurate if the variance of labour's share is large, but "while it is thus obvious that a low variance of labor's share is a necessary condition for a good set of wage predictions, it is by no means obvious that this is also a sufficient condition. Yet, by and large, we find this to be the case" (Fisher, 1971, p. 314). This result occurs even when it can be shown unequivocally that the "underlying technical relationships do not look anything like an aggregate Cobb-Douglas (or indeed *any* aggregate production function) in any sense" (p. 314, emphasis in the original). Fisher came to the conclusion that the point of our results, however, is not that an aggregate Cobb-Douglas fails to work well when labor's share ceases to be roughly constant, it is that an aggregate Cobb-Douglas will continue to work well so long as labor's share continues to be roughly constant, *even though that rough constancy is not itself a consequence of the economy having a technology that is truly summarized by an aggregate Cobb-Douglas.* (Fisher, 1971, p. 307, emphasis added)

Why did Fisher get such surprising results? We may explain this as follows.[10] Consider n firms or industries, each of which has a "true" production function given by $Q_{it} = A_{it}K_{it}^{\alpha_i}L_{it}^{(1-\alpha_i)}$ where $i = 1, \ldots n$, and the output elasticities differ. K is the firm-specific capital stock (in terms, of say, numbers of identical machines). To generate an aggregate capital stock, Fisher notes that Euler's theorem holds:[11]

$$V_t = w_t L_t + \sum_{i=1}^{n} \rho_{it} K_{it} \tag{14}$$

where ρ_t is again the rental price of capital, that is, the competitive cost of hiring a machine for one period. "This means that at any moment of time, the sum of[12] the right-hand side of [14] makes an excellent capital index" (p. 308). Fisher therefore runs the model for the individual firms over the 20-year period, and then obtains the sum of gross profits from the accounting identity for the firm. Then summing the number of machines for each firm, he obtains an average rental price of capital for each firm, which by definition is constant over the period:

$$\bar{\rho}_i \equiv \frac{\sum_{t=1}^{20} \rho_{it} K_{it}}{\sum_{t=1}^{20} K_{it}} \tag{15}$$

The index of the aggregate capital stock is then given by:

$$J_t^* \equiv \sum_{i=1}^{n} \bar{\rho}_i K_{it} \tag{16}$$

It should be noted that this index does not fulfil the necessary aggregation conditions.

The problem, of course, occurs because the relative magnitudes of the $[\rho_i(t)]$ not only do not remain constant over time but also are not independent of the magnitude of $L(t)$; this is the essence of the capital-aggregation problem.
Nevertheless, it seems clear that an aggregate production function will do best if its capital index comes as close as possible to weighting different capital goods by their rentals. (Fisher, 1971, p.308, omitting a footnote)

The definition of value added for the ith firm is:

$$V_{it} \equiv w_{it}L_{it} + \rho_{it}K_{it} \equiv w_{it}L_{it} + \frac{\rho_{it}}{\bar{\rho}_{it}}J_{it}^* \tag{17}$$

We may sum equation (17) over the n firms to give

$$V_t \equiv \sum_{i}^{n} V_{it} \equiv w_t L_t + \delta_t J_t^* \tag{18}$$

where w_t is the (weighted) average wage rate and $\delta_t \equiv (V_t - w_t L_t)/J_t^*$. The variable δ_t will be approximately equal to unity to the extent that the deviations of ρ_{it} from $\bar{\rho}_{it}$ tend to wash out when aggregated across firms. In other words, for every firm for which $\bar{\rho}_{it}$ overstates ρ_{it} there is a firm (or group of firms) where the ρ_{it} understates the rental price by approximately the same amount. A stronger assumption that gives the same result is that the rental price of capital for each firm does not greatly vary over time so $\rho_{it} \cong \bar{\rho}_{it}$.[13] It may be seen that the aggregate share of labour will be $(1 - a_t) = \sum_{i=1}^{n}(1 - a_i)\theta_{it}$ where $\theta_i = V_{it}/V_t$ and a_i is constant over time. $(1 - a_t)$ will be constant if θ_{it} is assumed either to be roughly constant or to vary in such a way as to make $(1 - a_t)$ constant.[14] We can now explain why an aggregate production function will give a good fit to the data. Even though the factor shares differ between firms, if in aggregate they are roughly constant, then assuming that $\delta = 1$ or is constant over time, differentiating equation (18) and integrating will give

$$V_t = Bw_t^{(1-a)}J_t^{*a}L_t^{(1-a)} \text{ or } V_t = A_0 e^{\lambda t}J_t^{*a}L_t^{(1-a)} \qquad (19)$$

where λ is the constant growth rate of w_t weighted by $(1 - a)$ and B is again the constant of integration. Thus, as Fisher (1971, p. 325) concludes, it is

> very plausible that in these experiments rough constancy of labor's share should lead to a situation in which an aggregate Cobb-Douglas gives generally good results including good wage predictions, even though the underlying technical relationships are not consistent with the existence of any aggregate production function and even though there is considerable relative movement of the underlying firm variables.

However, our interpretation is that the underlying micro-production functions will give constant firm-level factor shares for purely neoclassical reasons. It will be recalled that the firms are assumed to have Cobb-Douglas production functions which will give constant factor shares. Although the weights (the firms' shares in total output) attached to them for aggregation may change over time, this does not prevent the shares from being roughly constant. Solow (1958) discussed why an aggregate factor share often shows less volatility than the individual shares that constitute it. Fisher himself does not find this explanation convincing (p. 325, fn. 23),[15] but it is hard to see what logically could be a more plausible explanation. Of course, it could be argued that if we are correct, the aggregate production function could be viewed as being a reasonable approximation for the underlying Cobb-Douglas technology, *pace* Fisher. We shall next turn to three simulations where this clearly is not the case.

3.2   The evolutionary growth model of Nelson and Winter (1982)

The next example we shall consider is the evolutionary model of Nelson and Winter (1982, Chapter 9). While, perhaps unnecessarily, conceding that the neoclassical approach to growth has served to give coherence to many individual research projects, Nelson and Winter (1982, p. 206) nevertheless consider that "the weakness of the theoretical structure is that it provides a grossly inadequate vehicle for analysing technical change". What is particularly interesting is that they develop a model where individual firms have a *fixed-coefficients* production function and, as we shall see, their underlying behaviour is far from the usual neoclassical assumptions of the theory of the firm.

Their simulation model is one where a hypothetical economy is made up of a number of firms producing a homogeneous good. The technology available to each firm is, as we have said, one of fixed-coefficients, but with a large number of possible ways of producing the good given by different input coefficients (φ_L, φ_K) of differing efficiencies. However, the firm does not know the complete set of the input–output coefficients that are available to it, and so cannot immediately choose the best-practice technology. It only learns about the different techniques by engaging in a search procedure. The firms are not profit maximisers, but are satisficers and will only engage in such a search for a more efficient technique if the actual rate of profit falls below a certain satisfactory minimum, set at 16 per cent.

There are two ways by which the firm may learn of other fixed-coefficients techniques. The first is the *innovation* process. The firm engages in a localised search in the input-coefficient space. This potentially comprises the complete set of possible existing techniques, but the firm will be only concerned with a particular subset. This is because it is assumed that the probability of a firm identifying a new technique is a declining function of the "distance" in terms of efficiency between any particular new technique and the firm's existing technology. Consequently, the firm only searches locally in the input-coefficient space near its existing technique. The "distance" between the efficiency of a technique h' compared with the current technique h is a weighted average of $\ln(\varphi_K^h/\varphi_K^{h'})$ and $\ln(\varphi_L^h/\varphi_L^{h'})$ with the weights summing to unity. It follows that altering the weights on the distance measure will affect whether search is easier in a capital-saving or in a labour-saving direction, and this will influence the evolution of the capital–labour ratio.

Second, there is the *imitation* process where the firm discovers the existence of, and adopts, a more efficient technique because other firms are already using it. It is assumed that the probability of discovering this technique is positively related to the share of output produced by all the firms using this technique. This is similar to diffusion models where a firm that is not using the current best-practice technique learns of it with an increasing probability as more and more firms adopt it.

The overall probability of a firm finding a new technique h' is modelled as a weighted average of the probability of finding the technique by local search and by imitation. The exact values of the weights chosen in calibrating the model will determine whether the firm engages in local search or in imitation. The firm will adopt h' only if it gives a higher rate of profit than that obtained by the existing technique, but it is also possible for the firm to misjudge the input coefficients of an alternative technique. The model is sufficiently flexible for new firms to appear.

The wage rate is endogenously determined by labour demand and supply conditions in each time period. The labour supply is constructed to grow at 1.25 per cent per annum. The prevailing wage rate affects the profitability of each firm, given the technique it is using. The behaviour of the industry as a whole also affects the wage rate. Each firm is assumed to always operate at full capacity, and so in effect Say's law operates and there is no lack of effective demand.

The simulations show that the increase in wages has the effect of moving firms towards techniques that are relatively capital intensive. As a firm checks the profitability of the technique when there is an increased wage rate, it will be the more capital-intensive techniques that will pass the test. While a rising wage rate will make all techniques less profitable, those that are labour-intensive will be more adversely affected. However, as Nelson and Winter (1982, p. 227) point out, "while the explanation has a neoclassical ring, it is not based on neoclassical premises". The firms are not maximising profits.

> The observed constellations of inputs and outputs cannot be regarded as optimal in the Paretian sense: there are always better techniques not being used because they have not yet been found and always laggard firms using technologies less economical than current best practice.

The model was simulated with a view to comparing the outcome with Solow's (1957) results from fitting an aggregate production function to US data. To achieve this, the input-coefficient pairs space was derived from Solow's historical data – the US non-farm private business sector from 1909 to 1949. The simulation results produce industry data very similar to Solow's historical data. Indeed, if aggregate Cobb-Douglas production functions are fitted to Nelson and Winter's generated data, very good fits are obtained with the R^2s often over 0.99 and the estimated aggregate "output elasticity with respect to capital" (which, in fact, does not exist) often close to capital's share, although there are one or two exceptions. As Nelson and Winter (1982, p. 226) observe, "the fact that there is no production function in the simulated economy is clearly no barrier to a high degree of success in using such a function to describe the aggregate series it generates."

For our purposes, it is worth emphasising that the simulated macroeconomic data suggests an economy characterised by factors being paid their marginal products and an elasticity of substitution of unity, even though we know that every firm is subject to a fixed-coefficients technology.[16] The reason why the good fit to the Cobb-Douglas production function is found is once again because the factor shares produced by the simulation are relatively constant. Nelson and Winter (1982, p. 227) summarise their findings as follows:

> On our reading, at least, the neoclassical interpretation of long-run productivity change is sharply different from our own. It is based on a clean distinction between "moving along" an existing production function and shifting to a new one. In the evolutionary theory, substitution of the "search and selection" metaphor for the maximization and equilibrium metaphor, plus the assumption of the basic improvability of procedures, blurs the notion of a production function. In the simulation model discussed above, there was no production function – only a set of physically possible activities. The production function did not emerge from that set because it was not assumed that a particular subset of the possible techniques would be "known" at each particular time. The exploration of the set was treated as a historical, incremental process in which nonmarket information flows among firms played a major role and in which firms really "know" only one technique at a time.

3.3 Shaikh's (2005) non-linear Goodwin growth model and the Cobb-Douglas production function

Shaikh (2005) provides further evidence of the difficulty of estimating an aggregate production function by elaborating on his 1987 entry in the *New Palgrave*. He generates hypothetical data by simulating a slightly modified version of the Goodwin (1967) growth model, which is based on a fixed-coefficients production function with Harrod-neutral technical change. However, as the data set has the property that factor shares are roughly constant, not surprisingly, he is able, eventually, with a judicious choice of a time path for technical change, to show that the Cobb-Douglas production function gives an excellent fit to the data. The regressions using the hypothetical data are also contrasted with those using actual data for the US economy over the postwar period. (The latter are from the Bureau of Economic Analysis's National Income and Product Accounts and associated wealth stocks.)

The simulation model may be described as follows. The level of output is given by a fixed-coefficients production function:

$$V = \min\left(\frac{L}{\phi_L(t)}, \frac{J}{\phi_K}\right) \tag{20}$$

where $\phi_L(t) = \phi_{L0}e^{-\lambda t}$. Consequently, over time, the amount of labour required to produce a given volume of output falls at the rate λ, or, what comes to the same thing, labour productivity increases at the rate λ, which is taken to be 2 per cent per annum. Thus, machines of more recent vintages require less labour than, but the same amount of capital as, earlier machines. The capital coefficient (ϕ_K), however, is constant over time, so technical change is labour augmenting. It follows from the conditions of production that $\hat{V} - \hat{L} = \lambda$ and $\hat{V} - \hat{J} = 0$ and as $\hat{L}$ is assumed to grow at 2 per cent per annum, output and capital grow in equilibrium at 4 per cent (recalling that λ equals 2 per cent). This assumes that the economy is moving along its warranted path. Thus, we have two of Kaldor's stylised facts, namely, a constant growth of labour productivity and a constant capital–output ratio.

Shaikh constructs a hypothetical data set generated by the Goodwin model. The growth of the real wage rate is determined by the employment ratio (the ratio of employment to the labour force) and labour's share and has nothing to do with the technical conditions of production (as in the marginal productivity theory of factor pricing). A property of the production function is that a change in the wage rate will not affect the choice of technique; all it will do is alter the distribution of income. The fact that we are dealing with a fixed-coefficients technology means that the marginal products cannot be defined. As Shaikh (2005, p. 451, italics in the original) emphasises, *"it follows that the technological structure of this control group [Goodwin] model is entirely distinct from that of neoclassical production theory and associated marginal productivity rules"*.

In steady-state growth, the parameters of the real wage growth function are such that the growth of the real wage is 2 per cent per annum, that is, equal to the growth of labour productivity and this means that labour's (and, hence, capital's share) is constant. The model is stable in that after a shock, the growth of output converges to 4 per cent per annum and labour's share to a constant (approximately 0.84) and the employment ratio to a steady 95 per cent. Consequently, the simulated data series, like the actual US data, have factor shares that do not vary greatly over time. Nevertheless, when a Cobb-Douglas is estimated with a linear time trend (in the log-level specification) or with a constant intercept (in the growth rate form), the results are poor regardless of whether the simulated or the actual US data are used, and whether the Cobb-Douglas is freely estimated or has constant returns to scale imposed on the coefficients.

The reason is that notwithstanding the constancy of the factor shares, if the growth of the weighted wage rate and profit rate is not sufficiently constant, this can lead to poorly determined and biased coefficients of the factor inputs. In fact, both data sets show a pronounced fluctuation in the rate of profit, which has generally been found to be the main cause of other poor fits of the Cobb-Douglas (the wage rate is not so volatile around its trend). Shaikh notes that the *Solow Residual* is nothing other than the weighted average of the growth of the wage rate and the rate of profit, so that $\hat{A}_t = a_t \hat{r}_t + (1 - a)\hat{w}_t$ and, if factor shares are constant, $A_t = B_0 r_t^a w_t^{(1-a)}$. Consequently, the only difference between the Cobb-Douglas and the identity is the restriction usually imposed on the Cobb-Douglas that the weighted growth of the wage rate and rate of profit is a linear function of time with a random error term. (If shares are not exactly constant over time, then this will provide another difference.) But even in the neoclassical schema, there is no reason why this should be the case. The actual time path of A_t can be approximated to any required degree of precision by a complex time trend such as a Fourier series. Shaikh further notes that if one wishes to use a smooth path of technical change, then it is always possible to construct a series $\hat{F}_t = \psi \hat{A}_t$ where, if $\psi < 1$, this dampens, or smooths, the fluctuations.[17] Defining $\hat{A}_t$ as $(\hat{V}_t - \hat{L}_t) - a(\hat{J}_t - \hat{L}_t)$ and taking ψ as either 0.2 or 0.6, Shaikh, not surprisingly, gets a very good fit to the data with the estimated coefficients of the inputs almost precisely the same as the factor shares.

3.4   Felipe and McCombie's (2006) simulations: "The tyranny of the accounting identity"

Fisher (1971, p. 325) concluded his paper with the remarks, which could equally be the conclusions of the other two simulation studies, that

> the suggestion is clear, however, that labor's share is not roughly constant because the diverse technical relationships of modern economies are truly representable by an aggregate Cobb-Douglas but rather that such relationships appear to be representable by an aggregate Cobb-Douglas *because* labor's share happens to be roughly constant. If this is so, then the reason for such constancy becomes an important subject for further research. (Emphasis in the original)

This was one of the starting points of Felipe and McCombie's (2006)[18] simulations. A major difference between their explanation and the others is that Felipe and McCombie draw an explicit and important distinction between a micro-production function, which is an engineering relationship with output and capital measured in physical terms, and the aggregate production function where they are measured in constant-price monetary terms. Consequently, some set of base-year prices has to be used to construct a constant-price monetary measure of output and capital to allow aggregation.

Felipe and McCombie adopted an approach different from those discussed above, in that they constructed two types of data for the firm. They postulated that there were well-defined firm micro-production functions, with output and the capital stock specified in physical terms, as ideally they should be. These micro-production functions were Cobb-Douglas, but the output elasticity of capital was deliberately chosen to be 0.75 and of labour, 0.25. This stands in marked contrast to the usual values found of 0.25 and 0.75, respectively. Then they constructed constant-price data for output for firm i using a mark-up pricing model:

$$p_i = (1 + \pi)wL_i/Q_i \qquad (21)$$

where p is the price (£ per unit output), π is the mark-up, taken as 0.333, and w is the exogenously given money wage rate, which was assumed to be the same for each firm. The profit rate r took a value of 0.10 for each firm. The *value* of the capital stock was calculated residually through the accounting identity as $J_i \equiv (V_i - wL_i)/r$, where V_i is value added, constructed as $V_i = p_iQ_i$ by using equation (21) for each firm. The values of the factor shares are directly calculated using these value data. Labour's share is calculated as $(1 - a_i) = (wL_i/V_i)$ and capital's share as a_i. It should also be noted that $(1 - a_i) = 1/(1 + \pi)$, and so it takes a value of 0.75 for each firm, with a small variation because of an added random variable to prevent perfect multicollinearity. The researcher is assumed to know only the value data, that is, V and J and not Q and K. Using these data and running a cross-firm regression gives:[19]

$$\ln V = 2.867 + 0.250 \ln J + 0.750 \ln L \quad \bar{R}^2 = 0.999$$
$$(478.77)\,(45.41) \qquad (136.40) \qquad \text{s.e.r.} = 0.0025$$

Consequently, it can be seen that the estimated output elasticity of labour is 0.75 (and not the "true" value of 0.25) and of capital is 0.25 (and not 0.75).

Indeed, it is the constant mark-up that is solely responsible for generating the very good fit to the spurious Cobb-Douglas. To demonstrate this, the physical values of the three series Q, L and K were next generated as *random numbers*. V and J were calculated as before. Nevertheless, the estimation yielded a very good fit to the Cobb-Douglas with the values of the "output elasticities" the same as before. This does not necessarily mean that Felipe and McCombie are postulating that output is actually a random function of factor inputs. However, when one considers the complex production processes of any modern firm, there may be some individual parts of the process subject to fixed coefficients, whereas others are subject to differing elasticities of substitution, to say nothing of differences between plants in managerial and technical efficiencies. Thus, the randomness may simply be a reflection of the severe misspecification error inherent in specifying the micro-production function as a Cobb-Douglas. But the important point to note is that even in this case, where there is no well defined micro-production function, the use of value-added data will give the impression that there exists a well-behaved aggregate Cobb-Douglas production function.

When the true micro-production functions exhibit strong increasing returns (the degree of homogeneity was set equal to 1.20), but the value of the mark-up is the same as before, estimating the unrestricted Cobb-Douglas production function gives a result that is virtually identical to that for constant returns to scale, and reported above, except for a change in the value of the intercept. This shows that even when there are increasing returns to scale at the micro level, using value data will mean that this is captured in the "level of technology" of the aggregate production function and estimates of the latter will suggest constant returns to scale.

Felipe and McCombie also used these hypothetical data to calculate the growth of total factor productivity (or the size of the Solow residual) for an industry which consisted of ten firms. It was assumed that each firm experiences the same rate of technical progress of 0.5 per cent per annum. The output elasticities in physical terms were the same as before, as was the mark-up.

As the rate of technical progress was the same for each firm, we can talk about the rate of technical progress being 0.5 per cent per annum; even in the case where we assume that the physical outputs of the various firms are not homogeneous. The values of the individual firm's value added, constant price capital stock and employment were summed to give the industry values.

However, it was again assumed that all that can be used in empirical work, as is usually true in practice, is the constant-price value of output and of the capital stock. The growth of total factor productivity is given by:

$$TFPG \equiv \hat{V} - a\hat{J} - (1 - a)\hat{L} \tag{22}$$

where the shares of capital and labour are 0.25 and 0.75, respectively.

The rate of total factor productivity growth obtained by using the aggregated value data of the ten firms and equation (22) came to 1.48 per cent per annum. The reason for the marked difference between these values and the "true" rate of technical progress of 0.5 per cent per annum is that labour's share of output in value terms is 0.75, while the "true" output elasticity of the firms' production functions is 0.25. Consequently, the true rate of technical progress cannot be determined using constant-price monetary values, as is the universal practice.

4 Conclusions

Fisher (1971, p. 305) noted that Solow once remarked to him that, "had Douglas found labor's share to be 25 per cent and capital's 75 per cent instead of the other way around, we would not now be discussing aggregate production functions". In this chapter, we have shown that Douglas, by using monetary values in his estimations of the aggregate production function, could never have found this result. Indeed, with knowledge of Kaldor's stylised facts and the accounting identity linking total value added to the sum of wages and profits, we can predict the results of estimating various production functions before a single regression has been run. This has been shown, for example, by Felipe and McCombie (2005b) in the case of Mankiw et al.'s (1992) well-known study, which actually tells us nothing we did not already know. It certainly cannot be interpreted as a test of the factors that determine economic growth or of the augmented Solow model.

Our nihilistic conclusion is that because theoretically the aggregate production function does not exist, and empirically it cannot be meaningfully estimated, it can shed no light on how real economies work. Consequently, neoclassical growth theory, which relies on the aggregate production function, can shed little, if any light, on "why growth rates differ". We have also shown in section 3.4 above how the concept of total factor productivity growth (or multifactor productivity growth as it is sometimes called) is equally flawed, even though it is now widely used by such bodies as the OECD as a well-established and accepted measure of productivity growth.

Notes

1. The chapter reflects solely the opinions of the authors and does not necessarily reflect those of the Asian Development Bank, its Executive Directors, or those of the countries that they represent. We are grateful to Mark Setterfield for his helpful comments. The usual disclaimer applies.
2. For a survey of these issues see Felipe and Fisher (2003).
3. The argument equally applies to gross output, when materials are included as an input.
4. For expositional ease we ignore capital gains/losses and obsolescence.
5. We ignore the aggregation problems.
6. Fisher (1971) showed using simulation analysis that constant aggregate factor shares are not the result of an aggregate Cobb-Douglas production function. See the discussion of Fisher's simulation in the next section.

7. For reasons of space, we do not discuss the Monte-Carlo simulation experiments of Felipe and Holz (2001) that give some interesting insights into the econometric issues involved in the estimation of the Cobb-Douglas.
8. See also the discussion in Shaikh (1980).
9. Note that as output is assumed to be homogeneous by Fisher, we could equally have used the notation Q.
10. See Shaikh (1980) for an explanation along different lines.
11. Note that as equation (14) is an accounting identity, it will hold in all circumstances.
12. Fisher clearly means "on" here rather than "of".
13. Equation (18) differs from the identity derived from the national accounts $V_t \equiv w_t L_t + r_t J_t$, where r_t is the rate of profit. J_t is the value of the capital stock calculated by the perpetual inventory method and equals the number of machines multiplied by their purchase price appropriately deflated (not their rental price, which is the price per period). As we demonstrated above, if we assume for expositional purposes that r_t equals the rate of interest, then $J_{it} = (\rho_{it}/r_{it}) K_{it}$ and $V_t \equiv w_t L_t + \delta_t J_t^* \cong w_t L_t + r_t J_t$. (For expositional ease, we again abstract from capital gains and depreciation.) Consequently, if $\delta_t \cong 1$ then $J_t^* \cong r_t J$ or the total compensation of capital (see equation (14)).
14. With two firms, the firms' shares in total output have to be constant for aggregate labour's share (or the aggregate output elasticity of labour) to be constant. (This assumes that the individual firm's labour shares are constant.) But this is not true if there are more than two firms. Take the four-firm case where the labour shares are 0.6, 0.7, 0.8 and 0.9. At time t, if the firms' shares in total output are 0.25, 0.25, 0.25 and 0.25, the aggregate value of labour's share will be 0.75. It will, however, still take the same value at time $t + 1$ if the firms' shares change to 0.167, 0.333, 0.333 and 0.167.
15. Fisher argues that in his simulations "relative outputs do not seem to be very constant", but as we have seen in Note 14, this is not necessary for aggregate labour's share to be constant if the number of firms exceeds two.
16. Houthakker (1955–56) shows that if firms have a fixed-coefficients technology and firm size is distributed as a Pareto distribution, then the aggregate production function will be a Cobb-Douglas with diminishing returns to scale.
17. Shaikh uses the notation F_t instead of $\hat{F}_t$ and also allows its mean to differ from that of $\hat{A}_t$.
18. See also McCombie (2001).
19. The goodness of fit is determined by the random variable introduced into the construction of the value data to prevent perfect multicollinearity.

References

Barro, R.J and Sala-i-Martin, X. (2004), *Economic Growth*, 2nd edn, Cambridge, MA: MIT Press.

Bronfenbrenner, M. (1944), "Production functions: Cobb-Douglas, interfirm, intrafirm", *Econometrica*, **12**, 35–44.

Cohen, A.J. and Harcourt, G.C. (2003a), "Whatever happened to the capital controversies?", *Journal of Economic Perspectives*, **17**, 199–214.

Cohen, A. and Harcourt, G.C. (2003b), [Cambridge Capital Controversies] "Response", *The Journal of Economic Perspectives*, **17**, 227–232.

Cramer, J.S. (1969), *Empirical Econometrics*, Amsterdam: North-Holland.

Douglas, P.H. (1948), "Are there laws of production?", *American Economic Review*, **38**, 1–41.

Douglas, P.H. (1976), "The Cobb-Douglas production function once again: its history, its testing, and some new empirical values", *Journal of Political Economy*, **84**, 903–15.

Felipe, J. (2001a), "Endogenous growth, increasing returns, and externalities: an alternative interpretation of the evidence", *Metroeconomica*, **52**, 391–427.

Felipe, J. (2001b), "Aggregate production functions and the measurement of infrastructure productivity: a reassessment", *Eastern Economic Journal*, **27**, 323–44.

Felipe, J. and Adams, F.G. (2005), "'A theory of production'. The estimation of the Cobb-Douglas function: a retrospective view", *Eastern Economic Journal*, **31**, 427–45.

Felipe, J. and Fisher, F.M. (2003), "Aggregation in production functions: what applied economists should know", *Metroeconomica*, **54**, 208–62.

Felipe, J. and Holz, C. (2001), "Why do aggregate production functions work? Fisher's simulations, Shaikh's identity, and some new results", *International Review of Applied Economics*, **15**, 261–85.

Felipe, J. and McCombie, J.S.L. (2001), "The CES production function, the accounting identity, and Occam's Razor", *Applied Economics*, 33, 1221–32.

Felipe, J. and McCombie, J.S.L. (2003), "Methodological problems with neoclassical analyses of the East Asian miracle", *Cambridge Journal of Economics*, **54**, 695–721.

Felipe, J. and McCombie, J.S.L. (2005a), "How sound are the foundations of the aggregate production function?", *Eastern Economic Journal*, **31**, 467–88.

Felipe, J. and McCombie, J.S.L. (2005b), "Why are some countries richer than others? A sceptical view of Mankiw–Romer–Weil's test of the neoclassical growth model", *Metroeconomica*, **56**, 360–92.

Felipe, J. and McCombie, J.S.L. (2006), "The tyranny of the accounting identity: growth accounting revisited", *International Review of Applied Economics*, **20**, 283–99.

Felipe, J. and McCombie, J.S.L. (2007), "On the rental price of capital and the profit rate: the perils and pitfalls of total factor productivity growth", *Review of Political Economy*, **19**, 317–345.

Ferguson, C.E. (1971), "Capital theory up to date: a comment on Mrs. Robinson's article", *Canadian Journal of Economics*, **IV**, 250–54.

Fisher, F.M. (1971), "Aggregate production functions and the explanation of wages: a simulation experiment", *Review of Economics and Statistics*, **53**, 305–25.

Fisher, F.M. (1992), in F.M. Fisher and J. Monz (eds), *Aggregation. Aggregate Production Functions and Related Topics*, Cambridge, MA: MIT Press.

Fisher, F.M (2003), "Comment on Cohen and Harcourt", *Journal of Economic Perspectives*, **17**, 227–32.

Fisher, F.M. (2005), "Aggregate production functions – a pervasive, but unpersuasive, fairytale", *Eastern Economic Journal*, **31**, 489–91.

Friedman, M. (1951), "The methodology of positive economics", in M. Friedman (ed.), *Essays in Positive Economics*, Chicago: Chicago University Press.

Goodwin, R.M. (1967), "A growth cycle", in C.H. Feinstein (ed.), *Socialism, Capitalism and Economic Growth, Essays Presented to Maurice Dobb*, Cambridge: Cambridge University Press.

Houthakker, H.S. (1955–56), "The Pareto distribution and the Cobb-Douglas production function in activity analysis", *Review of Economic Studies*, **23**, 27–31.

Intriligator, M.D. (1978), *Econometric Models, Techniques and Applications*, Englewood Cliffs, NJ: Prentice Hall.

McCombie, J.S.L. (1987), "Does the aggregate production function imply anything about the laws of production? A note on the Simon and Shaikh critiques", *Applied Economics*, **19**, 1121–36.

McCombie, J.S.L. (1998a), "'Are there laws of production?': An assessment of the early criticisms of the Cobb-Douglas production function", *Review of Political Economy*, **10**, 141–73.

McCombie, J.S.L. (1998b), "Paradigms, rhetoric, and the relevance of the aggregate production function", in P. Arestis (ed.), *Method, Theory and Policy in Keynes. Essays in Honour of Paul Davidson*, Vol. III, Cheltenham, UK and Lyme, NH, USA: Edward Elgar.

McCombie, J.S.L. (2000–01), "The Solow residual, technical change and aggregate production functions", *Journal of Post Keynesian Economics*, **23**, 267–297. (Errata, **23**(3), 544.)

McCombie, J.S.L. (2001), "What do aggregate production functions show? Second thoughts on Solow's 'Second thoughts on growth theory'", *Journal of Post Keynesian Economics*, **23**, 589–615.

McCombie, J.S.L. and Dixon, R. (1991), "Estimating technical change in aggregate production functions: a critique", *International Review of Applied Economics*, **5**, 24–46.

McCombie, J.S.L. and Thirlwall, A.P. (1994), *Economic Growth and the Balance-of-Payments Constraint*, Basingstoke: Macmillan.

Mankiw, N.G., Romer, D. and Weil, D.N. (1992), "A contribution to the empirics of economic growth", *Quarterly Journal of Economics*, **107**, 407–37.

Marshak J. and Andrews, W.H. (1944), "Random simultaneous equations and the theory of production", *Econometrica*, **12**, 143–205.

Nelson, R.R and Winter, S.G. (1982), *An Evolutionary Theory of Economic Change*, Cambridge, MA: Harvard University Press.

Phelps Brown, E.H. (1957), "The meaning of the fitted Cobb-Douglas function", *Quarterly Journal of Economics*, **71**, 546–60.

Samuelson, P.A. (1979), "Paul Douglas's measurement of production functions and marginal productivities", *Journal of Political Economy*, **87**, 923–39.

Shaikh, A. (1974), "Laws of production and laws of algebra, the humbug production function", *Review of Economics and Statistics*, **56**, 115–20.

Shaikh, A. (1980), "Laws of production and laws of algebra: humbug II", in E.J. Nell (ed.), *Growth, Profits and Property*, Cambridge: Cambridge University Press.

Shaikh, A. (1987), "Humbug Production Function", in J. Eatwell, M. Milgate and P. Newman (eds), *The New Palgrave. A Dictionary of Economic Theory and Doctrine*, London: Macmillan.

Shaikh, A. (2005), "Nonlinear dynamics and pseudo-production functions", *Metroeconomica*, **31**, 447–66.

Simon, H.A. (1979a), "On parsimonious explanations of production relations", *Scandinavian Journal of Economics*, **81**, 459–74.

Simon, H.A. (1979b), "Rational decision-making in business organizations", *American Economic Review*, **69**, 493–513. (Nobel Memorial Lecture, 8 December 1997)

Simon, H.A. and Levy, F.K. (1963), "A note on the Cobb-Douglas function", *Review of Economic Studies*, **30**, 93–4.

Solow, R.M. (1957), "Technical change and the aggregate production function", *Review of Economics and Statistics*, **39**, 312–20.
Solow, R.M. (1958), "A skeptical note on the constancy of relative shares", *American Economic Review*, **48**, 618–63.
Solow, R.M. (1974), "Laws of production and laws of algebra: the humbug production function: a comment", *Review of Economics and Statistics*, **56**, 121.
Solow, R.M. (1987), "Second thoughts on growth theory", in A. Steinherr and D. Weiserbs (eds), *Employment and Growth: Issues for the 1980s*, Dordrecht: Martinus Nijhoff Publishers.
Wallis, K.F. (1979), *Topics in Applied Econometrics*, London: Gray-Mills Publishing.
Walters, A.A. (1963), "Production and cost functions", *Econometrica*, **31**, 1–66.

10 The endogenous nature of the "natural" rate of growth

Miguel A. León-Ledesma and Matteo Lanzafame

1 Introduction

Traditional growth models along neoclassical lines are built around the presumption that fluctuations do not affect the steady state equilibrium of the economy. These models define a rational expectations equilibrium that is achieved through a transitional dynamics path which is independent of any shocks that affect the economy. In its more standard version, initial conditions do not affect the equilibrium either. The view that the "actual" rate of growth can affect the "natural" or *potential* output growth rate, challenges these assumptions. This view implies that some large and persistent shocks during the transition towards equilibrium can move the equilibrium itself, hence inducing a relation between short-run fluctuations and long-run growth.

This proposition was articulated by León-Ledesma and Thirlwall (2002a) (LLT hereafter), who provide evidence on the sensitivity of a statistically defined "natural" rate of growth to economic fluctuations. The intuition behind this approach encapsulates many existing ideas about growth through cumulative causation.[1] It contrasts with traditional real business cycle theories and also Keynesian and new-Keynesian theories, which view long-run trends and short-run fluctuations as separate phenomena.

In this chapter we review the literature on the endogeneity of the natural rate of growth. The aim is, on the one hand, to survey the empirical evidence to date. On the other hand, we want to discuss the theoretical mechanisms that could link growth and fluctuations, with a view to emphasizing recent developments in the growth literature that can help understanding the potential forces at work behind this link.

Section 2 reviews the concept of the endogenous natural rate of growth. Section 3 analyses the theory and Section 4 the empirical evidence. Section 5 takes stock and concludes with an emphasis on future directions for research in this area.

2 The endogeneity of the natural rate

LLT argued that, because of the endogenous nature of productivity and labour supply, the so-called Harrodian *natural* rate of growth (g_N) would be endogenous to economic fluctuations reflected in the *actual* rate of growth (g_t).[2] In order to provide evidence on this idea, they devised a statistical technique based on the estimation of a simple form of Okun's Law (see Thirlwall, 1969). If the actual growth rate falls below the natural rate, the unemployment rate will rise, and if it rises above, the unemployment rate will fall. This implies that the natural rate of growth is the actual rate of growth that keeps unemployment constant. One can then estimate the natural rate by using the regression:

$$\Delta \% U_t = a_1 - b_1 \cdot g_t + \varepsilon_t, \tag{1}$$

where $\Delta\%U_t$ is the change in the percentage level of the unemployment rate and g_t is the rate of growth of output. When $\Delta\%U_t = 0$, the natural rate of growth is defined as a_1/b_1. It is also possible to obtain this estimate from the inverse of (1), which would be desirable to avoid estimation biases induced by labour hoarding:

$$g_t = a_2 - b_2 \cdot \Delta\%U_t + \varepsilon_t. \tag{2}$$

It should be noted, however, that this is *not* a *theory* of the natural rate, but a statistical device to calculate its value given an economic definition.

Once the natural rate of growth has been estimated, deviations of the actual growth rate from the natural rate can be calculated, and equation (2) can be estimated introducing a dummy variable (*D*) equal to one for periods when the actual rate of growth is above the natural rate and zero otherwise, as in equation (3)

$$g_t = a_3 + b_3 \cdot D - c_3(\Delta\%U_t) + v_t. \tag{3}$$

If the coefficient on the dummy (b_3) plus the constant (a_3) is significantly higher than the original constant (a_2) in equation (2), this means that the rate of growth to keep unemployment constant in booms must have risen. This is then interpreted to mean that the natural rate of growth must have been affected by the actual growth rate.

Dealing with a sample of 15 OECD countries and annual data over the 1961–95 period, LLT relied on time-series techniques to test the endogeneity hypothesis.[3] The OLS estimates of the natural rates from both (1) and (2) turned out to be always significant (except in a few cases associated with estimation of (1)), and both the equations produced similar results. Thus, LLT went on to use the more reliable estimates obtained from (2) as a basis for the estimation of equation (3), which produced significant results.[4] In particular, the coefficient on the dummy variable *D* turned out to be always positive and significant at the 5 per cent level, and implied an average increase of the natural rate in boom periods of about 50 per cent with respect to the estimate of g_N from (2).[5] Overall, therefore, the empirical evidence in LLT provided robust support for the hypothesis that the natural rate of growth is endogenous to actual growth.[6]

This conclusion was soon questioned by Boggio and Seravalli (2002) and rebutted by León-Ledesma and Thirlwall (2002b), in an exchange that appeared in the *Banca Nazionale del Lavoro Quarterly Review*. The exchange followed a paper previously published in the same journal by León-Ledesma and Thirlwall (2000), in which the authors presented a layman's version of their theory. The points raised by Boggio and Seravalli (2002) were essentially: (i) that a natural rate of growth cannot be a continuous function of the actual rate, otherwise it would contradict the very definition of the natural rate; and (ii) that the results in LLT are a product of statistical biases. In their reply, León-Ledesma and Thirlwall (2002b) proved that these criticisms were unfounded. First, LLT's argument considers the existence of two regimes (high and low growth) and not a continuum of natural rates. LLT's method is a statistical device and not a theory of the natural rate per se. Hence, Boggio and Seravalli misrepresented LLT's framework. Second, the results to which Boggio and Seravalli (2002) pointed as evidence of statistical bias concerned primarily the case of Italy which, as observed in LLT, was an exceptional case. In their reply, LLT show that, when using UK or US data, the estimation bias is of a much smaller magnitude and even insignificant.

3   What lies behind the endogenous natural rate?

As mentioned in the introduction, the idea that fluctuations can affect equilibrium is encapsulated in much of the Kaldorian tradition of growth theory. These theories emphasize the cumulative nature of economic development, the importance of path-dependency (Setterfield, 1998), and the role of increasing returns, and dispense with the traditional idea of equilibrium (Kaldor, 1966).

Two mechanisms explaining the endogeneity of the natural rate were emphasized by LLT. The first is the endogenous nature of labour supply. There are many ways in which labour supply is endogenous to cycles. Two of the most important are the "discouraged" worker effect and (internal and external) migration. The discouraged worker effect (Long, 1953) is the idea that groups of secondary workers have a tendency to move in and out of the labour force in response to the business cycle, looking for jobs when they are available, while giving up job search during recessions. The evidence in Benati (2001), for instance, shows a clear pro-cyclical pattern of labour supply in the US economy. Migration, on the other hand, is also strongly pro-cyclical and determined by the availability of job vacancies and wages, which are heavily cyclical variables. Much of the evidence reviewed by Cornwall (1977) on this matter stands up to the passage of time.

The second mechanism emphasized by LLT is the endogeneity of productivity growth, in what has come to be known as the Verdoorn effect (Verdoorn, 1949). This effect, central to many cumulative growth models, implies that productivity growth is induced by output growth as a consequence of the existence of increasing returns (static and dynamic). The relation is understood to be a structural, long-run phenomenon rather than just reflecting the short-run pro-cyclicality of labour productivity. As the size and scope of the market increase, plants become more productive through the exploitation of scale economies and, most importantly, learning-by-doing and innovation (dynamic effects) are also related to the rate of expansion of output. The findings of a large empirical literature on the Verdoorn effect consistently report a remarkably stable 0.5 per cent increase in productivity per 1 per cent expansion of output. A thorough review of this literature and empirical evidence can be found in the edited volume of McCombie et al. (2002) and recent evidence at the regional level in Angeriz et al. (2008) and McCombie and Roberts (2007).

These two factors taken together imply that expansions and recessions could potentially have an important impact on the natural rate of growth. In fact, LLT go beyond this and argue that factor inputs, far from being temporally causal of output, are *caused by* it, and provide empirical evidence supporting this claim. It is obvious that, being a purely technical (engineering) relationship, inputs have to have a causal impact on output, but it may well be that these are employed *as a consequence* of actual and expected output expansions.

The evidence on the endogenous rate of growth is usually taken to imply that so-called post-Keynesian theories of growth have the upper hand over neoclassical ones.[7] Certainly, the standard Ramsey-Solow and RBC models fail to account for any of the mechanisms discussed above. This would also be the case in mechanical Keynesian and new-Keynesian models of fluctuations. Indeed, the theoretical approach based on dynamic stochastic general equilibrium (DSGE) models with price rigidities, currently dominant in macroeconomics, assumes that potential output is not affected by output gap (or marginal cost) changes. If it was, equilibrium indeterminacy could easily dominate determinate solutions. However, the recent evolution of growth theory has moved substantially beyond this thinking, opening up a welcome opportunity for new ideas on the interplay of cycles and growth. This is a positive development that has brought two separate traditions in economics closer to each other. As we argue below, several models of "equilibrium" growth would also imply an endogenous natural rate of growth.

There are two main strands of the literature that could imply an endogenous natural rate: the restructuring/opportunity cost strand and the learning-by-doing strand.

3.1 Restructuring and opportunity costs

According to this strand of the literature, Schumpeterian selection occurs in markets with important implications for productivity growth. The two mechanisms through which this occurs are the "liquidationist" effect and the "pit-stop" or opportunity cost effect.

Caballero and Hammour (1994) present a model in which recessions have "cleansing" effects.[8] Because of innovative ideas, old production techniques are replaced by new ones in a process of creative destruction, as in Aghion and Howitt (1992). However, for some periods old and new vintage technologies can coexist. During recessions the old technologies become less profitable and they are pushed out of the market, hence liquidating older, less productive firms and jobs. According to this view, recessions can have positive effects on productivity, as productive efficiency increases because of the acceleration of selection in recessions. Caballero and Hammour (2005), however, show that this countercyclical behaviour of restructuring can be reversed. This is because the cleansing mechanism relies on the fact that the path of creation of new technologies is not affected by the recession. In fact, however, this is not the case: although recessions increase the pace of liquidations, recoveries do not increase sufficiently the path of creation. Hence, recessions can have permanent negative effects.

The second mechanism is related to the "pit-stop" view of recessions: this view states that recessions are times when productivity-improving activities are undertaken because of their temporarily low opportunity costs (see, e.g., Aghion and Saint-Paul, 1991, and Hall, 1991). The reorganization of activities within firms, such as the introduction of new technologies, takes place during recessions because the opportunity cost of restructuring is lower, given that the costs of forgone production and lost asset values are lower.

In all, this view recognizes the potentially permanent effects of business cycles on trend growth: either productivity or efficiency could be permanently affected by recessions (and expansions) because of a discipline mechanism embedded in markets. Note, however, that this market mechanism can be heavily influenced by institutional factors, such as labour and product market structures, credit market access, the development of innovation structures and the sectoral composition of output. Hence, the impact of fluctuations on growth cannot be expected to be uniform.

3.2 Learning-by-doing

The idea that cyclical booms can affect long-run growth has its initial roots in the *learning-by-doing* (LBD) hypothesis proposed by Arrow (1962), that played an important role in early endogenous growth models. Expansions resulting from demand or supply shocks increase the size of the market, inducing division of labour and investment in capital, which in turn generates a learning curve that enhances productivity and long-run growth. Modern models, such as Stadler (1990), have focused on the impact of expansions on R&D activity. If firms face financial constraints, boom periods will allow them to finance R&D through retained profits. This pro-cyclicality of R&D, also emphasized by Stiglitz (1993), would induce an impact of demand shocks on long-run productivity. There is no need, however, to resort to explicit R&D for generating this mechanism, as we know that R&D is usually carried out by large firms or else small firms that are highly dependent on large ones. If financing constraints à la Fazzari et al. (1988) are predominant, expansionary periods will induce higher investment in capital. Since capital embodies technical progress or is complementary to human capital, firms' productivity will increase without explicit expenditures on R&D. There is, however, another related link. As booms expand the size of the market, the scope for division of labour and *roundaboutness* increases productivity in the way that was originally pointed out by Young (1928).

What emerges from this literature? A common theme emerging from these contributions is the recognition, within more standard equilibrium models, that cycles and growth are interdependent. This amounts to stating that the natural rate can be endogenous to the actual rate, which can have important consequences for issues such as stabilization policies. This is true because in these models the trend (equilibrium) rate of growth *is* the potential (natural) rate of growth – so that demonstrating the influence of transitory shocks (departures from trend) on the trend itself is necessarily equivalent to demonstrating that the actual rate of growth affects the natural rate. More importantly, recent evidence in Cerra and Saxena (2008) shows that recessions appear to leave permanent scars on economies, with recovery being only partial after crises. In other words, the "trend" level of per capita GDP is not independent from the cycle, a statement that comes very close to LLT's results.

4 The empirical evidence

Empirical testing of the endogeneity hypothesis as originally advanced by LLT has so far received fairly little attention in the literature. Recently, however, this trend has been reversed with the appearance of a new study by León-Ledesma (2006) and a number of other papers providing new and much-needed empirical evidence – for example, Ciriaci (2007), Lanzafame (2009, 2010), Libânio (2009), Oreiro and Nakabashi (2007), Vogel (2009). The results from these studies are synthesized in Table 10.1.

The above-named authors have focused their attention on two (geographically) well-defined objects of investigation – the Latin American countries and the Italian regions. Though different in almost all other respects, the developing economies of Latin America and the regions of Italy do share a history of often poor growth performance, uneven economic development and persistent inequality. In this context, the question of whether or not the natural rate of growth (g_N) is in fact endogenous to the actual growth rate (g_t) becomes all the more relevant.

One clear example of this is Brazil, which is the object of investigation chosen by Oreiro and Nakabashi (2007). As part of a wider study aimed at analysing the determinants of the disappointing growth performance of the Brazilian economy for most of the last three

Table 10.1   Summary of selected studies on the endogeneity hypothesis

Study	Object	Data	Estimation technique	Support for LLT
Ciriaci (2007)	Italian regions	Annual data, 1980–2003	Pooled panel regressions	Yes
Lanzafame (2009)	Italian regions	Annual data, 1977–2003	TAR and SUR	Mixed
Lanzafame (2010)	Italian regions	Annual data, 1977–2003	Fixed-effects and SUR	Yes
León-Ledesma (2006)	Germany, UK, US	Quarterly data, 1960:1–2001:2	TAR	Mixed
Libânio (2009)	Latin American countries	Annual data, 1980–2004	OLS	Yes
Oreiro and Nakabashi (2007)	Brazil	Quarterly data, 1980:1–2002:4	OLS	Yes
Vogel (2009)	Latin American countries	Annual data, 1986–2003	SUR	Yes

decades and the role of demand as a constraint on growth, these authors use quarterly data over the period 1980:1–2002:4 to test the endogeneity hypothesis. The estimates of Brazil's quarterly natural rate of growth from equations (1) and (2) are both about 0.6 per cent, adding up to an annualized natural rate of about 2.5 per cent.[9] Moreover, OLS estimation of equation (3) indicates that, on an annual basis, the natural rate rises by a remarkable 11.4 percentage points when $g_t > g_N$. This result, however, may be a result of the use of quarterly data and, thus, may reflect business cycle dynamics more than the long-run relationship linking the actual and natural rates. This view is reinforced by the negative and strongly significant constant in equation (3), implying an implausible value of about -3.36 per cent for the natural rate in the slow-growth regime. Thus, Oreiro and Nakabashi (2007) also perform a second regression of (3) using three-month moving averages of the data to smooth out cyclical effects. This exercise results in still notable but lower estimates of the increase in the natural rate of growth in response to $g_t > g_N$ (equal to an annualized 6.24 per cent), and of the boom value of g_N (which is about 5.2 per cent).[10]

By and large, the strong endogeneity of the natural rate ascertained by Oreiro and Nakabashi (2007) for an emerging economy such as Brazil is confirmed in a more comprehensive study carried out by Libânio (2009), who focuses on the 12 largest Latin American economies (i.e. Argentina, Brazil, Chile, Colombia, Costa Rica, Dominican Republic, Ecuador, Guatemala, Mexico, Peru, Uruguay and Venezuela). Using annual data over the 1970–2004 period, the author starts by performing panel unit root tests on GDP and finds strong support for the hypothesis that GDP is non-stationary, thus suggesting that temporary shocks will have permanent effects. Libânio (2009) notes that, contrary to the mainstream view based on the dichotomy between trend and cycle, this result is entirely consistent with an environment in which demand-driven cyclical fluctuations affect long-run growth. (It has to be pointed out, nevertheless, that standard Solow-type growth models in stochastic environments can generate non-stationary output if technology follows a non-stationary generating process.)

To investigate the issue further, Libânio performs OLS regressions of equations (1) and (2) to obtain an estimate of the natural rate of growth and, hence, of equation (3) to test for its endogeneity. Though the estimates of a_3 in (3) (i.e. the natural rate) often turn out to be insignificant in the slow-growth regime, overall the results provide strong support for the endogeneity hypothesis. In particular, with the sole exception of Venezuela in one case, the intercept dummy D in (3) is always significant and the natural rate of growth in the sample of Latin American countries under consideration rises by an average of either 103 per cent or 73 per cent (depending on the specification used in response to $g_t > g_N$).[11] This is a significantly stronger increase than that ascertained by LLT for their sample of industrialized (OECD) countries. Moreover, Libânio's estimates indicate that the natural rate changes asymmetrically over the cycle, with the average fall in recessions being more pronounced than its increase in expansions. The author suggests both results are likely to depend on the structural features of the emerging economies under analysis, in particular the existence of a large informal sector (giving rise to significant labour force variation over the cycle) and "immature" industrial sectors, implying stronger Verdoorn effects between output and labour productivity growth (Kaldor, 1966). This interpretation accords with that provided by LLT to explain the cross-country variation in their own estimates of the sensitivity of g_N to g_t.

The evidence presented by Libânio (2009), however, may suffer some statistical problems. While in the first part of the paper the author makes use of panel data methods to assess the potential non-stationarity of the GDP series, the tests of the endogeneity hypothesis conducted in the second part are based on single-equation estimation techniques. This may be problematic since, given that the time-series dimension of his data is short, the efficiency of his estimates would be increased by the use of estimation methods based on cross-section pooling to test for the endogeneity hypothesis.

Vogel (2009) recognizes this and relies on a system of seemingly unrelated regressions (SUR) to test for the endogeneity hypothesis, using annual data covering the 1986–2003 period and a sample of Latin American countries similar to Libânio's.[12] The SUR estimates of the natural rate obtained from equation (2) are always strongly significant and the cross-equation restriction that Argentina, Bolivia, Brazil, Columbia and Peru share the same g_N (equal to about 3 per cent) cannot be rejected. Moreover, SUR regression of (3) supports the endogeneity hypothesis, as the dummy variable D is always significant at the 1 per cent level. Interestingly, as in Libânio (2009), the average increase of g_N in boom periods is remarkable (about 64 per cent), and even more so in the case of Argentina (137.6 per cent) and Venezuela (159.5 per cent). As stated above, this outcome supports the view that the natural rate may be more sensitive to actual growth in emerging economies than in industrially "mature" countries. *Ceteris paribus*, this implies that the potential long-run impact of demand-side policies may be larger as well.[13] However, one should interpret these results with some degree of caution given the large variance in output growth in emerging economies. Biased estimation results may be present the larger this variance becomes, as shown in the exchange between LLT and Boggio and Seravalli (2002).

Overall, it appears that for Latin American countries there is significant support for the hypothesis that the natural rate of growth is endogenous and remarkably sensitive to the actual rate of growth. The picture is somewhat different in the case of studies regarding the Italian regions.

One such study is that of Ciriaci (2007), who adopts panel data techniques and uses a dataset of regional annual data over the years 1980–2003. Based on a Breusch-Pagan test indicating the absence of significant fixed effects, the author proceeds to pooled OLS regressions of equation (2), both for the entire panel of the 20 Italian regions and for two sub-panels including the Centre-North and the Southern regions. In all cases, the estimates of g_N are significant at the 1 per cent level, but the regression R-squared turns out to be quite low. The introduction of the dummy variable D boosts the R-squared to a value of about 60 per cent and estimation of (3) supports the endogeneity hypothesis, as the natural rate rises significantly in all cases when $g_t > g_N$. In particular, for the average Italian region, the boom value of g_N is about 3.3 per cent, substantially higher than its value of 1.73 per cent during periods of slow growth.[14]

Referring to a slightly longer time-span (i.e. 1977–2003), Lanzafame (2010) presents a wider set of estimations, using both fixed-effects and SUR techniques. Moreover, the version of equation (3) employed includes a slope dummy on $\Delta\%U_t$, so that the relation between unemployment and growth is allowed to change when $g_t > g_N$. The endogeneity hypothesis is largely supported by the data, as both estimators provide fairly homogeneous results as regards the change in the natural rate when $g_t > g_N$. The intercept dummy D is always positive and strongly significant, with values ranging between about 3 and 3.7 per cent.[15]

A second study by Lanzafame (2009), however, provides different results. The dataset used is the same, but the methodology is different and primarily based on the threshold autoregressive (TAR) model proposed by Hansen (1997). The TAR approach fits well the goal of ascertaining whether there exists a significant relationship between cyclical and long-run growth, as it allows the parameters of an autoregressive (AR) model to change according to whether the value of a particular variable is above or below a certain threshold, which is jointly estimated with the other parameters of the model. Based on this approach, Lanzafame (2009) fits a TAR model to an AR1 process for g_t, considering two threshold variables: the first is a standard delay lag g_{t-j}, where j indicates the lag length; the second is Δg_{t-j}, which corresponds to the Momentum-TAR or M-TAR model proposed by Enders and Granger (1998).[16] The results provide evidence of significant non-linearities in g_t for only 8 out of the 20 Italian regions. This indicates that for most of the Italian regions growth is not endogenous, at least in terms of the endogeneity hypothesis as defined in LLT. The estimated thresholds are then used in equation (3) to further investigate the implications for the endogeneity hypothesis. Again, the SUR estimates of the model provide mixed results. For two out of eight regions for which growth appears to be endogenous, there is evidence of a higher natural rate when g_t is in the slow-growth regime. This is in line with the "restructuring/opportunity cost" approach to the endogeneity of growth and runs contrary to the LLT hypothesis.[17,18]

On the whole, therefore, in the case of the Italian regions the empirical evidence on the endogeneity hypothesis is mixed. On one hand, adopting the standard LLT approach, Ciriaci (2007) and Lanzafame (2010) provide qualified support for the hypothesis. But on the other, when, as in Lanzafame (2009), the non-linear relation between the actual and natural growth rates is assessed via a TAR model, the results are mixed. In particular, to the extent that regional natural growth rates in Italy appear to be endogenous, there is significant regional heterogeneity as regards the precise nature and sign of the relationship between g_t and g_N.

Interestingly, mixed evidence is also provided by León-Ledesma (2006), who also advocates the use of TAR models to assess the relationship between cyclical fluctuations and long-run growth. This study employs quarterly data on Germany, the UK and the US over the period 1960:1–2001:2 and, rather than using the LLT framework, focuses solely on the level of GDP implementing the TAR methodology developed by Caner and Hansen (2001) to test for non-linearities. Three different specifications for the threshold variable are adopted: the first is the change in GDP over a number of quarters which, as mentioned above, corresponds to the M-TAR model; the second and third rely on output gap measures that consider, respectively, whether the output gap is higher or lower than a certain threshold and whether it is higher or lower than zero.

Given the possible non-stationarity of GDP, León-Ledesma (2006) tests simultaneously for asymmetries and unit roots. He finds that GDP appears to be stationary in recessions and non-stationary in expansions, so that there is strong asymmetry in the output series analysed. Moreover, while in the UK trend output is not affected by the cycle, cyclical fluctuations appear to have a significant impact on the output trend for the other two countries, but with a different sign. For the US, the trend component of output is higher during recessions, suggesting that the opportunity-cost approach may be more relevant than the LBD effect. On the other hand, in the case of Germany the opposite is true, that is, the output trend increases during expansions in accordance with the endogeneity hypothesis.[19]

Taking stock of these results, as well as those provided by Lanzafame (2009), it can be said that the use of TAR models has brought new and more nuanced evidence to the empirical literature on the endogeneity hypothesis. This, together with the variable sensitivity of the natural rate of growth across countries and regions, suggests that structural features of economies (e.g. their sectoral composition, labour markets, and/or financial systems) are the main determinants of the sign of the relationship between g_t and g_N. Further research is needed to accumulate additional empirical evidence and deepen our understanding of how and to what extent these factors shape the endogeneity of the natural rate of growth.

5   Conclusions

The hypothesis that the natural rate of growth is endogenous to the actual rate calls into question the standard assumption that cycles and growth are two separate phenomena. We have reviewed the empirical evidence and theoretical arguments behind this hypothesis. Two main conclusions arise.

First, empirical evidence, although still scarce, provides significant support for the LLT hypothesis. This is especially the case for Latin American countries. Further evidence using regional datasets would contribute greatly to this evidence, as the mechanisms underlying the endogeneity of the natural rate are more likely to be operative when there are no barriers to factor and technology movements.

Second, the theoretical literature on the effects of cycles on growth is by now well developed. The original Kaldorian arguments employed by LLT are only one part of this literature. Recent growth models incorporating features such as output and employment relocation, opportunity costs of restructuring, and learning-by-doing have made important contributions to our understanding of the relationship between fluctuations and growth. We see this as a welcome convergence in views that can only enrich the debate on the endogeneity of the natural rate, and that will hopefully lead to important policy conclusions.

Future empirical work should be directed at understanding not only whether or not the natural rate is endogenous, but through which mechanisms. This objective is perhaps best achieved by using more disaggregated data on industries and firms, and by comparing the behaviour of output, employment, productivity and structural change over different stages of the cycle.

Notes

1. See, for instance, Kaldor (1966), McCombie and Thirlwall (1994), Toner (1999), Targetti and Foti (1997) and León-Ledesma (2002).
2. In what follows, we will sometimes refer to this as the "endogeneity hypothesis".
3. The countries included in the sample are: Australia, Austria, Belgium, Canada, Denmark, France, Germany, Greece, Italy, Japan, the Netherlands, Norway, Spain, the UK and the US.
4. As an alternative to estimating (3), LLT also took the natural rate to be equal to a 3- to 5-year moving average of the actual growth rate. Their results remained fundamentally unchanged.
5. For countries such as Greece, Italy and Japan, characterized by large reserves of labour and less than fully developed industrial sectors in the period under analysis, the sensitivity of the natural rate turned out to be higher. As will be seen later on, this outcome is confirmed in studies applying the LLT approach to emerging economies.
6. Granger causality tests between input and output growth reinforced this conclusion. Contrary to the mainstream view suggesting unidirectional causality from input to output growth, the results indicated bidirectional causality for 13 out of the 15 countries in the sample, and causality running solely from output to input growth in the remaining 2 countries.
7. Some prefer the use of "orthodox" vs "heterodox", but we believe orthodoxy to be related to the rigidity of one's views and the willingness to accept new ideas. In that sense, much of the so-called "heterodox" literature is actually deeply "orthodox". A good dose of self-criticism from the critics is much needed if these theories are to be generally accepted.
8. This, the authors emphasize, does not necessarily imply the *desirability* of recessions.
9. However, the intercept in equation (1) is not significant and Oreiro and Nakabashi (2007) do not perform a Wald test on a_1/b_1 to check whether or not their estimate of the natural rate is significant.
10. The estimate of g_N in the slow-growth regime is still negative and equal to about -1 per cent, but now significant only at the 10 per cent level.
11. Because of the lack of data for some countries, the sample period is reduced to 1980–2004 and both the Dominican Republic and Guatemala are excluded from the analysis.
12. Vogel (2009) takes a sample of 11 countries – Argentina, Bolivia, Brazil, Chile, Costa Rica, Colombia, Mexico, Nicaragua, Paraguay, Peru and Venezuela.
13. As in LLT, Vogel (2009) runs Granger causality tests to ascertain the direction of causation between input and output growth but, because of the lack of data for many countries, the analysis is limited to Brazil, Colombia, Mexico and Peru. The results show that there exists causality from output to input growth in all four countries, whereas the opposite relation can be proven reliably only in the case of Brazil.
14. As in other studies, Ciriaci (2007) also presents estimates of equation (3) relying on a three-year moving-average proxy of the natural rate and, in addition, performs feasible generalized least squares (FGLS) estimations. In both cases, the results do not change significantly.
15. This is close to the comparable figure of 4.2 per cent estimated for Italy as a whole by LLT (Table 3, p. 449). Moreover, it is worth noting that, in line with recent findings in the literature (e.g. Crespo Cuaresma, 2003), the SUR estimations reveal the presence of significant asymmetries in the relation between output growth and unemployment, which even becomes pro-cyclical in some cases during expansions.
16. The M-TAR model reflects the idea that the appearance of non-linearities in output growth might be triggered by an acceleration or deceleration of growth faster than a certain threshold rate.
17. Drawing on evidence of the structural composition of the regional economies in question, Lanzafame (2009) argues that the negative relationship between the actual and natural growth rates of these two regions (Liguria and Sicilia) can be explained by the preponderance of service activities over a small industrial sector.
18. As in Lanzafame (2010), in the eight regions in which growth does appear to be endogenous, the results also indicate the presence of significant non-linearities in Okun's Law, with unemployment switching from a counter- to a pro-cyclical (or acyclical) pattern during booms. This reinforces the view that both labour productivity and labour force participation react endogenously to growth.

19. León-Ledesma (2006) suggests differences in labour market structures and financial systems between the three countries may explain these results. In particular, promoting adjustment to shocks via changes in quantities rather than prices (e.g. wages, interest rates), Germany's more rigid labour market and bank-based financial system may go a long way to determining the pro-cyclical behaviour of potential GDP.

References

Aghion, P. and Howitt, P. (1992). "A model of growth through creative destruction", *Econometrica*, **60**, 323–51.

Aghion, P. and Saint-Paul, G. (1991). "On the virtue of bad times: an analysis of the interaction between economic fluctuations and productivity growth", DELTA Working Papers 91–23, DELTA.

Angeriz, A., McCombie, J.S.L. and Roberts, M. (2008). "Some new estimates of returns to scale for EU regional manufacturing 1986–2002", *International Regional Science Review*, **31**, 62–87.

Arrow, K.J. (1962). "The economic implications of learning-by-doing", *Review of Economic Studies*, **29**, 155–73.

Benati, L. (2001). "Some empirical evidence on the 'discouraged worker' effect", *Economics Letters*, **70**, 387–95.

Boggio, L. and Seravalli, G. (2002). "Is the natural rate of growth endogenous? A comment", *Banca Nazionale del Lavoro, Quarterly Review*, **221**, 219–27.

Caballero, R.J. and Hammour, M. (1994). "The cleansing effects of recessions", *American Economic Review*, **84**, 1350–68.

Caballero, R.J. and Hammour, M. (2005). "The cost of recessions revisited: a reversed-liquidationist view", *Review of Economic Studies*, **72**, 313–41.

Caner, M. and Hansen, B.E. (2001). "Threshold autoregressions with a unit root", *Econometrica*, **69**, 1555–96.

Cerra, V. and Saxena, S.C. (2008). "Growth dynamics: the myth of economic recovery", *American Economic Review*, **98**, 439–57.

Ciriaci, D. (2007). "Tasso di crescita naturale e crescita cumulativa nelle regioni Italiane", *Moneta e Credito*, **LX**, 287–310.

Cornwall, J. (1977). *Modern Capitalism: Its Growth and Transformation*. London: Martin Robertson.

Crespo Cuaresma, J. (2003). "Okun's law revisited", *Oxford Bulletin of Economics and Statistics*, **65**, 439–51.

Enders, W. and Granger, C.W.J. (1998). "Unit root tests and asymmetric adjustment with an example using the term structure of interest rates", *Journal of Business and Economic Statistics*, **16**, 304–11.

Fazzari, S., Hubbard, R.G. and Petersen, B. (1988). "Finance constraints and corporate investment", *Brookings Papers on Economic Activity*, **1**, 141–95.

Hall, R.E. (1991). "Recessions as reorganizations", in *NBER Macroeconomics Annual*. Cambridge, MA: MIT Press.

Hansen, B.E. (1997). "Inference in TAR models", *Studies in Nonlinear Dynamics and Econometrics*, **2**, 1–14.

Kaldor, N. (1966). *Causes of the Slow Rate of Economic Growth of the UK*. An Inaugural Lecture. Cambridge: Cambridge University Press.

Lanzafame, M. (2009). "Is regional growth in Italy endogenous?", *Regional Studies*, **43**, 1001–13.

Lanzafame, M. (2010). "The endogeneity of the natural rate of growth in the regions of Italy", *International Review of Applied Economics*, forthcoming.

León-Ledesma, M.A. (2002). "Accumulation, innovation and catching-up: an extended cumulative growth model", *Cambridge Journal of Economics*, **26**, 201–16.

León-Ledesma, M.A. (2006). "Cycles, aggregate demand and growth", in P. Arestis, J. McCombie and R. Vickerman (eds), *Growth and Economic Development: Essays in Honour of A.P. Thirlwall*. Cheltenham, UK and Northampton, MA, USA: Edward Elgar.

León-Ledesma, M.A. and Thirlwall, A.P. (2000). "Is the natural rate of growth exogenous?", *Banca Nazionale del Lavoro, Quarterly Review*, **53**, 433–46.

León-Ledesma, M.A. and Thirlwall, A.P. (2002a). "The endogeneity of the natural rate of growth", *Cambridge Journal of Economics*, **26**, 441–60.

León-Ledesma, M.A. and Thirlwall, A.P. (2002b). "The endogeneity of the natural rate of growth: a reply to Boggio and Seravalli", *Banca Nazionale del Lavoro, Quarterly Review*, **55**, 228–30.

Libânio, G.A. (2009). "Aggregate demand and the endogeneity of the natural rate of growth: evidence from Latin American economies", *Cambridge Journal of Economics*, **33** (5), 967–84.

Long, C. (1953). "Impact of effective demand on the labor supply", *American Economic Review, Papers and Proceedings*, **43**, 458–67.

McCombie, J.S.L. and Roberts, M. (2007). "Returns to scale and regional growth: the static–dynamic Verdoorn Law paradox revisited", *Journal of Regional Science*, **47**, 179–208.

McCombie, J.S.L. and Thirlwall, A.P. (1994). *Economic Growth and the Balance of Payments Constraint.* Basingstoke: Macmillan.

McCombie, J.S.L., Pugno, M. and Soro, B. (2002). *Productivity Growth and Economic Performance: Essays on Verdoorn's Law.* Basingstoke: Palgrave Macmillan.

Oreiro, J.L.C. and Nakabashi, L. (2007). "The economics of demand-led growth theory and evidence for Brazil", Curitiba: Centro de Pesquisas Econômicas (CEPEC/UFPR), Texto para Discussão.

Setterfield, M. (1998). "History versus equilibrium: Nicholas Kaldor on historical time and economic theory", *Cambridge Journal of Economics*, **22**, 521–37.

Stadler, G.W. (1990). "Business cycles models with endogenous technology", *American Economic Review*, **80**, 763–78.

Stiglitz, J. (1993). "Endogenous growth and cycles", NBER Working Paper No. 4286.

Targetti, F. and Foti, A. (1997). "Growth and productivity: a model of cumulative growth and catching-up", *Cambridge Journal of Economics*, **21**, 27–43.

Thirlwall, A.P. (1969). "Okun's Law and the natural rate of growth", *The Southern Economic Journal*, **36**, 87–89.

Toner, P. (1999). *Main Currents in Cumulative Causation: The Dynamics of Growth and Development.* Basingstoke: Macmillan.

Verdoorn, P.J. (1949). "Fattori che regolano lo sviluppo della produttività del lavoro", *L'Industria*, **1**, 45–53.

Vogel, L. (2009). "The endogeneity of the natural rate of growth – an empirical study for Latin American countries", *International Review of Applied Economics*, **23**, 41–53.

Young, A. (1928). "Increasing returns and economic progress", *Economic Journal*, **38**, 527–42.

11 Reconciling the growth of aggregate demand and aggregate supply
*Amitava Krishna Dutt**

1 Introduction

Theories of economic growth can be classified into two main types according to whether they view economic growth as being determined by the expansion of aggregate supply or that of aggregate demand.

The former have generally dominated growth theory. The classical economists – including Smith and Ricardo – emphasized aggregate supply by viewing growth as being determined by capital accumulation and technological change, both of which augment the economy's capacity to produce more goods; aggregate demand was not an issue because of what has subsequently been called Say's law, that is, aggregate supply created its own aggregate demand.[1] There were dissidents, of course: Malthus recognized the possibility of a general glut and Marx recognized the possibility of realization crises: insufficient demand for goods (perhaps because of low wages) could lead to production beyond what could be "realized" through sales. However, Marx did not develop an actual theory of crisis as a result of the lack of aggregate demand, let alone a theory of growth that emphasized the role of aggregate demand. Instead, he continued in the classical tradition of emphasizing capital accumulation and technological change (with labor being in unlimited supply from the reserve army of the unemployed at a real wage determined by the state of class struggle or by subsistence, broadly defined).

It was not until the development of the theory of aggregate demand by Kalecki (1971) and Keynes (1936) that the role of aggregate demand in the growth process came to be clearly recognized. While Keynes was mainly interested in the short-period theory of unemployment and Kalecki in the dynamics of the business cycle, this work inspired several theories of economic growth in which aggregate demand determines the growth rate (Harrod, 1939; Kahn, 1959; Robinson, 1962). According to these theories, it is possible to affect long-run growth by changing conditions on the demand side, for instance, by exciting animal spirits that induce firms to invest.

The neoclassical response to these theories was to develop growth theories in which all factors of production are always fully employed because of perfect price flexibility. Solow's (1956) growth model, which laid the foundations of neoclassical growth theory, *assumed* away the problem of aggregate demand by postulating that all saving (that is, income that was not spent on consumption) is automatically invested. Assuming a constant returns to scale technology that allowed smooth capital–labor substitution, Solow showed that the economy would converge to a balanced growth path in which all factors are fully employed and the growth rate is determined by the exogenously given rate of growth of labor supply (or, if one allows for labor augmenting technological change at an exogenously given rate, by the rates of growth of labor productivity and labor supply). The so-called "new" growth theory, which has now become dominant, emphasizing the roles of externalities, increasing returns, and the purposeful creation of knowledge, continues to assume that all saving is automatically invested and that all labor (and capital) is fully employed, while dispensing with the "old" neoclassical growth theory assumption of diminishing returns to capital (or more accurately, with the assumption that the marginal product of capital falls to zero when the capital–labor ratio becomes very large). Economic growth is thus determined by the rate of growth of labor supply and the growth of labor productivity: aggregate demand plays no role in the theory. The influence of aggregate demand on economic growth is emphasized only by those heterodox growth theorists who continue in the tradition of Kalecki, Keynes and Robinson.[2]

This division of growth theory between those invoking aggregate supply or aggregate demand while ignoring the other, and the dominance of theories emphasizing aggregate supply, may be disconcerting to those who believe that both aggregate supply and aggregate demand have some role in determining economic growth. Solow (1956, p. 91) clearly noted that his model

> is the neoclassical side of the coin. Most especially it is full employment economics – in the dual aspect of equilibrium condition and frictionless, competitive, causal system. All the difficulties and rigidities which go into modern Keynesian income analysis have been shunted aside. It is not my contention that these problems don't exist, nor that they are of no significance in the long run. My purpose was to examine what might be called the tight-rope view of economic growth and to see where more flexible assumptions about production would lead in a simple model. Underemployment and excess capacity or their opposite can still be attributed to any of the old causes of deficient or excess aggregate demand, but less readily to any deviation from a narrow "balance".

Later, Solow (1988, p. 309) admitted that "I think I paid too little attention to the problems of effective demand", and criticized "a standing temptation to sound like Dr. Pangloss, a very clever Dr. Pangloss. I think that tendency has won out in recent years". Similarly, some heterodox economists have argued, in essence, that those heterodox growth theorists who emphasize the role of aggregate demand neglect the role of aggregate supply in the sense that it was highlighted by the classical economists and Marx, and have suggested ways of combining the two sides in the analysis of economic growth.[3]

The purpose of this chapter is to provide simple characterizations of the two kinds of growth theories, to discuss some attempts to integrate the two approaches and criticize them for ultimately neglecting the role of aggregate demand in the growth process, and to suggest some avenues for a better reconciliation of aggregate demand and aggregate supply in the theory of growth. The rest of this chapter proceeds as follows. Section 2 attempts to define precisely the meaning of aggregate demand and aggregate supply growth and to examine how some growth theories have related them to the actual rate of growth. Section 3 evaluates some influential approaches for integrating aggregate demand and supply in growth theory. Section 4 presents simple models that are argued to provide a better reconciliation of the two approaches to growth theory. Section 5 summarizes and makes some concluding comments.

2 Aggregate supply versus aggregate demand

This section defines aggregate demand and aggregate supply in a general way, and then reviews some influential approaches to the treatment of their growth to illustrate more concretely the separation of growth theories between those that focus exclusively on the expansion of either aggregate supply or aggregate demand.

2.1   Aggregate demand and aggregate supply

We distinguish between aggregate demand (AD) and aggregate supply (AS) as follows.

AD is the real magnitude of *effective* planned expenditures by purchasers of final goods and services (consumers, firms, government or foreigners) and can be denoted by

$$Y_d = D(Y, A, Z_d) \tag{1}$$

where Y denotes real output and income, A is a vector of components of autonomous demand (such as autonomous investment, government expenditure on goods and services), and Z_d is a vector of other possible determinants of AD (such as the interest rate, money wage and the price level). For this function we have $D_Y > 0$ and $D_A > 0$ (where partials are denoted by subscripts).

AS is the *maximum* real output that can be produced by the economy given determinants of factor supplies, R, technological parameters, T, and Z_s, a vector of all other possible determinants of AS (most typically parameters relating to labor market conditions and industrial structure), and can be denoted by the function

$$Y_s = S(R, T, Z_s) \tag{2}$$

This is a very general formulation, since there may be some elements common to both Z_d and Z_s (though there are likely to be some elements which will be in only one of them). The only restrictions on these formulations are that: Y must enter the AD function to suggest that AD must be effective and supported by income, and that actual income does not affect AS; components of A do not enter the aggregate supply function; and (at least some) components of R (for instance, given supplies of factors) and T must enter the aggregate supply function (although some of them may also be included in Z_d). Note also that the definition of AS is broader than one that makes it depend only on technology and factor supplies. Although for some approaches these may indeed be the only determinants of Y_s, in others, expectations and characteristics of labor markets and industrial structure that are normally thought of as supply-side factors may also be relevant.

Using these definitions we can determine the growth rates of AD and AS, which involve the levels and/or rates of growth of some of the arguments of these equations. Note that, as will become clear below, the latter may depend on factors that do not enter in the level functions.

2.2   The classical-Marxian approach

A simple version of the classical-Marxian approach assumes that a single good is produced with a fixed-coefficients production technology with constant returns to scale, with a_0 the unit labor requirement and a_1 the unit capital requirement. Labor is assumed to be in unlimited supply (because of endogenous population growth or the existence of a reserve army), so that AS is given by

$$Y_s = K/a_1 \tag{3}$$

Note that Y_s is determined by the supply of just one resource (capital), and one techno-logical parameter, the unit capital requirement. If Y_s is actually produced, it results in income flows – to wage and profits – which may be consumed or saved. The classical-Marxian model assumes that all saving is automatically invested, so that

$$I \equiv S \tag{4}$$

Workers consume their entire income from wages, while capitalists, who receive profits, save a fraction of their income and consume the rest. Capitalists then invest their entire saving in order to expand their business and maintain their competitive position against other capitalists. The implication is that all income flows lead to planned expenditure flows and actual output is equal to AS. Thus, in this approach,

$$Y_s \equiv Y_d = Y \tag{5}$$

The rate of profit is given by

$$r = (1 - a_0 w)/a_1 \tag{6}$$

where w is the real wage. With the real wage given at "subsistence", this equation deter-mines the rate of profit. With s_c being the saving rate of capitalists out of profits we have

$$S = s_c r K \tag{7}$$

Assuming away depreciation of capital, for simplicity, this implies, using equations (4), (6) and (7),

$$\hat{K} = s_c \frac{1 - a_0 w}{a_1} \tag{8}$$

where overhats denote rates of growth, that is $\hat{x} = (dx/dt)/(x)$. Equations (3) and (8) imply, with technological parameters given, that

$$\hat{Y}_s = s_c \frac{1 - a_0 w}{a_1} \tag{9}$$

which shows that the growth rate of AS depends on technological parameters, labor market conditions and the saving rate. Since actual output and AD are equal to aggre-gate supply, this also determines the growth rate of AD and output.

   Three comments on this model are in order. First, it seems that unemployment in this model is the result of fixed coefficients of production. The stock of capital fixes output at a point in time, and this output is insufficient to fully employ all workers. While this interpretation is correct as far as this simple version of the model is concerned, it can also be justified in terms of constant-returns to scale technology that allows smooth substitu-tion between capital and labor, which, for the given exogenously fixed real wage, fixes the capital–labor ratio, and hence the unit capital and labor requirements. Thus, for a given real wage the model behaves just like the fixed-coefficients model.

   Second, it is not clear what makes saving identically equal to investment. One rationale may be that capitalists save in order to invest, so that all the income they do not consume is invested. But this rationale raises two questions. One, what prevents capitalists from first making saving plans and then deciding not to invest their entire saving because they expect future sales conditions to be poor? If they decide to use their unused saving to consume, then all goods will be sold. But what if they decide not to increase their consumption but instead hoard it in the form of non-produced wealth? Or, will capitalists *always* invest all their saving to compete with other capitalists? Clearly, as mentioned earlier, Marx thought otherwise, as suggested by his discussion of the realization crisis and money hoarding by capitalists. Two, what if capitalists who are producers borrowed from financiers (as Marx discussed), and wanted to invest more than what savers planned to save? What then brings saving and investment to equality?

Third, actual output and hence actual employment (in the absence of labor productivity growth) grow at the rate given by equation (9). What, then, prevents the unemployment rate of workers rising or falling indefinitely (tending to infinity or zero), if labor supply grows at an exogenously fixed rate, say n? Is this consistent with a long-run equilibrium theory of growth?

2.3   The neoclassical approach

This approach, as developed by Solow (1956), uses the production function with smooth substitution and constant returns to scale given by

$$Y = F(K, L) \tag{10}$$

Labor supply, N, is assumed to be given at a point in time and prices and wages adjust to clear all markets (in contrast to the fixed real wage of the previous model). Thus, labor and capital are fully employed at an instant of time, and the full employment output is produced. Thus, AS is given by

$$Y_s = F(K, N) \tag{11}$$

A fraction, s, of total income, is saved, so that

$$S = sY \tag{12}$$

As in the classical-Marxian approach, all saving is invested, so all output is demanded. Thus, equation (5) is satisfied, and there is no AD independent of AS. Writing the production function in intensive form,

$$y = f(k) \tag{13}$$

where $k = K/L = K/N$, we get the dynamic equation for the Solow model, given by

$$\frac{dk}{dt} = sf(k) - nk, \tag{14}$$

where n, as before, is the exogenously fixed rate of growth of labor supply. As is well known, this dynamic equation implies, with some restrictions on the production function (called the Inada conditions, which imply that both labor and capital are essential for production) that the economy converges to a long-run steady state at which capital, labor supply and output all grow at the same rate, determined by the rate of labor supply growth. Out of steady state the economy can grow at, say, a higher rate because of more saving and higher capital accumulation, than labor supply allows, but in the long run the economy grows at rate n, since diminishing returns to capital pushes growth back to this rate. All along the growth path, AS determines AD.

Nothing related to the status of AS and AD and their growth are changed by modifying the assumption that the saving rate is fixed (allowing, for instance, intertemporal optimization given preferences) and allowing technological change. With intertemporal optimization, the saving rate is replaced by more "fundamental" preference parameters as a determinant of (short-run) aggregate supply growth. Meanwhile, if technological change is assumed to be labor augmenting at an exogenously fixed rate, AS growth will be determined by n plus the rate of change of technology. Once the economy is in long-run steady state growth equilibrium, AS and output grow at the rate of growth of the effective supply of labor (that is, labor supply plus the rate of labor productivity growth). Nor is anything changed in "new" growth theory. Its only real departure from the "old" neoclassical approach is in violating the Inada conditions, by introducing a lower limit to the extent of diminishing returns to capital. This allows the long-run rate of AS and output growth to depend on saving and other parameters, in addition to labor supply growth and purely technological parameters.

2.4 The Kalecki–Keynes approach

Arguably the simplest growth model in the Kalecki–Keynes tradition assumes that saving is a fraction of real income so that equation (12) holds, and that output is produced with fixed coefficients technology as in the basic classical-Marxian model with given technology. Thus, real consumption, C, as a ratio of capital stock, is given by

$$C/K = (1 - s)u \tag{15}$$

where $u = Y/K$ is a measure of capacity utilization (given that $1/a_1$ is a constant). The model assumes that planned investment (as a ratio of capital stock) is a positive function of capacity utilization, so that, adopting a simple linear form,

$$I/K = \gamma + \beta u \tag{16}$$

where γ is the autonomous component of investment, and $\beta > 0$ is the response of the investment rate to changes in capacity utilization. The investment function states that higher capacity utilization makes firms want to invest more because they expect more buoyant markets and higher profits in the future. With no government fiscal activity, for a closed economy, AD is given by

$$Y_d = \gamma K + (1 - s + \beta) Y \tag{17}$$

which depends on Y, on autonomous expenditure γ, on K, and on other demand parameters. Now assume that the goods market clears through variations in the actual level of output in response to AD, and that $s > \beta$ (that is, the response of saving to changes in capacity utilization is higher than that of the response of investment, a standard stability condition in such macro-models). Thus, goods market equilibrium is achieved when

$$Y_d = Y \tag{18}$$

which implies that

$$u = \gamma/(s - \beta) \tag{19}$$

The level of output is determined at $Y = uK$. Continuing to assume away depreciation, the growth rate of capital is given by $g = I/K$, where

$$g = s\gamma/(s - \beta) \tag{20}$$

Abstracting from technological change, the growth rate of output (with output given by $Y = uK$) is also given by g since u is determined by (19).

Growth in this model is determined by the growth of AD and is independent of AS. This can be seen by examining AS in the two senses discussed above. In the classical-Marxian sense, AS is given by equation (3). In the model of this section, the output–capital ratio is determined in equilibrium by equation (19), that is, by AD parameters. There is no reason whatever that equation (3) is also satisfied, that is, that the economy is at full capacity utilization. Thus, AD will not, in general, be equal to AS. In equilibrium, AS will grow at the same rate as AD and output since capacity utilization is constant, but this will not be true if demand parameters, such as γ or autonomous investment, change over time. In this case, u will change over time, and AS will change according to the rate of growth of the capital stock, while output and AD will grow according to the rate of growth of capital stock and the rate of growth of u. To make this possible we have to assume that the level of u determined by equation (19) is less than or equal to the maximum output–capital ratio, that is, $u \leq 1/a_1$, that is, the AD parameters do not make u "too" high. In the neoclassical sense AS is given by the level of output at which labor is fully employed. Therefore, continuing to assume a fixed coefficients technology, if there is a fixed supply of labor at a point in time, N, which grows at the exogenously given rate n, AS is given by $Y_s = N/a_0$, and the growth of AS is given by n. Again, AS will in general not be equal to AD, since there is no reason for u as determined by equation (19) to be equal to $N/(Ka_0)$; and there is also no reason for the growth of AD and actual output, determined by equation (20), to be equal to the growth of AS, given by n. Thus with output growing at the rate g, unemployment will rise (if $g < n$) or fall (if $g > n$) indefinitely over time.

This basic model has been extended in a number of directions to incorporate a number of features left out of the simple model discussed here, including income distribution, differential saving propensities from wages and profits, inflation, open economy features, and debt of various kinds.[4] Two features in particular are relevant for present purposes, one regarding the relation between distribution and growth, and the other concerning technological change. If we assume that a fixed share of income, λ, goes to workers as wages, and make the classical-Marxian assumption about saving behavior, the model implies that an increase in λ increases the rate of growth of the economy, by increasing consumption demand, capacity utilization, and hence investment demand. This has been called the case of wage-led growth. If we assume that a_0 falls at the constant rate τ over time, the rate of growth of employment is given by $l = y - \tau$. There is, again, no reason why this l is going to be equal to n, and hence why the unemployment rate is constant in long-run equilibrium. Note also that if there is an increase in the rate of technological change, so that τ rises, unemployment will merely rise at a faster rate, leaving the rate of growth of output and per capita output unchanged.[5]

The two features of the model that imply that growth is determined by AD and is independent of AS, have been the subject of criticism. One criticism is that the model allows the rate of capacity utilization, u, to be endogenous even at long-run growth equilibrium, rather than requiring it to converge to the full capacity level or even, taking into account the possibility of firms wanting to maintain some excess capacity to meet unanticipated increases in demand and to take advantage of scale economies, some desired or planned level, which may be considered to be a requirement of long-run equilibrium. It may be asked why firms would continue investing at a rate that does not allow them to achieve their planned level of capacity utilization. Another criticism is that the model does not require the unemployment rate to arrive at some equilibrium level in long-run equilibrium. As noted before, the model implies that there is nothing to ensure that the unemployment rate does not rise or fall indefinitely at long-run equilibrium. The model may be considered to be problematic, both because one does not observe indefinite increases or decreases in the unemployment rate in reality, and also because it seems theoretically implausible to have a long-run equilibrium in which the rate of unemployment does not arrive at some equilibrium value.

3   Some proposed integrations of aggregate demand and aggregate supply

Several ways of integrating aggregate demand and aggregate supply in the analysis of growth have been suggested. This section examines two such influential suggestions, one integrating the classical-Marxian and the Kalecki–Keynes approaches, and the other the neoclassical and the Kalecki–Keynes approaches, and discusses their common features and shortcomings. Both integrations model the short run following the Kalecki–Keynes approach. Thus, planned investment is given by equation (16) and saving by equation (12). Thus, the short-run equilibrium level of u is shown by equation (19). The two models deviate in their analysis of long-run dynamics.

3.1   Classical-Marxian aggregate supply

The synthesis using the classical-Marxian AS story follows the approach developed by Duménil and Lévy (1999) and the one-sector model of Michl (2008), and incorporates inflation and a Central Bank response function which changes the real rate of interest to achieve inflation and utilization targets.[6] The model assumes that the inflation rate, p, depends on the gap between actual capacity utilization and desired capacity utilization, that is,

$$dp/dt = \Theta[u - u_d], \qquad (21)$$

where $\Theta > 0$ is a speed of adjustment constant. This is a modified Phillips curve that makes changes in the rate of inflation depend on the capacity utilization gap (rather than the unemployment rate): firms are portrayed as raising inflation at a faster rate when there is a high demand for goods so that actual capacity utilization exceeds desired capacity utilization. The Central Bank is assumed to change the real interest rate according to the policy-rule equation

$$dR/dt = (R_n - R) + \iota(p - p^T) \tag{22}$$

where R is the real interest rate, p^T is its target inflation rate, R_n is the real interest rate it targets in order to ensure that the economy achieves the firms' desired degree of capacity utilization, and $\iota > 0$ is a policy parameter. We slightly modify the desired investment rate of firms to make the "autonomous" component depend negatively on the real interest rate, or, $\gamma = \gamma_0 - \gamma_1 R$, so that we replace equation (16) by

$$I/K = \gamma_0 - \gamma_1 R + \beta u \tag{23}$$

where γ_i are positive investment parameters.

In the short run we assume that in addition to K, p and R are given. Setting aggregate demand, that is, the sum of consumption and investment demand, to total output, we get the equilibrium condition for the goods market in the short run, which implies

$$u = \frac{\gamma_0 - \gamma_1 R}{s - \beta} \tag{24}$$

Note that since the Central Bank sets R_n to ensure that $u = u_d$, we get

$$R_n = \frac{\gamma_0 - (s - \beta)u_d}{\gamma_1} \tag{25}$$

In the long run p and R adjust according to equations (21) and (22), and K grows according to the investment rate, I/K. Substituting equations (24) and (25) into equation (21) we get

$$dp/dt = \frac{\Theta\gamma_1}{s - \beta}(R_n - R) \tag{21'}$$

Using this equation and equation (22), we can see that the long-run dynamics of the model are given by Figure 11.1. The long-run equilibrium of the economy is globally stable, and at this long-run equilibrium, $u = u_d$, and capital, output and employment all grow at the rate

$$g = su_d \tag{26}$$

To make the model closer to the classical-Marxian model we would need to write $s = s_c(1 - \lambda)$ where $\lambda = a_0 w$ is the wage share and $1 - \lambda$ the profit share, assumed to be constant.

This model achieves an integration of sorts of the Kalecki–Keynes and the classical-Marxian approaches. As can be verified from equations (23) and (24), in the short run it behaves like the Kalecki–Keynes model: a rise in exogenous demand, γ_0, increases capacity utilization and growth; a rise in the saving propensity, s, reduces capacity utilization and growth (the paradox of thrift); and a rise in the wage share, λ (noting that $s =$

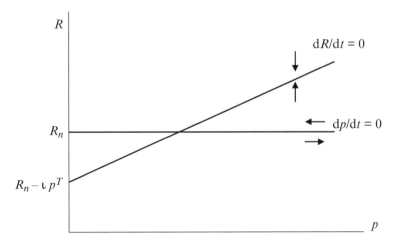

Figure 11.1   Dynamics of the classical-Marxian model

$s_c(1 - \lambda)$), increases capacity utilization and growth (wage-led growth). However, in the long run the model behaves like a classical-Marxian one, as can be verified from equation (26): the effect on the growth rate is zero for a rise in exogenous demand, positive for a rise in the saving rate, and negative for a rise in the wage share (profit-led growth); capacity utilization, of course, is equal to u_d, which is exogenously given.

This model can be criticized on several grounds, of which four are relevant for the purposes of our discussion. First, the model relies strongly on the Central Bank's policy stance as reflected in the reaction function given in equation (22), rather than on "natural" market forces involving the invisible hand that produces the long-run convergence to full or desired capacity utilization. What if the Central Bank does not follow a specific rule, but instead follows its instincts, not knowing – for instance – whether changes in the underlying parameters, and hence variables of the model, are permanent or transitory? The economy will then not necessarily converge to the desired capacity utilization rate. If persistent excess capacity induces firms to reduce investment, and this reduces γ_0, capacity utilization will be further reduced, implying Harrodian knife-edge instability. If the Central Bank does not have a real interest target but only an inflation target, the economy will exhibit limit cycle fluctuations instead of converging to the level of desired capacity (although it would still be true that on average the economy would hover around its desired rate of capacity utilization and its supply-determined growth rate). Second, adjustment relies strongly on the negative effect of the real interest rate on aggregate demand. While the mechanism may work during the upswing, it is less obvious that during the downswing interest rate reductions will systematically increase aggregate demand, as implied by empirical findings on the interest inelasticity of investment, especially when the interest rate falls. Third, the model – like the Kalecki–Steindl model – does not ensure that the rate of unemployment is constant (if labor supply grows at an exogenously fixed rate). Finally, the model assumes that income distribution is unaffected by inflation because the money wage adjusts fully to the inflation rate, keeping the real wage constant. These weaknesses result in what can be called a weak integration of AD and AS in which AD is relevant in the short run, but irrelevant in affecting the long-run rate of growth of the economy, which is determined solely by AS.

3.2   Neoclassical aggregate supply
An even more popular attempt at the integration of AS and AD is found in the standard textbook neoclassical-synthesis Keynesian model and in the new consensus and new neoclassical synthesis models (see, for instance, Woodford, 2003), where there is wage rigidity and unemployment in the short run and wage flexibility and full employment (or at least unemployment at the natural rate) in the long run. In the short run, with some degree of wage rigidity, the labor market does not clear, and output can grow at a rate that does not make the growth of labor demand equal to the growth of labor supply. However, in the longer run, with wage flexibility, this condition cannot persist, and growth can occur only with the demand and supply of labor growing at the same rate. Since these models are well known, we present a simple, reduced-form version that, rather than modeling inflation and asset markets explicitly, assumes that investment reacts to labor market conditions.

For the short run we use the saving and investment functions given by equations (12) and (16) and assume that output (and hence capacity utilization) adjustments clear the goods market to determine short-run equilibrium levels of capacity utilization and the rate of growth of capital stock given by equations (19) and (20), given K and γ.

For the long run we assume that

$$\hat{\gamma} = -\theta[l - n] \tag{27}$$

where l, as defined earlier, is the rate of growth of employment, n the exogenously given growth of labor supply and $\theta > 0$ is a speed of adjustment parameter. Two mechanisms can explain this adjustment, which shows that if the rate of growth of labor supply exceeds that of labor demand, so that the unemployment rate increases, the autonomous investment rate will fall. One, an increase in the unemployment rate reduces wages and prices, increases the real money supply, reduces the interest rate and increases investment. Two, a rise in the unemployment rate induces expansionary monetary and fiscal policies, which increase the investment rate.

Assuming that the productivity of labor is constant, the rate of growth of output, $y = l$. From the definition of u, we have

$$y = \hat{u} + g \tag{28}$$

From equations (19), (20), (27) and (28) we get

$$\hat{\gamma} = \frac{\theta}{1 + \theta}\left[n - \frac{s\gamma}{s - \beta}\right] \tag{29}$$

This equation of motion for the model implies that the long-run equilibrium rate of growth of the model, at which $\hat{\gamma} = 0$, is given by

$$g = n \tag{30}$$

and is stable. In long-run equilibrium, since $g = y = l$, the rate of unemployment is constant, and output grows at the rate of growth of labor supply, implying no growth in per capita income.

If we introduce technological change, reflected in a constant rate of labor productivity growth, τ, $y = l + \tau$, equation (29) must be modified to

$$\hat{\gamma} = \frac{\theta}{1 + \theta}\left[n + \tau - \frac{s\gamma}{s - \beta}\right] \tag{31}$$

In long-run equilibrium – which is again stable – the unemployment rate becomes constant and we have $y = g = n + \tau$. The rate of growth of per capita income is τ, as in the Solovian neoclassical growth model with exogenous technological change.

This model differs from the standard neoclassical synthesis model in that its long-run equilibrium rate of unemployment is *some* constant, rather than a *particular* exogenously specified full employment rate.[7] This follows from the assumption that investment varies with *changes* in – and not *levels* of (as in standard models) – the unemployment rate. Dependence on changes can be explained by what has been called hysteresis in labor markets. A high level of unemployment need not exert downward pressure on wages and lead to increases in investment because outsiders in the wage negotiation process may have no influence on wage bargains, and because workers who lose their skills are not relevant to the wage determination process. Thus it is only when unemployment increases that wages will tend to fall, because it takes time to lose skills or become outsiders, and this exerts downward wage pressures.[8] Fiscal and monetary policy may also change only when there are changes in the unemployment rate, with policy makers getting used to any level of unemployment by calling it the natural rate of unemployment consistent with price stability.

If these arguments are not found convincing, we may make alternative assumptions to make the model imply that the economy arrives at some exogenously specified natural rate of unemployment, $1 - e_n$ in long-run equilibrium. For instance, we could replace equation (27) by

$$\hat{\gamma} = q(e - e_n) \tag{32}$$

where $e = L/N$ is the employment rate, $q' < 0$ and $q(0) = 0$. Since $e = a_0uK/N$, with $\kappa = Ka_0/N$, we have

$$e = u\kappa \tag{33}$$

Substituting from equations (19) and (33) into equation (32) we can write

$$\hat{\gamma} = q\left(\frac{\gamma\kappa}{s - \beta} - e_n\right) \tag{34}$$

The definition of κ implies

$$\hat{\kappa} = g - n - \tau \tag{35}$$

which implies, substituting from equation (20),

$$\hat{\kappa} = \frac{s\gamma}{s - \beta} - n - \tau \tag{36}$$

With all parameters, including τ, given, equations (34) and (36) give us a two-dimensional dynamic system involving γ and κ. In $<\gamma, \kappa>$ space we can show the $\hat{\gamma} = 0$ locus as a rectangular hyperbola and the $\hat{\kappa} = 0$ locus as a horizontal line, that the long-run equilibrium is a stable one, and that the long-run equilibrium rate of growth of output is $n + \tau$ and of per-capita output is τ.

These synthesis models therefore produce Kalecki–Keynesian properties in the short run: output expands with an increase in autonomous demand, but in the long run they behave in the standard neoclassical manner, with AS determining growth. The property of these models that makes the economy grow at the rate determined by AS in the long run is that components of AD change in response to labor market conditions. For the market-mediated adjustment, this requires both that wages and prices are flexible in the long run, and that changes in the price level lead to increases in investment spending (because of, for instance, changes in the interest rate or, alternatively, the real balance or wealth effects). That such an adjustment may be aborted by a variety of factors, including wage and price rigidity, the endogeneity of credit money, uncertainty (which prevents investment from responding to a reduction in the rate of interest rate), and debt deflation, has been pointed out by Keynes (1936) and many Keynesian and post-Keynesian economists (see Dutt and Amadeo, 1990). Furthermore, the government policy adjustment may also be aborted by the unwillingness – for political reasons, for instance (see Kalecki, 1943) – or the inability of governments to adjust AD to AS. These problems may well interfere with the economy converging to positions of full employment or a constant unemployment rate. In this case, it is possible for the economy to grow – for considerable lengths of time – with a rate of growth of output determined by AD, as in the model of section 2.4. But if these problems are exceptional and the economy normally does converge to an equilibrium growth path with full employment or at least a constant unemployment rate, AS determines long-run growth.

4   Towards a reconciliation of aggregate demand and aggregate supply

The synthesis models discussed in the previous section imply that although aggregate demand can affect the level of output and the growth rate of the economy in the short run, in the long run growth is determined only by AS. If this view is correct, we may as well exclude AD considerations from the theory of growth, which is in fact what mainstream and other influential growth theories do. This section modifies the two models of the previous section to show that the conditions under which AD considerations are irrelevant for the determination of long-run growth are very stringent and that, if these conditions are not met, as is likely, this neglect of AD is inappropriate.

4.1   Endogenous distribution in the classical-Marxian synthesis model

As noted in section 3.1, the synthesis model with the classical-Marxian AS side assumed that the distribution of income is unaffected by inflation. Here we amend that model to take into account the possibility that wages do not fully adjust to price changes. More specifically, we assume the money wage changes according to the equation

$$\hat{W} = p^T + \delta(p - p^T)$$

with $\delta < 1$, which states that the money wage adjusts fully to the target inflation rate, but incompletely to deviations of actual inflation and this target rate, which guides inflation expectations. The real wage, w, therefore changes according to the equation

$$\hat{W} = (1 - \delta)(p^T - p)$$

Since the labor share in income is given by $\lambda = wa_0$, with given technology that keeps a_0 constant, we therefore have

$$\hat{\lambda} = (1 - \delta)(p^T - p) \qquad (37)$$

which shows that a higher rate of inflation is associated with a fall in the wage share since workers are not able to fully defend their real wage from erosion when inflation is higher. In other respects the model is the same as the earlier one, that is, we use the investment function given by equation (23), and take inflation dynamics and the Central Bank's policy rule to be given by equations (21) and (22). We write saving as a ratio of the capital stock in the form

$$S/K = s_c(1 - \lambda)u \qquad (38)$$

to make explicit the assumption about differential saving behavior of capitalists and workers. The only difference between this model and the earlier model is that in this one the distribution of income is endogenous.

In the short run we have R, p and λ given, and the model solves for the short-run equilibrium value of u given by equation (24), although with $s = s_c(1 - \lambda)u$. Since λ is fixed in the short run, the short-run properties of this model are exactly the same as its predecessor – that is, like a Kalecki–Keynes model. In the long run, however, the model has three dynamic equations involving the dynamics of three state variables, R, p and λ. The long-run dynamics can be shown to be stable. However, there is no unique long-run equilibrium for this model, but a continuum of equilibria. This can be seen by noting that in long-run equilibrium, with p and R stationary, equations (21) and (22') imply $R = R_n$ and $p = p^T$. But equation (37) is satisfied when the second of these conditions is satisfied: this model adds a new long-run variable, λ, without adding a new *independent* long-run equilibrium condition. It follows that the model cannot be solved to find a unique equilibrium for the three long-run variables: it is a zero-root model with a continuum of equilibria. In long-run equilibrium, $p = p^T$ which is uniquely determined since p^T is exogenously fixed. However, in long-run equilibrium R and λ can take any positive values as long as they satisfy the condition

$$R = \frac{\gamma_0 - (s_c - \beta)u_d}{\gamma_1} + \frac{s_c u_d}{\gamma_1}\lambda$$

This equation is obtained by substituting equations (25) and (38) into the condition $R = R_n$ that must be satisfied for a stationary level of p, as shown by equation (21'). The equation shows that a higher labor share, λ, increases the level of capacity utilization, which requires a higher interest rate, R, to reduce capacity utilization in order to bring down the rate of inflation to its target level. Since the long-run equilibrium value of λ is indeterminate, as shown by equation (38) for $u = u_d$, so is S/K, which implies, since the goods market always clears so that the saving-investment equality holds, that g is also indeterminate.

The problem is that there are three processes – changes in distribution and policy-induced changes in the real interest and the inflation rate – which respond to only two disequilibria in the short run, that is, the gap between the long-run inertial (or the Central Bank's target) rate of inflation and the short-run rate of inflation, and the gap between the real rate of interest and the Central Bank's target real rate of interest, which is designed to keep actual capacity utilization equal to desired capacity utilization. Since at long-run equilibrium the inflation rate is equal to its exogenously determined target level, how much adjustment in distribution and the real interest rate will occur to remove the disequilibra will depend not only on the speeds of adjustment of the three variables, but also from where the economy starts. History (represented by the model's initial conditions) matters for the final equilibrium of the economy.

This model implies that, in general, AD affects the long-run growth rate of the economy. This can be seen by considering a special case of the model in which the interest rate adjustment is very slow compared to the distributional and inflation adjustments, so that we can examine the dynamics of the model by assuming R to be fixed and using only equations (21) and (37).[9] In this case the long-run equilibrium value of inflation is equal to p^T, implying that distribution does not change, and the labor share is given by

$$\lambda^* = \frac{(s_c - \beta) u_d - \gamma_0 + \gamma_1 R}{s_c u_d} \tag{39}$$

implying that the rate of inflation does not change. Starting from this level, if the labor share increases, capacity utilization will increase because of an increase in consumption spending, and hence investment spending, given the fact that growth is wage-led in the short run, which makes the rate of inflation increase since capacity utilization exceeds its desired level. This version of the model takes a simple form that results in concentric limit cycles: an increase in the inflation rate resulting from a high wage share reduces the wage share and brings about a decline in capacity utilization, which then brings down the inflation rate, and so on.[10] The rate of accumulation for the economy also fluctuates, since a higher labor share implies a higher rate of growth. However, as can be verified from equations (38) and (39), the fluctuation occurs around the growth rate given by

$$g^* = \gamma_0 - \gamma_1 R + \beta u_d \tag{40}$$

Thus, the average rate of growth for the economy is affected positively by autonomous demand, and negatively by the rate of interest. Hence, AD parameters have long-run effects. If the growth rate increases, it can do so by reducing the labor share, so that growth is not wage-led. The model, in fact, bears a close resemblance to Robinson's (1962) model, referred to in the literature as the neo-Keynesian model, in which higher growth is possible through forced saving, that is, by an inflation-induced reduction in the wage share.[11]

4.2 Long-run endogeneity of the capacity utilization rate

The model just discussed does not allow for the possibility of wage-led growth and assumes that in long-run equilibrium actual capacity utilization is at its exogenously fixed desired level.[12] However, there is no particular reason why the capacity utilization rate in the long run must be equal to such a fixed desired level. This issue has been debated extensively, and we need only summarize some of the main arguments in favor of this view, and their implications.

First, there may be no such thing as a long-run equilibrium in which all relevant adjustments have been completed, so that one can analyze the long run simply as an average of short-run positions. If this is the case, there is no particular reason why the long-run equilibrium (a hypothetical construction) need be qualitatively different from short-run equilibria. The short-run result of wage-led growth will therefore carry over to the longer run. This argument essentially rejects the classical-Marxian long-run equilibrium notion.

Second, although firms may have some planned or desired levels of capacity utilization, in uncertain environments, they may not choose a specific level, and may be content if actual capacity utilization falls within a band. If the long-run equilibrium occurs within a band, firms will not be surprised in Shackle's (1955) sense, their attention will not be arrested, and they will not be induced to change their investment behavior. In this case the classical-Marxian long-run equilibrium is not being abandoned, but is being interpreted in a flexible manner. As long as the economy remains within this band (the width of which may be taken to depend positively on the extent of uncertainty faced by firms) AD will have long-run effects and growth can be wage-led.

Third, although firms may have a target level of the degree of capacity utilization, they may have other targets as well, such as their desire to maintain their share of the value added in their bargains with workers, and to meet the demands of financial capitalists. When such multiple targets are taken into account, firms are likely to behave in a way in which they do not precisely meet any particular target, so that the degree of capacity utilization can be endogenous. This approach does not reject the classical-Marxian equilibrium notion but broadens it to incorporate multiple pressures on the firm.

Finally, firms may have a desired rate of capacity utilization, but this rate may be endogenous. If firms maintain excess capacity as a defensive weapon against potential entrants, and if they choose to increase their desired amount of excess capacity when they expect the economy to grow at a higher rate than at present, it is possible to have a model with multiple equilibria in which changes in expectations affect both investment and desired capacity utilization. In long-run equilibrium, the actual and desired levels of capacity utilization will be equal, but the desired level is endogenous, and long-run growth is affected by AD and may be wage led (see Dutt, 1997 and Lavoie, 1995). This approach accepts the classical-Marxian long-run equilibrium notion but extends it by endogenizing firms' plans.

If we give up the classical-Marxian notion that firms must achieve a fixed desired level of capacity utilization in the long run – by accepting any one of these arguments – not only will long-run growth be affected by AD factors, but growth can also be wage-led.

4.3   Endogenous technological change in the neoclassical-synthesis model

The neoclassical approach to growth theory makes the long-run growth rate of the economy depend on AS factors such as the rate of growth of labor supply and of labor productivity. If the long-run rates of change in these variables are independent of AD, then the actual growth rate is not affected by AD. There are, however, a number of reasons why the growth rates of labor supply and labor productivity may depend on what happens in the short run, which in turn depend on AD.[13] There may be changes in labor supply or aggregate labor productivity because of shifts from low to high productivity sectors. However, in terms of growth rates, technological change is likely to have the more important role. We consider simple extensions of the models with neoclassical AS to incorporate endogenous technological change into them.

A simple formulation (see Dutt, 2006) assumes that labor productivity growth, τ, changes according to the equation

$$\hat{\tau} = \Phi\,[l - n] \tag{41}$$

where $\Phi > 0$.[14] In this approach an expansion in aggregate demand leads to a faster rate of growth of employment, which results in a faster rate of labor-augmenting technological change, allowing an increase in the rate of growth without creating a labor shortage. This view is different from that of mainstream growth models, which do not distinguish between employment and labor supply and which explain technical progress in terms of research and development activities, human capital accumulation and learning by doing. In the view adopted here, firms are assumed to experience an increase in the rate of labor productivity growth in response to shortages of labor by adopting at a faster rate technology that economizes labor use. The approach follows Marx's (1867, Chapter 15.5) analysis of technological change – which involves the adoption of labor-displacing machines – as a weapon in the hands of capitalists in class struggle and is also consistent with the views of Robinson (1956). This view of technological change differs from the new growth theory approach by emphasizing the demand side of the economy rather than the supply side, and the diffusion of technology among firms who are driven to adopt the technology by labor shortages, rather than the process of invention (although it is also consistent with the innovation view).

As in section 3.2 we assume that investment adjusts according to equation (31), where τ is given in the short run, but changes according to equation (41) in the long run. Equation (41) implies, using equations (19), (20), (28) and (31),

$$\hat{\tau} = \frac{\Phi}{1 + \theta}\left[\frac{s\gamma}{s - \beta} - n - \tau\right] \tag{42}$$

The dynamic system given by equations (31) and (42) is a zero-root system which can be represented by the phase diagram shown in Figure 11.2, where the $\hat{\gamma} = 0$ and $\hat{\tau} = 0$ loci are both given by the equation $\tau = -n + (s\gamma/(s - \beta))$. Note that at long-run equilibrium the rate of unemployment is a constant, since $l = n$.

Instead of a unique long-run equilibrium, the economy has a continuum of equilibria along the $\hat{\gamma} = 0$ and $\hat{\tau} = 0$ loci, which happen to coincide. It can be shown that these equilibria are all stable (see Dutt, 2006). This implies that the long-run equilibrium position of the economy will depend on the initial conditions. Starting from a long-run

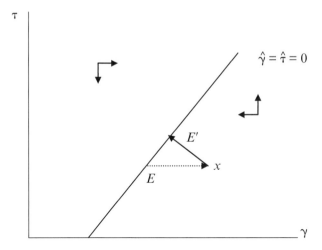

Figure 11.2   Dynamics of the neoclassical-synthesis Keynesian model with endogenous technological change

equilibrium, say at E, an exogenous increase in γ, brought about by expansionary fiscal or monetary policy, or an autonomous boost in animal spirits, will imply a move to a position like x (since a is given in the short run). In the long run there will be a movement along the diagonal arrow to E' resulting in a higher rate of growth than at the initial equilibrium at E. Hence, expansionary policies and other positive aggregate demand shocks have long-term expansionary effects, although not as strong as short-run expansionary effects. Likewise, contractionary policies have long-run contractionary effects. Third, the path of the economy from any point in the diagram will depend on the relative sizes of the two adjustment parameters: θ, which denotes the adjustment of investment to deviations of the rate of growth of demand for labor from the supply of labor, and Φ, the response of technological change to the same deviation. If technological change is not very responsive to conditions in the labor market, Φ will be close to zero, τ will adjust very little, so that the economy will move from point x back to a point close to E. If, on the other hand, investment is not very responsive – because of the rigidity of wages and prices or because of slow adjustments in investment to asset market conditions, or because government policy is not contractionary when the economy begins to heat up, θ will be close to zero, and γ will adjust very little, and the economy will move from point x to a point on the $\hat{\gamma} = \hat{\tau} = 0$ line vertically above x. Thus, the path of the economy depends on the technological responsiveness of the economy (captured by Φ) and by the policy stance of the government, or by labor and asset market characteristics (captured by θ).

A second model uses equation (32) to formalize changes in investment and assumes that technological change adjusts according to labor shortages as measured by the *levels* of labor supply and demand rather than rates of change in the employment rate, so that we have

$$\hat{\tau} = h(e - e_n) \tag{43}$$

where $h' > 0$ and $h(0) = 0$, that is, labor productivity growth grows more rapidly when the labor market is tighter, and is constant when the economy is at its "natural" rate of unemployed, when there is no upward pressure on the real wage. As in the second model of section 3.2, investment dynamics are given by (32), the dynamics of κ by equation (35), and e by equation (33).

We therefore obtain a three-dimensional dynamic system involving γ, κ and τ given by equations (34), (36) and

$$\hat{\tau} = h'\left(\frac{\gamma\kappa}{s - \beta} - e_n\right) \tag{44}$$

A glance at equations (34) and (44) reveals that this model again produces a zero-root system with a continuum of equilibria. It can be shown that the equilibria are stable, provided that h' is not too large.[15] The results of our simple two-variable model presented earlier in this subsection therefore carry over to this model – although we do not have hysteresis in unemployment, only in growth rates. In particular, an exogenous increase in γ, representing AD, will result in an increase in the long-run equilibrium value of γ, which will increase the rate of growth of the economy in the long run.

5   Conclusion

The dominant view in growth theory is that long-run growth is affected by factors on the aggregate supply side, and that aggregate demand is irrelevant in determining the rate of growth in the long run. Attempts by those with classical-Marxian and neoclassical orientations to synthesize aggregate demand and supply in the analysis of growth have resulted in models in which aggregate demand can have short-run growth effects, but in the long run growth is determined by factors on the supply side. This chapter has made precise what is meant by aggregate demand and aggregate supply, examined these attempted syntheses, and shown that if these models are slightly modified to take into account important aspects of the economy (such as the roles of distributional dynamics and technological change, and the possible long-run endogeneity of the rate of capacity utilization) they imply that aggregate demand can have an effect on growth not only in the short run but also in the long run. Thus, our reconciliation of aggregate demand and aggregate supply suggests that both affect long-run growth.

This analysis has obvious and important policy implications. For instance, contractionary aggregate demand policies that attempt to stabilize the economy in the short run, or that attempt to reduce government deficits and debt, can have long-run negative effects on economic growth, and improvements in income distribution can have positive long-run effects on growth.

Notes

* * I am grateful to Mark Setterfield for his useful comments and suggestions on an earlier draft.
1. Labor supply was also not an issue because it was assumed that increases in population growth (when wages rise above subsistence) remove labor shortages.
2. See, for instance, Taylor (1983), Dutt (1990) and Lavoie (1992) for discussions of neo-Keynesian and other Keynesian and post-Keynesian models.
3. See, for instance, Duménil and Lévy (1999).
4. See, for instance, Dutt (1990), Lavoie (1992) and Taylor (1983, 2004).
5. Some models – see Rowthorn (1982) and Dutt (1990), for instance – assume that investment depends positively on technological change. In these models an increase in the rate of technological change can –

but need not, if the response of investment to technological change is small – increase the rate of growth of per capita output. But it does so by increasing aggregate demand, and not because it increases aggregate supply.

6. While these presentations use a discrete-time framework, here, for convenience, a continuous-time framework is used.

7. Full employment here can be generalized to a natural rate of unemployment or NAIRU.

8. See for instance, Dutt and Ros (2007).

9. The model of section 3.1 can be thought of as another special case, in which $\delta = 1$ and in which p and R are the long-run variables. A third possibility – in which p does not change and in which R and λ vary in the long run cannot be considered because unless $p = p^T$ equation (37) will not hold. Note that in the special case being considered here, since there is no Central Bank target for the inflation rate, p^T has to be interpreted as inertial inflation because of inflation expectations (determined perhaps by historical factors).

10. The stability of the more general model with three variables comes from the stabilizing influence of changes in R as seen in the model of section 3.2.

11. See Marglin (1984) and Dutt (1990). Such a model can be considered a special case in which inflation adjustment occurs infinitely fast, so that $u = u_d$ always holds, and λ is determined by equation (39) even in the short run. The growth rate of the economy is, again, seen to depend on aggregate demand.

12. See, for instance, Lavoie (1995, 2003), Dutt (1997), and Skott (2008).

13. There is a small literature, with contributions from post-Keynesian economists (see, for instance, Cornwall and Cornwall, 1994, Palley, 1997 and Setterfield, 2002) that examines these and other possibilities and argues for the long-run relevance of AD. For a brief discussion of these contributions and a comparison to the model that follows, see Dutt (2006).

14. An alternative expression of this is given by the equation

$$\tau = \xi (L/N)^\Phi$$

where ξ is a positive constant, and where L and N refer to employment and labor supply, which shows that labor productivity growth depends positively on the employment rate.

15. The trace of the system is given by $q' \, k/(s - \beta) < 0$, and the sum of the principal diagonal minors is given by $[\gamma/(s - \beta)][h' - q' \, (s/(s - \beta))]$. Since stability requires that this is positive, we require h' to be small. Note that the determinant is zero, which makes the system lack a unique equilibrium. The model is discussed in more detail in Dutt (2006).

References

Cornwall, John and Cornwall, Wendy (1994). "Growth theory and economic structure", *Economica*, **61**, 237–51.

Duménil, Gerard and Lévy, Dominic (1999). "Being Keynesian in the short term and classical in the long term: the traverse to classical long-term equilibrium", *Manchester School*, **67**(6), 684–716.

Dutt, Amitava Krishna (1990). *Growth, Distribution and Uneven Development*, Cambridge: Cambridge University Press.

Dutt, Amitava Krishna (1997). "Equilibrium, path dependence and hysteresis in post-Keynesian models", in P. Arestis and M. Sawyer (eds), *Essays in Honour of G.C. Harcourt, Vol 2: Markets, Unemployment and Economic Policy*, London: Routledge.

Dutt, Amitava Krishna (2006). "Aggregate demand, aggregate supply and economic growth", *International Review of Applied Economics*, **20**(3), 319–36.

Dutt, Amitava Krishna and Amadeo, Edward J. (1990). *Keynes's Third Alternative? The Neo-Ricardian Keynesians and the Post Keynesians*, Aldershot, UK and Brookfield, USA: Edward Elgar.

Dutt, Amitava Krishna and Ros, Jaime (2007). "Aggregate demand shocks and economic growth", *Structural Change and Economic Dynamics*, **18**(1), 75–99.

Harrod, Roy F. (1939). "An essay in dynamic theory", *Economic Journal*, **49**, 14–33.

Kahn, Richard F. (1959). "Exercises in the analysis of growth", *Oxford Economic Papers*, **11**, 143–56.

Kalecki, Michal (1943). "Political aspects to full employment", *Political Quarterly*, reprinted in M. Kalecki (1971). *Selected Essays on the Dynamics of the Capitalist Economy*, Cambridge: Cambridge University Press.

Kalecki, Michal (1971). *Selected Essays on the Dynamics of the Capitalist Economy*, Cambridge: Cambridge University Press.

Keynes, John Maynard (1936). *The General Theory of Employment, Interest and Money*, London: Macmillan.

Lavoie, Marc (1992). *Foundations of Post-Keynesian Economic Analysis*, Aldershot, UK and Brookfield, USA: Edward Elgar.

Lavoie, Marc (1995). "The Kaleckian model of growth and distribution and its neo-Ricardian and neo-Marxian critiques", *Cambridge Journal of Economics*, **19**(6), 789–818.
Lavoie, Marc (2003). "Kaleckian effective demand and Sraffian normal prices: towards a reconciliation", *Review of Political Economy*, **15**(1), 53–74.
Marglin, Stephen A. (1984). *Growth, Distribution and Prices*, Cambridge, MA: Harvard University Press.
Marx, Karl (1867). *Capital*, Vol. 1, New York: International Publishers, 1967.
Michl, Thomas R. (2008). "Tinbergen rules the Taylor rule", *Eastern Economic Journal*, **34**, 293–309.
Palley, Thomas I. (1997). "Aggregate demand and endogenous growth: a generalized Keynes-Kaldor model of economic growth", *Metroeconomica*, **48**(2), 161–76.
Robinson, Joan V. (1956). *The Accumulation of Capital*, London: Macmillan.
Robinson, Joan (1962). *Essays in the Theory of Economic Growth*, London: Macmillan.
Rowthorn, Robert (1982). "Demand, real wages and growth", *Studi Economici*, **18**, 3–54.
Setterfield, Mark (ed.) (2002). *Economics of Demand-Led Growth. Challenging the Supply-Side Vision of Long-Run Growth*, Cheltenham, UK and Northampton, MA, USA: Edward Elgar.
Shackle, G.L.S. (1955). *Uncertainty in Economics*, Cambridge: Cambridge University Press.
Skott, Peter (2008). "Theoretical and empirical shortcomings of the Kaleckian investment function", unpublished, Department of Economics, University of Massachusetts, Amherst.
Solow, Robert M. (1956). "A contribution to the theory of economic growth", *Quarterly Journal of Economics*, **70**, 65–94.
Solow, Robert M. (1988). "Growth theory and after", *American Economic Review*, **78**, 307–17.
Taylor, Lance (1983). *Structuralist Macroeconomics. Applicable Models for the Third World*, New York: Basic Books.
Taylor, Lance (2004). *Reconstructing Macroeconomics*, Cambridge, MA: Harvard University Press.
Woodford, M. (2003). *Interest and Prices. Foundations of a Theory of Monetary Policy*, Princeton: Princeton University Press.

PART III

ECONOMIC GROWTH AND TECHNICAL CHANGE

12 The classical-Marxian evolutionary model of technical change: application to historical tendencies

Gérard Duménil and Dominique Lévy

Introduction

Central to the classical and Marxian analyses of technical change is the idea that capitalists choose among competing techniques of production, depending on their comparative profitability. A new technique is implemented if it increases the profit rate of the firm. This idea is common to Ricardo and Marx. It is also part of Sraffa's framework.[1] Although capitalists do not "maximize" their profit rate on the basis of a given production function, as within neoclassical models, they seek to obtain the best possible profit rate by choosing the most appropriate technology. The wage rate is an important parameter in this selection (see the reference to Marx below, in the description of section 3).

This very simple principle should not be mistaken for a theory of technical change or innovation in general. Why does a firm or an economy generate new and better performing techniques whereas others do not? What determines the pattern of innovation? Why does technical change display favorable features in some periods, and not in others, and so on? All these issues relate to major aspects of the analysis of technical change. The choice of the most profitable techniques of production per se is in no way sufficient to answer these questions.

Nonetheless, many properties of technical change can be derived from the mere principle of the selection of the most profitable techniques, provided that it is embedded within an appropriate framework of analysis. It is the purpose of this chapter to define such a model and to investigate its properties. There is no denying the fact that this framework is, in a sense, reminiscent of the neoclassical production function, but with the significant difference that no such function is considered!

This model can be called the *classical-Marxian evolutionary model of technical change*,[2] since it interprets the classical-Marxian analysis of technical change in a framework analogous to many evolutionary models. It is difficult to devise a more straightforward approach to innovation. Innovations appear randomly in a vicinity of actual techniques. They are selected if the profit rates that they would yield at existing prices if they were implemented, are larger than prevailing rates. This process is repeated period after period in a stochastic dynamical model. This model is presented in section 1.

In spite of its simplicity, this framework of analysis yields several interesting theoretical and empirical applications. In section 2, we use what could be called the "*aggregate* classical-Marxian evolutionary model of technical change" to interpret the secular profile of the main variables accounting for technology and distribution in the US since the Civil War. Three periods can be distinguished, corresponding roughly to the late nineteenth century, the first half of the twentieth century, and the second half of the twentieth century. The model suggests an interpretation of these three periods as an effect of a steady variation of *the conditions of innovation*. The first and third periods can be characterized by unfavorable conditions of innovation and the downward trend of the profit rate, in sharp contrast with the intermediate period. The model can also be applied to the investigation of the catching-up of European economies and Japan with the US.

Section 3 is devoted to understanding Marx's analysis in Volume III of *Capital* concerning the specific properties of technical and distributional change in capitalism. Marx's tendency for the profit rate to fall is part of a broader system of laws including labor productivity, the composition of capital, the rate of surplus value, and accumulation. With specific assumptions concerning wages, the model allows for the derivation of these tendencies. Finally, we attribute the tendency for the profit rate to fall to the specific features of innovation – in general and within capitalism in particular. These features echo Marx's idea of the increasing composition of capital inherent to mechanization (see Box 12.1). They can be expressed in various forms, such as the "difficulty of innovating" or an intrinsic labor-saving capital-consuming "bias" of innovation. The assumption that this difficulty increases tendencially over time increases its consistency with Marx's overall picture of historical tendencies within capitalism.[3]

Section 4 abandons the global approach of the previous sections to concentrate on meso or micro mechanisms and disequilibrium. It shows that the model can be used in frameworks analyzing firms or industries, in which technology is heterogeneous. A subsection introduces endogenous properties of innovation and technical change.

Section 5 is devoted to the discussion of the nature of this model. On what grounds can it be called Marxian and classical? How does it differ from the neoclassical production function? In what sense and to what extent can it find roots in evolutionary approaches?

1 Modeling technical change

The model is presented in section 1.1. Section 1.2 uses this framework to discuss the features of innovation and technical change.

1.1 The basic model

We present in this section the simplest possible form of the model. Only one good exists and it is produced by a representative firm. At a given point in time, the production of one unit of this commodity requires a certain amount of itself, A, used as fixed capital, and a quantity of labor (also assumed homogeneous), L. Thus, a technique is denoted (A, L). The ratio of output to either one of the inputs is the productivity of this input. The productivity of capital is $P_K = 1/A$, and labor productivity is $P_L = 1/L$.

A new technique, (A_+, L_+), appears at each period. It can be compared to the existing technique by the rates, a and l, of saving on each input:

$$A_+ = A/(1 + a) \text{ and } L_+ = L/(1 + l) \tag{1}$$

If the new technique is adopted, a and l are also the growth rates of the two productivities:

$$\rho(P_K) = a \text{ and } \rho(P_L) = l \tag{2}$$

12.1 THE IMPACT OF LABOR COST ON TECHNNICAL CHANGE

It is explicit in Marx's analysis that innovations are implemented depending on a comparison between the cost of the equipment and the cost of labor saved. In the following extract from a chapter of *Capital*, entitled *Machinery and Large-Scale Industry*, Marx compares the labor time embodied in the machine (which will be transferred to the product) to the labor time saved as a result of the use of the machine. However, he then explains that the capitalist only pays the value of the labor power. This is what matters in this comparison. Marx finally considers the actual wage which may diverge from the value of labor power. The reference to *competition* indicates a transition to an approach based on prices.

> The use of machinery for the exclusive purpose of cheapening the product is limited by the requirement that less labor must be expended in producing the machinery than is displaced by the employment of that machinery. For the capitalist, however, there is a further limit on its use. Instead of paying for the labor, he pays only for the value of the labor-power employed; the limit to his using a machine is therefore fixed by the difference between the value of the machine and the value of the labor-power replaced by it. Since the division of the day's work into necessary labour and surplus labour differs in different countries, and even in the same country at different periods, or in different branches of industry; and further, since the actual wage of the worker sometimes sinks below the value of his labor power, and sometimes rises above it, it is possible for the difference between the price of the machinery and the price of the labour-power replaced by that machinery to undergo great variations, while the difference between the quantity of labour needed to produce the machine and the total quantity of labour replaced by it remains constant. But it is only the former difference that determines the cost to the capitalist producing a commodity, and influences his actions through the pressure of competition.(a)

The circulation of capital (the existence of capital stock and the progressive transfer of its value to the product) is not discussed in this extract. Using the framework of Volume II, it is clearly the profit rate which is at issue. This is explicit in Volume III:

> No capitalist voluntarily applies a new method of production, no matter how much more productive it may be or how much it might rise the rate of surplus value, if it reduces the rate of profit.(b)

(a) K. Marx, *Capital, Volume I*, New York: First Vintage Book Edition (1867), Ch. 15, pp. 515–16.
(b) K. Marx, *Capital, Volume III*, New York: First Vintage Book Edition (1894), Ch. 15, p. 373.

In panel (a) of Figure 12.1, the horizontal and vertical axes measure the quantity of the good and the quantity of labor used as inputs respectively. The existing technique, (A, L), is represented by the black dot ($\cdot$). A new technique, (A_+, L_+), can be located on this figure, and falls within any one of the four regions [1] to [4]. Within region [1] the amount of each input is reduced. Conversely, both inputs are increased in region [4]. Within regions [2] and [3], the amount of one input is reduced whereas the other is increased.

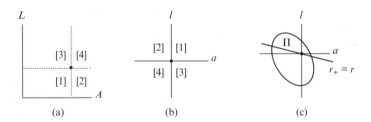

Figure 12.1   The choice of technology

A similar image is displayed in panel (b), where the performances of the new technique are described in terms of variations, using the variables, a and l defined in equations 1. Thus, the two axes account respectively for the growth rates of capital and labor productivities (positive or negative).

Technical change can be decomposed into two distinct steps: innovation and selection. We will consider these steps successively:

1. New techniques result from R&D activities. We make the following assumptions: (1) the outcome of R&D is to a large extent unpredictable; (2) new techniques are devised on the basis of the existing technology, which is only modified gradually (innovation is local). Thus, innovation is modeled as a random process, which follows a *probability distribution*, $\pi(a, l)$, whose support is bounded and denoted as the *innovation set* (see panel (c)). Maintaining the actual technique is always a possibility, and the origin belongs to the innovation set.
2. The criterion used in the decision to adopt a new technique is whether it yields a larger profit rate at prevailing prices (including the wage rate). If the innovation falls within region [1] the result is obvious and independent of prices: Since the new technique saves on both inputs, it is adopted. If it falls in region [4], increased amounts of the two inputs would be required, and the new technique is rejected. A computation must be made in order to compare the profit rates of the old and new techniques whenever the innovation falls in regions [2] or [3]. We call the *selection frontier* the line which separates the adopted ($r_+ > r$) from the rejected techniques ($r_+ < r$). This line represents the points satisfying the condition $r_+ = r$. As shown in panel (c) of Figure 12.1, it is a downward sloping line crossing the origin. We denote as the *profitable innovation set*, Π, the subset of the innovation set which lies above this line. Only innovations falling in this region are selected.

The equation of the selection frontier can be determined as follows. Only one relative price is required in this model in which a single good is considered. It is the unit wage deflated by the price of the good ("labor cost" for short), denoted w. The corresponding profit rates are:

$$r = \frac{1 - Lw}{A} \text{ and } r_+ = \frac{1 - L_+w}{A_+} \tag{3}$$

If the innovation set is small, the profit rate, r_+ of the new technique can be developed linearly in the vicinity of the prevailing profit rate r:

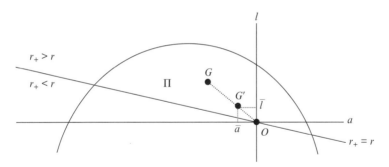

Figure 12.2   The average features of technical change $(\bar{a}, \bar{l})$

$$r_+ = r\left(1 + \frac{\mu a + l}{\mu}\right) \tag{4}$$

where μ is the ratio of profits to wages, or the "rate of surplus value", with $\mu = (1 - Lw)/Lw$, and Lw is the *wage share*, later denoted as ω. The equation for the selection frontier is:

$$\mu a + l = 0 \tag{5}$$

The slope of this frontier is $-\mu$.

This framework defines a dynamical model that determines the technique in any period from the technique prevailing in the previous period. The labor cost, w, is the only exogenous variable. More generally, beginning with a technique (A_0, L_0), one can derive a sequence of techniques, A_t, L_t (with $t = 1, 2, \ldots$), from a given sequence of labor costs w_t (with $t = 0, 1, 2, \ldots$). We denote such a sequence as a *technical trajectory*. Formally, a *stochastic dynamical model* has been defined.

In the investigation of the properties of this model, it is useful to consider the *average values* of variables a and l. Considering only innovations which are selected, their average value corresponds to G, the center of gravity of the innovation set, as shown in Figure 12.2. When innovations are not retained because they are less profitable than the prevailing technique, the origin, O, continues to represent the technique used during the new period. Thus, the average value of the random variable is a weighted average, G', of these two cases (located on GO). The coordinates of G' are denoted $\bar{a}$ and $\bar{l}$.[4]

1.2   The features of innovation and of technical change
Figure 12.3 illustrates four types of properties of innovation:

1.   Panels (a) and (b) show how the *difficulty* of innovating can be expressed in this model. In panel (a), finding profitable innovations is easy in comparison to the situation in panel (b), as a result of the reduction of the innovation set (a homothetical transformation centered in the origin).
2.   Panels (c) and (d) suggest another interpretation of the difficulty of innovating. In these two diagrams the radius of the circle is the same, and the two centers are located on the first bisector. It is the location of the center, its distance from the origin, which accounts for the difficulty of innovating.

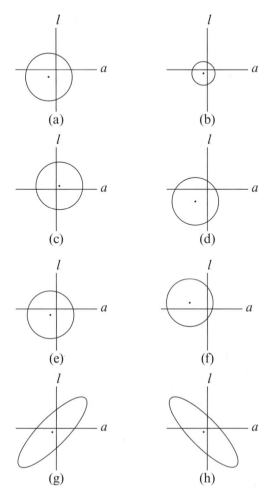

Figure 12.3   Alternative properties of innovation

3. Panels (e) and (f) are devoted to the notion of *bias*. In panel (e), the circle is centered on the first bisector, and innovations economizing on each input are equally probable. There is, therefore, no bias. The converse is true of panel (f), where the circle has been shifted toward the upper left-hand side. Consequently, the probability of finding labor-saving capital-consuming innovations ($l > 0$ and $a < 0$) is larger ($\bar{a} \searrow$ and $\bar{l} \nearrow$).

4. Panels (g) and (h) describe two distinct patterns concerning the direction of variation of the two inputs when innovations occur. The circle has been replaced by an ellipse. In panel (g), the use of the two inputs tends to vary in the same direction. In panel (h), the use of one input tends to increase while the use of the other tends to diminish.[5] The pattern in panel (g) matches, for example, the complementary features of structures and labor (like an office environment), while panel (h) may correspond to the case of equipment and labor.

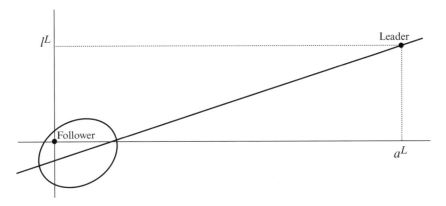

Figure 12.4   Catching-up

Obviously, these various features of innovation can be combined.

The characteristics of technical change, in an enterprise, industry or country, may also be influenced by the existence of competitors. Firms producing the same good tend to copy one another. New organizational and management patterns spread from one enterprise to another, from one industry to another. Countries that confront one another on the world market must adapt to their competitors' performances.

Catching-up represents an interesting special case of the above. The overall idea is that technical change in one country, the follower, is *influenced* by the technology of a more advanced country, the leader. For obvious reasons, switching immediately to the technology of the leader is impossible (assuming that it would be justified on account of the difference in wages). This was, in particular, true of competition between the European countries and Japan on the one hand, and the US on the other, after World War II.

The existence of a leader has an impact on the conditions of innovation. Innovations that tend to reproduce the technology of the leader are favored. This can be captured in the model by giving the innovation set a particular shape, for example an ellipse, whose main axis points toward the technique of the leader (Figure 12.4).

The intersect of the axes represents the technology of the follower (A, L). The technology, (A^L, L^L), in the leading country can be located in this plane by its two coordinates, (a^L, l^L), which measure the distance between the two technologies:

$$A^L = \frac{A}{1 + a^L} \text{ and } L^L = \frac{L}{1 + l^L}$$

As is evident from Figure 12.5, the leader dominates the follower on account of the higher productivities of both labor and capital,[6] and the ellipse points toward the upper-right side.[7]

We now turn to the analysis of the second step in the process of technical change: the selection of profitable innovations. Even on the basis of an unbiased pattern of innovation as in panel (e) of Figure 12.3, technical change will usually be biased as a result of the effect of distribution on the slope of the selection frontier. The profitable innovation set in panel (a) of Figure 12.5 is not symmetrical with respect to the first bisector, although the innovation set is symmetrical. Obviously, this bias may coexist with the

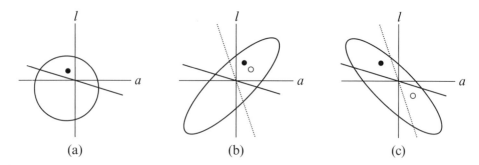

Figure 12.5   Biased technical change: the effects of distribution

bias in innovation as in panel (f) of Figure 12.3. In an empirical study, we estimated the average annual growth rate of the capital–labor ratio in the United States over the period 1869–1992 at 1.39 percent, of which 0.89 percent could be attributed to the bias of the innovation set, and the remainder to the effect of distribution.[8]

The size of the impact of distribution on technical change depends on the properties of innovation. Consider, for example, the two cases described in panels (g) and (h) of Figure 12.3. Two alternative selection frontiers are drawn in panels (b) and (c) of Figure 12.5. In panel (b), the average features [(•) or (∘)] of technical change depend only slightly on the slope of the selection frontier, that is, on distributional outcomes, but the converse is true in panel (c) of Figure 12.5.

2   The historical trends of technology and distribution
The above model is capable of many applications. This section is devoted to the historical profile of technology and distribution. Section 2.1 provides an interpretation of the evolution of technology and distribution in the US since the Civil War. Section 2.2 shows how the catching-up of less "advanced" countries toward a leader modifies such patterns of evolution.

It is important to emphasize from the outset, that the model is only one tool among many. It cannot alone provide a comprehensive interpretation of any particular phenomenon. Take, for example, the actual features of technical and distributional change in the US: the model points to a set of basic observations, which must in turn be interpreted within a larger social and political framework. Similarly, in the discussion of catching-up, the explanatory power of the model is real, but limited. In particular, it does not account for the reasons why one country did catch up, whereas another did not.

2.1   Secular trends in the US
Four variables are used in the analysis of the secular trends of technology and distribution in the US: labor cost, labor productivity, the productivity of capital, and the rate of profit (for the total private economy). *Labor cost*, w, is the total compensation per hour worked deflated by the net national product (NNP) deflator. *Labor productivity*, P_L, is NNP (in constant dollars) divided by the number of hours worked. The *productivity of capital*, P_K, is NNP divided by the net capital stock (equipment and structures). The

Table 12.1   Average annual growth rates (% per year)

	1869–1920	1920–60	1960–97	1869–1997
$\rho(w)$	1.45	2.34	1.56	2.01
$\rho(P_L)$	1.29	2.51	1.53	2.03
$\rho(P_K)$	−0.97	0.85	−0.49	0.03
$\rho(r)$	−1.25	1.07	−0.58	0.01

profit rate is the ratio of *NNP minus labor remuneration* and the *net stock of fixed capital.*[9]
A wage-equivalent for the self-employed is included within labor income.

The last column in Table 12.1 displays the average annual rate of growth of these variables over the entire period (1869–1997). It is clear from these figures that the four variables can be separated into two groups. Labor cost and labor productivity display a clear upward historical trend, whereas the trend of the profit rate is approximately horizontal, as is the case for the productivity of capital.

The evolution of each of the four variables around its trend conforms to a common pattern of fluctuation. Hence three subperiods can be distinguished in the table, with the breaks in 1920 and 1960:

1. Beginning with the Civil War and stretching up to the early twentieth century, the growth rates of labor cost and labor productivity remain comparatively low (lower than the average for the entire period), while the productivity of capital and the profit rate display a downward trend.
2. From the early twentieth century to the 1950s, the growth rates of labor cost and labor productivity are higher (larger than the average for the entire period), and the trends of the productivity of capital and the profit rate are upward. Thus, this intermediate period appears very favorable: technical progress is rapid and a comparatively large growth rate of labor cost coincides with a rising profit rate.
3. From the 1960s onward, the trends of the first period are reasserted. The similarity between the first and third periods is striking.

The notion of technical progress is ambiguous during the first and third periods since labor productivity rises and the productivity of capital declines. This observation recalls the importance of the simultaneous consideration of labor and capital in relation to output, not simply labor productivity.

The model of section 1 can easily account for such patterns of evolution. Considering the labor cost as exogenous, we interpret the succession of these three periods as the expression of a continuous transformation in the conditions of technical change. Using the terminology defined in section 1.2, we contend that the *difficulty* of innovating varied over time.

Our hypothesis is that innovation was relatively difficult, then easy, and then difficult. Within the framework of panels (c) and (d) of Figure 12.3 (where innovation is unbiased, that is, the coordinates, δ_a and δ_l, of the center of the circle are equal), this is equivalent to saying that the innovation set was comparatively low (a large negative common value, δ, as in panel (d)) at the beginning of the period, moved progressively upward ($\delta \nearrow$), thus

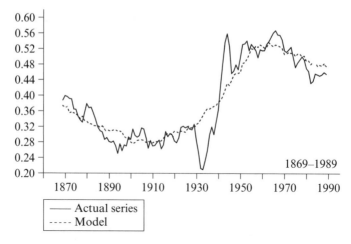

Figure 12.6   The productivity of capital in the US (1869–1989)

creating the favorable conditions prevailing in the intermediate period (as in panel (c)), and returned progressively to its original position ($\delta \searrow$ back to (d)).[10] A similar result can be obtained considering a transformation such as that between panels (a) and (b).

Figure 12.6 illustrates the ability of such a model to account for the evolution of the productivity of capital (for the period 1869–1989).[11] The actual series displays more fluctuations than the model because of short-term perturbations (notice, for example, the effect of the Great Depression). The other variables in Table 12.1 can be reproduced in a similar manner. *These results show that changes in labor cost together with gradual variation in the difficulty of innovating, account convincingly for trends in the main variables associated with technical and distributional change in the US since the Civil War.* The reconstruction of the series in Figure 12.6 was made without assuming any a priori bias in innovation. Other assumptions were made in other studies.[12]

The main results of the investigation thus far can be summarized as follows:

1. Technical change results from a random neutral innovation process, followed by the selection of techniques that appear to be the most profitable (the most able to allow for survival within competitive markets).
2. Labor productivity and wages evolve in concert, because of the effect of the wage share in the selection of new techniques.
3. Depending on the difficulty of innovating, rising labor costs may be associated with distinct patterns of variation of the productivity of capital and the profit rate: (1) If innovation is difficult, the two variables decline, (2) If it is comparatively easier, they rise.
4. Since the Civil War, the first configuration has prevailed twice, during the earlier and latter decades of this period. The second was observed from the early twentieth century to the 1950s.
5. Overall, the secular trends of the variables correspond to a situation close to the boundary between the two cases above, with nearly horizontal trends in the profit rate and of productivity of capital.

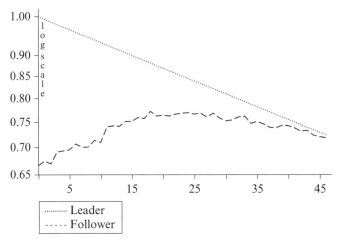

Figure 12.7   Catching-up in two fictitious countries: the productivities of capital of the leader and the follower

The specific profile of the intermediate period relates, in our opinion, to the transformations of relations of production and class patterns at the turn of the century. They correspond to what has been called the *corporate revolution* and the *managerial revolution*. A new efficiency was achieved within large corporations because of the revolution in technology and organization, a revolution in management in the broad sense of the term.[13]

2.2   Catching up with the US
An important feature of technical change since World War II has been the propensity of European countries and Japan to catch up with the US. The effects of this catching-up combined with the decline of the profit rate in a complex pattern of events. In a sense, this tendency of the profit rate to decline can be described as a world phenomenon, but trends in technology in Europe and Japan were also historically specific during the first few decades of the postwar period, displaying differences among countries. As these countries were progressively converging toward the US economy, similar evolutions were observable in all countries. The overall picture is difficult to untangle.[14]

It is possible to illustrate this pattern of events using the framework of Figure 12.4. The results of two simulations are presented in Figures 12.7 and 12.8:

1. We first assume that the leader has reached a smooth trajectory with a declining productivity of capital and a constant wage share. An assumption must be made concerning wages in the follower country. We arbitrarily assume that the wage share is equal to that of the leader. Figure 12.7 shows the patterns of evolution of the two productivities of capital. During a first phase, the productivity of capital of the follower rises, as a result of the favorable conditions created by the existence of the leader (from the point of view of the availability of new techniques, abstracting, in particular, from the effects of international competition[15]).
2. The realism of the picture is increased in Figure 12.8 by using the actual evolution of technology in the US to represent the leader, and the actual series of labor cost in

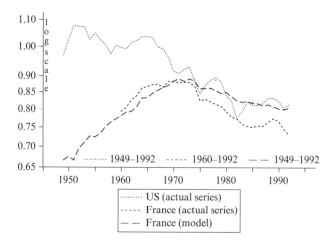

Note: The actual series for France have been multiplied by a constant, since the the two definitions are not coherent. Data for the US are from the BEA, and for France, from the OECD.

Figure 12.8   *France catching up with the US: the productivities of capital in the US and in France*

France, to denote the follower. A similar evolution results. Although the parameters accounting for the conditions of innovation in France have been determined more or less arbitrarily, the profile of the productivity of capital deriving from the simulation for France is not significantly different from the actual series (also plotted in the figure for comparison). In particular, the productivity of capital, as simulated, reaches its maximum in the early 1970s as in the actual series.

The model illustrates an intuitive property of catching-up. With a configuration such as that of Figure 12.4, the impact of labor cost is small in the economy of the follower as long as it remains at a considerable distance from the leader.

3 Marx's analysis of historical tendencies

The tendency for the profit rate to fall is only one component of a larger framework of analysis in which technology, distribution and accumulation are involved. Section 3.1 recalls the main features of Marx's presentation. In the remainder of this section, we use the framework of section 1 to interpret Marx's analysis. The simplest case, in which the rate of growth of the labor cost is exogenous, is discussed in section 3.2. Section 3.3 adds to the model a feedback relationship linking changes in labor cost to changes in the profit rate. Accumulation is introduced in section 3.4. Section 3.5 provides a brief synthesis of these results. Last, section 3.6 suggests an interpretation of Marx's thesis of a falling profit rate, associated with specific "unfavorable" conditions of innovation or their tendencial deterioration – in general and within capitalism in particular.

3.1 A system of tendencies

At least five "laws of motion" are considered by Marx in his famous analysis of Volume III of historical tendencies: (1) the diminishing value of use-values (the progress of labor productivity); (2) the rising value composition of capital; (3) the rising rate of surplus value; (4) the falling profit rate; (5) accelerated accumulation.

As is well known, Marx first addresses the issue of the falling profit rate under the assumption of a constant rate of surplus value: "[. . .] a gradual fall in the general rate of profit, given that the rate of surplus value, or the level of exploitation of labour by capital, remains the same".[16] How can the profit rate decline whereas the rate of surplus value is constant? Marx's answer is straightforward: this is the effect of the rising composition of capital, the fact that more and more constant capital is required compared to variable capital. The assumption of a constant rate of surplus value is used by Marx to contend that the fall of the profit rate is not a result of excessive wages, but of a given feature of technical change. This analysis sharply contrasts with Ricardo's analysis that locates the declining profitability of capital in the rise of the relative price of corn, and, thus, of the nominal wage and of the wage share. In a contemporary formulation, Marx contends that the downward trend of the profit rate must not be interpreted as a *wage squeeze*.

This configuration is very relevant factually. In the account that we provided of the features of technical and distributional change in the US, a falling profit rate prevailed in the late nineteenth century and in the second half of the twentieth century. During these two periods the share of wages, that is, the rate of surplus value,[17] remained more or less constant.

As one progresses into the chapters of *Capital* devoted to the falling profit rate, it becomes clear that Marx is not content with the assumption of a constant rate of surplus value. The fall of the profit rate is said to be compatible with a rising rate of exploitation. At the end of Chapter 14, one can read: "The tendential fall in the profit rate is linked with a tendential rise in the rate of surplus value".[18]

Last, Marx was conscious of the link between the falling profit rate and accumulation: "A fall in the profit rate, and accelerated accumulation, are simply different expressions of the same process, [. . .]. In this way there is an acceleration of accumulation as far as its mass is concerned, even though the rate of this accumulation falls together with the rate of profit".[19] Thus, the rate of accumulation tends to fall with the profit rate, while the mass of capital accumulated rises: $\rho(K) = (\Delta K)/(K) \searrow$ and $\Delta K \nearrow$.

There is no denying the fact that Marx's analysis is also deficient in several respects. Five problem areas are discussed below:

1. Why would a declining profit rate be paralleled by a rising rate of exploitation? Marx is not explicit in this respect. Since labor productivity increases, capitalists can impose a larger rate of exploitation on the workers without lowering their real wage. But why is this tendency so strongly linked to the downward trend of the profit rate?

2. Although Marx insists repeatedly on the tendency of the composition of capital to rise, he is not very explicit concerning the origin of this tendency. Is mechanization a feature of technical change in general, not only within capitalism? Does such a mechanization always require the rise of the technical and organic compositions of capital? Marx repeatedly asserts that the perpetuation of capitalist relations of production impacts on the rhythms of mechanization, but the direction of this effect is not always the same. He sometimes contends that capitalists push the use

of machinery even beyond purely technical requirements in order to control the workers. He sometimes points to the fact that exploitation (the low cost of labor) limits the incentive to employ more mechanized processes, since capitalists only pay a fraction of the labor time expended by the workers.[20]

3. The formalism in Chapter 13 of Volume III of *Capital* is not really appropriate. The tendency for the profit rate to fall is presented within the framework used in Volume I to account for the theory of surplus value. Capital, $c + v$, is the sum of two flows. As is well known, the profit rate is written: $s/(c + v)$ or $s'/(1 + \gamma)$, with s' denoting the rate of exploitation and γ the organic composition of capital. This framework abstracts from the circulation of capital introduced (later) in Volume II. In Volume III, surplus value is designated as *profit*, π, and capital is actually a stock, the sum of three components: productive, commodity, and money capitals. Thus the profit rate should be: π/K. Within K, it should be possible to distinguish two components, one resulting from the financing of variable capital, and one from constant capital. In addition to the difficulties inherent to Marx's presentation, for practical reasons because of the availability of data, one must substitute the productivity of capital or its inverse, the capital–output ratio, for Marx's organic composition of capital. Marx's statements concerning the rise of the organic composition of capital can be translated into *a declining productivity of capital*.[21]

4. In his analysis of historical tendencies, Marx is reluctant to refer to wages, nominal or real. He only considers the rate of exploitation: "We entirely leave aside here the fact that the same amount of value represents a progressively rising mass of use-values and satisfactions, with the progress of capitalist production".[22] If labor productivity increases, a constant rate of surplus value results in a rising real wage. In other parts of his work, Marx quite explicitly refers to the movement of the real wage (see for example, the quotations at the beginning of this study, or the famous Chapter 25 of Volume I of *Capital*).

5. It is also necessary to recall that Marx's description of the mechanisms leading to a diminished average profit rate is problematic. Marx's account is well known: (1) Individual producers may introduce a new technique on account of the incremental profit that it yields prior to its diffusion to all producers; (2) Once it is generalized to all producers and a uniform profit rate is re-established, the average profit rate is diminished. In order to reach a conclusion concerning the comparison between the profit rate prevailing before the introduction of the new process of production and the eventual profit rate after its diffusion, one additional assumption must actually be made concerning distribution. Nobuo Okishio has shown, in his famous theorem, that the profit rate must rise if the real wage is maintained,[23] that is, if capitalists absorb the entire advantage of the new improved conditions of production. The profit rate can decline only if the workers benefit from at least a portion of the progress accomplished, that is, if the real wage increases to an extent. It is therefore not possible to establish a falling profit rate under the assumption of a constant real wage rate.[24]

Overall, Marx's analysis of the historical tendencies of capitalism is fascinating. Its relevance is still obvious after more than a century. But it is also, in several important respects, deficient.

3.2   The falling profit rate with an exogenous growth rate of labor cost

In this section, we interpret historical tendencies as asymptotic trajectories of the dynamical model. This means that, under certain assumptions, beginning with any technique and any level of labor cost, the model converges toward a trajectory à la Marx. We use in turn two sets of assumptions:

1.   *We first assume that the innovation set, the probability distribution, and the growth rate, ρ_w, of the labor cost are all given.*

The average features of technical change are described by $\bar{a}$ and $\bar{l}$, the coordinates of G' (see Figure 12.2). They are functions of the innovation set, of the probability distribution (which is given), and of the slope of the selection frontier (the rate of surplus value), μ, and, thus, of the wage share ω: $\bar{a} = \bar{a}(\omega)$ and $\bar{l} = \bar{l}(\omega)$. The following properties are intuitive: (1) The average growth rate of the productivity of capital, $\bar{a}(\omega)$, is a decreasing function of ω; (2) The average growth rate of labor productivity, $\bar{l}(\omega)$, is an increasing function of ω.

After substituting the average values of innovation, $\bar{a}$ and $\bar{l}$, for their stochastic values, a and l, into equation 2, a deterministic dynamical system is obtained for the two variables which describe technology, A and L (or equivalently P_K and P_L). Replacing L (or P_L) by the wage share $\omega = Lw$, the dynamical system can be written as:

$$\rho(\omega) = \rho_w - \bar{l}(\omega)$$
$$\rho(P_K) = \bar{a}(\omega) \tag{6}$$

The first equation can be studied independently of the second.

The equilibrium value of the wage share, ω^*, is the solution of the following implicit equation:

$$\bar{l}(\omega^*) = \rho_w$$

Since $\bar{l}(\omega)$ is a monotonically increasing function of ω, a unique fixed point, ω^*, exists, if ρ_w belongs to the interval $[\bar{l}(0), \bar{l}(1)]$. At the fixed point, the wage share is constant and, thus, the growth rate of labor productivity is also constant and equal to that of wages:

$$\rho(P_L) = \rho_w \tag{7}$$

In continuous time, the local stability of this fixed point is easy to prove.[25]

Consider now the second of the equations in 6. The fixed point of the first equation corresponds to an asymptotic trajectory in which the productivity of capital, P_K, and the profit rate, r, increase or diminish at the same constant rate:

$$\rho(P_K) = \rho(r) = \bar{a}(\omega^*) \tag{8}$$

Thus, the profile of the series over time can be derived from their initial values in period 0:

$$P_L = \frac{w}{\omega^*} = P_L(0)e^{\rho_w t} \text{ and } P_K = P_K(0)e^{\bar{a}(\omega^*)t}$$

This allows for the derivation of the trajectories for r and the organic composition of capital, γ:

$$r = (1 - \omega^*)P_K \text{ and } \gamma = \frac{1}{\omega^* P_K}$$

The direction of the variation of the profit rate or of the productivity of capital along this trajectory is determined by the sign of $\bar{a}(\omega^*)$ and depends on the exogenous growth rate of the cost of labor, the innovation set, and the probability distribution. This sign is discussed in section 3.6. Thus, trajectories à la Marx may obtain, but are subject to certain conditions.

2. *We now assume that the innovation set, the probability distribution, and the growth rate of the labor cost vary over time: the innovation set is gradually reduced as in panel (b) of Figure 12.3.*

We assume that this variation of the innovation set is a homothety centered in the origin, whose ratio is $1/t^\alpha$. Thus, the average values, $\bar{a}$ and $\bar{l}$, can be written:

$$\bar{a} = \frac{\bar{a}(\omega)}{t^\alpha} \text{ and } \bar{l} = \frac{\bar{l}(\omega)}{t^\alpha}$$

in which the functions $\bar{a}(\omega)$ and $\bar{l}(\omega)$ are independent of time. The assumption made about the wage rate is: $\rho(w) = \rho_w/t^\alpha$.

With these assumptions, the system in 6 becomes:

$$\rho(\omega) = \frac{\rho_w - \bar{l}(\omega)}{t^\alpha}$$

$$\rho(P_K) = \frac{\bar{a}(\omega)}{t^\alpha}$$

The implicit equation for ω^* is formally unchanged. Equations 7 and 8 become respectively:

$$\rho(P_L) = \frac{\rho_w}{t^\alpha} \text{ and } \rho(P_K) = \rho(r) = \frac{\bar{a}(\omega^*)}{t^\alpha}$$

The growth rates of the variables along their asymptotic trajectories diminish with time:[26]

$$P_L = \frac{w}{\omega^*} = P_L(t_0)\left(\frac{t}{t_0}\right)^{\rho_w} \text{ and } P_K = P_K(t_0)\left(\frac{t}{t_0}\right)^{a(\omega^*)} \text{ if } \alpha = 1$$

$$P_L = \frac{w}{\omega^*} = P_L(t_0)\exp\left(\frac{\rho_w}{1-\alpha}(t^{1-\alpha} - t_0^{1-\alpha})\right)$$

$$\text{and } P_K = P_K(t_0)\exp\left(\frac{\bar{a}(\omega^*)}{1-\alpha}(t^{1-\alpha} - t_0^{1-\alpha})\right) \text{ if } \alpha < 1$$

It is interesting to compare the properties of the asymptotic trajectory with those obtained under the previous set of assumptions:

1. Again, the rate of surplus value is constant (ω is constant).
2. A productivity slowdown is observed, with $\rho(P_L) = \rho_w/t^\alpha$.
3. The condition required to obtain a downward trend of the profit rate is unchanged: $\bar{a}(\omega^*) < 0$, with ω^* still given by $\bar{l}(\omega) = \rho_w$.
4. What changes is the rapidity of the decline of the profit rate and of the productivity of capital. For example, if $\alpha = 1$, power trajectories are substituted for exponential trajectories.

The results obtained in this section under two different sets of assumptions (given conditions of innovation and a constant rate of growth real wages, or the gradual decline of these parameters at the same rate) are well in line with Marx's analysis at the beginning of Chapter 13 of Volume III of *Capital*. Stable trajectories with a downward trend of the profit rate and a constant rate of surplus value can be reproduced under certain conditions.

3.3 Exploitation: a feedback effect of the profit rate on labor cost

We have already noted in section 3.1 that Marx is not explicit concerning the reasons for the coexistence of a declining profit rate and a rising rate of exploitation. The underlying idea could, in our opinion, be more adequately expressed by referring to the rate of growth of the real wage rate or labor cost.

A declining (or low) profit rate will strengthen the resistance of firms to any further rise of the labor cost. The recurrence of recessions, associated with a declining profit rate, forces down wage increases. Accumulation is slowed and unemployment increases during a structural crisis. The converse is true when the profit rate rises and is high: Accumulation is rapid, the labor market is tight, and this is a favorable environment for rising wages. Such a relationship between the trend of the profit rate and that of wages was clearly manifested during the twentieth century, and this confirms that Marx's insight should be taken seriously.[27]

As suggested by Figure 12.9, the relationships investigated in the previous sections can be supplemented by a feedback effect of the profit rate on wages. The first two arrows, [1], recall that the profit rate is determined, by definition, by technology and wages. The second arrow [2] denotes the effect of the profit rate on the selection of new techniques. The third arrow [3] represents the new relationship: the impact of the profit rate on the growth rate of the labor cost. Such a model can be fitted to the data.[28]

As suggested by historical observation, both the variation of the profit rate and its level can play a role in this relationship.[29] In the first set of assumptions considered in the previous section, this feedback effect of the profit rate on wages can be modeled simply as follows:

$$\rho(w) = f + g\rho(r) + h\,log(1 + r) \qquad (9)$$

In this equation, parameter f accounts for an exogenous historical trend, and g and h for the fluctuations of w around this trend.[30]

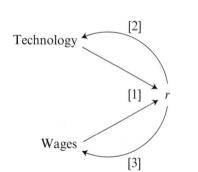

Figure 12.9   The dynamics of distribution and technical change

Equation 9 does not suggest that wages are not determined by the struggle between workers and capitalists. First, the secular growth rate of the labor cost remains exogenous. Second, this equation only accounts for an observable, rather stable, quantitative pattern in the outcome of this struggle. It is because of the fact that the effect of class struggle on wages depends to a considerable extent on underlying economic conditions. The model emphasizes the importance of the profit rate and its movement in the determination of this outcome of class struggle.

When we first introduced this model, the relationship between the movement of wages and the profit rate was not recognized as such. The standard analysis among the "left" linked the movement of wages to that of labor productivity, as if the relevant variable was the share of profits instead of the profit rate. Even if it was not explicitly considered by Marx himself, the establishment of this relationship plays, in our opinion, a significant role in the restoration of the centrality of the profit rate to the analysis of capitalism.

Examining the properties of the asymptotical trajectories of our variables shows that the third term in equation 9, $h \log(1 + r)$, plays an important role:

1. If this term is deleted ($h = 0$), the feedback of the variation of the profit rate on that of labor cost only impacts on the growth rates of variables.[31] The properties of the asymptotic trajectories are not changed.
2. If the second term is included, the feedback of the variation of the profit rate on that of labor cost stabilizes the profit rate at a certain level. A stationary state à la Mill obtains.[32] As shown in Figure 12.10, the trajectory described by Marx could only be interpreted as a pre-asymptotic state, preliminary to the convergence of the profit rate toward its limit.

In spite of the feedback effect of the profit rate on the movement of wages, these models always lead to a stabilization of the share of wages, along the asymptotic trajectory, at a certain level. They are not compatible with a rising rate of surplus value except during pre-asymptotic stages.

3.4   Accumulation

The behavior of accumulation is also a component of the description of historical tendencies, and this connection is explicit in Marx's analysis.

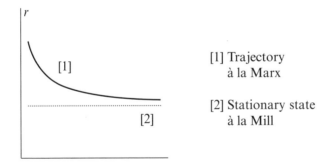

Figure 12.10   Trajectories à la Marx and à la Mill

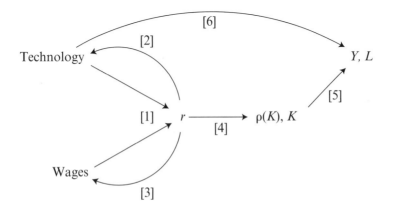

Figure 12.11   The dynamics of distribution, technical change, and accumulation

A central aspect of the classical-Marxian analysis is that the rate of accumulation is a function of the profit rate. This is traditionally represented by the relationship between the growth rate of the capital stock, $\rho(K)$, and the profit rate:[33]

$$\rho(K) = sr \qquad (10)$$

Beginning with a given stock of capital, the entire series of capital can be derived. As shown in Figure 12.11, new relationships must be introduced in Figure 12.9. The above expression of accumulation as a function of the profit rate is depicted by the arrow [4]. Output and employment can be derived from the capital stock, [5], and technology, [6]:

$$Y = KP_K \text{ and } L = K\frac{P_K}{P_L}$$

The overall dynamics described in Figure 12.11 correspond to a model with four variables (P_L, P_K, w and r), to which three other variables are added (K, Y, and L). It goes without saying that this model emphasizes a number of relationships which are of primary importance, abstracting from other possible interactions of lesser influence. This model can be fitted to the data for the US economy.[34]

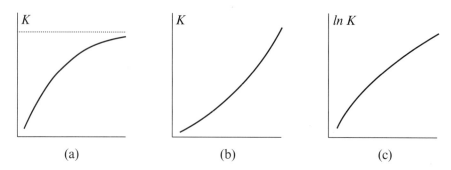

Figure 12.12   Accumulation along a trajectory à la Marx

Whether or not it is possible to recover Marx's statements concerning accumulation depends on the set of assumptions considered in section 3.2:

1.   *Constant innovation set and growth rate of wages.*

Along a trajectory on which the profit rate declines, the growth rate of the capital stock also diminishes (equation 10). Its trajectory can be made explicit:

$$K = K(0)\ exp\left(\frac{sr(0)}{\bar{a}(\omega*)}(exp(\bar{a}(\omega*)t) - 1)\right)$$

On a trajectory à la Marx, one has $\bar{a}(\omega*) < 0$, and the capital stock tends toward a constant (see panel (a) of Figure 12.12). Since the productivity of capital declines, output must also decline. The amount of capital accumulated in each period also declines.

In spite of its simple and apparently basic characteristics, this first interpretation of Marx's analysis is not consistent with his views concerning accumulation. It is clear that the eventual decline of output is inappropriate.

2.   *The gradual reduction of the innovation set and of the growth rate of wages.*

It is also possible to determine explicitly the profile of the capital stock using the second set of assumptions with $\gamma = 1$:[35]

$$K = C_1 exp\ (C_2 t^{\bar{a}(\omega*) + 1})$$

The case $\gamma < 1$ is more complex.

Since $\bar{a}(\omega*) > -1$, the capital stock rises indefinitely, as well as production and the amount of capital accumulated in each period. These profiles are described in panels (b) and (c) of Figure 12.12. Panel (b) illustrates the fact that the capital stock increases more and more ($\Delta K \nearrow$). The logarithm of the capital stock in panel (c) shows that the growth rate of the capital stock is gradually diminished.

Abstracting from the tendency for the rate of surplus value to rise, this second set of assumptions is in line with Marx's analysis. Therefore, his view of historical tendencies seems more consistent with the thesis of *a gradual increase in the difficulty of innovating* in the sense of panels (a) and (b) of Figure 12.3. The downward trend of the profit rate obtains in spite of the gradual reduction of the growth rate of the real wage, at the same rate as the difficulty of innovating increases. It is not possible to attribute the tendency for the profit rate to fall, in this model, to a wage squeeze: (1) the share of wages is constant; (2) the deterioration of the conditions of innovation is paralleled by a similar decline of the rate of growth of the real wage rate.

3.5 A summing up

Two basic sets of assumptions concerning technical change have been considered in the previous sections in order to discuss Marx's analysis of historical tendencies:

1. In a first group of models, the conditions of innovation are assumed constant. Three variants of this model have been discussed, that differ according to the assumed growth rate of the real wage.[36] The growth rate of the real wage can alternatively:
   - be constant.
   - respond to the variations of the profit rate. (A rising profit rate allows for a larger variation of the real wage, and a declining profit rate diminishes the capacity of the real wage to rise.)
   - react to the variations of the profit rate as above *and* to its level. (A high profit rate is favorable to a rise in the real wage rate, and a low profit rate unfavorable to this increase.)
2. A second model assumes that the conditions of innovation are subject to a constant deterioration, and that the growth rate of the real wage diminishes at the same rate.

The results can be summarized as follows:

1. None of these models vindicates the tendency for the rate of surplus value to rise (a decline of the share of wages in the model). All asymptotic trajectories display a constant share of wages.[37]
2. A declining profit rate may prevail in each model under certain assumptions. However, in the third variant of the first group of models, because of the strong adjustment of the growth rate of real wages, the profit rate tends toward a constant.
3. Consider now accumulation and output. A problem with the two first variants of the first group is that the declining profit rate leads to the stagnation of the capital stock, which results in a declining output because of the falling productivity of capital. In the third variant, the growth rates of the capital stock and of output both tend to stabilize with the profit rate. Only the second set of assumptions, with the simultaneous deterioration of the conditions of innovation and of the growth rate of the real wage (at the same rate), allows for: (1) a declining profit rate; (2) an acceleration of accumulation as far as the mass investment in each period is considered, and a decline of the rate of accumulation with respect to the stock of capital; (3) a declining (but still positive) growth rate of output. As stated in section 3.4, this model is in line with Marx's insights in his analysis of historical tendencies, the tendency for the rate of surplus value to rise being the only exception.

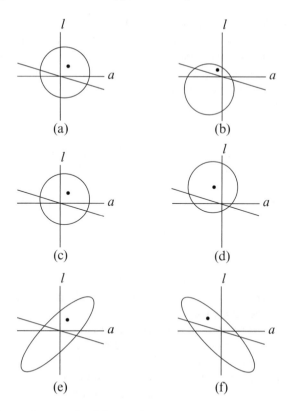

Figure 12.13   Alternative trends of the profit rate

3.6   The conditions of innovation: the roots of the tendency for the profit rate to fall
At the beginning of Chapter 13 of Volume III of *Capital*, Marx presents the rise of the technical or organic composition of capital, in combination with a constant rate of surplus value, as the *cause* of the tendency for the profit rate to fall. As stated in section 3.1, Marx is, however, not clear concerning the origin of the rise of the composition of capital.

We interpret Marx's analysis of the *tendency* for the profit rate to fall as a thesis concerning the features of innovation. According to Marx, innovation displays certain conditions such that the profit rate will tend to decline, even if the growth of the labor cost remains moderate. For a given growth rate of the labor cost, the economy will enter into a trajectory à la Marx, if certain features become manifest.

We must therefore confront two questions: (1) What are these conditions? (2) Why do they prevail, in particular within capitalism?

Figure 12.3 can assist in this discussion. We add the selection frontiers for a given wage share, as well as the center of gravity of the innovation set. (We abstract from the difference between G and G'.) Thus, Figure 12.3 can be transformed into Figure 12.13. It is easy to locate visually on these panels the cases corresponding to a falling profit rate. Whenever, the coordinate, $\bar{a}$, of the center of gravity on the horizontal axis is negative, the profit rate falls along an asymptotic trajectory. It is clear that this configuration is observed for each panel in the right-hand column. The profit rate is more inclined to decrease whenever: (1) the difficulty of innovating is larger, (a) → (b); (2) innovation is biased, (c) → (d); (3) inputs are substitutes, (e) → (f).

This discussion can be easily translated into the second set of assumptions of the model (the gradual reduction of the innovation set and of the growth rate of wages). As a result of the assumption of a homothetical transformation centered on the origin, the diagrams in the first column are unchanged with the exception that the scale of the axes is reduced over time.

The configurations described in panels (d) and (f) are quite reflective of Marx's insight concerning the composition of capital. Innovations can be found which diminish the productivity of capital (signaling heavy mechanization). Other cases are possible, but rare. The first configuration in panel (b) is interesting, since it signals that this propensity of innovations to display characteristics à la Marx can result from the *difficulty* of finding profitable innovations in general, independently of any a priori bias.

Consider this later case. Is it a property of capitalism in particular (which could be avoided within "socialism")? Obviously, R&D activities are intrinsically costly and risky. However, one interpretation could be that the limits set by private property within capitalism pose specific barriers to innovation, or at least some forms of it. These problems arise from the contradiction between the cost of R&D, and the difficulty of privately capturing the total profit from the innovation. Either patent legislation is too narrow, or it is protective and patents claims are too broad, making the diffusion of inventions or follow-on innovations too costly. In the first case, R&D will be weak; in the second case, new innovations cannot spread rapidly. In this respect, private interest contradicts collective interest.[38]

Independently of the exact nature of the problem with technical change within capitalism, the tendency for the profit rate to fall points to some limitation of capitalism. A configuration such as that in panel (a) of Figure 12.13, characteristic of what we called the *intermediate period* in section 2.1, is favorable. Technical progress can be rapid, and wages can rise in concert with the profit rate. Conversely, Marx's analysis points to an unfavorable pattern, a kind of contradictory process – possibly increasing over time. Technical progress is paralleled by a decline of the profit rate, which tends to diminish the workers' chances of obtaining wage increases. Accumulation is slowed. The outcome is a structural crisis, following which the dynamic of the mode of production can only be restored as a result of important transformations. Overall, capitalism does "revolutionize" technology and organization, but in a convulsive manner.

4 A broader framework of analysis

In the previous sections, the model of section 1 is used within very simple frameworks of analysis. The economy is generally considered globally and in equilibrium. Only section 2.2 contrasts the features of technical change within two distinct economies. This framework also abstracts from traditional determinants of technical change, such as growth or competition. Obviously, nothing restricts the use of the model to such frameworks or forbids the consideration of other mechanisms that affect technical change. It is the purpose of this section to sketch two such possible developments. Section 4.1 uses the model in a disaggregated economy, where disequilibrium may prevail. Section 4.2 briefly suggests a number of developments concerning endogenous technical change.

4.1 Heterogeneity and disequilibrium

The model presented in section 1 can be used to account for the behavior of firms, industries, larger sectors of the economy, or the total economy. Significant heterogeneities may prevail and impact considerably on the functioning of the economy. A number of potentially important phenomena are a priori linked to the fact that decisions are actually made by individual agents in a decentralized manner and within the context of disequilibrium. Supply may differ from demand, and productive capacities are not necessarily fully utilized.

The heterogeneity of the economy may be crucial. An important aspect of the historical transformations described in section 2.1 is that the favorable profile of technical change observed during the intermediate period was concentrated, in the US, within a given segment of the economy: large corporations backed up by the new finance. Far from affecting the economy uniformly, the corporate and managerial revolutions of the early twentieth century left aside a large segment of the economy, composed of smaller firms still dependent on traditional technology and management.

Instead of the simple characterization of an average transformation of the conditions of innovation described in section 2.1, one can contemplate a model in which two sectors are considered. One sector evolved along the traditional lines of evolution, whereas new organization and technology prevailed in the emerging corporate managerial sector. The resulting new sector was more efficient. Consequently, two technologies and patterns of technical change must be described, even assuming for simplicity that wages are identical. This model generates two distinct technical trajectories. The total economy can be described as a weighted average of the two sectors, with changing weights mirroring the rise to dominance of the new sector, and the progressive elimination of the other. Such a model is studied in one of our recent papers.[39] Note that this heterogeneous character of technology is not merely a hypothetical extension of the analysis. It was, in our opinion, a key factor in the occurrence of the Great Depression.[40]

The model of section 2.2 only considers the impact of a leader on the conditions of innovation faced by a follower. It is, however, clear that the actual process is one of reciprocal interaction. Various countries compete on an international basis, and tend to borrow innovations from one another. The *catching-up* corresponds to the case in which a leader can be distinguished from a follower, and imitation denotes reciprocal interaction. Obviously, there would be nothing wrong with a model that takes into account a reciprocal influence of innovation sets.

Heterogeneous techniques also coexist among firms, within a given product line, in the same country. It is clear that the diffusion of innovations can also be treated in a framework such as that outlined above.

The consideration of individual agents in interaction opens our analysis to the field of microeconomics and disequilibrium. Elsewhere, we have presented in other works what we call *disequilibrium microeconomics* to be substituted for neoclassical microeconomics, and a general disequilibrium model.[41]

The framework of analysis in such *general disequilibrium models* can be briefly sketched as follows. A straightforward meaning is given to the notion of disequilibrium: markets do not clear, productive capacities are not fully utilized, and so on. Decisions are decentralized. When production decisions are made, demand is still unknown. At the close of the market, inventories of unsold commodities may exist, and are transmitted to the next period. Rationing may occur. Prices are also decided by individual firms, and they are not necessarily uniform. The demands facing the various producers of the same good depend on their individual prices. The issuance of money by the banking system is endogenous to the model, and responds to the general level of activity and inflation. The demand for fixed capital (investment) follows from the accumulation of profits and new loans. Investment is also influenced by the capacity utilization rate and the profit rate of the various industries. Consumption is determined by wages, a fraction of profits devoted to consumption, and the stock of money held by potential consumers. Technology is heterogeneous (among the producers of the same good). Decisions are modeled in terms of *adjustment*, that is, reaction to disequilibrium. For example, any firm that produces and does not sell its output as expected, reduces production in the next period.

In such models, one can determine a classical long-term equilibrium with a uniform profit rate among industries (averaging the various techniques in each industry). It is usually stable. A short-term equilibrium also exists. It can be stable or unstable, and the economy remains generally in the vicinity of short-term equilibria. The succession of periods of stability and instability accounts for business-cycle fluctuations.

We studied a model in which two goods are produced, each by two firms, using the framework of section 1.[42] Each of the four firms is described by seven variables: the capacity utilization rate, inventories, the price of output, the stock of capital and its growth rate, and the two technical parameters A and L. To this one must add the money stock, its growth rate and inflation. (The number of variables is 27.)

The properties of this model can only be investigated through a simulation approach. It appears that the model has several interesting properties:

1. It reproduces the usual properties obtained in other classical dynamical models, in particular, a tendency toward a uniform profit rate among industries.[43]
2. Tendencies such as those studied in section 2.1 may prevail.
3. A number of additional results are observed. For example, the technical heterogeneity among firms can be maintained over time, or even increase. However, firms lagging behind tend to disappear since less capital flows into them.

Overall, the adoption of a disaggregated framework of analysis does not question the relevance of the aggregate analysis, but many industry- or firm-specific traits can be identified. Clearly, such analysis opens a broad research field for future investigation.

4.2 Endogenous technology and endogenous technical change

In the model used in this chapter, the pattern of innovation (the innovation set) is given or varies exogenously, but technology is determined endogenously:

1. The profit rate, which is used as a criterion in the selection among new innovations, is an endogenous variable of the model. In a more complex model, as in section 4.1, the profit rate is a function of a broad set of circumstances: demand, competition, and so on. All these circumstances will impact on the trajectory of technical change.
2. Although the random variables a and l are exogenous, the technique in one period is always derived from the technique prevailing in the previous period, and is, therefore, endogenous.

Moreover, in a vintage model,[44] the average technology in a given year is a function of the rate of accumulation. If the growth rate of the fixed capital stock is large, the average technology is closer to the most recent technology embodied in the later investments.

There would be no difficulty in treating the *innovation set* itself as endogenous:

1. In a model in which the innovation set is a circle, the conditions of innovation are described by a set of parameters, the radius of the circle, the coordinates of the center, and the probability distribution. All of these parameters can be expressed as functions of time or of economic variables. For example, they can be modeled as functions of the growth rate of output (as in the Kaldor–Verdoorn Law), of the growth of the capital stock per worker (as in Kaldor's technical progress function), or of the accumulation of "human capital", if such a variable is introduced into the model.

2. In addition to the traditional sources of endogenous of technical change listed above, the model itself suggests new developments. For example, the entire innovation set, rather than just the profitable innovation set, can be linked to distribution. One can, for example, assume that R&D is oriented in specific directions by prevailing prices. Firms search along lines that are more likely to produce large gains. This could be dealt with in a model in which the innovation set is oriented in a direction perpendicular to the selection frontier, and then constantly redirected depending on the prevailing distribution of income.

Only empirical analysis can determine the relevance of such extension of the model.

5 Classical-Marxian, evolutionary, and neoclassical perspectives

In what sense can the framework of section 1 be called *classical-Marxian*, when considered in isolation independently of the analysis of historical tendencies or disequilibrium microeconomics (for example, the allocation of capital as a function of comparative profit rates)? In a very simple and limited sense, the answer is straightforward: techniques of production are selected if they provide larger profit rates at prevailing prices.[45] The specificity of the neoclassical framework lies in the next component of the analysis: the production function. Neoclassical models assume that the set of techniques available, that is, the innovation set, can be described by a production function, and that firms maximize their profits along such functions.

Figure 12.14 compares technical change in one period in our model, and using a production function. It clearly illustrates the limitation of technical change (its local features) in our model, in sharp contrast with the production function. The plane is (A, L) as in panel (a) of Figure 12.1. Consider first panel (a) of Figure 12.14. The dot represents the technique actually used in the current period. The line describes the set of technical combinations available for the next period with a Cobb-Douglas production function (with a shift factor). Depending on the variation of the real wage (such that $0 < w < \infty$), technical change can be very large. Panel (b) illustrates the possibilities available in our approach, assuming a broad innovation set ($R = 0.4$). The dotted line (······) is the image in (A, L), of a circular innovation set in (a, l). The tiny curve close to the dot depicts the positions of the centers of gravity (G') of the profitable innovation set for all possible values of the real wage. (Panel (c) simply enlarges the picture in panel (b).) Even if the real wage rate

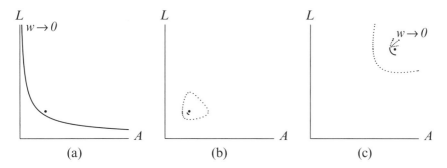

Figure 12.14 A comparison with the production function

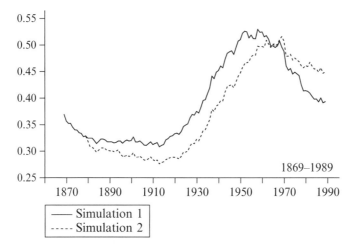

Figure 12.15 Path-dependence: two simulations of the productivity of capital in the US for the same labor costs in the first and last periods, but two different patterns of evolution in between

varies tremendously, the extent of technical change in one period is quite limited. In this framework, the effect of a decrease of wages on employment remains weak in the short run, in sharp contrast with the neoclassical model.

The neoclassical framework incorporates the idea that the production function evolves over time as a result of technical progress, allowing a number of parameters of the function to vary. This variation can be exogenous in the simplest models, or endogenous, as within *endogenous growth models*.

Although path-dependence can be incorporated in a neoclassical model within an endogenous-growth framework, it is typically excluded from the analysis. Conversely, it is easy to illustrate the path-dependence that prevails in our model by running simulations. Consider, for example, the investigation whose results are displayed in Figure 12.6. We reran a similar simulation, conserving the actual values of the labor cost in 1869 and 1989, but assuming that the cost of labor grew at a constant rate throughout the period, that is, a pattern of evolution similar to that actually observed. As shown in Figure 12.15,

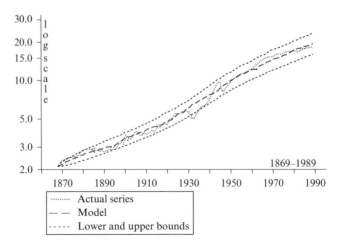

.... Actual series
— — Model
----- Lower and upper bounds

Figure 12.16   *The impact of random variables: a set of 1000 runs for labor productivity in the US*

the technology obtained toward the end of the period is significantly different. Not just the current value of labor cost but its entire trajectory matters.

The modeling of technical change in the present chapter is closer to evolutionary models. This explains why we refer to the model as a *classical-Marxian evolutionary model of technical change*. The framework of analysis used by Nelson and Winter is similar to our approach in several important respects.[46] Innovation is random and local. Techniques are selected depending on their profitability. The model also allows for wages to affect the choice of technology, without resorting to the neoclassical production function. There are also a number of differences. Nelson and Winter refer to *satisficing*: reducing the profit rate below a certain minimum triggers the adoption of new techniques. They also distinguish between innovation and imitation, in a manner that is significantly different from what we call *catching-up*.

The general disequilibrium model of section 4.1 is also "evolutionary" in several respects. Rationality is bounded (behaviors are *sensible* but distinct from neoclassical optimization): agents react to disequilibrium. Heterogeneity is crucial in the model. Several producers of the same good are considered, and they use different techniques. Technology and behaviors evolve only gradually.

There is no denying the fact that the classical notion of *economic law* is a priori alien to the evolutionary train of thought, or even contrary to one of its fundamental tenets. Between an excessively deterministic approach and total contingency, it is very difficult to find a satisfactory compromise. This problem is well known to Marxist economists. The *law* of the tendency of the profit rate to fall, and its host of countertendencies is probably the most famous example of this conflict.

The simulation presented in Figure 12.6 provides an interesting illustration of this problem. Since innovation is a random process in this model, one may wonder to what extent the reconstruction of the series depends on the exact sequence of innovations randomly determined (within the innovation set). We reran our model 1000 times, for the same conditions of innovation and the same series of labor costs. Figure 12.16 presents the results of these simulations for labor productivity. The dotted lines mark the upper and lower bounds of a band within which lies 95 percent of the possible outcomes. As would be expected, the distance between these two lines increases with time. An interval of ±20 percent obtains in the last year. It is clear that the exact sequence of innovation impacts on the profile of the series, but the same basic evolution is nevertheless observed. This is a form of what could be called *mild determination*. This is how we should always look at historical tendencies.

Notes

1. P. Sraffa, *Production of Commodities by Means of Commodities*, Cambridge: Cambridge University Press (1960), Ch. XII.
2. This is how Duncan Foley named the model we presented a few years ago in various papers (D. Foley, "Simulating Long-Run Technical Change", Department of Economics, Barnard College, Columbia University, New York (1998); G. Duménil, D. Lévy, "A Stochastic Model of Technical Change, Application to the US Economy (1869–1989)", *Metroeconomica*, 46 (1995), pp. 213–45).
3. In this study, we leave aside discussion of the use of variables measured in terms of value (as in Marx's analysis) or prices (as in data bases). What is, for example, the relationship between the rate of surplus value and the ratio of profits to wages? What is the importance of the distinction between productive and unproductive labor?
4. One has:

$$\bar{a} = \iint_\Pi a \, d\pi(a, l) \text{ and } \bar{l} = \iint_\Pi l \, d\pi(a, l)$$

   in which the integrals are limited to selected innovations, that is, the profitable innovation set Π.
5. All techniques in this model are represented by fixed coefficients. The patterns of variation described in panels (g) and (h) are, however, evocative of the notions of complementary and substitutable factors.
6. For example, for the productivity of capital:

$$a^L > 0 \Leftrightarrow \frac{1}{A^L} > \frac{1}{A}.$$

7. The equation of the ellipse is:

$$bx^2 + 2cxy + dy^2 = 1 \text{ with } x = a - \delta_a \text{ and } y = l - \delta_l$$

   The parameters are:

$$c = \frac{m}{1 + m^2}\left(\frac{1}{R^2} - \frac{1}{R'^2}\right), \ b = \frac{1}{1 + m^2}\left(\frac{m^2}{R^2} - \frac{1}{R'^2}\right), \text{ and } d = \frac{1}{1 + m^2}\left(\frac{1}{R^2} - \frac{m^2}{R'^2}\right)$$

   δ_a and δ_l are the coordinates of the center of the ellipse, $m = (l^L - \delta_l)/(a^L - \delta_a)$ is the slope of the main axis, and R and R' are half the lengths of the axes.
8. G. Duménil, D. Lévy, "The Acceleration and Slowdown of Technical Progress in the US since the Civil War: The Transition Between Two Paradigms", *Revue Internationale de Systémique*, 10 (1996), pp. 303–21.
9. Such a measure of the profit rate is appropriate in the analysis of technical and distributional change. To obtain the profit rate garnered by firms, it would be necessary to subtract taxes and interests. The measure of capital could also be made more precise, to include, in particular, inventories.
10. More specifically, we used the following analytical form (the derivative of a logistic function):

$$\delta(t) = \delta_0 + 4\delta_1 \exp\left(-\frac{t - \bar{t}}{\Delta}\right) \Big/ \left(1 + \exp\left(-\frac{t - \bar{t}}{\Delta}\right)\right)^2$$

   In this expression, $\bar{t}$ denotes the year in which the maximum value of $\delta(t)$ was reached, and Δ provides a measure of the duration of this movement. It is easy to verify that the curve is symmetrical with respect to $\bar{t}$.
11. This analysis is borrowed from G. Duménil, D. Lévy, "Complexity and Stylization: An Evolutionary Model of Technical Change in the US Economy", in R. Delorme, K. Dopfer (eds), *The Political Economy of Diversity: Evolutionary Perspectives on Economic Order and Disorder*, Aldershot, UK and Brookfield, USA: Edward Elgar (1994), pp. 229–51.
12. G. Duménil, D. Lévy, "The Acceleration and Slowdown", op. cit. Note 8.

13. A.D. Chandler, *The Visible Hand. The Managerial Revolution in American Business*, Cambridge: Harvard University Press (1977); G. Duménil, D. Lévy, *The Economics of the Profit Rate: Competition, Crises, and Historical Tendencies in Capitalism*, Aldershot, UK and Brookfield, USA: Edward Elgar (1993); *La dynamique du capital. Un siècle d'économie américaine*, Paris: Presses Universitaires de France (1996).

14. Robert Brenner locates mistakenly, in our opinion, the *cause* of the decline of the profit rate in the catching-up (R. Brenner, "The Economics of Global Turbulence", *New Left Review*, 229 (1998), pp. 1–264).

15. Obviously excess exposure to international competition can kill the follower.

16. K. Marx, *Capital, Volume III*, New York: First Vintage Book Edition (1894), Ch. 13, p. 318.

17. Still abstracting from a number of difficulties.

18. K. Marx, ibid., Ch. 14, p. 347.

19. K. Marx, ibid., p. 348.

20. See K. Marx, ibid., Ch. 15, section IV.

21. Instead of $r = s'/(1 + \gamma)$, we use $r = P_K(1 - \omega)$.

22. K. Marx, ibid., Ch. 13, p. 325.

23. N. Okishio, "Technical Change and the Rate of Profit", *Kobe University Economic Review*, 7 (1961), pp. 86–99.

24. Or a basic assumption must be abandoned. For example, one can assume that capitalists choose, for some reason, techniques that do not maximize the profit rate (A. Shaikh, "Marxian Competition versus Perfect Competition: Further Comments on the So-Called Choice of Technique", *Cambridge Journal of Economics*, 4 (1980), pp. 75–83).

25. These properties are rather intuitive. If labor productivity grows at a slower rate than the exogenous labor cost, $(\bar{l}(\omega) < \rho_w)$, a rising labor share follows. The rotation of the selection frontier provokes, in turn, a larger growth rate of labor productivity. Conversely, labor productivity growing faster than labor cost rotates the selection frontier toward a more vertical position, and initiates a decline in the growth rate of labor productivity. Equilibrium is reached when the two growth rates are equal.

26. The first period corresponds to $t_0 > 0$. If $\alpha > 1$, the slowdown is too strong: Labor productivity tends toward a constant.

27. In the structural crisis of the 1970s, the decline of the profit rate slowed, or even stopped, the rise of wages, even if the share of wages was not considerably increased. Conversely, during the first half of the twentieth century, the evolution of technology, favorable to the rise of the profit rate, allowed for a larger rate of growth of wages. (In spite of this increased growth rate of the labor cost, the profit rate still rose.)

28. G. Duménil, D. Lévy, *The Economics of the Profit Rate*, op. cit. Note 13, Ch. 15.

29. Consider, for example, the situation in the US, at the beginning of the twentieth century. The low profitability of capital prolonged the slow growth of wages while the profit rate was already beginning to recover. In a similar manner, the effects of the high profit rates of the 1960s on wages were still felt in the 1970s, when the decline of the profit rate was already well established. A situation similar to that observed at the beginning of the century seems to prevail presently: a rising profit rate and continuing wage stagnation.

30. The case $g = h = 0$ corresponds to the exogenous growth rate of labor cost of the previous section.

31. The equation accounting for ω^* becomes: $l(\omega^*) = f + g\bar{a}(\omega^*)$.

32. The equilibrium wage share is given by: $\bar{a}(\omega^*) = 0$.

33. In this long-term analysis, we abstract from business-cycle fluctuations.

34. G. Duménil, D. Lévy, ibid.

35. With:

$$C_1 = K(t_0)exp(-C_2 t_0^{\bar{a}(\omega^*)+1}) \text{ and } C_2 = \frac{sr(t_0)}{t_0^{\bar{a}(\omega^*)}(\bar{a}(\omega^*) + 1)}.$$

36. These variants correspond to the number of terms conserved in equation 9: (1) only the first term; (2) the two first terms; (3) the three terms.

37. Tom Michl obtains trajectories with a declining profit rate and a rising rate of surplus value ("Biased Technical Chance and the Aggregate Production Function", *International Review of Applied Economics*, 13 (1999), pp. 193–206). In his model, the growth rates of labor productivity and capital productivity, that we denote $\bar{l}$ and $\bar{a}$, are assumed constant, and positive and negative respectively. Thus, they do not respond to variations in wages. In our model, l and $\bar{a}$ are functions of wages, and the tendency for the rate of surplus value to rise, that is, the decline of the share of wages toward 0, results in a vertical selection frontier. In this situation, $\bar{a}$ is positive and the profit rate necessarily rises asymptotically.

38. Note that what is at issue concerning the falling profit rate is *process innovation*, not *product innovation*. Product innovation is not a counter-tendency to the falling profit rate. A priori a new product results from any kind of technique, with a low or high composition of capital.

39. G. Duménil, D. Lévy, "The Acceleration and Slowdown", op. cit. Note 8.

40. G. Duménil, D. Lévy, "The Great Depression: A Paradoxical Event?", Cepremap, num. 9510, Paris (1995).
41. G. Duménil, D. Lévy, *The Economics of the Profit Rate*, op. cit. Note 13; *La dynamique du capital*, op. cit. Note 13.
42. G. Duménil, D. Lévy, "Complexity and Stylization", op. cit. Note 11.
43. As usual these results are subject to conditions. For a discussion of these conditions, see G. Duménil, D. Lévy, *The Economics of the Profit Rate,* op. cit. Note 13 and *La dynamique du capital*, op. cit. Note 13.
44. G. Duménil, D. Lévy, "Stylized Facts about Technical Progress since the Civil War: A Vintage Model", *Structural Change and Economic Dynamics*, 5 (1994), pp. 1–23.
45. Obviously, we abstract here from other features of the neoclassical framework which cannot be accepted (for example, innovation is not local).
46. R.R. Nelson, S.G. Winter, "Factor Prices Changes and Factor Substitution in an Evolutionary Model", *Bell Journal of Economics*, 6 (1975), pp. 466–86; *An Evolutionary Theory of Economic Change*, Cambridge, MA: Harvard University Press (1982).

PART IV

MONEY, FINANCE AND GROWTH

13 "Financialisation" in post-Keynesian models of distribution and growth: a systematic review*

Eckhard Hein and Till van Treeck

1 Introduction

Recent decades have seen major changes in the financial sectors of developed and developing countries.[1] Generally, we have observed a rapid development of new financial instruments, triggered by national and international liberalisation of legal systems and by the development of new communication technologies. The overall importance of financial factors for distribution, consumption, investment and growth seems to have increased considerably. These developments and the related consequences and effects have been broadly summarised as "financialisation" by some authors (Epstein, 2005; Hein, 2010; Krippner, 2005; Lavoie, 2008; Palley, 2008; Skott and Ryoo, 2008a, 2008b; Stockhammer, 2004; van Treeck, 2009a, 2009b).[2] However, a major part of this literature remains somewhat opaque when it comes to the precise meaning of "financialisation". Epstein (2005, p. 3), for example, argues rather broadly that "[. . .] financialization means the increasing role of financial motives, financial markets, financial actors and financial institutions in the operation of the domestic and international economies". In this chapter we start with a more precise meaning and analytical definition of what "financialisation" involves. This will help us to review recent attempts to incorporate these developments into post-Keynesian models of distribution and growth in a systematic way.

Seen from a post-Keynesian macroeconomic perspective, and limiting our attention to closed private economies, we suggest that "financialisation" has the following potential implications:[3]

1. Both the objectives and the constraints of firms as a whole may be affected. On the one hand, increasing shareholder power will subordinate managements' and workers' preferences for (long-run) accumulation to shareholders' preference for (short-term) profitability. On the other hand, increasing dividend payments, share buybacks and so on will restrict the availability of finance for firms' investment projects.
2. New opportunities (and longer term risks) for households in terms of wealth-based and debt-financed consumption may arise. The reasons for this are financial asset price booms associated with the shareholder value orientation of firms on the one hand, and new credit instruments made available to households by profit-seeking banks on the other.
3. The distribution of income may be affected because of changes in power relations between shareholders, managers and workers. Distribution effects will then feed back on investment and consumption.

The remainder of the chapter is structured as follows. In the second section we draw on the existing literature in order to develop a general post-Keynesian framework for the analysis of "financialisation". In particular, we attempt to coherently link the microeconomic foundations of shareholder value orientation at the firm level with the possible macroeconomic outcomes. In the third section, we discuss different possible "regimes", showing why financialisation may have either contractionary or expansionary effects, and raising some stock-flow as well as financial fragility and instability issues. The fourth section summarises and concludes.

2   A general post-Keynesian framework for the analysis of "financialisation"

2.1   "Financialisation" and the post-Keynesian theory of the firm

In the traditional post-Keynesian theory of the firm, rentiers are seen as playing only a minor role in corporate governance. The typical post-Keynesian firm is a large corporation, operating in imperfectly competitive markets (Eichner's, 1976, "megacorp"). The main interest of the management of such firms (Galbraith's, 1967, "technostructure") has traditionally been seen to be the growth of the firm, subject to only loose profitability constraints enforced by owners. In light of recent developments in financial markets and corporate governance, this post-Keynesian theory of the firm needs to be reconsidered.[4]

More recently, post-Keynesians, such as Crotty (1990), Dallery (2009), or Stockhammer (2005–06), have highlighted the importance of the "owner–manager conflict" inherent to large corporations. This conflict arises from a postulated "growth–profit trade-off", implying that shareholder value orientation is likely to be associated with a high preference for short-term profitability and with a low propensity to invest in real capital stock by firms. Because of diversified portfolios, "stockholders typically have only a fleeting relation with any particular enterprise" (Crotty, 1990, p. 534) and care much more about the current profitability than the long-term expansion and survival of a particular firm.[5] In fact, with "financialisation", various mechanisms have been designed to, on the one hand, impose restrictions on management's ability to seek expansion, and, on the other hand, change management's preferences themselves and align them to shareholders' profit maximisation objective. Management's desire for growth is nowadays contained through, in particular, higher dividend payouts demanded by shareholders, a weaker ability of firms to obtain new equity finance through stock issues (which tend to decrease share prices), a larger dependence on leverage, and an increased threat of hostile takeovers in a liberalised market for corporate control. Simultaneously, financial market-oriented remuneration schemes have been developed to align management preferences to shareholders' objectives. It has been argued that the traditional managerial policy of "retain and invest" has been replaced by the shareholder-oriented strategy of "downsize and distribute" (Lazonick and O'Sullivan, 2000).

Graphically, these new developments can be analysed on the basis of Figure 13.1. The lines given by FF_i reflect different finance constraints faced by the managers of the firm in their investment decision. These finance frontiers indicate the maximum rate of accumulation (g) that firms can finance with a given profit rate (r). In other words, they determine the profit rate that is necessary for firms to be able to finance the desired accumulation rate. The finance frontier can be derived algebraically as follows. Notice first that investment (I) can be financed either by retained earnings or by external finance:

$$I = s_f(\Pi - i_b K_b) + x_b I + x_s I. \tag{1}$$

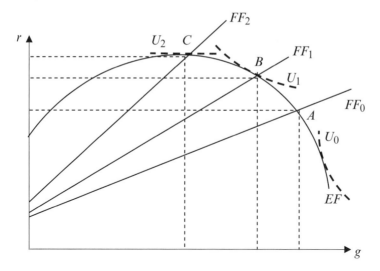

Figure 13.1   Shareholder value orientation and investment decisions at the firm level

with Π as profits, s_f as the share of retained profits in profits net of interest payments (the retention ratio), i_b as the interest rate paid by firms, K_b as firms' outstanding bonds or loans, and x_b and x_s respectively as the proportions of investment financed by bond issues/bank credit and equity issues. Defining the profit rate as $r = \Pi/K$, and the leverage ratio as $LEV = K_b/K$, from equation (1) it follows that

$$g = \frac{I}{K} = \frac{s_f(r - i_b LEV)}{1 - x_b - x_s}. \tag{2}$$

This implies that for a given profit rate (r) managers can finance a higher accumulation rate, the lower are dividend payments and interest obligations and the higher is the proportion of externally financed investment that is tolerated by creditors as well as the firm itself under conditions of asymmetric information, considering Kalecki's (1937) "principle of increasing risk". Graphically, if creditors and/or firms tolerate a higher proportion of investment financed by external means and/or the leverage ratio, the interest rate or the required dividend payout ratio declines, the firm's finance frontier in Figure 13.1 rotates clockwise and/or shifts downwards.

The second constraint faced by managers is the expansion frontier (*EF*). It indicates the profit rate that can be realised with a particular growth strategy. The expansion frontier is assumed to be upward sloping for low accumulation rates (because of efficiency gains resulting from the implementation of new production technologies, etc.), and downward sloping for higher rates (because of technical and logistical inefficiencies, etc.) (Lavoie, 1992, pp. 114–16).

In the traditional post-Keynesian analysis of the firm, the accumulation decision is determined by the point of intersection of the finance frontier and the expansion frontier (Lavoie, 1992, p. 117). In this view, firms are interested in the profit rate only insofar as a higher profit rate eases the finance constraint and hence allows for faster expansion. As suggested by Lavoie (1992, p. 106): "Put briefly, growth is the objective, and profits are the means to realize this objective." In contrast, with "financialisation" it seems more appropriate to consider the possibility that the desired accumulation rate, given by preferences, is below the maximum rate, given by the finance constraint: "profits are no longer a means to an end but have become an end in itself" (Dallery, 2009, p. 495). Therefore, Figure 13.1 is completed by a set of indifference curves, U_i, reflecting different preferences of managers faced with the growth-profitability trade-off in the downward-sloping segment of the expansion frontier (see also Dallery, 2009; Stockhammer, 2005–06).[6]

With higher shareholder value orientation, one may expect two things to happen:

1.   Shareholders impose a higher distribution of profits by firms: (higher required dividend payout ratio and hence lower rentention ratio and lower contribution of new equity issues to the financing of investment, or share buybacks.
2.   Managers' (firms') preference for growth is weakened as a result of remuneration schemes based on short-term profitability and financial market results.

The first effect will imply a counter-clockwise rotation and an upward shift of the finance frontier in Figure 13.1. These movements may even be more pronounced in the longer run, because the leverage ratio may increase as a result of lower profit retention and lower equity issues. This, however, can be expected to further reduce firms' ability to secure external means of finance. The second effect can be represented in Figure 13.1 as a flattening of the indifference curve.

Starting from a situation (point A) in which shareholders' influence on the firm's preferences is very weak (U_0) and the firm's accumulation decisions are restricted only by a relatively loose finance constraint (FF_0), the effects of increasing shareholder value orientation can be interpreted as follows. The new accumulation decision will be determined either by the new preferences alone (U_2 with FF_0 or FF_1 (point C) or U_1 with FF_0 (point B)), or by the new finance constraint alone (U_0 with FF_1 (point B) or U_0 or U_1 with FF_2 (point C)), or by preferences fully compatible with constraints (U_1 with FF_1 (point B) or U_2 with FF_2 (point C)). Note that when the finance constraint remains binding (e.g. U_1 with FF_2), shareholders are not able to impose their preferred investment strategy as a result of a shareholder–creditor conflict, with banks refusing to provide the required amount of credit necessary to realise shareholders' claims in terms of both profit distribution and investment policy.

2.2   "Financialisation" and aggregate demand

The growth–profitability trade-off postulated at the firm level in the previous subsection does not simply carry over to the macroeconomic level. Here, a lower accumulation rate leads to a lower profit rate, *ceteris paribus*. This is clearly expressed in the macroeconomic profit equation emphasised by Kalecki (1954, pp. 45–52) and also follows strictly from national income accounting:

$$\Pi = I + C_\Pi - S_W. \tag{3}$$

In a closed private economy, profits (Π) must always be exactly equal to investment (I) plus consumption out of profits (C_Π) minus saving out of wages (S_W). When many firms simultaneously attempt to move to the left along their individual expansion frontiers, they will experience a downward shift of these expansion frontiers, because of the adverse aggregate demand effect. This fallacy of composition seems to be neglected in much of the political economy and even macroeconomics literature on financialisation (see Skott and Ryoo, 2008a, van Treeck, 2009b, and Hein and van Treeck, 2010 for a critique). In what follows, we develop a general framework describing the macroeconomic implications of financialisation in terms of private investment and consumption decisions.

Equation (4) is a general investment function, relating net investment to the capital stock, which can be seen as grounded in the "microfoundations" outlined in the previous subsection.

$$g^i = \frac{I}{K} = \gamma_0 - \gamma_1 r_{sf} - \gamma_2 LEV + \gamma_3 u + \gamma_4 q, \qquad (4)$$

where r_{sf} is firms' target rate of profit, u is the rate of capacity utilisation, and $q = (K_b + K_s)/K$ is Tobin's q, with K_s being stock market capitalisation. The term $-\gamma_1 r_{sf}$ expresses the degree to which (shareholders') profitability targets affect firms' investment decisions: in terms of Figure 13.1, it can be seen as based on a set of indifference curves along a linearised downward sloping expansion frontier. Similarly, the term $-\gamma_2 LEV$ proxies the degree to which investment is finance constrained, because firms' access to external means of finance is negatively and interest obligations are positively related to the leverage ratio.[7] In terms of Figure 13.1, the points of intersection between a linear expansion frontier and a set of finance constraints also yield a downward sloping line in r–g space. The rate of capacity utilisation and Tobin's q are proxies for current and expected future demand and profitability conditions faced by firms, respectively. In Figure 13.1, an increase in either of these variables can be represented by an upward shift of the expansion frontier. For a given u and q, the accumulation policy of an individual firm is thus determined by either its preferences or the finance constraint, as previously argued. Financial asset prices, and hence Tobin's q, are jointly determined by firms' financing decisions and households' portfolio choices, which are not modelled explicitly here.[8]

Equation (4) encompasses various views on the effects of shareholder value orientation that can be found in the literature. Some authors, such as Boyer (2000), Cordonnier and Van de Velde (2008), Firmin (2008), and Stockhammer (2004, 2005–06), have focused on the effects on firms' preferences in terms of the growth–profit trade-off. In terms of Figure 13.1, as r_{sf} (the "financial norm" in Boyer, 2000) increases, the indifference curve representing firms' preferences becomes flatter and firms wish to move to the left along the expansion frontier. Other authors have emphasised the financial effects of shareholder value orientation, based on the idea that a higher rate of distributed profits reduces managers' ability to invest (Hein, 2006, 2007; Lavoie, 1995, 2008; Ndikumana, 1999; van Treeck, 2009a). Finally, some authors have considered both effects to be relevant (Dallery and van Treeck, 2010; Hein, 2008b, 2009, 2010; Skott and Ryoo, 2008a). In our view, for the business sector as a whole, it seems plausible to assume non-zero coefficients on both the financial norm set by shareholders and on distributed profits, implying that accumulation may be restricted exclusively by preferences in some firms, and by financing constraints in others. Also, in practice, it may be almost impossible to clearly distinguish between preferences and constraints: as the shareholder value orientation of management increases, their preference for profitability (linked to performance-oriented remuneration schemes) should increase together with their propensity to distribute profits, which may then further restrict investment decisions from the financing side.

The role of Tobin's q in the investment function is very controversial. In some models, it plays a crucial role allowing for positive effects of shareholder value orientation on accumulation (Skott and Ryoo, 2008a, 2008b; van Treeck, 2009a). In others, it is explicitly excluded from the investment function because it is argued that when firms themselves intervene in the stock market (e.g. by buying back shares), the resulting increase in Tobin's q will not be taken by them as a signal to invest more (Hein, 2009, 2010; and the discussion and literature review in van Treeck, 2009a).

A general saving function can be formulated as follows:

$$g^s = \frac{S}{K} = r - \beta_1[(1 - s_f)(r - i_bLEV) + i_bLEV] - \beta_2 q - \beta_3\frac{\Delta L_w}{K} - \beta_4\frac{\Delta L_r}{K}, \quad (5)$$

with

$$\Delta L_w = f(\overset{+}{W}, \overset{-}{L_w}, \overset{-}{i}_l, rep)$$

and

$$\Delta L_r = f(\overset{+}{\Pi}, \overset{+}{K_b}, \overset{+}{K_s}, \overset{-}{L_r}, \overset{-}{i}_l, rep).$$

It is assumed that there is no saving out of wage income. Saving in relation to the capital stock (g^s) is therefore determined by firms' retained profits and saving out of profits distributed to creditors and shareholders: $r - \beta_1[(1 - s_f)(r - i_bLEV) + i_bLEV]$. Saving may be reduced if consumption out of financial wealth (q) and out of new loans granted to workers (ΔL_w) and to rentiers (ΔL_r), each relative to the capital stock, is included. Net new loans are granted to workers and rentiers respectively on the basis of wage (W) or profit (Π) income, financial wealth, outstanding loans, the interest rate on personal loans (i_l), and the rate of loan repayment (rep).

Equation (5) encompasses different views of "financialisation" in terms of its implications for private consumption. In a pure flow model, Cordonnier (2006) argues that when firms increase dividend payments at the expense of accumulation, the macroeconomic profit rate may nevertheless increase, provided that shareholders have a large propensity to consume out of distributed profits, given by β_1 in the saving function above (see also Hein, 2008b, 2009, 2010; Van de Velde, 2005, p. 184; van Treeck, 2009a). The likelihood of such a scenario increases when the potentially positive effects of higher financial wealth on consumption are also taken into account ($\beta_2 > 0$), as in Boyer (2000), Lavoie and Godley (2001–2), Skott and Ryoo (2008a, 2008b), and van Treeck (2009a). Finally, debt-financing of consumption ($\beta_3 > 0$ and/or $\beta_4 > 0$) is a further channel facilitating the divorce of profits and investment at the macroeconomic level. However, some authors have pointed to the potentially longer-term risks of debt-financed consumption. In particular, Bhaduri et al. (2006) recall that a positive wealth effect, if it is to operate, also implies rising personal indebtedness, because financial wealth is by definition notional and cannot be realised at a macroeconomic scale. However, although rising wealth initially increases households' collateral, allowing for an expansion of credit [$\Delta L_r = f(\overset{+}{K_b}, \overset{+}{K_s})$], the accumulation of debt may, in the longer run, undermine households' creditworthiness and increase their burden of debt servicing, forcing them to increase saving again [$\Delta L_r = f(\overset{-}{L_r}, \overset{-}{i}_l, rep)$]. In a somewhat different vein, Dutt (2005, 2006) emphasises the distributional effects of credit-financing of consumption by workers. While the initial effects are clearly expansionary [upward shift in $\Delta L_w = f(\overset{+}{W}, \overset{-}{L_w}, \overset{-}{i}_l, rep)$], in the longer run, as workers accumulate debt and interest and repayment obligations increase, income is redistributed from workers towards rentiers, which causes the overall personal saving rate to rise. Palley (1996) has also analysed such conflicting effects of credit and debt over the business cycle.

Finally, the effects of financialisation on income distribution can be specified with the following general profit share equation:

$$h = \frac{\Pi}{Y} = \frac{m}{1 + m}, \text{ with } m = f(\overset{+}{r}_{sf}, \overset{-}{s}_f, \overset{-}{x}_s, \overset{+}{BUR}_W),$$ (6)

$$\text{with } BUR_W = \frac{(i_l + rep)L_W}{Y}$$

where h is the profit share, m is firms' mark-up, and BUR_W is workers' burden of debt, here defined as debt servicing by workers as a ratio of national income. According to equation (6), firms attempt to pass through higher profitability requirements as well as any rentier-imposed drain of retained profits (higher dividend payouts and share buy-backs) onto workers, by means of increasing the mark-up in their goods market pricing decisions. Also, the profit share increases as workers' debt servicing obligations increase relative to income. Such mechanisms have been discussed by, for example, Boyer (2000), Dallery and van Treeck (2010), Hein (2008b, 2009, 2010), and Palley (2008). Furthermore, Lavoie (2009) and Palley (2006) consider the effects of "cadrisme", imply-ing an increasingly unequal distribution of white collar (or management) salaries and blue collar wages (see also the empirical work by Piketty and Saez, 2003). In our view, as management's remuneration is increasingly pegged to firms' financial results, it is nowa-days increasingly of the nature of profit income rather than ordinary wage income (see the empirical work by Mohun, 2006).

3   Different "regimes"

Elsewhere, we have developed and solved full macroeconomic models of financialisa-tion (Hein, 2008b, 2009, 2010; van Treeck, 2009a; Dallery and van Treeck, 2010). Here, our purpose is to summarise less formally the potential overall effects of "financialisa-tion" in the general framework outlined above. Based on the discussion in the previous section, Figure 13.2 illustrates the potential macroeconomic effects of (a) an increasing shareholder value orientation of firms, which means a higher profitability norm, a larger dividend payout ratio, and a lower rate of equity issues, and (b) easier access to credit for private households, that is, rentiers as well as workers.[9] As can be seen in Figure 13.2, the effects of financialisation on the endogenous variables of the model are ambiguous throughout. Different authors have therefore come to different conclusions regarding the macroeconomic effects of financialisation.

3.1   Macroeconomic effects of changes in firms' preferences

The upper left part of Figure 13.2 describes the effects of a higher profitability norm. In terms of Figure 13.1, the individual firm attempts to move leftwards along its expansion frontier. However, in the absence of compensating macroeconomic forces (i.e. impacting on the saving function), the resulting decline in accumulation will clearly be contrac-tionary and induce a decrease, not an increase, in firms' profit rates. This fundamental

(a)   Shareholder value orientation, investment and saving

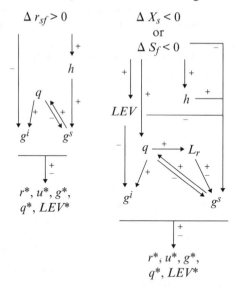

(b)   Personal borrowing and saving

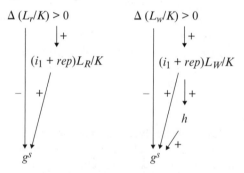

Figure 13.2   "Financialisation", income distribution and aggregate demand

micro–macro divide has been recalled by, among others, Cordonnier (2006), Cordonnier and Van de Velde (2008), Dallery (2009), Firmin (2008), Hein (2008b, 2009, 2010), Hein and van Treeck (2010), Skott and Ryoo (2008a), and van Treeck (2009b).

Some authors have, however, argued that there may indeed be important macroeconomic forces that may allow shareholders to realise their microeconomic objectives. One widely noted attempt in this direction has been made by Boyer (2000) in his analysis of the viability of a "finance-led growth regime". In this model, when employees are assumed to be "clearly aware of the favourable effect of wage restraint on their wealth" (Boyer, 2000, p. 125), an increase in the financial norm may have overall expansionary macroeconomic effects, as a result of the stimulating impact of higher financial wealth on consumption, and despite the direct negative effect in the investment function, as well as the indirect negative effect on consumption via the redistribution of income from wages to profits. Yet, Boyer's (2000) model is incomplete in a number of respects, and it is not clear, for instance, how exactly a change in the financial norm affects financial wealth (Tobin's q is assumed to be constant in his model, and wealth is calculated on the basis of Tobin's q, profits and the interest rate) (see Skott and Ryoo, 2008a, and van Treeck, 2009b, for a critique). In a full macroeconomic model, one would have to model financial wealth (or Tobin's q) as the result of households' saving and portfolio decisions as well as firms' financing decisions. In the framework developed above, an increase in the financial norm can be expansionary if it is linked to an increase in the profit share which then, via its effect on saving, stimulates Tobin's q and thereby investment (Figure 2a).[10]

A further mechanism that may countervail the depressive impact of higher profit-ability claims by shareholders has been analysed by Dallery and van Treeck (2010). They argue that when managers realise that increased profitability claims are not being met, they may have incentives to buy back shares and/or to distribute higher dividends in order to satisfy shareholders. Paradoxically, this may then stimulate profitability, utilisation and accumulation, because of rentiers' consumption out of capital income and wealth, and shareholders' microeconomic claims may hence eventually be realised at the macroeconomic level, provided that banks accept the associated increase in firms' indebtedness. A similar approach has been taken by Cordonnier (2006), who also consid-ers the possibility that a higher preference for profitability will be accompanied by higher dividend payments. Yet, according to this view, there is no direct causal relationship between dividend payments and investment, because dividend payments are not seen as a restriction, but rather as the result of shareholders demanding managers to distribute those profits that are not "needed", given the preferred investment strategy. However, as argued above on the basis of Figure 13.1, dividend payments and share buybacks also worsen firms' financial position and may therefore further affect investment adversely. This mechanism is discussed next.

3.2 Macroeconomic effects of changes in financial constraints faced by firms
Some authors have discussed the effects of shareholder value orientation in terms of its implications for firms' financing constraints. Some of these contributions are extensions of post-Keynesian growth models incorporating the impact of interest payments on invest-ment and consumption (Lavoie, 1995; Lavoie and Godley, 2001–02; Hein, 2006, 2007, 2008b, 2009, 2010; Skott and Ryoo, 2008a, 2008b; van Treeck, 2009a). Here, we discuss the effects of an increasing dividend payout ratio ($\Delta s_f < 0$) and of a reduction in the contri-bution of new equity issues to the financing of investment ($\Delta x_s < 0$) (Figure 2a). The two effects are essentially similar: both a higher dividend payout ratio, and hence a decreas-ing retention ratio, and share buybacks tend to increase firms' dependence on debt (thus increasing their leverage[11]), but they also stimulate share prices and Tobin's q because of larger household saving in both cases and by reducing the stock of equities in the case of share buybacks. Some authors (Hein 2008b, 2009, 2010; Palley, 2008; van Treeck, 2009a) have also argued that a decrease in firms' retention ratio may lead to an increase in the profit share, as firms attempt to pass through higher profit payouts and financing costs to workers. The overall effects on growth will be ambiguous, therefore, depending on the relative strengths of various partial effects (see Figure 13.2a): the negative impact of higher leverage and a lower retention ratio on accumulation (via the finance frontier in terms of Figure 13.1); the positive effect of a higher Tobin's q on accumulation (an upward shift of

the expansion frontier in Figure 13.1); the negative effect of a higher profit share on consumption; and the positive effect of higher financial wealth on consumption (directly and indirectly via the increase in collateral and household borrowing).

Therefore, it comes as no surprise that different authors have come to different conclusions regarding the overall impact of more shareholder-friendly financing decisions by firms. Lavoie and Godley (2001–02) find, in a stock–flow consistent (SFC) model, that both a lower retention rate and lower equity issues have expansionary effects given their chosen model specification and parameter values. Skott and Ryoo (2008a, 2008b) come to the same conclusion, and also provide a general analytical treatment: they conclude that for systems with relatively "inelastic stock–flow ratios" (financial wealth-to-income ratios), the effects of higher dividends and lower equity issues can be expected to be expansionary, while in the case of "elastic stock–flow ratios", the results may be contractionary.[12] They also argue that it is empirically more plausible to assume stock–flow inelastic systems. Somewhat different results have been derived by Hein (2009, 2010) and van Treeck (2009a), who distinguish between contractionary ("normal"), intermediate, and expansionary ("puzzling") cases, following Lavoie's (1995) discussion of the ambiguous effects of increases in the interest rate on the rates of capacity utilisation, profit, and accumulation. In the contractionary (expansionary) case, the endogenous variables are negatively (positively) affected throughout, while in the intermediate case the accumulation rate declines while the rates of capacity utilisation and profit increase, which corresponds to Cordonnier's (2006) "profits without investment" and Stockhammer's (2005–06) "investment-profit puzzle". The somewhat more complex model by Godley and Lavoie (2007, Chapter 11, pp. 435–9) and the experiments based on this model by Lavoie (2008) also produce contractionary results: an increase in the target proportion of investment financed by retained earnings, corresponding to a decrease in the proportion of investment financed by new equity issues, has negative effects on economic activity and growth, because it increases firms' costing margins and conflict inflation, and it decreases real wages. Although Tobin's q rises, this does not impact on investment in this model. In Lavoie (2008), an increase in the fraction of profits distributed as dividends has negative effects on output and employment for the same reasons: firms' target costing margin and conflict inflation increase, real wages decline and the increase in Tobin's q has no positive feedback effect on investment.

As discussed by Skott and Ryoo (2008a, 2008b) and van Treeck (2009a), the overall results depend crucially on the coefficients attached to the leverage ratio and Tobin's q in the investment function and to the wealth effect in the consumption function. The plausibility of the different regimes is thus an empirical matter. While Skott and Ryoo see wealth effects on investment and consumption as empirically important, Hein (2009, 2010) and van Treeck (2009a) argue that Tobin's q may be an unreliable indicator for investment decisions when firms intervene themselves in the stock market and, for instance, actively reduce the supply of equities.[13] Also, while it is acknowledged that the wealth effect on consumption has been empirically very important in some countries (in particular in the US), they maintain that this is less the case in other countries (e.g. continental Europe) and argue that an initially wealth- and credit-driven system may eventually come to an end when it is linked to rising corporate and personal debt ratios. In the terminology applied by Taylor (2004), an initially "debt-led" system may eventually become "debt-burdened".

In the end, however, it seems that there is widespread agreement that shareholder value orientation potentially has overall contractionary effects, when its implications for both firms' preferences and financing constraints are taken together (see e.g. the concluding discussion in Skott and Ryoo, 2008a).

3.3   Macroeconomic effects of easier access to credit for private households

In Figure 13.2b, some potential implications of easier access to credit for private households are discussed. The reasons for the ambiguous effects of increased borrowing opportunities on saving are linked to the interaction between (the flow of) credit and (the stock of) debt. An increase in household borrowing is initially expansionary because it stimulates consumption. In the longer run, however, debt servicing obligations increase and tend to depress consumer spending. Bhaduri et al. (2006) even consider the possibility of a negative wealth effect on consumption, which is based on the idea that the wealth effect can only operate through increases in household debt, because notional wealth cannot be realised collectively but only serve as collateral for consumers.

Note that the magnitude of the conflicting flow and stock effects of higher debt will be particularly large when lower income households (workers) increase their borrowing ($\Delta L_w > 0$) and are assumed to have a higher marginal propensity to consume (MPC) than higher income households (rentiers). As emphasised by Palley (1996, p. 202) in an early contribution: "increases in debt initially stimulate aggregate demand by transferring spending power from creditors to debtors, but the interest payments on accumulated debt stocks become a burden on aggregate demand since they transfer income from high MPC households to low MPC households" (see also Palley, 1994). Dutt (2006) has confirmed this mechanism in a growth context.

3.4   "Financialisation" and macroeconomic instability

It is beyond the scope of this review to extensively discuss the literature on financial fragility. Here, we only briefly touch on the potential links between macroeconomic instability and financialisation.

To begin with, as argued above, both shareholder value orientation and the deregulation of credit markets are likely to contribute to rising debt ratios in both the corporate and the private household sectors, which in turn seems to increase financial fragility. As recently observed by Palley (2008, p. 2) in his overview of financialisation in the US:

> The last two decades have been marked by rapidly rising household debt–income ratios and corporate debt–equity ratios. These developments explain both the system's growth and increasing fragility [. . .]. The risk is when this happens the economy could be vulnerable to debt-deflation and prolonged recession.

While these observations may not look very new to adherers of Minsky's financial fragility hypothesis (Minsky, 1975, 1982), the existing literature also shows that increasing leverage ratios and/or Tobin's *q* are not necessarily associated with economic expansions. Rather, when the economy is "debt-burdened", higher leverage ratios go in line with lower utilisation, profit and accumulation rates (see also Lavoie and Seccareccia, 2001). Similarly, as shown by Bhaduri et al. (2006, p. 418), it is possible to perceive situations in which "the level of real income and, of virtual wealth may [. . .] move in opposite directions". Lavoie (1995) and Hein (2006, 2007, 2009, 2010), referring to Steindl's

(1952) "paradox of debt", also emphasise that increasing interest or dividend obligations for firms may even be associated with exploding debt– or outside finance–capital ratios, despite (or because of) their contractionary effects on capacity utilisation and capital accumulation.

A different type of instability potentially linked to shareholder value orientation has recently been highlighted by Cordonnier and Van de Velde (2008). They start their argument by noting that a larger (microeconomic) preference for profitability will induce a declining profit rate at the macroeconomic level (see Figure 13.2a). In a closed private economy, the only remedy to this macroeconomic realisation problem seems to be a higher rate of distributed profits that then stimulates consumption and hence profits. This, however, also requires higher leverage of firms, and as soon as lenders refuse to expand the flow of credit to firms, the process of adjusting the realised profit rate to shareholders' target comes to an end. While Dallery and van Treeck (2010) have envisaged the possibility that, despite failing to resolve this shareholder–creditor conflict, the economy converges to a steady state consistent with the maximum leverage ratio targeted by banks, Cordonnier and Van de Velde (2008, p. 14) point at the potentially "depressionary pathos of financialised capitalism": when firms are systematically disappointed with their realised profit rate, they may become ever more selective in their investment projects in an attempt to move leftwards on their expansion frontier (see Figure 13.1). This, however, may lead into a deflationary spiral by further reducing aggregate demand and realised profitability.

The bottom line is that financialisation may be quite compatible with strong economic activity and may be very successful (under certain conditions) in providing firms with high profit rates. But the associated risks are equally obvious: rising debt ratios in both the corporate and personal sectors may increase financial fragility, and when profitability claims by shareholders become overly demanding, the credit system may at some point refuse to accommodate the associated rise in private debt-to-income and debt-to-capital ratios.

4   Summary and conclusions

In the present chapter we have reviewed the integration of financialisation processes into post-Keynesian distribution and growth models and distinguished three principal channels of influence: changing preferences of and tougher financial restrictions on firms; new opportunities for households' wealth-based and debt-financed consumption; and the redistribution between capital and labour, on the one hand, and between management and workers, on the other hand. Starting from a reinterpretation of the post-Keynesian theory of the firm we have bridged the gap between micro- and macro-analysis of financialisation and have traced the main characteristics and effects of financialisation from the micro to the macro level taking into account stock–flow interactions. Our review of the theoretical literature on financialisation shows that expansionary effects may arise under certain conditions, in particular when there are strong wealth effects in firms' investment decisions (via Tobin's q) and in households' consumption decisions. However, our review also suggests that even an expansionary finance-led economy may build up major financial imbalances – such as increasing debt–capital or debt–income ratios – which make such economies prone to financial instability.

Post-Keynesian models of growth and distribution, and in particular stock–flow consistent models, are well suited for analysis of the complex interactions between the conflicting claims of shareholders, managers and workers, aggregate demand and the financial sphere of the economy. Given the renewed topicality of these issues, further research, both theoretical and empirical, is highly warranted.

Notes

*   This work started when we were visiting Marc Lavoie in Ottawa in May/June 2008. We would like to thank the University of Ottawa for its hospitality and the IMK at Hans Boeckler Foundation for the supply of travel funding. We have greatly benefited from the discussions with Marc Lavoie and the participants of the workshop "Financialisation: Post Keynesian Approaches" at the University of Lille 1 in April 2008, from helpful comments by Thomas Dallery on an earlier version of this chapter, and from comments and suggestions by Mark Setterfield at the final stage. However, we alone are responsible for remaining errors.

1.   See for example the overview in Eatwell and Taylor (2000) for an early analysis, Krippner (2005) and the contributions in Epstein (2005) for a detailed treatment of developments in the US and other countries, van Treeck et al. (2007) and van Treeck (2009b) for a comparison of the macroeconomics of "financialisation" in the US and Germany, and Stockhammer (2008) for developments in Europe.

2.   Other authors have used different terms, with sometimes different meanings: "finance-led growth regime" (Boyer, 2000), "financial wealth-induced growth regime" (Aglietta, 2000), "finance-dominated regime" (Stockhammer, 2008), "neo-liberalism" (Duménil and Lévy, 2005), "shareholder value orientation" (Hein, 2008b, 2009; Stockhammer, 2005–06), "maximizing shareholder value" (Lazonick and O'Sullivan, 2000).

3.   Whereas earlier post-Keynesian and Kaleckian models of distribution and growth were missing explicit monetary and financial variables (with the exception of Pasinetti's, 1974, pp. 139–41, natural rate of growth models) these variables have been introduced into post-Keynesian models since the late 1980s/ early 1990s by various authors. However, the focus in these models has mainly been on the introduction of the rate of interest, as an exogenous distribution parameter determined by central bank policies, and bank credit, created endogenously by a developed banking sector in response to demand from creditworthy borrowers. See the surveys by, among others, Hein (2008a), Lavoie (1992, pp. 347–71, 1995), and Taylor (2004, pp. 272–8).

4.   For a review of the post-Keynesian theory of the firm, as developed by, amongst others, Galbraith (1967), Eichner (1976), and Wood (1975), see Lavoie (1992, pp. 94–118), who could still argue in 1992 that: "Whether the owners are still in control or not is irrelevant: those individuals taking decisions within the firm are in search of power; and their behaviour and motivations will reflect that fundamental fact" (Lavoie, 1992, p. 102).

5.   In the New Institutional Economics literature, the "owner–manager conflict" is interpreted as a "principal–agent problem" involving shareholders and managers. In this literature, however, the focus is not primarily on managers' preference for growth and on the related effects on aggregate demand, but on management's shirking and interest in "benefits in kind", such as "physical appointments of the office", the "attractiveness of the secretarial staff", or "a larger than optimal computer to play with" (Jensen and Meckling, 1976, p. 312).

6.   One may also interpret the indifference curves as reflecting the preferences of the firm as a whole, determined by a compromise between shareholders and managers.

7.   Many authors also include the rate of retained profits, given by $s_f(r-i_bLEV)$, in the investment function (e.g. recently Lavoie and Godley, 2001–02; Ndikumana, 1999; Skott and Ryoo, 2008a, 2008b; van Treeck, 2009a). Here we wish to keep things simple and to explicitly ground the investment function in the post-Keynesian theory of the firm as exposed in Figure 13.1. While the leverage ratio affects only the finance constraint, the rate of retained profits is also directly influenced by aggregate demand, which also affects the position of the individual firm's expansion frontier. Note that with our chosen specification an increase in the dividend–payout ratio will have only an indirect negative effect on investment through an increase in the leverage ratio.

8.   See Godley and Lavoie (2007) for the integration of financial decisions of firms and households in stock–flow consistent models. In these models, $q=1$ is not an equilibrium condition.

9.   The effects of financialisation working through the third channel discussed earlier (changes in income distribution) are subsumed in the upper and lower panels of Figure 13.2, by virtue of the endogeneity of the profit share (h) to factors that fall under the rubric of (a) and (b).

10.   Another possibility would be that a higher financial norm increases households' preference for equities and hence Tobin's q and accumulation and consumption.

11.   In Hein (2009, 2010), however, a higher dividend rate (a higher rentiers' rate of return in his model) is not necessarily associated with a higher equilibrium leverage ratio. In his "finance-led growth" regime,

the stable equilibrium leverage ratio may actually decline, when its initial value is already large. In the unstable "contractive" and "profits without investment" regimes the equilibrium value of the leverage ratio may rise or decline too, but the actual value will increase and explode because of a cumulative disequilibrium process involving a continued decline of the rate of capital accumulation.

12. Skott and Ryoo (2008a, 2008b) distinguish between Harrodian and Kaleckian economies with and without labour constraints. In the Harrodian labour constrained case, the expansionary effects of higher dividend payments and share buybacks on growth occur only in the short run, but in the long run investment decisions are adjusted such that the economy grows at a rate given by the growth rate of labour supply. The postulated adjustment mechanism is a deterioration of firms' animal spirits in the face of increasing workers' militancy triggered by low unemployment.

13. See Medlen (2003) for empirical support for our doubts. According to his observations there is a positive correlation between Tobin's q, on the one hand, and the ratio of mergers to new real investment, on the other hand, the exact opposite of what Tobin's q would suggest. Generally, empirical studies have difficulties in finding a statistically significant and empirically relevant effect of Tobin's q on investment. See, for example, Bhaskar and Glyn (1995), Chirinko (1993), and Ndikumana (1999).

References

Aglietta, M. (2000), "Shareholder value and corporate governance: some tricky questions", *Economy and Society*, **29**, 146–59.

Bhaduri, A., K. Laski, and M. Riese (2006), "A model of interaction between the virtual and the real economy", *Metroeconomica*, **57**, 412–27.

Bhaskar, V. and A. Glyn (1995), "Investment and profitability: the evidence from the advanced capitalist countries", in G.A. Epstein and H.M. Gintis (eds), *Macroeconomic Policy after the Conservative Era*, Cambridge: Cambridge University Press, pp. 175–96.

Boyer, R. (2000), "Is a finance-led growth regime a viable alternative to Fordism? A preliminary analysis", *Economy and Society*, **29**, 111–45.

Chirinko, R.S. (1993), "Business fixed investment spending: modelling strategies, empirical results and policy implications", *The Journal of Economic Literature*, **31**, 1875–911.

Cordonnier, L. (2006), "Le profit sans l'accumulation: la recette du capitalisme dominé par la finance", *Innovations, Cahiers d'économie de l'innovation*, **23** (1), 51–72.

Cordonnier, L. and F. Van de Velde (2008), "Financial claims and the glass ceiling of profitability", Paper presented at the Workshop "Financialization: Post-Keynesian Approaches", University of Lille, April.

Crotty, J. (1990), "Owner–management conflict and financial theories of investment instability: a critical assessment of Keynes, Tobin, and Minsky", *Journal of Post Keynesian Economics*, **12**, 519–42.

Dallery, T. (2009), "Post-Keynesian theories of the firm under financialization", *Review of Radical Political Economics*, **41**, 492–515.

Dallery, T. and T. van Treeck (2010), "Conflicting claims and equilibrium adjustment processes in a stock-flow consistent macro model", forthcoming in *Review of Political Economy*.

Duménil, G. and D. Lévy (2005), "Costs and benefits of neoliberalism: a class analysis", in G.A. Epstein (ed.), *Financialization and the World Economy*, Cheltenham, UK and Northampton, MA, USA: Edward Elgar, pp. 17–45.

Dutt, A.K. (2005), "Conspicuous consumption, consumer debt and economic growth", in M. Setterfield (ed.), *Interactions in Analytical Political Economy. Theory, Policy and Applications*, Armonk, NY: M.E. Sharpe, pp. 155–78.

Dutt, A.K. (2006), "Maturity, stagnation and consumer debt: a Steindlian approach", *Metroeconomica*, **57**, 339–64.

Eatwell, J. and L. Taylor (2000), *Global Finance at Risk*, Cambridge: Polity Press.

Eichner, A. (1976), *Megacorp and Oligopoly: Micro Foundations of Macro Dynamics*, Cambridge: Cambridge University Press.

Epstein, G.A. (ed.) (2005), *Financialization in the World Economy*, Cheltenham, UK and Northampton, MA, USA: Edward Elgar.

Firmin, C. (2008), "Financialization and income distribution: a post-Keynesian interpretation of the French case", Paper presented at the Workshop "Financialization: Post-Keynesian Approaches", University of Lille, April.

Galbraith, J.K. (1967), *The New Industrial State*, Harmonsworth: Pelican Books.

Godley, W. and M. Lavoie (2007), *Monetary Economics. An Integrated Approach to Credit, Money, Income, Production and Wealth*, Basingstoke: Palgrave Macmillan.

Hein, E. (2006), "Interest, debt and capital accumulation – a Kaleckian approach", *International Review of Applied Economics*, **20**, 337–52.

Hein, E. (2007), "Interest rate, debt, distribution and capital accumulation in a post-Kaleckian model", *Metroeconomica*, **57**, 310–39.

Hein, E. (2008a), *Money, Distribution Conflict and Capital Accumulation. Contributions to "Monetary Analysis"*, Basingstoke: Palgrave Macmillan.

Hein, E. (2008b), "Rising shareholder power – effects on distribution, capacity utilisation and capital accumulation in Kaleckian/post-Kaleckian models", in E. Hein, T. Niechoj, P. Spahn and A. Truger (eds), *Finance-led Capitalism? Macroeconomic Effects of Changes in the Financial Sector*, Marburg: Metropolis, pp. 89–120.

Hein, E. (2009), "Shareholder value orientation, distribution and growth: short- and medium-run effects in a Kaleckian model", *Metroeconomica*, Early view DOI: 10.1111/j.1467-999X.2009.04071.x.

Hein, E. (2010), "A (post-)Keynesian perspective on 'financialisation'", in P. Arestis and M. Sawyer (eds), *21st Century Keynesian Economics*, London: Palgrave.

Hein, E. and T. van Treeck (2010), "Financialization and rising shareholder power in Kaleckian/post-Kaleckian models of distribution and growth", forthcoming in *Review of Political Economy*.

Jensen, M.C. and W.H. Meckling (1976), "Theory of firm – managerial behavior, agency costs and ownership structure", *Journal of Financial Economics*, **3** (4), 305–60.

Kalecki, M. (1937), "The principle of increasing risk", *Economica*, **4**, 440–47.

Kalecki, M. (1954), *Theory of Economic Dynamics*, London: George Allen & Unwin.

Krippner, G.R. (2005), "The financialization of the American economy", *Socio-Economic Review*, **3**, 173–208.

Lavoie, M. (1992), *Foundations of Post Keynesian Economic Analysis*, Aldershot, UK and Brookfield, USA: Edward Elgar.

Lavoie, M. (1995), "Interest rates in post-Keynesian models of growth and distribution", *Metroeconomica*, **46**, 146–77.

Lavoie, M. (2008), "Financialisation issues in a post-Keynesian stock–flow consistent model", *Intervention. European Journal of Economics and Economic Policies*, **5**, 331–56.

Lavoie, M. (2009), "Cadrisme within a Kaleckian model of growth and distribution", *Review of Political Economy*, **21**, 369–91.

Lavoie, M. and W. Godley (2001–02), "Kaleckian models of growth in a coherent stock–flow monetary framework: a Kaldorian view", *Journal of Post Keynesian Economics*, **22**, 277–311.

Lavoie, M. and M. Seccareccia (2001), "Minsky's financial fragility hypothesis: a missing macroeconomic link?", in R. Bellofiore and P. Ferri (eds), *Financial Fragility and Investment in the Capitalist Economy, The Economic Legacy of Hyman Minsky*, Vol. 2, Cheltenham, UK and Northampton, MA, USA: Edward Elgar, pp. 76–96.

Lazonick, W. and M. O'Sullivan (2000), "Maximizing shareholder value: a new ideology for corporate governance", *Economy and Society*, **29**, 13–35.

Medlen, C. (2003), "The trouble with Q", *Journal of Post Keynesian Economics*, **25**, 693–98.

Minsky, H. (1975), *John Maynard Keynes*, New York: Columbia University Press.

Minsky, H. (1982), *Can "It" Happen Again? Essays on Instability and Finance*, Armonk, NY: M.E. Sharpe.

Mohun, S. (2006), "Distributive shares in the US economy, 1964–2001", *Cambridge Journal of Economics*, **30**, 347–70.

Ndikumana, L. (1999), "Debt service, financing constraints, and fixed investment: evidence from panel data", *Journal of Post Keynesian Economics*, **21**, 455–78.

Palley, T. (1994), "Debt, aggregate demand, and the business cycle: an analysis in the spirit of Kaldor and Minsky", *Journal of Post Keynesian Economics*, **16**, 371–90.

Palley, T. (1996), *Post Keynesian Economics. Debt, Distribution and the Macro Economy*, Basingstoke: Macmillan.

Palley, T. (2006), "Class conflict and the Cambridge theory of income distribution", in E. Hein, A, Heise and A. Truger (eds), *Wages, Employment, Distribution and Growth. International Perspectives*, Basingstoke: Palgrave Macmillan, pp. 223–46.

Palley, T. (2008), "Financialization: what it is and why it matters", in E. Hein, T. Niechoj, P. Spahn and A. Truger (eds), *Finance-led Capitalism? Macroeconomic Effects of Changes in the Financial Sector*, Marburg: Metropolis, pp. 29–60.

Pasinetti, L.L. (1974), *Growth and Income Distribution*, Cambridge: Cambridge University Press.

Piketty, T and E. Saez (2003), "Income inequality in the United States, 1913–1998", *Quarterly Journal of Economics*, **118** (1), 1–39.

Skott, P. and S. Ryoo (2008a), "Macroeconomic implications of financialization", *Cambridge Journal of Economics*, **32**: 827–62.

Skott. P. and S. Ryoo (2008b), "Financialization in Kaleckian economics with and without labor constraints", *Intervention. European Journal of Economics and Economic Policies*, **5**, 357–86.

Steindl, J. (1952), *Maturity and Stagnation in American Capitalism*, Oxford: Blackwell.

Stockhammer, E. (2004), "Financialisation and the slowdown of accumulation", *Cambridge Journal of Economics*, **28**, 719–741.

Stockhammer, E. (2005–06), "Shareholder value orientation and the investment–profit puzzle", *Journal of Post Keynesian Economics*, **28**, 193–215.

Stockhammer, E. (2008), "Some stylized facts on the finance-dominated accumulation regime", *Competition and Change*, **12**, 189–207.

Taylor, L. (2004), *Reconstructing Macroeconomics. Structuralists Proposals and Critiques of the Mainstream*, Cambridge, MA and London: Harvard University Press.

Van de Velde, F. (2005), *Monnaie, Chômage et Capitalisme*, Villeneuve d'Ascq: Septentrion.

van Treeck, T. (2009a), "A synthetic, stock–flow consistent macroeconomic model of financialisation", *Cambridge Journal of Economics*, **33** (3), 467–93.

van Treeck, T. (2009b), "The political economy debate on 'financialisation' – a macroeconomic perspective", *Review of International Political Economy*, **16**, 907–44.

van Treeck, T., E. Hein and P. Dünhaupt (2007), "Finanzsystem und wirtschaftliche Entwicklung: neuere Tendenzen in den USA und in Deutschland", IMK Studies 5/2007, Düsseldorf, Macroeconomic Policy Institute (IMK) at Hans Boeckler Foundation.

Wood, A. (1975), *A Theory of Profits*, Cambridge: Cambridge University Press.

14 Inside debt and economic growth: a neo-Kaleckian analysis

Thomas I. Palley

1 Introduction: inside debt, macroeconomics and growth

Recently, there has been a surge of interest in the economic effects of inside (private sector) debt owing to rising indebtedness in many countries. The current chapter explores the effects of inside debt on economic growth within a neo-Kaleckian framework.[1] The foundation of the neo-Kaleckian framework is the model of economic growth developed by such authors as Rowthorn (1982), Taylor (1983) and Dutt (1984, 1990). In these models growth is determined by the rate of capital accumulation, which depends on the profit rate and the rate of capacity utilization. That core model is then supplemented by a model of income distribution in which the profit share and rate of profit depend on the rate of capacity utilization (Lavoie, 1995).

After long being ignored, inside debt effects have become a major focus of interest in macroeconomics. One strand of literature explores Fisher's (1933) debt-deflation theory of depressions, whereby debt causes price level reductions and deflation to be destabilizing (Tobin, 1980; Caskey and Fazzari, 1987; Palley, 1991–92, 1996, 1997a, 1999, 2008a, 2008b).[2]

A second strand of literature concerns the effect of inside debt on the business cycle. Most of this literature has focused on the effect of corporate debt, which creates balance sheet congestion that limits investment spending. This congestion mechanism applies to both Keynesian (Gallegati and Gardini, 1991; Jarsulic, 1989; Semmler and Franke, 1991; Skott, 1994) and new Keynesian models (Bernanke et al., 1996, 1999; Kiyotaki and Moore, 1997). In Keynesian models corporate debt congestion effects operate via the aggregate demand channel, whereas in new Keynesian models they operate via the aggregate supply channel with lower investment lowering the capital stock and output.

Household debt is another channel whereby debt affects the business cycle. The mechanism here is transfer of interest service from free spending debtors to thrifty creditors, which lowers aggregate consumption (Palley, 1994, 1997b). Debt is therefore a double-edged sword: borrowing is initially expansionary but it leaves behind a debt burden that is contractionary.

Palley (2004/2008) presents a corporate debt model of the business cycle that also uses an interest transfer mechanism, only now interest transfers are between firms and households. In that model, debt can be expansionary or contractionary, depending on the relative size of households' propensity to consume versus firms' propensity to invest.

The current chapter applies these insights regarding the macroeconomic effects of interest transfer payments to the economics of growth and examines how debtor–creditor interest service transfers affect steady state growth. The chapter adds a new dimension to the burgeoning literature on "financialization" that argues changes in the financial system over the last 25 years may have lowered growth (Hein and van Treeck,

2007; Skott and Ryoo, 2007; Stockhammer, 2004). The existing financialization literature tends to focus on the growth effects of higher asset prices and an increased profit share, whereas the current chapter focuses on the growth effect of higher indebtedness.

The effect of debt on growth operates primarily through its impact on saving, which in turn affects capacity utilization and the profit rate. These latter two variables then impact investment and thereby affect growth.

The chapter is structured as follows. Section 2 examines an economy with consumer debt issued through a bond market. Section 3 examines an economy with consumer debt financed by an endogenous money banking system. Section 4 examines an economy with corporate debt financed by an endogenous money banking system. Section 5 discusses the implications of alternative specifications of the mark-up. Section 6 concludes the chapter. One major take-away is that intuitions derived from short-run macroeconomics can be misleading for growth theory. Thus, in short-run macro models higher inside debt levels lower economic activity, but in a growth context higher debt can theoretically raise growth rates.

2   A growth model with loanable funds consumer debt

The first model to be considered is an economy in which there is consumer debt provided through a loanable funds credit market (i.e. a bond market) where debtor households borrow from creditor households. The bond market therefore transfers income claims from creditors to debtors.

The model that is developed is related to one presented by Dutt (2006). However, his analysis is conducted under conditions of a fixed income distribution, whereas the current model has an endogenous income distribution that is affected by the level of debt.

2.1   The basic model

The equations of the short-run static macro model are:

$$Y = C + I \tag{1}$$

$$C = C_W + C_C \tag{2}$$

$$C_W = \gamma_1\{[1 - \phi]Y + [1 - z]\phi Y\} - ziD + zB \qquad 0 < \gamma_1 < 1, 0 < \phi < 1 \tag{3}$$

$$C_C = \gamma_2 z\{\phi Y + iD\} \qquad 0 < \gamma_2 < \gamma_1 < 1, 0 < \phi < 1 \tag{4}$$

where Y is real output; C is aggregate consumption; I is investment; C_W is consumption of worker households; C_C is consumption of capitalist households; φ is the profit share and $1 - \varphi$ the wage share; $[1 - z]$ is the share of wealth owned by workers and z the share owned by capitalists; i denotes the interest rate and D is the level of debt; B is current period borrowing; γ_1 is the marginal propensity to consume (MPC) of worker households and γ_2 is the MPC of capitalist households. Workers have a higher MPC than capitalists.

Workers receive all wage income and a share of profit income equal to their ownership share. They also make interest payments to capitalists on the share of debt owned by capitalists and they borrow from capitalists. There is implicitly some lending between worker households so that worker households on aggregate only pay interest on that portion of inside debt owned by capitalists. Capitalists own the same share of capital and debt, and the share of borrowing funded by capitalists equals their ownership share of the debt.

The level of aggregate saving is given by:

$$S = Y - C_W - C_C \tag{5}$$

Substituting equations (3) and (4) into (5) and collecting terms yields:

$$S = Y\{1 - \gamma_1\{1 - \phi + [1 - z]\phi\} - \gamma_2 z\phi\} - [\gamma_2 - 1]ziD - zB \tag{6}$$

Aggregate saving is a positive function of Y. It is increased by debt service transfers to capitalists (ziD) and decreased by worker household borrowing (zB). Increases in the wage share reduce aggregate saving by transferring income to worker households who have a higher MPC than capitalist households ($\gamma_1 > \gamma_2$).

The rate of capital accumulation and growth is determined as follows:

$$I/K = g = \alpha_0 + \alpha_1 p + \alpha_2 u = g(p, u) \qquad \alpha_0, \alpha_1, \alpha_2 > 0; g_p > 0, g_u > 0 \tag{7}$$

where I denotes investment spending; K is the capital stock; g is rate of growth; p is the profit rate; and u is the rate of capacity utilization that is defined as Y/K. According to equation (7), the rate of capital accumulation is a positive function of the profit rate and the rate of capacity utilization.[3]

Income distribution is determined in accordance with standard Kaleckian theory. The profit share is a positive function of the mark-up and given by:

$$\phi = \phi(m) \qquad \phi_m > 0 \tag{8}$$

where m denotes the mark-up. The mark-up is in turn a positive function of the rate of capacity utilization and given by:

$$m = m(u, \beta) \qquad m_u > 0, m_\beta > 0 \tag{9}$$

where β denotes a shift factor reflecting the overall economic power of firms, both with regard to pricing of goods and bargaining of real wages with workers. An increase in corporate power raises the mark-up. Combining equations (8) and (9) yields:

$$\phi = \phi(m(u, \beta)) = \Phi(u, \beta) \qquad \Phi_u > 0, \Phi_\beta > 0, \tag{10}$$

The profit rate can be expressed as the profit share multiplied by the rate of capacity utilization. Given this, the profit rate is determined by:

$$p = \phi u = \rho(u, \beta) \qquad \rho_u > 0, \rho_\beta > 0 \tag{11}$$

The profit rate is a positive function of the rate of capacity utilization and corporate economic power.

Short-run equilibrium requires the goods market to clear, which imposes the condition:

$$I/K = S/K \tag{12}$$

Steady state equilibrium imposes an additional condition that the debt stock grows at the rate of capital accumulation, which implies:[4]

$$B/D = I/K \tag{13}$$

Cross-multiplying by D, substituting for $I/K = g$, and dividing both sides by K, yields an expression for steady state borrowing given by:

$$B/K = gD/K \tag{14}$$

Dividing equation (6) by the capital stock yields the rate of saving with respect to the capital stock:

$$S/K = s = u[1 - \gamma_1\{1 - \phi + [1 - z]\phi\} - \gamma_2 z\phi] - [\gamma_2 - 1]zid - zgd \tag{15}$$

where $d = D/K$. The saving rate can then be expressed in general form as:

$$s = \sigma(u, d, \beta, \gamma_1, \gamma_2, z, i) - zgd$$
$$\sigma_u > 0, \sigma_d > 0, \sigma_\beta > 0, \sigma_{\gamma 1} < 0, \sigma_{\gamma 2} < 0, \sigma_z > 0, \sigma_i > 0 \tag{16}$$

The saving rate is positively related to capacity utilization, there being two channels of effect. First, higher capacity utilization raises overall income (Y/K). Second, higher capacity utilization raises the mark-up and profit share (φ), shifting income distribution toward higher saving capitalist households.[5]

The effect of higher debt on aggregate saving is ambiguous. On one hand, higher debt raises saving by increasing the interest transfer payment to higher saving capitalist households (σ_d). On the other hand, it also increases steady state borrowing by worker households (zgd), which reduces aggregate saving.

Increased corporate economic power increases saving by raising the profit share, which disproportionately benefits capitalists who have a higher propensity to save. Increases in the MPC of either worker or capitalist households reduce aggregate saving.

Increases in the ownership share of capitalists have an ambiguous impact on aggregate saving. On one hand, profit income is shifted to capitalists, which increases aggregate saving because they have a higher propensity to save. On the other hand, workers must borrow more from capitalists, which reduces aggregate saving. Lastly, a higher interest rate increases aggregate saving since worker households pay more debt service to higher saving capitalist households.

The steady state solution to the model is obtained by simultaneous solution of the following two equations:

$$p = \rho(u, \beta) \qquad \rho_u > 0, \rho_\beta > 0 \tag{17}$$

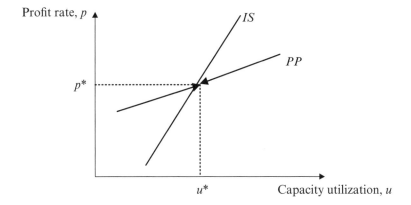

Figure 14.1   The stable case of the ISPP model

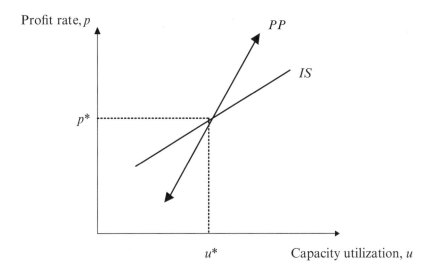

Figure 14.2   The unstable case of the ISPP model

$$[1 + zd]g(p, u) = \sigma(u, d, \beta, \gamma_1, \gamma_2, z, i)$$

$$g_p > 0, g_u > 0, \sigma_u > 0, \sigma_d > 0, \sigma_\beta > 0, \sigma_z > 0, \sigma_i > 0 \qquad (18)$$

The endogenous variables are p and u. Equation (17) determines the profit rate and it traces out a profit rate function in $[u, p]$ space that is denoted *PP*. Equation (18) is an *IS* equation obtained from equations (7), (12), and (16). The appendix provides a formal analysis of the stability conditions and comparative statics results. Figures 14.1 and 14.2 provide a graphical analogue of the model. Figure 14.1 corresponds to the stable case, while Figure 14.2 corresponds to the unstable case. The condition for stability is that the *IS* schedule be steeper than the *PP* schedule.

The slopes of the *PP* function and *IS* schedule are given by:

$$dp/du|_{PP} = \rho_u > 0$$

$$dp/du|_{IS} = \{\sigma_u - [1 + zd]g_u\}/[1 + zd]g_p \underset{<}{>} 0 \quad \text{if} \quad \sigma_u^> \underset{<}{} [1 + zd]g_u$$

In principle, the slope of the *IS* schedule is ambiguous. Henceforth, it is assumed that $\sigma_u - zdg_u > g_u$, making the *IS* positively sloped. This assumption implies that saving is more responsive to capacity utilization than investment, which corresponds to the conventional Keynesian stability condition restricting the expenditure multiplier to be less than unity. Consequently, points to the left of the *IS* schedule correspond to conditions of excess demand. The logic is that a reduction in capacity utilization, holding the profit rate constant, causes a larger decline in saving than investment, thereby creating excess demand.

The dynamics of the system are as follows. Output increases in response to excess demand and decreases in response to excess supply. Furthermore, firms are assumed to always be on the profit rate function, with their mark-up set according to equation (9). Adjustment in response to disequilibrium conditions therefore takes place along the *PP* function. Putting the pieces together, this yields the pattern of stability and instability shown in Figures 14.1 and 14.2. The model is stable if the *IS* schedule is steeper than the *PP* function, and it is unstable if the *IS* schedule is flatter than the *PP*.[6]

The comparative statics can be understood in terms of the *ISPP* diagram. An increase in the propensity to consume of either worker or debtor households lowers aggregate saving. With capacity utilization unchanged, a lower profit rate is needed to get firms to reduce investment. Consequently, the *IS* shifts down, resulting in a new equilibrium with a higher profit rate and higher capacity utilization.

An increase in capitalists' ownership share or the interest rate both increase saving. That shifts the *IS* up and lowers the equilibrium profit rate and rate of capacity utilization.

An increase in the debt ratio (*d*) has ambiguous effects. On one hand it results in higher interest payments to higher saving capitalist households, which increases aggregate saving. However, it also means higher steady state borrowing by higher consuming worker households, which lowers aggregate saving. If the former effect dominates, the *IS* shifts left and the equilibrium rates of profit and capacity utilization fall. If the latter effect dominates, the *IS* shifts right and the equilibrium rates of profit and capacity utilization increase. Increased steady state debt can therefore be contractionary or expansionary, or it may have little effect at all.

An increase in corporate economic power (β) also has ambiguous effects. Higher β raises the mark-up and profit rate, shifting the *PP* function up. However, a higher β also increases the profit share and shifts income to capitalists, which raises saving and shifts the *IS* up. The net effect of these twin shifts on *p* and *u* is ambiguous. If the upward *PP* shift effect dominates, the rate of profit and capacity utilization both increase. If the leftward *IS* shift dominates, the rate of profit and capacity utilization both fall. The former outcome corresponds to the "exhilarationist" or "profit-led" scenario identified by Bhaduri and Marglin (1990). The latter outcome corresponds to their "stagnationist" or "wage-led" scenario.

The effects on growth are given by:

$$dg/d\gamma_1 = g_p p_{\gamma 1} + g_u u_{\gamma 1} > 0$$

$$dg/d\gamma_2 = g_p p_{\gamma 2} + g_u u_{\gamma 2} > 0$$

$$dg/dz = g_p p_z + g_u u_z^{\gtrless} \lessgtr 0$$

$$dg/di = g_p p_i + g_u u_i < 0$$

$$dg/dd = g_p p_d + g_u u_d^{\gtrless} \lessgtr 0$$

$$dg/d\beta = g_p p_\beta + g_u u_\beta^{\gtrless} \lessgtr 0$$

Increased steady state debt has an ambiguous effect on growth, which may increase, fall, or remain essentially little changed. This shows that the intuitions of short-run macroeconomics do not automatically carry over to growth economics. In short-run macro, where borrowing is held constant, higher debt levels are contractionary owing to the Fisher (1933) debt effect. However, higher debt does not necessarily lower growth, and may even raise it. Higher debt raises interest transfers to creditors, which lowers p and u in a manner consistent with short-run macro. But balanced against this, higher debt increases steady state consumption borrowing by debtors, which raises p and u.

2.2 Endogenous debt ratios

So far the model has assumed exogenous debt ratios. However, debt can be endogenized by assuming households are borrowing constrained and that their constraint varies with economic activity. Given debtors are always constrained by their debt ceiling, actual debt is then determined by the debt ceiling, which is endogenous.

One possibility is credit markets impose on debtors a maximum debt interest service to income ratio given by:[7]

$$iD/\{[1 - \phi]Y + [1 - z]\phi Y\} \le \psi \qquad z > 0 \qquad (19)$$

where ψ is the debt ceiling ratio. Rearranging, expressing in terms of capacity utilization, substituting for ϕ then implies a maximum D/K ratio given by:

$$D/K = d_{MAX} = d(u, \beta, \psi, i, z) \qquad d_u^{\gtrless} \lessgtr 0, d_\beta < 0, d_\psi > 0, d_i < 0 d_z < 0 \qquad (20)$$

The effect of capacity utilization on the debt ceiling is ambiguous. On one hand, higher capacity utilization raises aggregate income. On the other hand, it raises the mark-up and profit share, shifting income away from worker/debtor households. Increased corporate economic power unambiguously decreases the debt ceiling by raising the mark-up and shifting income away from debtors. A higher permissible debt service to income ratio unambiguously raises the debt ceiling. A higher interest rate and higher capitalist ownership share both lower the debt ceiling.

Substituting equation (20) into equation (18) yields a new configuration of the model given by:

$$p = \rho(u, \beta) \tag{21}$$

$$[1 + zd(u, \beta, \psi, i, z)]g(p, u) = \sigma(u, d(u, \beta, \psi, i, z), \beta, \gamma_1, \gamma_2, z, i) \tag{22}$$

The *PP* function is unaffected but the *IS* schedule is changed. The slope of the *IS* schedule is given by:

$$dp/du|_{IS} = \{\sigma_u + \sigma_d d_u - [1 + zd]g_u - zgd_u\}/[1 + zd]g_p^{>}{}_{<}0$$

$$\text{if } \sigma_u + \sigma_d d_u^{>}{}_{<} [1 + zd]g_u + zgd_u$$

Now, there are two additional terms ($\sigma_d d_u$ and zgd_u) in the numerator, but their sign is ambiguous. If their combined impact is positive, the slope of the *IS* steepens. If their combined effect is negative, the slope of the *IS* flattens. If this latter effect is sufficiently large, the *IS* schedule could become flatter than the *PP* function, rendering the model unstable.

Financial innovation and financialization can be viewed as increasing the parameter ψ that determines the permissible debt service to income ratio. The effect of a higher ψ operates via the *IS* schedule, but its impact is ambiguous. On one hand a higher ψ increases aggregate saving ($\sigma_d d_\psi$) by increasing the debt ratio, which increases interest transfers to high saving capitalist households. On the other hand, it reduces aggregate saving by increasing the steady state borrowing of low saving worker households (zgd_ψ). If the former effect dominates, the *IS* shifts up and p and u fall. If the latter effect dominates, the *IS* shifts down and p and u rise. If they offset there is no impact. The implication is that consumer debt effects of financialization can theoretically raise growth, lower growth, or have little impact at all on growth.

3   Growth with endogenous money bank financed consumer debt
The previous section examined the growth effects of debt when debt is financed through a bond market. This section presents a model in which there is endogenous money and debt is financed through the banking sector, which creates loans. Previously, Palley (1997b) has examined the business cycle effects of such arrangements.

The critical feature of a model with endogenous money is that lending creates money balances. Loans are issued to borrowers and the process of loan issuance creates money. Those money balances are spent by debtors and accumulated by creditors who own the businesses that produce the goods and services debtor households purchase.

This simple schema results in a re-specified short-run model given by:

$$Y = C + I \tag{23}$$

$$C = C_W + C_C \tag{24}$$

$$C_W = \gamma_1\{[1 - \phi]Y + [1 - z]\phi Y\} - ziD + zB + \gamma_3[1 - z]M \quad 0 < \phi < 1, 0 < z < 1 \tag{25}$$

$$C_C = \gamma_2 z\{[1 - \phi]Y + iD\} + \gamma_4 zM \quad 0 < \gamma_4 < \gamma_2 < \gamma_1 < 1; 0 < \gamma_3 < \gamma_1 < 1 \tag{26}$$

$$M = D \tag{27}$$

where M is the money supply. Debtor and creditor consumption is given by equations (25) and (26) and both are amended to include a wealth effect from money. The wealth effect (γ_3 and γ_4) is less than the MPC out of income and it operates on that share of the money stock owned by each class. That share is equal to their ownership share of the capital stock. Equation (27) has the money supply determined by bank lending.

Aggregate saving is now given by:

$$S = Y\{1 - \gamma_1(1 - \phi + [1 - z]\phi) - \gamma_2 z\phi\} - [\gamma_2 - 1]ziD - zB - [\gamma_3 + \gamma_4]M \tag{28}$$

Saving is therefore reduced by the aggregate wealth effect, $[\gamma_3 + \gamma_4]M$. Substituting equations (14) and (27) and dividing by the capital stock yields:

$$s = u\{1 - \gamma_1(1 - \phi + [1 - z]\phi) - \gamma_2 z\phi\} - [\gamma_2 - 1]zid - zgd - [\gamma_3 + \gamma_4]d$$
$$= \sigma(u, d, \beta, z, i, \gamma_1, \gamma_2, \gamma_3, \gamma_4) - zgd \quad \sigma_{\gamma3} < 0, \sigma_{\gamma4} < 0 \tag{29}$$

The wealth effect therefore reduces aggregate saving (s) and it also diminishes the magnitude of σ_d. The diminished magnitude of σ_d means an increase in steady state debt will result in a smaller increase in saving because higher debt now generates a positive consumption wealth effect that damps saving.

The above description of saving in an endogenous credit money economy can then be combined with the model of capital accumulation given by equation (7) and the model of the profit rate given by equation (11). This yields an *ISPP* model that is structurally similar to the model described in section 2. The *PP* function is exactly as before, and the *IS* schedule has the same slope as before.

The only change is that for a given level of debt, saving will be lower in an endogenous money economy owing to the wealth effect from endogenous money. Consequently, the *IS* schedule will be shifted to the right compared to the loanable funds economy. That means u and p will be higher, which in turn means growth will be higher since $g = g(u, p)$ and $g_u > 0$ and $g_p > 0$.

4   Growth effects of corporate debt

Corporations also issue debt and that gives rise to transfers between corporations and creditor households (Lavoie and Godley, 2001–02; Palley 2004/2008). This section presents a simple growth model with corporate debt. Once again debt financing can be through bond markets or through banks, or a combination of both. The model that is presented assumes bank financing.

The major innovation in the model is re-specification of the investment function to include a corporate cash flow effect, an effect that has been emphasized in the empirical literature on investment (Fazzari et al., 1988). On one hand, corporate debt has a positive growth effect because it increases household income through payment of interest. That spurs consumption, raising capacity utilization and investment. On the other hand, interest payments on corporate debt reduce corporate cash flows, which in turn reduce investment spending.

In a model with corporate debt, the corporate sector constitutes the debtor while the household sector is the creditor. This structure means there is no need to disaggregate the household sector into debtor and creditor households, and instead consumption can be represented by a single consumption function given by

$$C = [1 - \phi]Y + \gamma_1\{[1 - \lambda]\phi Y + iD\} + \gamma_2 M$$

$$0 < \gamma_2 < \gamma_1 < 1, 0 < \phi < 1, 0 < \lambda < 1 \tag{30}$$

where λ is the share of profits retained by firms. Households are assumed to adopt a "rule of thumb" approach to saving, whereby they consume all wage income and save out of dividends and interest income as originally assumed by Kalecki (1943/1971) and Kaldor (1955–56).

Aggregate saving consists of saving by the household sector and corporate sector, and it is given by:

$$S = S_H + S_F = Y - C \tag{31}$$

Corporate sector saving is equal to retained profits and is given by:

$$S_F = \lambda \phi Y \tag{32}$$

Substituting equations (30) into (31), collecting terms, and using equation (27) yields:

$$S = \phi Y\{1 - \gamma_1[1 - \lambda]\} - [\gamma_1 i + \gamma_2]D \tag{33}$$

Dividing by the capital stock yields aggregate saving per unit of capital:

$$s = S/K = \phi u\{1 - \gamma_1[1 - \lambda]\} - [\gamma_1 i + \gamma_2]d$$

$$= \sigma(u, d, \beta, \lambda, i, \gamma_1, \gamma_2) \quad \sigma_u > 0, \sigma_d < 0, \sigma_\beta > 0, \sigma_\lambda > 0, \sigma_i < 0, \sigma_{\gamma 1} < 0, \sigma_{\gamma 2} < 0 \tag{34}$$

Higher capacity utilization increases aggregate income and increases aggregate saving. Higher debt and a higher interest rate both lower aggregate saving. The logic is that a higher interest rate increases interest transfer incomes of households, which raises their consumption and lowers saving. Higher debt also increases household interest transfer income, thereby raising consumption and lowering saving. Furthermore, higher debt increases the money supply and money wealth giving rise to a wealth effect that further lowers household saving. Increased corporate power raises the profit share and increases aggregate saving.

The second change to the model concerns investment and the determination of the rate of capital accumulation, which is given by:

$$I/K = g = \alpha_0 + \alpha_1 p + \alpha_2 u + \alpha_3 F/K \quad \alpha_0, \alpha_1, \alpha_2, \alpha_3 > 0 \tag{35}$$

where F is real retained cash flows. The only change from the earlier model is the addition of a positive cash flow effect on investment. Cash flows are defined as:

$$F = \lambda \phi Y - iD + B \tag{36}$$

Substituting equations (10), (14), and (36) into (35) and collecting terms then yields:

$$g = \{\alpha_0 + \alpha_1 p + [\alpha_2 + \alpha_3 \lambda \Phi(u, \beta)]u - \alpha_3 id\}/[1 - \alpha_3 d]$$

$$= g(u, p, i, d, \lambda, \beta, \alpha_0, \alpha_1, \alpha_2, \alpha_3,) \quad g_u > 0, g_p > 0, g_i < 0, g_\lambda > 0, g_\beta > 0, g_d^> {}_< 0,$$

$$g_{\alpha 0} > 0, g_{\alpha 1} > 0, g_{\alpha 2} > 0, g_{\alpha 3} > 0 \tag{37}$$

It is assumed that $1 > \alpha_3 d$ so that investment increases if the profit rate and capacity utilization increase. Explanation of the signing of the partial derivatives for equation (37) is as follows. A higher interest rate reduces capital accumulation because it reduces firms' cash flow. A higher retained profit ratio increases capital accumulation because it increases cash flow. Increased corporate economic power also increases capital accumulation by increasing the mark-up and profit share, which increases cash flow. The only ambiguous partial derivative concerns d and it is given by:

$$dg/dd = \alpha_3[g - i]/[1 - \alpha_3 d] {}^>_< 0 \text{ if } g {}^>_< i$$

If $g > i$, then steady state borrowing (gd), which increases cash flow and investment, exceeds the interest payment on debt (id), which reduces cash flow and investment. In this case higher debt raises steady capital accumulation.

As before the model reduces to a two-equation *ISPP* framework given by:

$$p = \rho(u, \beta) \tag{38}$$

$$[1 + zd]g(u, p, i, d, \lambda, \beta \alpha_0, \alpha_1, \alpha_2, \alpha_3,) = \sigma(u, i, d, \lambda, \beta, \gamma_1, \gamma_2) \tag{39}$$

The slopes of the *PP* function and *IS* schedule are given as before by:

$$dp/du|_{PP} = \rho_u > 0$$

$$dp/du|_{IS} = \{\sigma_u - [1 + zd]g_u\}/[1 + zd]g_p {}^>_< 0 \qquad \text{if } \sigma_u^> {}_< [1 + zd]g_u$$

Comparative statics are as follows. An increase in the interest rate has an ambiguous effect. On one hand it lowers investment by squeezing corporate cash flow. On the other hand it reduces aggregate saving by increasing interest transfers to households, and households consume part of those transfers, lowering aggregate saving. If the lower investment effect dominates, the *IS* shifts left and p and u fall. If the lower saving effect dominates, the *IS* shifts right and p and u rise. The critical issue is the sensitivity of investment to reduced cash flows owing to higher interest payments versus the sensitivity of consumption to increased interest transfer income.

The effect of an increase in d, which can be identified with financialization, has a similar ambiguous effect owing to the conflicting investment and consumption effects of increased interest transfers from firms to households. However, higher debt is more likely to be expansionary than higher interest rates for two reasons. First, higher debt increases the money supply giving rise to a positive consumption wealth effect. Second, higher debt increases steady state borrowing for investment.

An increase in retained profits is also ambiguous. On the expansionary side, investment increases because of increased cash flow for firms, which shifts the *IS* right. On the contractionary side, aggregate saving increases as firms increase saving and households reduce consumption because of lower dividend income. This shifts the *IS* left. If α_3 is large, then increased investment owing to increased cash flow may exceed the increase in saving. In that case, increased retained profits are expansionary and shift the *IS* right, causing *p* and *u* to increase.

Lastly, an increase in firms' economic power is also ambiguous. Increased power increases the mark-up and profit share. This increases firms' cash flow, which increases investment. However, an increased profit share also increases both firms' saving and household saving. The *IS* schedule can therefore shift left or right. A leftward shift reduces *u* and *p* and corresponds to a "stagnationist" or wage-led regime. A right shift increases *u* and *p* and corresponds to an exhilarationist or profit-led regime.

The effect on growth of these comparative static experiments depends on their combined effect on *u* and *p*, operating via equation (37). If *u* and *p* increase, steady state growth increases. If *u* and *p* fall, steady state growth falls. If *u* and *p* move in opposite directions, steady state growth may rise or fall depending on the relative size of the changes in *p* and *u*, and on the magnitude of the partial derivatives g_p and g_u. Since the effect of debt on *u* and *p* is ambiguous, the effect of debt on growth is once again ambiguous.

5 Further considerations regarding the mark-up

The behavior of the mark-up plays a critical role in the model. Equation (9) assumed the mark-up increased in response to higher capacity utilization. However, an alternative possibility is that the mark-up falls with capacity utilization, as has been argued by Rotemberg and Saloner (1986). In this case the slope of the *PP* function is:

$$dp/du|_{PP} = \phi_u u + \phi \quad \text{where } \phi_u < 0$$

The slope is flatter than the case when $\varphi_u > 0$ and the slope could even be negative.

A counter-cyclical mark-up also has implications for the *IS* schedule. As capacity utilization increases the mark-up falls, which lowers the profit share and increases the wage share. That will tend to lower saving. At the same time, the profit rate rises more slowly, which will tend to lower investment for a given rate of capacity utilization. If the former effect dominates the *IS* schedule will tend to shift right relative to an economy with a pro-cyclical mark-up, which will raise *u*, *p*, and *g*. If the latter effect dominates, the reverse holds and the *IS* will tend to shift left relative to an economy with a pro-cyclical mark-up.

Another possibility is that firms set their mark-up to achieve a target rate of profit. In this case the *PP* function is horizontal at the target rate of profit and the economy moves along the horizontal *PP* in response to *IS* shocks.

6   Conclusion

Inside debt is a fundamental feature of capitalist economies. This chapter has examined the growth effects of consumer and corporate debt using a neo-Kaleckian growth framework. According to this framework inside debt has an ambiguous effect on growth. This is counter to the intuition of static short-run macro models in which higher debt levels always lower economic activity, and it shows that intuitions of short-run macroeconomics do not always carry over to growth theory.

Growth is faster in endogenous money economies than in pure credit economies, *ceteris paribus*. That is because lending in endogenous money economies creates money wealth that increases spending and lowers saving, resulting in higher capacity utilization and faster growth.

Interest payments from debtors to creditors are a critical channel whereby debt affects growth. In the consumer debt model this interest transfer mechanism exerts an unambiguous negative influence on growth by transferring income from low saving debtor households to higher saving creditor households. However, in the corporate debt model the effect of higher interest rates is ambiguous. Increased interest transfers can raise growth if the marginal propensity to consume of households out of interest transfer income exceeds firms' marginal propensity to invest out of cash flow. In the neo-Kaleckian growth model with corporate debt, higher interest rates can therefore be expansionary, again challenging the conventions of short-run macroeconomics.

Notes

1. The issue of government (outside) debt is a separate question that requires a treatment of its own.
2. Tobin (1975) and De Long and Summers (1986) are widely cited articles on deflation but they do not have debt effects. Instead, the destabilizing impact of deflation operates via the Tobin–Mundell real interest rate effect whereby deflation increases the return to money. That increases the money demand, raising the real interest rate and lowering aggregate demand.
3. Equation (7) specifies investment as a positive function of the profit rate. A theoretically superior specification is to specify investment as a positive function of the ratio of the profit rate and the interest rate in a vein similar to Tobin's q (Tobin and Brainard, 1968). However, because the interest rate is assumed to be exogenous, it is suppressed in equation (7) to simplify algebraic manipulations.
4. Debtor consumption, C_D, must also grow at the rate of output growth in steady state to ensure constant consumption shares. This condition is satisfied if debtor borrowing grows at the rate of output growth.
5. The effect of capacity utilization on saving is given by $ds/du = [s_u + s_\varphi \varphi_u] = \sigma_u > 0$.
6. If $\sigma_u - z dg_u < g_u$ the *IS* schedule is negatively sloped. This signing implies investment is more responsive to capacity utilization than aggregate saving. Consequently, points to the left of the *IS* represent conditions of excess supply, while points to the right represent conditions of excess demand. This configuration renders the model unstable and output diverges from equilibrium, moving along the *PP* schedule, which remains positively sloped.
7. Palley (1994) has a condition $D/\varphi Y = k$. Since the interest rate is constant, that specification is equivalent to embedding the interest rate in the constant, k.

References

Bernanke, B., M. Gertler and S. Gilchrist (1996), "The financial accelerator and the flight to quality," *Review of Economics and Statistics*, **78**, 1–15.

Bernanke, B., M. Gertler and S. Gilchrist (1999), "The financial accelerator in a quantitative business cycle framework," in J.B. Taylor and M. Woodford (eds), *Handbook of Macroeconomics*, Vol. 1, Amsterdam: Elsevier Science, pp. 1341–93.

Bhaduri, A. and S. Marglin (1990), "Unemployment and the real wage: the economic basis for contesting political ideologies," *Cambridge Journal of Economics*, **14**, 375–93.

Caskey, J. and S. Fazzari (1987), "Aggregate demand contractions with nominal debt commitments: is wage flexibility stabilizing?," *Economic Inquiry*, **25**, 583–97.

De Long, B. and L. Summers (1986), "Is increased price flexibility stabilizing?," *American Economic Review*, **76**, 1031–44.

Dutt, A.K. (1984), "Stagnation, income distribution, and monopoly power," *Cambridge Journal of Economics*, **8**, 25–40.

Dutt, A.K. (1990), *Growth, Distribution and Uneven Development*, Cambridge: Cambridge University Press.

Dutt, A.K. (2006), "Maturity, stagnation and consumer debt: a Steindlian approach," *Metroeconomica*, **57**, 339–64.

Fazzari, S., R.G. Hubbard and B.C. Petersen (1988), "Financing constraints and corporate investment activity," *Brookings Papers on Economic Activity*, **1**, 141–95.

Fisher, I. (1933), "The debt–deflation theory of great depressions," *Econometrica*, **1**, 337–57.

Gallegati, M. and L. Gardini (1991), "A non-linear model of the business cycle with money and finance," *Metroeconomica*, **42**, 1–32.

Hein, E. and T. van Treeck (2007), "Financialization in Kaleckian/post-Kaleckian models of distribution and growth," IMK Working Paper 7/2007.

Jarsulic, M. (1989), "Endogenous credit and endogenous business cycles," *Journal of Post Keynesian Economics*, **12**, 35–48.

Kaldor, N. (1955–56), "Alternative theories of distribution," *Review of Economic Studies*, **7**, 83–100.

Kalecki, M. (1943/1971), "Studies in economic dynamics," in J. Osiatynski (ed.), *Collected Works of Michael Kalecki*, Vol. 2, Oxford: Clarendon Press, pp. 207–338.

Kiyotaki, N. and J. Moore (1997), "Credit cycles," *Journal of Political Economy*, **105**, 211–48.

Lavoie, M. (1995), "The Kaleckian model of growth and distribution and its neo-Ricardian and Marxist critiques," *Cambridge Journal of Economics*, **19**, 789–818.

Lavoie, M. and W. Godley (2001–02), "Kaleckian models of growth in a coherent stock–flow monetary framework: a Kaldorian view," *Journal of Post Keynesian Economics*, **24**, 277–312.

Palley, T.I. (1991–92), "Money, credit, and prices in a Kaldorian macro model," *Journal of Post Keynesian Economics*, **14**, 183–204.

Palley, T.I. (1994), "Debt, AD and the business cycle: a model in the spirit of Kaldor and Minsky," *Journal of Post Keynesian Economics*, **16**, 371–90.

Palley, T.I. (1996), *Post Keynesian Economics: Debt, Distribution, and the Macro Economy*, London: Macmillan Press.

Palley, T.I. (1997a), "Keynesian theory and AS/AD analysis: further observations," *Eastern Economics Journal*, **23**, 459–68.

Palley, T.I. (1997b), "Endogenous money and the business cycle," *Journal of Economics*, **65**, 133–49.

Palley, T.I. (1999), "General disequilibrium analysis with inside debt," *Journal of Macroeconomics*, **21**, 785–804.

Palley, T.I. (2004/2008), "The simple analytics of debt-driven business cycles," paper presented at the Post-Keynesian Conference, University of Missouri, Kansas City, Kansas, June 2004 and revised 2008.

Palley, T.I. (2008a), "The macroeconomics of aggregate demand and the price level," *Investigacion Economica*, **LXVII**(263), 49–66.

Palley, T.I. (2008b), "Keynesian models of deflation and depression revisited," *Journal of Economic Behavior and Organization*, **68**, 167–77.

Rotemberg, J.J. and G. Saloner (1986), "A supergame-theoretic model of price wars during booms," *American Economic Review*, **76**, 390–407.

Rowthorn, R. (1982), "Demand, real wages and growth," *Studi Economici*, **18**, 3–54.

Semmler, W. and R. Franke (1991), "Debt financing of firms, stability, and cycles in a dynamical macroeconomic growth model," in E. Nell and W. Semmler (eds), *Nicholas Kaldor and Mainstream Macroeconomics*, London: Macmillan.

Skott, P. (1994), "On the modeling of systemic financial fragility," in A.K. Dutt (ed.), *New Directions in Analytical Political Economy*, Aldershot, UK and Brookfield, USA: Edward Elgar.

Skott, P. and S. Ryoo (2007), "Macroeconomic implications of financialization," Economics Department, University of Massachusetts, Amherst, MA.

Stockhammer, E. (2004), "Financialization and the slowdown of accumulation," *Cambridge Journal of Economics*, **28**, 719–41.

Taylor, L. (1983), *Structuralist Macroeconomics*, New York: Basic Books.

Tobin, J. (1975), "Keynesian models of recession and depression," *American Economic Review*, **65**, 195–202.

Tobin, J. (1980), *Asset Accumulation and Economic Activity*, Chicago: Chicago University Press.

Tobin, J. and W. Brainard (1968), "Pitfalls in financial model building," *American Economic Review*, **58**, 99–122.

Appendix
The equations of the model with loanable funds consumer debt presented in section II are

$$p = \rho(u, \beta) \tag{A.1}$$

$$[1 + zd]g(p, u) = \sigma(u, d, \beta, \gamma_1, \gamma_2, z, i) \tag{A.2}$$

The stability of the model can be understood via graphical phase diagram analysis constructed in $[u, p]$ space. Equation (A.1) generates a profit rate function in $[u, p]$ space that is denoted PP. Equation (A.2) generates a goods market equilibrium schedule in $[u, p]$ space that is denoted IS.

Points to the left of the IS schedule represent points of excess demand. For such points, capacity utilization is too low for goods market equilibrium given the rate of profit. The logic is that saving is more sensitive to capacity utilization than investment, reflecting the Keynesian expenditure multiplier stability assumption. Consequently, there is excess demand at low rates of capacity utilization.

Assuming firms always charge a mark-up as determined by equation (9), the economy is always on the PP function. In that case, capacity utilization adjustment proceeds along the PP schedule.

Let the speed of capacity utilization adjustment be governed by:

$$du/dt/u = \Lambda[U(p(u),...) - u] \qquad \Lambda > 0 \tag{A.3}$$

where u = actual rate of capacity utilization and $U(p(u),...)$ = rate of capacity utilization consistent with goods market clearing given a profit rate of $p(u)$. According to this mechanism, capacity utilization expands when $U(p(u),...) > u$ and contracts when $u > U(p(u),...)$.

Putting the pieces together, stability requires that the PP function be flatter than the IS schedule in $[u, p]$ space. This condition requires:

$$dp/du|_{IS} = \{\sigma_u - [1 + zd]g_u\}/[1 + zd]g_p > dp/du|_{PP} = \rho_u > 0$$

This implies $\{\sigma_u - [1 + zd]g_u\} > \rho_u[1 + zd]g_p$. Collecting terms on the left-hand side and multiplying by minus one, the condition becomes $\rho_u[1 + zd]g_p - \sigma_u + \rho_u[1 + zd]g_p < 0$
Totally differentiating equations (A.1) and (A.2) and arranging in matrix form yields:

$$
\begin{vmatrix} 1 & -\rho_u \\ [1 + zd]g_p & [1 + zd]g_u - \sigma_u \end{vmatrix}
\begin{vmatrix} dp \\ du \end{vmatrix}
=
\begin{vmatrix} \rho_\beta & 0 & 0 & 0 & 0 & 0 \\ \sigma_\beta & \sigma_d - zg & \sigma_{\gamma 1} & \sigma_{\gamma 2} & \sigma_z - dg & \sigma_i \end{vmatrix}
\begin{vmatrix} d\beta \\ dd \\ d\gamma_1 \\ d\gamma_2 \\ dz \\ di \end{vmatrix}
$$

The Jacobian is given by:

$$|J| = [1 + zd]g_u - \sigma_u + \rho_u[1 + zd]g_p < 0 \text{ if the above stability condition holds.}$$

The comparative statics are then given by:

$$dp/d\beta = \begin{vmatrix} \rho_\beta & -\rho_u \\ \sigma_\beta & [1 + zd]g_u - \sigma_u \end{vmatrix} / |J| \gtrless 0$$

$$du/d\beta = \begin{vmatrix} 1 & \rho_\beta \\ [1 + zd]g_p & \sigma_\beta \end{vmatrix} / |J| \gtrless 0$$

$$dp/dd = \begin{vmatrix} 0 & -\rho_u \\ \sigma_d - zg & [1 + zd]g_u - \sigma_u \end{vmatrix} / |J| \gtrless 0$$

$$du/dd = \begin{vmatrix} 1 & 0 \\ [1 + zd]g_p & \sigma_d - zg \end{vmatrix} / |J| \gtrless 0$$

$$dp/d\gamma_1 = \begin{vmatrix} 0 & -\rho_u \\ \sigma_{\gamma 1} & [1 + zd]g_u - \sigma_u \end{vmatrix} / |J| > 0$$

$$du/d\gamma_1 = \begin{vmatrix} 1 & 0 \\ [1 + zd]g_p & \sigma_{\gamma 1} \end{vmatrix} / |J| > 0$$

$$dp/d\gamma_2 = \begin{vmatrix} 0 & -\rho_u \\ \sigma_{\gamma 2} & [1 + zd]g_u - \sigma_u \end{vmatrix} / |J| > 0$$

$$du/d\gamma_2 = \begin{vmatrix} 1 & 0 \\ [1 + zd]g_p & \sigma_{\gamma 2} \end{vmatrix} / |J| > 0$$

$$dp/dz = \begin{vmatrix} 0 & -\rho_u \\ \sigma_z - dg & [1 + zd]g_u - \sigma_u \end{vmatrix} / |J| \gtrless 0$$

$$du/dz = \begin{vmatrix} 1 & 0 \\ [1 + zd]g_p & \sigma_z - dg \end{vmatrix} / |J| \gtrless 0$$

$$dp/di = \begin{vmatrix} 0 & -\rho_u \\ \sigma_i & [1 + zd]g_u - \sigma_u \end{vmatrix} / |J| < 0$$

$$du/di = \begin{vmatrix} 1 & 0 \\ [1 + zd]g_p & \sigma_i \end{vmatrix} / |J| < 0$$

PART V

GROWTH AND DISTRIBUTION

15 Feasible egalitarianism: demand-led growth, labour and technology
C. W. M. Naastepad and Servaas Storm

1 Introduction

When it comes to analysing unemployment and, more generally, macroeconomic performance in the OECD, the standard – mainstream – analysis is predicated upon a "one-size-fits-all" approach – usually some variant of the non-accelerating inflation rate of unemployment (NAIRU) model – and does not recognize, let alone incorporate, systemic differences between OECD economies. In this approach, high unemployment (and lacklustre macro performance in general) is a result of labour market rigidities, caused by "excessive" regulation. It follows that, to reduce unemployment and revive growth, labour markets have to be deregulated and welfare states have to be scaled down. There thus exists an in-built conflict (or trade-off) between economic growth and low unemployment, on the one hand, and egalitarian outcomes (based on high wage growth and relatively pro-worker labour market regulation), on the other hand. *Egalitarianism*, in other words, comes at the cost of slow growth, high unemployment and limited technological dynamism. However, although the NAIRU view that labour market regulation explains OECD unemployment has become widely accepted, particularly in policy circles, it is by no means universally accepted. Serious problems remain. Specifically, empirical evidence suggesting an association between unemployment and regulatory institutions in OECD labour markets has been shown to be statistically non-robust (Baker et al., 2005a, 2005b; Baccaro and Rei, 2005; Howell et al., 2006). We argue that this non-robustness (or weakness) of the association between unemployment and regulation must be accepted as a stylized fact in itself, because it reflects the fact that policies of real wage growth restraint and labour market *de*regulation do not generate uniform reactions, but rather produce a variety of growth, productivity and unemployment responses as a result of systemic differences between countries. Hence, the standard "one-size-fits-all" NAIRU approach is wrong.

Building on the macro models of Bhaduri and Marglin (1990), Naastepad (2006), Naastepad and Storm (2006/07), and Storm and Naastepad (2007a, 2009a), we present, in section 2, a demand-led growth model which does allow for systemic diversity. Our growth model integrates neo-Kaleckian growth theory (in which the interaction of growth and distribution assumes centre-stage, but technological progress is overlooked) and neo-Kaldorian growth theory (in which long-run growth is accompanied by endogenous technological progress, but there is no discussion of the impact of distribution on growth). The diversity in outcomes is in a large measure a result of differences in *demand regimes* – aggregate demand being either profit-led or wage-led. The recognition of the variety in growth regimes, based on systemic differences between economies, leads us to conclude that the trade-off between growth and unemployment and egalitarian outcomes does not apply universally and, accordingly, that the consequences of real wage restraint and labour market deregulation (both intended to raise profitability) are not unambiguously beneficial. This we explain in sections 2 and 3. Further, we show in section 4 – building on Storm and Naastepad (2008, 2009a) – that the standard NAIRU model must be regarded as a *special case* of our more general model of equilibrium unemployment, in which aggregate demand, investment and demand-induced endogenous technological progress do play a major role. Equilibrium unemployment does not constitute a fixed centre of gravity towards which the economy automatically tends, but instead is sensitive to (changes in) autonomous demand and endogenous technological progress. In this view of the NAIRU, there need not exist a conflict between growth and equality. In section 5 we briefly evaluate the empirical relevance of our theoretical analysis.

2 The growth model

To analyse the (longer-run) interactions between demand, productivity, the real wage, unemployment and labour market regulation we use and extend the model developed in Naastepad (2006). This model constitutes a general Keynesian growth model, which integrates (a reformulated version of) the wage-led or profit-led aggregate demand system and a neo-Kaldorian supply system incorporating the productivity-growth enhancing effects of higher demand and higher real wages. Our unifying framework can be summarized in three curves:

- The *productivity regime* (PR) curve, according to which labour productivity growth $\hat{\lambda}$ is a positive function of demand-determined output growth $\hat{x}$, real wage growth $\hat{w}$ and labour market regulation z.

$$\hat{\lambda} = \beta_0 + \beta_1 \hat{x} + \beta_2 \hat{w} + \beta_3 z \qquad \beta_0, \beta_2, \beta_3 > 0; 0 < \beta_1 < 1. \qquad (1)$$

  where a superscript "hat" ($\wedge$) indicates the relative rate of change (or growth rate). Coefficient β_1 is the Kaldor–Verdoorn coefficient, which reflects static and dynamic increasing returns to scale (McCombie et al., 2002).[1] Coefficient β_2 reflects the degree of wage-led (or wage-cost induced) technological progress, that is, the extent to which more expensive labour induces firms to intensify their search for and adoption of labour productivity-raising techniques (Foley and Michl, 1999). Coefficient β_3 captures the impact of labour market regulation on labour productivity growth. The more regulated, coordinated and pro-worker is labour market regulation, the higher is z. We assume (based on empirical evidence, see Storm and Naastepad, 2007b, 2009b) that a higher z is associated with more rapid labour productivity growth, that is, $\beta_3 > 0$.
- The *demand regime* curve: (demand-determined) output growth is a function of real wage growth and productivity growth; in addition, aggregate demand growth is a function of autonomous demand growth (including world demand and the real interest rate).

$$\hat{x} = \Theta + C[\hat{w} - \hat{\lambda}] \qquad (2)$$

  where Θ = the contribution to output growth of autonomous factors, and $C = (d\hat{x}/d[\hat{w} - \hat{\lambda}])$. The derivation of (2) is given in the Appendix. We note that coefficient C is the net effect of two opposing effects on output growth. On the one hand, a rise in $[\hat{w} - \hat{\lambda}] = \hat{v}$, or the growth of labour costs per unit of output, reduces investment growth and export growth, consequently lowering output growth. But on the other hand, it increases the size of the multiplier, because it entails a redistribution of income from profits towards wage income and a consequent decline in the aggregate savings propensity (because the propensity to save out of wages is smaller than the propensity to save out of profits). Following convention, the *demand regime* is *wage-led*, if

$$\frac{d\hat{x}}{d\hat{v}} = C > 0 \tag{3}$$

The positive impact on consumption of higher real wage growth (or lower labour productivity growth) is larger (in absolute terms) than the negative effects on output of reduced investment and export growth (see the Appendix). In contrast, the *demand regime* is *profit-led*, if

$$\frac{d\hat{x}}{d\hat{v}} = C < 0 \tag{4}$$

Higher real wage growth (or lower productivity growth) raises unit labour costs, which reduces investment and export growth more than it raises consumption growth.

- The *employment regime* curve: by definition, employment growth (i.e. labour demand growth) $\hat{\ell}$ is equal to:

$$\hat{\ell} = \hat{x} - \hat{\lambda} \tag{5}$$

Substituting (1) into this expression gives us:

$$\hat{\ell} = (1 - \beta_1)\hat{x} - \beta_0 - \beta_2\hat{w} - \beta_3 z \tag{5'}$$

(This is the relationship underlying the employment regime curve in Figures 15.1, 15.2 and 15.3, below.) Unemployment u, in turn, is a negative function of employment growth (assuming that labour supply growth is exogenous).[2]

$$u = f(\hat{\ell}) = \Omega - \gamma\hat{\ell} \tag{6}$$

Finally, in line with the standard (NAIRU) approach to wage bargaining, we assume that

$$\hat{w} = \alpha_0 - \alpha_1 u + \alpha_2\hat{\lambda} + \alpha_3 z \qquad \alpha_0, \alpha_2 > 0. \tag{7}$$

Coefficient α_1 reflects the (negative) impact on the real wage of a rise in unemployment: because higher unemployment weakens workers' bargaining power, they are forced to accept a lower real wage. Coefficient α_2 represents the extent to which labour productivity growth is reflected in the real wage bargain (Hatton, 2007). According to recent econometric evidence for 15 OECD countries during 1961–96,

α_2 is statistically significantly smaller than unity (Carter, 2007). A higher z reflects a strengthened bargaining position of workers, which increases real wage growth demanded by workers at a given unemployment rate, hence $\alpha_3 > 0$.

Let us for the moment ignore equation (7), however, and assume that real wage growth is exogenously given as the outcome of institutionalized negotiation and bargaining between unions and employers' associations. Combining equations (1), (2) and (5), we can solve for the equilibrium rates of output and labour productivity growth $\hat{x}$, $\hat{\lambda}$ and equilibrium employment growth $\hat{\ell}$:

$$\hat{x} = \frac{\Theta - \beta_0 C}{1 + \beta_1 C} + \frac{(1 - \beta_2) C}{1 + \beta_1 C} \hat{w} - \frac{\beta_3 C}{1 + \beta_1 C} z = \overline{\Theta} + \Xi \, \hat{w} - \Phi z \tag{8}$$

$$\hat{\lambda} = \beta_0 + \beta_1 \overline{\Theta} + [\beta_2 + \beta_1 \Xi] \, \hat{w} + [\beta_3 - \beta_1 \Phi] \, z \tag{9}$$

$$\hat{\ell} = -\beta_0 + (1 - \beta_1) \overline{\Theta} + [(1 - \beta_1) \Xi - \beta_2] \hat{w} - [\beta_3 + (1 - \beta_1) \Phi] z \tag{10}$$

where

$$\overline{\Theta} = \frac{\Theta - \beta_0 C}{1 + \beta_1 C}; \Xi = \frac{(1 - \beta_2) C}{1 + \beta_1 C}; \text{ and } \Phi = \frac{\beta_3 C}{1 + \beta_1 C}.$$

These equilibrium expressions can be used to analyse how output, productivity and employment growth are affected by changes in real wage growth ($\Delta \hat{w}$) and by changes in the extent of labour market regulation (Δz). Let us here consider the effects of real wage restraint, operationalized as a reduction of real wage growth ($\Delta \hat{w} < 0$). The total impact of the decline in real wage growth on output growth is given by:

$$\frac{d \hat{x}}{d \hat{w}} = \frac{(1 - \beta_2) C}{1 + \beta_1 C} = \Xi \tag{11}$$

We note that $(1)/(1 + \beta_1 C)$ represents an "endogenous-technology" multiplier, which captures the process of cumulative causation implied by the Kaldor–Verdoorn relationship; note that if the Kaldor–Verdoorn coefficient $\beta_1 = 0$, the endogenous-technology multiplier vanishes. It follows from the model's stability conditions that the denominator $1 + \beta_1 C$ of (11) is positive (Naastepad, 2006). Accordingly, the sign of $(d\hat{x}/d\hat{w})$ depends on whether the numerator $(1 - \beta_2) C$ is positive or negative.

When the demand regime is *wage-led* ($C > 0$), the numerator will be positive if $0 \le \beta_2 < 1$, that is, the elasticity of productivity with respect to the real wage (the "wage-cost induced technological progress effect") is smaller than unity. In this case, lower real wage growth unequivocally lowers output growth, as in earlier models in which productivity growth is exogenously given (Taylor, 1991). However, if $\beta_2 \to 1$, $(d\hat{x}/d\hat{w}) \to 0$, that is, the impact on output growth of reduced real wage growth becomes smaller (in absolute terms) and eventually vanishes, the more β_2 approaches a value of one. This leads us to an important conclusion: a higher sensitivity to real wage growth of labour productivity growth reduces the strength of the wage-led nature of aggregate demand.[3]

Turning to (9), what is the impact of reduced real wage growth on equilibrium productivity growth when demand is wage-led? From (9), it follows that

$$\frac{d\hat{\lambda}}{d\hat{w}} = \beta_2 + \beta_1 \frac{d\hat{x}}{d\hat{w}} = \beta_2 + \frac{\beta_1(1 - \beta_2)C}{1 + \beta_1 C} = \frac{\beta_2 + \beta_1 C}{1 + \beta_1 C} \tag{12}$$

A reduction in real wage growth has direct and indirect effects on productivity growth. The direct effect equals $\beta_2 > 0$. The indirect effect is equal to the change in long-run demand growth, caused by the decrease in real wage growth $(d\hat{x}/d\hat{w})$ multiplied by the Kaldor–Verdoorn elasticity β_1. If the economy is wage-led, $(d\hat{\lambda}/d\hat{w})$ is always positive, because $C > 0$; consequently, reduced real wage growth always depresses long-run productivity growth – directly (providing less inducement to improve technology) and indirectly (by reducing demand, which reduces productivity growth via the Kaldor–Verdoorn channel).

From (11) and (12), we can derive the employment growth effect of reduced real wage growth:

$$\frac{d\hat{e}}{d\hat{w}} = \frac{d\hat{x}}{d\hat{w}} - \frac{d\hat{\lambda}}{d\hat{w}} = (1 - \beta_1)\frac{d\hat{x}}{d\hat{w}} - \beta_2 = \frac{(1 - \beta_1 - \beta_2)C - \beta_2}{1 + \beta_1 C} \tag{13}$$

It can be seen that the total impact on employment growth is the net result of three separate effects of reduced real wage growth: (i) a decrease in output growth $(d\hat{x}/d\hat{w} > 0$ because demand is wage-led); (ii) a direct decline in productivity growth via β_2; and (iii) a decrease in labour productivity growth via the Kaldor–Verdoorn coefficient β_1. The sign of $d\hat{e}/d\hat{w}$ depends on the magnitude of each of these three effects and, hence, employment growth may rise or fall in response to the fall in real wage growth. Formally, if $d\hat{e}/d\hat{w} > 0$, then $C > (\beta_2)/(1 - \beta_1 - \beta_2)$. Under wage-led demand $(C > 0)$, this condition is always met if we assume that $\beta_2 = 0$; hence, in the absence of induced technological progress, lower wage growth results in lower employment growth under wage-led demand. The picture changes when $\beta_2 > 0$; for high values of β_1 and especially β_2, the sign of $d\hat{e}/d\hat{w}$ will become negative: in other words, a decline in real wage growth may lead to a rise in employment growth, mainly because of its negative impact on induced labour-saving technological progress and productivity growth, and the consequent positive effect on the growth of demand. To conclude, as equation (13) shows, in a wage-led system, the employment effect of increased real wage growth is inherently ambiguous.

When, in contrast, the demand regime is *profit-led* $(C < 0)$, the numerator of equation (11) will be negative if $0 \leq \beta_2 < 1$; hence, a fall in real wage growth increases output growth (as in the standard, exogenous technology, models). But we note again that if $\beta_2 \to 1$, $(d\hat{x}/d\hat{w}) \to 0$, that is, the growth promoting impact of lower real wage growth becomes smaller, the more β_2 approaches unity. Hence, aggregate demand growth becomes less profit-led when productivity growth becomes more sensitive to real wage growth.[4] What happens to productivity growth in the profit-led case? Going back to equation (12), we note that – given that $C < 0$ – the numerator can be positive, zero, or negative depending on the size of the coefficients. If $0 \leq \beta_2 < -\beta_1 C$, the numerator is negative and a decline in real wage growth raises productivity growth, because the wage-cost induced productivity growth decline is more than offset by the increase in productivity growth because of higher (profit-led) demand growth (the Kaldor–Verdoorn effect). But if $\beta_2 > -\beta_1 C$, then $(d\hat{\lambda}/d\hat{w})$ is positive and lower wage growth leads to reduced productivity growth. Employment growth in a profit-led system will – most likely – increase because of lower real wage growth, because $C < (\beta_2)/(1 - \beta_1 - \beta_2)$.[5]

From our discussion so far, we conclude that the effects of real wage growth restraint on output, productivity and employment growth (and consequently on unemployment) vary – depending on the nature of the demand regime as well as the nature of the productivity regime. Based on the above approach, Naastepad (2006) provides a useful detailed classification of (OECD) growth trajectories, which we do not reproduce here for reasons of space. To empirically illustrate the relevance of the growth model, Naastepad (2006) applies it (econometrically) to assess the effects of the policy of (voluntary) real wage growth restraint, as pursued in the Netherlands after the early 1980s. The main conclusions of this analysis are:

- Dutch aggregate demand growth is relatively insensitive to changes in real wage growth: $(d\hat{x}/d\hat{w}) = C = + 0.06$, which is positive, but close to zero. This finding is the result of a – perhaps surprisingly – limited responsiveness of investment growth to profitability and of export growth to unit labour costs.
- Dutch labour productivity, in contrast, is significantly affected by changes in real wage growth. In fact, real wage growth restraint explains – both directly (by retarding induced technological progress) and indirectly (through Kaldor–Verdoorn effects) – 85 per cent of the decline in Dutch labour productivity growth after 1984.
- Owing to this slowdown of productivity growth, Dutch employment increased tremendously. Because C is almost zero, $C < (\beta_2)/(1 - \beta_1 - \beta_2)$, which implies that the decline in real wage growth did raise employment growth, mainly by reducing productivity growth. Dutch high employment growth has therefore been the by-product of wage-led technological regression.

These findings show that real wage restraint is not a necessary condition for adequate long-run macroeconomic performance in all OECD countries, as the NAIRU approach claims. It may lead to increased employment growth, but by depressing productivity growth (rather than raising profitability, investment and export and output growth). The negative consequences for GDP growth of the productivity growth crisis (caused by real wage restraint) are obvious, once it is recognized that the export performance of OECD countries depends on embodied technology, quality and innovativeness. Seen in this light, the case for the more egalitarian and technologically dynamic policy alternative, based on higher real wage growth, becomes more persuasive.

3 The macroeconomic effects of labour market deregulation

The main implication of the NAIRU approach is that a restoration of profitability is necessary for a revival of OECD growth and a reduction of unemployment, and that this can be achieved by a policy of real wage growth restraint in combination with a more general policy of labour market deregulation. This view of the effects of deregulation does not stand up to closer scrutiny, however. Empirical research has shown that the association between unemployment and labour market regulation is generally (statistically) weak, or even insignificant. We do not want to review this important empirical literature here. Rather, we point out two theoretical flaws built into the NAIRU approach: (1) it presupposes that all OECD economies are profit-led, which is not the case; labour market regulation works out differently in wage-led economies; and (2) it – rather one-sidedly – ignores potential beneficial effects of regulation, for example more regulation may induce more rapid labour-saving technological change and more rapid productivity growth. What, then, are the effects on growth, productivity and employment of labour market deregulation in our (arguably more general and realistic) growth model?

To explore the macro effects of labour market regulation and to illustrate our two main points, while keeping the derivations tractable, we assume (without loss of generality) that $\alpha_0 = \alpha_1 = \alpha_2 = 0$ in equation (7); real wage growth thus becomes a function of regulation only:

$$\hat{w} = \alpha_3 z. \tag{14}$$

Labour market deregulation is operationalized by a decline in our variable z. This has two effects. First, real wage growth will decline (from (14)). Second, from equation (1), we can see that less regulation reduces pressures to economize on labour cost and hence, productivity growth declines – via coefficient β_3. To determine the impact of a decline in z on output growth, we first substitute (14) into equation (8) and next totally differentiate the resulting equation with respect to z as follows:

$$\frac{d\hat{x}}{dz} = \frac{\alpha_3(1 - \beta_2)C - \beta_3 C}{1 + \beta_1 C} \tag{15}$$

The sign of $(d\hat{x})/(dz)$ is ambiguous and depends on the nature of the demand regime. If demand is wage-led $(C > 0)$, $(d\hat{x})/(dz) > 0$ if $\alpha_3 > \alpha_3\beta_2 + \beta_3$, that is, the decline in real wage growth resulting from a decline in z is smaller (in absolute terms) than the corresponding decline in productivity growth. Hence, output growth declines if z is reduced, because unit (real) labour cost growth declines; in contrast, if $\alpha_3 < \alpha_3\beta_2 + \beta_3$, a reduction of z will raise output growth. Alternatively, if demand is profit-led $(C < 0)$, $(d\hat{x})/(dz) > 0$ if $\alpha_3 < \alpha_3\beta_2 + \beta_3$, that is, output growth will now rise if z is reduced, because real wage growth declines less than productivity growth, which means that income is being redistributed from wages to profits; the consequent increase (decline) in the profit (wage) share raises output. In contrast, if $\alpha_3 > \alpha_3\beta_2 + \beta_3$, a reduction of z reduces output growth. This shows that one-and-the-same policy change (a decline in z) may provoke very diverse output responses. The same holds true for the productivity growth effects.

The impact of a decline in z on productivity growth can be determined by substituting (14) into (9) and totally differentiating with respect to z:

$$\frac{d\hat{\lambda}}{dz} = \frac{\alpha_3\beta_2 + \alpha_3\beta_1 C + \beta_3}{1 + \beta_1 C} \tag{16}$$

Because the denominator is positive (by assumption), the sign of $(d\hat{\lambda}/dz)$ depends on the sign of the numerator. If the economy is wage-led, the numerator is positive: as a result, productivity growth will always decline as a result of labour market deregulation, because (by depressing wage growth) this leads to less rapid induced technological change and negative Kaldor–Verdoorn effects. However, if the demand regime is profit-led $(C < 0)$, the sign of $(d\hat{\lambda}/dz)$ becomes ambiguous. We can see that the numerator is positive only if $\alpha_3\beta_2 + \beta_3 > -\alpha_3\beta_1 C$; in this case, the decline in z reduces productivity growth, because the productivity-growth augmenting (Kaldor–Verdoorn) effect of higher output growth as a result of the lower real wage growth $(-\alpha_3\beta_1 C)$ is more than offset by the productivity-growth depressing effect of the reduced rate of technological progress $(\alpha_3\beta_2 + \beta_3)$. But if, in contrast, $\alpha_3\beta_2 + \beta_3 < -\alpha_3\beta_1 C$, the decline in z raises labour productivity growth. Accordingly, the impact on productivity growth of labour market deregulation can be positive or negative when demand is profit-led.

In view of the diversity in output and productivity growth responses, it comes as no surprise that the impact of deregulation (a lower z) on employment growth $\hat{\ell}$ is equally ambiguous – and contingent on the nature of the demand regime. The claim of the conventional NAIRU approach is that $(d\hat{\ell})/(dz) < 0$: a *decline* in z (i.e. deregulation) leads to *increased* employment growth. From equation (5), it follows that $(d\hat{\ell})/(dz) < 0$ *if* $(d\hat{x})/(dz) < (d\hat{\lambda})/(dz)$. Using (15) and (16), we can derive the following condition for $(d\hat{\ell})/(dz) < 0$:

$$C \left[\alpha_3 - \beta_2\alpha_3 - \beta_3\right] < \alpha_3\beta_2 + \alpha_3\beta_1 C + \beta_3 \tag{17}$$

The left-hand-side of (17) gives the impact of a change in z on output growth; the right-hand-side equals the corresponding change in productivity growth.

Consider first the case of wage-led demand. If $C > 0$, the right-hand-side is positive, indicating that productivity growth will fall in response to a decline in z. The left-hand-side can be positive or negative. If $\alpha_3 > \alpha_3\beta_2 + \beta_3$, the left-hand-side is positive, meaning $(d\hat{x})/(dz) > 0$, hence a decline in z reduces $\hat{x}$. If the decline in $\hat{x}$ is smaller than the decline in $\hat{\lambda}$ (i.e. $0 < (d\hat{x})/(dz) < (d\hat{\lambda})/(dz)$, or condition (17) is satisfied), employment growth will rise in response to deregulation – and unemployment will decline (from 6), because productivity growth declines more than output growth; this is what happened in the Netherlands in the 1980s and 1990s (Naastepad, 2006) and in Spain after 1995 (Dew-Becker and Gordon, 2007). Condition (17) need not be satisfied, however, if $\alpha_3 > \alpha_3\beta_2 + \beta_3$; in that case, $0 < (d\hat{\lambda})/(dz) < (d\hat{x})/(dz)$ and employment growth under wage-led demand will decline as a result of a reduced z (and unemployment will rise). We note that employment growth must rise if $\alpha_3 < \alpha_3\beta_2 + \beta_3$, because then $(d\hat{x})/(dz) < 0 < (d\hat{\lambda})/(dz)$: output growth increases, while productivity growth declines in the wake of labour market deregulation. On the face of it, this is a NAIRUvian outcome (less regulation being associated with higher employment growth and lower unemployment), but we emphasize that the employment growth is the result more of technological stagnation than of economic dynamism.

Likewise, a decline in z provokes a similar multitude of outcomes when the demand regime is profit-led $(C > 0)$. Table 15.1 shows a complete classification of macroeconomic responses to labour market deregulation. Let us look at two sharply contrasting trajectories. First, we know from (15) that output growth will decline in response to a decline in z if $\alpha_3 > \alpha_3\beta_2 + \beta_3$. This output growth decline coincides with an increase in productivity growth if (at the same time) $\alpha_3\beta_2 + \beta_3 > -\alpha_3\beta_1 C$; as a consequence, employment growth $\hat{\ell}$ must decline. Accordingly, under the stipulated conditions, labour market deregulation reduces employment growth and *increases unemployment*, even though the system is profit-led – a finding that squarely contradicts the standard NAIRU claim. Second, the opposite outcome – higher output growth, lower productivity growth and consequently higher employment growth – will come about if $\alpha_3 < \alpha_3\beta_2 + \beta_3$ and simultaneously $\alpha_3\beta_2 + \beta_3 < -\alpha_3\beta_1 C$. Unemployment will fall in reaction to deregulation, as

Table 15.1   Classification of macro responses to labour market deregulation (a decline in z)

Output growth response:	Wage-led demand	Profit-led demand Productivity growth response:	
		$\alpha_3\beta_2 + \beta_3 > -\alpha_3\beta_1 C$	$\alpha_3\beta_2 + \beta_3 < -\alpha_3\beta_1 C$
$\alpha_3 > \alpha_3\beta_2 + \beta_3$	(W1) $\hat{x}\downarrow; \hat{\lambda}\downarrow; \hat{\ell}?$	(P1) $\hat{x}\uparrow; \hat{\lambda}\downarrow; \hat{\ell}\uparrow$	(P3) $\hat{x}\uparrow; \hat{\lambda}\uparrow; \hat{\ell}?$
$\alpha_3 < \alpha_3\beta_2 + \beta_3$	(W2) $\hat{x}\uparrow; \hat{\lambda}\downarrow; \hat{\ell}\uparrow$	(P2) $\hat{x}\downarrow; \hat{\lambda}\downarrow; \hat{\ell}?$	(P4) $\hat{x}\downarrow; \hat{\lambda}\uparrow; \hat{\ell}\downarrow$

Note: ↑ = increase in growth rate; ↓ = decline in growth rate; ? = ambiguous response.

in the NAIRU approach, but again the underlying cause is a significant slowdown of productivity growth (because of technological regression). Thus, unlike the NAIRU approach, our demand-led growth model not only (realistically) allows for a variety of macro responses to labour market deregulation, but also – by uncovering the mechanisms through which a decline in z affects demand growth as well as productive capacity and productivity – highlights the (often substantial, opportunity) costs of deregulation in terms of productivity growth forgone.

The *productivity regime, demand regime* and *employment regime* curves are given in Figure 15.1 (for a profit-led economy) and Figures 15.2 and 15.3 (for a strongly wage-led and a marginally wage-led economy, respectively). Note that output growth is measured on the vertical axis and labour productivity growth on the horizontal axis. The productivity regime is always upward-sloping, which reflects the Kaldor–Verdoorn relation that faster output growth is associated with higher productivity growth. The profit-led demand regime curve is upward sloping in the $(\hat{\lambda}, \hat{x})$ plane, because faster productivity growth stimulates output expansion (mainly because higher productivity reduces unit labour costs and thus stimulates investment and exports). The wage-led demand regime curve is downward-sloping. Employment growth is presented as a function of output growth as in (5). The intersection of the productivity regime and demand regime curves determines the equilibrium rates of labour productivity growth $\hat{\lambda}_0$ and output growth $\hat{x}_0$.[6] The (dynamic) stability conditions, derived in Naastepad (2006), require that the slope of the productivity regime curve exceeds the slope of the demand regime curve. Figures 15.1, 15.2 and 15.3 show what happens to growth, productivity and (un-) employment when labour markets are deregulated, that is, z is reduced.

Consider first the case of profit-led demand P1 (from Table 15.1), illustrated in Figure 15.1. Because of the decline in z (and the consequent decline in real wage growth), the productivity regime shifts upwards (toward the left), which means that the initial rate of output growth $\hat{x}_0$ now "warrants" a lower rate of labour productivity growth. At the same time, the profit-led demand regime will shift upward, because the decline in wage growth (given $\hat{\lambda}_0$ and given that $C < 0$) leads to an increased profit share and hence to higher output growth. The eventual result is an *increase* in equilibrium output growth (from $\hat{x}_0$ to $\hat{x}_1$) and a *fall* in labour productivity growth (from $\hat{\lambda}_0$ to $\hat{\lambda}_1$). Employment growth must rise, as is illustrated in Figure 15.1, and unemployment (from (6)) declines. Hence, in the profit-led case P1, labour market deregulation leads to lower unemployment – as is also predicted by the NAIRU model – but this comes at the cost of declining productivity

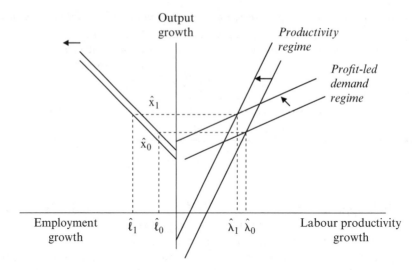

Note: The arrows indicate shifts in the demand, productivity and employment regime curves caused by a decline in real wage growth, which is in turn a result of a weakening of the bargaining power of workers caused by labour market deregulation (a decline in z). In this profit-led economy, labour market deregulation will lead to a rise in employment growth. Unemployment will fall as a result, which is a NAIRUvian outcome, but brought about by a long-run increase in profit-led output growth.

Figure 15.1   Determination of productivity growth $(\hat{\lambda})$, output growth $(\hat{x})$ and employment growth $(\hat{\ell})$: profit-led demand

growth. We emphasize that the macro behaviour of the profit-led system will resemble that of the standard NAIRU model somewhat less, once we assume that $\alpha_1 \neq 0$ (lower unemployment leads to higher real wage growth). In this case, real wage growth will not decline as much as in Figure 15.1, because there is upward wage pressure because of lower unemployment; in terms of Figure 15.1 (but not illustrated in the figure), shifts in the positions of all curves will be smaller (but still in the same direction).

Figure 15.2 illustrates the case of an economy in which demand growth is strongly wage-led (the demand regime curve is steeply downward sloping). As in Figure 15.1, the productivity regime curve shifts upwards (and to the left) because of a decline in z. But now the demand regime shifts downwards, because of the decline in real wage growth (since $C > 0$). This reflects the fact that the decline in the wage share (caused by the decline in wage growth at the initial rate of productivity growth $\hat{\lambda}_0$) forces down equilibrium output growth in a wage-led system. The result of these shifts in productivity and demand regimes is a *decline* in output growth (from $\hat{x}_0$ to $\hat{x}_1$) and a *decline* in labour productivity growth (from $\hat{\lambda}_0$ to $\hat{\lambda}_1$). Because the output growth decline is larger (in absolute terms) than the productivity growth decline (as we assume in Figure 15.2), employment growth will decline and unemployment (from (6)) will rise. Hence, under a strongly wage-led demand regime, labour market *de*regulation leads to declining output and productivity growth and higher unemployment – which is an outcome diametrically opposed to NAIRU predictions. What is important to our argument is that employment growth is more likely to decline if the slope of the demand regime curve, given by C, is

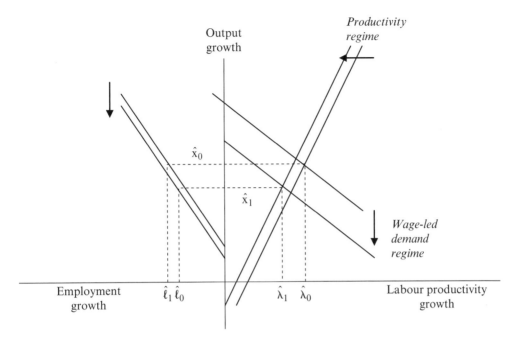

Note: The arrows indicate shifts in the demand, productivity and employment regime curves caused by a decline in real wage growth, caused by labour market deregulation (a decline in z). In this wage-led economy, labour market deregulation leads to lower employment growth and higher unemployment – a non-NAIRUvian outcome – because GDP growth declines more than labour productivity growth.

Figure 15.2   Determination of productivity growth ($\hat{\lambda}$), output growth ($\hat{x}$) and employment growth ($\hat{\ell}$): wage-led demand (strong)

small (in absolute terms). Finally, we point out that the negative macroeconomic effects of a reduction of z are augmented, if we assume that $\alpha_1 \neq 0$ (higher unemployment leads to lower real wage growth). The reason is that, under wage-led demand, lower employment growth and the consequent rise in unemployment depress real wage growth even further – which again reduces output growth more than productivity growth, in turn raising unemployment even more. It will be evident that the macro responses to reduced z of this strongly wage-led system are diametrically opposed to the reactions implied by the standard NAIRU model.

Figure 15.3 illustrates what happens in a marginally wage-led economy (i.e. C is close to zero) when z is reduced. The downward shift of the demand regime is small (compared to the leftward shift of the productivity regime) and the result is an increase in employment growth from $\hat{\ell}_0$ to $\hat{\ell}_1$. Clearly, unemployment is reduced because of the deregulation of the labour market, even though the economy is wage-led. This shows that a weakly wage-led economy (unlike the strongly wage-led case) may exhibit unemployment responses to policies of labour market deregulation that are in accordance with the outcomes of similar changes in the NAIRU model. But the underlying mechanisms are very different: here, it is the larger slowdown of labour productivity growth (than in demand and output growth) that brings about more job growth and reduced

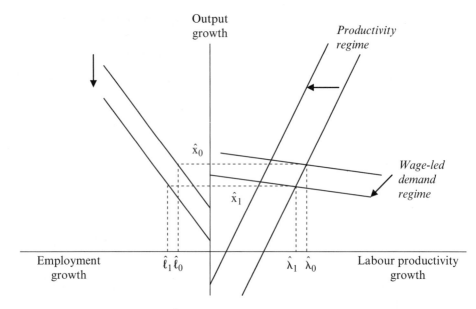

Note: The arrows indicate shifts in the demand, productivity and employment regime curves caused by a reduction in real wage growth, which is in turn a result of labour market deregulation. In this (marginally) wage-led economy, labour market deregulation leads to a rise in employment growth and lower unemployment – which is in line with NAIRU theory – because productivity growth declines more than output growth.

Figure 15.3   Determination of productivity growth ($\hat{\lambda}$), output growth ($\hat{x}$) and employment growth ($\hat{\ell}$): wage-led demand (weak)

unemployment. Technological stagnation and a productivity growth crisis are therefore the flipside of low unemployment in this system.

4   The NAIRU, demand growth and technology

We can use our (general) model to determine the non-accelerating inflation rate of unemployment (NAIRU), also called equilibrium unemployment, u. By combining the productivity regime (1), the demand regime (2), and the real wage growth equation (7), we obtain a system of three equations in four unknowns: $\hat{\lambda}$, $\hat{x}$, $\hat{w}$, and u^*.[7] One additional restriction needs to be imposed to "close" the system. We assume that in the long run real wages must grow at the same rate as labour productivity, so that

$$\hat{\lambda} = \hat{w} \tag{18}$$

Condition (18) implies that both inflation and the distribution of income across wages and profits are constant. Using (18) and equation (A.14) from the Appendix, we can immediately obtain the reduced form expression for long-run equilibrium income growth $\hat{x}^*$ from equation (2):

$$\hat{x}^* = \Theta = \frac{\psi_i \phi_0 \hat{b} + \psi_g \hat{g}^* + \psi_e \hat{e} - \psi_i \phi_3 r_k}{1 - \psi_i \phi_2} \tag{19}$$

The right-hand-side expression is derived and explained in the Appendix. Interestingly, the wage-led or profit-led nature of the demand regime, while being of crucial importance in the medium run, turns out to be immaterial for long-run income growth; this is not surprising, however, since we are keeping the distribution of income between wages and profits unchanged by imposing restriction (18). Long-run growth thus depends on (autonomous) investment growth $\hat{b}$ and export growth $\hat{e}$, the growth of net public expenditure $\hat{g}^*$ (the fiscal policy stance), and the real interest rate r_k (the monetary policy stance). Substitution of equation (19) into the productivity regime (1) gives us the reduced form expression for equilibrium labour productivity growth $\hat{\lambda}^*$:

$$\hat{\lambda}^* = \frac{\beta_0}{1 - \beta_2} + \frac{\beta_1}{1 - \beta_2} * \frac{\psi_i \phi_0 \hat{b} + \psi_g \hat{g}^* + \psi_e \hat{e} - \psi_i \phi_3 r_k}{1 - \psi_i \phi_2} + \frac{\beta_3}{1 - \beta_2} z \qquad (20)$$

Provided $\beta_1 > 0$, that is, the Kaldor–Verdoorn coefficient is positive, long-run productivity growth depends positively on the growth of autonomous demand and negatively on the real interest rate (assuming that $1 - \beta_2 > 0$). In addition, if $\beta_3 > 0$, any rise in the extent of labour market regulation (captured by a rise in z) will raise productivity growth – through inducing labour-saving technological progress.

Turning to unemployment, we first note that the equilibrium unemployment rate u^* that satisfies restriction (18) equals:

$$u^* = \frac{\alpha_0 - (1 - \alpha_2)\hat{\lambda} + \alpha_3 z}{\alpha_1} \qquad (21)$$

Substitution of (20) into (21) finally gives the following reduced-form expression for u^*:

$$u^* = \frac{\alpha_0(1 - \beta_2) - \beta_0(1 - \alpha_2)}{\alpha_1(1 - \beta_2)} + \left[\frac{\alpha_3(1 - \beta_2) - (1 - \alpha_2)\beta_3}{\alpha_1(1 - \beta_2)}\right] z$$

$$- \left[\frac{(1 - \alpha_2)\beta_1}{\alpha_1(1 - \beta_2)}\right] * \left[\frac{\psi_i \phi_0 \hat{b} + \psi_g \hat{g}^* + \psi_e \hat{e} - \psi_i \phi_3 r_k}{1 - \psi_i \phi_2}\right] \qquad (22)$$

Two insights follow directly from (22). First, unlike in the NAIRU model, demand factors $\hat{b}$, $\hat{g}^*$, $\hat{e}$ and r_k do have permanent effects on equilibrium unemployment. If $\alpha_1 > 0$; $0 < \alpha_2 < 1$; $0 < \beta_1 < 1$; and $0 \leq \beta_2 < 1$, it follows that an increase in the growth rate of autonomous investment, net public expenditure and exports will reduce equilibrium unemployment, whereas a rise in the real rate of interest will reduce u^* (by depressing investment demand):

$$\frac{\partial u^*}{\partial \hat{g}^*} = -\left[\frac{(1 - \alpha_2)\beta_1}{\alpha_1(1 - \beta_2)}\right]\left[\frac{\psi_g}{1 - \psi_i \phi_2}\right] < 0 \qquad (23A)$$

$$\frac{\partial u^*}{\partial \hat{e}} = -\left[\frac{(1 - \alpha_2)\beta_1}{\alpha_1(1 - \beta_2)}\right]\left[\frac{\psi_e}{1 - \psi_i \phi_2}\right] < 0 \qquad (23B)$$

$$\frac{\partial u^*}{\partial r_k} = \left[\frac{(1 - \alpha_2)\beta_1}{\alpha_1(1 - \beta_2)}\right]\left[\frac{\psi_i \phi_3}{1 - \psi_i \phi_2}\right] > 0 \qquad (23C)$$

According to (23A)–(23C), demand manipulation by means of fiscal and/or monetary policy causes the NAIRU itself to change over time.[8] The reason is that the inflationary impact of demand expansions is (at least partly) mitigated because they lead to faster productivity growth (via the Kaldor–Verdoorn effect, captured by β_1); hence output growth, wage growth and employment growth can be increased permanently in a non-inflationary manner.

Second, from (22), it can be seen that the sign of the impact on equilibrium unemployment of an increase in z is ambiguous. It follows that increased regulation leads to higher equilibrium unemployment (as conventional wisdom holds) only if

$$\frac{\partial u^*}{\partial z} = \frac{\alpha_3(1 - \beta_2) - (1 - \alpha_2)\beta_3}{\alpha_1(1 - \beta_2)} > 0 \tag{24}$$

Assuming that $\alpha_1 > 0$ and $(1 - \beta_2) > 0$, condition (24) can be restated as:

$$\frac{\partial u^*}{\partial z} > 0 \text{ if } \frac{\alpha_3}{(1 - \alpha_2)} > \frac{\beta_3}{(1 - \beta_2)}. \tag{25}$$

This inequality has a straightforward interpretation. Its right-hand-side is the impact of an increase in z on productivity growth from (20): $(\partial\hat{\lambda}^*)/(\partial z) = (\beta_3)/(1 - \beta_2) > 0$. Because of the increase in productivity growth, equilibrium real wage growth can also increase while keeping the rate of inflation constant. Accordingly, we can define $\Delta\hat{w}_W = (\partial\hat{\lambda}^*)/(\partial z) = (\beta_3)/(1 - \beta_2)$ as the increase in real wage growth warranted by increased productivity growth. The left-hand-side of (25) reflects the extra real wage growth *demanded* by workers in response to an increase in z. To see this, we rewrite equation (7) in terms of real wage growth (using equation (18)):

$$\hat{w} = \frac{\alpha_0}{1 - \alpha_2} - \frac{\alpha_1}{1 - \alpha_2}u + \frac{\alpha_3}{1 - \alpha_2}z \tag{7'}$$

From (7'), it follows that $(\partial\hat{w})/(\partial z) = (\alpha_3)/(1 - \alpha_2) > 0$. Let us denote the additional wage growth demanded by $\Delta\hat{w}_D$. According to condition (25), $\Delta\hat{w}_D > \Delta\hat{w}_W$, that is, the extra wage growth claimed exceeds the wage growth increase warranted by the increased productivity growth. This can only be reconciled by a rise in equilibrium unemployment, which – as shown by equation (7') – forces workers to reduce their wage growth demands until, in equilibrium, $\Delta\hat{w}_D = \Delta\hat{w}_W = \Delta\hat{w}^*$. But condition (25) need not be satisfied and hence it is equally possible that

$$\frac{\partial u^*}{\partial z} < 0 \text{ if } \frac{\alpha_3}{(1 - \alpha_2)} < \frac{\beta_3}{(1 - \beta_2)}. \tag{26}$$

Now, $\Delta\hat{w}_D < \Delta\hat{w}_W$, that is, the extra wage growth claimed by workers is less than the wage growth increase warranted by the increased productivity growth. This means that in this case – and in contrast to what the standard NAIRU model predicts – increased labour market regulation will lead to a permanent *decline* in u^* (Storm and Naastepad, 2008, 2009a).[9]

5   Empirical relevance

The theoretical results of Sections 2, 3 and 4 are relevant in light of the statistical findings by Baker et al. (2005a, 2005b), Baccaro and Rei (2005) and Howell et al. (2006) that the association between higher unemployment and more extensive labour market regulation is not at all statistically robust. The non-robustness and the lack of uniformity of the statistical evidence are (in our view) related to a misspecification of the NAIRU model, which underlies most econometric analyses. To see this, let us look again at the impact of labour market regulation on employment growth. From equations (5) and (17), it follows that $(d\hat{\ell})/(dz) < 0$ *if* $(d\hat{x})/(dz) < (d\hat{\lambda})/(dz)$: if the rise in output growth resulting from a higher z is smaller than the corresponding rise in labour productivity growth, employment growth will fall (and unemployment will increase). $(d\hat{\ell})/(dz) < 0$ requires that:

$$C\,[\alpha_3 - \beta_2\alpha_3 - \beta_3] < \alpha_3\beta_2 + \alpha_3\beta_1 C + \beta_3 \qquad (17')$$

The standard NAIRU model assumes (without any testing) that $\beta_1 = 0$; $\beta_2 = 1$; and $\beta_3 = 0$. If we impose these restrictions on $(17')$, we get $0 < \alpha_3$, which is a condition always satisfied (irrespective of whether demand is wage-led or profit-led) if there is a positive and statistically significant impact of regulation on real wage growth claims. Further, $(d\hat{\ell})/(dz) < 0$ if we assume that $\beta_1 = 0$ and $\beta_3 = 0$ and if $C < 0$ (demand is profit-led), because in that case $C < [\beta_2/(1 - \beta_2)]$. But under all other configurations of β_1, β_2, and β_3, it is not guaranteed that $(d\hat{\ell})/(dz) < 0$. Using their more general approach and based on a statistical analysis for 20 OECD countries (1984–2004), Storm and Naastepad (2009a) obtain (statistically significant) values for β_1, β_2 and β_3 such that $(d\hat{\ell})/(dz) > 0$; hence, contrary to conventional wisdom, they find that labour market regulation leads to higher employment growth and lower unemployment in the OECD.

Our theoretical analysis of the determinants of equilibrium unemployment is important in a second respect – namely by showing that there exists a mechanism by which (autonomous) demand expansions can produce permanent (long-run) decreases in unemployment (again, in contrast to NAIRU predictions). Corroborating evidence suggesting that there exists a statistically significant negative relationship between long-run unemployment and demand is provided by Rowthorn (1995, 1999) and Arestis et al. (2007). Storm and Naastepad (2009a), in their empirical (cross-country) analysis of the determinants of equilibrium unemployment in 20 OECD countries during the period 1984–2004, find that two-thirds of the actual long-term increase in OECD unemployment between 1960–80 and 1980–2000 must be attributed to declining demand growth (caused by lower export growth and higher real rates of interest). This result highlights the seriousness of omitting demand from the analysis of long-run unemployment.

6 Conclusions

NAIRU-based macroeconomics mistakenly presupposes that the trade-off between growth (and low unemployment) and equality applies to all OECD economies. It rejects *egalitarianism* by pointing to its supposed costs – slow growth, high unemployment and limited technological dynamism – and claims that, to reduce unemployment and revive growth, labour markets have to be deregulated and wage growth has to be kept below productivity growth. This chapter has argued that the NAIRU view is wrong: (1) real wage restraint and labour market deregulation may work out differently than expected if the economy is wage-led (as many OECD economies are); and (2) because higher wage growth and more regulation both induce more rapid labour-saving technological change and productivity growth, these need not necessarily lead to increased (steady-inflation) unemployment. *Feasible egalitarianism* (featuring high output and productivity growth, low unemployment, high real wage growth and pro-worker labour market regulation) requires strongly wage-led aggregate demand as well as rapid wage-led technological progress. Our general conclusion is that macroeconomic analysis and policymaking cannot ignore the systemic differences highlighted in this chapter by insisting on the one-size-fits-all policy of labour market flexibilization without creating major social costs and negligible benefits. NAIRU-based anti-inflation, pro-profit policies, presuming profit-led systems, have not only raised inequality and lowered real wage growth, but have also increased unemployment and slowed down labour productivity growth in the wage-led OECD countries. Hence, economists should urgently face the facts of systemic diversity and reconstruct their thinking about the causes of (output and productivity) growth and unemployment from the ground up.

Notes

1. Static returns refer to the well-known technical (and other) economies of scale associated with mass production. Dynamic returns are multifarious, based on learning by doing, induced capital accumulation embodying technological progress, and economies that arise from the overall expansion of an interrelated cluster of industries.
2. Deriving (6), we start from the identities that (i) $u = 1 - e$; and (ii) $e = \ell/n$, where e is the employment rate and n is the labour force. It follows that $\Delta u = -e(\Delta e)/(e) = -e\hat{e} = -e[\hat{\ell} - \hat{n}]$. Because $u = u_{-1} + \Delta u$, we obtain $u = [u_{-1} + e\hat{n}] - e\hat{\ell}$, which is equation (6). All the comparative static exercises start from a situation in which $\hat{\ell} = \hat{n}$ initially.
3. It follows that if $\beta_2 > 1$, $(d\hat{x}/d\hat{w}) < 0$, that is, a decline in real wage growth leads to a rise in output growth notwithstanding the *wage-led* nature of the demand regime. The productivity regime in this case dominates the demand regime.
4. It follows that if $\beta_2 > 1$, $(d\hat{x}/d\hat{w}) > 0$, that is, a fall in wage growth leads to a fall in profit-led output growth, because the productivity regime dominates the demand regime.
5. Only when $1 - \beta_1 - \beta_2 < 0$ it may occur that $C > (\beta_2)/(1 - \beta_1 - \beta_2)$ in which case lower real wage growth would reduce employment growth in a profit-led economy.
6. Note that these are not long-run equilibrium values (in a classical sense), because the model is predicated on $\hat{w} \neq \hat{\lambda}$ which is not sustainable in the limit. Hence, $\hat{\lambda}_0$, $\hat{x}_0$ must be regarded as a conditional or provisional equilibrium as defined by Setterfield (2002).
7. Note that equation (6) must now be dropped.
8. The results here are because $0 < \alpha_2 < 1$, that is, workers do not fully index productivity gains into real wage growth; but we note that this assumption still implies that the wage share (or profit share) is constant in the longer term. Empirical evidence that $\alpha_2 < 1$ is provided by Hatton (2007), Carter (2007) and Storm and Naastepad (2009a, 2009b). Roberts (2002) provides a similar theoretical argument as ours. The fact that $\alpha_2 < 1$ can be interpreted as the outcome of a wage bargaining process in which workers (unions) not only care about (insiders') wage gains but also (outsiders') employment (opportunities) – as has been true of Dutch unions post 1982 (see for example Naastepad, 2006).
9. For a comparison of our model with more standard NAIRU models, see Storm and Naastepad (2008, 2009a). For evidence on the productivity regime, see Storm and Naastepad (2009b).

References

Arestis, Philip, Michelle Baddeley and Malcolm Sawyer (2007). "The relationship between capital stock, unemployment and wages in nine EMU countries". *Bulletin of Economic Research*, 59 (2): 125–48.

Baccaro, Lucio and Diego Rei (2005). "Institutional determinants of unemployment in OECD countries: a time-series cross-section analysis (1960–1998)". *International Institute for Labour Studies Discussion Paper* 160/2005, Geneva: ILO.

Baker, Dean, Andrew Glyn, David Howell and John Schmitt (2005a). "Labor market institutions and unemployment: a critical assessment of the cross-country evidence", in David Howell (ed.), *Questioning Liberalization: Unemployment, Labor Markets and the Welfare State*. Oxford: Oxford University Press, pp. 72–118.

Baker, Dean, Andrew Glyn, David Howell and John Schmitt (2005b). "Unemployment and labor market institutions: the failure of the empirical case for deregulation". Working Paper, CEPA, New School University, New York.

Bhaduri, Amit and Stephen Marglin (1990). "Unemployment and the real wage: the economic basis for con-testing political ideologies". *Cambridge Journal of Economics*, **14** (4): 375–93.

Carter, Scott (2007). "Real wage productivity elasticity across advanced economies, 1963–1996". *Journal of Post Keynesian Economics*, **29** (4): 573–600.

Dew-Becker, Ian and Robert J. Gordon (2007). "The role of labor-market changes in the slowdown of European productivity growth". Paper presented at NBER Productivity Program Meeting, 7 December, Cambridge, MA.

Foley, Duncan K. and Thomas R. Michl (1999). *Growth and Distribution*. Cambridge, MA: Harvard University Press.

Hatton, Timothy J. (2007). "Can productivity growth explain the NAIRU? Long-run evidence from Britain, 1871–1999". *Economica*, **74**(295): 475–91.

Howell, David, Dean Baker, Andrew Glyn and John Schmitt (2006). "Are protective labor market institu-tions really at the root of unemployment? A critical perspective on the statistical evidence". CEPR Report 200607A.

McCombie, John S.L., Maurizio Pugno and Bruno Soro (2002). *Productivity Growth and Economic Performance: Essays on Verdoorn's Law*. London: Macmillan.

Naastepad, C.W.M. (2006). "Technology, demand and distribution: a cumulative growth model with an appli-cation to the Dutch productivity growth slowdown". *Cambridge Journal of Economics*, **30** (3): 403–34.

Naastepad, C.W.M. and Servaas Storm (2006/07). "OECD demand regimes (1960–2000)". *Journal of Post Keynesian Economics*, **29** (2): 211–46.

Roberts, Mark (2002). "Cumulative causation and unemployment", in John McCombie, Maurizio Pugno and Bruno Soro (eds), *Productivity Growth and Economic Performance*, London: Palgrave Macmillan, pp. 165–96.

Rowthorn, Robert E. (1995). "Capital formation and unemployment". *Oxford Review of Economic Policy*, **11** (1): 26–39.

Rowthorn, Robert E. (1999). "Unemployment, wage bargaining and capital–labour substitution". *Cambridge Journal of Economics*, **23** (4): 413–25.

Setterfield, Mark (ed.) (2002). *The Economics of Demand-Led Growth. Challenging the Supply-Side Vision of the Long Run*. Cheltenham, UK and Northampton, MA, USA: Edward Elgar.

Storm, Servaas and C.W.M. Naastepad (2007a). "It is high time to ditch the NAIRU". *Journal of Post Keynesian Economics*, **29** (4), 531–54.

Storm, Servaas and C.W.M. Naastepad (2007b). "Why labour market regulation may pay off. Worker moti-vation, co-ordination and productivity growth". *Economic and Labour Market Analysis Discussion Paper* 2007/2. Geneva: ILO.

Storm, Servaas and C.W.M. Naastepad (2008). "The NAIRU reconsidered: why labour market deregulation may raise unemployment". *International Review of Applied Economics*, **22** (5): 527–44.

Storm, Servaas and C.W.M. Naastepad (2009a). "The NAIRU, demand and technology". *Eastern Economic Journal*, **35** (3): 309–37.

Storm, Servaas and C.W.M. Naastepad (2009b). "Labour market regulation and productivity growth: evi-dence for 20 OECD countries (1984–2004)". *Industrial Relations*, **48** (1), 629–54.

Taylor, Lance (1991). *Income Distribution, Inflation, and Growth. Lectures on Structuralist Macroeconomic Theory*. Cambridge, MA: MIT Press.

Appendix   The demand regime

We assume that aggregate output x is determined by effective demand:

$$x = c + g + i + e - m, \tag{A.1}$$

where c is private consumption, g is public current expenditure, i is aggregate investment, e is exports, and m is imports; all are measured at constant prices. We define the real labour cost per unit of output or the real wage share as:

$$v = (W/P)\lambda^{-1} = w\lambda^{-1} \tag{A.2}$$

W is the nominal wage (per hour of work), P is the aggregate price level, and λ is the level of labour productivity (real value added per hour worked). We express (A.2) in growth rates:

$$\hat{v} = \hat{w} - \hat{\lambda} \tag{A.3}$$

From (A.2), and at a given level of labour productivity λ, it follows that there exists a negative relationship between the real wage rate and the profit share π. To see this, note that, by definition, the (real) profit share is equal to 1 minus the wage share:

$$\pi = 1 - \frac{W\lambda^{-1}}{P} = 1 - v \tag{A.4}$$

Expressed in growth rates this gives:

$$\hat{\pi} = \frac{\Delta\pi}{\pi} = -\frac{v}{\pi}\frac{\Delta v}{v} = -\theta(\hat{w} - \hat{\lambda}) \tag{A.5}$$

where θ is defined as $(v/\pi) = v/(1 - v) > 0$. Profit share growth thus declines as a result of real wage growth in excess of labour productivity growth. Consumption is a function of wage income and capital income. Denoting the saving propensity by σ and using the subscripts w and π to refer to wage and profit income, respectively, wage earners consume $(1 - \sigma_w)$ of their income, while capitalists' average consumption propensity equals $(1-\sigma\pi)$. Suppose further that $\sigma_w < \sigma\pi$, as a result of the retention of a significant portion of profits by corporations. Accordingly, consumption is determined as follows:

$$c = (1 - \sigma_w)w\lambda^{-1}x + (1 - \sigma_\pi)\pi x - t = [(1 - \sigma_w)v + (1 - \sigma_\pi)(1 - v)]x - t \tag{A.6}$$

t is aggregate direct tax payments. Import demand depends on output:

$$m = \zeta x \tag{A.7}$$

where ζ is the (average) import propensity. Substituting equations (A.6) and (A.7) into (A.1) and rearranging, we get:

$$x = \frac{(g - t) + i + e}{[1 - (1 - \sigma_w)v - (1 - \sigma_\pi)(1 - v) + \zeta]} = \mu^{-1}(g^* + i + e) \tag{A.8}$$

We define $g^* = g - t$ as government current expenditure *net* of direct tax payments. Note that $\mu^{-1} = 1/[1 - (1 - \sigma_w)v - (1 - \sigma_\pi)(1 - v) + \zeta]$ is the Keynesian multiplier ($\mu^{-1} > 1$), the magnitude of which depends, via v on the distribution of income and on the real wage and the level of labour productivity, in particular. Totally differentiating (A.8) with respect to time, dividing through by x, and rearranging give:

$$\hat{x} = -\hat{\mu} + \frac{\mu^{-1}g^*}{x}\hat{g}^* + \frac{\mu^{-1}i}{x}\hat{i} + \frac{\mu^{-1}e}{x}\hat{e} = -\hat{\mu} + \psi_g\hat{g}^* + \psi_i\hat{i} + \psi_e\hat{e}, \qquad (A.9)$$

where ψ_g, ψ_i and ψ_e are the (multiplier-adjusted) shares in GDP of net government current expenditure, investment and exports, respectively. It must be noted that the multiplier is endogenous, because any change in real labour cost per unit of output will directly affect its denominator μ, which equals $\sigma_\pi - v(\sigma_\pi - \sigma_w) + \zeta]$. Using this expression for μ, we can derive its growth rate as a function of unit labour cost growth as follows

$$\hat{\mu} = -\frac{v}{\mu}(\sigma_\pi - \sigma_w)\hat{v} = -\xi(\sigma_\pi - \sigma_w)(\hat{w} - \hat{\lambda}) \qquad (A.10)$$

where ξ is the positive fraction (v/μ). We now turn to investment and export growth. The growth rate of investment i depends positively on the growth of π and x, and negatively on the real interest rate (or cost of capital) r_k:

$$\hat{i} = \phi_0\hat{b} + \phi_1\hat{\pi} + \phi_2\hat{x} - \phi_3 r_k \qquad \phi_0, \phi_1, \phi_2, \phi_3 > 0 \qquad (A.11)$$

$\hat{b}$ represents other factors (mainly "animal spirits" of entrepreneurs) influencing investment decisions. Coefficient Φ_1 is the elasticity of investment with respect to the profit share; the positive effect on investment of π can be justified by reference to the use of corporate retained profits for relieving financial constraint on investment. The positive effect of x reflects the accelerator effect; Φ_2 is the elasticity of investment with respect to demand. Φ_3 is the sensitivity of the growth of investment demand with respect to the real interest rate. Exports e are a negative function of relative unit labour cost and a positive function of exogenous exports e_0:

$$e = e_0\left[\frac{v}{v_{row}}\right]^{-\varepsilon_1} \qquad (A.12)$$

v_{row} is the real labour cost (in domestic currency) associated with one unit of world exports; and ε_1 is the elasticity of export volume with respect to change in (relative) real unit labour cost. For simplicity and without loss of generality, we assume that $v_{row} = 1$; linearizing (A.12) in growth rates gives

$$\hat{e} = \hat{e}_0 - \varepsilon_1\hat{v} \qquad (A.13)$$

Substitution of (A.5), (A.10), (A.11) and (A.13) into (A.9) yields the following reduced form equation for the demand regime:

$$\hat{x} = \frac{\psi_i\phi_0\hat{b} + \psi_g\hat{g}^* + \psi_e\hat{e} - \psi_i\phi_3 r_k}{1 - \psi_i\phi_2} + \frac{[\xi(\sigma_\pi - \sigma_w) - \psi_i\phi_1\theta - \psi_e\varepsilon_1]}{1 - \psi_i\phi_2}[\hat{w} - \hat{\lambda}] \quad (A.14)$$

Note that for (A.14) to be economically meaningful we must assume that $[1 - \psi_i\phi_2] > 0$, that is, given that $0 < \psi_i < 1$, the "accelerator elasticity" has to fall within the following range: $0 \leq \phi_2 < (1/\psi_i)$. (A.14) is equation (2) in the main text, if we assume that

$$\Theta = \frac{\psi_i\phi_0\hat{b} + \psi_g\hat{g}^* + \psi_e\hat{e} - \psi_i\phi_3 r_k}{1 - \psi_i\phi_2} \quad \text{and} \tag{A.15}$$

$$C = d\hat{x}/d[\hat{w} - \hat{\lambda}] = \frac{[\xi(\sigma_\pi - \sigma_w) - \psi_i\phi_1\theta - \psi_e\varepsilon_1]}{1 - \psi_i\phi_2} \tag{A.16}$$

Θ thus represents the (positive) effects on output of the growth of autonomous investment $\hat{b}$, net public current expenditure $\hat{g}^*$, and autonomous exports $\hat{e}_0$, and the negative impact of a higher real interest rate r_k. C gives the impact of labour cost growth on output growth and it can be seen that C is ambiguous in sign. This is so, because any excess of real wage growth over labour productivity growth (i.e. $\hat{v} > 0$ or $\hat{w} > \hat{\lambda}$) has two opposing effects on output growth. On the one hand, it will reduce investment and export growth, and consequently lower output growth. But on the other hand, it will increase the size of the multiplier, because it entails a redistribution of income from profits towards wage income and a consequent decline in the aggregate savings propensity. To derive the sign of $C = d\hat{x}/d[\hat{w} - \hat{\lambda}]$ from (A.16), recall that $[1 - \psi_i\phi_2] > 0$, $\xi = (v/\mu)$, $\psi_i = i/(\mu x)$ and $\psi_e = e/(\mu x)$. It then follows that C is positive and the economy *wage-led*, if

$$\frac{d\hat{x}}{d\hat{v}} = C > 0 \text{ if } (\sigma_\pi - \sigma_w) > \left(\frac{i}{\pi x}\right)\phi_1 + \left(\frac{e}{vx}\right)\varepsilon_1 \tag{A.17}$$

Alternatively, demand will be *profit-led* if

$$\frac{d\hat{x}}{d\hat{v}} = C < 0 \text{ if } (\sigma_\pi - \sigma_w) < \left(\frac{i}{\pi x}\right)\phi_1 + \left(\frac{e}{vx}\right)\varepsilon_1 \tag{A.18}$$

16 Dissent-driven capitalism, flexicurity growth and environmental rehabilitation*

Peter Flaschel and Alfred Greiner

1 Sustainable social evolution through recurrent mass unemployment?

This chapter starts from the hypothesis that Goodwin's (1967) Classical Growth Cycle, modeling the Marxian Reserve Army Mechanism, does not represent a process of social reproduction that can be considered adequate and sustainable in a social and democratic society in the long run. The chapter derives from this background a basic macrodynamic framework in which cyclical growth and the reproduction of capitalism à la Goodwin is replaced by an employer of "first" resort, added to an economic reproduction process that is highly competitive and flexible and thus not of the type characteristic of former Eastern socialist economies. Instead, there is a high degree of capital and labor mobility (particularly with respect to "hiring" and "firing"), and thus flexibility, but fluctuations of employment in this first labor market (the private sector) are made socially acceptable through the security aspect of the flexicurity concept by a second labor market where all remaining workers (and even pensioners) find meaningful occupation. The resulting model of flexicurity capitalism with its detailed transfer payment schemes is in its essence comparable to the flexicurity models developed for the Nordic welfare states and Denmark in particular. We show that this economy exhibits a balanced growth path that is globally attracting. We add here that credit financed investment, and thus more flexible investment behavior, can be easily added without disturbing the prevailing situation of full capacity growth (see Flaschel et al., 2008 for details). In this chapter, however, we model only supply-driven business fluctuations with both factors of production always fully employed.[1] The resulting model combines flexible factor adjustments in the private sector with high employment security for the labor force and shows that the flexicurity variety of a capitalist economy, protected by the government, can work in a fairly balanced manner.

Solow's (1956) famous growth model is to a certain degree also of the flexicurity type, since competitive firms always operate at their profit-maximizing activity level and since the labor market is assumed to always guarantee full employment. We thus have employment flexibility again coupled with income security, through the assumed behavior of firms and through the assumption of perfectly flexible money wages. The monetarist critique of Keynesianism and recent work by Blanchard and Katz (1999) in particular suggests, however, a wage Phillips curve which, when coupled with the assumption of myopic perfect foresight regarding the price inflation rate, implies a real wage Phillips curve where the growth rate of real wages depends positively on the employment rate and negatively on the level of the real wage rate. Adding such empirically supported real wage rigidity to the Solow model then gives rise to two laws of motion (for labor intensity and the real wage) – a dynamical system which imitates the situation of the overshooting feature of Goodwin's growth cycle mechanism if factor substitution in production is

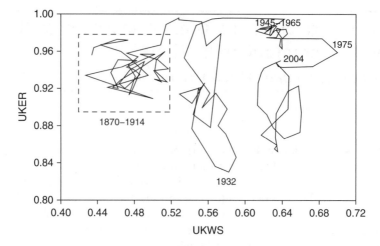

Figure 16.1   Distributive cycles 1870–2004 (WS = wage share, ER = employment rate)

sufficiently inelastic and if the Blanchard and Katz (1999) real wage error correction term in the Phillips curve is sufficiently weak. Solow's growth model thus becomes a variant of the classical distributive growth cycle with its overshooting reserve army mechanism, the adequacy of which for a democratic society is questioned in this chapter. An illustration of what is meant by this latter statement is provided by Figure 16.1.

The important insight that can be obtained from Figure 16.1 for the UK economy 1855–1965 is that the Goodwin cycle must have been significantly shorter before 1914 (with larger fluctuations in employment during each business cycle), and that there has been a major change in it after 1945. This may be explained by significant changes in the adjustment processes of market economies for these two periods: primarily price adjustment before 1914 and quantity adjustments after 1945. Based on data up to 1965 one could have claimed that the growth cycle had become obsolete (and maybe even the business cycle as it was claimed in the late 1960s). Yet, with the sample extended by the data shown in Figure 16.1 (taken from Groth and Madsen, 2007), it is now obvious that nothing of the sort took place in the UK economy. In fact, we see in Figure 16.1 two periods of excessive over-employment (in the language of the theory of the NAIRU) which were followed by periods of dramatic underemployment, both begun by periods of more or less pronounced stagflation.

Generating order and economic viability in market economies through large swings in the unemployment rate (thus degrading members of families that make up the society), as shown above, is one way to make capitalism work, but this must surely be rejected because of its social consequences. Such a reproduction mechanism is not compatible with an educated and democratic society in the long run, as we shall describe in this chapter, which is supposed to provide equal opportunities to all of its citizens.

This situation must therefore be contrasted with an alternative social structure of accumulation that allows the combination of a highly competitive market economy with a human rights bill that includes the right (and the obligation) to work, and to get income from this work that at least supports basic needs and basic happiness. The

Danish flexicurity system may provide an example of the path towards such an alternative. By contrast, a laissez-faire capitalistic society that ruins family structures to a considerable degree (through alienated work, degrading unemployment and education- and value-decomposing visual media) cannot be made compatible with a democratic society in the long run, since it produces conflicts ranging from social segmentation to class- and race-based disturbances. By contrast, we argue in this chapter that stable balanced reproduction is possible under a socially responsible regime of flexicurity capitalism that is backed by educational principles conducive to skill formation and citizenship education in a democratic society.

2 Dissent-driven capitalism and the evolution of its infrastructure[2]

In this section we briefly discuss the implications of a Goodwin (1967) representation of the growth cycle of capitalist economies that is enhanced by the effects of infrastructure consumption or rehabilitation. We are able to treat in this framework two fundamental problems of the process of capital accumulation, namely the partial degradation of workers through recurrent situations of mass unemployment (in the depression phase) and the partial destruction of the infrastructure through the recurrent overexploitation of "nature" (in the boom phase). We emphasize that the Goodwin model does not imply that capitalists are solely responsible for the occurrence of such effects. Instead, the long-phased overshooting nature of the conflict over income distribution between capital and labor drives the results. We will show in later sections that it is by no means necessary to create order in Western type market economies in this way. Instead, structures of economic and social reproduction can be designed where order is created in a way that preserves the flexibility of Western type market economies, but that is consent-based through its provision of security in the labor markets. This possibility implies that the crude reserve army based reproduction mechanism of most current capitalist economies can be overcome by institutional reforms in the labor markets that may lead at least advanced capitalist democracies from the welfare state through workfare arrangements towards flexicurity and beyond.

We begin with a brief formulation of the model. The growth rate $\hat{w}$ of the money wage of workers is assumed to be given by a conventional money wage Phillips curve (where the rate of employment, e, replaces the unemployment rate, $\bar{e}$ the employment rate that corresponds to the NAIRU unemployment rate):

$$\hat{w} = \beta_w(e - \bar{e}) + \hat{p} + \hat{z}, \quad \hat{w} = \dot{w}/w$$

Workers negotiate real wages as in Goodwin (1967), since the inclusion of the actual rate of inflation $\hat{p}$ on the right hand side reduces this nominal wage Phillips curve to a real wage Phillips curve. Moreover, the additional 1–1 passthrough of the growth rate of labor productivity z into nominal wage growth in fact leads immediately to a law of motion for the wage share $v = w/p/z$ given by $\hat{v} = \beta_w(e - \bar{e})$.

Goodwin's accumulation equation, based on the basis of a linear technology with no technical change (i.e. given input–output proportions $y^p = Y^p/K = $ const., $z = Y^p/L^d = $ const.) and classical savings and investment assumptions ($s_c = 1$; $s_w = 0$), can be stated as follows:

$$\hat{K} = \dot{K}/K = \frac{Y^p - \delta K - \omega L^d}{K} = y^p(1 - \omega/z) - \delta, \qquad \omega = w/p$$

with δ the depreciation rate of the capital stock. If we add Harrod neutral technical change ($\hat{z} = $ const.) to this fixed proportions technology, we must replace the variable K (which is now growing over time) with a new state variable K_z, the law of motion of which is given by:

$$\hat{K}_z = \hat{K} - \hat{z} = y^p(1 - v) - \delta - \hat{z}, \qquad K_z = K/z$$

in order to get a trendless magnitude. In what follows, we use g_z in place of $\hat{z}$ to denote the trend growth rate in labor productivity.

We now add a third law of motion for the infrastructure N of the economy to the otherwise standard Goodwin (1967) growth cycle model above. Here we assume the following dynamic equation:

$$\dot{N} = -\alpha_n(y^p(n) - y^p(n_o))K, \qquad n = N/K, \ y^{p'}(n) > 0,$$

$$\text{i.e.,} \qquad \hat{n} = -\alpha_n(y^p(n) - y^p(n_o))/n - \hat{K}$$

We are thus now further modifying the Goodwin model by assuming that the output capital ratio is no longer constant, but in fact a function of the ratio n of the infrastructure N to the capital stock K. There is a natural level n_o for this ratio and a corresponding output capital ratio where the existing infrastructure remains intact (unchanged). Higher output capital ratios reduce the existing infrastructure N as shown, while lower ones will lead to its recovery. These output capital ratios in turn depend on the ratio n between "nature" N and capital K, with higher n allowing for higher y^p because of an abundance of "nature".

This new feedback structure also modifies the first two laws of motion of the model, since we now have:

$$e = \frac{L^d}{L} = \frac{y^p(n)K_z}{L}$$

For simplicity we assume a given labor supply L (no natural growth) and thus concentrate on productivity growth in this variant of the Goodwin model.

From the above we thus get an autonomous 3D system of differential equations in the state variables v, K_z, n, giving us the dynamics:

$$\hat{v} = \beta_w(y^p(n)K_z/L - \bar{e})v, \qquad v = w/p/z \tag{1}$$

$$\dot{K}_z = [y^p(n)(1 - v) - \delta - g_z]K_z, \qquad K_z = K/z \tag{2}$$

$$\hat{n} = -g_z n - \alpha_n(y^p(n) - y^p(n_o)) - [y^p(n)(1 - v) - \delta - g_z]n, \qquad n = N/K \tag{3}$$

The uniquely determined interior steady state solution of this system is (if we assume for simplicity that function $y^p(n)$ is given by γn):

$$v^* = 1 - \frac{\delta + g_z}{y^p(n^*)}, \qquad K_z^* = \bar{e}L/y^p(n^*), \qquad n^* = \frac{n_o}{1 + g_z/(\gamma\alpha_n)} < n_o$$

Note that the steady state level of n is below its natural level, a result that also holds for all other admissible types of functions $y^p(n)$. Note also that the steady wage share is lower than it would be at the natural level of the infrastructure. With respect to this steady state position the following holds:

Proposition
The steady state of the Goodwinian dynamics (1)–(3) with environmental feedback channels is always surrounded by centrifugal forces, that is, this economy is not viable in the long run.

Proof: The Jacobian matrix of the dynamics we are considering reads at the steady state:

$$J = \begin{pmatrix} J_{11} & J_{12} & J_{13} \\ J_{21} & J_{22} & J_{23} \\ J_{31} & J_{32} & J_{33} \end{pmatrix} = \begin{pmatrix} 0 & + & + \\ - & 0 & + \\ + & 0 & - \end{pmatrix}.$$

Remark: As the distribution of signs in the matrix J shows we have conventional Goodwin type cross-dual dynamics with respect to the state variables v, K_z coupled with a feedback structure between the state variables v and n which is of a cumulative nature.

In order to get convergence of the orbits of the dynamics to the steady state we have to show for the characteristic polynomial $\lambda^3 + a_1\lambda^2 + a_2\lambda + a_3$ of the matrix J that $a_i > 0$, $i = 1, 2, 3$ and $a_1a_2-a_3 > 0$.[3] Since the term $-[y^p(n)(1 - v) - \delta - g_z]$ in the third law of motion is proportional to the second law of motion it does not matter for the calculation of the determinant of the Jacobian J. In this calculation of the determinant we can therefore artificially assume $J_{31} = 0$ which gives us:

$$a_3 = -\det J = J_{33}J_{12}J_{21} > 0, \quad \text{i.e., } a_1a_2 - a_3 = J_{33}J_{31}J_{13} < 0$$

This simple result is because of the fact that we have only one entry in the trace of $J(= -a_1)$ and since the top left principal minor of order 2 of J (when multiplied with a_1) cancels against det $J(= -a_3)$.

We thus have the result that the positive feedback channel between the wage share v and the nature capital ratio n through the first and third laws of motion always destabilizes the growth cycle of this model, leading to fluctuations of income distribution and employment of increasing amplitude. The economy therefore faces the twofold dilemma of partial workforce degradation and partial waste of infrastructure. These two problems are not easily overcome in a market economy that is based on overshooting distributional conflict between capital and labor and an accumulation process that is of a strongly cyclical nature. In a democratic society there is therefore a compelling need to find means that transcend such cyclical accumulation dynamics in order to make it sustainable in the long run.

3   Flexicurity capitalism: national accounts
We now design as an alternative to the Goodwin growth cycle a model of economic growth that rests not on overaccumulation (in the prosperity phase) and mass unemployment (in the stagnant phase), but on a second labor market, which through its institutional setup guarantees full employment in its interaction with the first labor market, the

Table 16.1   Firms: production and income account

Uses	Resources
δK	δK
$\omega_1 L_1^d, L_1^d = Y^p/z$	$C_1 + C_2 + C_r$
$\omega_2 L_{2f}^w$	G
$\Pi - g_z N$	I
$\delta_1 R + \dot{R}$	S_1
Y^p	Y^p

employment in the industrial sector of the economy, which is modeled as highly flexible and competitive. An excellent introduction into the literature with which such a flexicurity modeling approach is compatible can be found in Tcherneva (2007), which also provides the backdrop for Flaschel et al.'s (2008) discussion of credit, money and Keynesian demand problems. The basic difference is that we interpret the flexicurity model developed below as resting on the concept of an employer of first – not last – resort, where education, skill formation and the principle of equal opportunities allow for a highly educated workforce (see Flaschel, 2008, Ch.10 on these latter issues).

We first reconsider the corporate sector of the economy, as shown in Table 16.1.

This account is a simple one. Firms use their capital stock (at full capacity utilization as we shall show later on) to employ the amount of labor (in hours): L_1^d, at the real wage ω_1, the law of motion of which is again determined from a model of wage–price interaction in the manufacturing sector. In addition they employ a labor force $L_{2f}^w = \alpha_f L_1^d, \alpha_f = $ const. from the second labor market at the wage ω_2, which is a constant fraction α_ω of the market wage in the first labor market. This labor force L_{2f}^w works the normal hours of a standard workday, while the workforce L_1^w from the first labor market may be working overtime or undertime depending on the size of the capital stock in comparison to that of this "primary" workforce. The variable $u_w = L_1^d/L_1^w$ is the utilization rate of the workforce in the first labor market, the industrial workers of the economy (all other employment originates from the work of households occupied in the second labor market).

Firms produce full capacity output[4] $Y^p + \delta_1 R = C_1 + C_2 + C_r + g_z N + I + \delta K + G$, that is sold to the two types of consumers (and retired households), used for infrastructure rehabilitation, and sold to investing firms and the government. The demand side of the model is formulated in a way such that this full capacity output can indeed be sold. Deducting from this output Y^p, firms' real wage payments to workers from the first and the second labor market and infrastructure preservation efforts (together with depreciation)[5] we get the profits of firms which are here assumed to be invested fully into capital stock growth $\dot{K} = I = \Pi$. We thus have classical (direct) investment habits in this model with an employer of first resort. We assume again a fixed proportions technology with $y^p = Y^p/K$ the potential output–capital ratio and with $z = Y^p/L_1^d$ the given value of labor productivity (which determines the employment L_1^d of the workforce L_1^w of firms).

Compared to Flaschel et al. (2008) the model here is augmented by efforts to preserve the infrastructure of the economy, a cost that is paid by firms and which therefore appears in the above production account as a deduction from firms' profit. Because of

Table 16.2   Households I and II (primary and secondary labor market)

(a) Income account (households I)

Uses	Resources
$C_1 = c_{h1}(1 - \tau_h)\omega_1 L_1^d$	
$\omega_2 L_{2h}^w = c_{h2}(1 - \tau_h)\omega_1 L_1^d$	
$T = \tau_h \omega_1 L_1^d$	
$\omega_2(L - (L_1^w + L_{2f}^w + L_{2h}^w + L_{2g}^w))$	
$\omega_2 L^r, L^r = \alpha_r L$	
S_1	$\omega_1 L_1^d$
$Y_1^w = \omega_1 L_1^d$	$Y_1^w = \omega_1 L_1^d$

(b) Income account (households II)

Uses	Resources
C_2	$\omega_2 L_2^w, L_2^w = L - L_1^w$
Y_2^w	Y_2^w

this, the law of motion for N, from the preceding section, is augmented as follows (where again $n = N/K$):

$$\dot{N} = g_z N - \alpha_n(y^p(n) - y^p(n_o))K, \; y'(n) > 0, \text{ i.e.,} \quad \hat{n} = g_z - \alpha_n(y^p(n) - y^p(n_o))/n - \hat{K}$$

Firms therefore introduce in this model of flexicurity capitalism a trend growth term into the reproduction of the infrastructure, which is here set equal to the trend in labor productivity g_z.

We assume as in the preceding case of classical capitalism that output per unit of capital depends positively on the ratio n. The law of motion of this state variable now takes the form:

$$\dot{n} = -\alpha_n(y^p(n) - y^p(n_o)) - [y^p(n)(1 - (1 + \alpha_\omega \alpha_f)v_1) - \delta - g_z n - g_z]n$$

because of the environmental protection efforts of firms. This removes the trend term in the law of motion for $\hat{K}$ since

$$\hat{K} = y^p(n)(1 - v_1 - \alpha_f v_2) - \delta - g_z n = =y^p(n)(1 - (1 + \alpha_\omega \alpha_f)v_1) - \delta - g_z n$$

is again to be replaced by the growth rate $\hat{K}_z = \hat{K} - g_z$ of the detrended capital stock.[6] We next consider the household sector, which is composed of worker households working in the first labor market together with those working in the second labor market (see Table 16.2).

Households of type I consume manufacturing goods of amount C_1 and services from the second labor market L_{2h}^w. They pay (all) income taxes T and they pay in addition – via further tax transfers – all workers' income in the labor market that does not come from the services they employ, from firms and in an active way from the

Table 16.3   Income account (retired households)

Uses	Resources
C_r	$\omega_2 L^r + \delta_1 R,\ L^r = \alpha_r L$
Y^r	Y^r

government (which is by and large therefore equivalent to an unemployment insurance). Moreover, they pay the pensions of retired households ($\omega_2 L^r$) and accumulate their remaining income S_1 in the form of company pensions into a fund R that is administrated by firms (with inflow S_1 from these households and with outflow $\delta_1 R$ to pensioners).

The transfer $\omega_2 (L - (L_1^w + L_{2f}^w + L_{2h}^w + L_{2g}^w))$ can be interpreted as solidarity payment, since workers from the first labor market that lose their job will automatically be employed in the second labor market where full employment is guaranteed by the government (as employer of first resort). We consider this employment as skill preserving, since it can be viewed as ordinary office or handicraft work (subject only to learning by doing when such workers return to the first labor market).

The second sector of households is modeled in the simplest way possible: Households employed in the second labor market, that is, $L_2^w = L_{2f}^w + L_{2h}^w + L_{2g}^w$ pay no taxes and totally consume their income. We thus have classical saving habits in this household sector, while households of type I may have positive or negative savings S_1 as residual from their income and expenditures. The law of motion for pension funds R is:

$$\dot{R} = S_1 - \delta_1 R$$

where δ_1 is the rate at which these funds are depreciated through company pension payments to the "officially retired" workers L^r, assumed to be a constant fraction of the "active" workforce $L^r = \alpha_r L$. These worker households are not really inactive in our model, but offer work according to their still existing capabilities that can be considered as an addition to the supply of work organized by the government $L - (L_1^w + L_{2f}^w + L_{2h}^w)$. In other words, the working potential of officially retired persons remains a valuable contribution to the total working hours that are supplied by all members of the society. It is obvious that the proper allocation of the work hours under the control of the government needs thorough reflection from both the microeconomic and the social point of view, but this topic is beyond the scope of this chapter.

The income account of retired households shows that they receive pension payments as if they are working in the second labor market and they also get individual transfer income (company pensions) from the accumulated funds R in proportion to the time they have been active in the first labor market, as a portion of $\delta_1 R$ by which the pension funds R are reduced in each period (Table 16.3).

Finally there is the government sector, which is also formulated in a very simple fashion as shown in Table 16.4.

The government receives income taxes, the solidarity payments (employment benefits) for the second labor market paid by workers in the first labor market, and old-age pension payments. It uses the taxes to finance government goods demand G and the surplus of

Table 16.4 *The government: income account: fiscal authority/employer of first resort*

Uses	Resources
$G = \alpha_g T$	$T = \tau_h \omega_1 L_1^d$
$\omega_2 L_{g2}^w = (1 - \alpha_g) T$	
$\omega_2 (L - (L_1^w + L_{2f}^w + L_{2h}^w + L_{2g}^w))$	$\omega_2 L_r^w$
$\omega_2 L^r$	$\omega_2 \alpha_r L$
Y^g	Y^g

taxes over these government expenditures to actively employ workers in the government sector. In addition it employs the workers receiving unemployment benefits and also employs "retired" persons to the extent they can still contribute to employment activities. The total labor force in the second labor market is thus employed by firms, by type I households and the government. The income payments to workers in the second labor market ($\omega_2 L_2^w$) that do not originate from their services to firms, to type I households or from an excess of income taxes over government commodity expenditures are thus paid out of transfers from type I households to the government, and on the basis of these payments the remaining work in the second labor market is organized by government.

In sum, workers are employed either in the first labor market and/or by performing auxiliary work within firms, services for type I households or services in the government sector associated with public administration, infrastructure services, educational services or other public services. In addition there is the potential labor supply $\alpha_r L$ from retired households, which because of the long-life expectancy in modern societies can remain effective suppliers of specific work over a considerable span of time. In this way the whole workforce is always fully employed in this model of social growth (including retired persons who work according to their capabilities and willingness) and so does not suffer from human degradation through unemployment. Of course, there are a variety of issues concerning state organized work that point to problems with the organization of such work, but such problems already exist in actual industrialized market economies in one way or another. We thus have a classical growth model of the economy where full employment is not assumed, but actively constructed and where –because of the assumed expenditure structure – Say's law holds true, that is, the capital stock of firms is also always fully utilized.

4 Dynamics: convergence towards balanced reproduction

Since the labor market has been redesigned in this approach to flexicurity growth, we assume the adjusted law of motion for the deflated and detrended wage dynamic to be:[7]

$$\hat{v} = \beta_w (u_w - \bar{u}_w),$$

where $\bar{u}_w$ is the NAIRU utilization rate of type I workers. Wage negotiations are now conducted by type I workers (the insider core), according to their utilization rate $u_w = L_1^d = L_1^w$. Since demand pressure on the external labor market no longer exists in this model, it is simply replaced in the equation above by the extent of over- or under-utilization of the workers L_1^w.

The growth law of the capital stock moreover now reads ($\omega_i = w_i/p$, $v_i = \omega_i/z$):

$$\hat{K} = \rho = \frac{Y^p - \delta K - \omega_1 L_1^d - \omega_2 L_{2f}^w - g_z N}{K} = y^p(n)(1 - (1 + \alpha_\omega \alpha_f) v_1) - \delta - g_z n.$$

The important dynamic innovation in this model is that we now have a law of motion for the stock of type I workers employed by firms. This law of motion describes the recruitment policy of firms, that is, their hiring and firing decisions concerning type I workers, and is given by:

$$\hat{L}_1^w = \beta_u (u_w - \bar{u}_w),$$

i.e., the growth rate of this part of the workforce depends on the extent to which type I workers are over- or underemployed because of the current state of capital accumulation, that is, the size of the capital stock. Note that type II workers are assumed to be skilled enough to enter the type I workforce if they are demanded by firms, that is, training costs are neglected for simplicity. This assumes that education and life-long learning are organized accordingly in our model.

The above three laws of motion can be easily reformulated in terms of the state variables $v_1 = \omega_1/z$, $l_1^w = zL_1^w/K = L_1^w/K_z$ and $n = N/K$ and give rise to the following autonomous system of differential equations, expressed in growth rate terms:

$$\hat{v}_1 = \beta_w (y^p/l_1^w - \bar{u}_w) \tag{4}$$

$$\hat{l}_1^w = \beta_u (y^p/l_1^w - \bar{u}_w) - [y^p(n)(1 - (1 + \alpha_\omega \alpha_f) v_1) - \delta - g_z n] \tag{5}$$

$$\hat{n} = -\alpha_n (y^p(n) - y^p(n_o))/n - \hat{K}_z, \quad \hat{K}_z = y^p(n)(1 - (1 + \alpha_\omega \alpha_f) v_1) - \delta - g_z n - g_z$$

$$= g_z - \alpha_n (y^p(n) - y^p(n_o))/n - [y^p(n)(1 - (1 + \alpha_\omega \alpha_f) v_1) - \delta - g_z n] \tag{6}$$

since we have $\omega_2 = \alpha_\omega \omega_1$, $L_{2f}^w = \alpha_f L_1^d$, $L_1^d/K = y^p/z$.

The uniquely determined interior steady state solution of this system is

$$v^* = 1 - \frac{\delta + g_z}{y^p(n^*)(1 + \alpha_\omega \alpha_f)}, \quad l_1^{w*} = y^p(n^*)/\bar{u}_w, \quad n^* = n_o$$

Note that the steady state level of n is now at its natural level. Note also that the steady wage share is higher now than it would be under classical capitalism (if $\alpha_\omega \alpha_f = 0$ holds). Under the assumed infrastructure rehabilitation efforts of firms there is therefore an improved steady state solution for the dynamics under consideration. With respect to this steady state position the following holds:

Proposition
Assume that the growth rate of labor productivity g_z is sufficiently small (in order to preserve the condition $J_{33} < 0$). Then the above 3D flexicurity growth dynamic with environmental protection is convergent to its interior steady state, that is, is viable, if the hiring and firing parameter β_u is chosen sufficiently large, that is, if the employment policy of firms is sufficiently flexible.

Proof: The Jacobian matrix of the dynamics under consideration reads, at the steady state:

$$J = \begin{pmatrix} J11 & J12 & J13 \\ J21 & J22 & J23 \\ J31 & J32 & J33 \end{pmatrix} = \begin{pmatrix} 0 & - & + \\ + & - & + \\ + & 0 & - \end{pmatrix}.$$

Remark: As the distribution of signs in the matrix J shows we now have conventional Goodwin type cross-dual dynamics with respect to the state variables v, l_1^w, coupled with a feedback structure between the state variables v and n which is of a cumulative nature. In contrast to the preceding section we now however have a negative feedback effect of the size of the type I workforce on its rate of growth (through the recruitment policy of firms) and a new slightly positive influence of the ratio n on its time rate of change. This latter effect is however of no importance if the parameter g_z (a growth rate) is chosen sufficiently small.

In order to get convergence of the orbits of the dynamics to the interior steady state we must again show that for the characteristic polynomial $\lambda^3 + a_1\lambda^2 + a_2\lambda + a_3$ of the matrix J the conditions $a_i > 0$, $i = 1, 2, 3$ and $a_1a_2 - a_3 > 0$. Since the term $\hat{K}_z$ can again be removed from the third law of motion without altering det J, we again have det $J = -J_{33}J_{12}J_{21} < 0$. This makes $a_1a_2 - a_3$ positive if the parameter β_u is chosen sufficiently large, since this parameter appears with a positive coefficient in a_1, a_2, and a_3, but of course in a_1a_2 in squared form that will dominate a_3 sooner or later. But $a_1a_2 - a_3$, a_1, a_3 > 0 implies $a_2 > 0$, which proves the asymptotic stability of the interior steady state.

We thus have the result that the positive feedback channel between the wage share v_1 and the nature capital ratio n through the first and the third law of motion is dominated by the central flexibility parameter in our model of flexicurity growth, leading (possibly) to fluctuations of income distribution, but that are now damped, depending on the degree of employment flexibility. The economy therefore no longer faces the twofold dilemma of partial workforce degradation and partial waste of infrastructure as was the case in the model with an active reserve army mechanism. These two problems are now overcome in a market economy that is based on employment (not job) security, free entry and exit in the employment of the factors of production, and infrastructure regulation that commits firms to finance a constant rate of growth of infrastructural rehabilitation in order to mitigate the effects of production on the infrastructure of the economy.

5 Company pension funds

There is a further law of motion in the background of the model that needs to be considered in order to provide a complete statement on the viability of our model of flexicurity capitalism. This law of motion describes the evolution of the pension fund per unit of the capital stock $\eta = R/K$ and is obtained from the defining equation $\dot{R} = S_1 - \delta_1 R$ as follows:

$$\hat{\eta} = \hat{R} - \hat{K} = \frac{\dot{R}K}{KR} - \rho = \frac{S_1 - \delta_1 R}{K} \Big/ \eta - \rho,$$

$$\dot{\eta} = \frac{S_1}{K} - (\delta_1 + \rho)\eta = s_1 - (\delta_1 + \rho)\eta$$

i.e.: with savings of households of type I and profits of firms per unit of capital being given by:

$$s_1 = (1 - (c_{h1} + c_{h2})(1 - \tau_h) - \tau_h)v_1y^p - \alpha_\omega v_1(l_x^w + l^r)$$

$$l_x^w = 1 - (l_1^w + l_{2f}^w + l_{2h}^w + l_{2g}^w)$$

$l^r = \alpha_r l,$ i.e., due to the financing of the employment terms $l_{2h}^w + l_{2g}^w$:

$$s_1 = (1 - c_{h1}(1 - \tau_h) - \alpha_g\tau_h)v_1y^p - ((1 + \alpha_r)l - (l_1^w + l_{2f}^w))\alpha_\omega v_1, \quad l_{2f}^w = \alpha_f y^p$$

$$\rho = y^p[1 - (1 + \alpha_\omega\alpha_f)v_1] - \delta - g_z n$$

For analytical simplicity we assume that all state variables up to η have already reached their steady state position. Moreover we also assume for simplicity $\delta_1 = \delta$. This gives us the following law of motion of the pension–capital ratio, η:

$$\dot\eta = (1 - c_{h1}(1 - \tau_h) - \alpha_g\tau_h)v_1^*y^{p^*} - ((1 + \alpha_r)l^* - (l_1^{w^*} + \alpha_f y^{p^*}))\alpha_\omega v_1^* - (\delta + \rho^*)\eta$$

This reduced form dynamic is globally asymptotically stable and exhibits the steady state value:

$$\eta_o = \frac{(1 - c_{h1}(1 - \tau_h) - \alpha_g\tau_h)v_1^*y^{p^*} - ((1 + \alpha_r)l^* - (1 + \alpha_f)y^{p^*})\alpha_\omega v_1^*}{\delta + \rho^*}$$

where ρ^* denotes the steady state rate of profit of firms.

The steady state level of η is positive – and the economy is therefore viable – if and only if the full employment labor intensity ratio is such that:

$$l^* < \frac{(1 - c_{h1}(1 - \tau_h) - \alpha_g\tau_h)v_1^*y^{p^*} + ((1 + \alpha_f)y^{p^*})\alpha_\omega v_1^*}{(\delta + \rho^*)(1 + \alpha_r)\alpha_\omega v_1^*}$$

6   Conclusions

We have shown in this chapter that there is a (model) alternative to the classical growth cycle analysis of overshooting income distribution dynamics proposed by Goodwin (1967), which overcomes the degradation of part of the workforce in the depressed part of the growth cycle and which also mitigates workers overshooting income claims in the prosperity phase of the growth cycle. In addition, we have shown that the environmental implications of unrestricted capitalist accumulation make the Goodwin growth cycle a (mildly) explosive dynamical process (at an unnaturally low infrastructure level) and thus a non-viable reproduction process in the long run. However, this can be overcome by an infrastructure rehabilitation policy where firms use part of their profits for environmental reconstruction.

The overall outcome is not only a better steady state position for the economy, but also a stable dynamics in place of the unstable feedback mechanisms that characterize a reserve army led reproduction process. Combining flexibility in the adjustment of the workforce of firms with employment (but not job) security allows us to formulate a model where stable reproduction can be successfully combined with environmental protection in a consent-driven socioeconomic framework, in place of dissent-driven recurrently overshooting income claims.

The approach chosen in this chapter requires further refinement in order to show that it truly represents a viable social structure of accumulation. We refer the reader here to Flaschel et al. (2008) for generalizations of this model of flexicurity growth to credit relationships and Keynesian demand problems in particular, where the preservation of full employment becomes an even more important issue in an environment where flexibility and social security are reconciled with each other.

Notes

*   We have to thank Mark Setterfield for many very useful comments on the chapter. Of course, usual caveats apply.
1.   See however Flaschel et al. (2008) for the occurrence of Keynesian business cycles in such a framework.
2.   Note that the term "infrastructure" is used throughout this chapter to denote environmental quality.
3.   See Flaschel (2008, Mathematical Appendix) for details.
4.   As augmented by company pension payments $\delta_1 R$.
5.   The term S_1 is equal to $\delta_1 R + \dot{R}$.
6.   See also section 4 in this regard.
7.   Augmenting this Phillips curve by Blanchard and Katz (1999) error correction terms would further improve the results obtained in this section, but is left out here for reasons of comparability with the dissent-driven Goodwin (1967) model.

References

Blanchard, O.J. and Katz, L. (1999): "Wage dynamics: reconciling theory and evidence". *American Economic Review. Papers and Proceedings*, **89**, 69–74.

Flaschel, P. (2008): *The Macrodynamics of Capitalism. Elements for a Synthesis of Marx, Keynes and Schumpeter*. Heidelberg: Springer.

Flaschel, P., Greiner, A., Luchtenberg, S. and Nell, E. (2008): "Varieties of capitalism. The flexicurity model", in P. Flaschel and M. Landesmann (eds), *Mathematical Economics and the Dynamics of Capitalism*. London: Routledge.

Goodwin, R. (1967): "A growth cycle", in C.H. Feinstein (ed.), *Socialism, Capitalism and Economic Growth*. Cambridge: Cambridge University Press, pp. 54–8.

Groth, C. and Madsen, J.B. (2007): "Medium-term fluctuations and the 'Great Ratios' of economic growth". Working Paper, University of Copenhagen.

Solow, R. (1956): "A contribution to the theory of economic growth". *Quarterly Journal of Economics*, **70**, 65–94.

Tcherneva, P. (2007): "What are the relative macroeconomic merits and environmental impacts of direct job creation and basic income guarantees?" The Levy Economics Institute of Bard College, Working Paper 517.

17 Profit sharing, capacity utilization and growth in a post-Keynesian macromodel

*Gilberto Tadeu Lima**

1 Introduction

Though Weitzman's (1983, 1984, 1985) claim that profit sharing is able to generate full employment and low inflation has not led to its widespread adoption, alternative employee compensation mechanisms have nonetheless become increasingly common in industrialized economies since the 1980s. Weitzman argued that while a wage economy is prone to unemployment in the short run, a profit-sharing economy experiences excess demand for labor. If some part of workers' compensation is received as a profit share and if, as a result, the base wage is lower than otherwise, firms face a lower marginal cost of labor. Profit-maximizing monopolistically competitive firms will then be willing to hire more workers and given a sufficient degree of profit sharing, an excess demand for labor results. As the marked up price is lower than in a wage economy, a resulting real balance effect leads to a higher aggregate demand and therefore to a higher desired output.[1]

Weitzman's propositions about the macroeconomic benefits of profit sharing have often been criticized by economists of different persuasions, and a common heterodox criticism is that Weitzman ignored the truly Keynesian factors of uncertainty and deficient effective demand and implicitly assumed that involuntary unemployment is caused by downward wage inflexibility (see, e.g., Davidson, 1986–87; Rothschild, 1986–87). However well taken these criticisms may be, and the one just mentioned surely is, they do not imply that profit sharing per se should necessarily be dismissed up front. It is therefore the purpose of this chapter to develop a post-Keynesian short-run macromodel of capacity utilization and growth, in which distribution features a profit-sharing arrangement. Indeed, given the prominent role played by income distribution in the post-Keynesian approach, it is only natural to investigate the potential benefits of profit sharing for macroeconomic performance in a model that conforms to the essential tenets of post-Keynesian economics. For the sake of demonstrating the robustness of the results, several different specifications of the consumption and investment demand functions are considered, including one in which workers save some of the compensation they receive from profit sharing. And in line with the empirical evidence, the possibility that labor productivity varies positively with profit sharing is also considered.

The empirical literature on profit sharing is actually quite extensive, and a considerable body of evidence suggests that its introduction increases the productivity of the firm.[2] Though the estimated size of the productivity gain varies considerably from case to case, it is usually substantial. However, the evidence for the proposition that profit sharing leads to stronger employment performance is more mixed.

Weitzman and Kruse (1990) examine 16 studies showing that profit sharing raises productivity. Only 6 percent of the 218 estimated profit-sharing coefficients are negative, and none significantly so, while 60 percent of them are significantly positive. Employing meta-analysis, which formalizes the notion that a large number of independent, though relatively weak, results can add up to a strong statistical case, they conclude that the null hypothesis of no productivity effect can be rejected at infinitesimal levels of significance. Bhargava (1994), using UK data, finds a positive impact of profit-sharing on profitability (measured by total profits and the return on capital), while Conyon and Freeman (2004), also using UK data, find that firms that adopt profit-related pay tend to outperform other firms in terms of productivity and financial performance. Cahuc and Dormont (1997), employing French data, find that profit-sharing firms perform better as regards labor productivity, employment, output and profitability. Estrin et al. (1997), using UK data, find that firms that have introduced profit sharing produced more output from a given set of factor inputs, while Azfar and Danninger (2001), employing US data, find that workers participating in profit-sharing plans have (on average) more human capital.

Meanwhile, D'Art and Turner (2004), using data for 11 European countries, find that the relationship between profit sharing and financial performance is statistically and strongly significant. Firms with a profit-sharing scheme are 1.8 times more likely to report that their gross revenue over the past three years is well in excess of costs. The authors also find that profit sharing is significantly (though less strongly) associated with productivity and technological innovation, as firms with a profit sharing scheme are 1.3–1.4 times more likely to rate their performance in the top 10 percent of companies in terms of innovation rates and productivity levels. More recently, Kraft and Ugarkovic (2006), using German data, also find that the adoption of profit sharing positively affects profitability.

The remainder of this chapter is organized as follows. First, the structure of the model is described and the equilibrium values of capacity utilization and growth are derived. Next, the same equilibrium values are derived under alternative specifications of the consumption and investment demand functions. Finally, the impact of profit sharing on employment when labor productivity also varies with the profit-sharing coefficient is briefly investigated.

2 Structure of the model

The economy is a closed one and with no government activities, producing only one good for both investment and consumption. Two (homogeneous) factors of production are used, capital and labor, which are combined through a fixed-coefficient technology. Labor employment is therefore determined by production:

$$L = aX \tag{1}$$

where L is the employment level, a is the labor-output ratio and X is the output level. Capitalist firms in oligopolistic markets carry out production. They produce (and hire labor) according to demand, which is assumed to be insufficient for firms to produce at full capacity at prevailing prices.

The economy is inhabited by two classes, capitalists and workers. Following the tradition of Kalecki (1971), Kaldor (1956), Robinson (1962), and Pasinetti (1962), we assume that these classes have different consumption and saving behaviors. Workers, who are always in excess supply, provide labor and earn a base wage income. In line with the literature on profit sharing reviewed in the preceding section, workers also receive a share of profit income, which is the entire surplus over the base wage. We start by assuming that workers' total compensation is all spent on consumption, although later on we extend the model to consider the possibility that workers save a fraction of their share of profits. This initial assumption that workers as a class do no saving does not, of course, rule out the possibility that individual workers might save. What this view amounts to is the assumption that for workers as a class, the saving of some households is matched by the dissaving of others. Meanwhile, capitalists receive that part of total profit income which is not distributed to workers, of which they save a fraction, s_c. Division of real income is then given by:

$$X = (W/P)L + \lambda R + (1 - \lambda)R \qquad (2)$$

where W is the nominal base wage, P is the price level, R is the flow of real profits and $0 < \lambda < 1$ is the profit-sharing coefficient. Workers' total compensation as a proportion of real income, σ, can therefore be expressed as:

$$\sigma = \frac{VL + R_w}{X} = Va + \pi_w \qquad (3)$$

where $V = (W/P)$ stands for the real base wage, $R_w = \lambda R$ is the amount of real profits that accrue to workers as a result of profit-sharing, and $\pi_w = \lambda \pi$ denotes workers' profits as a proportion of real income, with $\pi = (R/X)$ standing for total profits as a proportion of real income. We refer to the two components of workers' total income share as the base wage share, $\sigma_1 = Va$, and the surplus wage share, $\sigma_2 = \pi_w$, respectively. As total profits are given by $R = R_w + R_c$, where R_c denotes the amount of real profits that accrue to capitalists, and (1) and (2) imply that the ratio of total profits to income is given by $\pi = (1 - Va)$, workers' total compensation as a proportion of real income can be alternatively expressed as:

$$\sigma = Va + \lambda(1 - Va) \qquad (4)$$

which implies that capitalists' compensation as a proportion of real income, $\pi_c = (1 - \sigma)$, is given by:

$$\pi_c = (1 - \lambda)\pi = (1 - \lambda)(1 - Va) \qquad (5)$$

Hence capitalists' compensation as a proportion of income, given the labor–output ratio, varies negatively with the real base wage and the profit-sharing coefficient. Since a proportion of profit income accrues to workers, the rate of profit of the economy, r, which is the flow of real profits divided by the capital stock, K, is likewise divided in the following way:

$$r = \frac{R_w + R_c}{K} = r_w + r_c = (\pi_w + \pi_c)u \qquad (6)$$

where r_w and r_c are the components of the general rate of profit corresponding to the profits that accrue to workers and capitalists, respectively, while $u = X/K$ is the rate of capacity utilization. As we assume that the ratio of capacity output to the capital stock is constant, we can therefore identify capacity utilization with the output–capital ratio. Using equation (5), we can therefore express the capitalists' rate of profit, r_c, as follows:

$$r_c = (1 - \lambda)(1 - Va)u \tag{7}$$

The price level is determined à la Kalecki (1971), being set by firms as a markup over prime costs:

$$P = zWa \tag{8}$$

where $z > 1$ is the markup factor. Firms also make capital accumulation plans which can be represented by a standard post-Keynesian desired investment function with profitability and capacity utilization as arguments. We start by assuming that the relevant measure of profitability is the capitalists' rate of profit, r_c, although later on we extend the model to consider capitalists' share in income, π_c, as the relevant variable. Firms' desired capital accumulation is therefore initially given by:

$$g^d = \beta_0 + \beta_1 r_c + \beta_2 u \tag{9}$$

where β_i are positive parameters of the desired investment function, g^d, which measures desired capital accumulation as a ratio of the existing capital stock. We follow Rowthorn (1981) and Dutt (1984, 1990), who in turn follow Kalecki (1971) and Robinson (1962), by making desired accumulation depend positively on the profit rate. The rationale is that the current profit rate is not only an index of expected future earnings, but also provides internal funding for capital accumulation plans and makes it easier for firms to obtain external funding. In this model a proportion of profit income accrues to workers as a result of profit sharing, though, so that it is more reasonable to make desired investment depend on the component of the general rate of profit which corresponds to the profits that accrue to capitalists, given by r_c.[3] Meanwhile, we also follow Rowthorn (1981) and Dutt (1984, 1990), who in turn follow Steindl (1952), in assuming that investment depends positively on capacity utilization as a result of accelerator-type effects.

Since the model is demand-driven, the macroeconomic equality between investment and saving will be brought about by changes in output through changes in capacity utilization. As we start by assuming that none of workers' total compensation is saved, while capitalists save a fraction, s_c, of the profit income that is not distributed to workers, aggregate saving as a proportion of the capital stock (g^s) is given (from equation (7)) by:

$$g^s = \frac{s_c R_c}{K} = s_c(1 - \lambda)(1 - Va)u \tag{10}$$

3 Equilibrium capacity utilization and growth in the short run

The short run is first defined as a time frame in which the capital stock, K, the labor supply, N, the profit-sharing coefficient, λ, the labor–output ratio, a, the markup factor, z, the nominal base wage, W, and hence the price level, P, can all be taken as given.[4] The existence of excess capacity implies that output will adjust to remove any excess demand or supply in the economy, so that in short-run equilibrium, $g^s = g^d$. Substituting from (7), (9) and (10), we can solve for the equilibrium value of u to obtain:

$$u^* = \frac{\beta_0}{(1 - \lambda)(s_c - \beta_1)(1 - Va) - \beta_2} \tag{11}$$

We assume a Keynesian short-run adjustment mechanism stating that capacity utilization will change in proportion to the excess demand in the goods market. This means that u^* will be positive and stable provided that aggregate saving is more responsive than desired investment to changes in capacity utilization, which in turn requires that the denominator of the expression in (11) is positive. As the pricing equation given by (8) implies meaningful values for the ratio of total profits to income given by $0 < (1 - Va) < 1$, it follows that $s_c > \beta_1$ is a necessary condition for the equilibrium value of u to be positive and stable.

An issue worth addressing at this point is the impact of changes in the real base wage on capacity utilization, which is given by:

$$\partial u^*/\partial V = u_V^* = \frac{(1 - \lambda)(s_c - \beta_1) a \beta_0}{A^2} > 0 \tag{12}$$

where A is the denominator in the expression in (11). Hence an increase in the real base wage, which actually translates into a rise in the share of workers' total compensation in income, as shown by (4), leads to an increase in capacity utilization. As in the canonical post-Keynesian model developed independently by Rowthorn (1981) and Dutt (1984), which does not feature a profit-sharing arrangement, an increase in the real base wage, by redistributing income from capitalists who save to workers who do not, raises consumption demand, increases investment spending through the capacity utilization effect on capital accumulation, and hence raises the level of activity. Moreover, an increase in the real base wage will also lead to an increase in the short-run equilibrium levels of the general rate of profit, r^*, the capitalists' rate of profit, r_c^*, and the growth rate, g^*, as shown by the corresponding expressions obtained through substitution from equations (6)–(7) and (10)–(11):

$$g^* = s_c r_c^* = s_c(1 - \lambda)r^* = s_c(1 - \lambda)(1 - Va)u^* \tag{13}$$

and

$$\frac{\partial g^*}{\partial V} = s_c \frac{\partial r_c^*}{\partial V} = s_c(1 - \lambda)\frac{\partial r^*}{\partial V} = \frac{s_c(1 - \lambda) a \beta_0 \beta_2}{A^2} > 0 \tag{14}$$

Hence a rise in the real base wage, by leading to an increase in aggregate effective demand, makes for an increase not only in capacity utilization, but also in the general profit rate and the growth rate, as in the canonical post-Keynesian model of Rowthorn (1981) and Dutt (1984). Note also that the equilibrium capitalists' rate of profit is increasing in the real base wage, despite the fact that the equilibrium value of the component of the general rate of profit that accrues to workers (which according to (5)–(7) and (11) is given by $r_w^* = \lambda r^*$) is increasing in the profit-sharing coefficient.

Another issue that is worthy of notice concerns the impact of changes in the profit-sharing coefficient on capacity utilization, which is given by:

$$\partial u^*/\partial \lambda = u_\lambda^* = \frac{(s_c - \beta_1)(1 - Va)\beta_0}{A^2} > 0 \tag{15}$$

Hence an increase in the profit-sharing coefficient, which actually translates into a rise in the share of workers' total compensation in income (as shown by (4)) leads to an increase in capacity utilization. An increase in the profit-sharing coefficient, by redistributing income from capitalists who save to workers who do not, raises consumption demand, increases investment spending through the capacity utilization effect on capital accumulation and hence raises the levels of output and employment. As it turns out, the equilibrium general profit rate, which according to (5)–(7) and (11) is given by $r^* = (1 - Va)u^*$, is also increasing in the profit-sharing coefficient. Now, an issue that remains to be addressed is whether a rise in the profit-sharing coefficient will also lead to an increase in the equilibrium value of the capitalists' rate of profit, which according to (13) is given by $r_c^* = (1 - \lambda)r^*$, and therefore in the equilibrium growth rate, which also according to (13) is given by $g^* = s_c r_c^*$. Formally, we have:

$$\frac{\partial g^*}{\partial \lambda} = s_c \frac{\partial r_c^*}{\partial \lambda} = \frac{s_c(1 - Va)\beta_0\beta_2}{A^2} > 0 \tag{16}$$

Therefore, a rise in the profit-sharing coefficient leads to an increase in the general rate of profit, which is large enough to also make for an increase in both the capitalists' rate of profit and the growth rate. This is so despite the fact that the equilibrium value of the component of the general rate of profit that accrues to workers, $r_w^* = \lambda r^*$, is increasing in the profit-sharing coefficient.

4   Alternative specifications of the desired investment function
While equation (9) makes desired capital accumulation depend on capitalists' rate of profit and the rate of capacity utilization, equation (7) shows that these two arguments are functionally related in a way that might eventually make it more reasonable to have desired investment depending only on the former. Formally, this alternative specification of the desired capital accumulation function is given by:

$$g^d = \beta_0 + \beta_1 r_c \tag{9A}$$

Substituting from (7), (9A) and (10), we can solve for the corresponding equilibrium value of u to obtain:

$$u^* = \frac{\beta_0}{(1 - \lambda)(s_c - \beta_1)(1 - Va)} \tag{17}$$

Assuming again a Keynesian short-run adjustment mechanism stating that capacity utilization will change in proportion to excess demand in the goods market, this equilibrium rate of capacity utilization will be positive and stable provided the denominator of the expression in (17) is positive. By comparing the denominators of the expressions in (11) and (17), it can be seen that the conditions for positivity and stability of the corresponding equilibrium values of u are less stringent when capacity utilization is not a separate argument in the desired investment function. As in the previous specification, meanwhile, an increase in either the real base wage or the profit-sharing coefficient, which again translates into a rise in the share of workers' total compensation in income (as shown by (4)) leads to an increase in capacity utilization, and hence in output and employment. Formally, we have:

$$\partial u^*/\partial V = u_V^* = \frac{a\beta_0}{(1 - \lambda)(s_c - \beta_1)(1 - Va)^2} > 0 \tag{18}$$

and

$$\partial u^*/\partial \lambda = u_\lambda^* = \frac{\beta_0}{(s_c - \beta_1)(1 - Va)(1 - \lambda)^2} > 0 \tag{19}$$

It is now the case, however, that the general profit rate, the capitalists' profit rate and the growth rate cease to depend on the share of total profits in income, and hence on the real base wage, while the capitalists' profit rate and the growth rate cease to depend on the profit-sharing coefficient as well. The corresponding equilibrium expressions can be obtained through substitution from (6)–(7), (10) and (17):

$$g^* = s_c r_c^* = s_c(1 - \lambda)r^* = s_c(1 - \lambda)(1 - Va)u^* = \frac{s_c\beta_0}{s_c - \beta_1} \tag{20}$$

Hence the general profit rate, the capitalists' profit rate and the growth rate become insensitive to changes in distribution resulting from changes in the real base wage, while the latter two become insensitive also to changes in distribution resulting from changes in the profit-sharing coefficient. Meanwhile, the impact of changes in the profit-sharing coefficient on the general profit rate is given by:

$$\partial r^*/\partial \lambda = \frac{\beta_0}{(s_c - \beta_1)(1 - \lambda)^2} > 0 \tag{21}$$

Hence an increase in the profit-sharing coefficient, by raising aggregate effective demand and therefore capacity utilization, while leaving the share of total profits in income unchanged, makes for an increase in the general profit rate. It does so, however, to an extent that leaves the capitalists' profit rate, and hence the growth rate, unchanged. Indeed, with desired investment being determined by (9A), an increase in the general profit rate brought about by an increase in the profit-sharing coefficient will fully translate into an increase in the component of the general rate of profit that accrues to workers. As the latter, according to (5)–(7) and (17), is given by $r_w^* = \lambda r^*$, it follows from (20) that $\partial r_w^*/\partial \lambda$ is also given by (21). Meanwhile, the reason why a change in the real base wage will not have any impact on the general profit rate, which is given by $r^* = \pi u^*$, and hence on the capitalists' profit rate and the growth rate, is that it will lead to a change in capacity utilization that exactly offsets the accompanying change in the share of total profits in income.[5]

Meanwhile, Marglin and Bhaduri (1990) argue that it is theoretically unsound to make investment depend on both capacity utilization and the general rate of profit, because it is not clear that an increase in capacity utilization will induce additional investment when the general profit rate is held constant. This is because if capacity utilization increases while the general profit rate remains constant, it must be the case that the share of total profits in income falls. They claim that to use the rate of profit is therefore tantamount to assuming that a given rate of profit will produce the same level of investment regardless of whether it results from a high rate of capacity utilization and a low profit share, or from a low rate of capacity utilization and a high profit share. Marglin and Bhaduri (1990) then argue for a formulation of desired investment as a function of the profit share, rather than the profit rate, on the grounds that this clearly separates the two influences at work, whereas the rate of profit reflects the dual influences of both the profit share and the rate of capacity utilization.

As intimated earlier, Marglin and Bhaduri (1990) start by assuming that desired investment depends positively on the expected general profit rate, r^e. They then further assume that since the expected general profit rate is positively affected by the same two variables – capacity utilization, u, and the share of total profits in income, π – that determine the general rate of profit, r, desired capital accumulation should be made to depend separately and positively on u and π. In the model developed in this chapter, however, a proportion of profit income accrues to workers through profit sharing, so it is more reasonable to make desired investment depend on the component of the share of total profits which actually accrues to capitalists, given by π_c. A linear version of the corresponding investment function is therefore given by:

$$g^d = \beta_0 + \beta_1\pi_c + \beta_2 u \tag{9B}$$

Substituting from (9A) and (10), we can solve for the equilibrium value of u to obtain:

$$u^* = \frac{\beta_0 + \beta_1\pi_c}{s_c\pi_c - \beta_2} \tag{22}$$

where we have used (5) to express aggregate saving, given by (10), in terms of the capitalists' profit share, π_c. For purposes of algebraic simplicity, the corresponding comparative-static analysis will be performed with respect to the capitalists' profit share, which according to (5) varies negatively with the real base wage *and* the profit-sharing coefficient when the labor–output ratio is given (as we have assumed it to be so far). We assume again a Keynesian short-run adjustment mechanism, where capacity utilization changes in proportion to excess demand in the goods market. This means that the equilibrium capacity utilization given by (22) will be positive and stable provided that aggregate saving is more responsive than desired investment to changes in capacity utilization, which in turn requires that the denominator of the expression in (22) is positive. The impact of a change in the capitalists' profit share on equilibrium capacity utilization is given by:

$$\partial u^*/\partial \pi_c = u^*_{\pi_c} = \frac{-(s_c\beta_0 + \beta_1\beta_2)}{B^2} \tag{23}$$

where B denotes the denominator of the expression in (22). An increase in either the real base wage or the profit-sharing coefficient, by raising workers' total compensation as a proportion of income, will raise consumption demand by more than the accompanying fall in investment spending, with the resulting increase in aggregate demand leading to a rise in capacity utilization, output and employment. However, while a decrease in the capitalists' profit share, by raising capacity utilization, will indirectly exert an upward pressure on the rates of capitalists' profit and growth, it will also exert a direct downward pressure on the same variables. The resulting ambiguous impact of an increase in either the real base wage or the profit-sharing coefficient on the growth rate is described by the formal expressions for the short-run equilibrium growth rate, g^*, and the corresponding partial derivative of this growth rate, which, using (7), (10) and (22), are given by:

$$g^* = s_c r_c^* = s_c \pi_c u^* = \frac{(\beta_0 + \beta_1 \pi_c) s_c \pi_c}{s_c \pi_c - \beta_2} \tag{24}$$

and

$$\partial g^*/\partial \pi_c = g_{\pi_c}^* = s_c (\partial r^*/\partial \pi_c) = \frac{s_c (s_c \beta_1 \pi_c^2 - 2\beta_1 \beta_2 \pi_c - \beta_0 \beta_2)}{B^2} \tag{25}$$

The numerator of the expression in (25) is non-linear in π_c, with $\pi_c^* = \beta_2/s_c$ being the minimum point of this concave-up parabola. Meanwhile, stability of the equilibrium values of capacity utilization and growth requires that $s_c \pi_c > \beta_2$, which in turn requires that $\beta_2 \ll s_c$ along the economically meaningful domain of the capitalists' profit share given by $0 < \pi_c < 1$, so that $0 < \pi_c^* \ll 1$. As the value of the numerator of the expression in (25) is equal to $-s_c \beta_0 \beta_2$ at $\pi_c = 0$, it follows that one of the roots of that parabola is negative, and therefore that $g_{\pi_c}^* < 0$ for sufficiently low levels of the capitalists' profit share given by $0 < \pi_c < \pi_c^*$. Now, since the absolute value of the negative impact of a higher capitalists' profit share on capacity utilization, given by (23), is decreasing in that share, it is intuitive that the possibility that a rise in the capitalists' profit share leads to a rise in both the capitalists' profit rate and the growth rate turns out to be increasing in that share. Indeed, suitable restrictions in the parameters would ensure that the other root of the corresponding concave-up parabola is given by some $\pi_c^* < \pi_c'' < 1$, so that the meaningful subset of the distributive domain would be divided into two regions. More precisely, a rise (fall) in either the real base wage or the profit-sharing coefficient, which makes for a fall (rise) in the capitalists' profit share, leads to a rise in both the capitalists' profit rate and the growth rate when $\pi_c < \pi_c'' (\pi_c > \pi_c'')$. To put it alternatively, as implied by (4) and (5), a rise (fall) in either the real base wage or the profit-sharing coefficient, and hence a rise (fall) in the share of workers' total compensation, leads to a rise in both the capitalists' profit rate and the growth rate when that share is high (low) enough, that is, when $\pi_c < \pi_c'' (\pi_c > \pi_c'')$.

A special case of the specification of the desired rate of capital accumulation in (9B) makes it depend only on the capitalists' profit share, and a linear version of this investment function is given by:

$$g^d = \beta_0 + \beta_1 \pi_c \tag{9C}$$

Substituting from (5), (9C) and (10), we can solve for the corresponding equilibrium value of u to obtain:

$$u^* = \frac{\beta_1}{s_c} + \frac{\beta_0}{s_c(1 - \lambda)(1 - Va)} \tag{26}$$

We assume again a Keynesian short-run adjustment mechanism where capacity utilization changes in proportion to excess demand in the goods market, which implies that the stability of this equilibrium value of capacity utilization is automatically ensured by virtue of desired investment being independent of the level of capacity utilization. As in the previous specification, meanwhile, an increase in either the real base wage or the profit-sharing coefficient, which again translates into a rise in the share of workers' total compensation in income leads to an increase in capacity utilization, and hence in output and employment. The reason is that a rise in the share of workers' total compensation in income raises consumption demand by more than it lowers investment demand, thus leading to a rise in aggregate demand. Formally, we have:

$$\partial u^*/\partial V = u_V^* = \frac{a\beta_0}{s_c(1 - \lambda)(1 - Va)^2} > 0 \tag{27}$$

and

$$\partial u^*/\partial \lambda = u_\lambda^* = \frac{\beta_0}{s_c(1 - Va)(1 - \lambda)^2} > 0 \tag{28}$$

Now, (3)–(6) imply that the general profit rate, $r = \pi u$, is affected by the profit-sharing coefficient only through the impact of the latter on capacity utilization, while it is affected by the real base wage through the impact of the latter both on capacity utilization and on the share of total profit income, $\pi = (1 - Va)$. Therefore, while a rise in the profit-sharing coefficient, by raising capacity utilization, unambiguously raises the general rate of profit as well, a rise in the real base wage may raise capacity utilization to an extent that does not compensate for the accompanying fall in the share of total profits in income. Indeed, this is precisely the case when the desired capital accumulation function is given by (9C), featuring only the capitalists' profit share, as revealed by the corresponding expressions:

$$\partial r^*/\partial V = r_V^* = -\frac{a\beta_1}{s_c} < 0 \tag{29}$$

and

$$\partial r^*/\partial \lambda = r_\lambda^* = \frac{\beta_0}{s_c} > 0 \tag{30}$$

Meanwhile, an increase in either the real base wage (by reducing the general rate of profit) or the profit-sharing coefficient (despite raising the general rate of profit) leads to a fall in both the capitalists' profit rate and the growth rate, as revealed by the corresponding expressions:

$$\partial g^*/\partial V = s_c(\partial r_c^*/\partial V) = -a\beta_1(1 - \lambda) < 0 \tag{31}$$

and

$$\partial g^*/\partial \lambda = s_c(\partial r_c^*/\partial \lambda) = -\beta_1(1 - Va) < 0 \tag{32}$$

5 Workers' positive saving out of shared profits

Let us now extend the model to consider the possibility that workers save a fraction, s_w, of their share of profits, while capitalists still save a fraction, s_c, of the profit income which is not shared with workers. Given the variable nature of the shared profit income (even in the short run), workers are assumed to behave in such a precautious manner when planning consumption out of it. However, we do not impose any a priori restriction on the value of these saving propensities other than that $0 < s_c, s_w < 1$. Using (5)–(7), aggregate saving as a proportion of the capital stock, g^s, is now given by:

$$g^s = \frac{s_c R_c + s_w R_w}{K} = [s_c(1 - \lambda) + s_w\lambda](1 - Va)u \qquad (10A)$$

As the aggregate saving rate applies solely to profit income, it is a weighted average of the functional saving rates, with weights being the shares of profits that accrue to capitalists and workers, respectively. In order to focus on the implications for labor employment of workers saving a fraction of their share of profits, in this section we solve solely for the equilibrium capacity utilization, and again take the labor–output ratio as given. Moreover, we consider only some of the specifications of the desired investment function explored in the preceding sections.

We start by considering the determination of desired investment given by (9), which is close to the most commonly used specification in the post-Keynesian literature associated with the Kalecki–Steindl tradition. Substituting from (7), (9) and (10A), we can solve for the corresponding equilibrium value of u to obtain:

$$u^* = \frac{\beta_0}{[(s_c - \beta_1)(1 - \lambda) + s_w\lambda](1 - Va) - \beta_2} \qquad (33)$$

We assume again a Keynesian short-run adjustment mechanism where capacity utilization varies positively with excess demand in the goods market. This implies that u^* is stable if aggregate saving is more responsive than desired investment to changes in capacity utilization, which in turn requires that the denominator of the expression in (33) is positive. As compared to the equilibrium rate of capacity utilization given by (11) (where workers save nothing) the expression in (33) suggests that capacity utilization, output and hence employment will all be lower. However, and for the very same reason (which is the increase in the aggregate saving rate) the stability condition of the equilibrium capacity utilization rate given by (33) is less stringent. Indeed, $s_c > \beta_1$ is no longer a necessary condition for stability of the equilibrium value of u. All that is now required is that the term in brackets in the denominator of (33) be positive. Moreover, this new condition ensures that capacity utilization, output and labor employment again vary positively with the real base wage, as revealed by the corresponding formal expression:

$$\partial u^*/\partial V = u_V^* = \frac{a\beta_0[(s_c - \beta_1)(1 - \lambda) + s_w\lambda]}{C^2} > 0 \qquad (34)$$

where C denotes the denominator of the expression in (33). The impact of a change in the profit-sharing coefficient on capacity utilization is, however, ambiguous:

$$\partial u^*/\partial \lambda = u_\lambda^* = \frac{\beta_0(s_c - s_w - \beta_1)(1 - Va)}{C^2} \qquad (35)$$

Hence an increase in the profit-sharing coefficient, which translates into a rise in the share of workers' total compensation in income by redistributing the same share of *total* profits in income towards workers, reduces capacity utilization when $s_c - s_w < \beta_1$. Note that this condition is immediately satisfied when capitalists and workers share the same saving propensity, $s_c = s_w = s$.[6] In this case, an increase in the profit-sharing coefficient will leave consumption demand unchanged, while it will lower investment demand by reducing capitalists' rate of profit, which will reduce capacity utilization and employment. Moreover, the same qualitative result is obtained when $s_c < s_w$.[7] In this case, a rise in the profit-sharing coefficient, by translating into a rise in the share of workers' total compensation in income, will reduce both consumption demand and investment expenditure, and hence capacity utilization and employment. Meanwhile, note that $s_c > s_w$, a possibility that is also compatible with the stability of the equilibrium capacity utilization rate, is not a sufficient condition for a rise in the profit-sharing coefficient to raise capacity utilization. The reason is that $s_c > s_w$ implies only that a rise in the profit-sharing coefficient will make for a rise in consumption demand, while an ultimate rise in aggregate demand (which will lead to a rise in capacity utilization) requires that this rise in consumption is large enough. Capacity utilization and employment vary positively with the profit-sharing coefficient, therefore, when $s_c - s_w > \beta_1$.[8]

Another specification of the desired investment function for which positive saving by workers has implications that are worth exploring is (9C), where capitalists' profit share is the only argument. Substituting from (5), (9C) and (10A), we obtain the equilibrium capacity utilization rate:

$$u^* = \frac{\beta_0 + \beta_1(1 - \lambda)(1 - Va)}{[s_c(1 - \lambda) - s_w\lambda](1 - Va)} \tag{36}$$

Since we assume again a short-run adjustment mechanism stating that capacity utilization varies positively with excess demand in the goods market, the stability of u^* is automatically ensured by virtue of desired investment being independent of capacity utilization. Note that equilibrium capacity utilization and employment again vary positively with the real base wage, as the resulting rise in the share of workers' total compensation raises consumption demand by more than it lowers investment demand. Formally, we have:

$$\partial u^*/\partial V = u_V^* = \frac{a\beta_0}{[s_c(1 - \lambda) + s_w\lambda)](1 - Va)^2} > 0 \tag{37}$$

Meanwhile, the impact of a change in the profit-sharing coefficient on capacity utilization and employment is again ambiguous:

$$\partial u^*/\partial \lambda = u_\lambda^* = \frac{\beta_0(s_c - s_w)\pi - \beta_1 s_w\pi^2}{D^2} \tag{38}$$

where D denotes the denominator of the expression in (36). An increase in the profit-sharing coefficient unambiguously reduces equilibrium capacity utilization and employment when $s_c \leq s_w$. When $s_c = s_w$ ($s_c < s_w$), an increase in the profit-sharing coefficient will make for an unchanged (a lower) level of consumption demand, while it will lower investment demand by reducing the capitalists' profit share. But note that $s_c > s_w$ is not a sufficient condition for a rise in the profit-sharing coefficient to raise equilibrium capacity utilization and employment, since the numerator of the expression in (38) is non-linear in π, the share of total profits in income. As the two roots of this concave-down parabola are $\pi' = 0$ and $\pi'' = \beta_0(s_c - s_w)/\beta_1 s_w$, the numerator of the above expression is unambiguously positive, and hence capacity utilization and employment vary positively with the profit-sharing coefficient, at least in some part of the economically meaningful domain given by $0 < \pi < 1$. In fact, $\pi'' \geq 1$, and therefore $u^*_\lambda > 0$ throughout $0 < \pi < 1$, when $(s_c/s_w) \geq (\beta_0 + \beta_1)/\beta_0$. It is intuitive that, given the autonomous component of investment, β_0, the extent to which s_c has to be greater than s_w to ensure $u^*_\lambda > 0$ throughout $0 < \pi < 1$, varies positively with β_1. This is because $s_c > s_w$ implies that a rise in the profit-sharing coefficient, by leading to a redistribution of profits from capitalists to workers, will make for a rise in consumption demand, while the resulting fall in the capitalists' profit share will lead to a fall in investment. Now, (9C) shows that the investment effect is given by $\partial g^d/\partial \lambda = -\beta_1\pi$, while the consumption effect is given by $\partial g^s/\partial \lambda = (s_w - s_c)\pi u$. This implies that, given the parameters of the investment function and the savings rate differential, the resulting impact of a rise in the profit-sharing coefficient on aggregate demand depends on the levels of the share of total profits in income, π, and capacity utilization. If $\pi'' < 1$, therefore, a rise in the profit-sharing coefficient will raise (lower) capacity utilization and labor employment for levels of the share of total profits in income given by $\pi < \pi'' (\pi > \pi'')$.

6   Short-run equilibrium with variable productivity

As a final extension, let us consider the possibility that labor productivity varies positively with the profit-sharing coefficient in the short run. As this alternative assumption will not affect any of the previous qualititative results related to changes in the real base wage, we confine attention to the impact of changes in the profit-sharing coefficient on the equilibrium rate of capacity utilization and employment. Formally, we consider the possibility of localized technical change defined by $a = a(\lambda)$, with $a(0) > 0$ and $a'(\lambda) = -\delta$. As it turns out, the share of workers' total compensation, given by (4), will no longer necessarily vary positively with the profit-sharing coefficient:

$$\partial\sigma/\partial\lambda = \sigma_\lambda = (1 - Va) - \delta V(1 - \lambda) \tag{39}$$

which is ambiguous in sign. The intuition is that while an increase in the profit-sharing coefficient, by reducing the labour–output ratio, raises both the share of total profits and the fraction of this share which accrues to workers, and therefore raises the surplus wage share, it also reduces the base wage share.

Assuming for simplicity that $s_w = 0$, let us start by considering the desired capital accumulation function given by (9), featuring the capitalists' rate of profit and capacity utilization, which gives rise to the equilibrium capacity utilization rate given by (11). The impact of a rise in the profit-sharing coefficient on equilibrium capacity utilization is now given by:

$$\partial u^*/\partial\lambda = u^*_\lambda = \frac{\beta_0(s_c - \beta_1)[(1 - Va) - \delta V(1 - \lambda)]}{A^2} \tag{40}$$

which is ambiguous in sign. Since $s_c > \beta_1$ is a necessary condition for the stability of u^*, it follows that u^*_λ and σ_λ share the very same sources of sign ambiguity, as revealed by comparison of (39) and (40). In line with the intuition behind (15), a rise in the profit-sharing coefficient leads to a rise (fall) in capacity utilization if it makes for a rise (fall) in the share of workers' total compensation in income. In fact, the very same sign ambiguity arises when any of the other desired investment functions are considered. Formally, we have:

$$\partial u^{*}/\partial \lambda = u_{\lambda}^{*} = \frac{\beta_0 [(1 - Va) - \delta V(1 - \lambda)]}{(s_c - \beta_1)[(1 - Va)(1 - \lambda)]^2} \tag{41}$$

and

$$\partial u^{*}/\partial \lambda = u_{\lambda}^{*} = \frac{(s_c \beta_0 + \beta_1 \beta_2)[(1 - Va) - \delta V(1 - \lambda)]}{B^2} \tag{42}$$

and

$$\partial u^{*}/\partial \lambda = u_{\lambda}^{*} = \frac{\beta_0 [(1 - Va) - \delta V(1 - \lambda)]}{s_c [(1 - Va)(1 - \lambda)]^2} \tag{43}$$

with these expressions corresponding to the desired investment functions given by (9A), (9B) and (9C), respectively.

As labor productivity now varies positively with the profit-sharing coefficient, the impact of a change in the latter on equilibrium employment becomes ambiguous. Using (1), and normalizing the capital stock to one to economize on notation, we can express the equilibrium level of employment as $L^* = au^*$. Since the impact of a change in the profit-sharing coefficient on equilibrium employment is given by $\partial L^*/\partial \lambda = L_{\lambda}^* = au_{\lambda}^* - \delta u^*$, it follows that $u_{\lambda}^* < 0$ will make for $L_{\lambda}^* < 0$. Hence a necessary condition for a rise in the profit-sharing coefficient to lead to a rise in equilibrium employment is that $u_{\lambda}^* > 0$, which (going back to (40)–(43)) in turn requires that $(1 - Va) > \delta V(1 - \lambda)$.

7   Concluding remarks

This chapter has developed several specifications of a post-Keynesian macromodel in order to investigate the impact of profit sharing on capacity utilization, employment and growth. It was found that the way in which a change in the profit-sharing coefficient affects output and employment depends not only on the specification of aggregate (consumption and investment) demand, but also on the accompanying impact on labor productivity. As a comparative static framework is used throughout, a natural line of extension would be to incorporate dynamic forces, thus addressing some major issues from which this chapter has abstracted. For instance, the profit-sharing coefficient, and eventually the sharing mechanism itself, is likely to change endogenously over time. Another issue that is left for future research is the impact of profit sharing on conflicting-claims inflation – which may interact with the determination of equilibrium capacity utilization and growth (see, for example, Lavoie, 2002; Cassetti, 2002).

Notes

*   I am grateful to Mark Setterfield for his extensive and quite useful comments on an earlier version of this chapter. Any remaining errors are my own, though.
1. Profit-sharing arrangements vary considerably, and some major ways in which they differ concern what is shared (e.g. total profits or profits above a certain target), how and when compensation is made (e.g. in cash or company stocks, in a deferred or non-deferred way) and to whom compensation is paid (e.g. directly to workers or to some workers' retirement plan). Mitchell et al. (1990) provide a detailed history of thinking on and experience with profit sharing (which traces its roots back to the nineteenth century) and other alternative pay systems.
2. Two reasons offered in the literature for the productivity-enhancing effect of profit sharing are its inducement of higher worker effort levels and its reduction of labor turnover, which stimulates firm-specific investment in human capital.
3. Alternatively, following Kalecki (1935) and Robinson (1962), we could assume that it is the expected profit

rate that matters for desired investment, so that (9) would feature the expected capitalists' rate of profit, r_c^e, instead. Hence the specification in (9) can be taken as making the implicit assumption (often made by Kalecki and Robinson themselves) of static profit expectations, $r^e = r$, so that $r_c^e = r_c$. Another alternative would be to follow the claim made by Marglin and Bhaduri (1990) that, since profit expectations given by r^e are positively affected by the two variables – capacity utilization, u, and the share of total profits in income, π – which determine the general rate of profit, r, desired capital accumulation should be made to depend separately and positively on u and π. We explore this alternative later in the chapter. A further alternative to these assumptions, following Lima (2009), would be to assume that because expected capacity utilization (which depends on the expected demand) depends on the expected distribution of income, the expected general profit rate is ultimately – and conceivably non-linearly – determined by expected distribution. However, this alternative is not explored in this chapter.

4. Nonetheless, we extend the model subsequently to consider the possibility that the labor–output ratio varies negatively with the profit-sharing coefficient, in line with the empirical literature briefly reviewed in the introduction.
5. Another special case of the desired accumulation function in (9) involves accumulation depending solely on capacity utilization. Though the implications of this alternative specification are not explored here, it can be shown that they include capacity utilization (and hence output and employment) and the rates of general profit, capitalists' profit and growth all varying positively with both the real base wage and the profit-sharing coefficient.
6. It can be verified that a necessary condition for stability of the equilibrium rate of capacity utilization in this case is $s > (1 - \lambda)\beta_1$.
7. It can be shown that this possibility need not compromise the necessary condition for the stability of the equilibrium capacity utilization rate in (33), as long as s_c or λ is high enough or β_1 is low enough.
8. It can be verified that this is also the condition for capacity utilization and employment to vary positively with the profit-sharing coefficient when desired capital accumulation depends solely on the capitalists' profit rate, as in (9A). As the corresponding expression for u^* will be a special case of (33) with $\beta_2 = 0$, and hence will imply a lower u^* since the accelerator effect has been removed from the investment function, the comparative-statics with respect to both the real base wage and the profit-sharing coefficient will have the same signs as those given by (34) and (35), respectively.

References

Azfar, O. and S. Danninger (2001), "Profit sharing, employment stability, and wage growth", *Industrial and Labour Relations Review*, **54**(3), 619–30.

Bhargava, S. (1994), "Profit sharing and the financial performance of companies: evidence from U.K. panel data", *Economic Journal*, **104**(426), 1044–56.

Cahuc, Pierre and B. Dormont (1997), "Profit-sharing: does it increase productivity and employment? A theoretical model and empirical evidence on French micro data", *Labour Economics*, **4**, 293–319.

Cassetti, M. (2002), "Conflict, inflation, distribution and terms of trade in the Kaleckian model", in M. Setterfield (ed.), *The Economics of Demand-Led Growth*, Cheltenham, UK and Northampton, MA, USA: Edward Elgar.

Conyon, Martin J. and R. Freeman (2004), "Shared modes of compensation and firm performance: U.K. evidence", in Richard Blundell, David Card and Richard Freeman (eds), *Seeking a Premier League Economy: The Economic Effects of British Economic Reforms, 1980–2000*, Chicago: University of Chicago Press.

D'Art, Daryl and T. Turner (2004), "Profit sharing, firm performance and union influence in selected European countries", *Personnel Review*, **33**(3), 335–50.

Davidson, P. (1986–87), "The simple macroeconomics of a nonergodic monetary economy vs a share economy: is Weitzman's macroeconomics too simple?", *Journal of Post Keynesian Economics*, **9**(2), 212–25.

Dutt, A.K. (1984), "Stagnation, income distribution and monopoly power", *Cambridge Journal of Economics*, **8**(1), 25–40.

Dutt, A.K. (1990), *Growth, Distribution and Uneven Development*, Cambridge: Cambridge University Press.

Estrin, S., V. Pérotin, A. Robinson and N. Wilson (1997), "Profit-sharing in OECD countries: a review and some evidence", *Business Strategy Review*, **8**(4), 27–32.

Kaldor, N. (1956), "Alternative theories of distribution", *Review of Economic Studies*, **23**(2), 83–100.

Kalecki, M. (1935), "A macrodynamic theory of the business cycle", *Econometrica*, **3**(3), 327–44.

Kalecki, M. (1971), *Selected Essays on the Dynamics of the Capitalist Economy*, Cambridge: Cambridge University Press.

Kraft, K. and M. Ugarkovic (2006), "Profit sharing and the financial performance of firms: evidence from Germany", *Economics Letters*, **92**, 333–8.

Lavoie, M. (2002), "The Kaleckian growth model with target return pricing and conflict inflation", in M.

Setterfield (ed.), *The Economics of Demand-Led Growth*, Cheltenham, UK and Northampton, MA, USA: Edward Elgar.

Lima, G.T. (2009), "Functional distribution, capital accumulation and growth in a non-linear macrodynamic model", *Journal of Income Distribution*, **18**(1), 3–19.

Marglin, S.A. and A. Bhaduri (1990), "Profit squeeze and Keynesian theory", in Stephen A. Marglin and Juliet B. Schor (eds), *The Golden Age of Capitalism*, Oxford: Clarendon Press, pp. 153–86.

Mitchell, Daniel J.B., David Lewin and Edward E. Lawler (1990), "Alternative pay systems, firm performance, and productivity", in Alan S. Blinder (ed.), *Paying for Productivity*, Washington, DC: Brookings Institution, pp. 15–88.

Pasinetti, L. (1962), "The rate of profit and income distribution in relation to the rate of economic growth", *Review of Economic Studies*, **29**(4), 267–79.

Robinson, Joan (1962), *Essays in the Theory of Economic Growth*, London: Macmillan.

Rothschild, K.W. (1986–87), "Is there a Weitzman miracle?", *Journal of Post Keynesian Economics*, **9**(2), 198–211.

Rowthorn, B. (1981), "Demand, real wages and economic growth", in *Thames Papers in Political Economy*, London: Thames Polytechnic, pp. 1–39.

Steindl, J. (1952), *Maturity and Stagnation in American Capitalism*, New York: Monthly Review Press.

Weitzman, M.L. (1983), "Some alternative implications of alternative compensation systems", *Economic Journal*, **93**, 763–83.

Weitzman, M.L. (1984), *The Share Economy*, Cambridge, MA: Harvard University Press.

Weitzman, M.L. (1985), "The simple macroeconomics of profit sharing", *American Economic Review*, **95**, 937–53.

Weitzman, M.L. and D. Kruse (1990), "Profit sharing and productivity", in Alan S. Blinder (ed.), *Paying for Productivity*, Washington, DC: Brookings Institution, pp. 95–140.

18 Gender equality and the sustainability of steady state growth paths
Stephanie Seguino and Mark Setterfield

1 Introduction

The basic concern that motivates this chapter is the potential trade-off between gender wage equality and economic growth in developing countries. While some evidence suggests that gender equality may enhance long-run growth prospects (e.g. Hill and King, 1995; Tzannatos, 1999; Klasen, 2002; Knowles et al., 2002), in the short run, higher female wages can be contractionary (Blecker and Seguino, 2002; Seguino, 2000a, 2000b). And yet ideally, we would like to observe both more equality and more growth in developing economies. But if more of the former in fact causes less of the latter, then clearly this can become an obstacle to advocating for increased gender wage equality on the grounds of other criteria, such as equity (see Seguino, 2010 for further discussion).

This chapter draws attention to a possible solution to this dilemma. It shows that, if we begin with a sufficiently high rate of growth (relative to potential),[1] then even if increasing gender wage equality *does* reduce growth, this can be an unequivocally good thing if the growth rate is thus made more *sustainable* in the long run, in the sense that potential and real output grow at the same rate. In other words, we can find ourselves in a "win–win" situation where increasing gender wage equality results in increased *sustainability* of the growth rate, making it easier to advocate for increased equality as an end in itself.

The remainder of the chapter is organized as follows. The next two sections construct developing country models of balance of payments equilibrium growth, technical progress, and potential output. They incorporate salient features of gender differences in household behavior and labor market outcomes. The subsequent section demonstrates how gender equality can be used as an adjustment mechanism to achieve sustainable long-run growth, while the penultimate section addresses political economic concerns associated with reducing male relative economic power. The final section concludes with some observations on the contributions of this modeling exercise to current debates in the gender and macroeconomics literature.

2 A balance of payments constrained growth model for developing countries

The analysis in this section develops a model of balance of payments constrained growth (BPCG) that is modified from the form originally described by Thirlwall (1978, 1979) to allow for certain features of production, pricing and import demand that are specific to developing economies. We begin by specifying export, import and pricing equations as follows:

$$X = A\left(\frac{EP_f}{P}\right)^{\psi} Y_w^{\varepsilon} \tag{1}$$

$$M = B\left(\frac{P}{EP_f}\right)^{\eta}\left(\frac{W_M}{W_F}\right)^{\theta} Y^{\sigma} \tag{2}$$

$$P = (1 + \tau)\frac{W_F N_F}{Y_F} \tag{3}$$

where X denotes total exports (in real terms), A and B are positive constants, E is the nominal exchange rate (specifically, the price in domestic currency of one unit of foreign currency), P_f and P are the price of foreign and domestically produced tradables, respectively, Y_w denotes world income (in real terms), ψ is the (foreign) price elasticity of demand for exports, ε is the (foreign) income elasticity of demand, η is the price elasticity of imports, θ is the elasticity of imports with respect to the gender distribution of income, and σ is the income elasticity of import demand. M is total imports (in real terms), W_M and W_F are male and female nominal wages, respectively, Y is domestic (real) income, N_F denotes total employment in the tradable sector and Y_F is the real output of the tradable sector.

The export and import demand functions in equations (1) and (2) respectively differ from their canonical form in BPCG theory in just one key respect: the inclusion of a direct effect of relative nominal wages (W_M/W_F) on imports in equation (2). The inclusion of this term is explained by: (i) the "consumption effect" found in semi-industrialized economies (SIEs), according to which men spend proportionally more of their income on luxury goods that are more likely to be imported, so that a redistribution of wage income towards men will boost imports (Seguino, 2010);[2,3] and (ii) the "production effect" found in low-income agriculturally dependent economies (LIAEs), as a result of which increasing women's bargaining power in the household (proxied by a rise in women's relative wages), allows women to augment the time they devote to production of their own (import substituting) subsistence crops (Darity, 1995; Udry et al., 1995; Blackden and Bhanu, 1999; Quisumbing, 2005).

Equation (3), meanwhile, is a simplified version of the pricing equation for domestically produced tradables found in Blecker and Seguino (2002, p. 104). Equation (3) assumes for simplicity that export industries rely exclusively on female labour (i.e. that men are employed only in the production of non-tradables),[4] and that intermediate goods do not feature in the calculation of unit prime cost to which the mark-up is applied in the determination of prices. Inspection of equations (1) and (3) reveals an indirect relationship between female wages and exports because of a "cost effect": increasing female wages will increase the cost and hence (assuming the mark-up is fixed) the price of domestically produced tradables, thus lowering exports.[5] Note that we deliberately overlook the possibility of a strong efficiency wage effect here, as a result of which an increase in female wages leads to a more-than-proportional increase in the efficiency of female labor, so that unit labor costs (and hence the price of tradables) ultimately *decline*.[6] This is because the resulting stimulus to exports provided by such an efficiency wage effect will ultimately boost growth in the model derived from equations (1)–(3) below. This, in turn, would make it "too easy" to advocate for reduced gender wage inequality, because, by creating a direct relationship between equality and the equilibrium rate of growth, it would mean that any reduction in gender wage inequality is necessarily *also* conducive to increasing the equilibrium rate of growth.[7]

As the preceding discussion suggests, our model appeals to features of both SIEs and LIAEs. The results that follow, then, can be thought of as applying to a less developed region (LDR) comprising both SIEs and LIAEs, rather than to a single less developed country (LDC) (which presumably can be either an SIE or a LIAE, but not both).

Using lower case letters to denote the proportional rates of growth of variables, it follows from (1)–(3) that:

$$x = \psi(e + p_f - p) + \varepsilon y_w \tag{4}$$

$$m = \eta(p - e - p_f) + \theta(w_M - w_F) + \sigma y \tag{5}$$

$$p = w_F - q \tag{6}$$

where q denotes the rate of growth of labour productivity and (in the formulation of equation (6)) we assume for simplicity that $q_F = q_M = q$.[8] Substituting equation (6) into equations (4) and (5), we arrive at:

$$x = -\psi w_F + \psi(q + e + p_f) + \varepsilon y_w \tag{7}$$

$$m = (\eta - \theta)w_F - \eta(q + e + p_f) + \theta w_M + \sigma y \tag{8}$$

These equations help to isolate the impact of male and female nominal wage growth on export and import growth. Hence note that:

$$\frac{\partial x}{\partial w_F} = -\psi < 0$$

$$\frac{\partial m}{\partial w_F} = (\eta - \theta)$$

$$\frac{\partial m}{\partial w_M} = \theta > 0$$

The first of these partial derivatives reflects the cost effect discussed earlier, while the third reflects the workings of the consumption and production effects. The second partial derivative – the sign of which is ambiguous – depends on all three effects. If $\eta > \theta$, the cost effect dominates and increasing female wage growth will raise the growth of imports. But if $\eta < \theta$, increasing female wage growth will *reduce* the growth of imports, as the consumption and production effects dominate the cost effect.

Our BPCG model is completed by introducing the familiar balance of payments constraint:

$$XP = EP_f M$$

which states that the value of exports must equal the value of imports. It follows from this equality that:

$$x + p = m + e + p_f \tag{9}$$

When combined with equation (6), this last expression yields:

$$x + w_F = m + (q + e + p_f) \tag{10}$$

Finally, substituting equations (7) and (8) into (10) and solving for y yields:

$$y = \frac{(\eta + \psi - 1)(q + e + p_f) - (\eta + \psi - 1 - \theta)w_F - \theta w_M + \varepsilon y_w}{\sigma} \tag{11}$$

where we assume that $\eta + \psi > 1$ – that is, that the Marshall–Lerner conditions hold.[9] Equation (11) is the balance of payments constrained equilibrium growth rate.

Two interesting comparative static results follow from (11). First:

$$\frac{\partial y}{\partial w_M} = -\frac{\theta}{\sigma} < 0$$

This tells us that raising the rate of growth of male wages *ceteris paribus* will unambiguously reduce the rate of growth, because of the consumption and production effects. Note, however, that:

$$\frac{\partial y}{\partial w_F} = -\frac{(\eta + \psi - 1 - \theta)}{\sigma}$$

The sign of this second partial derivative is ambiguous. If $\eta + \psi - 1 > \theta$, then the cost effect dominates the consumption and production effects, and *ceteris paribus*, raising the rate of growth of female wages will cause the rate of growth to decline. But if $\eta + \psi - 1 < \theta$, then the cost effect is dominated by the consumption and production effects. In this case, raising the rate of growth of female wages (*ceteris paribus*) will cause the rate of growth to *increase*.[10] These results point to an important conclusion regarding gender equality and economic growth in the BPCG framework developed thus far: it is always possible to reconcile faster growth with increased gender wage equality as long as the latter is achieved by depressing the rate of growth of male wages (which will raise y) rather than increasing the rate of growth of female wages (which will have an ambiguous effect on y).[11] However, we are not convinced that reducing the rate of growth of male wages is the best strategy for reducing gender wage inequality. This is because, given the foreign rate of inflation and the exchange rate, a reduction in the rate of growth of male wages will depress the rate of growth of the male consumer real wage – possibly to the point that the *level* of the male consumer real wage will fall. And this sequence of events poses three potential problems. First, it may give rise to real wage resistance on the part of males, which may negate the efforts to reduce male wage growth (and hence gender wage inequality) in the first place. Second, if this real wage resistance does not occur, the result may be increased gender conflict (especially if men's standards of living fall in absolute terms), from which women will suffer.[12] Finally, even if neither real wage resistance nor increased gender conflict materialize, we would prefer to enhance gender equality without reducing the rate of growth (much less the level) of real income for men, bearing in mind the relatively low levels of per capita real income earned by *all* workers in LDRs and the desire to enhance these incomes over time.

3   Technical progress and the potential rate of growth

In this section, we extend the growth model developed in the previous section by adding descriptions of technical progress, the potential (Harrodian natural) rate of growth, and the relationship between the actual and potential rate of growth. These are as follows:[13]

$$q = \beta + \gamma y \tag{12}$$

$$y_p = q + l \tag{13}$$

$$y = y_p \tag{14}$$

where y_p is the potential or natural rate of growth, l is the (assumed given) rate of growth of the labor force and all other variables are as previously defined. Equation (12) is the Verdoorn Law, describing technical progress as a function of the actual rate of growth (because of dynamic increasing returns – the Smith–Young–Kaldor dictum that "the division of labor depends on the extent of the market") and the parameter β. The latter can be understood as capturing influences on productivity other than the actual rate of growth – including variables that measure female relative economic status at the household level. Gender equality's impact on long-run productivity growth occurs via several channels. As women's control over economic resources rises, their bargaining power in the household increases. That power, in turn, has been found to have a positive impact on the share of household expenditures on children's health, nutrition and education, improving the quality of the labor supply in the long run (Haddad et al., 1997). Greater gender equality in education also raises productivity as a result of allocative efficiency. Hence increased educational investments in females reduces selection distortion, by reducing investments in males with lower aptitudes. Finally, note that technical progress in equation (12) is Harrod neutral, which is consistent with the assumption that production is characterized by a fixed capital–output ratio, v.

Equation (13), meanwhile, describes the potential rate of growth as the sum of the rates of growth of productivity and of the labour force. This follows from the identity:

$$Y_p \equiv \frac{Y_p}{N^{FE}} \frac{N^{FE}}{L} \frac{L}{POP} POP$$

where Y_p denotes the maximum level of output that can be produced at full employment (N^{FE}),[14] L is the total labor force, POP denotes population, and it is assumed that both the full employment rate of employment (N^{FE}/L) and the labor force participation rate (L/POP) are constant so that $\hat{POP} = l$.[15,16] Finally, equation (14) is the "golden rule" for sustainable steady state growth. This golden rule is derived from the following measure of capacity utilization:

$$u = \frac{Y}{Y_p}$$

from which it follows that:

$$\dot{u} = u(y - y_p)$$

It can now be seen that the golden rule in (14) will result in $\dot{u}/u = 0$. This is the only plausible steady state rate of growth of u, since u is bounded above and below and thus cannot expand or contract indefinitely at a constant rate.

The first thing to note is that our introduction of the technical progress function in equation (12) modifies the BPCG equilibrium growth rate derived in the previous section (equation (11)). Hence combining equations (7), (8), (10) and (12) yields:

$$y = \frac{\mu(\beta + e + p_f) - (\mu - \theta)w_F - \theta w_M + \varepsilon y_w}{\sigma - \mu\gamma} \tag{15}$$

where $\mu = (\eta + \psi - 1) > 0$ is the Marshall–Lerner condition. Note that it follows from (15) that:

$$\frac{\partial y}{\partial w_M} = -\frac{\theta}{\sigma - \mu\gamma}$$

and:

$$\frac{\partial y}{\partial w_F} = -\frac{\mu - \theta}{\sigma - \mu\gamma}$$

In other words (and assuming that $\sigma > \mu\gamma$) introducing equation (12) into the solution for the BPCG equilibrium growth rate affects the *size* but not the *sign* of the key comparative static results relating to gender wage inequality derived in the previous section.[17] However, the introduction of equations (12)–(14) has a second and more serious impact on our BPCG model: the model is now over-determined. Hence note that, in addition to equation (15), we can also solve equations (12)–(14) to derive a *second* expression for the equilibrium rate of growth:

$$y = \frac{\beta + l}{1 - \gamma} \tag{16}$$

This means that the BPCG equilibrium growth rate (given by equation (15)) and the equilibrium rate of growth that satisfies the golden rule (given by equation (16)) will only be equal if:

$$\frac{\mu(\beta + e + p_f) - (\mu - \theta)w_F - \theta w_M + \varepsilon y_W}{\sigma - \mu\gamma} = \frac{\beta + l}{1 - \gamma} \tag{17}$$

It is possible, but highly unlikely, that this condition will be satisfied. Figure 18.1 – in which y_B denotes the BPCG equilibrium growth rate corresponding to the particular rate of growth of world income, $\bar{y}_w$, and:

$$\Omega = \frac{\mu(\beta + e + p_f) - (\mu - \theta)w_F - \theta w_M}{\sigma - \mu\gamma}$$

– illustrates an initial situation in which the condition in (17) is *not* met.

4 Gender wage equality to the rescue?
Palley (2002) and Setterfield (2006) specify a variety of adjustment mechanisms capable of solving the problem identified in the previous section by ensuring that either y and/

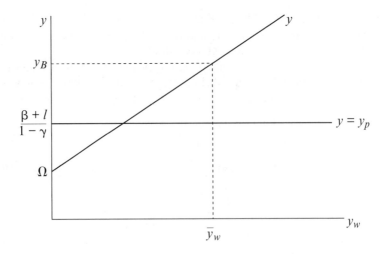

Figure 18.1 *Violating the golden rule: example of an unsustainable BPCG equilibrium growth rate*

or y_p adjusts in response to $y \neq y_p$ until the condition in (17) is satisfied. The point of this section is to propose a new adjustment mechanism that, if operative, is capable of achieving the same end, but this time in a manner that *also* involves an increase in gender wage equality.

The mechanism in question operates in the labor market. To begin with, suppose that:

$$w_F = w_F(u), \, w_F' > 0 \tag{18}$$

and

$$\dot{w}_M = \varphi(w_F - w_M), \, \varphi < 1 \tag{19}$$

According to equation (18), the rate of growth of female wages is increasing in u, our measure of capacity utilization. Recall that:

$$u = \frac{Y}{Y_p}$$

so that:

$$\dot{u} = u(y - y_p)$$

So u rises whenever $y > y_p$. Given equation (13) and the fact that:

$$y \equiv q + n$$

where n denotes the rate of growth of employment, it follows that:

$$y > y_p$$
$$\Rightarrow q + n > q + l$$
$$\Rightarrow n > l$$

which, in turn, implies that the rate of employment (N/L) is rising. In other words, equation (18) simply says that female wage growth increases as the labor market tightens – as in a traditional wage inflation Phillips curve.

Meanwhile, equation (19) suggests that the rate of growth of male wages will increase by some fraction, φ, of any difference between female and male wage growth. The idea behind equations (18) and (19) is that a tightening of the labor market will *first* lead to an increase in female wage growth (equation (18)), *followed* by an (eventually) commensurate increase in male wage growth (equation (19)) – so women are the "wage leaders" and men the "wage followers" in the labor market. For the transitory period during which $w_F > w_M$, $W_R = W_M/W_F$ will fall and hence ω_F – the female wage share – will rise (as demonstrated earlier). But as soon as the equality of w_M and w_F is restored by equation (19) and steady state conditions (with $\dot{w}_M = 0$) are regained, relative wages and the female wage share will cease to change.[18] In short, the dynamics of equations (18) and (19) ensure that whenever $y > y_p$ so that $\dot{u} > 0$ and the labor market tightens, there will be a general increase in wage growth (male and female) consistent with a once-over but permanent compression of male–female relative wages and hence a once-over but permanent increase in women's share of wage income.[19]

It is important to note at this point that we are not necessarily suggesting that equations (18) and (19) are *already* features of most LDRs. Instead, our analysis in this section is designed to identify a mechanism in the labour market which, *if operative*, will resolve the problem of reconciling the actual and potential rates of growth identified in section 3, and in a manner that involves an increase in gender wage equality. To the extent that this mechanism is not already operative the obvious question that arises is: what policy interventions could we entertain that would instate equations (18) and (19) and thus *make* the mechanism operative? We will return to discuss this question in greater detail in section 5 below.

In the meantime, we are now in a position to demonstrate the significance of augmenting our growth model with equations (18) and (19). Consider once again the outcome depicted in Figure 18.1, where the condition in (17) is clearly not satisfied. The equilibrium rate of growth y_B is not sustainable since, with $y = y_B > (\beta + l)/(1 - \gamma) = y_p$, we will observe $\dot{u}/u > 0$ which, as discussed earlier, is not feasible as a steady state outcome. But now consider what will happen to growth as a result of equations (18) and (19). Recall that:

$$\dot{u} = u(y - y_p)$$

so that in response to the situation in Figure 18.1, both female and (subsequently) male wage growth will increase in equations (18) and (19). Now note that:[20]

$$\frac{d\Omega}{dw_F} = \frac{\partial\Omega}{\partial w_F} + \frac{\partial\Omega}{\partial w_M}\frac{dw_M}{dw_F} = \frac{-(\mu - \theta)}{\sigma - \mu\gamma} + \frac{-\theta}{\sigma - \mu\gamma}$$

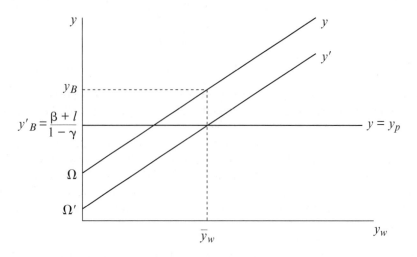

*Figure 18.2   Narrowing the gender gap with demand-side adjustment to a sustainable
BPCG equilibrium growth rate*

$$\Rightarrow \frac{d\Omega}{dw_F} = -\frac{\mu}{\sigma - \mu\gamma}$$

Notice that, regardless of whether or not the cost effect outweighs the consumption and production effects – that is, regardless of the sign of $\partial\Omega/\partial w_F$ – the total impact on growth of an increase in the rate of growth of female wages (as captured by $d\Omega/dw_F$ above) is now unambiguously negative. In other words, thanks to the operation of equations (18) and (19), the problem of $y > y_p$ illustrated in Figure 18.1 is self-correcting. Whenever the actual (BPCG equilibrium) rate of growth is greater than the potential rate of growth, the labor market will tighten, resulting in an increase in the rates of growth of female and (with a lag) male wages. These latter outcomes will have two effects. First, there will be a once-over reduction in gender wage inequality, as the temporarily faster rate of growth of female wages relative to male wages reduces $W_R = W_M/W_F$ and thus increases the female wage share. Second, there will be a reduction in the actual rate of growth, as a result of the increase in the rates of growth of both female *and* male wages. This, in turn, will reduce the (unsustainable) gap between the actual and potential rates of growth.

   The various processes outlined above (tightening of the labor market, falling gender wage inequality and a falling rate of growth) that unfold in response to $y > y_p$ will continue until the gap between the actual (BPCG equilibrium) and potential rate of growth is eliminated. At this point, the condition for sustainable steady state growth in equation (17) will be realized, and the associated BPCG equilibrium growth rate – now equal to the natural rate of growth – will be a sustainable long-run equilibrium growth rate. This situation is illustrated in Figure 18.2, where Ω' corresponds to the rates of growth of female and male wages associated with the steady state value of u, and y'_B denotes the BPCG equilibrium growth rate that now corresponds to the particular rate of growth of world income, $\bar{y}_w$.[21]

   However, Ω is not the only parameter of our model that may be affected by the

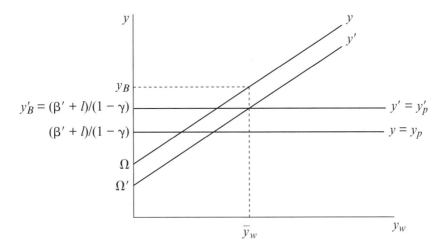

Figure 18.3   Demand- and supply-side adjustments in response to a narrowing gender wage gap

operation of equations (18) and (19), and the impact of these equations on gender wage equality. Hence following on from our earlier discussion of the determinants of β in the Verdoorn Law, suppose that we write:

$$\beta = \beta(W_R), \beta' < 0 \tag{20}$$

where (as before) $W_R = W_M/W_F$ is the relative male–female wage rate. Suppose further that we begin again with the situation depicted in Figure 18.1, where the condition in equation (17) is not satisfied. We have already established above that with $y = y_B >$ $(\beta + l)/(1 - \gamma) = y_p$, we will observe $\dot{u} = u(y - y_p) > 0$, as a result of which both female and male wage growth will increase (via equations (18) and (19)) resulting in a reduction in Ω and hence the BPCG equilibrium growth rate. However, because equations (18) and (19) will also reduce the male–female relative wage, W_R (and hence raise the female wage share), equation (20) ensures that a second mechanism will also be at work. Specifically, by increasing W_R, the response of the economy to $y > y_p$ will also involve an increase in β and hence (via equation (16)) the rate of growth that satisfies the golden rule. The gap between y and y_p is now being closed both by reductions in the actual (BPCG equilibrium) rate of growth, *and* by increases in the potential rate of growth. As a result, the condition for sustainable steady state growth in (17) will eventually be realized at a growth rate that lies somewhere between y_B and $y_p = (\beta + l)/(1 - \gamma)$. This situation is depicted in Figure 18.3.[22]

The upshot of this extension to our analysis is that increasing gender wage equality may increase the sustainability of long-run growth by reducing the actual rate of growth *and* by raising the potential rate of growth. As such, and taking as given the effects of equations (18) and (19) on the actual rate of growth discussed earlier, the price to be paid for sustainable growth (in terms of reductions in the actual rate of growth) is lower the stronger is the mechanism in equation (20). As we will see below, this result may be of some significance when we come to reflect on the practical possibility of instituting equations (18) and (19) in LDRs.

5   The political economy of increasing the sustainability of growth by reducing gender wage inequality

The results above describe a reconciliation of the actual and potential rates of growth (and hence an increase in the sustainability of long-run equilibrium growth) consistent with (indeed, resulting from) a decrease in gender wage inequality – specifically, a decrease in the steady state value of $W_R = W_M/W_F$ and an accompanying increase in the steady state female wage share, ω_F. Hence although increased gender wage equality reduces the rate of growth, this is not altogether a bad thing: since $y > y_p$ initially, a decline in the rate of growth will help to make the growth process more sustainable in the long run. Moreover, the extent to which the actual rate of growth must fall in order to reconcile y and y_p is mitigated by the positive impact of gender wage equality on the potential rate of growth. Rather than observing a simple trade-off between gender equality and growth, then, we instead observe a new type of positive sum outcome, wherein increased gender equality increases the *sustainability* of the long-run equilibrium growth rate. This direct relationship between gender equality and the sustainability of growth makes it easier to advocate for increased gender equality as an end in itself.

One potentially interesting policy implication of all this is as follows. In the analysis above, the coincidence of increased gender wage equality and increased sustainability of the equilibrium growth rate is crucially dependent (inter alia) on the operation of equations (18) and (19) (the female wage inflation Phillips curve and the male wage growth "catch up" equation). If the mechanisms in equations (18) and (19) are not sufficiently strong in actually existing economies, then the results above provide a rationale for using policy interventions to boost female wage growth ahead of male wage growth whenever the labor market is tightening. Several mechanisms might be used to achieve this goal. Higher minimum wages differentially impact workers in low wage industries and these tend to employ a disproportionately large share of women. Protections that allow workers to organize would have a similar effect, especially if these rights were extended to workers in export processing zones. Unemployment insurance that extends to the types of jobs women hold would raise their reservation wage, increasing their bargaining power vis-à-vis employers. Though not exclusively under the control of national governments, labor standards and decent work agreements would also help (Berik and Rodgers, 2007).[23]

In this way, the model developed above can be thought of as a *prescriptive* rather than a *descriptive* device: it draws attention to mechanisms that, if they did exist, would reconcile increased gender wage equality with increased sustainability of the long-run growth rate – a positive sum outcome that facilitates promotion of gender equality as an end in itself. Ultimately, then, the model can be interpreted as a basis for advocating for policies that make the labor market work in conformity with equations (18) and (19), which basically describe an institutionalist-type "leader–follower" labor market, in which better organized workers lead with wage claims, and others follow the pattern established by the leading sector. The essential purpose of policy in this case would be to empower women in LDRs sufficiently to make them the wage leaders in the labor market.

But can gender inequality be reduced without creating a male backlash? This is a ponderous question. Gender norms that ratify male social dominance can inhibit progress towards gender equality if men resist the loss of authority and control that results from females' greater control over resources. Aside from the social norms that inhibit change, men's superior economic position enhances their bargaining power, thus enabling them to collect rents from female labor – whether from their greater access to the best paid jobs, or their ability to shift unpaid labor in the household onto women, who therefore bear the greatest burden for the production of children as "public goods" (Folbre, 1994a; Braunstein, 2008).

That said, gradual closure of gender gaps may not be strongly conflictual because of imperfect information (the time lag in identifying shifts in average wages). Further, such shifts may be more palatable so long as closing wage gaps is not contractionary, with men losing both absolutely (as employment declines) and relatively.[24] It may take a good deal more effort, however, to ensure that men accept the reduction in the actual rate of growth that accompanies increased sustainability of growth.[25] This trade-off between the rate of growth and the sustainability of growth, with redistribution towards women reducing the former but increasing the latter, suggests a knife's edge of social relations. For it to be successful as a strategy, it would require males to have a long time horizon in evaluating their individual well-being. Such an attitude would be easier to cultivate in countries with sound social safety nets, reducing the degree of economic insecurity that can fuel distributional conflicts.

6 Conclusions

Despite the growing international interest in promoting gender equality, little research has been conducted into the macroeconomic feasibility of policies that would close gender wage gaps. More generally, the role of gender wage inequality in influencing macroeconomic outcomes has only recently begun to receive attention. This chapter attempts to address that lacuna by developing a long-run growth model that incorporates both supply- and demand-side effects of changes in the gender wage gap. The result is a very different type of endogenous growth model that highlights the real world problems of inequality and distributional conflict.

Numerous economists have exclusively emphasized the supply-side benefits of greater equality – as, for example, when higher relative female wages that increase women's bargaining power improve the quality of the next generation of workers.[26] But these analyses do not assess the potentially negative effect of increased gender equality on the demand-side, and, in particular, on the balance of payments constraint on growth. Where women are concentrated heavily in labor-intensive export sectors, efforts to promote gender equality can harm the trade balance. This poses a serious macroeconomic constraint to greater equality. However, the model developed in this chapter shows that, even so, gender equality can actually play a salutary role in promoting sustainable growth.

While the model is developed with the structure of developing economies and gender divisions of labor in those countries in mind, we recognize that the adjustment mechanisms proposed here have not been studied previously. Nor do we fully understand the extent to which male resistance might subvert their workings. How to best attenuate male resistance to loss of economic dominance is a question that requires careful consideration and more research. Our goal here is more limited – and that is, to identify mechanisms by which gender equality may play a positive macroeconomic role in the long run.

Notes

1. It may seem unrealistic to characterize the poorest developing countries as falling into this category, but some do (to wit, China and Vietnam) as do numerous middle income countries such as South Korea, Taiwan, Malaysia and Singapore.
2. The evidence that men spend more of their income on luxury goods than women is surprisingly consistent across a varied set of developing economies (Haddad et al., 1997; Hoddinott and Haddad, 1995; Quisumbing and Maluccio, 2003; Xu, 2007). Luxury goods are both domestically produced (e.g. alcohol, cigarettes, gambling), and imported (consumer electronics, automobiles, cell phones). While we hypothesize that a redistribution to men worsens the import bill via consumption effects based on some class-based evidence (Dutt, 1984), firm conjectures require empirical evidence. As yet, however, we know of no empirical evidence that directly links higher relative male income to an increase in the import bill.
3. Note that if:

$$W = W_F N_F + W_M N_M$$

represents the total wage bill, then the female wage share can be written as:

$$\omega_F = \frac{W_F N_F}{W} = \frac{W_F N_F}{W_F N_F + W_M N_M} \Rightarrow \omega_F = \frac{1}{1 + \alpha \dfrac{W_M}{W_F}}$$

where $\alpha = N_M/N_F$ is taken as given. This assumption reflects a kind of gendered fixed coefficients production process, because of job segregation by gender, rigidified by gender norms and stereotypes. It then follows that:

$$\frac{d\omega_F}{d(W_M/W_F)} = \frac{-\alpha}{\left(1 + \alpha \dfrac{W_M}{W_F}\right)^2} < 0$$

   In other words, the female share of the total wage bill is decreasing in the male–female wage ratio: any increase in the latter will result in a redistribution of wage income away from women and towards men, *ceteris paribus*. Hence $\theta > 0$ in equation (2) will pick up the "consumption effect" described above.
4. Equation (3) thus better reflects the structure of a SIE than a LIAE. See Seguino (2010).
5. A flexible mark-up, sensitive to foreign price competition, may be lowered as female wages rise, thus resulting in a profit squeeze effect on investment. For Kaleckian models with a flexible mark-up on export goods see Blecker (1989) and Blecker and Seguino (2002). In this model, for simplicity, we ignore this possibility, although it should be noted that such a response could attenuate the negative effect of higher female wages on export demand. The capacity of a flexible mark-up to cushion the negative demand-side effect of higher female wages is, however, likely to be quite small for two reasons. First, a lower mark-up will depress investment spending and, second, many export firms in developing countries are integrated as small producers into the global commodity chain, and operate with already very small profit margins.
6. We could, of course, include an efficiency wage effect that increases the efficiency of female labor less than proportionally with respect to the female wage, so that the cost effect identified above (which associates rising female wages with rising unit labor costs in the tradables sector) is still observed. But this would add nothing of value to our analysis here. See, however, the discussion at the end of Section 4 below.
7. Of course, if this *is* in fact the case, then developing countries should immediately and unequivocally act to reduce gender wage inequality by raising female wages as a straightforward mechanism for raising the equilibrium rate of growth and hence the growth of the standard of living of all members of their societies.
8. The reader is reminded that we are assuming a fixed mark-up in the derivation of (6).
9. For many developing countries that are import dependent, the Marshall–Lerner condition does *not* hold, and devaluations can be contractionary (see, for example, Krugman and Taylor, 1978). Indeed, there seems to be evidence that at least in the short run, contraction is likely. As will be made clear below, however, failure of the Marshall–Lerner conditions to hold means that reducing gender wage inequality will be conducive to the equilibrium rate of growth – making it easier to advocate for reductions in inequality. Once again, then, the purpose of our assuming here that the Marshall–Lerner conditions *do* hold is to avoid constructing a model in which it is "too easy" to advocate for reduced gender wage inequality because there is a straightforward, direct relationship between equality and the equilibrium rate of growth.
10. Note that we will always observe this inequality if the Marshall–Lerner condition does not hold. Hence

the claim made in the previous note – that our purpose in assuming that the Marshall–Lerner conditions *do* hold is to avoid making it "too easy" to advocate for reduced gender wage inequality by creating a direct relationship between gender wage equality and the equilibrium rate of growth.

11. If we define the relative wage as:

$$W_R = \frac{W_M}{W_F}$$

then as has already been demonstrated, the female wage share will rise if W_R falls. In a dynamic context, this requires that:

$$w_R = w_M - w_F < 0$$

Hence in order to increase gender wage equality (as alluded to in the text), we must observe either a reduction of w_M or an increase in w_F sufficiently large to render $w_R < 0$.

Note that in a long-run, steady state equilibrium, we would expect to observe $w_R = 0$; that is, constancy of the relative price of male and female labor. Otherwise (given a constant value of α) the female wage share will rise/fall continuously. Since the female wage share is bounded above and below, there are only certain conditions under which this is logically possible. Moreover, the stylized facts of growth in LDCs are not consistent with a continuously rising or falling female wage share: our reading of the empirical evidence is that there is no unambiguous trend in the female wage share in developing countries (UNRISD, 2005). The effects of changing the rates of growth of male or female wages *ceteris paribus* as discussed above are therefore best considered short-run results.

12. We label this case "conflictive gender equality," whereby improvements in women's relative status come about through absolute declines in male economic status. Evidence on the gender effects of achieving gender equality by this route is sparse and tends to be context-specific. Chant (2000), for example, notes the negative effect on gender relations of falling male wages and access to employment in Costa Rica in the 1990s. Susan Faludi's (1991) *Backlash* underscores the negative response to women's economic empowerment in the United States. Naila Kabeer (2000) describes the efforts that Bangladeshi women who take up work in garment manufacturing make to maintain a demeanor of subservience in the home toward the male head of household so as not to disrupt patriarchal norms of male authority. Each of these cases speaks to the underlying dominance of patriarchal norms which, when contested, produce gender conflict. While there is as yet no empirical evidence to our knowledge on the conditions that shape the intensity of backlash, intuitively, it would seem that female economic advancements are likely to face less resistance under either of two conditions. The first is if higher female wages (or a higher female wage share) are achieved in the context of a stable rate of growth of male wages and employment. The second (and less ideal) is if increased gender wage equality is attained without provoking a decline in average real male wages or increases in unemployment.

13. This extension of the BPCG framework is based on the work of Palley (2002). See also Setterfield (2006).

14. Note that the association of Y_p with N^{FE} here involves the implicit assumption that $K/Y_p \geq v$, where K is the total capital stock in existence. In other words, output is never capital constrained, but is instead only ever constrained by the effective demand for goods and hence labor.

15. There is evidence that greater gender equality lowers fertility, and because women's unpaid labor burden declines, female labor force participation rates rise. Labor force participation could then be modeled as a positive function of the female wage rate. The latter's effect on potential output via the labor force participation rate is analogous to its effect via β. For simplicity, we omit this complication from our model as it does not qualitatively alter the results.

16. Note that combining equations (12) and (13) yields:

$$y_p = \beta + l + \gamma y.$$

In other words, our model involves an endogenous natural rate of growth in the style of Leon-Ledesma and Thirlwall (2000, 2002). The positive impact of gender equality on both β and l reflects the supply-side effect that has been emphasized in much of the gender and macroeconomics literature (Folbre, 1994a, 1994b; Blackden and Bhanu, 1999; Elson, 1991).

17. Note that the inequality stated above is empirically plausible, given that it is commonly understood that $\gamma < 1$ and since we may even observe $\mu = (\eta + \psi - 1) \approx 0$. Bahmani-Oskooee and Kara (2005) provide estimates of export and import price elasticities for a number of developed and developing economies. For most developing countries in the sample (e.g. Colombia, Pakistan, and Turkey) estimates of μ range from 0.27 to 0.65.

18. As noted earlier, this ensures that the results of our model are consistent with sustainable steady state growth outcomes. See the discussion in Note 11.

19. Wage inflation Phillips curves in open, developing countries are likely to have a flatter slope than in more closed economies (Gruben and McLeod, 2003). Firm mobility plays a role: higher wages cause mobile firms (which tend to be labor-intensive exporters) to relocate or buyers in the global commodity chain to source from lower wage countries (Seguino, 2007).
20. The derivative that follows is evaluated at a point consistent with the labour market having regained steady state equilibrium conditions – that is, $\dot{w}_M = 0$. At this point, the total change in w_M is equivalent to the total change in w_F created by equation (18), so that $dw_M = dw_F \Rightarrow dw_M/dw_F = 1$.
21. In the parlance of Setterfield (2006), the resulting model is one of quasi-supply-determined growth, since y adjusts towards y_p in the process of satisfying the golden rule.
22. The model may now be referred to as one of quasi-demand-determined growth, since some (but not all) of the burden of adjustment involved in reconciling the actual and potential rates of growth is borne by the latter (rather than by the demand-determined actual rate of growth alone). Note that if, as we hypothesized earlier, greater gender equality raises the labor force participation rate (l rises), potential output bears an even greater share of the burden of adjustment. Such an outcome would make gender equality more palatable to men, easing as it does the negative effect on aggregate demand and thus employment.
23. "Better Factories Cambodia" is an example of a trade-linked scheme that offered increased US market access to Cambodia in return for the government improving labor standards enforcement. The program focused on the garments and textiles industries in which, as elsewhere, workers are largely female. Berik and Rodgers (2007) find evidence that such schemes can improve labor standards adherence without hindering export growth or job growth.
24. Note that this problem does not emerge in our model. In the transition towards a sustainable steady state equilibrium, the unemployment rate will continue to fall as long as actual rate of growth exceeds the potential rate, and will then become stationary. Unemployment will not therefore increase, but will instead stabilize at an indeterminate rate. This may still produce gender conflicts if the male unemployment remains very high, as it has, for example, in the Caribbean.
25. The situation described here is analogous to Bhaduri and Marglin's (1990) conflictive stagnationism, whereby a redistribution towards wages boosts short-run macro performance but decreases the rate of growth. The question we confront is: will men be sufficiently far sighted to accept a lower but sustainable rate of growth in place of higher but unsustainable growth?
26. In a departure from others in this area of inquiry, Seguino (2000a, 2000b) emphasizes the role of gender *inequality* in stimulating exports, thus generating foreign exchange to import technology-intensive imports that raise productivity and stimulate long-run growth.

References

Bahmani-Oskooee, M. and O. Kara (2005) "Income and price elasticities of trade: some new estimates." *International Trade Journal*, **19**, 165–78.
Berik, G. and Y. Rodgers (2007) "The debate on labor standards and international trade: lessons from Cambodia and Bangladesh." Department of Economics Working Paper No. 2007-03, University of Utah.
Bhaduri, A. and S. Marglin (1990) "Unemployment and the real wage: the economic basis for contesting political ideologies." *Cambridge Journal of Economics*, **14** (4), 375–94.
Blackden, C.M. and C. Bhanu (1999) "Gender, growth, and poverty reduction. Special program of assistance for Africa, 1998 status report on poverty in sub-Saharan Africa." World Bank Technical Paper No. 428.
Blecker, R.A. (1989) "International competition, income distribution and economic growth." *Cambridge Journal of Economics*, **13**, 395–412.
Blecker, R.A. and S. Seguino (2002) "Macroeconomic effects of reducing gender wage inequality in an export-oriented, semi-industrialized economy." *Review of Development Economics*, **6** (1), 103–19. (Reprinted in 2007)
Braunstein, E. (2008) "The feminist political economy of the rent-seeking society: An investigation of gender inequality and economic growth." *Journal of Economic Issues*, **42** (4), 959–80.
Chant, S. (2000) "Men in crisis? Reflections on masculinities, work, and family in Northwest Costa Rica." *The European Journal of Development Research*, **12** (2), 199–218.
Darity, W. Jr (1995) "The formal structure of a gender-segregated low-income economy." *World Development*, **23** (11), 1963-8.
Dutt, A. (1984) "Stagnation, income distribution, and monopoly power." *Cambridge Journal of Economics*, **8**, 25–40.
Elson, D. (ed.) (1991) *Male Bias in the Development Process*. Manchester and New York: Manchester University Press.
Faludi, S. (1991) *Backlash: The Undeclared War Against American Women*. New York: Crown.
Folbre, N. (1994a) "Children as public goods." *American Economic Review*, **84** (2), 86–90.

Folbre, N. (1994b) *Who Pays for the Kids? Gender and the Structures of Constraint.* London and New York: Routledge.

Gruben, W. and D. McLeod (2003) "The openness-inflation puzzle revisited." Center for Latin America Working Papers 0203.

Haddad, L., J. Hoddinott and H. Alderman (1997) *Intrahousehold Resource Allocation in Developing Countries.* Baltimore, MD: Johns Hopkins University.

Hill, M.A. and E. King (1995) "Women's education and economic well-being." *Feminist Economics*, 1 (2), 21–46.

Hoddinott, J. and L. Haddad (1995) "Does female income share influence household expenditures? Evidence from Cote d'Ivoire." *Oxford Bulletin of Economics and Statistics*, 57 (1), 77–96.

Kabeer, N. (2000) *The Power to Choose: Bangladeshi Women and Labour Market Conditions in London and Dhaka.* London and New York: Verso.

Klasen, S. (2002) "Low schooling for girls, slower growth for all? Cross-country evidence on the effect of gender inequality in education on economic development." *The World Bank Economic Review*, 16 (3), 345–73.

Knowles, S., P. Lorgelly and P.D. Owen (2002) "Are educational gender gaps a brake on economic development? Some cross-country empirical evidence." *Oxford Economic Papers*, 54 (1), 118–49.

Krugman, P. and L. Taylor (1978) "Contractionary effects of devaluation." *Journal of International Economics*, 8 (3), 445–56.

Leon-Ledesma, M. and A.P. Thirlwall (2000) "Is the natural rate of growth exogenous?" *Banca Nazionale del Lavoro Quarterly Review*, 215, 433–45.

Leon-Ledesma, M. and A.P. Thirlwall (2002) "The endogeneity of the natural rate of growth." *Cambridge Journal of Economics*, 26, 441–59.

Palley, T.I. (2002) "Pitfalls in the theory of growth: an application to the balance-of-payments-constrained growth model," in M. Setterfield (ed.) *The Economics of Demand-Led Growth: Challenging the Supply-Side Vision of the Long Run.* Cheltenham, UK and Northampton, MA, USA: Edward Elgar.

Quisumbing, A. (ed.) (2005) *Household Decisions, Gender, and Development: A Synthesis of Recent Research.* Baltimore, MD: Johns Hopkins University Press–International Food Policy Research Institute.

Quisumbing, A. and J.A. Maluccio (2003) "Resources at marriage and intrahousehold allocation: evidence from Bangladesh, Ethiopia, Indonesia, and South Africa." *Oxford Bulletin of Economics and Statistics*, 65 (3), 283–328.

Seguino, S. (2000a) "Accounting for gender in Asian economic growth." *Feminist Economics*, 6 (3), 22–58.

Seguino, S. (2000b) "Gender inequality and economic growth: a cross-country analysis." *World Development*, 28 (7), 1211–30.

Seguino, S. (2007) "Is more mobility good?: Firm mobility and the low-wage low-productivity trap." *Structural Change and Economic Dynamics*, 18 (1), 27–51.

Seguino, S. (2009) "Gender, distribution and balance of payments constrained growth in developing countries," forthcoming in *Review of Political Economy*, 22 (2).

Setterfield, M. (2006) "Thirlwall's law and Palley's pitfalls: a reconsideration," in P. Arestis, J. McCombie and R. Vickerman (eds) *Growth and Economic Development: Essays in Honour of A.P. Thirlwall*, Cheltenham, UK and Northampton, MA, USA: Edward Elgar, pp. 47–59.

Thirlwall, A.P. (1978) "The UK's economic problem: a balance of payments constraint?" *National Westminster Bank Quarterly Review*, February, 24–32.

Thirlwall, A.P. (1979) "The balance of payments constraint as an explanation of international growth rate differences," *Banca Nazionale del Lavoro Quarterly Review*, 128, 45–53.

Tzannatos, Z. (1999) "Women and labor market changes in the global economy: growth helps, inequalities hurt and public policy matters." *World Development*, 27 (3), 551–69.

Udry, C., J. Hoddinott, H. Alderman and L. Haddad (1995) "Gender differentials in farm productivity: implications for household efficiency and agricultural policy." *Food Policy*, 20 (5), 407–23.

United Nations Research Institute for Social Development (UNRISD) (2005) *Gender Equality: Striving for Justice in an Unequal World.* Geneva: UNRISD.

Xu, Z. (2007) "A survey on intra-household models and evidence." Munich Personal RePEc Archive Paper No. 3763.

PART VI

INTERNATIONAL AND REGIONAL DIMENSIONS OF GROWTH

19 Export-led growth, real exchange rates and the fallacy of composition

Robert A. Blecker and Arslan Razmi

1 Introduction

In the past two decades, developing countries have significantly increased both their export orientation and the proportion of their exports that consists of manufactured goods.[1] These shifts have been driven by several motivations, including the perceived inefficiencies of inward-oriented, import-substitution industrialization, a desire to avoid the historically recurring problem of falling terms of trade for primary commodities and a belief that manufactures offer superior long-run development prospects compared to primary commodities. The increasing reliance on manufactured export-oriented growth strategies has had some stunning successes, particularly in the so-called "four tigers" (South Korea, Taiwan, Hong Kong and Singapore) in the 1970s and 1980s and China in the 1990s and early 2000s. Nevertheless, for a large number of countries that have sought to jump on this bandwagon, the results have been disappointing. While a small group of East Asian nations have used manufactured exports to propel themselves into a process of convergence with the industrialized economies of the global "North", most of the countries in the "South" that have specialized in manufactured exports over the past two decades have not achieved similar success.

The uneven growth performance of the developing countries most specialized in manufactured exports in the past three decades is shown in Table 19.1. The growth of the four tigers ("newly industrialized Asian economies"), which averaged 7.7 percent per year in the 1980s, slowed down in the 1990s and 2000s, when many other developing countries began to enter the market for manufactured exports. China grew at rates of about 10 percent per year throughout all the periods shown, and India accelerated to 7.1 percent in 2000–07. However, the 12 other emerging and developing economies specialized in manufactures increased their average growth rates only marginally (from 3.8 percent in 1980–89 to 4.5 percent in 2000–07) in spite of the fact that many of them were plagued by the debt crisis in the 1980s, and never came close to the earlier rapid growth of the four tigers or the more recent success of China and India. Between 2000 and 2007, these 12 economies actually grew more slowly than the average for all emerging and developing economies (6.4 percent) as the countries that were specialized in primary commodities benefited from the commodity price boom during that period.

Undoubtedly, many factors impact on countries' growth rates, and domestic policies contribute to the success or failure of export-led growth strategies. Nevertheless, the inability of so many countries to fully emulate the rapid export-led growth of the East Asian countries and to withstand growing Chinese competition raises the possibility of what has come to be known as the "fallacy of composition", that is, an adding-up constraint on the efforts of numerous developing countries to simultaneously export similar types of manufactured goods to the same industrialized country markets. In theory, the

Table 19.1   Average annual growth rates, selected countries and years

	1980–89	1990–99	2000–07
Asian newly industrialized economies (four tigers)[a]	7.7	6.1	4.9
China (People's Republic)	9.7	10.0	10.0
India	5.6	4.6	7.1
Other emerging and developing economies specialized in manufactures[b]	3.8	4.2	4.5
Average for all emerging and developing economies (excluding the four tigers)	3.5	3.2	6.4

Notes:
Averages are calculated using GDP at purchasing power parity as weights.
[a]   Republic of Korea, Taiwan Province of China, Hong Kong, and Singapore.
[b]   Bangladesh, Dominican Republic, Jamaica, Malaysia, Mauritius, Mexico, Pakistan, Philippines, Sri Lanka, Thailand, Tunisia, and Turkey. These are the 12 other countries, besides China, India, and the four tigers, for which manufactures constituted more than 70 percent of their merchandise exports in either 1990 or 2001.

Source: International Monetary Fund, *World Economic Outlook*, October 2008 Database, http://www.imf. org/external/pubs/ft/weo/2008/02/weodata/index.aspx, and authors' calculations.

exporting nations need not face demand-side constraints, under certain optimistic conditions: (1) the industrialized countries grow rapidly enough to accommodate increasing volumes of developing country exports of manufactures without depressing the prices of those goods (or alternatively, the income elasticity of demand for developing country exports is very high); (2) the developing nations provide increasing amounts of reciprocal demand for each other's exports via "South–South" trade to relieve the constraints emanating from limitations on industrialized countries' demand; or (3) the developing countries as a group move in a "flying geese formation" in which the relatively more advanced ones move on to more capital-intensive and technologically sophisticated products, thereby making room for new entrants exporting more labor-intensive, standardized products. Although there is some evidence for conditions (2) and (3) holding for certain countries in some time periods, there is little evidence for condition (1). Furthermore, a growing body of research suggests that these optimistic conditions do not hold generally and, as a result, most developing country exporters of manufactures are subject to significant demand-side constraints arising from their competition over the same export markets in similar products. The rest of this chapter reviews this mounting evidence and discusses its policy implications.

2   Previous literature
Many of the arguments in favor of manufacturing export-led growth have implicitly assumed a "small country" paradigm, in which each country's exports can increase without quantitative limit and without putting downward pressure on their prices. These arguments do not consider what happens if a large number of developing countries pursue export-led growth by targeting the same industrialized country markets simultaneously. In other words, what are the consequences when a large number of small

countries add up and essentially act as a "large country" in the global market for manu-factured exports? Studies that have addressed this issue can be divided into two broad groups and several sub-categories.[2] In the broadest terms, the two main types of studies are those that have tested for negative effects of intra-developing competition on export performance and those that have examined the impact of that competition on growth rates. We shall consider each group briefly in turn.

The literature that has focused on exports contains three main branches: (1) studies of quantitative crowding-out or displacement; (2) studies of negative effects on prices of manufactured exports; and (3) studies of price competition limiting export growth among the developing countries. Empirical studies of quantitative displacement began with the pioneering work of Cline (1982), who suggested that it would be difficult for very many countries to emulate the success of the four tigers from the 1970s. Blecker (2002) and Palley (2003) found evidence of crowding out of imports from certain countries in the US market in certain periods, but did not study global competition or control for other variables. More recently, several studies (for example, Eichengreen et al., 2007) have sought to identify the effects of China's entry into the global economy on the exports of other developing countries (including exporters of primary commodities, who generally benefit, as well as exporters of manufactures, who tend to lose). Razmi (2007b) improved on the earlier econometric studies of the displacement hypothesis by control-ling for exchange rates and total demand, and his work is summarized below.

With regard to negative price effects, Kaplinsky (1993, 1999) has suggested that many manufactured export products have become "commoditized" and now behave more like primary commodities in the sense that they are prone to declining terms of trade when exported in increasing volumes. He also suggests that the need to compete via low prices pressures developing countries to suppress real wages and devalue their curren-cies, thereby limiting the income gains from exports. Evidence about trends in the terms of trade for developing country exports of manufactures is mixed overall, but using disaggregated EU import data Kaplinsky and Santos-Paulino (2006) have found that less technologically advanced exports from lower-income countries are falling in rela-tive price. US import data show a general decline in the relative price of imports of all manufactured goods from developing countries compared with manufactured imports from industrialized countries from 1991 to 2007, and this is just as true for the East Asian newly industrializing countries as it is for all developing countries (see Figure 19.1).[3]

Turning to price effects on export demand, Faini et al. (1992) and Muscatelli et al. (1994) were the first to identify significant price-substitution effects in competition among developing nations for manufactured export markets in the industrialized coun-tries. While these studies estimated export demand functions for individual developing nations, Razmi and Blecker (2008) – in addition to providing estimates for individual countries using more recent data and better price indexes – also tested for overall price competition effects using panel data methods. Dividing their sample of 18 countries into panels of low- and high-technology exporters, they found that price competition was more significant among the low-technology exporters while the income elasticity of export demand was higher for the high-technology exporters. An updated version of these results is presented below.

Turning to the second broad group, only a small number of recent studies have tested for growth or output impacts of competition among developing countries for export

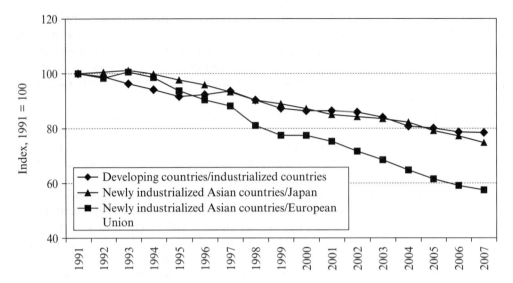

Note: The price indexes are for manufactured imports only, except the index for the newly industrialized Asian countries is for total imports.

Source: US Department of Labor, Bureau of Labor Statistics, Import Price Indexes, www.bls.gov, and authors' calculations.

Figure 19.1 *Indexes of relative prices of manufactured goods imported by the US, annual averages, 1991 to 2007*

markets. These studies have mainly focused on whether relative prices or real exchange rates of developing country exporters of manufactures have a significant impact on their overall macroeconomic performance. Before discussing this empirical research, a brief summary of the underlying theoretical issues is in order. Traditionally, mainstream macroeconomics has downplayed the role of the real exchange rate as a policy instrument, considering it to be a variable whose equilibrium value is given at a point in time by factors such as technology, factor endowments and tastes. Any temporary deviations are counteracted by the tendency of relative prices of tradables to move towards maintaining (absolute or relative) purchasing power parity. Classical neutrality of money allegedly ensures the insulation of real variables from changes in their nominal values beyond the short run.

Many development economists have also often taken a skeptical view of the utility of the real exchange as a development tool, although on different grounds. Traditionally, developing countries were categorized as exporters of primary commodities and agricultural products, the demand for which is relatively price-inelastic. The nonsatisfaction of the Marshall–Lerner condition implies that exchange rate devaluations could result in undesirable and destabilizing consequences.[4] Considering that manufactures now constitute the largest share of exports from developing countries as a whole, this concern has become of less importance. Indeed, given the increasing competition among developing country manufacturers, one might expect to see relatively high cross-price elasticities of demand for such products.

The post-Keynesian balance-of-payments-constrained growth (BPCG) model provides a convenient theoretical framework for thinking about demand-side constraints on export-led growth.[5] However, the original BPCG model assumed that each individual country's export performance was independent of other countries' exports, and it also assumed that demand was relatively price-inelastic (or else that purchasing power parity prevented relative prices from changing in the long run). Blecker (2002) addressed the first problem by synthesizing the "almost ideal demand system" (AIDS) developed by Deaton and Muellbauer (1980) with the BPCG framework to create a model in which relative price changes among a large number of countries can affect the output growth rates of the exporting nations, on the assumption that their growth is constrained by the requirement of maintaining balanced trade. The AIDS specification allows for the incorporation of an adding-up constraint on the growth of exports from a group of countries that compete for shares in the same industrialized country markets. Since the growth of exports places a constraint on output growth in the BPCG framework, an adding-up constraint on export growth, in turn, translates into an adding-up constraint on output growth. Blecker also dropped the assumption that relative price (real exchange rate) effects are negligible, especially when considering competition by countries exporting similar products to the same markets. Subsequently, Razmi (2004) extended Blecker's model to incorporate capital flows. The presence of capital flows (thus relaxing the assumption of balanced trade) and the focus on relative price changes render the model more suitable for application to short-run changes in output.[6]

Recent empirical work has generated a fair amount of evidence that the real exchange rate does, in fact, play a significant role in influencing output growth. This, along with the refusal of China to let its currency rapidly appreciate or freely float – presumably on the grounds that it will harm China's investment- and export-led growth strategy – has led to a renewed interest in the role of the exchange rate as a development policy tool. In a comprehensive study that identifies more than 80 episodes of sustained growth since the 1950s (that is, growth spurts that lasted more than eight years), Hausmann et al. (2005) find few statistically significant economic indicators of growth accelerations. They do, however, find that depreciated real exchange rates are robust correlates of such episodes. Similarly, using econometric techniques to identify structural breaks in growth paths, Berg et al. (2008) find that competitive exchange rates are one of the few factors that are robustly correlated with prolonged growth spells.

Levy-Yeyati and Sturzenegger (2007) hypothesize a "fear of appreciation", as opposed to the "fear of floating" originally suggested by Calvo and Reinhart (2002). While the latter term was coined to refer to the fear of dramatic depreciations preceding or during currency crises, Levy-Yeyati and Sturzenegger argue that the rapid growth of foreign exchange reserves in developing countries reflects a fear of floating in reverse, which leads them to (successfully) intervene in foreign exchange markets to maintain a depreciated real exchange rate. Furthermore, these authors explore the relationship between real exchange changes and growth econometrically, finding that undervaluation is correlated with faster employment and output growth. Notably, the positive relationship appears to go beyond short-term cyclical changes to long-run growth. However, the boost to long-run growth seems not to work through greater export volumes or import substitution, but rather through greater investment and savings.

Polterovich and Popov (2002) find that the accumulation of foreign exchange reserves contributes to developing country economic growth.[7] Moreover, the reported estimates suggest that only reserve accumulation under positive external balances (as opposed to reserves following from foreign borrowing) result in beneficial undervaluation of the exchange rate. They explain these results partly by hypothesizing that the accumulation of reserves leads to exchange rate undervaluation, which in turn results in external surpluses, higher investment and savings, and export-led growth. Razin and Collins (1997) found that low-to-moderate real exchange rate undervaluations are correlated with accelerated growth. The relationship displays important nonlinearities, however. For example, large undervaluations are not associated with more rapid growth.[8]

While this emerging body of literature has renewed interest in the phenomenon of real exchange rate management, it does not distinguish between real exchange rate changes relative to other industrialized countries versus those relative to other developing countries. Blecker and Razmi (2008) addressed this problem by constructing separate real exchange rate indexes for each developing country exporter in their sample relative to (a) the industrialized countries' currencies and (b) the currencies of rival developing country exporters.[9] Using panel data methods, they found that real depreciations relative to the industrialized countries generally have contractionary effects – as hypothesized in the large literature on "contractionary devaluations"[10] – but that real depreciations relative to competing developing countries generally have expansionary effects on output growth. These results, which differ in some subtle respects between different groups of developing country exporters, are summarized below.

3   Empirical hypotheses and econometric results

As the preceding discussion makes clear, there are a number of ways of specifying the fallacy of composition (FOC) hypothesis that have different empirical implications. In this section, we consider three specific FOC hypotheses and corresponding econometric tests.[11] The three hypotheses are:

- **FOC-quantity**: This is the simplest version of FOC, which is the idea of quantitative displacement or crowding out of the exports of some developing countries by exports from other developing countries.
- **FOC-price**: This refers to intra-developing country price competition over export markets in the industrialized countries, which is usually tested by estimating export demand functions for developing country exports of manufactures.
- **FOC-growth**: This refers to positive output or growth effects of real depreciations (lower relative prices of exports) with respect to rival developing countries competing in the same industrialized country markets. This is the strongest version of FOC, which is motivated by the theoretical model of Blecker (2002) and Razmi (2004) discussed earlier.

In the remainder of this section, we discuss the econometric models used to test each of these hypotheses and the results thereof in turn. In all cases, we define manufactures as consisting of products falling under standard international trade classification (SITC) categories 5 (chemicals and related products), 6 (manufactured goods classified chiefly by material, including rubber, textiles, iron and steel), 7 (machinery and transport equipment, including telecommunications, electrical, computers, other electronics and automobiles) and 8 (miscellaneous manufactured articles, including furniture, apparel, footwear and instruments), excluding category 68 (non-ferrous metals). In all of the econometric estimates presented below, endogeneity issues are addressed by using the general method of moments (GMM) approach, which utilizes the lagged values of the dependent and independent variables as instruments.

3.1   Crowding out (FOC-quantity)

The most basic idea of FOC is the notion that exports of manufactures from one developing country can be crowded out or displaced by the growth of similar exports from competing developing countries. If this is true, then the quantity of one country's manufactured exports should be inversely related to the quantity of other developing countries' exports, after controlling for relative price and income effects. One advantage of pursuing this quantitative approach is that the quantitative data, unlike the price data, are available at more disaggregated levels, allowing us to explore the presence of crowding-out effects at the two-digit SITC level.

To test this hypothesis, we specify the following empirical model:[12]

$$X_{it} = a_0 + a_1 Z_{it}^N + a_2 R_{it}^N + a_3 X_{it}^L + e_{it} \tag{1}$$

where X_{it} is the volume of exports of manufactured goods from country i at time t, Z_{it}^N is total real expenditures on imports of manufactured goods by the industrialized countries, $R_{it}^N = P_{it}^N/P_{it}$ is the relative price of domestically produced manufactured goods in the industrialized countries (measured by the index P_{it}^N) to country i's own export price index (P_{it}), X_{it}^L is an index of the volume of exports from other developing countries that compete with exports from each country i and e_{it} is the error term. The FOC-quantity or quantitative displacement hypothesis implies $a_3 < 0$.

Table 19.2 summarizes the results of estimating equation (1) for the period 1984–2004 using a sample of 22 developing countries and 13 industrialized countries, using annual data measured in natural logarithms.[13] In estimating equation (1), we used an autoregressive distributed lag specification with one lag each of the dependent and independent variables, that is, ARDL (1,1). The long-run coefficients reported in Table 19.2 were derived by dividing the sum of the current and lagged coefficients for each variable by one minus the coefficient on the lagged dependent variable. The results in the first column (for the "ALL" panel) show evidence of crowding out at the aggregate level including all developing countries in the sample. The estimates for the other panels, which are disaggregated by industry (SITC categories), suggest that displacement effects (negative coefficients on X^L) are strongest in categories 6, 8 and associated sub-categories, but they are also found in category 7, which includes some of the products that, because of their relatively high-tech nature, have traditionally been considered to be relatively immune to cut-throat competition. This may be explained by two factors. First, the term "high-tech" may be misleading as a substantial proportion of the production falling under these categories consists of labor-intensive assembly operations requiring relatively few skills and exhibiting relatively low barriers to entry. Second, and on a related note, a number of developing countries have established a presence in the sectors classified under SITC 7, owing in no small measure to the vertical disintegration of global production processes.[14] Thus, some of the SITC categories traditionally seen

Table 19.2 GMM estimates of export equation (1), tests for FOC-quantity. Sample period after lags and differences, 1987–2004

Dependent variable: (logged value of) real exports, X

Panel	ALL	SITC 5	SITC 6	SITC 7	SITC 8	SITC 65	SITC 75	SITC 77	SITC 84	SITC 85
Cross-sections	22	22	22	22	22	22	22	22	22	22
Total panel observations	390	390	390	390	390	390	388	390	390	390
Long-run coefficients on:										
Z^N	2.383	-0.755	2.841	3.887	0.677*	1.244	5.240	3.412	3.219	-0.356
	(0.004)	(0.029)	(0.000)	(0.000)	(0.169)	(0.000)	(0.000)	(0.000)	(0.001)	(0.060)
R^N	1.774	1.492	0.842	1.819	1.301	2.671	2.633	1.312	3.808	4.051
	(0.081)	(0.000)	(0.000)	(0.000)	(0.019)	(0.000)	(0.000)	(0.005)	(0.000)	(0.000)
X^L	-0.699	1.257	-1.486	-0.791	-0.896	-1.657	-0.945	-0.561	-2.534	-3.174
	(0.081)	(0.000)	(0.000)	(0.001)	(0.040)	(0.000)	(0.014)	(0.060)	(0.003)	(0.000)
Sargan test (p-value)	0.589	0.497	0.545	0.367	0.610	0.561	0.525	0.357	0.737	0.784

Notes:

p-values in parentheses, based on White period standard errors and variance (degrees of freedom corrected). All variables were measured in natural logarithms using annual data. Constants and lagged dependent variables were included in all equations. The reported coefficients are the "long-run" coefficients, that is, the sums of the current and one-year lagged variables divided by one minus the coefficient of the lagged dependent variable. Second and third lags of the dependent variable and lagged instances of the regressors were used as instruments. Period SUR weighted matrices were used to correct for both period heteroskedasticity and general correlation of observations within cross-sections. Orthogonal deviations were used to remove individual specific effects. The Sargan test is for the validity of overidentifying restrictions. SITC 65 includes textile yarn, fabrics, made-up articles and related products, SITC 75 includes office machines and automatic, data-processing machines, SITC 77 includes electrical machinery, apparatus and appliances, SITC 84 includes articles of apparel and clothing accessories, SITC 85 includes footwear.

* Denotes variables that were not significant at the 10 per cent level, but which were included based on Wald tests for joint exclusion.

Source: Razmi (2007b), reproduced with permission.

as relatively high-tech may not be immune to what Kaplinsky (1993) has called the commoditization of manufactures.

Alternative estimates of this model, which are not shown here for reasons of space,[15] yield additional insights into where and when the greatest displacement effects are found. Dividing the industrialized countries into three blocs – the US, EU and Japan – reveals that crowding-out effects are significant only in the US market, which is also the largest destination. Splitting the sample period into two halves shows that the crowding-out coefficient is statistically significant only for the second half of the sample period, 1994–2004. Notably, this period includes the formation of the North American Free Trade Agreement, the creation of the World Trade Organization (WTO) and the rise of China as a major exporting power (as well as China's accession to the WTO in 2001). Furthermore, the results suggest the presence of a "China effect" in the sense that the crowding-out coefficient turns statistically insignificant once the effects of Chinese export competition are excluded from the sample.[16] This China effect seems to exert the most influence in SITC 7, where displacement effects become insignificant both at the one- and two-digit SITC levels once China is excluded.

3.2   Price competition (FOC-price)

A second approach is to test for the existence of significant relative price effects on export demand, indicating a high degree of substitutability between manufactures produced in different developing nations. This requires estimating an export demand function in which, as discussed earlier, we distinguish relative prices or real exchange rates with the industrialized countries and with competing developing countries:

$$X_{it} = b_0 + b_1 Z_{it}^N + b_2 R_{it}^N + b_3 R_{it}^L + u_{it} \tag{2}$$

where $R_{it}^L = P_{it}^L/P_{it}$ is the relative price of manufactured exports from competing developing countries (measured by price index P_{it}^L) to home country exports of manufactures (with price index P_{it}),[17] u_{it} is the error term and all other variables are defined as before. In this specification, the FOC-price hypothesis of strong substitution effects between developing country exports implies $b_3 > 0$.

When estimating equation (2), in order to ensure that changes in export prices reflect those of manufactured exports, only those developing countries for which manufacturing exports constituted at least 70 percent of total exports in at least one of two years, 1990 and 2001, were included in the sample. This gave us a sample of 18 developing countries plus the 10 largest importing industrialized countries.[18] Although we could not obtain disaggregated price indexes for different types of exports, we were able to group the developing countries into several different panels according to their structural characteristics including their export composition (see Table 19.3). Some of these panels (country groups) were motivated more by considerations related to testing the FOC-growth hypothesis rather than FOC-price, but for the sake of consistency the same panels were used for both sets of estimates.

The panel "ALL" includes all 18 developing countries in the sample. We then classified any country with a trade share in GDP of greater than 50 percent and a GDP of less than US$100 billion in the SMALLOPEN panel and put all other countries in the LARGE panel. An alternative criterion that could be used to select the developing countries

Table 19.3   Countries included in the panels for testing FOC-price and FOC-growth

ALL: Bangladesh, China, Dominican Republic, Hong Kong,[a] India, Jamaica, Korea, Malaysia, Mauritius, Mexico, Pakistan, Philippines, Singapore, Sri Lanka, Taiwan, Thailand, Tunisia, Turkey

SMALLOPEN (total trade share of GDP over 50% and GDP less than US$100 billion in 2000): Dominican Republic, Hong Kong,[a] Jamaica, Malaysia, Mauritius, Philippines, Singapore, Sri Lanka, Tunisia

LARGE (total trade share of GDP under 50% or GDP greater than US$100 billion in 2000): Bangladesh, China, India, Korea, Mexico, Pakistan, Taiwan, Thailand, Turkey

HIMFRGDP (ratio of manufactured exports to GDP greater than 25%): Hong Kong,[a] Korea, Malaysia, Mauritius, Philippines, Singapore, Taiwan, Thailand

LOMFRGDP (ratio of manufactured exports to GDP less than 25%): Bangladesh, China, Dominican Republic, India, Jamaica, Mexico, Pakistan, Sri Lanka, Tunisia, Turkey

HITECH (share of high technology imports greater than 30%): China,[b] Hong Kong,[a] Korea, Malaysia, Mexico,[b] Philippines, Singapore, Sri Lanka, Taiwan

LOTECH (share of high technology imports less than 10%): Bangladesh, China,[b] Dominican Republic, India, Jamaica, Malaysia, Mauritius, Mexico,[b] Sri Lanka, Tunisia, Turkey

HIDEBT (ratio of external debt to GDP greater than 33%): Bangladesh, Dominican Republic, Jamaica, Malaysia, Mauritius, Mexico, Pakistan, Philippines, Sri Lanka, Thailand, Tunisia, Turkey

LODEBT (ratio of external debt to GDP less than 33%): China, Hong Kong,[a] India, Korea, Singapore, Taiwan

Notes:
[a]   Hong Kong is omitted from all regressions in the tests of FOC-growth in Table 19.5, because of a lack of foreign capital inflow data prior to 1999, but it is used in the FOC-price tests in Table 19.4.
[b]   China and Mexico are included in both HITECH and LOTECH because of their intermediate status, with high technology shares around 20% and rising during the sample period.

in the sample is manufactured exports measured as a percentage of GDP, rather than as a percentage of total exports. We therefore divide the panel into two sub-panels of countries that are above and below a 25 percent threshold for this indicator, referred to as HIMFRGDP and LOMFRGDP, respectively. We expect FOC-price effects to be stronger in the SMALLOPEN and HIMFRGDP panels compared with LARGE and LOMFRGDP, respectively. Another possible classification is one based on the nature of a country's exports. We designated countries with 30 percent high-technology exports or above in 2000 as "high-technology" (HITECH) exporters and those with less than 10 percent as "low-technology" (LOTECH) exporters;[19] China and Mexico were included in both panels because of their intermediate status (they each had approximately 20 percent high technology exports in 2000 and in each case this share rose rapidly in the 1990s) and on the assumption that they compete with countries in both groups. We expect that the FOC hypothesis is more likely to apply to countries that are specialized in less technologically sophisticated, more "commoditized" exports, such as textiles and apparel. Finally, we distinguish between countries based on their external debt-to-GDP ratios using a 33 percent cut-off for the debt to GDP ratio, resulting in the two panels HIDEBT and LODEBT. This gives us a total of eight sub-panels consisting of more structurally homogeneous countries, as compared with the whole sample in the ALL panel.

Table 19.4 shows the results of estimating equation (2). As before, we used an

Table 19.4 GMM estimates of export equation (2), tests for FOC-price. Sample period after lags and differences, 1987–2004

Dependent variable: (logged value of) real exports, X

Panel	ALL	SMALLOPEN	LARGE	HIMFRGDP	LOMFRGDP	HITECH	LOTECH	HIDEBT	LODEBT
Cross-sections included	18	9	9	8	10	9	11	12	6
Total panel observations	336	165	171	146	190	165	209	222	114
Long-run coefficients on:									
Z^N	0.780	0.383	1.124	1.879	−0.122	1.109	−0.137	0.199	0.527
	(0.033)	(0.148)	(0.000)	(0.000)	(0.000)	(0.000)	(0.458)	(0.492)	(0.000)
R^N	−0.730	−0.669	−0.764	−3.757	2.524	−4.024	2.523	0.215	−1.474
	(0.211)	(0.355)	(0.000)	(0.000)	(0.000)	(0.000)	(0.000)	(0.756)	(0.000)
R^L	2.456	3.126	1.901	6.468	−1.562	4.918	−1.456	1.285	1.940
	(0.003)	(0.000)	(0.000)	(0.000)	(0.000)	(0.000)	(0.001)	(0.023)	(0.000)
Sargan test (p-value)	0.105	0.568	0.771	0.809	0.386	0.327	0.233	0.276	0.699

Notes: Same as for Table 19.2, except that the panels used here are the ones described in Table 19.3.

Source: Authors' calculations.

ARDL(1,1) specification with annual data and all variables measured in natural logarithms; long-run coefficients were calculated the same way as in Table 19.2.[20] In general, the results indicate that the developing country exporters in our sample mainly compete with each other, and not with domestic producers in the industrialized countries (this can be observed from the positive coefficients on R^L compared with the mostly negative coefficients on R^N in most of the panels shown in Table 19.4). The main exceptions are the LOMFRGDP and LOTECH panels. While we don't have strong prior expectations about the LOMFRGDP panel, the negative sign for R^L for the LOTECH panel is contrary to our priors – we would have expected exporting developing countries specialized in low-technology manufactures to face more competition from other developing countries, not less, as we originally found in Razmi and Blecker (2008). In that earlier article (in which the sample period covered only 1983–2001), we found that the LOTECH countries mainly competed with other developing countries, while the HITECH countries mainly competed with industrial country producers. A result that is more consistent with expectations is that the expenditure elasticity (coefficient on Z^N) is highly positive and significant for the HITECH countries, but negative and statistically insignificant for the LOTECH countries.

3.3   Output effects (FOC-growth)

To test for effects of intra-developing country competition in export markets on the growth of output, we estimate an econometric model that incorporates the same independent variables as in the export equation (2) but also controls for net financial inflows:[21]

$$\hat{Y}_{it} = c_0 + c_1\hat{Z}^N_{it} + c_2\hat{R}^N_{it} + c_3\hat{R}^L_{it} + c_4\hat{F}_{it} + v_{it} \tag{3}$$

where $\hat{Y}_{it}$ is the growth rate of real domestic output in country i at time t, $\hat{F}_{it}$ is the growth rate of real capital inflows (measured as a percentage of GDP) into country i at time t and v_{it} is the error term. All other variables are defined as before, except that ^s are used to indicate growth rates (measured as log differences).

We expect the expenditure effect c_1 and the financial inflows effect c_4 to be positive, while the signs of the relative price (real exchange rate) effects c_2 and c_3 are theoretically ambiguous as they depend on the degree to which the products of different countries are substitutes. The FOC-growth hypothesis rests on the assumption that developing countries' manufactured exports are close substitutes for each other, and that sales in the same industrialized country markets imply the possibility of mutual crowding out. Such crowding out can restrain the growth of exports and, in the presence of a balance of payments constraint, the growth of output as well. If these effects are significant, we would expect $c_3 > 0$, otherwise $c_3 \leq 0$.

This leaves the sign of c_2, which is the effect of a real depreciation of the home currency relative to the industrialized countries' currencies on the home country's growth rate. Although we hypothesize that the substitution effects of relative price changes are likely to dominate other effects when developing countries devalue relative to each other, if developing country manufactures do not compete to a significant extent with industrialized country products, then other channels may assume added importance when developing nations devalue relative to industrialized countries.[22] For example, recent studies have emphasized balance sheet effects. If a developing country's foreign debt is mostly denominated in industrialized country currencies, then a real devaluation relative to these countries could have a contractionary effect as the country suddenly has to scrounge for further resources to deal with the inflated debt burden. Also, many developing countries are dependent on industrialized countries for capital goods and equipment. A devaluation relative to those countries, by rendering these critical goods harder to buy, could have a negative impact on output. For these and other reasons, a real devaluation vis-à-vis industrialized countries may depress national income, as has been recognized in the large literature on contractionary devaluations.[23] In that case, $c_2 < 0$, which (following Blecker and Razmi, 2008) we call the "COD" (for contractionary devaluation) hypothesis. In the alternative case, $c_2 \geq 0$.

The estimates of equation (3) are summarized in Table 19.5, using the same panels of countries as in Table 19.4 (except that Hong Kong is omitted for lack of financial inflow data). The model is estimated in ARDL(1,1) form and only long-run coefficients are reported in the table as before. The estimates in Table 19.5, however, use different price measures: instead of the export price indexes used in the regressions in Tables 19.2 and 19.4, the regressions in Table 19.5 use consumer price indexes to adjust nominal exchange rates in calculating real exchange rates (results using the export price indexes, which are generally similar but suffer from certain econometric problems, are reported in Blecker and Razmi, 2008). The results in Table 19.5 reveal significant COD effects (i.e. negative coefficients on $\hat{R}^N$) in all of the panels shown and significant FOC-growth effects (i.e. positive coefficients on $\hat{R}^L$) in most of them. FOC-growth effects are strongest for the SMALLOPEN and LOTECH panels, but they were also found to be statistically significant in most of the other panels. As expected (based on the balance sheet effects discussed above), COD effects are stronger in HIDEBT panel compared with LODEBT. The only anomaly in these results is the negative coefficient on $\hat{R}^L$ for the HIMFRGDP panel, which in principle might be expected to have a relatively strong FOC-growth effect.

These findings suggest that the expanding group of developing countries that are pursuing an export-led growth strategy may face a dilemma. If any given exporting nation becomes more price-competitive in global export markets relative to competing developing nations (whether through a nominal currency depreciation, wage cuts, or other cost reductions), that country may obtain short-run growth benefits, but these are offset to the extent that its real exchange rate also depreciates relative to the industrialized countries at the same time. If other developing nations match the lower prices, then the competitive benefits vis-à-vis those nations are lost, while the contractionary effects of the depreciation relative to the industrialized countries are then felt by all the developing countries involved. Also, if a rival developing country cheapens its exports of manufactures and the home country is unable to match this depreciation, the latter may experience a growth slowdown as a result of the FOC-growth effect (there will not be a COD effect in the home country in this situation).

4 Conclusions and future prospects

In a recent newspaper editorial, Dani Rodrik writes that "there are signs that we are at the cusp of the transition to a new regime in which the rules of the game will not be nearly as accommodating for export-led strategies" (Rodrik, 2008). The reasons he cites for this prediction are the growth slowdown in the advanced economies associated with the financial crisis of 2007–08, the likely unwinding of global current account imbalances, and the

Table 19.5 GMM estimates of output equation (3), tests for FOC-growth and COD. Sample period after lags and differences, 1987–2004

Panel	ALL	SMALLOPEN	LARGE	HIMFRGDP	LOMFRGDP	HITECH	LOTECH	HIDEBT	LODEBT
Dependent variable: growth rate (log difference) of real GDP, $\hat{Y}$									
Cross-sections included	17	8	9	7	10	8	11	12	5
Total panel observations	297	142	155	124	173	191	142	209	89
Long-run coefficients on:									
$\hat{Z}^N$	0.122	0.122	0.118	0.111	0.059	0.221	0.039	0.073	0.118
	(0.000)	(0.000)	(0.000)	(0.000)	(0.000)	(0.000)	(0.000)	(0.021)	(0.000)
$\hat{R}^N$	−0.337	−0.376	−0.165	−0.301	−0.167	−0.121	−0.174	−0.272	−0.128
	(0.000)	(0.000)	(0.000)	(0.000)	(0.000)	(0.000)	(0.000)	(0.000)	(0.000)
$\hat{R}^L$	0.165	0.202	0.134	−0.212	0.086	−0.093	0.110	0.105	−0.086*
	(0.008)	(0.000)	(0.000)	(0.000)	(0.001)	(0.011)	(0.003)	(0.002)	(0.198)
$\hat{F}$	0.579	0.190	1.226	0.370	0.258	0.790	0.217	0.501	0.152
	(0.000)	(0.000)	(0.000)	(0.000)	(0.000)	(0.000)	(0.004)	(0.000)	(0.003)
Sargan test (p-value)	0.208	0.593	0.806	0.681	0.402	0.737	0.375	0.117	0.690

Notes: Same as for Table 19.2, except that all variables are measured in first differences of natural logarithms and the panels used here are the ones described in Table 19.3.

Source: Blecker and Razmi (2008), reproduced with permission.

threat of increased protectionism in the advanced countries. While these potential obstacles to future export-led growth are real, the research cited in this chapter shows that the export-led growth model already suffered from a significant internal contradiction even before these new problems arose. While such a model could work well for a small number of countries without too many competitors, such as the four Asian tigers in the 1970s and 1980s, the diffusion of the model to a large number of countries in the 1990s and 2000s made it likely that together they would face an adding-up constraint or FOC.

The econometric estimates discussed in this chapter find evidence in support of three variants of the FOC hypothesis. First, we found evidence of significant quantitative displacement of manufactured exports from some developing countries by similar types of exports from other developing countries. Second, we found that exports from different developing countries are strong substitutes for each other, in the sense that price competition over market shares in the industrialized countries enables the developing countries with relatively lower-priced exports to succeed at the expense of others. Third, and most strikingly, we found that developing countries obtain significant growth benefits by maintaining low real exchange rates relative to competing developing countries, in spite of the fact that real depreciations relative to the industrialized countries have contractionary effects. This suggests that the export-led growth model was not a panacea for many developing nations even under the more favorable global conditions that prevailed prior to 2008.

If industrialized country markets do not grow rapidly enough, even in prosperous times, to accommodate all of the desired increases in manufactured exports from the developing countries, one of the obvious solutions is to increase "South–South" or intra-developing country trade. Such trade has grown rapidly in recent years, especially in Asia (less so in other global regions). One recent study (Akin and Kose, 2008) finds that the more advanced emerging market nations have begun to "decouple" from the industrialized nations in the sense that the impact of Northern economic activity (GDP growth) on the growth of what they call "the emerging South" was reduced during the 1986–2005 period compared with earlier years. Nevertheless, the impact of Northern growth on the emerging South economies remains positive and significant after 1986, implying that the latter countries are not immune from a growth slowdown in the North. Moreover, regionally disaggregated results show that this apparent (and partial) "decoupling" is found only in the Asia-Pacific region, while in Latin America and the Caribbean the effect of Northern growth becomes larger and more significant after 1986, and for the "developing South" (i.e. the less developed nations) the effects of Northern growth remain strong and there is no structural break after 1986.[24] Thus, although the Asia-Pacific region has become relatively less dependent on Northern growth than in the past, it and all other parts of the "developing" and "emerging" South remain significantly constrained by the growth of their primary export markets, which continue to be located mainly in the advanced industrial economies. Finally, one should note that a significant part of South–South trade consists in the exchange of intermediate goods for further assembly, and to this extent Southern exports still depend ultimately on final consumer demand in the North (see Athukorala, 2008).

Our analysis thus leads inexorably to the conclusion that, for most developing or emerging nations, the path toward sustainable long-run development must emphasize internal markets and domestic demand much more than it has during the ascendancy of export-led strategies in the past few decades. Although those strategies produced several notable success stories in Asia, it does not appear feasible for all countries in the developing world to emulate their success – and if it was not feasible even during the years of relatively rapid global growth in the 1990s and mid-2000s, it will be even less so in the aftermath of the global financial crisis and recession of 2008–09. Perhaps one of the few silver linings of the latter will be the impetus it may give to a rethinking of development strategy, in the direction of a better balance of internal and external sources of demand, rather than the extreme pendulum swings of the import-substitution and export-promotion eras. Such a redirection of development policy may also permit a return to growth with equity, as labor income becomes seen as a crucial element of aggregate demand and not merely a cost to be minimized in the interest of external competitiveness.

Notes

The authors wish to thank Greg Seymour for capable reaearch assistance.

1. See Razmi (2007b) and Razmi and Blecker (2008) for more detailed statistics.
2. For surveys covering a wide range of studies see Blecker (2002, 2003), Mayer (2002), and Blecker and Razmi (2008).
3. The idea of using US import data to calculate terms of trade for developing country exports is due to Maizels (2000). The data shown in this figure are not available prior to 1991 on a comparable basis from the source used here.
4. Of course, the implication that ought to have been derived is that real exchange rate overvaluations would constitute a beneficial development policy objective, but, as pointed out by Williamson (2008), this implication was seldom or never translated into a serious policy recommendation.
5. See McCombie and Thirlwall (2004) for a collection of the main contributions.
6. The extended model including capital mobility is presented in the unpublished theoretical appendix to Blecker and Razmi (2008), which is available from the authors on request.
7. The result does not appear to hold for developed countries.
8. Other papers that have recently explored the real exchange rate–growth nexus include Aguirre and Calderón (2005), Prasad et al. (2007), Johnson et al. (2007), Eichengreen (2007), Williamson (2008), Frenkel and Ros (2006), and Montiel and Serven (2008).
9. These indexes use a dual weighting scheme previously utilized in Razmi and Blecker (2008) which, in spite of the common publication date, was written earlier than Blecker and Razmi (2008).
10. This literature originated with classic articles by Díaz-Alejandro (1963) and Krugman and Taylor (1978). For references to more recent literature as well as new empirical tests, see Razmi (2007a) and Blecker and Razmi (2008). It should be noted that the possibility of a devaluation being contractionary does not necessarily depend on short-run "J-curve" effects, in which the trade balance initially worsens and then eventually improves following a devaluation. Even if the J-curve eventually turns up and the trade balance improves, a devaluation can still be contractionary if the increase in the trade balance is offset by other consequences of the devaluation, such as the balance sheet effects discussed below.
11. This section draws on the authors' previously published findings in Razmi (2007b) and Blecker and Razmi (2008), and also presents updated and revised estimates similar to those in Razmi and Blecker (2008). For reasons of space, our discussion here is limited to the main panel data results. Readers are referred to the original articles for details of the index construction, sample selection criteria, individual country estimates, and sensitivity tests.
12. See Razmi (2007b) for the underlying theoretical specification of export demand that implies equation (1) as a method of testing for quantitative displacement. We ignore lags here in order to focus on the main motivation behind the specification; the lag structure is discussed below.
13. The developing countries, which were chosen because of the relatively high percentage of manufactures in their exports, are: Bangladesh, Brazil, China, Costa Rica, Hungary, India, Indonesia, Jordan, Korea (Rep.), Malaysia, Mauritius, Mexico, Morocco, Pakistan, the Philippines, Poland, South Africa, Sri Lanka, Taiwan, Thailand, Tunisia, and Turkey. The industrialized countries, which were chosen because of their size, are: Austria, Belgium, Canada, France, Germany, Italy, Japan, Netherlands, Spain, Sweden, Switzerland, the UK, and the US.
14. Notice that SITC 7 is also the category in which the growth of global production networks and vertical intra-industry trade was the most rapid during this period. See, for example, Lall et al. (2004) and UNCTAD (2004).
15. See Razmi (2007b) for complete results.

16. Both the China effect and the importance of the US market as a locus of competition are corroborated by other recent studies. For example, Arnold (2008) finds that a large part of the increase in Chinese imports into the US has come at the expense of imports from other Asian countries, rather than US domestic products. However, Hanson and Robertson (2008) find only a small impact of Chinese exports on exports of other developing countries using a gravity model. Also, Wang and Wei (2008) find evidence of increasing similarity of Chinese exports to domestic products in the US and other advanced economies.

17. See Razmi and Blecker (2008) and Blecker and Razmi (2008) for more details on how these price indexes were constructed and how the empirical model maps onto the theoretical framework alluded to in Note 6, above.

18. These 18 developing countries are Bangladesh, China, the Dominican Republic, Hong Kong, India, Jamaica, South Korea, Malaysia, Mauritius, Mexico, Pakistan, the Philippines, Singapore, Sri Lanka, Taiwan, Thailand, Tunisia and Turkey; the ten largest industrialized countries are Belgium, Canada, France, Germany, Italy, Japan, Netherlands, Switzerland, the UK and the US.

19. These panels largely correspond to the percentages of the countries' exports in the four major SITC classifications for manufactures. Especially, the countries that export largely products in SITC 7, which includes electronics, computers, automobiles and other types of machinery and equipment, are all in the HITECH category. In contrast, the countries whose exports are mostly in SITC 6 (mainly textiles and steel) and 8 (mostly apparel and footwear) are all in the LOTECH group.

20. Thus, the underlying specification is of a log-linear Cobb-Douglas form, which assumes that developing countries export products that are imperfect substitutes.

21. This empirical specification was used previously in Blecker and Razmi (2008) and is inspired by the theoretical models of Blecker (2002) and Blecker and Razmi (2004), discussed earlier.

22. See Razmi (2007a) and Blecker and Razmi (2008) for more detailed discussions of these other channels.

23. Another reason is that a devaluation tends to redistribute income away from labor, thereby reducing consumer demand. See the sources cited in Note 10, above.

24. The countries included in Akin and Kose's "emerging South" are Argentina, Brazil, Chile, Colombia, Mexico, Peru, Venezuela, China, Hong Kong, India, Indonesia, Korea, Malaysia, Pakistan, Philippines, Singapore, Thailand, Turkey, Egypt, Israel, Jordan, Morocco, and South Africa. These are largely the same countries we have included in this study as the developing nations most specialized in manufactured exports, with only a few exceptions (compare Notes 13 and 18, above).

References

Aguirre, A. and C. Calderón (2005), "Real exchange rate misalignments and economic performance", Working Paper Number 315, Central Bank of Chile, Santiago, April.

Akin, C. and M.A. Kose (2008), "Changing nature of North–South linkages: stylized facts and explanations", *Journal of Asian Economics*, **19** (1), 1–28.

Arnold, B. (2008), "How changes in the value of the Chinese currency affect U.S. imports", US Congressional Budget Office, July.

Athukorala, P. (2008), "China's integration into global production networks and its implications for export-led growth strategy in other countries in the region", Australian National University, Working Paper No. 2008/04, April.

Berg, A., J. Ostry and J. Zettelmeyer (2008), "What makes growth sustained?", IMF Working Paper Series 08/59, International Monetary Fund, Washington, DC, March.

Blecker, R.A. (2002), "The balance-of-payments-constrained growth model and the limits to export-led growth", in P. Davidson (ed.), *A Post Keynesian Perspective on Twenty-First Century Economic Problems*, Cheltenham, UK and Northampton, MA, USA: Edward Elgar, pp. 69–88.

Blecker, R.A. (2003), "The diminishing returns to export-led growth", in W.R. Mead and S.R. Schwenninger (eds), *The Bridge to a Global Middle Class: Development, Trade, and International Finance*, Boston: Kluwer, pp. 259–98.

Blecker, R. and A. Razmi (2008), "The fallacy of composition and contractionary devaluations: output effects of real exchange rate shocks in semi-industrialised countries", *Cambridge Journal of Economics*, **32** (1), 83–109.

Calvo, G. and C. Reinhart (2002), "Fear of floating", *Quarterly Journal of Economics*, **117** (2), 379–408.

Cline, W.R. (1982), "Can the East Asian model of development be generalized?", *World Development*, **10** (2), 81–90.

Deaton, A. and J. Muellbauer (1980), "An almost ideal demand system", *American Economic Review*, **70** (3), 312–26.

Díaz-Alejandro, C. (1963), "A note on the impact of devaluation and the redistributive effects", *Journal of Political Economy*, **71**, 577–80.

Eichengreen, B. (2007), "The real exchange rate and economic growth", unpublished manuscript, University of California, Berkeley, July.

Eichengreen, B., Y. Rhee and H. Tong (2007), "China and the exports of other Asian countries", *Review of World Economics*, **143** (2), 201–26.

Faini, R., F. Clavijo and A. Senhadji-Semlali (1992), "The fallacy of composition argument: is it relevant for LDCs' manufactures exports?", *European Economic Review*, **36** (4), 865–82.

Frenkel, R. and J. Ros (2006), "Unemployment and the real exchange rate in Latin America", *World Development*, **34** (4), 631–46.

Hanson, G.H. and R. Robertson (2008), "China and the manufacturing exports of other developing countries", Working Paper, University of California, San Diego, and Macalester College, January.

Hausmann, R., L. Pritchett and D. Rodrik (2005), "Growth accelerations", *Journal of Economic Growth*, **10**, 303–29.

Johnson, S., J. Ostry and A. Subramanian (2007), "The prospects for sustained growth in Africa: benchmarking the constraints", IMF Working Paper Series 07/52, International Monetary Fund, Washington, DC, March.

Kaplinsky, R. (1993), "Export processing zones in the Dominican Republic: transforming manufactures into commodities", *World Development*, **21**, 1851–65.

Kaplinsky, R. (1999), "If you want to get somewhere else, you must run at least twice as fast as that! The roots of the East Asian crisis", *Competition and Change*, **4**, 1–30.

Kaplinsky, R. and A.U. Santos-Paulino (2006), "A disaggregated analysis of EU imports: the implications for the study of patterns of trade and technology", *Cambridge Journal of Economics*, **30**, 587–611.

Krugman, P. and L. Taylor (1978), "Contractionary effects of devaluation", *Journal of International Economics*, **8** (3), 445–56.

Lall, S., M. Albaladejo and J. Zhang (2004), "Mapping fragmentation: electronics and automobiles in East Asia and Latin America", *Oxford Development Studies*, **32** (3), 407–32.

Levy-Yeyati, E. and F. Sturzenegger (2007), "Fear of appreciation", World Bank Policy Research Working Paper No. 4387, Washington, DC, 1 November.

Maizels, A. (2000), "The manufactures terms of trade of developing countries with the United States, 1981–97", Working Paper No. 36, Finance and Trade Policy Research Centre, Queen Elizabeth House, Oxford.

Mayer, J. (2002), "The fallacy of composition: a review of the literature", *World Economy*, **25** (6), 875–94.

McCombie, J.S.L. and A.P. Thirlwall (eds) (2004), *Essays on Balance of Payments Constrained Growth: Theory and Evidence*, London: Routledge.

Montiel, P. and L. Serven (2008), "Real exchange rates, saving and growth: is there a link?", Policy Research Working Paper, World Bank, Washington, DC, May.

Muscatelli, V.A., A.A. Stevenson and C. Montagna (1994), "Intra-NIE competition in exports of manufactures", *Journal of International Economics*, **37** (1), 29–47.

Palley, T. (2003), "Export-led growth: evidence of developing country crowding-out", in P. Arestis, M. Baddeley, and J. McCombie (eds), *Globalisation, Regionalism and Economic Activity*, Cheltenham, UK and Northampton, MA, USA: Edward Elgar, pp. 175–97.

Polterovich, V. and V. Popov (2002), "Accumulation of foreign exchange reserves and long term growth", unpublished manuscript, New Economic School, Moscow.

Prasad, E., R. Rajan and A. Subramanian (2007), "Foreign capital and economic growth", *Brookings Papers on Economic Activity*, **1:2007**, 1–57.

Razin, O. and S. Collins (1997), "Real exchange rate misalignments and growth. International economic integration: public economics perspectives", in A. Razin and E. Sadka (eds), *International Economic Integration: Public Economics Perspectives*, Cambridge: Cambridge University Press.

Razmi, A. (2004), "Three essays on balance of payments-related constraints on the growth of developing economies", unpublished PhD thesis, American University, Washington, DC.

Razmi, A. (2007a), "The contractionary short-run effects of nominal devaluation in developing countries: some neglected nuances", *International Review of Applied Economics*, **21** (5), 577–602.

Razmi, A. (2007b), "Pursuing manufacturing-based export-led growth: are developing countries increasingly crowding each other out?", *Structural Change and Economic Dynamics*, **18** (4), 460–82.

Razmi, A. and R. Blecker (2008), "Developing country exports of manufactures: moving up the ladder to escape the fallacy of composition?", *Journal of Development Studies*, **44** (1), 21–48.

Rodrik, D. (2008), "Is export led growth passé?", *Daily News Egypt*, 12 September, http://dailystaregypt.com/printerfriendly.aspx?ArticleID=16429.

United Nations Commission on Trade and Development (UNCTAD) (2004), *Trade and Development Report*, Geneva: UNCTAD.

Wang, Z. and S. Wei (2008), "What accounts for the rising sophistication of China's exports?", National Bureau of Economic Research, Working Paper No. 13771, February.

Williamson, J. (2008), "Exchange rate economics", Working Paper Number 08-3, Peterson Institute for International Economics, Washington, DC, February.

20 Trade and economic growth: a Latin American perspective on rhetoric and reality

Juan Carlos Moreno Brid and Esteban Pérez Caldentey[1]

1 Introduction

There is a longstanding tradition of analysing trade and growth in economics, going back to the discipline's founders. But for Latin America, the debate on the significance of this relationship has had much more than academic relevance. It has been one of the central components of the different approaches to development that have shaped the region's economic history, the other (closely related) component being the roles of the state and of the market in economic development.

In Latin America, the dominant understanding of the relationship between trade and growth has evolved radically over time. Starting from the position that foreign trade should be managed with the objective of promoting industrialization and domestic development, around the mid-1980s it changed to an opposing view based on the notion that free trade and privatization are the fundamental guarantors of sustainable economic growth. In the last ten years, however, the consensus view has shifted again, to a more critical, sceptical view of the benefits of trade as an automatic and dynamic engine of economic growth.

More precisely, the analysis of the trade–growth relationship in Latin America since World War II (WWII) has passed through various stages. The first, which lasted until the early 1960s, was associated with the dominance of the Structuralist school of economic thought. It was marked by a rejection of free trade policies, an emphasis on primary commodity exports and inward, state-led industrialization. In the second stage, which lasted from 1960 to the mid-1970s, the policies associated with "structuralism" were called into question. But many professional economists remained committed to state-led industrialization while also recognizing the role of manufacturing exports in promoting growth. The third and fourth stages were characterized by the dominance of orthodox economists and the unconditional support within the economics profession for free trade and free market policies. Finally the fifth stage, associated with the erosion of the Washington Consensus, reflects the end of the region's fascination with free trade as an unequivocal and strong promoter of development. It has its roots, on the one hand, in Latin America's failed quest to enter a path of high and sustained economic expansion after the drastic elimination of trade protection implemented across the continent since the mid-1980s. On the other hand, it is also rooted in the fact that the resumption of high rates of economic expansion in many countries of the region in the last five years has resulted mainly from the worldwide commodity and mineral boom – a boom whose cause and effects have nothing to do with the adoption of the trade liberalization reforms in the region.

The approaches to the relationship between trade and growth described above were embedded in particular rhetorics meant to persuade and win converts to their causes.[2]

The terms "center–periphery", "dependency", "external strangulation" and "secular decline in the terms-of-trade" were introduced and became integral parts of the development literature in the region during the inward industrialization stage. The expressions "import-substitution industrialization" (ISI), "export oriented industrialization" (EOI) and "rent-seeking behaviour" were widely used thereafter, especially in the third stage. As we will see, in spite of their theoretical difference, the rhetoric of the alternative approaches to trade and growth that have prevailed in Latin America shared a common feature. Each emphasized the allegedly dynamic, growth oriented character of their own interpretation of the determinants of growth and underscored their close correspondence to the Latin American reality. Opposing theoretical perspectives and their implicit economic policies were portrayed as flawed, based on an incorrect or unrealistic identification of the determinants of growth, and even as inapplicable to the Latin American case.

This chapter analyses the different approaches to trade and growth in Latin America from the end of WWII to the present day. Specifically, it examines the underlying rhetoric of these alternative approaches and the extent to which their rhetorics matched their understanding of Latin American reality. It is shown that throughout the period under study, the relationship between trade and growth was far from robust. In other words, the region has been unable to make exports the lynchpin of rapid long-run growth. Addressing this failure is one of the most urgent tasks confronting Latin America, and one that has received insufficient attention.

2   The Latin American rhetoric on trade and growth: Part I

At the time of the initial formulation of development as an economic discipline following WWII, the prevailing theory of international commerce advocated unrestricted trade on the grounds that it is a mutually beneficial activity for both rich and poor nations. Using as its centre-piece the doctrine of comparative advantage developed by David Ricardo, the theory asserted that free trade enables trading countries to specialize in the production of the commodities they are able to produce at home at the lowest real cost, in accordance with their factor endowments. Free trade thus facilitates the optimal use of resources. These benefits were compounded by the freedom of choice in consumption allowed for by free trade.[3]

The argument for free trade was very persuasive. It showed that any country – independently of its relative endowment of resources and its productive structure – would benefit from free trade. The free trade doctrine was part of the general argument for laissez-faire, which was lauded for its promotion of both economic efficiency and social equity. The latter was a crucial component of laissez-faire and free trade rhetoric. As asserted by Viner (1960, p. 66): "no modern people will have zeal for the free market unless it operates within a setting of 'distributive justice' with which they are tolerably content."[4]

The analytical argument for free trade required very stringent assumptions. It assumed market clearing in the labour market (full employment), and that all trading nations have equal access to the same technology and to all markets.[5] The majority of development economists dealing with the Latin American case, including Raúl Prébisch (1901–86), Ragnar Nurske (1907–59), W. Arthur Lewis (1915–91), Gunnar Myrdal (1898–1987) and Paul Rosenstein-Rodan (1902–85), adopted an opposite view. They maintained that the expansion of trade hindered economic growth and development. Their arguments were prefaced on the fact that the assumptions required by the argument for free trade theory were not applicable to developing countries. For this opposing perspective, the fact that developed and developing countries did not have access to the same technology and that there were no mechanisms to ensure that all countries could equally share the fruits of technological progress constituted the basis on which to question the mainstream view of the trade–growth–development nexus.

The above-named economists identified several mechanisms through which trade generated and compounded international inequality. Such mechanisms included (among others) the combination of inelastic world demand for primary products, the existing mix of monopolistic markets for manufactures and competitive markets for primary products, and the enclave nature of primary commodity production.

The view that trade could be a fetter to economic growth justified the implementation of state-led inward industrialization and development policies. From the mid-1940s until the 1960s, excluding trade as an automatic engine for growth meant that the problem of industrialization and development had to be understood as crucially dependent on achieving a sufficient rate of capital accumulation.[6] The process of capital accumulation would lead to development by the absorption of excess labour into the more productive sectors and by raising overall productivity (Lewis, 1954; Rosenstein-Rodan, 1943). Also, a rapid process of capital accumulation would allow the populations of developing countries to break away from the "vicious circle of poverty" or the "poverty trap" (Nurske, 1953; Nelson, 1956).

This alternative theoretical framework implied on the one hand that development could not be attained unless a significant effort was made to accumulate capital. On the other hand this framework presupposed that the existing "automatic market forces" would keep the economic system entrenched in a low level of development. Industrialization was not to be left to the market, but was rather to be the product of government intervention.[7] In fact, the state was called on to take a leading role in the inward industrialization process.

In the specific case of Latin America, the case for inward state-led industrialization found its most complete formulation in Prébisch (1949, 1951 and 1959).[8] It rested mainly on a division between the structure and function of countries in the centre (developed) and those in the periphery (developing). The former are self-sustained in their technological progress, which is the dynamic force in the growth process. The countries of the periphery supply food and raw materials to the countries of the centre but do not manage to benefit equally from the fruits of the technological progress achieved at the centre. In fact, the benefits of increased productivity in the periphery are transferred to the centre. Countries in the periphery are thus caught in a poverty trap. The suggested solution was inward state-led industrialization. As Prébisch (1984, p. 179) argued:

> import substitution stimulated by a moderate and selective protection policy was an economically sound way to achieve certain desirable effects. Such a policy would help correct the tendency toward a foreign constraint on development resulting from the low income elasticity of demand for imports of primary product by the centers, compared with the high income elasticity of demand at the periphery for manufactures from the centers. Import substitution by protection counteracts the tendency toward the deterioration in the terms of trade by avoiding the allocation of additional productive resources to primary export activities and diverting

them instead to industrial production. Industrialization, in addition to assisting the overall penetration of technology and creating employment, promotes changes in the structure of production in response to this high demand elasticity for manufactures . . . industrialization and increased productivity in primary production are complementary. The more intense the latter, the greater the need for industrialization.

The existing complementarities between primary production and industrialization meant that the manufacturing sector could not develop at the expense of agriculture. It also implied that state-led industrialization required the expansion of primary exports. Exports of primary products were to be encouraged as they provided the finance to buy imported capital goods – machinery and equipment – at this stage indispensable to sustain the industrialization effort.[9]

These arguments and theoretical constructs and their associated rhetoric did not in fact induce the adoption of import substitution policies by Latin America countries. Rather the opposite was the case. That is, the adoption of import substitution policies preceded the formulation of the approach associated with import substitution and its rhetoric. As stated by Prébisch (1984, p. 177):

> In reality my policy proposal provided a theoretical justification for the industrialization process which was already being followed (especially by the large countries of Latin America), to encourage others to follow it too, and to provide all of them with an orderly strategy for carrying this out.

In short, state-led industrialization was a fact before it became a policy and a policy before it became a theory.[10] Moreover, the political discourse that advocated this policy was dominated by the belief that industrialization, much more than a coherent set of economic measures with the aim of boosting growth and employment, was the way to overcome economic "backwardness".[11] In short, inward state-led industrialization policies were not derived from a theory and were not part of a standard economic strategy adopted by all or most Latin American economies. Rather they were a practical reality in the large economies of the region (Argentina, Brazil, Chile, Mexico and Venezuela).

In the nations that adopted this development strategy the state used a variety of instruments to promote industrialization, including its legal authority to control the major natural resource based industries (i.e. the "crown jewels"). It undertook the promotion of new industries through fiscal, monetary and commercial means. Such instruments included a variety of subsidies ranging from fiscal transfers and tax exemptions, and also the use of a selective tariff policy that aimed to increase effective protection. Most important, the state established national or development banks to channel credit under favourable circumstances – including below market and/or fixed nominal rates of interest – to targeted sectors.[12]

3   The Latin American rhetoric on trade and growth: Part II

The inward oriented development strategy evolved into one that highlighted the role played by the external sector in promoting growth. This change in orientation was in part a result of the perception that the strategy of inward industrialization did not provide the required foreign exchange, and that developing countries faced an impending foreign exchange gap. At the more general level, this change in orientation responded to the limitations of the inward industrialization process.[13] The strategy

Table 20.1   *Latin American real GDP per capita, average growth rates, 1941–59*
           (percentages)

Countries	Time periods	
	1941–49	1950–59
Argentina	2.3	0.8
Bolivia	0.6	−1.7
Brazil	1.6	3.6
Chile	1.5	1.3
Colombia	1.6	1.8
Costa Rica	4.7	2.8
Dominican Republic	3.0	3.4
Ecuador	4.1	2.4
El Salvador	9.3	1.8
Guatemala	0.3	0.5
Honduras	1.5	−0.1
Mexico	3.7	3.1
Nicaragua	4.2	2.4
Panama	−2.2	1.8
Paraguay	0.6	−0.7
Peru	2.5	3.0
Uruguay	2.5	1
Venezuela	6.7	2.9
Average	2.7	1.7

Source: Authors' own elaboration based on official figures.

gradually reached a point where it was unable to significantly develop the manufacturing industry and thus improve the growth prospects of Latin American economies (see Tables 20.1 and 20.2).

Between 1941–49 and 1950–59, the average growth rate for Latin America declined from 2.7 per cent to 1.7 per cent. At the same time the composition of Latin American GDP did not alter greatly. The share of most industries in economic activity (mining, transportation and communication, electricity, gas and water, and services) remained essentially unchanged, although between 1950 and 1960 the share of manufacturing increased slightly from 19 per cent to 22 per cent of GDP while that of agriculture declined from 25 per cent to 22 per cent. In terms of the distribution of the labour force, manufacturing maintained its share between 1950 and 1960, while that of agriculture fell from 54 per cent to 48 per cent.

The contribution of the inward industrialization process to growth and development during this period was hampered by several factors. Tax and investment incentives were provided to foreign firms, but these firms contributed little by way of value added and employment to the economies in which they operated and had rather regressive effects on the distribution of income. Moreover the strategy failed to create a robust domestic capital goods industry. As such, developing economies never really broke their dependency on imports of foreign machinery, equipment and intermediate goods. Finally, the

Table 20.2   Percentage distribution of gross domestic product and labour force by economic sector in Latin America, 1950–64

Sector	Distribution of gross product				Distribution of labour force			
	1950	1955	1960	1964	1950	1955	1960	1962
Agriculture	24.7	23.9	21.8	20.8	53.5	50.4	47.7	46.5
Mining	4.0	4.4	4.9	5.0	1.1	1.1	1.0	0.4
Manufacturing	**18.9**	**19.9**	**21.8**	**22.8**	**14.4**	**14.2**	**14.2**	**13.8**
Construction	3.4	3.4	3.3	3.3	3.7	4.5	4.8	4.6
Electricity, gas and water	0.7	0.8	1.0	1.2	4.2	4.7	5.2	5.3
Transportation and communication and other services	48.3	47.6	47.2	46.9	23.1	25.1	27.1	29.4
Total	100	100	100	100	100	100	100	100

Source: United Nations (1966); Grunwald (1970).

repatriation of profits by foreign firms and the substantial import requirements of domestically produced consumer goods compounded the balance of payments constraint.[14]

In Latin America, the limitations of this "closed economy" development strategy were soon recognized. In the late 1950s, the initial concern was the growing import requirement of capital and intermediate goods, which exceeded the capacity of exports thus creating a "foreign exchange gap". ECLA economists understood that to avoid what they termed the "external strangulation" of Latin American economies, the persistent rise in net imports of capital goods had to be offset by large volumes of financial flows, be they foreign investment or external debt.

During the 1960s, criticisms of the inward industrialization strategy became more general. It was argued that the strategy: (i) was not conducive to the development of manufacturing (ECLA, 1964), (ii) had failed to weaken the import requirements of capital and intermediate goods (Tavares, 1964), (iii) had failed to generate sufficient employment, and (iv) had created inefficient industries incapable of competing in the international markets (Macario, 1964).[15] Such recognition of the limits of the inward industrialization strategy opened the way for a shift towards a new "growth through trade" strategy. This shift was reinforced by the growing importance granted to trade by multilateral organizations, as reflected in the adoption in 1961 of resolution 1707, "International Trade as the Primary Instrument for Development" by the UN General Assembly. In this regard, the creation of the United Nations Conference on Trade and Development (UNCTAD) and the nomination of Raúl Prébisch as its first Director General provided a unique opportunity to articulate the new development strategy.

Prébisch criticized the strategy of industrialization, arguing that it was bringing about the creation of inefficient industries, leading Latin America to adopt on average the highest tariffs in the world, preventing the generation of economies of scale and thus hindering overall growth prospects.[16] In his words, it had:

Table 20.3   Composition of exports of Latin America (percentages), 1934–62

	1934–38	1946–51	1955–56	1961–62
Agricultural products	66	70	52	53
Minerals and fuels	33	28	44	43
Total raw material exports[a]	**99**	**98**	**96**	**96**
Manufactured products	1	2	4	4
Total	100	100	100	100

Note: [a] Total raw materials = sum of agricultural products and minerals and fuels.

Source: Grunwald (1970) p. 839.

generally insulated national markets from external competition, weakening and even destroying the incentive necessary for improving the quality of output and lowering costs under the private-enterprise system. It has thus tended to stifle the initiative of enterprises as regards both the internal and external market exports.[17]

The revised strategy was formulated by UNCTAD for the developing world as a whole.[18] However, it reflected foremost the evolution of Latin American thinking on the relationship between trade and growth. As noted by Love (2005), pp. 170–1: "The original UNCTAD programme . . . was that of ECLA *mutatis mutandis* at the global level. Prébisch's reports to the organization in 1964 and 1968 if not fully *cepalismo*, were definitely international adaptations of the regional agency as it had evolved by the early 1960s."[19] From this new perspective exports of primary commodities were seen as necessary to finance imports. It also emphasized the need for developing countries to export manufactured products. In the case of Latin America, manufactured export products accounted for only 4 per cent of total exports in 1961–62 (see Table 20.3). Moreover, it also argued that non-reciprocal treatment should be granted by developed to developing countries to "promote specialization in industrial and primary commodities". Such treatment was justified on the basis of the infant industry argument. Trade – and more specifically managed trade – was considered a "primary instrument for growth". Within this strategy the government had a key role to play in the management of trade, by implementing selected measures to monitor the evolution of imports and promoting exports.

4   The Latin American rhetoric on trade and growth: Part III

The Latin American rhetoric on trade changed remarkably from the 1980s onwards. The main event behind this shift was the international debt crisis that plunged the whole region into a deep financial collapse. Indeed, following the onset of the crisis in 1980, Latin American GDP per capita growth contracted in 1981, 1982 and 1983 by 1.8 per cent, 3.6 per cent and 4.7 per cent respectively (Figure 20.1). The varying intensity of the debt crisis within Latin America produced large disparities of GDP per capita variation at the country level. In 1981, eight out of 18 Latin American countries suffered contractions, including three of the largest economies of the region: Argentina, Brazil and Venezuela (where GDP fell 7.1 per cent, 6.6 per cent and 3.4 per cent respectively). In 1982, all Latin American economies, with the exception of Panama, experienced contraction. In 1983, the region contracted once again with the exceptions of Argentina and three Central American countries (Costa Rica, El Salvador and Nicaragua). In spite of the slow recovery process that began in 1984, these three consecutive years of massive downturns produced the worst decadal growth performance in Latin America and the 1980s were termed the "Lost Decade" (see Figure 20.1).

The "Lost Decade" and the codification of free market oriented policies into the so-called Washington Consensus became the main pillars on which to launch a devastating critique of the developmental policies followed previously in Latin America. Countries were urged and pressured to follow the mantra: "Stabilize, privatize and liberalise."[20]

The policies followed prior to the 1980s were all classified under the label of import substitution industrialization (ISI). This label permeated the development vocabulary, and was interpreted (or caricatured) as an autarkic strategy seeking to substitute domestic goods for imports through a plethora of price distorting incentives, in particular in the area of trade policy. A recent textbook description is provided in Dunn and Mutti (2000, pp. 264–65):

> During 1950–1970, the governments of many developing countries encouraged by a few academic economists, concluded that international trade was unlikely to benefit poor countries and that they should design policies to minimize their reliance on trade. Instead of stressing export growth, tariffs and other trade barriers were used to encourage the growth of local industries in order to produce substitutes for products that had previously been imported. This inward-looking, or autarkic, approach was designed to sharply reduce the role of trade in a nation's economy . . . the export sector could be ignored or even taxed, a strategy that promoted the shift of resources out of primary production.[21]

Mainstream economists and orthodox policy makers consider ISI as having had only detrimental consequences for growth. They argue that ISI is at the root of many of the ills of developing economies including: the decline of primary sector output and exports; the excessive promotion of capital-intensive techniques coupled with low capac-

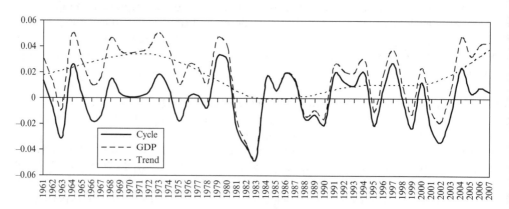

Source: Authors' calculations based on data from World Bank Development Indicators (2009).

Figure 20.1   Per capita GDP growth in Latin America, decomposed into trend and cycle (Hodrick-Prescott method), 1961–2007

ity utilization and high levels of unemployment and informality; unequal distribution of incomes and high poverty rates.[22]

The intellectual origins of such anti-ISI rhetoric can be traced back to a series of empirical studies aimed at measuring the effects of the distortions brought about by trade protection. Perhaps the most influential one in this regard was Little et al. (1970). The book argued that countries that pursued import substitution policies beyond certain limits suffered adverse impacts. Import substitution led to an inefficient and high cost industrial sector incapable of facing foreign competition, and that could only survive by absorbing resources from other sectors, inter alia agriculture. They emphasized that the administrative controls necessary to keep in place this "distorted" incentive structure led firms to operate below potential capacity and thus to generate unemployment.

A key empirical measure of the distortion introduced by ISI policies presented by these and subsequent authors is the rate of effective protection.[23] This measures the percentage by which the value added at a particular stage of processing in a domestic industry can exceed what it would be without protection.[24] The greater the effective rate of protection the greater the level of distortion introduced by a given tariff regime. Their empirical studies concluded that the rates of effective protection in Latin America were high and that they exhibited great variance by type of good, among economic sectors and even within countries (see Tables 20.4 and 20.5 below). As an example, the average rate of effective protection in Brazil in the year 1966 ranged from 31 per cent in capital goods industries to 230 per cent in the consumption goods industries. But in Mexico, the rate of effective protection was much lower and the dispersion narrower, varying from 22 per cent in the consumption goods industries to 55 per cent in capital goods industries. Moreover, while Brazil afforded the highest rate of protection to consumption goods, Mexico provided it to its capital goods industries (see Table 20.4).

The argument based on the concept of effective protection turned out to be weak. First, as shown in Table 20.5, estimates of effective protection rates exhibited a wide range of variation. While Little et al. (1970) calculated a rate of 162 per cent for Argentina for the manufacturing sector, Cohen (1971) computed a rate of just 55 per cent. These computations also required stringent assumptions that call into question their veracity. Most important, empirical studies that followed the pioneering study by Little et al. (1970) showed that the role of the rate of effective protection in obstructing export development, industrialization and growth was in fact ambiguous. As explained by Bruton (1998) p. 912:

Table 20.4   *Average rate of effective protection for manufacturing by type of good in selected Latin American countries (percentages)*

Country	Year	Consumption	Intermediate	Capital	All manufactures
Argentina	1958	164	167	133	162
Brazil	1966	230	68	31	118
Mexico	1960	22	34	55	27

Source: Little et al. (1970), p. 174.

Table 20.5   *Estimates of average rates of effective protection in selected Latin American countries*

Country	Little et al. (1970)[a,b]	Cohen (1971)[b]	Anjaria et al. (1985)[b]	Greenaway and Milner (1987)	World Bank (1987)
Argentina	162	55	27	. . .	. . .
Brazil	118	58	66	63	23
Chile	. . .	. . .	217	. . .	217
Colombia	. . .	. . .	29	19	55
Costa Rica	. . .	. . .	22	. . .	. . .
Dominican Republic	. . .	. . .	124	. . .	. . .
El Salvador	. . .	. . .	44	. . .	. . .
Guatemala	. . .	. . .	31	. . .	. . .
Honduras	. . .	. . .	59	. . .	. . .
Mexico	27	61	49	. . .	. . .
Nicaragua	. . .	. . .	53	. . .	. . .
Uruguay	. . .	. . .	384	384	. . .

Notes:
. . . denotes not available.
[a]   The rates of effective protection in Little at al. refer to the years 1958, 1966 and 1960 for Argentina, Brazil and Mexico. The rates of effective protection in Cohen are for the years 1953, 1966 and 1960 for Argentina, Brazil and Mexico respectively. The rates of effective protection for World Bank (1987) correspond to the years 1980–81, 1967 and 1979 for Brazil, Chile, Colombia.
[b]   Rates of effective protection in the manufacturing sector.

Sources: Little et al. (1970), Greenaway and Milner (1987) and World Bank (1987).

> A particularly interesting point about the ERP [effective rate of protection] as it evolved is that a number of countries, later achieving outstanding success, showed the same sort of protection picture as did later failures. An obvious example is Taiwan. . . . Taiwan's ERP for consumer goods was higher than that of the Philippines and vastly higher than that of Mexico . . . Evidently the role of ERP is still ambiguous.

This initial ISI criticism based on empirical measures such as the rate of effective protection was surpassed by an argument that emphasized the inefficient and rent-seeking character of government and government officials. Rent seeking was highlighted as a wasteful, inefficient and costly activity inherent to any regime based on strong intervention of the state in the economy. This criticism – based on the New Political Economy (NPE) – argued for a minimalist state as its proponents argued that governments were "almost universally prone to failure".[25]

The argument was potent because it stated that the most serious detrimental consequence of ISI for growth and development stemmed not from the distortion of resource allocation and its effects on output. Rather, the most important consequence was that it led to rent seeking, thus destroying the very foundations for growth and development. Indeed, ISI was seen as merely transforming the main agents of production and growth, namely firms and entrepreneurs, into rent-seeking entities. The argument was already present in Little et al.:

The most serious results of these policies, however, is that the nascent industries have come to depend for their profits on government decisions, and so have formed the habit of devoting their efforts to obtaining privileges by pressure on the government rather than by cutting their costs.[26]

Nonetheless, the NPE rent-seeking ISI argument was developed to its full extent during the 1980s drawing on the work of Buchanan and Tullock (1962).[27]

Either forced by necessity or convinced by the weight of argument, most Latin American economies adopted trade liberalization policies in the late 1980s and 1990s. In a sense, the free trade discourse and associated rhetoric represented a return to the arguments traditionally espoused in favour of such policies. First, that free trade improves resource allocation and stimulates employment and growth. Second, free trade is fair trade as it provides equal trading opportunity to all countries according to their respective capacities and endowments. Third, free trade helps countries to achieve development, rewarding economic agents and sectors with comparative advantage. Fourth, free trade benefits households and firms by widening the supply of products and lowering their costs. And finally, free trade prevents rent-seeking behaviour and promotes good government.[28]

During this period Latin American countries completed their adhesion to the GATT and World Trade Organization (WTO), reduced their tariff rates and opened up their economies. Following trade liberalization and taking the 1980s as a reference point, the average regional tariff rate declined from 37 per cent to 12 per cent during the trade liberalization period.[29] The openness coefficient, measured as the sum of export and imports over GDP, almost doubled, increasing from 23 per cent to 40 per cent between the periods 1970–80 and 2002–06 (see Tables 20.6 and 20.7).

The Latin American stance on free trade was enhanced by the region's active participation in promoting the Free Trade Area of the Americas,[30] and more importantly in the region's involvement in the proliferation in bilateral free trade agreements (BFTA). The number of BFTAs – just four prior to the North American Free Trade Agreement signed by Mexico, the US and Canada in 1994 – increased thereafter to more than 20 (see Table 20.8).

5   The Latin American rhetoric on trade and growth: Part IV

The proliferation of BFTAs has without doubt deepened Latin America's free market orientation by significantly reducing the scope for public policy and government intervention, and by bringing under the sphere of the market other areas such as labour and the environment. This trend, present in NAFTA, is epitomized by the BFTA signed between the United States and Chile (2004). Both agreements have provided the structure and legal model for the majority of free trade agreements signed (or in the process of negotiation) by Latin American countries.

In these agreements, trade in goods is governed by the principle of non-discrimination and provides for the phasing out and elimination of tariffs between the signatory countries. While tariffs are for the most part programmed to be immediately eliminated, the text often contemplates their gradual phasing out for selected products over a specified period. Contrary to WTO legal texts, the services provisions require the granting of national and most-favoured-nation treatment (i.e. non-discriminatory treatment) to service suppliers of contracting parties. The WTO General Agreement on Trade in Services (GATS) text permits the imposition of "discriminatory subsidies." However,

Table 20.6   Year of adhesion to GATT and WTO, and pre and post trade liberalization tariff rates and tariff dispersion in Latin America

Country	GATT	WTO	Year of trade liberalization	Pre trade liberalization		Post trade liberalization	
				Tariff rate	Tariff dispersion	Tariff rate	Tariff dispersion
Argentina	1967	1995	1991	42.0	15–115	12.5	5–22
Bolivia	1990	1995	1985	12.0		10.3	5–10
Brazil	1948	1995	1991	51.0	0–105	17.32	0–65
Chile	1949	1995	1976	35.0	35	11.33	11
Colombia	1981	1995	1986	61.0	0–220	10.60	5–20
Costa Rica	1990	1995	1986	53	0–1400	14.30	5–20
Dominican Republic	1948	1995	1992	. . .	. . .	16.70	. . .
Ecuador	–	1996	1991	37.0	0–338	11.29	2–25
El Salvador	1991	1995	1989	20.0		9.38	5–20
Guatemala	1991	1995	1988	50.0	5–90	10.27	5–20
Honduras	1994	1995	1991	41.0	5–90	8.90	5–20
Mexico	1966	1995	1986	24.0	0–100	12.53	0–20
Nicaragua	1950	1995	1991	15.9	. . .	9.90	0–20
Panama	–	1997	1996	. . .	. . .	10.67	. . .
Paraguay	1994	1995	1989	. . .	. . .	10.91	3–86
Peru	1951	1995	1991	37.6	0–120	16.80	5–25
Uruguay	1953	1995	1990	32.0	10–55	14.00	12–24
Venezuela	1990	1995	1996	37.0	0–135	14.31	0–50

Notes:
. . . denotes not available.
The pre trade liberalization years are 1984 for Chile, 1985 for Bolivia, Costa Rica, Guatemala, Honduras and Mexico, 1987 for Brazil and Uruguay, 1986 for Argentina, 1988 for Paraguay and Peru, 1989 for Ecuador and Venezuela, 1978–84 for Nicaragua, 1980 for El Salvador. The post trade liberalization year is 1990 for Mexico, 1991 for Argentina, Bolivia, Chile, Paraguay and Venezuela and 1992 for the rest of the countries.

Sources: Wacziarg and Welch (2003); Henry (2007); WTO (2008b); Alam and Rajapatirana (1993); Cardoso and Helwege (1992).

within the framework of the most perfected bilateral BFTA, these measures are not allowed once the agreement enters into force.

The more recent bilateral agreements include an investment chapter. Its provisions are without doubt one of the most important pillars of the BFTAs.[31] It seeks to provide protection for foreign investors, or more specifically, "a secure, predictable, legal framework for foreign investors". This chapter is also one of the more controversial ones. First, the definition of investment is broad enough to cover tangible and intangible assets (property rights are considered an investment). Second, the investment chapter generally accords foreign investors national treatment and most-favoured-nation treatment. Both national and most-favoured-nation provisions refer to the equality of treatment accorded to national and foreign investors in "like circumstances".[32] The term "like circumstances" is, however, broad and difficult to define and delimit.

Table 20.7 Trade openness in selected regions (percentages of GDP), 1970–2006

	1970–80	1981–91	1992–2006
Latin America & Caribbean	23.5	28.3	40.3
East Asia & Pacific	22.1	37.9	66.2
Europe & Central Asia	. . .	45.4	69.8
Euro area	46.2	54.6	64.5
Middle East & North Africa	60.4	51.1	57.2
South Asia	15.6	18.3	30.9
Sub-Saharan Africa	53.9	53.2	61.7
World	32.5	37.4	45.5

Note: Openness was measured as the sum of imports and exports divided by GDP.

Source: *World Bank Development Indicators* (2008a).

Table 20.8 Existing trade agreements in the Americas

Agreement	Date of entry into force	Type of agreement
Central American Common Market	1961	Customs Union
Latin American Integration Association	1981	Preferential Trade Agreement
Andean Community of Nations	1988	Customs Union
MERCOSUR	1991	Customs Union
NAFTA	1994	Free Trade Area
Costa Rica–Mexico	1995	Free Trade Area
Canada–Chile	1997	Free Trade Area
Mexico–Nicaragua	1998	Free Trade Area
Chile–Mexico	1999	Free Trade Area
EFTA–Mexico	2000	Free Trade Area
Israel–Mexico	2000	Free Trade Area
EC–Mexico	2000	Free Trade Area
Guatemala–Mexico	2001	Free Trade Area
El Salvador–Mexico	2001	Free Trade Area
Honduras–Mexico	2001	Free Trade Area
Chile–Costa Rica	2002	Free Trade Area
Chile–El Salvador	2002	Free Trade Area
Canada–Costa Rica	2002	Free Trade Area
EC–Chile	2003	Free Trade Area
Panama–El Salvador	2003	Free Trade Area
United States–Chile	2004	Free Trade Area
Korea–Chile	2004	Free Trade Area
EFTA–Chile	2004	Free Trade Area
Japan–Mexico	2005	Free Trade Area
CAFTA–DR	2006	Free Trade Area
Panama–Singapore	2006	Free Trade Area
Chile–China	2006	Free Trade Area
Chile–Japan	2007	Free Trade Area

Source: WTO (2008b).

Third, the level of generality of the investment chapter is enhanced by the call for minimum standards of treatment for foreign investors. The minimum standard of treatment means that investment should be treated according to the canons of customary international law. In turn, customary international law is defined as including "fair and equitable treatment" and "full security and protection".[33] Fourth, the investment chapter explicitly decouples investment flows from performance requirements (such as requirements that activity involve a given level or percentage of domestic content, or generate a certain level of foreign exchange earnings).

The most controversial provisions of the investment chapter are those related to the issues of expropriation and compensation. The free trade agreements prohibit direct or indirect expropriation (or nationalization). Direct expropriation is a well-defined term that refers to the nationalization, transfer of title or seizure of private property by the host government.[34] However, the term indirect expropriation (or nationalization) can be interpreted in different ways.[35] The legal texts mention the phrase "indirect expropriation by measures equivalent (or tantamount) to expropriation or nationalization".[36] In order to determine whether an action constitutes "indirect expropriation" it needs to be assessed on a case-by-case basis. The evidence includes the economic impact of government action, the degree of interference of government action with investment-backed expectations.[37]

All BFTAs are similar in their structure and content, with some chapters having identical provisions. It can be easily argued that the negotiations are in fact a gradual piecemeal approach to a single BFTA with the rest of the world, whereby countries are added on a gradual basis. In this view, the bilateral agreements will eventually converge to an overall encompassing multilateral agreement, giving credence to the consequent improvement in welfare and growth hypothesized by free trade advocates. In short, the BFTAs represent the last step towards the outright liberalization of the movement of goods and services and the full implementation of free trade policies. They also imply the quasi-complete abandonment of domestic policies to stimulate growth.

6   The pattern of export development 1970–2006

Following the trade liberalization initiatives of the 1990s, Latin America did improve its export performance. The average annual rate of growth of exports of goods and services jumped from 4.8 per cent in 1970–91 to 7.3 per cent in 1992–2006 (see Figure 20.2). However, this dynamism of exports barely enhanced Latin America's participation in world trade.

As shown in Figure 20.3, Latin America increased, albeit modestly, its share of world exports of goods and services from 4.5 per cent in 1990 to 5 per cent in 2006. But its share of world trade in the post trade liberalization period (1990–2006) never managed to reach the levels attained during the pre-liberalization era (1960–70). Moreover, the region has not improved its position in relation to other emerging economies in the East Asian bloc. It is worth noting that the economies of East Asia and the Pacific and Latin America had similar shares of world trade in the periods 1970–80 and 1980–90 (4.4 per cent and 4.6 per cent, and 4.9 per cent and 4.6 per cent respectively). However, during 1990–2006 (the period of trade liberalization), East Asia and the Pacific augmented their share in world trade to 8 per cent, surpassing that attained by Latin America (5 per cent).

Latin America's export performance can be better explained by examining the com-

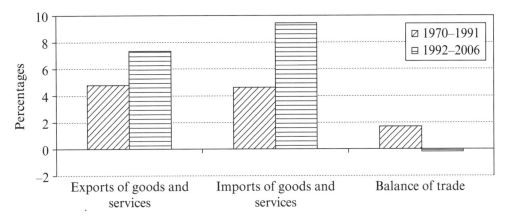

Source: *World Development Indicators* (World Bank, 2008a) and ECLAC (2008).

Figure 20.2 *Latin America. Exports and imports of goods and services (annual average rates of growth), 1970–2006*

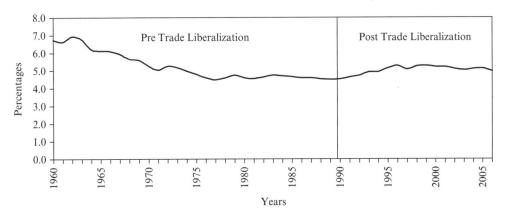

Source: *World Development Indicators* (World Bank, 2008a).

Figure 20.3 *Latin America's share of world exports (percentages), 1960–2006*

position of its exports. To this end, we compute the composition of exports of Latin America by factor intensity and compare it to that of world imports. If the Latin American factor intensity composition of exports differs substantially from that of world imports, then Latin America's pattern of specialization does not meet the conditions of external demand.

Table 20.9 shows the exports of Latin America to the rest of the world, classified by factor intensity into five categories using the SITC classification for the period 1980–2006. The categories are: (i) primary commodities, (ii) labour intensive and resource-based manufactures, (iii) manufactures with low skill and technology intensity, (iv) manufactures with medium skill and technology intensity, and (v) manufactures with high skill and technology intensity.

Table 20.9   Merchandise exports of Latin America to the rest of the world and world merchandise imports classified by group according to factor intensity, 1980–2006 (in percentage of the total)

Product group	1980	1985	1990	1995	2000	2002	2005	2006
Exports of Latin America to the rest of the world classified by group according to factor intensity								
Primary commodities	78.9	64.7	55.2	40.6	28.4	29.3	34.8	37.4
Labour-intensive and resource-based manufactures	8.8	9.8	10.9	12.2	12.1	11.8	10.0	8.4
Manufactures with low skill and technology intensity	2.4	9.0	8.7	6.9	5.6	6.0	7.1	6.2
Manufactures with medium skill and technology intensity	3.8	7.9	13.5	22.6	28.4	27.8	25.6	25.2
Manufactures with high skill and technology intensity	4.8	7.9	10.3	15.3	23.6	23.1	20.3	20.2
Not classified	1.2	0.8	1.4	2.4	1.9	2.1	2.3	2.5
World imports classified by group according to factor intensity								
Primary commodities	26.1	22.1	18.6	16.9	13.4	13.5	13.6	14.3
Labour-intensive and resource-based manufactures	18.2	17.9	20.1	19.4	18.6	18.7	17.1	16.4
Manufactures with low skill and technology intensity	8.8	7.2	6.6	6.5	5.8	5.7	6.9	7.0
Manufactures with medium skill and technology intensity	32.3	37.3	38.8	41.6	46.5	44.8	44.6	44.7
Manufactures with high skill and technology intensity	11.7	12.0	12.3	12.4	12.5	13.9	14.5	14.4
Not classified	2.9	3.5	3.6	3.2	3.2	3.4	3.3	3.1
Coefficient of adaptation of Latin America's exports to world import demand								
Primary commodities	3.02	2.93	2.97	2.41	2.12	2.16	2.55	2.61
Labour-intensive and resource-based manufactures	0.49	0.55	0.54	0.63	0.65	0.63	0.59	0.51
Manufactures with low skill and technology intensity	0.27	1.24	1.31	1.06	0.95	1.05	1.03	0.88
Manufactures with medium skill and technology intensity	0.12	0.21	0.35	0.54	0.61	0.62	0.57	0.56
Manufactures with high skill and technology intensity	0.41	0.65	0.84	1.23	1.89	1.66	1.40	1.40

Note: Authors' own computations based on the classification provided by UNCTAD (2002) and data obtained from WITS (World Bank, 2008b).

Table 20.9 shows a change in the composition of Latin American exports to the rest of the world, which has affected mainly primary commodities and manufactures with medium and high skill and technology intensity. Since 1980 the share of both manufactures with medium skill and technology intensity and manufactures with high skill and technology intensity has increased. Their respective export shares rose from 3.8 per cent and 4.8 per cent in 1980 to 25 per cent and 20 per cent of the total in 2006. During the same period the share of commodity exports declined from 79 per cent to 37 per cent. The shares of the two remaining categories, manufactures that are labour-intensive and resource-based, and those with low skill and technology intensity, have not changed significantly over time. But these changes in the composition of exports began prior to the trade liberalization period. As a result, trade liberalization per se may not have produced any change with respect to the share of commodities in Latin America's export basket, but merely reinforced a previously existing trend. Furthermore, in spite of the decline in the commodity share of exports, the export structure remains predominantly commodity oriented. This characteristic is even more pronounced when the analysis is carried out at a more detailed and disaggregated level on a country-by-country basis.

Table 20.10 shows the ten leading traditional Latin American export products on a country-by-country basis for 1995 and 2006, classified by major categories. The categories include food and agriculture, beverages, oils and seeds, raw materials, mining and energy. The ten major commodity exports accounted on average for 56 per cent of the total for Latin America.

At the country level, the data reveal that a subset of countries (Paraguay, Uruguay, Panama and Nicaragua) are highly specialized in the export of traditional commodities and have strengthened their pattern of specialization over time. For this group of countries, the ten major leading commodities represented 64 per cent and 71 per cent of total exports of goods in 1995 and 2006.

The exceptions to this pattern of specialization are mainly Central American countries (Costa Rica, El Salvador, Guatemala, Honduras), which have markedly decreased their degree of specialization in primary commodities (from 54 per cent to 29 per cent of the total). With the exception of Costa Rica, Central American countries have switched to the export of textiles. At the country level in 1990 textile exports represented 22.8 per cent, 24.0 per cent, and 22.9 per cent of the total exports to the United States for El Salvador, Guatemala and Honduras, respectively. In 2006, textile exports represented 76 per cent, 54 per cent, and 68 per cent for the same countries respectively (see Table 20A.1 in the appendix).

Comparison of the composition of Latin America's exports with that of world imports shows that the region's specialization in manufactures with high skill and technological intensity and more importantly commodities is greater than that required by the rest of the world. In the case of commodities, the ratio of Latin America's share of commodities as a percentage of its total exports relative to the share of world commodity imports in total world imports is roughly 2.5 per cent for the whole period. That is, Latin America's specialization in commodities exports is more than twice as great as that required by the composition of imports in the rest of the world.

Meanwhile, Latin America's export specialization in labour-intensive and resource-based manufactures and manufactures with medium skill and technology intensity falls

Table 20.10 Export share of the ten leading products in selected Latin American countries, 1995–2006 (percentages)

	Food and agriculture		Beverages		Oil and seeds		Raw materials		Mining		Energy		Total traditional		Other		Total	
	1995	2006	1995	2006	1995	2006	1995	2006	1995	2006	1995	2006	1995	2006	1995	2006	1995	2006
Argentina	18.0	9.5			17.4	21.0				2.9	7.6	16.2	43.0	49.6	0.0	0.0	43.0	49.6
Bolivia		2.6			7.3	11.5			38.3	16.7	11.9	46.3	57.5	77.1	13.0	2.4	70.5	79.5
Brazil	7.3		4.2	2.1	4.4	6.9	3.5		8.2	6.2		7.6	27.6	22.8	6.2	11.7	33.8	34.5
Chile	10.7	6.8					6.8	2.7	45.7	52.3		2.0	63.2	63.8	1.5	4.1	64.7	67.9
Colombia	22.2	9.4							7.4	14.5	21.4	26.1	51.0	50.0	13.5	13.0	64.5	63.0
Ecuador	39.8	21.3	6.2	1.2		1.2			2.2		35.1	56.9	83.3	80.6	1.8	4.7	85.1	85.3
Paraguay	40.7	33.9			29.8	44.7							70.5	78.6	7.9	2.1	78.4	80.7
Peru	13.3	7.1	5.3						38.0	49.3	5.0	7.2	61.6	63.6	0.0	5.8	61.6	69.4
Uruguay	36.3	42.8				3.0						4.4	36.3	50.2	15.4	5.6	51.7	55.8
Venezuela									3.9	2.3	76.3	87.2	80.2	89.5	4.9	3.5	85.1	93.0
Costa Rica	34.4	14.5	15.5	3.5									49.9	18.0	5.3	37.2	55.2	55.2
El Salvador	10.4	7.1	37.7	9.9								2.9	48.1	19.9	11.3	21.6	59.4	41.5
Guatemala	23.2	16.8	28.1	13.8		3.0					1.7	6.7	53.0	40.3	7.1	13.3	60.1	53.6
Honduras	34.8	17.2	28.6	17.5		3.0			2.2				65.6	37.7	8.5	19.4	74.1	57.1
Nicaragua	32.2	45.5	23.5	15.1						5.3			55.7	65.9	15.7		71.4	65.9
Panama	58.6	75.1	5.8						3.2				67.6	75.1	7.1	2.2	74.7	77.3
Mexico											9.3	13.2	9.3	13.2	33.5	35.2	42.8	48.4

Source: Own computations based on the anuario estadístico de la CEPAL (2007).

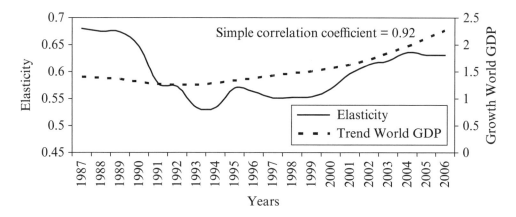

Source: Authors' elaboration based on data from *World Development Indicators* (World Bank, 2008a).

Figure 20.4   *Trends in the income elasticity of demand for Latin American exports (Kalman filter) and world real GDP growth (Hodrick-Prescott filter), 1987–2006*

below that required by world imports. The ratio of Latin America's exports of labour-intensive and resource-based manufactures and manufactures with medium skill and technology intensity to that of imports of these goods by the rest of the world is on average 0.5. In short, trade liberalization has not managed to change the composition of Latin America's exports to adequately meet the conditions of demand from the rest of the world. As a result the region has not been able to boost exports on a sufficient scale to gain world market share. In this sense it is important to note that, contrary to free trade rhetoric, increasing exports is not equivalent to changing their composition towards products with a higher value added, but means rather changing their composition to meet external demand. Latin America's failure to adjust its export basket to world demand is reflected in the fact that the world income elasticity of demand for its exports is less than unity.

Figure 20.4 shows the income elasticity of demand for Latin American exports and the trend of the rate growth of world GDP. The export elasticity was computed from a standard export equation using space-state econometric techniques. That is, exports (in real terms) are posited as a function of the terms-of-trade and world real GDP per capita. The trend in real world GDP growth was obtained using the Hodrick-Prescott method.

Figure 20.4 shows that the income elasticity of Latin America's exports somewhat follows the trend of world GDP growth. The correlation coefficient between both series is 0.92 for the whole period considered and is statistically significant. However, the trajectory of the moving elasticity coefficient indicates that its final value is equal to 0.63, and that the maximum and minimum values are 0.68 and 0.63.[38] Most important is the fact that the growth in exports of goods and services has not been able to keep pace with the rise in imports that accompanied trade liberalization. As indicated above, exports of goods and services expanded at an average annual rate of 4.8 per cent and 7.3 per cent in

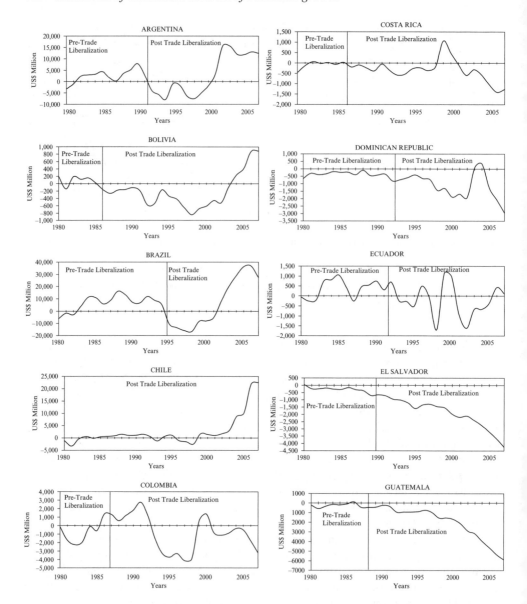

Source: ECLAC. *Statistical Yearbook for Latin America and the Caribbean.* Santiago: ECLAC. Several issues.

Figure 20.5   *Latin America. Evolution of the trade balance of goods and services in pre and post trade liberalization period (on a country basis), 1980–2006 (US$ million)*

1970–91 and 1992–2006. But imports of goods and services expanded at rates of 4.6 per cent and 9.4 per cent respectively for the same periods.

Figure 20.5 shows that the balance of trade in goods and services thus deteriorated during the trade liberalization period. Indeed, the balance of trade was positive during

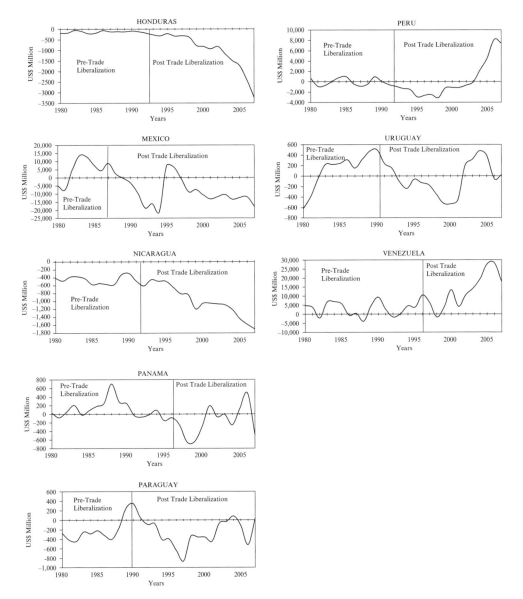

Figure 20.5 (continued)

the pre-trade liberalization period 1980–90 (2.6 per cent of GDP), but turned negative on average for the post-liberalization period 1991–2006 (–0.2 per cent of GDP) (see Table 20A.3 in the appendix). Country-by-country analysis for Latin American economies reveals, with very few exceptions, similar results.

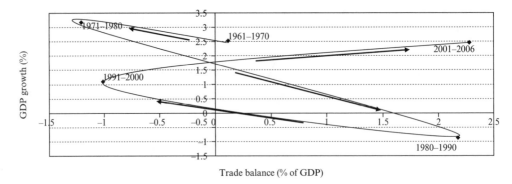

Source: Based on *World Development Indicators* (World Bank, 2008a) and UNCTAD (1999).

Figure 20.6   *Relationship between the balance of trade in goods and services (percent of GDP) and the rate of growth of per capita GDP in Latin America, 1961–2006*

7   An analysis of the relationship between trade and growth 1970–2006

The current pattern of trade in Latin America has two major implications for economic growth. It has limited the potential for growth and has imparted volatility to the growth trajectory. As a result and as shown above, the export elasticity for Latin American products from the rest of the world is less than unity. That is, export growth in Latin America is not commensurate with the growth of demand in the rest of the world.

Also, the negative trade balances that characterize the external positions of most Latin American countries imply that trade acts as a net leakage from rather than an injection into the economy.[39] The balance-of-payments constrained nature of these economies is illustrated in Figure 20.6. It shows that with the exception of the import substitution and recent commodity boom periods (1960–70 and 2001–06 respectively), Latin American economies have been forced to reduce their rates of growth in order to maintain external balance.[40]

The pattern of export specialization has also enhanced the volatility of Latin American growth. Indeed, the main export category (i.e. commodities) is acutely affected by not only foreign demand, but also the terms-of-trade. *Ceteris paribus*, the frequency and size of terms-of-trade fluctuations will affect the evolution of exports. Figure 20.7 below shows the evolution of the cyclical components of exports of goods and services and of the terms-of-trade for the period 1960–2006, together with correlation coefficients for the entire period and the sub-periods 1960–70, 1970–80, 1980–90, 1990–2000 and 2001–06.

The evidence shows that starting in 1980, the correlation coefficient between the cyclical components of the terms of trade and exports becomes significant and remains so throughout the trade liberalization period. For 1980–90, the correlation coefficient is equal to 0.75; for 1990–2000 and 2001–06, the coefficient is 0.49 and 0.83 respectively.

More to the point, the correlation coefficient between the volatility of the terms of trade and that of exports is positive and statistically significant for all periods under consideration. Thus the greater and/or more frequent the fluctuations in the terms of trade (that is, the more volatile they are), the greater and more frequent will be fluctuations in exports. In turn, the cyclical component of exports is significantly associated with the cyclical component of Latin America per capita GDP, both in levels and growth rates.

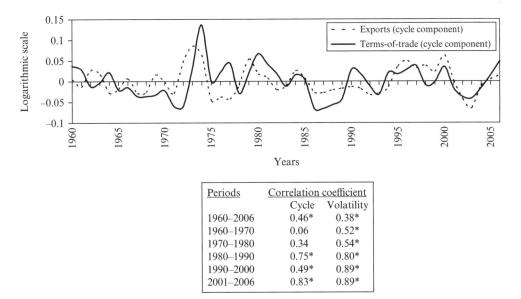

Periods	Correlation coefficient	
	Cycle	Volatility
1960–2006	0.46*	0.38*
1960–1970	0.06	0.52*
1970–1980	0.34	0.54*
1980–1990	0.75*	0.80*
1990–2000	0.49*	0.89*
2001–2006	0.83*	0.89*

Note: * denotes significant at the 95% confidence level.

Source: Based on *World Development Indicators* (World Bank, 2008a).

Figure 20.7   *Evolution of the cyclical component of exports of goods and services in real terms and terms of trade in Latin America 1960–2006 (Hodrick-Prescott filter), and correlation coefficients for selected periods*

The volatility imparted by terms-of-trade fluctuations on the growth trajectory of the Latin American economy is compounded by two factors. The first is financial volatility, which became prominent during the 1980s debt crisis and especially in the 1990s, because of the greater degree of financial openness of Latin American economies. The second is the policy reaction of Latin American governments and policy makers to real and financial volatility.

Figure 20.8 shows an index of openness in capital account transactions developed by Chinn and Ito (2008). The higher the value of the index, the greater is the degree of openness of an economy to cross-border capital transactions. As Figure 20.8 shows, the level of financial openness rose above zero and systematically increased throughout the 1990s, reflecting the fact that Latin American countries became on average more "financially open" during this decade.

At the same time the region experienced various episodes when capital inflows came to a sudden stop ("sudden capital stops"). Recent empirical evidence shows that Latin American countries experienced 25 episodes of sudden capital stops in the 1990s – double that of the 1980s. In addition, the evidence indicates that the average magnitude of financial shocks rose from 0.7 per cent of regional GDP in the 1980s to 3.5 per cent of GDP in the 1990s. In other words, financial shocks not only became more frequent in the 1990s but also more significant relative to GDP.

The response of Latin American governments to real and financial volatility (terms of

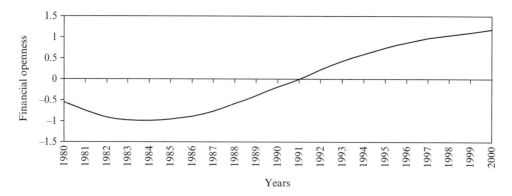

Figure 20.8   Evolution of financial openness in Latin America, 1980–2000

Table 20.11   Average contraction in domestic demand as a result of financial and terms-of-trade shocks in Latin America, 1980–2006 (percentages of regional Latin American GDP)

	Financial shocks	Terms-of-trade shocks (real shocks)
Latin America	6.99	2.64
South America	3.26	1.49
Central America	0.15	0.23
Mexico	3.58	0.92

trade and sudden capital stops) has been rather uniform. It consists of a contraction of internal demand as the main response to any significant terms-of-trade decline or sudden capital stop. Table 20.11 shows that the average contraction in absorption as a result of both financial and terms-of-trade shocks for the period 1980–2006 was equivalent to roughly 10 per cent of regional GDP.

The terms-of-trade volatility and abrupt cessations in the inflow of foreign capital that have accompanied economic liberalization – together with the policy reactions that follow – have had important effects on both the trend and fluctuations of GDP growth in Latin America. In terms of its trend, GDP growth in the 1990s was on average half that registered in the protectionist-cum-ISI period. For 1960–79, the average rate of growth of Latin American GDP was 2.8 per cent. This pattern also holds with few exceptions at the country level where 13 of 18 countries experienced lower rates of growth of GDP per capita in the 1990s than in 1960–80. Meanwhile, evidence shows that the volatility of GDP growth – as measured by the coefficient of variation – increased in the 1990s. In 1960–80, the coefficient of variation was 0.47, rising to 2.25 in the 1990s.

More precisely, during the 1990s Latin America witnessed more frequent periods of acceleration and deceleration in its growth of GDP per capita. In the period running from 1960 to 1980, it experienced an acceleration/deceleration in its rate of per capita

Table 20.12   Selected macroeconomic indicators for Latin America, 1960–2006

	1960–2006	1960–79	1980–90	1991–2001	2002–06
Rate of growth of actual GDP per capita (percentages)	1.6	2.8	-0.4	1.4	2.2
Rate of growth of the trend component of GDP per capita (percentages)[a]	1.6	2.6	0.2	1.0	2.2
Frequency of GDP per capita cycles (number of years)	. . .	4	4	2	2
Coefficient of variation of GDP per capita growth					
Latin America	1.56	0.47	5.75	2.25	1.26
East Asia and the Pacific	0.50	0.88	0.26	0.36	0.08
Middle East and North Africa	1.77	1.10	8.47	0.78	0.59
South Asia	0.94	3.28	0.36	0.46	0.37
Amplitude of cycles[b]	3.14	3.08	2.93	3.41(4.42[c])	3.81

Notes:
[a]   The trend and cycle components of the rate of growth of GDP per capita were obtained through the use of the Hodrick-Prescott filter.
[b]   The amplitude of the cycle was computed as the distance in percentage growth points between peak and trough.
[c]   Amplitude of cycle for the period 1995–2001.

Source: Titelman et al. (2008).

GDP growth every four years. Thereafter, the region experienced such a phenomenon every two years. Moreover, the amplitude of the GDP fluctuations became more pronounced during trade liberalization. The distance between peak and trough measured in percentage terms averaged 3.1 per cent for the period 1960–79, increasing to 3.4 per cent in 1991–2001 and 3.8 per cent for 2002–06 (see Table 20.12).[41]

8   Conclusions

In Latin America the dominant understanding of the relationship between trade and growth, and its accompanying rhetoric, has radically evolved over time.

Initially the relationship was conceived as one of managed trade to promote industrialization and growth. This view was based on the belief that development could not be attained unless a significant effort was made to accumulate capital. At the same time it presupposed that the existing "automatic market forces" would keep the economic system entrenched in a low level of development. Industrialization was not to be left to the market, but was rather to be the product of government intervention.

As a result, the state was called on to take a leading role in the inward industrialization process. This inward industrialization approach, originally developed in the period 1940–60 and framed in terms of concepts such as "centre-periphery", "dependency" and "external strangulation", came to recognize the role of the external sector and of trade policies in promoting domestic industrialization efforts. The concepts of "infant industry", "managed trade" and "special and differential treatment" took centre stage.

By the 1980s, the debt crisis that caused the largest drop in output growth in the region's history and affected most Latin American countries, was used as the leitmotif to launch a devastating critique of earlier developmental policies and to recommend policies based on the mantra "stabilize, privatize and liberalize". All pre-1980 policies were labelled import substitution industrialization (ISI) strategies and were identified as being at the root of the economic evils of Latin America. Export outward oriented (EO) policies, responsible for the economic success of Asian countries according to the mainstream view, were then contra-posed to ISI policies. Free market beliefs and policies dominated the Latin American landscape during the 1990s and early 2000s.

The implementation of free market policies notwithstanding, Latin America failed to overcome its external constraints, became highly vulnerable to the contagion effects of financial crisis, and became increasingly volatile. In short, a decade or more of free market policies did not lead Latin America onto a path of high and sustained rates of economic expansion. Moreover, the resumption of high rates of growth in many countries of the region in the last five years has resulted mainly from the worldwide commodities and minerals boom – the cause and effects of which have nothing to do with the adoption of trade liberalization reforms in the region.

The erosion of the Washington Consensus, reflecting the end of the region's fascination with free trade as a strategy for development, has led to a fifth stage in the understanding of the relationship between trade and growth. The characteristic feature of this stage is scepticism with the notions that either free market or state intervention policies alone will ensure sustainable growth in Latin America. While there is a perceived need for a third way combining market and state intervention, the fifth stage has failed to produce any clearly defined alternative development strategy. This failure has been heightened by the unfolding of the global financial crisis that, because of the strong expected contraction in external demand, threatens to significantly limit the role of trade as an engine of growth in Latin America.

Notes

1. The opinions here expressed are the authors' own and may not coincide with those of ECLAC. The authors wish to acknowledge the comments and suggestions provided by Mark Setterfield on an earlier version of this chapter.
2. According to McCloskey (1986, 1987) rhetoric is the study and practice of persuasive expression. The rhetoric of economics examines how economists persuade. In his paper, "The intellectual history of laissez-faire", Jacob Viner, one of the early and prominent critics of state-led inward industrialization in Latin America, also gave his views on the rhetoric of economics and how economists persuade (Viner, 1960).
3. See Allen (1958) for an exposition and defence of free trade theory and policy. The properties of the standard mainstream free trade model based on comparative advantage – the Heckscher–Ohlin (H–O) or Heckscher–Ohlin–Samuelson (H–O–S) model – are found in four well-known theorems: (i) the Heckscher–Ohlin theorem; (ii) the Stolper–Samuelson theorem; (iii) the Rybczynski theorem; and (iv) the factor-price equalization theorem. The Heckscher–Ohlin theorem establishes a relationship between factor scarcity and factor embodiment in a commodity, such that countries export the commodity that intensively uses the abundant factor. It provides the basis for the gains from trade argument. These refer to the increase in output and real income for a given set of inputs or domestic resources that result from trade. The Stolper–Samuelson theorem complements the above theorem by stating that the intensive use of a factor of production for export (i.e. the abundant factor) raises its rate of return above all other prices. In turn, the consequent increase in the supply of that factor of production will lead to an increase in the output of the commodity intensive in that factor of production (the Rybczynski theorem). Finally, the factor-price equalization theorem states that trade equalizes commodity and factor prices across countries. Under conditions of perfect competition, trade in goods acts as a substitute for factor mobility.

Under conditions of imperfect competition, free trade does not result in the full equalization of commodity and factor prices. However, free trade reduces commodity and factor-price differentials among countries and thus acts as a force of convergence. See Evans (1989).

4. As put by Speigel (1987, p. 814) "The article in which Viner developed these ideas was ostensibly an exposition of the rhetoric of laissez faire, an early exercise in an approach that D.N. McCloskey was to apply on a wider scale more than a quarter century later."

5. See Eatwell (1987), Robinson (1979, pp. 102–104).

6. The identification of development with economic growth and industrialization was entrenched in the thought of early development theorists. In this regard, it is interesting to note that Arthur Lewis's *The Theory of Economic Growth* – first published in 1955 – dealt with development issues and not with what economists currently understand as "growth theory".

7. See Nurske (1953), p. 10, Meier (2005), pp. 61–67 and Arndt (1987) p. 57.

8. In 1950, Raúl Prébisch was appointed Executive Secretary of the Economic Commission for Latin America (ECLA, later renamed as ECLAC to officially include the Caribbean in its denomination). However, some of the main concepts that became associated with ECLAC, such as the "centre–periphery" dichotomy or the "secular decline in the terms-of-trade", were developed in the mid-1940s. It is to be noted that ECLA was created in 1948 and the outcome of its first meeting was a resolution requesting a study of Latin America's terms-of-trade. See Love (2005), pp. 162–63.

9. See, Prébisch (1949), p. 2 and Frankenhoff (1962), p. 192.

10. Love (1994), p. 395 cited in Ocampo (2004).

11. See FitzGerald (2005), p. 107.

12. Brazil provides one of the best examples of formal, organized government intervention in the economy. It adopted the first formal government development plan in Latin America, the Target Plan of 1956–60. Chile's guided industrialization efforts by the *Corporación de Fomento* (CORFO) is another case in point. CORFO was created in 1939 to take a leading role in the establishment of several manufacturing industries and the diversification of the productive structure (Collier and Sater, 1996, pp. 235–7). This interventionist view was, in general, widespread in the region at the time, and also accepted internationally. Hence the General Agreement on Trade and Tariffs (GATT) included provisions allowing countries to impose tariff protection and import restrictions in order to safeguard their balance of payments position (articles 12 and 18) – see WTO (1999) and Meier (2005, pp. 74–5) – while not imposing specific trade rules on government procurement or prohibiting subsidies of services.

13. See Arndt (1987), p. 76, who also states that the "Soviet efforts to neutralise the role of GATT, reinforced by the emerging political muscle of the Third World" were also a factor that influenced this change of orientation.

14. The over-valued currencies in many countries that adopted this strategy further stimulated imports and deterred exports, thus weakening their trade balance positions.

15. Prébisch (1986) pp. 212–13 asserts that the criticism of import substitution can be dated at least to 1959, but is careful to state that the first severe critique of the industrialization policy followed in Latin America was put forward in 1961 in his document "Economic development, planning and international cooperation".

16. Prébisch (1986) states: "In ECLAC we maintained from the very outset that protection was indispensable as a means of standing up to the centres' technical and economic superiority. Unfortunately protection as a general rule has been greatly exaggerated if not abusive and has been kept in force for a very long time, affording industries no incentive to reduce their production costs." See Prébisch (1967) and Love (2005, pp. 170–3).

17. See Prébisch (1984) and (1986).

18. See Prébisch (1964).

19. See also Prébisch (1967 and 1968).

20. See Rodrik (2006). The original Washington Consensus consisted of ten reform policies: (1) fiscal discipline; (2) reorientation of public expenditure; (3) tax reform; (4) liberalization of financial markets; (5) competitive exchange rate; (6) liberalization of trade policies; (7) openness to foreign direct investment; (8) privatization; (9) deregulation; and (10) secure property rights. See Williamson (1990).

21. A similar interpretation can be found in the case of Latin America in the study undertaken by *El Colegio de México*, the *Fundacao Getulio Vargas* and the Washington Institute for International Economics published in the early 1980s. The study asserts: "The early post-war years saw a policy shift from export orientation to import substitution in Latin America. The intellectual underpinnings of this shift were provided by the United Commission for Latin America that saw scant possibilities for export growth through export expansion. The view was expressed that, due to a secular decline in their import coefficients, the developed industrial countries would not provide a sufficient stimulus for economic growth through primary exports; that Latin American countries were not in a favourable position to develop manufactured exports . . .". Prébisch terms this view "a purely arbitrary assertion". See, Prébisch (1986), p. 212.

22. See for example, Griffin (1989) pp. 109–11 and Todaro (1989), pp. 438–44.
23. The studies by Little et al. (1970) and Balassa (1971) are the most cited computations of effective rates of protection. Others include Cohen (1971), Anjaria et al. (1985), World Bank (1987) and Greenaway and Milner (1987).
24. The effective rate of protection is formally defined in the most simple terms as:

$$ERP = \frac{t_j - \sum a_{ij} t_j}{1 - \sum a_{ij}}$$

where,
t_j = nominal tariff on an importable product j.
t_i = nominal tariff rate on importable i.
a_{ij} = share of i in the cost of j under no tariffs.
See Corden (1987), p. 103.
25. The expression is from Stewart (2005).
26. Little et al. ibid., p. xviii.
27. Representatives of the New Political Economy include Lal (1983) and Bhagwati (1982).
28. See WTO (2008a). The mainstream literature argues that there is a wealth of empirical evidence showing that trade promotes growth and that the positive causal relationship between trade and growth has gained the status of a stylized fact in the literature. However, the transmission mechanisms between trade and growth have not received the required level of attention or study. As stated by Lewer and Van den Berg (2003) p. 163: "A serious weakness of the many statistical studies [of trade and growth] is that they have not yet shed much light on *why* the statistical relationship between trade growth holds so robust . . . studies have tried to distinguish the channels of influence through which trade enhances economic growth, but the results are so far merely suggestive." Ultimately the authors suggest that the main possible channel for trade to influence growth is through investment.
29. It should be noted that the nominal tariff estimates presented in Table 20.6 do not include para-tariffs. The inclusion of para-tariffs increases the rate of nominal protection. Edwards (1995, p. 200) reports for example that the pre-tariff rate of protection including para-tariffs was 92 per cent for Costa Rica and 80 per cent for Brazil, whereas in Table 20.6, the nominal level of protection is 53 per cent and 51 per cent, respectively.
30. The Free Trade Area of the Americas (FTAA, hereafter) negotiations, which were expected to be completed in the year 2005, involved 34 countries including all Latin American and Caribbean countries, the United States and Canada – countries with important differences in size, population, economic structure, economic performance, stability and welfare. The FTAA comprised nine negotiating groups. These are: market access, agriculture, government procurement, investment, competition policy, intellectual property rights, services, dispute settlement, subsidies, antidumping and countervailing duties. FTAA was negotiated on the belief that a free trade agreement will (i) widen and solidify market access leading countries to maintain their preferential market access and act as a springboard for export development and promotion; (ii) lead to greater foreign direct investment; (iii) allow for technological transfer; and (iv) improve labour mobility. See Roberts (2008) for a proposal to rethink and resuscitate the now-defunct FTAA.
31. Bilateral trade agreements and the investment chapters of the FTAs are meant to encourage investment flows in a context where foreign direct investment should fill the shortfall in official aid. This is particularly relevant for smaller economies. For an analysis of bilateral investment treaties and their impact on development policy, see Peterson (2004).
32. See articles 10.2, 15.2 and 10.3 of the US–Chile, US–Singapore and US–CAFTA free trade agreements. See also "U.S.–Chile Free Trade Agreement", *The American Journal of International Law* (July, 2003).
33. "Fair and equitable treatment" includes the obligation not to deny justice in criminal, civil or administrative adjudicatory proceedings in accordance with the principle of due process embodied in the principal legal systems of the world. "Full protection and security" requires each party to provide the level of police protection required under customary international law. See articles 10.4, 15.5 and 10.5 of the US–Chile, US–Singapore and US–CAFTA free trade agreements. See also *The American Journal of International Law* (October 2001a), pp. 881–85.
34. See "Expropriation in international law" by Professor B.A. Wortley. Mimeo, July 1947.
35. In some court cases the term "creeping expropriation" as a form of indirect expropriation is also utilized.
36. The issue of indirect expropriation was amply debated in the case of Metalcad Corporation vs Mexico and Mexico vs Metalcad Corporation in 2001 within the NAFTA framework. The tribunal that analysed the case decided that the term expropriation meant "not only open, deliberate, and acknowledged takings

of property . . . but also covert or incidental interference with the use of property which has the effect of depriving the owner of the actual or expected benefits of property . . ." See Dodge (2001) and *The American Journal of International Law* (October 2001b), pp. 910–19.

37. Exceptions include cases where expropriation or nationalization are carried out, among other reasons, for a public purpose, in a non-discriminatory manner, or in accordance with due process of law.

38. Formally, in the general case a state space model representation for an n x1 vector y_t, comprises two equations:

$$y_t = Z_t\alpha_t + c_t + \varepsilon_t$$

$$\alpha_t = d_t + T_t\alpha_{t-1} + v_t$$

Where Z_t is a conformable matrix, associated to the $(m \times 1)$ vector of unobserved state variables α_t. T_t is a matrix of parameters; d_t and c_t are vectors that include exogenous and observable variables. The error terms ε_t and v_t have the usual properties. By construction the $(m \times 1)$ vector of unobserved state variables α_t follows a first order autoregressive process. The most widely used algorithm to estimate the parameters of these equations is the Kalman filter. The statistical significance of the correlation coefficient was determined on the basis of the formula:

$$\rho = \frac{r\sqrt{n-2}}{\sqrt{1-r^2}}$$

where r is the simple correlation coefficient and n the number of observations. ρ follows a Student t distribution. In this particular case the computed t value is equal to 9.31 above the critical 1.64 at a 95 per cent level of confidence.

39. Within the non-mainstream literature this point has been made by Kalecki (1969), Minsky (1986), McCombie and Thirlwall (1994).

40. Figure 20.6 appeared originally in UNCTAD (1999). Its potent message has been emphasized by, among others, Ocampo (Ocampo and Martin, 2003; Ocampo, 2004) and ECLAC.

41. Note also that GDP growth is more volatile in Latin America than in other regions of the world, including East Asia and the Pacific, the Middle East and North Africa and South Asia.

Bibliography

Agénor, P.R. and Montiel, P.J. (1996) *Development Macroeconomics*. Princeton, NJ: Princeton University Press.

Alam, A. and Rajapatirana, S. (1993) "Trade policy reform in Latin America and the Caribbean in the 1980s". PRE Working Paper No. 1104. World Bank (February).

Allen, W.R. (1958) "International trade theory, comercial policy and the economist". *Political Science Quarterly*, **73**, (1), 47–56.

Anjaria, S.J., Kirmani, N. and A.B. Petersen (1985) "Trade policy issues and developments". IMF Occasional Paper. Washington, DC.

Arndt, H.W. (1987) *Economic Development. The History of an Idea*. Chicago: University of Chicago Press.

Baer, W. (2008) *The Brazilian Economy. Growth and Development*. Boulder, CO: Lynne Rienner Publishers.

Bagchi, A.K. (1982) *The Political Economy of Underdevelopment*. New York: Cambridge University Press.

Balassa, B. (1971) "Effective protection in developing countries", in J.N. Bhagwati, R.W. Jones, R.A. Mundell and J. Vanek (eds) *Trade Balance of Payments and Growth. Papers in International Economics in Honor of Charles P. Klindeberger*. Amsterdam: North Holland.

Bhagwati, J.N. (1982) "Directly unproductive, profit-seeking activities". *Journal of Political Economy*, **190** (5), 982–1002.

Bruton, H.J (1998) "A reconsideration of import substitution". *Journal of Economic Literature*, **36** (2), 903–36.

Buchanan, J.M. and Tullock, G. (1962) *The Calculus of Consent: Logical Foundations of Constitutional Democracy*. Ann Arbor: University of Michigan Press.

Cardoso, E. and Helwege, A. (1992) *Latin America's Economy*. Cambridge, MA: MIT Press.

Chinn, M.D. and Ito, H. (2008) "A new measure of financial openness." *Journal of Comparative Policy Analysis*, **10**, 309–22.

Cohen, B.I. (1971) "The use of effective tariffs". *Journal of Political Economy*, **79** (1), 128–141.

Collier, S. and Sater, W. (1996) *Historia de Chile 1808–1994*. Cambridge: Cambridge University Press. (Traducción Española, Cambridge University Press, Sucursal en España, 1998)

Collins, J. and Lear, J. (1995) *Chile's Free-Market Miracle: A Second Look*. Oakland, CA: Institute for Food and Development.

Corden, W.M. (1987) "Effective protection", in J. Eatwell, M. Milgate and P. Newman (eds) *The New Palgrave Dictionary of Economics*, Vol. 2. New York: Macmillan Press, pp. 102–105.

Dodge, W.S. (2001) *Metalcad Corporation v. Mexico*. ICSID Case No ARB (AF)/97/1.40 ILM 36 (2001).

Dunn, R.M. Jr and Mutti, J. (2000) *International Economics*. New York: Routledge.

Eatwell, J. (1987) "Import substitution and export-led growth", in J. Eatwell, M. Milgate and P. Newman (eds) *The New Palgrave Dictionary of Economics*, Vol. 2. New York: Macmillan Press, pp. 737–8.

ECLA (1964) *The Economic Development of Latin America in the Post-war Period*. New York: United Nations.

ECLAC (2007) *Statistical Yearbook for Latin America and the Caribbean*. Santiago, Chile: ECLAC.

ECLAC (2008) *Module to Analyse the Growth of International Commerce* (MAGIC, 2001). Santiago, Chile: ECLAC.

Edwards, S. (1995) "Trade and industrial policy reform in Latin America", in André Lara Resende (ed.) *Policies for Growth*. Washington: International Monetary Fund, pp. 182–250.

Evans, H.D. (1989) *Comparative Advantage and Growth*. New York: St Martin's Press.

FitzGerald, V. (2005) "The conflict of economic ideas in Latin America", in Valpy FitzGerald and Rosemary Thorp (eds) *Economic Doctrines in Latin America*. New York: Palgrave Macmillan, pp. 97–114.

Ffrench-Davis, R. (1999) *Reforming the Reforms in Latin America: Macroeconomics, Trade, Finance*. London: Macmillan.

Frankenhoff, Ch.A. (1962) "The Prebisch thesis: a theory of industrialism for Latin America". *Journal of Inter-American Studies*, 4 (2), 185–206.

Greenaway, D. and Milner, C. (1987) "Trade theory and the less developed countries", in Norman Gemmell (ed.) *Survey in Development Economics*. Oxford: Basil Blackwell.

Griffin, K. (1989) *Alternative Strategies for Economic Development*. New York: St Martin's Press.

Grunwald, J. (1970) "Some reflections on Latin American industrialization policy". *The Journal of Political Economy*, 78 (4), "Part 2: Key problems of economic policy in Latin America" (Jul–Aug 1979), pp. 826–56.

Ha-Joon C. (2002) *Kicking Away the Ladder. Development Strategy in Historical Perspective*. London: Anthem Press.

Ha-Joon, C. (2008) *Bad Samaritans. The Myth of Free Trade and the Secret History of Capitalism*. New York: Bloomsbury Press.

Henry, P.B. (2007) "Capital account liberalization: theory, evidence and speculation". *Journal of Economic Literature*, XLV (4), 887–935.

Kalecki, M. (1969) *Theory of Economic Dynamics*. New York: Kelley Publishers.

Krugman, P. (1993) "Protection in developing countries" in Rudiger Dornbusch (ed.) *Policy Making in the Open Economy*, New York: Oxford University Press, pp. 127–48.

Lal, D. (1983) *The Poverty of Development Economics*. London: Institute of Economic Affairs.

Lewer, J.L. and Van den Berg, H. (2003) "How large is international trade's effect on economic growth?", in D.A.R. George, L. Oxley and K.I. Carlaw (eds) *Surveys in Economic Growth*. Malden: Blackwell Publishing, pp. 137–70.

Lewis, W.A. (1954) "Economic development with unlimited supplies of labour." *The Manchester School*, 22, 139–91.

Little, I., Scitovsky, T. and Scott, M. (1970) *Industry and Trade in Some Developing Countries. A Comparative Study*. New York: Oxford University Press.

Love, J.L. (1994) "Economic ideas and ideologies in Latin America since 1930", in L. Berthel (ed.) *The Cambridge History of Latin America*, 6(1). Cambridge: Cambridge University Press.

Love, J.L. (2005) "The rise and fall of structuralism", in Valpy FitzGerald and Rosemary Thorp (eds) *Economic Doctrines in Latin America*. New York: Palgrave Macmillan, pp. 157–81.

Macario, S. (1964) "Protectionism and industrialization in Latin America". *Economic Bulletin for Latin America*, 9, 61–101.

MAGIC (2008) *Module to Analyze the Growth of International Commerce*. Santiago, Chile: ECLAC.

McCloskey, D. (1986) *The Rhetoric of Economics*. Madison: University of Wisconsin Press.

McCloskey, D. (1987) "Rhetoric" in J. Eatwell, M. Milgate and P. Newman (eds) *The New Palgrave Dictionary of Economics*, Vol 4. New York: Macmillan Press, pp. 173–4.

McCombie, J.S.L. and Thirlwall, A.P. (1994) *Economic Growth and the Balance-of-Payments Constraint*. New York: St. Martin's Press.

Meier, G.M. (2005) *Biography of a Subject. An Evolution of Development Economics*. New York: Oxford University Press.

Meier, G.M. and Seers, D. (eds) (1984) *Pioneers in Development*. New York: Oxford University Press.

Minsky, H.P. (1986) *Stabilizing and Unstable Economy*. New Haven, CT: Yale University Press.

Moreno-Brid, J.C. and Pérez Caldentey, E. (1993) "Trade liberalization and economic growth in Central America". *CEPAL Review*, 81, 151–68.

Nelson, E.R. (1956) "A theory of the low-level equilibrium trap in underdeveloped economies". *The American Economic Review*, **46** (5), 894–908.

Nurske, R. (1953) *Problems of Capital Formation in Underdeveloped Countries*. Oxford: Basil Blackwell.

Ocampo, J.A. (2004), "La América Latina y la economía mundial en el largo siglo XX". *El Trimestre Económico*, **LXXI**(4), 725–88. In Spanish.

Ocampo, J.A. and Martin, J. (2003) *Globalización y Desarrollo*. Comisión para América Latina y el Caribe. Bogotá: Alfaomega Colombiana. In Spanish.

Peterson, L.E. (2004) *Bilateral Investment Treaties and Development Policy-Making*. Winnipeg: International Institute for Sustainable Development.

Prébisch, R. (1949) *Economic Survey of Latin America*. New York: United Nations Economic Commission for Latin America.

Prébisch, R. (1950) *The Economic Development of Latin America and its Principal Problems*. New York: UN, for the Economic Commission of Latin America, United Nations Department of Economic Affairs.

Prébisch, R. (1951) "Interpretação do Processo de Desenvolvimento Econômico". *Revista Brasileira de Economía*, **5** (1), 7–101.

Prébisch, R. (1959) "Commercial policy in the underdeveloped countries", *American Economic Review*, **49** (2), 251–73.

Prébisch, R. (1964) *Towards a New Trade Policy for Development*. New York: UNCTAD.

Prébisch, R. (1967) *Hacia una Dinámica del Desarrollo Latinoamericano*. Montevideo: Banda Oriental.

Prébisch, R. (1968) *Towards a Global Strategy of Development*. UNCTAD Second Conference. New York: UNCTAD.

Prébisch, R. (1984) "Five stages in my thinking on development", in Gerald Meier and Dudley Seers (eds) *Pioneers in Development*. Washington, DC: World Bank, pp. 175–91.

Prébisch, R. (1986) "Notes on trade from the standpoint of the periphery". *CEPAL Review*, **28**, 203–14.

Roberts, J.M. (2008) "Rethinking the summit of the Americas and Advancing Free Trade in Latin America". *Backgrounder*, **2170**, Heritage Foundation.

Robinson, J. (1979) *Aspects of Development and Underdevelopment*. New York: Cambridge University Press.

Robinson, J. (1985) *Aspects of Development and Underdevelopment*. Cambridge: Cambridge University Press.

Rodlauer, M. and Schipke, A. (eds) (2005) "Central America: global integration and regional cooperation". IMF Occasional Paper 243.

Rodrik, D. (2006) "Goodbye Washington Consensus, hello Washington confusion? A review of the World Bank's economic growth in the 1990s: learning from a decade of reforms". *Journal of Economic Literature*, **XLIV** (4), 973–87.

Rosenstein-Rodan, P.N. (1943) "Problems of industrialization of Eastern and South-Eastern Europe". *Economic Journal*, **53**, 202–11.

Speigel, H.W. (1987) "Jacob Viner (1892–1979)". in J. Eatwell, M. Milgate and P. Newman (eds), *The New Palgrave Dictionary of Economics*, Vol 4. New York: Macmillan Press, pp. 812–14.

Stewart, F. (2005) "The evolution of economic ideas: from import substitution to human development". in Valpy FitzGerald and Rosemary Thorp (eds) *Economic Doctrines in Latin America*. New York: Palgrave MacMillan, pp. 48–71.

Tavares, M. da Conceiçaô (1964) "The growth and decline of import substitution in Brazil". *Economic Bulletin for Latin America*, **9**, 1–59.

The American Journal of International Law (October, 2001a), "U.S. interpretation of core NAFTA investment standards". **95** (4), 881–85.

The American Journal of International Law (October, 2001b), "*Mexico v. Metalcad Corporation, 2001*, B.C.S.C. 664". **95** (4). 910–19.

The American Journal of International Law (2003) "U.S.–Chile free trade agreement". **97** (3), 696–9.

The United States Office of the Trade Representative, Annual Trade Report, 2007.

Titelman, D., Pérez-Caldentey, E. and Minzer, R. (2008) "Comparación de la dinámica e impactos de los choques financieros y de términos de intercambio en América Latina en el período 1980–2006". *Serie financiamiento del desarrollo*, 203. Santiago, Chile: CEPAL.

Todaro, M.P. (1989) *Economic Development in the Third World*. New York: Longman.

UNCTAD (1999) *Trade and Development Report, 1999*. Geneva: UNCTAD.

UNCTAD (2002) *Trade and Development Report, 2002*. Geneva: UNCTAD.

United Nations (1966) *Economic Survey of Latin America, 1964*. New York: United Nations.

Viner, J. (1960) "The intellectual history of laissez-faire". *Journal of Law and Economics*, (3), 45–69.

Wacziarg, R.W. and Welch K.H. (2003) "Trade liberalization and growth: new evidence". NBER Working Paper 10152.

Williamson, J. (ed.) (1990) *Latin American Adjustment: How Much Has it Happened?* Washington, DC: Institute for International Economics.

World Bank (1987) *World Development Report 1987*. New York: Oxford University Press.

World Bank (2005) *Economic Growth in the 1990s: Learning from a Decade of Reform.* Washington, DC: World Bank.
World Bank (2008a). World Development Indicators. Washington, DC: World Bank.
World Bank (2008b). *World Integrated Solution (WITS)*, available at http://wits.worldbank.org/witsweb/
World Bank (2009) *World Development Indicators*. Washington, DC: World Bank.
World Trade Organization (1999) *The Legal Texts*. Cambridge: Cambridge University Press.
World Trade Organization (2008a) *10 Benefits of the WTO Trading System*, available at http://www.wto.org/
World Trade Organization (2008b) http://www.wto.org/
Wortley, B.A. (1947) "Expropriation in International Law". Mimeo, July.

Appendix

Table 20A.1   Central America: main export products to the United States as a percentage of the total, 1990–2006

	1990	1995	2000	2006
Costa Rica				
Edible fruits and nuts	22.8	20.7	15.0	19.3
Optical photographic	0.7	2.0	5.3	15.4
Electrical machinery and equipment	4.7	6.4	35.5	22.0
Textile and apparel	**37.5**	**40.9**	**23.3**	**12.1**
Coffee and tea spices	4.6	4.6	3.5	3.6
Total	70.3	74.6	82.6	72.4
El Salvador				
Textile and apparel	**22.8**	**71.7**	**82.9**	**75.8**
Beverages	0.1	1.8	0.6	5.4
Coffee and tea spices	36.1	6.3	7.0	3.7
Sugars	4.0	3.1	0.9	2.1
Total	62.9	82.9	91.4	87.1
Guatemala				
Textile and apparel	**24.0**	**44.8**	**57.1**	**53.8**
Edible fruits and nuts	15.3	10.7	9.7	12.0
Coffee and tea spices	23.7	21.0	11.8	9.0
Mineral fuels	2.9	2.4	5.9	7.1
Sugars	9.8	3.8	1.5	3.9
Total	75.6	82.7	86.0	85.9
Honduras				
Textile and apparel	**22.9**	**64.7**	**78.2**	**67.7**
Machinery	0.0	0.5	2.3	10.2
Edible fruits and nuts	32.0	12.7	3.6	4.1
Fish and crustaceans	12.6	6.9	4.2	3.9
Total	67.4	84.8	88.2	86.0
Nicaragua				
Textile and apparel	**0.0**	**57.2**	**51.7**	**57.6**
Electrical machinery and equipment	0.0	0.0	0.0	8.3
Mineral fuels	4.1	0.0	0.0	7.2
Coffee and tea spices	0.1	10.0	1.5	5.8
Fish and crustaceans	36.1	18.1	20.0	5.7
Meat	0.0	3.7	3.7	3.7
Tobacco	2.3	1.8	0.5	2.2
Pearls	0.0	1.5	3.0	2.1
Sugars	47.9	2.4	3.0	1.8
Total	90.6	94.8	83.4	94.4

Source: MAGIC (2008).

Table 20A.2   Rate of growth of GDP per capita (using a five year rolling window) in Latin America, 1960–2006

Countries	1960–70	1971–80	1981–90	1991–2001	2002–06
Argentina	2.5	1.4	−2.8	2.6	3.9
Bolivia	0.5	1.5	−2	1.3	1.6
Brazil	3.3	6	−0.4	0.9	1.8
Chile	1.8	1.5	2.2	4.6	3.2
Colombia	2.3	3.1	1.5	0.7	2.9
Costa Rica	2.8	3	−0.1	2.4	3.6
Dominican Republic	2.9	4.5	0.4	3.9	3.3
Ecuador	1.3	4	−0.5	0.4	3.5
El Salvador	2.2	0	−1.4	2.2	0.8
Guatemala	2.7	3	−1.5	1.6	0.5
Honduras	1.6	2.2	−0.7	0.5	2
Mexico	3.4	3.7	−0.2	1.6	1.7
Nicaragua	3.5	−2.2	−3.7	1.2	2.2
Panama	4.8	1.5	−0.6	2.6	3.9
Paraguay	1.8	5.9	−0.2	−0.5	1
Peru	2.4	0.9	−2.7	1.9	4.2
Uruguay	0.4	2.7	−0.5	1.9	3.3
Venezuela, RB	1.5	−0.7	−1.8	0.2	2.7
Latin America	2.6	3.2	−0.4	1.4	2.2
South America	1.8	2.6	−0.7	1.4	2.8
Central America	2.9	1.2	−1.3	1.8	2.2

Source: Own computations based on *World Bank Development Indicators* (World Bank, 2008a).

Table 20A.3   Current account indicators as a percentage of of GDP in Latin America, 1980–1992–2006

	1980–91	1992–2006
Current account balance	−1.88	−1.65
Exports of goods	12.81	16.34
Imports of goods	−10.09	−15.68
Balance of trade	2.72	0.66
Balance of goods and services	1.70	−0.19
Income balance	−4.12	−2.67
Net unilateral transfers	0.54	1.22
Capital and financial account	0.05	2.36
Reserves	2.26	−0.43

Sources: Based on ECLAC (2007) and *World Bank Development Indicators* (World Bank, 2008a/).

21 Endogenous regional growth: a critical survey
Mark Roberts and Mark Setterfield

1 Introduction

An important stylised fact of capitalist growth and development is large and persistent differences in per capita income growth between regions.[1] Theoretical and empirical analysis of the regional growth process has a history stretching back over more than 50 years, with neoclassical approaches dating back to Borts and Stein (1964) and an emphasis on increasing returns at the regional level going back to Kaldor (1970) and even Marshall (1890/1966). However, traditionally, the subject has been rather marginal to the mainstream of economics. This has begun to change in the last 20 years though, with the mid-1980s renaissance of interest in growth theory sparking a related rise of interest in regional and urban growth processes. In this context, Glaeser (2000) identifies the emergence of a new economics of urban and regional growth, which has been especially influenced by the work of Romer (1986, 1990) and the realisation that cities provide the most natural environment in which to look for evidence of the knowledge spillovers so emphasised by endogenous growth theory (Lucas, 1988).[2]

The "new economics" literature has mainly been a North American literature, having primarily involved North American academics and/or focused on US regional growth. By contrast, rising interest among European researchers in regional growth processes has come from a different angle. In particular, aided by the development of Eurostat's REGIO database[3] and stimulated by deepening European integration, European researchers have been quick to apply advances in spatial econometrics to the analysis of regional growth disparities in the EU. However, the focus has typically been at a higher level of spatial aggregation than in the "new economics" literature. Hence, the focus has been less on cities or metropolitan areas and more on broadly defined administrative regions. Nevertheless, both literatures share the feature of being mainly empirically driven. Only more recently have there been explicit theoretical attempts to incorporate geographic space into growth models to create *geographical or spatial models of endogenous growth* (Martin and Ottaviano, 1999).

Despite the paucity of explicit spatial models, endogenous growth theory as applied to the urban and regional levels is already having a substantial policy influence. This is exemplified by the UK's "new regional policy", which, partly inspired by endogenous growth theory, has identified five key drivers of local productivity growth – skills, investment, innovation, enterprise and competition (HM Treasury, 2001). Moreover, there is an (often implicit) presumption in regional development circles that universities and other research institutions can act as catalysts for localised growth. This proposition is consistent with the "new economics" argument that knowledge spillovers are geographically bounded and that, by driving productivity growth, they also drive regional growth.

Given the above, this chapter provides a critical survey of literature relating to the spatial application of endogenous growth theory. Both the North American and

European literatures that have come into being over the last 20 years are discussed.[4] By necessity, the chapter abstracts from much of the research on regional growth that has been done by geographers and other social scientists.[5] Furthermore, even within the domain of the economics literature, the survey is necessarily selective, focusing on work and issues that the authors consider to be of greatest importance.

The chapter is organised as follows. First, important issues of measurement and definition are briefly discussed. Second, the theoretical literature on endogenous growth is examined, with particular attention paid to arguments that have been used to link endogenous growth theory to the urban and regional levels. Third, consideration is given to empirical work on regional growth disparities. This includes a critical examination of both the North American new economics literature and the European spatial econometrics literature. Fourth, the chapter identifies remaining theoretical and empirical shortcomings with the spatial application of endogenous growth theory. In so doing, it suggests gaps in the literature that, in the opinion of the authors, future work should address. The chapter is brought to an end with some concluding remarks.

2   On the metric of regional growth and definition of the region

Before endogenous growth theory can be considered, an obvious and fundamental question that must be addressed is that of the relevant metric of regional growth. At the regional level, where factor mobility is high, it has been traditional since Alonso (1964) to argue that capital and labour will move until a spatial equilibrium is reached. In this equilibrium, utility levels across homogeneous agents will be equalised. *Ceteris paribus*, this will tend to make for the spatial equality of wages and profits, not to mention the spatial equality of productivity levels at the margin. In light of this, it has been argued that the relevant metric of growth at the regional or urban level is provided by *employment* or *population* growth rather than income/output per capita or productivity growth. In particular, this argument has been characteristic of the North American new economics literature (see, in particular, Glaeser et al., 1992; Glaeser, 2000).

But traditionally, levels of labour mobility have been much lower in Europe than in the United States (Cheshire and Magrini, 2005, p. 1). Consequently, empirical research on EU regional growth has overwhelmingly focused on output, income and productivity based measures of growth (see, inter alia, Cheshire and Magrini, 2005; Fingleton and McCombie, 1998; Le Gallo and Dall'erba, 2008). Even in the US context, it has been acknowledged that output, income and productivity based measures of growth might, in certain circumstances, provide information on localised sources of productivity – for example, if workers need to buy land to live or if congestion effects make crowded locations less pleasant (Glaeser, 2000, p. 86).[6, 7]

Having considered the question of the relevant metric of regional growth, the next question is that of how to define the region. The answer to this partly depends on the precise research question that is being addressed. Thus it might seem more obvious to look for evidence of the knowledge spillovers emphasised by endogenous growth theory in more tightly defined regional areas that correspond to individual cities.[8] This has been the practice of much of the new economics literature, which has made extensive use of plentiful data at the Standard Metropolitan Statistical Area (SMSA) level (see, for example, Beardsell and Henderson, 1999; Glaeser et al., 1992; Jaffe et al., 1993; Rauch, 1993). These regions have the advantage of corresponding to an analytical/functional definition of the region, representing relatively self-contained zones of economic activity.

By contrast, studies of European regional growth have typically utilised NUTS definitions of regions.[9] This is hardly surprising given that the NUTS classification was constructed by Eurostat to provide harmonised social and economic indicators across European regions. However, unlike US SMSAs, NUTS regions are defined according to *normative* rather than analytical criteria (corresponding to institutional/administrative boundaries) and therefore represent a less satisfactory definition of the region for the purposes of analysing regional growth.[10] Given the problems with the NUTS classification, a small number of studies on European regional growth have preferred to make use of data on functionally defined economic regions (Cheshire and Carbonaro, 1995, 1996; Cheshire and Magrini, 2005; Magrini, 1998, 1999). However, data on such regions are not publicly available, so it is likely that the majority of future European regional growth studies will continue to make use of the NUTS classification. This being the case, there needs to be awareness of the problems associated with the classification, and attempts should be made to test and control for problems of measurement error.[11]

3 Endogenous growth theory and its regional application

3.1 *Endogenous growth theory*

Although the *idea* of endogenous growth is not new (Roberts and Setterfield, 2007), endogenous growth as a mainstream theoretical concept dates back only to the mid-1980s. In particular, modern endogenous growth theory has its origins in the work of Paul Romer (Romer, 1983, 1986, 1990). Since then, important contributions to the literature have been made by, inter alia, Aghion and Howitt (1998), Grossman and Helpman (1991), and Lucas (1988).

The endogenous growth literature departs from traditional neoclassical growth theory (Solow, 1956; Swan, 1956) through its emphasis on the modelling of the creation and accumulation of knowledge. This is not to say that knowledge is not present in the Solow–Swan model; just that there is no explicit theory of the knowledge accumulation process. Knowledge is implicitly treated as a pure public good in Solow–Swan. Consequently, in contrast to endogenous growth theory, there can be no localised knowledge accumulation.

It is the endogenisation of knowledge creation and accumulation that, in part, explains the label "endogenous growth theory". However, there is also another, related, reason for this label. The endogenisation of knowledge creation and accumulation generates (either directly or indirectly) increasing returns to scale that render the equilibrium (steady-state) growth rate dependent on technological and preference parameters. Hence, growth is endogenous in the sense that it is not predetermined by an exogenous driving force.[12]

Endogenous growth models differ from one other in the precise mechanisms for knowledge creation and accumulation they describe. In the original model of Romer (1986), the mechanism is indirect: knowledge accumulation is an accidental byproduct of the investment decisions of individual firms. Capital accumulation indirectly generates intra-firm knowledge accumulation through learning-by-doing, and the knowledge so acquired spills over to other firms (so that, in the aggregate, knowledge remains a public good). Increasing returns thus arise from knowledge spillovers, which constitute a type of positive externality. The spillover mechanism reconciles endogenous growth with perfect competition, although the resulting equilibrium growth rate is suboptimal. This, in turn, justifies government intervention to encourage capital accumulation.[13]

In contrast, later endogenous growth models posit more direct mechanisms of knowledge creation and accumulation (Aghion and Howitt, 1998; Grossman and Helpman, 1991; Romer, 1990). Although these models differ in their details, they all portray knowledge accumulation as the intentional outcome of decisions to invest in research and development (R&D). Thus knowledge ceases to be a pure public good because, in order for firms to have the incentive to invest in R&D in the first place, knowledge must be, at least partially, excludable. The resulting monopoly control enables firms to earn abnormal profits which justify the cost (Romer, 1990) and risk (Aghion and Howitt, 1998) of their R&D. Clearly, in these models, endogenous growth presupposes imperfect competition.[14]

However, although firms in these later models can exclude others from directly copying their ideas, knowledge spillovers still occur. Thus, spillovers are posited in research activities: while intellectual property rights deter the outright theft of ideas, nothing prevents a firm from building on ideas implicit in existing goods or the accumulated stock of public knowledge. This gives rise to either horizontal innovation, whereby the existing stock of knowledge acts as an input into entirely new product varieties (as in Romer, 1990), or vertical innovation, whereby rival firms compete to improve the quality of existing product lines (as in Aghion and Howitt, 1998; Grossman and Helpman, 1991).[15] In the former case, knowledge spillovers are predominantly cross-industry in nature,[16] while, in the latter case, they are mainly within-industry in character. Note also the Schumpeterian nature of growth in the latter case, where monopoly profits earned by the incumbent firm stimulate market entry and the introduction of improved versions of the same product. The knowledge creation process is therefore characterised by "creative destruction", resulting in a business stealing effect.[17]

By focusing on intentional, profit-motivated, knowledge creation and accumulation, later models of endogenous growth highlight the importance of human capital in the growth process. Specifically, these models treat human capital as a key input into the knowledge creation process – a prerequisite for transforming a society's existing stock of knowledge into a continuous flow of new knowledge. Furthermore, the higher the level of human capital, the more effective the transformation process will be, the faster will be the rate of new knowledge creation and the higher will be the equilibrium growth rate. Note that by focusing on individuals involved in the knowledge creation process, the emphasis is not so much on an economy's average level of human capital, but on the availability of highly trained specialists.

Notice also that the treatment of human capital described above means that knowledge is embodied in the existing stock of goods and services that incorporate ideas arising from previous knowledge creation activities (see also Magrini, 1998, p. 44).[18] By contrast, the earlier Lucas (1988) model sees knowledge as being embodied within human capital itself, so that knowledge spillovers are dependent on direct human interaction. This being the case, encouraging human capital accumulation provides not just an indirect spur to growth (as in R&D-based models), but also a much more direct stimulus. Knowledge creation goes hand in hand with human capital accumulation (in fact, the two are basically indistinguishable), so facilitating the latter directly facilitates the former.

3.2   The regional application of endogenous growth theory

Given his treatment of the knowledge creation and accumulation processes, it is hardly surprising that the link from mainstream endogenous growth theory to the new economics of urban and regional growth starts with Lucas (1988) and his emphasis on the importance of direct human interaction. Simply put, direct human interaction requires proximity, meaning that knowledge spillovers are most likely to occur at a local level. This leads to the contention that cities provide the more obvious locus of such spillovers (Lucas, 1988, pp. 38–9). Since Lucas, authors working in the new economics have elaborated on the point that proximity facilitates knowledge spillovers by emphasising that knowledge is conceptually distinct from information (Feldman and Audretsch, 1999, p. 411). Thus, while information can be transmitted at a cost which is invariant to distance, knowledge can adopt a "sticky" character that prevents its easy codification and renders it largely tacit in nature. This is particularly the case when knowledge is of a highly contextual and uncertain nature, as is likely to be the case at the forefront of any knowledge creation process. Citing Von Hipple (1994), Feldman and Audretsch (1999, p. 411) state that such knowledge "is best transmitted via face-to-face interaction and through frequent contact". Consequently, it is "talk" and, in particular, the "quality of talk" (i.e. its relevance to productive knowledge creation) that matters.[19, 20] In this context, individuals can be imagined as supplementing their knowledge and human capital through "chance" pairwise meetings at which ideas are exchanged (Jovanovic and Rob, 1989). Given this, the higher the average level of human capital, the greater is the expected probability that a "chance" meeting results in an improvement in an individual's knowledge and human capital (Rauch, 1993, p. 381). Furthermore, it might be imagined that, in meeting and discussing, individuals not only transmit knowledge (thereby leading to a spillover), but also alter, and, therefore, *create*, knowledge.

While the above discussion fits most neatly with Lucas's treatment of knowledge, it has also been argued within the new economics that proximity "enables workers to acquire human capital by imitating a rich array of role models and learning by seeing" (Glaeser, 2000, p. 85). This implies that, even if the link from human capital to economic growth is only indirect, in the sense that human capital is merely an input into the creation of either embodied (e.g. in the quality of final goods) or disembodied knowledge, the local (urban and regional) dimension remains important in the knowledge creation and accumulation processes.[21]

Of course, imitation works both ways and can represent a double-edged sword for urban areas. Thus, "a rich array of role models" may include not only individuals with high levels of human capital who contribute to localised knowledge accumulation, but also individuals with little in the way of formal qualifications who engage in activity (e.g. crime) that only serves to redistribute and/or destroy existing economic activity. As such, history is likely to matter in the determination of regional growth processes and it is easy to imagine the operation of processes of "circular and cumulative causation" akin to those discussed by Myrdal (1957).

In sum, endogenous growth theory's potential role in explaining urban and regional growth disparities comes from the hypothesis that knowledge spillovers are geographically bounded because of their embodiment in human capital and/or because human capital accumulation itself has a regional dynamic (the role model effect). Thus, fast growing regions are predicted to be those in which the conditions for knowledge creation, accumulation and transmission are ripe. This means that the local entry cost into knowledge creating activities will be important, and variations in such costs will lead to interregional growth rate differences.[22] Likewise, variations in the local supply of inputs into knowledge production – such as the availability of human capital, and activities and institutions (universities and colleges, for example) that promote its acquisition – will be important in explaining interregional growth differences. The internal spatial structure of a region will also affect growth. Thus, to the extent that the spatial configuration of a city or region impedes human interactions that facilitate good-quality talk, growth will suffer. Consequently, the nature of a city's built environment will matter for growth, as will the degree of segregation between groups characterised by high and low levels of human capital.[23] Meanwhile, in a more broadly defined region that consists of multiple cities, it is possible that the distance between cities and the quality of transportation links between them will be important,[24] since these factors will impinge on the ability of individuals in different cities to engage in face-to-face interaction.

It is important to note, however, that the links between endogenous growth theory and regional analysis discussed above are not links that have typically been explicitly modelled.[25] Thus, although "new economics" authors have been quick to draw such links, this is typically done in a discursive rather than an analytical manner. As discussed below, this has led to a rather loose correspondence between ideas in endogenous growth theory and their representation in empirical work on urban and regional growth. It is also clear that there is some inconsistency between the "new economics" and the theoretical endogenous growth models on which it purports to build. For example, consider the way in which the geographical bounding of knowledge spillovers is invariably explained by the need for direct human contact. This is consistent with the Lucas (1988) treatment of knowledge, but not with that found in the R&D-based models of endogenous growth of Romer et al. The literature would therefore benefit from more theoretical work – in particular, theoretical work focusing on the explicit incorporation of space into endogenous growth models and which pays attention to the geographical mechanisms by which knowledge spillovers occur.[26, 27]

4   The regional application of endogenous growth theory: empirics

4.1   Empirical work associated with the "new economics of urban and regional growth"
The "new economics of urban and regional growth" claims endogenous growth theory as its inspiration, but is primarily an empirical literature led by North American researchers. The first seminal article in this literature is Glaeser et al. (1992). Three different "theories" of endogenous regional growth are identified and tested for a sample of 1016 city-industries using SMSA data, with regional growth measured by employment growth.[28] Given that all three theories concern different types of knowledge spillovers and emphasise human interaction as the mechanism for knowledge spillovers, the use of such data seems entirely appropriate. Thus, not only are SMSAs analytically/functionally defined regions, but they constitute a meaningful level of spatial aggregation at which to look for knowledge spillovers. The three theories tested are characterised by Glaeser et al. as:

(1) the Marshall–Arrow–Romer (MAR) theory, (2) the Porter theory, and (3) the Jacobs theory. In the MAR theory, knowledge spillovers are assumed to occur within industries through several different mechanisms. These include employees in different firms talking with each other, inter-firm labour mobility, and employees leaving established firms and using their acquired expertise to start up independently. Consequently, a high degree of specialisation is predicted to be good for a region's growth, while competition is predicted to be bad. This is because increased competition reduces the ability of firms to appropriate knowledge spillovers, therefore reducing the incentive to invest in activities that are, directly or indirectly, related to knowledge creation.

The Porter theory, like the MAR theory, predicts that specialisation is good for regional growth, because of within-industry knowledge spillovers. But unlike the MAR theory, competition is also predicted to be good. Hence although competition reduces the returns to knowledge creation, "it also increases pressure to innovate: firms that do not advance technologically are bankrupted by their innovating competitors" (Glaeser et al., 1992, p. 1131). This positive "stick" effect of increased competition is taken to outweigh the negative "carrot" effect.[29]

Finally, the Jacobs theory is associated by Glaeser et al. with the work of Jane Jacobs (in particular, Jacobs, 1969). It differs from both the MAR and Porter theories by assuming that knowledge spillovers are of the cross-industry variety. Particularly important is the cross-fertilisation of ideas between different industries, meaning that diversification of industry within a region is predicted to be good for growth. The Jacobs theory also shares with the Porter theory the notion that local competition is good for growth.

The link between formal endogenous growth theory and the three stylised theories of growth presented by Glaeser et al. (1992) is loose, which is in keeping with the empirical orientation of the new economics literature. Thus, while the MAR theory is clearly meant to apply Romer's (1986) model to the regions, there are no formal equivalents of the Porter and Jacobs theories in endogenous growth theory – although elements of both can be found. Hence Jacobs's idea that spillovers are of the cross-industry variety seems consistent with the notion of horizontal innovation found in some R&D-based models (notably, Romer, 1990). Meanwhile, the Jacobs–Porter idea that competition is good for regional growth is consistent with the modelling of the competition–growth nexus in neo-Schumpeterian models (see, for example, Aghion and Howitt, 1998, Chapter 7).

Moreover, the questions asked by Glaeser et al. are clearly important for improving our understanding of the regional growth process. In particular, whether it is specialisation or diversification that enhances regional growth, and whether or not competition boosts regional growth, clearly matters for both the theoretical modelling of knowledge spillovers and for policymaking. Given this, it is interesting that Glaeser et al.'s results come out decisively in favour of the Jacobs theory. Thus, conditional on a number of control variables,[30] both Glaeser et al.'s diversity and competition measures are found to have a significant positive influence on SMSA employment growth, while their specialisation measure is found to have a significant negative effect. However, it is important to beware of Glaeser et al.'s warning that their results should not be taken out of context. Thus, given their sample period of 1956–87, they state that "we are looking at a particular period of US history in which traditional manufacturing industries have fared poorly because of import competition" (Glaeser et al., 1992, p. 1151). They further note that their sample is limited to "very mature cities" in the US (p. 1151), meaning that the authors have little to say about the growth of small city-industries (Glaeser, 1994, p. 16). We might add that Glaeser et al.'s study focuses on industries that were highly concentrated in the 1950s: for any given city, they only include an industry in their sample if it was one of the six largest (see also Henderson et al., 1995, fn. 3, p. 1076).

The nature of their sample might explain why subsequent literature on the importance of diversification versus specialisation for regional growth has produced mixed support for Glaeser et al.'s findings.[31,32] Thus, while both Feldman and Audretsch's (1999) and Van Stel and Nieuwenhuijsen's (2004) results are similar to those of Glaeser et al., Beardsell and Henderson (1999) and Henderson et al. (1995) find that it is specialisation rather than diversity that is good for regional growth.[33] However, the sole focus of Beardsell and Henderson (1999) is the spatial evolution of the computer industry at the MSA level between 1977 and 1992. Hence, while their findings are clearly relevant to thinking about the future of regional growth and, in particular, to policymakers looking to base growth around the computer industry, they are not comparable with those of Glaeser et al. (1992). If anything, their focus on such different industries means the Beardsell and Henderson (1999) and Glaeser et al. (1992) studies should be thought of as complementary. Meanwhile, while Henderson et al.'s (1995) study seems more directly comparable to Glaeser et al. (1992), the differences in samples alone can plausibly explain the differences in results. Thus, for the shorter period 1970–87, Henderson et al.'s results again relate to individual industries rather than to a pool of industries. Indeed, Henderson et al. restrict themselves to consideration of eight individual industries, three of which are newer "high-tech" industries (computers, electronic components, and instruments). These industries were marketing products in 1987 that did not even exist in 1970. Furthermore, they did not have a significant presence in every city in Henderson et al.'s sample, in either the initial or the terminal year of the study.

Still, the fact that the results for the five traditional manufacturing industries that Henderson et al. consider are decisively against the idea that diversity is good and specialisation bad for local growth, does raise some concern. In particular, they call attention to the danger of relying on the "average" picture obtained from pooled estimation for implementing policy at a local level. This is especially important when local policy relates to a particular set of industries that are very different from the average. Furthermore, it leaves one to wonder whether, because of ignored heterogeneity, pooling itself results in bias in even the estimated "average" picture.[34] Finally, at the theoretical level, it suggests that endogenous growth theory is too aggregated to provide anything more than broad insight into the fact that knowledge creation and accumulation matters for regional growth. Thus, given that different regions are characterised by different industry-mixes, simple endogenous growth models are incapable of furnishing a proper understanding of the likely mosaic of regional growth patterns.

Given the above, it is hard to draw firm conclusions about the predominant nature of knowledge spillovers and thus decide on a single "flavour" of endogenous growth theory. However, within the new economics literature, there is much more agreement on the empirical importance of human capital for regional growth. Hence, even in some of the studies mentioned above, there is support for the importance of human capital. Henderson et al. (1995), for example, find that, for the computer and medical equipment industries, the presence of a local pool of highly qualified workers increases the probability that a region is a significant player. More generally, the importance of human capital has been borne out by both Rauch (1993) and Glaeser et al. (1995). Using data from the 1980 US Census for individuals and households in 237 SMSAs, Rauch (1993) estimates the average level of human capital within a city to have a highly significant positive impact on both wage and rent levels. This is consistent with the presence of human capital knowledge spillovers, and, therefore, with the regional application of endogenous growth theory.[35] Indeed, the fact that it is the average level (rather than the total stock) of human capital that appears important is consistent with Lucas's (1988) treatment of human capital and knowledge. From a practical viewpoint, this suggests that, *ceteris paribus*, rapid growth is more likely in a small city that is populated by highly educated people (e.g. Boulder, Colorado, in the US or Cambridge in the UK) than a large city that is mainly populated by the relatively uneducated.

Rauch's (1993) finding that it is years of schooling rather than years of experience that matters is also consistent with Lucas (1988). A major part of formal education is concerned with communication skills (Rauch, 1993, p. 391), and as seen in the previous section, the link from endogenous growth theory to the regions comes from the need for direct human communication for knowledge spillovers to occur.

Glaeser et al.'s (1995) results, meanwhile, are consistent with those of Rauch (1993). For a sample of 203 US cities, the authors find the initial level of human capital to have a significant (conditional) positive effect on city growth (as measured by both population and income per capita growth) between 1960 and 1990. Furthermore, it is again the average level of education that is important (p. 138).[36,37] However, some care is required with Glaeser et al.'s (1995) study because it employs the same type of Barro-style regression that has been subject to much criticism in cross-country convergence studies (see, for example, Temple, 1999). Hence Glaeser et al.'s simple cross-sectional regressions ignore the possibility of omitted city effects that could be correlated with both the initial level of human capital and subsequent city growth.[38] This could bias their results in favour of the human capital externality story.[39] Alternatively, as Glaeser (1994) admits, results indicating the importance of human capital could be attributable to an increasing skill-bias in technological progress over time rather than significant knowledge spillovers. Indeed, this alternative link between human capital and regional growth seems highly plausible in view of recent literature relating increases in income inequality in the US and UK to skill-biased technological progress (see, for example, Aghion and Williamson, 1999; Bresnahan, 1999). Of course, this alternative story does not imply that human capital is unimportant for city growth. After all, it implies that those US cities that have benefited most from the occurrence of skill-biased technological progress are precisely those with high average levels of education. However, it does mean that, while important in *distributing* growth between cities, human capital does not *drive* city growth.

The study by Glaeser et al. (1995) is also important for its focus on a number of potential social and political determinants of US city growth. These include measures of the degree of racial segregation within a city, which, as previously discussed, could be important from an endogenous growth perspective thanks to both role model effects and the nature of spatial knowledge flows. The authors find racial segregation has an important positive impact on city growth for cities with large non-white populations (p. 146). Whether or not this reflects role model and other endogenous growth theory type effects or econometric misspecification, however, is clearly something that requires further research. This is also the case for their finding of a significant positive relationship between government debt per capita in 1960 and subsequent city growth.

4.2   *Empirical work on European regions*

While North American research explicitly derives from the (imperfect) spatial interpretation of endogenous growth theory, it was noted earlier that research on EU regional growth disparities emerged from a different starting point. In particular, against the backdrop of increasing European integration, it arose from the increased availability of data for the EU regions stemming from the development of the REGIO database. Furthermore, unlike the new economics literature, it is distinguished by the widespread application of spatial econometric techniques. According to Abreu et al. (2005, p. 21), 68 per cent of all spatial econometric studies on growth published since 1995 make use of European regional data.[40]

Before examining this use of spatial econometric techniques, however, it is worth dividing studies of European regional growth into two different categories. The first category consists of studies concerned with the question of cross-regional convergence (see, inter alia, Armstrong, 1995a, 1995b and Le Gallo and Dall'erba, 2008). In the second category, exemplified by Fingleton and McCombie (1998) and Pons-Novell and Viladecans-Marsal (1999), are studies that test for localised increasing returns using the Verdoorn law.[41]

The studies in these categories originate from very different theoretical paradigms. Hence while the convergence literature is rooted in traditional neoclassical growth theory, the Verdoorn law literature is embedded within a Kaldorian vision of regional growth. Both approaches pose, in different ways, challenges to endogenous growth theory. Traditional neoclassical theory poses a challenge because it relies on the assumption of constant returns to scale. It, therefore, views the knowledge spillovers that are central to endogenous growth theory as being of little empirical importance. Kaldorian growth theory concurs with endogenous growth theory as to the importance of localised increasing returns, but takes a demand-oriented view of regional growth. Thus, in its simplest form, the Verdoorn law is specified as a positive causal relationship running from the growth of aggregate demand for regional output (as proxied by regional output growth) to regional labour productivity growth. In essence, therefore, and in contrast to endogenous growth theory, aggregate demand growth for local output is a prerequisite for the realisation of localised increasing returns to scale. The Verdoorn law is then seen as providing the linchpin of theoretical models of "circular and cumulative causation" (Dixon and Thirlwall, 1975) in which localised increasing returns help regions to maintain initial growth advantages, while, at the same time, making it difficult for lagging regions to catch up. Originally, the Verdoorn law was understood to operate only in manufacturing industries (Kaldor, 1966), but this position is difficult to maintain in the present day.[42]

Turning to the results of these literatures, convergence analyses find that, at the aggregate level, convergence between NUTS regions has slowed – indeed, virtually ceased – since the mid to late 1970s. This is the case regardless of whether the focus is absolute β-convergence (the tendency for poorer regions to grow faster than richer regions) or σ-convergence (a declining dispersion of per capita income levels). Underlying this aggregate pattern, however, exists a heterogeneity of experience across sectors (Le Gallo and Dall'erba, 2008) with, for example, the market and non-market service sectors experiencing σ-convergence while other sectors have experienced no such convergence or even, in the case of agriculture, divergence. Differences between core and peripheral regions have also been discovered (Le Gallo and Dall'erba, 2008).[43,44] These results concerning a lack of both absolute β- and σ-convergence at the aggregate level seem more consistent with an endogenous growth view of the world than with a traditional neoclassical view. Indeed, if knowledge spillovers in capital accumulation à la Romer (1986) are incorporated into the Solow–Swan model, the predicted speed of convergence in the model slows with divergence predicted if the knowledge spillovers are sufficiently strong.[45] However, the results concerning a diversity of experience across sectors seem more difficult to reconcile with simple spatial applications of endogenous growth theory. This is because of the highly aggregated nature of endogenous growth models. Once again, this suggests that such models are insufficient to furnish a proper understanding of the mosaic of regional growth experiences.

In the Verdoorn law literature, meanwhile, both Fingleton and McCombie (1998) and Pons-Novell and Viladecans-Marsal (1999) find evidence of substantial localised increasing returns to scale in EU manufacturing at the NUTS2 and NUTS1 levels, respectively.[46] These findings again provide support for endogenous growth theory, even though simple studies of the Verdoorn law are incapable of testing the specific emphasis of such theory on dynamic knowledge spillovers. However, the support found for the Verdoorn law also challenges the supply-side emphasis of endogenous growth theory.

Turning now to the use of spatial econometric techniques, this is predicated on the realisation that the assumption of an independently distributed error term is unlikely to hold in a cross-sectional regional setting. This is for two reasons: (1) the fact that NUTS regions in the EU are not defined on analytical/functional grounds and so do not delineate meaningful areas of economic activity; and (2) recognition that significant spillovers of the sort emphasised by endogenous growth theory may occur not only between agents *within* regions, but also between agents in *different* regions. Spatial autocorrelation arising for the first reason is considered to be a "nuisance", while that arising for the second reason is considered to be "substantive" on the grounds that it has a meaningful economic interpretation. To test for, and subsequently deal with, spatial autocorrelation, studies of European regional growth have typically adopted a "testing-up" strategy (see, for example, Fingleton and McCombie, 1998, and Pons-Novell and Viladecans-Marsal, 1999). This begins with standard OLS estimation of the growth equation under consideration. Spatial autocorrelation in the residuals of the equation is then tested for using an appropriate test statistic – for example, Moran's I statistic. If, using this test, spatial autocorrelation is detected, a decision is made between two different spatial specifications of the growth equation. These specifications are the spatial error model (SEM) and the spatial autoregressive (SAR) or spatial lag model:

$$\text{SEM specification: } g = X\delta_1 + \varepsilon_1 \tag{1}$$

$$\text{where } \varepsilon_1 = \eta W \varepsilon_1 + \mu$$

$$\text{SAR specification: } g = X\delta_2 + \rho Wg + \varepsilon_2 \tag{2}$$

where g is a $N \times 1$ vector of regional growth rates, X is a matrix of exogenous influences on growth, and W is a row-standardised spatial weights matrix that captures the spatial interaction between regions.[47] In the SEM specification it can be seen that the error term adopts a spatial structure with μ being well-behaved. By contrast, in the SAR specification, the spatial autocorrelation is modelled through the use of an extra regressor – namely, the spatially lagged growth rate, which captures the idea that the growth of one region depends directly on the growth of "neighbouring" regions.[48]

The choice between the SEM and SAR specifications is made on the basis of Lagrange Multiplier (LM) statistics. Specifically, following OLS estimation, two such statistics are calculated, one (LM_{SEM}) having greater power against the SEM specification and the other (LM_{SAR}) having greater power against the SAR specification. The specification selected is the one with the highest associated LM statistic.[49]

Clearly, the choice between the SEM and SAR specifications in European regional growth studies is of great importance, not least because the former is seen as capturing "nuisance" spatial autocorrelation and the latter "substantive" spatial autocorrelation. Hence the spatial autoregressive parameter ρ in the SAR specification is interpreted as capturing cross-regional knowledge spillovers. This has led to the conclusion that knowledge spillovers between agents in different European regions are substantial. For example, in estimating the Verdoorn law, Pons-Novell and Viladecans-Marsal (1999) find ρ to be 0.201 (Table 3, p. 448), implying that 20 per cent of growth in one NUTS1 region spills over into neighbouring NUTS1 regions. This would seem to provide considerable support to the spatial application of endogenous growth theory.

However, the "testing-up" strategy and the interpretation of ρ in equation (2) as capturing endogenous growth theory style spillovers is problematic (Abreu et al., 2005, pp. 32–5; Angeriz et al., 2008; Roberts, 2006a). Most notably, it is just as (if not more) likely that a significant value of ρ reflects the existence of spatially autocorrelated omitted variables as it does cross-regional spillovers. For example, there is a notable absence of comprehensive data on human capital at the various NUTS levels and so this variable is typically absent from European regional growth studies. However, if human capital levels are spatially autocorrelated, this omitted variable problem will show up as substantive spatial autocorrelation.[50] Additional problems relate to the difficulty of distinguishing between the SEM and SAR specifications when both the LM_{SEM} and LM_{SAR} statistics are significant (Angeriz et al., 2008) and the weakness of the links between the SAR specification and economic theory (Abreu et al., 2005, p33; Angeriz et al., 2008; Roberts, 2006a). With respect to the latter, if spillovers between regions are thought to operate through a particular variable rather than through income per capita or productivity growth per se, it is more appropriate to include a spatial lag of this variable as an extra regressor rather than the spatially lagged growth rate (as in the SAR specification). This approach has recently been adopted by, for example, Angeriz et al. (2008), who find that interregional spillovers are much smaller than suggested by Pons-Novell and Viladecans-Marsal (1999).

5   Remaining theoretical and empirical issues in the regional application of endogenous growth theory

It follows from the preceding discussion that both North American and European researchers can learn useful lessons from each other. Researchers working on European regional growth can learn from the new economics literature the value of a definition of the region that is appropriate to the issue being studied. They should also heed the lesson that a proper understanding of the causal forces underlying regional growth requires more than studying convergence or the Verdoorn law. In particular, it is important to "get inside" the "black box" of localised increasing returns to unpack the nature of any knowledge spillovers. Whether knowledge spillovers are, for example, within-industry or cross-industry in nature is critical from both theoretical and policy perspectives. But studies of European regional growth are at least aware of the importance that attaches to spatial autocorrelation. In contrast, this phenomenon has largely been ignored in the new economics literature. It is therefore possible that the estimating equations in some of this literature are seriously misspecified. Replicating some of the new economics research while paying explicit attention to the problem of spatial autocorrelation would appear worthwhile, if only to check the robustness of the results so far derived. A second important lesson that the new economics literature can learn comes from the European literature on the Verdoorn law. This literature highlights the potential importance of demand growth in driving regional growth processes, a possibility that has been ignored in the new economics literature. The importance of this lesson stems from the fact that, even if the knowledge spillovers highlighted by endogenous growth theory exist at the local level, policymakers may never be able to harness them unless they attend to conditions on both the supply *and* demand sides of the economy.

This leads to the first of several remaining issues in the spatial application of endogenous growth theory. The overwhelmingly supply-side focus of endogenous growth theory takes the demand-side of regional economies too much for granted. At both a theoretical and policy level, the neglect of the demand side needs to be reconsidered. In the UK, for instance, there is a need to think carefully about the adequacy of a regional policy that relies on five key supply-side drivers of growth with little or no attention paid to local demand conditions. Meanwhile, at the theoretical level, it should be recognised that endogenous growth models can be either "Keynesian" or "neoclassical" (Roberts and Setterfield, 2007). One example of a "Keynesian" endogenous growth model is the Dixon–Thirlwall model that is part of the Kaldorian tradition discussed in the previous section. While paying due attention to the demand side, however, the treatment of localised increasing returns in this model is primitive. It does not provide the detailed modelling of increasing returns that is characteristic of "neoclassical" endogenous growth theory. What is needed, then, is the development of "Keynesian" endogenous growth models that combine the strengths of conventional endogenous growth theory with more explicit treatment of the role and evolution of local demand.

Two questions help to highlight the potential importance of demand-side considerations for the analysis of regional growth. First, what does aggregate growth theory indicate about the ultimate source of growth? And, second, is this source of growth likely to be geographically confined, giving the growth process an inherently spatial dimension? In "neoclassical" endogenous growth models, the ultimate source of growth is the supply-side expansion of the availability and productivity of factor inputs. Meanwhile, the mechanism that geographically confines this source of growth is the Lucas (1988) theorem that knowledge spillovers require direct human interaction. But from a Keynesian viewpoint, the level and/or growth rate of aggregate demand is the ultimate source of growth. The potential for geographical confinement of demand conditions depends on the precise component of aggregate expenditures that is crucial to the growth process, and/or the growth-generating mechanism that characterises the model at hand. In the Dixon–Thirlwall model, for example, the demand for a region's exports is of ultimate importance. Moreover, any historical "accident" in the form of a positive idiosyncratic shock to regional export demand sets in motion cumulative processes that create persistence in the spatial pattern of future aggregate demand growth. Recent contributions to "Keynesian" endogenous growth theory have built on this, suggesting additional feedback mechanisms so that self-reinforcing growth can break down (Setterfield, 1997a, 1997b) or, alternatively, be kick-started where it has previously been absent (Roberts, 2006b).[51]

A second remaining issue relates back to the fact that, within the new economics literature, the application of endogenous growth theory to a spatial setting is mainly informal. This is problematic not only because the resulting application is sometimes rather loose, but also because the key endogenous growth models on which the new economics literature draws are closed economy models. This is only natural because such models were designed primarily with national economies in mind. However, when translated to a spatial setting, the closed economy assumption encourages a tendency to ignore systemic or "spatial general equilibrium" aspects of the working of regional economies. The danger of this is again highlighted by UK regional policy. Encouraged by a closed economy mentality, UK regional policy effectively assumes that all regions can achieve rapid growth and a high level of prosperity if they push the sorts of policy levers suggested by endogenous growth theory (e.g. skills, investment, innovation, enterprise and competition). But looking at regional economies as a system and acknowledging both the positive and negative linkages between them, is this really possible? Clearly, more theoretical and empirical research is required here. In particular, the development of more explicitly spatial models of endogenous growth would, once again, be useful. In order to facilitate the analysis of models with both multiple regions and sectors, this should draw on modern computer simulation techniques such as those already in use in the "new economic geography" literature.

The third outstanding issue concerns the fact that empirical work seems to reveal a considerable diversity of growth patterns and mechanisms in both the spatial and temporal dimensions. Thus, in the "new economics" literature, both within- and cross-industry knowledge spillovers have been found, depending on the industries and/or time periods studied. European work, meanwhile, has revealed that different sectors are characterised by different convergence patterns and that, over time, the aggregate speed of convergence has slowed. These results suggest that no single endogenous growth mechanism can explain all spatio-temporal growth rate differences. Instead, it would seem that different mechanisms operate simultaneously, with the exact combination of mechanisms (and their net effect) being context dependent. This being the case, it is useful to view regional growth processes as being characterised by different spatial and temporal growth regimes. Thus, for example, Roberts (2004) has argued that the late 1970s–early 1980s witnessed the emergence of a new growth regime for the system of UK regional economies. This new regime was characterised by a policy–technology mix that favoured certain types of human capital intensive industries. High human capital regions that were well placed to increase their specialisation in these industries benefited from this regime switch, while regions that were not suffered.[52]

A final remaining issue relates to spatial implications of endogenous growth theory that have, as of yet, gone largely unexplored. Some of the most interesting implications of endogenous growth theory concern the impact of the internal spatial organisation of regions on knowledge flows. This is because endogenous growth theory as applied to the regions, relies on human and social interactions for both the occurrence and geographic bounding of knowledge spillovers. The strength of knowledge spillovers can, therefore, be expected to depend on the physical layout of a city or region and the extent to which it encourages human and social interaction where the "talk is good". However, this is something that seems to have gone unnoticed in the "new economics" literature, save for Glaeser et al.'s (1995) inclusion of a measure of racial segregation in a Barro-style regression. Such regressions are ill-suited to "getting inside" the "black box" of social and human interaction, however. Research drawing on microeconomic data is likely to be much more fruitful in this regard.

6 Conclusion

This chapter has provided a critical survey of literature relating to the spatial application of endogenous growth theory. In so doing, it has covered both the "new economics of urban and regional growth" literature of Glaeser et al. and the European literature on convergence and the Verdoorn law. It has been shown that both of these literatures have something to learn from each other. Furthermore, important issues, both theoretical and empirical, remain regarding the spatial application of endogenous growth theory. Prime among these is the need to pay more attention to the demand side of local economies; to beware the pitfalls of drawing conclusions from closed economy models for a system of open regional economies; and to be conscious of the possible existence of different "growth regimes" across both time and space. Overall, we may conclude that while endogenous growth theory sheds light on the geographic transmission of knowledge, spatial application of this theory is not, by itself, enough to provide a full understanding of the regional growth process. Further theoretical and empirical work is yet required and one aim of this survey has been to identify areas of research that, in the opinions of the authors, should be given priority.

Notes

1. In Europe, for example, growth rates of gross value added (GVA) per capita for the period 1980–2002 averaged 2.13 per cent per annum for all NUTS2 regions, but the dispersion of growth rates around this average was considerable. Some 14 regions recorded growth rates in excess of 3.5 per cent per annum while, at the bottom of the distribution, 14 other regions grew at less than 1 per cent per annum.
2. Endogenous growth theory is associated here with neoclassical endogenous growth theory in the sense that the emphasis is on the supply-side determinants of growth. However, association of the concept of endogenous growth with supply-side macroeconomics does not automatically follow. Hence the origins of the concept of endogenous growth can be contested (Roberts and Setterfield, 2007) while, more importantly, there exist Keynesian as well as neoclassical endogenous growth models. The penultimate section of this chapter returns to the issue of the existence of both Keynesian and neoclassical endogenous growth models.
3. Also important in this context has been *Cambridge Econometrics's* extension of the REGIO database, which has been used as the basis for much empirical work (see http://www.camecon.com/services/europe/research2.htm).
4. In so doing, the chapter leaves to one side a number of interesting contributions focusing on developing countries (see, for example, Deichmann et al., 2005).
5. For a survey of work by geographers see Sheppard (2000).
6. The argument that congestion will lead to the bidding-up of factor prices has been used as the basis for a

notable test by Rauch (1993) for human capital knowledge spillovers in US metropolitan area data. This study is examined in more detail later in the chapter.

7.   More fundamentally, it might be argued that, even for the US, the argument that the appropriate metric of regional growth is provided by employment or population growth is theoretically contestable on the grounds that it presupposes a neoclassical (supply-side) view of the world. Thus, the argument that the choice of metric is influenced by the degree of spatial mobility of factors of production implies acceptance of the notion that the availability and productivity of factors are the key drivers of growth. However, what of the possibility that growth is instead driven by aggregate demand in circumstances in which geographical confinement of such growth is possible? Again, we return to this issue of "Keynesian" versus "neoclassical" regional growth in the penultimate section.

8.   This is so for theoretical reasons that will be elaborated on in the next section.

9.   NUTS is an acronym for Nomenclature of Units of Territorial Statistics. For details of the definition of the NUTS regions see http://europa.eu.int/comm/eurostat/ramon/nuts/basicnuts_regions_en.html.

10. See Magrini (1998, Chapter 3) for discussion of the difficulties posed by NUTS regions for the empirical analysis of regional growth.

11. Roberts (2004), for example, attempts to control for similar problems in the context of data on the UK counties. This he does by employing instrumental variable techniques such as Durbin's ranking method and paying careful attention to outliers. Additionally, where appropriate, researchers might consider orthogonal regression methods (on which, see Malinvaud, 1980).

12. More recently, this second sense in which growth is endogenous in mainstream endogenous growth models has been challenged (Jones, 1995, 2002; Mankiw et al., 1992). In particular, it has been claimed that such growth is crucially dependent on a knife-edge assumption and predictions of "scale effects" that are not observed internationally. This has led to the emergence of "semi-endogenous" growth models. Crucially from the current viewpoint however, these models share the same basic mechanisms for endogenous knowledge creation and accumulation as their "fully endogenous" counterparts.

13. Important aspects of the Romer (1986) model were anticipated by Arrow (1962).

14. In particular, competition in the intermediate goods sector is assumed to be monopolistic, typically being modelled in the Dixit–Stiglitz (1977) manner.

15. There also exist endogenous growth models that combine vertical and horizontal innovation (see, for example, Young, 1998; Won-Li, 2000).

16. This is reminiscent of Jacobs (1969)-style knowledge spillovers.

17. This business stealing effect acts as a negative externality, offsetting the positive externality resulting from within-industry knowledge spillovers.

18. Strictly speaking, in the Romer (1990) model, the stock of knowledge is embodied in a set of blueprints for the production of intermediate goods. These blueprints subsequently act as inputs to the production of new final goods.

19. Not all "new economics" authors have been so careful in making the distinction between knowledge and information (see, most notably, Glaeser, 1994).

20. This is consistent with work by the economic historians Simon and Nardinelli (1996) on the growth of English and Welsh cities over the late nineteenth and twentieth centuries. Thus, drawing inspiration from endogenous growth theory, they state that "People in cities talk; the talk leads to the creation of knowledge. Cities where the 'talk is good', meaning that it carries useful information, grow more rapidly than cities where the talk is mostly noise" (p. 385, footnote excluded). In this context, Simon and Nardinelli associate high-quality talk with information-oriented professionals such as brokers, accountants and lawyers. Regressing city population growth on the initial share of employment accounted for by such professions and various control variables, they find a strong positive relationship that is consistent with the "talk is good" hypothesis.

21. Not only might imitation by individuals be important, but so, too, might imitation by firms. Thus there is an interesting related literature on general-purpose technologies (GPTs) where a GPT is a new technological paradigm that has the potential to affect the entire economic and social system (Aghion and Williamson, 1999). When a new GPT is introduced to an economy, however, it is unclear what the best application of the GPT is. This being the case, firms look for examples of other firms that have successfully implemented the technology. In other words, they look for a "role model" firm from which they might be able to acquire a knowledge spillover by observation. It is easy to imagine this process having a local dimension, so that successful adoption of the GPT takes off in a single or small number of regions in the first instance, leading to a temporary period of very fast growth in these regions.

22. In the Romer (1990) model, for example, a reduced fixed cost of R&D stimulates entry into research activities, which, in turn, increases the equilibrium growth rate.

23. The effect of the degree of segregation on knowledge spillovers and human capital accumulation could potentially be negative or positive. Thus, imagine increased segregation between a group possessing high levels of human capital and a group possessing low levels. On the one hand, the individuals in the low

human capital group would get less chance to interact with individuals in the high human capital group, thereby providing a potential absence of access to positive role models. On the other, individuals in the high human capital group would have a greater tendency to interact with each other, which might better promote good quality talk and thus facilitate knowledge spillovers.

24. In this context, it may be hypothesised that significant non-linearities exist in terms of the impact of infrastructure projects to improve transportation links. Thus, for example, while initial improvements from a low base might yield increasing returns, improvements to an already highly developed transport system might only result in decreasing returns.

25. An exception is provided by Magrini (1998, Chapters 5 and 6).

26. Further reasons for the need for more theoretical work are highlighted later in the chapter.

27. As mentioned previously, there has been some theoretical work in this direction in the form of the explicit development of geographical or spatial models of endogenous growth (Martin and Ottaviano, 1999). In particular, these models look to combine the treatment of space provided by the "new economic geography" literature of, inter alia, Fujita et al. (1999) with endogenous growth mechanisms. However, the treatment of space in these models is very simple, while the geographical bounding of knowledge spillovers is assumed rather than explicitly modelled.

28. This is for reasons discussed earlier.

29. The Porter theory is attributed by Glaeser et al. to Michael Porter (in particular, Porter, 1990).

30. Namely, the 1956 log city-industry wage, the 1956 log city-industry employment level, national employment growth in an industry and a dummy variable for Southern city-industries.

31. Differences in empirical methodology also likely contribute to differences in results. For example, of the studies discussed below, Henderson et al. (1995) differs from Glaeser et al. (1992) by not controlling for competition. Meanwhile, Beardsell and Henderson (1999) make use of conditional Markov chain analysis as well as regression methods.

32. Glaeser et al.'s finding that competition is associated with fast regional growth has been subject to little subsequent controversy. Reflecting on this, Glaeser (2000, p. 93) states that "Every piece of research in this area that I am aware of finds a positive effect of competition on later growth." However, as Glaeser acknowledges, there are problems interpreting this relationship between competition and growth. Hence, one interpretation is that competition encourages innovation, while an alternative is that fast-growing cities have a lot of new plants and firms that are also small, in which case reverse causation from growth to competition exists.

33. The study by Feldman and Audretsch (1999) is interesting because it uses a direct measure of the innovative output of a city-industry as its dependent variable. Consequently, this study relates more directly to the object of interest – knowledge creation, accumulation and spillovers.

34. One possibility is that there may be an ecological inference problem. Alternatively, something akin to Simpson's paradox might be in operation. The latter arises when, for example, the probability of an event A occurring in a population X and in a population Y is in both cases greater than it not occurring. However, when the two populations are combined, the opposite is found (see McCombie and Roberts, 2007).

35. Rauch (1993) calculates that the size of the human capital knowledge externality is such that an additional year of average city level education will increase local TFP by 2.8 per cent (with a standard error of 0.8 per cent).

36. Glaeser et al. (1995) find that a one standard deviation increase in the median years of schooling in 1960 is associated with a 2.78 per cent increase in income over the sample period.

37. Glaeser et al. (1995) also find a significant negative impact of the initial unemployment rate on city growth. They interpret this as reinforcing the importance of human capital, because they view unemployment as proxying unobserved deficiencies in human capital. The alternative interpretation is that high initial unemployment indicates deficient aggregate demand for locally produced commodities, which, in turn, impacts negatively on city growth. This alternative interpretation is more consistent with Keynesian endogenous growth models.

38. To overcome such problems, a panel data approach to estimation allowing for city-specific fixed effects is recommended.

39. A second important econometric problem that could bias Glaeser et al.'s results is spatial autocorrelation. We return to this theme in the next subsection.

40. The widespread application of spatial econometric techniques by European researchers and their neglect in the new economics literature is somewhat ironic. This is because many of the major contributions to spatial econometric methodology have been made by North American based academics (see, most notably, Anselin, 1988).

41. This contrast between North American and European research is, of course, an oversimplification. Thus, the most notable early contributions to the regional convergence literature were made by Barro and Sala-i-Martin (for an overview see Barro and Sala-i-Martin, 2004, Chapter 11). Meanwhile, the first regional estimation of the Verdoorn law was for the US states (McCombie and de Ridder, 1984). However, clearly,

in recent years, interest in both regional convergence and the Verdoorn law has mainly been a European interest with a European focus.

42. For an extensive general overview of the Kaldorian growth literature and issues involved in the specification of the Verdoorn law see McCombie et al. (2002).

43. Le Gallo and Dall'erba (2005) make use of data for 145 NUTS2 regions for 1975–2000. The data cover five different sectors – agriculture, energy and manufacturing, construction, market services and non-market services.

44. Similar results to those of Le Gallo and Dall'erba (2008) hold within individual EU countries (see, for example, Roberts, 2004, in the case of the UK).

45. The predicted speed of convergence in the Solow–Swan model is given by $\beta \approx (1 - \alpha)(n + g + d)$ where α is the elasticity of real output with respect to capital, n is the rate of population growth, g is the rate of technological progress and d is the rate of capital depreciation. Under constant returns to scale, α is equal to the capital share (i.e. $\alpha \approx 0.30$), but with the inclusion of knowledge spillovers, α increases above this value, implying that $\beta \to 0$.

46. Fingleton and McCombie (1988) also find evidence of a significant technological diffusion effect.

47. Normally, the weights matrix takes the form of either a simple contiguity matrix in which only direct interaction between geographically neighbouring regions is allowed for (such a weights matrix is used by, inter alia, Armstrong, 1995a, 1995b, and Pons-Novell and Viladecans-Marsal, 1999) or an inverse square distance matrix with or without a critical cutoff distance above which direct interactions between regions are assumed to be negligible (used by, for example, Fingleton and McCombie, 1998). More recently, authors have turned to more sophisticated weights matrices based on, for instance, travel time by road between regions with a penalty for the crossing of a national border (Cheshire and Magrini, 2005). Nevertheless, the selection of the appropriate weights matrix remains a critical issue of specification in spatial econometric models. Although as yet unexploited in the growth context, developments in Bayesian spatial econometrics (see, in particular, Le Sage, 1999) may help tackle this issue.

48. The standard approach is to estimate both the SEM and SAR models using maximum likelihood (ML) techniques.

49. This "testing-up" strategy has its origins in the Monte Carlo study of Anselin and Rey (1991), which investigates the size and power properties of the LM_{SEM} and LM_{SAR} test statistics. A robust version of this strategy also exists in which the two tests are replaced by versions that are robust to local misspecification in the form of the existence of the type of spatial autocorrelation not being tested for. This version of the strategy has, however, been shown to be inferior in the context of Monte Carlo work by Florax et al. (2003).

50. Roberts (2004) finds that, for his sample of UK counties, including a proxy for human capital, along with population growth, removes any evidence of spatial autocorrelation in the estimation of convergence equations.

51. This relates to the important question of the ability of cities and regions to reinvent themselves, thereby allowing a locality that might have been depressed for decades to escape the seemingly inevitable trap of continuing economic decline. Recent examples of such successful reinvention within the UK include such cities as Manchester, Glasgow, Leeds and Newcastle, as well as parts of London.

52. Audretsch and Fritsch (2000) have also made use of the analytical device of growth regimes in studying the growth performances of the system of West German planning regions in the 1980s and 1990s. Further applications of the growth regimes device have taken place in the context of international growth disparities (see, most notably, Cornwall and Cornwall, 2001; Setterfield and Cornwall, 2002).

References

Abreu, M., H.L.F. De Groot and R.J.G.M. Florax (2005) "Space and growth: a survey of empirical evidence and methods", *Région et Développement*, **21**, 13–44.

Aghion, P. and J.G. Williamson (1999) *Growth, Inequality, and Globalisation: Theory, History, and Policy*, Cambridge: Cambridge University Press.

Aghion, P. and Howitt P. (1998) *Endogenous Growth Theory*, Cambridge, MA: MIT Press.

Alonso, W. (1964) *Location and Land Use*, Cambridge, MA: Harvard University Press.

Angeriz, A., J.S.L. McCombie and M. Roberts (2008) "New estimates of return to scale and spatial spillovers for EU regional manufacturing, 1986–2002", *International Regional Science Review*, **31**, 62–87.

Anselin, L. (1988) *Spatial Econometrics: Methods and Models*, Dordrecht: Kluwer.

Anselin, L. and S. Rey (1991) "Properties of tests for spatial dependence in linear regression models", *Geographical Analysis*, **23**, 112–31.

Armstrong, H.W. (1995a) "An appraisal of the evidence from cross-sectional analysis of the regional growth process within the European Union", in H.W. Armstrong and R.W. Vickerman (eds) *Convergence and Divergence among European Regions*, Vol. 5. London: Pion.

Armstrong, H.W. (1995b) "Convergence among regions of the European Union", *Papers in Regional Science*, **74**, 143–52.

Arrow, K.J. (1962) "The economic implications of learning by doing", *Review of Economic Studies*, **29**, 155–73.

Audretsch, D.B. and M. Fritsch (2002) "Growth regimes over time and space", *Regional Studies*, **36**, 113–24.

Barro, R.J. and X. Sala-i-Martin (2004) *Economic Growth*, 2nd edn., Cambridge, MA: MIT Press.

Beardsell, M. and V. Henderson (1999) "Spatial evolution of the computer industry in the USA", *European Economic Review*, **43**, 431–56.

Borts, G.H. and J.L. Stein (1964) *Economic Growth in a Free Market*, New York: Columbia University Press.

Bresnahan, T. (1999) "Computerisation and wage dispersion: an analytical reinterpretation", *Economic Journal*, **109**, F390–F415.

Cheshire, P.C. and G. Carbonaro (1995) "Convergence–divergence in regional growth rates: an empty black box?", in H.W. Armstrong and R.W. Vickerman (eds) *Convergence and Divergence among European Regions*, London: Pion.

Cheshire, P.C. and G. Carbonaro (1996) "Urban economic growth in Europe: testing theory and policy prescriptions", *Urban Studies*, **33**, 1111–28.

Cheshire, P.C. and S. Magrini (2005) "European urban growth: throwing some economic light into the black box", paper presented at Spatial Econometrics Workshop, Kiel Institute of World Economics, Germany, 8–9 April.

Cornwall, J. and W. Cornwall (2001) *Capitalist Development in the 20th Century: An Evolutionary-Keynesian Analysis*, Cambridge: Cambridge University Press.

Deichmann, U., K. Kaiser, S. Lall and Z. Shalizi (2005) "Agglomeration, transport, and regional development in Indonesia", World Bank Policy Research Working Paper 3477.

Dixit, A. and J.E. Stiglitz (1977) "Monopolistic competition and optimum product diversity", *American Economic Review*, **67**, 297–308.

Dixon, R. and A.P. Thirlwall (1975) "A model of regional growth rate differences on Kaldorian lines", *Oxford Economic Papers*, **27**, 201–14.

Feldman, M.P. and D.B. Audretsch (1999) "Innovation in cities: science-based diversity, specialisation and localised competition", *European Economic Review*, **43**, 409–29.

Fingleton, B. and J.S.L. McCombie (1998) "Increasing returns and economic growth: some evidence for manufacturing from the European Union regions", *Oxford Economic Papers*, **50**, 89–105.

Florax, R.J.G.M., H. Folmer and S.J. Rey (2003) "Specification searches in spatial econometrics: the relevance of Hendry's methodology", *Regional Science and Urban Economics*, **33**, 557–79.

Fujita, M., P. Krugman and A. Venables (1999) *The Spatial Economy: Cities, Regions, and International Trade*, Cambridge, MA: MIT Press.

Glaeser, E.L. (1994) "Cities, information and economic growth", *Cityscape*, **1**, 9–48.

Glaeser, E.L. (2000) "The new economics of urban and regional growth", in G.L. Clark, M.P. Feldman and M.S. Gertler (eds) *The Oxford Handbook of Economic Geography*, Oxford: Oxford University Press.

Glaeser, E.L., H.D. Kallal, J.A. Scheinkman and A. Shleifer (1992) "Growth in cities", *Journal of Political Economy*, **100**, 1126–52.

Glaeser, E.L., J.A. Scheinkman and A. Shleifer (1995) "Economic growth in a cross-section of cities", *Journal of Monetary Economics*, **36**, 117–43.

Grossman, G.M. and E. Helpman (1991) *Innovation and Growth in the Global Economy*, Cambridge, MA: MIT Press.

Henderson, V., A. Kuncoro and M. Turner (1995) "Industrial development in cities", *Journal of Political Economy*, **103**, 1067–90.

H.M. Treasury (2001) *Productivity in the UK, No. 3: The Regional Dimension*, London: H.M. Treasury.

Jacobs, J. (1969) *The Economy of Cities*, New York: Random House.

Jaffe, A.B., M. Trajtenberg and R. Henderson (1993) "Geographic localisation of knowledge spillovers as evidenced by patent citations", *Quarterly Journal of Economics*, **108**, 577–98.

Jones, C.I. (1995) "R&D-based models of economic growth", *Journal of Political Economy*, **103**, 759–84.

Jones, C.I. (2002) *Introduction to Economic Growth*, 2nd edn, New York: Norton.

Jovanovic, B. and R. Rob (1989) "The growth and diffusion of knowledge", *Review of Economic Studies*, **56**, 569–82.

Kaldor, N. (1966) *Causes of the Slow Rate of Growth of the United Kingdom*, Cambridge: Cambridge University Press.

Kaldor, N. (1970) "The case for regional policies", *Scottish Journal of Political Economy*, **17**, 337–48.

Le Gallo, J. and S. Dall'erba (2008) "Spatial and sectoral productivity convergence between European regions, 1975–2000", *Papers in Regional Science*, **87**, 505–25.

Le Sage, J. (1999) *The Theory and Practice of Spatial Econometrics*, available at: www.spatial-econometrics.com.

Lucas, R.E. (1988) "On the mechanics of economic development", *Journal of Monetary Economics*, **22**, 3–42.

McCombie, J.S.L. and J.R. De Ridder (1984) "The Verdoorn law controversy: some new empirical evidence using US state data", *Oxford Economic Papers*, **36**, 268–84.

McCombie, J.S.L., M. Pugno and B. Soro (2002) *Productivity Growth and Economic Performance: Essays on Verdoorn's Law*, Basingstoke: Palgrave.

McCombie, J.S.L. and M. Roberts (2007) "Returns to scale and regional economic growth: the static–dynamic Verdoorn law paradox revisited", *Journal of Regional Science*, **47**, 179–208.

Magrini, S. (1998) "Modelling regional economic growth: the role of human capital and innovation", unpublished PhD thesis, University of London.

Magrini, S. (1999) "The evolution of income disparities among the regions of the European Union", *Regional Science and Urban Economics*, **29**, 257–81.

Malinvaud, E. (1980) *Statistical Methods in Econometrics*, 3rd edn, Amsterdam: North-Holland Publishing Co.

Mankiw, G.N., D.N. Weil and D. Romer (1992) "A contribution to the empirics of economic growth", *Quarterly Journal of Economics*, **57**, 407–37.

Marshall, A. (1890/1966) *Principles of Economics*, London: Macmillan.

Martin, P. and G.I.P. Ottaviano (1999) "Growing locations: industry location in a model of endogenous growth", *European Economic Review*, **43**, 281–302.

Myrdal, G. (1957) *Economic Theory and Under-developed Countries*, London: Duckworth.

Pons-Novell, J. and E. Viladecans-Marsal (1999) "Kaldor's laws and spatial dependence: evidence for the European regions", *Regional Studies*, **33**, 443–51.

Porter, M.E. (1990) *The Competitive Advantage of Nations*, London: Free Press.

Rauch, J.E. (1993) "Productivity gains from geographical concentration of human capital: evidence from the cities", *Journal of Urban Economics*, **34**, 380–400.

Roberts, M. (2004) "The growth performances of the GB counties: some new empirical evidence for 1977–1993", *Regional Studies*, **38**, 149–65.

Roberts, M. (2006a) "Seek and you will (not) find: model specification and search in the presence of two-directional spatial autocorrelation", Cambridge Centre for Economic and Public Policy, University of Cambridge, mimeo.

Roberts, M. (2006b) "Modelling historical growth: a contribution to the debate", in P. Arestis, J.S.L. McCombie and R.W. Vickerman (eds) *Growth and Development*, Cheltenham, UK and Northampton, MA, USA: Edward Elgar.

Roberts, M. and M. Setterfield (2007) "What is endogenous growth?", in P. Arestis, M. Baddeley and J.S.L. McCombie (eds) *Understanding Economic Growth. New Directions in Theory and Policy*, Cheltenham, UK and Northampton, MA, USA: Edward Elgar.

Romer, P.M. (1983) "Dynamic competitive equilibria with externalities, increasing returns and unbounded growth", unpublished PhD thesis, University of Chicago.

Romer, P.M. (1986) "Increasing returns and long-run growth", *Journal of Political Economy*, **94**, 1002–37.

Romer, P.M. (1990) "Endogenous technological change", *Journal of Political Economy*, **98**, 71–101.

Setterfield, M. (1997a) "History versus equilibrium' and the theory of economic growth", *Cambridge Journal of Economics*, **21**, 365–78.

Setterfield, M. (1997b) *Rapid Growth and Relative Decline: Modelling Macroeconomic Dynamics with Hysteresis*, London: Macmillan.

Setterfield, M. and J. Cornwall (2002) "A neo-Kaldorian perspective on the rise and decline of the golden age", in M. Setterfield (ed.) *The Economics of Demand-led Growth: Challenging the Supply-side Vision of the Long-run*. Cheltenham, UK and Northampton, MA, USA: Edward Elgar.

Sheppard, E. (2000) "Geography or economics? Conceptions of space, time, interdependence, and agency", in G.L. Clark, M.S. Gertler and M.P. Feldman (eds) *Oxford Handbook of Economic Geography*, Oxford: Oxford University Press.

Simon, C.J. and C. Nardinelli (1996) "The talk of the town: human capital, information, and the growth of English cities, 1861 to 1961", *Explorations in Economic History*, **33**, 384–413.

Solow, R.M. (1956) "A contribution to the theory of economic growth", *Quarterly Journal of Economics*, **70**, 65–94.

Swan, T.W. (1956) "Economic growth and capital accumulation", *The Economic Record*, **32**, 334–61.

Temple, J. (1999) "The new growth evidence", *Journal of Economic Literature*, **37**, 112–56.

Van Stel, A.J. and H.R. Nieuwenhuijsen (2004) "Knowledge spillovers and economic growth: an analysis using data of Dutch regions in the period 1987–1995", *Regional Studies*, **38**, 393–407.

Von Hipple, E. (1994) "Sticky information and the locus of problem-solving: implications for innovation", *Management Science*, **40**, 429–39.

Won-Li, C. (2000) "Endogenous vs. semi-endogenous growth in a two-R&D-sector model", *Economic Journal*, **110**, C109–C122.

Young, A. (1998) "Growth without scale effects", *Journal of Political Economy*, **106**, 41–63.

Index